The Life And Letters Of Samuel Hahnemann

Thomas Lindsley Bradford

THE

LIFE AND LETTERS

OF

DR. SAMUEL HAHNEMANN,

BY

THOMAS LINDSLEY BRADFORD, M. D.

Author of Homœopathic Bibliography of the United States; Senior of the American Institute of Homœopathy; Member of Homœopathic Medical Society of Pennsylvania; Philadelphia County Homœopathic Medical Society.

PHILADELPHIA:
BOERICKE & TAFEL.
1895.

T. B. & H. B. COCHRAN, PRINTERS,
LANCASTER, PA.

This book is respectfully dedicated to

R. E. Dudgeon, M. D., of London, England,

than whom no one has done more to render the writings of

Hahnemann accessible to the English-speaking

world.

"Die milde Macht ist gross."

PREFACE.

In 1847, Dr. Constantine Hering, the Father of American Homœopathy, published in the *Hygea* an article, entitled "Requisites to a Correct Estimate of Hahnemann." In this he wrote that in order to worthily estimate the character of this man, belonging to history, it would be necessary to mention the age in which he lived; to depict the life at Meissen, the home life, the school days, the artist-father and the mother, the early training of the boy. After this to describe the life and labors up to 1790, the year of the discovery of the New Law of Healing, and then:

"The foundation being thus laid, and the man presented to us in his daily life, his thoughts and his labors, his time and his contemporaries, the second and most important part would be devoted to the consideration of his new opinions, and a statement of the origin and gradual development, step by step, of Homœopathy. From the note in Cullen's "Materia Medica," through all his subsequent writings, and even through the successive editions of the "Organon," the materials must be industriously sought and carefully brought together down to the latest words of the expiring sage.

"Through the whole of this, criticism should be silent, no partisanship should divert shallow readers with straight laced conventionalities, the day-spring of the discoverer's thought should appear in its true primordial form, in its progress and in its growth, exempt from all cavil.

"After his writings, after his published and his various unpublished correspondence and other productions, the inner moral state of the man, the heart and feelings must be developed as the hidden spring of all. Here, where, for us as for all men, lies the danger of error; yea, the greatest danger, that of being unjust—and where we would, least of all, dare to be unjust—here the greatest watchfulness and most rigorous care are but requirements of the lowest and commonest duty. Nothing in the shape of testimony should here be omitted, not, however, what others have said of him, but what he has said of himself and of others.

"Next to this should be given his character, his mode of thought as they concerned domestic, civic and political life, and his conduct as man, husband, father and citizen, and then his bearing as physician, preceptor, colleague and controversialist. We are all the children of our parents—circumstances, moulded by our proximate relations in proportion to their force and repetition—this consideration should not be without its weight in the present case.

"The multitude of calumnies against Hahnemann should not protract their brief existence by a place in such a volume. Where, however, they chafed or roused their noble mark (for in his venerable age he was at times galled even to tears) they might merit a passing notice.

"Thus should the historian accompany his hero to the time when a friendly beckoning hand withdraws him from things without; his senses close to page and speech, unfold to sources of joy and hope, and he departs, at peace with himself, with God and with the mantled world.

"Then let the estimate follow, not penned by the laborious biographer, but formed in the inmost soul of him who shall have read and weighed the whole."

It has been the intention to follow Dr. Hering's advice and to permit Hahnemann to speak by means of his writings; to avoid criticism of his motives and to be very chary of personal opinion; to narrate in a concise manner the romantic story of his wanderings, his persecutions, his discoveries, his triumphs and his peaceful death, with the hope that the reader may find in the letters and events of this long and remarkable existence reasons for correctly understanding the expounder of a doctrine believed by so many to be founded upon an eternal law of God.

While much has been published in the past, it has all been fragmentary, and only by delving within the covers of many rare and difficult volumes can it be found. It has been the aim to collect everything bearing any relation to the career of Hahnemann in this book. The German, French and English literature have been thoroughly examined, considerable of the matter being for the first time published in English.

The portrait of Hahnemann is taken from an oil painting now in the possession of the Hahnemann Medical College of Philadelphia. Mr. Enoch Pratt, of Baltimore, to whom it formerly belonged, says of it: "I was in Paris in 1855, at the request of Dr. Schmidt of this city (Baltimore), I found the widow of Dr. Hahnemann, who had, she considered, the best original likeness of her husband painted in his lifetime; she consented to my having it copied, which was done by Hathaway, a distinguished painter of that day, in her house, under her own supervision, and she pronounced it perfect, saying she could distinguish no difference in them. I consider yours an original and very valuable."

This compilation has been made so that not only the younger physicians and students of our school but other readers may readily gain access to the facts in the life of HAHNEMANN, brilliant chemist, learned physician, great reformer and cultured man, and that they may become more familiar with the story of his marvelous career.

And at this time when the people are finding out that there is truth behind the doctrines of Homœopathy, it is the hope of the compiler that this book may be accepted as a biographical monument to the memory of this man whose teachings and influence have done so much to rob sickness of its terrors and to restore health to humanity.

CONTENTS.

CHAPTER XCI.

CHAPTER XCII.

THE LIFE OF HAHNEMANN.

CHAPTER I.

MEISSEN, THE CAPITAL OF MISNIA.

In the days gone by, there was situated in Upper Saxony a beautiful town called Meissen; it was the capital of the Margravate of Misnia, and was located on the little river Meisse, near its junction, with the stately Elbe, in a fertile valley rich in corn and vineyards, and was about twelve miles northwest of the city of Dresden.

In the middle of the eighteenth century, the period of which we write, Meissen had about four thousand inhabitants, many of whom were expert artists, chemists and painters. It was a town of importance, for it contained a branch of the Electoral Academy of Sciences, various cloth factories, and a manufactory for the newly discovered and wonderful "China-glass," or porcelain.

This porcelain factory was in the ruins of an ancient castle, which stood on the side of a mountain near by. The main portion alone was standing; the wings, the former homes of the Burgraves of Saxony, had long been but a mass of ruins. This central building, known as the Albertsburg, had been for many years occupied by the Saxon Margraves, the rulers of the land, but when the Electoral Princes went to live in Dresden, this old and deserted palace of the Prince Albrecht was turned into a manufactory for the beautiful and rare porcelain.

In the town there was a Cathedral church, having a very lofty spire of stone, and within its chapel reposed the bones of the Saxon Princes, the descendents of Frederick the Warlike. An arched church belonging to the castle towered above the steeple of the town church, while over beyond, was the mountain of St. Afra, having upon its side a building that, until the middle of the sixteenth century, had been a Benedictine convent, but was now used as a private school, and was called the "Afraneum" or School of St. Afra. There was also the town school which was known as the "Franciscaneum."

At this time the new art of ornamenting the china-glass with colors, with gold, and with painted pictures, was a great secret, and, as such, was jealously guarded. All the chemists and artists engaged in this work were sworn to secrecy, and only men of well-tried integrity were employed.

Upon the outskirts of the village, not far from the old Albrecht Castle, stood a long, plain building of three stories in height, that towered high above its neighbors, and was known as the Eck-haus. This house, on the 6th of April, 1753, one Christian Gottfried Hahnemann bought from the master-smith Lohse, for the sum of 437 thalers, and set up his household gods within its walls. He was a painter on porcelain, and had come to Meissen to adorn the dainty ware made there. The Eck-haus stood at the junction of two streets, the Fleischstege and the Newmarket. On the ground floor, in a corner room whose two large shuttered windows looked out on the Market Place, there was born upon the 11th of April, 1755, to the wife of the painter Hahnemann, a son, whose wonderful fortunes in life are now to be related. The baptismal register of Meissen contains the following record:* "Christian Friedrich Samuel Hahnemann, born on the morning of the 11th of April, of 1755; baptized the thirteenth day of April of the same year, by M. Junghanns. Father, Christian Gottfried Hahnemann, painter. Mother, Johanna Christiana, born Spiess." The worthy pastor, M. Junghanns, was of the Lutheran faith, and the infant was baptized on the Sabbath after its birth according to those tenets. The date of Hahnemann's birth has usually been given as the 10th, and not the 11th of April. The town register gives the 11th, and at the celebration at Meissen, in 1855, of the hundredth birthday, the 11th was the day selected.

Fortunately we are enabled to obtain certain knowledge about the early days of this great man by means of his autobiography.

*British Journal Homœopathy, Vol. 13, p. 525.

CHAPTER II.

STORY OF THE EARLIER DAYS OF HAHNEMANN, TOLD BY HIMSELF.

I was born April 10, 1755, in the Electorate of Saxony, one of the most beautiful parts of Germany. This circumstance, as I grew up to manhood, doubtless contributed a great deal to my veneration for the beauties of nature. My father, Christian Gottfried Hahnemann, together with my mother, Johanna Christiana, born Spiess, for a pastime taught me to read and write. My father died four years ago (1787.) Without being deeply versed in science (he was a designer in a porcelain manufactory in his native place, and is the author of a brief treatise on painting in water colors) he had the soundest ideas of what may be considered good and worthy, and he implanted them deeply on my mind.

To live and to act without pretence or show was his most noteworthy precept, and his example was even more impressive than his words. He was always present, though often unobserved, in body and soul wherever any good was to be done. In his acts he discriminated with the utmost nicety between the noble and the ignoble, and he did it with a justness which was highly creditable to his tender feelings. In this respect, too, he was my preceptor. He seemed to have ideas of the first principles of creation, of the dignity of humanity, and of its ennobling destiny, that were not in the least inconsistent with his manner of acting. This gave direction to my moral training. To speak of my mental training, I spent several years in the public school of Meissen so as to go thence, in my sixteenth year, to the private school (Fürstenschule), in the same place, and four years thereafter to attend the University of Leipsic. There was nothing noteworthy respecting me at school, except that Master Muller, my teacher in ancient languages and German composition, who besides living a great deal for the world and me, was rector of the Meissen private school, and scarcely has had his equal in industry and honesty, loved me as his own child and allowed me liberties in the way of study, which I am thankful for to this day, and which had a perceptible influence upon my subsequent studies. In my twelfth year he intrusted to me to impart to others the rudiments of the Greek language. Moreover, in his

private classes with his boarders and myself, he listened attentively and lovingly to my critical exposition of the old writers,
and often preferred my meaning to his own. I was often over-
taxed and became ill from study, and was the only one who was
excused from lessons at times unsuitable for me, and who was
permitted to hand in written exercises or other work performed
subsequently, and to read foreign treatises on the lessons. I had
free access to him at all times of the day, and in many respects
was given the preference in public to many others; and, nevertheless, which is very strange, my fellow pupils loved me. All
this together speaks volumes in praise of a Saxony private school.

Here I was less solicitous about reading than about digesting
what was read, and was careful to read little, but to read correctly and to classify it in my mind before reading further. My
father did not wish me to study at all; he repeatedly took me
from the public school for a whole year, so that I might pursue
some other business more suited to his income. My teachers
prevented this by not accepting any pay for my schooling during
the last eight years, and they entreated him to leave me with
them and thus indulge my propensity for learning. He did not
resist their entreaty, but could do nothing more for me. On
Easter, 1775, he let me go to Leipsic, taking with me twenty
thalers for my support. This was the last money received
from his hand. He had several other children to educate from
his scanty income, enough to excuse any seeming negligence
in the best of fathers.

By giving instruction in German and French to a rich young
Greek from Jassy, in Moldavia, as well as by translating English
books, I supported myself for the time, intending to leave Leipsic after a stay of two years.

I can conscientiously bear testimony that I endeavored to
practice in Leipsic also, the rule of my father, never to be a
passive listener or learner. I did not forget here, however, to
procure for my body, by outdoor exercise, that sprightliness and
vigor by which alone continued mental exertion can be successfully endured.

During this stay in Leipsic I attended lectures only at such
hours as seemed best suited to me, although Herr Bergrath
Porner, of Meissen, had the kindness to furnish me with free
tickets to the lectures of all the medical professors. So I read

by myself, unweariedly of course, but always only of the best that was procurable, and only so much as I could digest. My fondness for practicing medicine, as there is no medical school at Leipzig, led me to go to Vienna at my own expense. But a malicious trick which was played upon me and which robbed me of my public reputation acquired in Leipsic (repentance demands atonement, and I say nothing about names and circumstances) was answerable for my being compelled to leave Vienna after a sojourn of three-fourths of a year. During these nine months I had had for my support only sixty-eight florins and twelve kreutzers. To the hospital of Brothers of Charity, in the Leopoldstadt, and to the great practical genius of the Prince's family physician, named Von Quarin, I am indebted for my calling as a physician. I had his friendship, and I might also say his love, and I was the only one of my age whom he took with him to visit his private patients. He respected, loved and instructed me as if I had been the first of his pupils, and even more than this, and he did all without expecting to receive any compensation from me.

CHAPTER III.

AUTOBIOGRAPHY, CONTINUED.

My last crumbs of subsistence were just about to vanish when the Governor of Transylvania, Baron von Bruckenthal, invited me under honorable conditions to go with him to Hermanstadt as family physician and custodian of his important library. Here I had the opportunity to learn several other languages necessary to me, and to acquire some collateral knowledge that was pertinent and still seemed to be lacking in me.

I arranged and catalogued his matchless collection of ancient coins as well as his vast library, practiced medicine in this populous city for a year and nine months and then departed, although very unwillingly, from these honorable people to receive at Erlangen the degree of doctor of medicine, which I was then able to do from my own attainments. To the Privy Councillor, Delius, and Councillors Isenflamm, Schreber and Wendt, I am indebted for many favors and much instruction.

Councillor Schreber taught me what I still lacked in Botany.

On August 10, 1779, I defended my dissertation, and, thereupon, received the honorable title of doctor of medicine.

The instinctive love of a Swiss for his rugged Alps cannot be more irresistible than that of a native of Saxony for his fatherland.

I went thither to begin my career as a practicing physician in the mining town of Hettstadt, in Mansfield county. Here it was impossible to develop either inwardly or outwardly, and I left the place for Dessau in the spring of 1781, after a sojourn of nine months. Here I found a better and more cultured society. Chemistry occupied my leisure hours and short trips made to improve my knowledge of mining and smelting filled up the yet quite large dormer windows in my mind.

Towards the close of the year 1791 I received an insignificant call as physician to Gommern, near Magdeburg. The size of the town being considerable, I looked for a better reception and business than I found in the two years and three-fourths which I passed in this place.

There had lived as yet no physician in this little place to which I had removed, and the people had no idea concerning such a person.

Now I began for the first time to taste the innocent joys of home along with the delights of business in the companionship of the partner of my life, who was the step-daughter of Herr Haseler, an apothecary in Dessau, and whom I married immediately after entering upon the duties of this position. Dresden was the next place of my sojourn.

I played no brilliant rôle here, probably because I did not wish to do so. However, I lacked here neither friends nor instruction. The venerable Doctor Wagner, the town physician, who was a pattern of unswerving uprightness, honored me with his intimate friendship, showed me clearly what legal duties belonged to the physician (for he was master in his art), and for a year delivered over to me on account of his illness, with the magistrate's consent, all of his patients (in the town hospitals), a wide field for a friend of humanity. Moreover, the Superintendent of the Electoral Library, Councillor Adelung, became very fond of me and, together with the Librarian, Dossdorf, contributed a great deal towards making my sojourn interesting and agreeable. Four years thus elapsed, more speedily to me in the bosom of my increasing family, than to the unexpected heir to great riches, and I went about the time of Michaelmas, 1789, to

Leipsic, in order to be nearer to the fountain of science. Here I quietly witness the Providence which Destiny assigns to each of my days, the number of which lies in her hand.

Four daughters and one son, together with my wife, constitute the spice of my life. In the year 1791 the Leipsic Economical Society, and on the second of August of the same year the Electoral Mayence Academy of Science elected me a fellow member. Dated Leipsic, August 30, 1791. A foot note in the Hildesheim History reads: "Since 1792 Doctor Hahnemann has lived as foreign resident in the Province of Gotha. He afterwards established an institute for the insane at Georgenthal in this province, but he soon gave it up again. He went to Pyrmont in 1794. (3d volume, page 53, 5th edition of S. Meusel's 'Germany,' 1797.)"*

CHAPTER IV.

SCHOOL DAYS.

The story of the early days of this wonderful man forms a key to all his future. The poor German lad, whose father simply desired for his son the same upright, careful life, as had been his own, was impelled by that irresistible force constituting genius to gain knowledge by every possible means, and to satisfy the demands of a mind eager to understand the many wonders of the world before it. When Hahnemann was five years of age, his father had a habit of giving his son what he called "thinking lessons." Dr. Hering mentions this several times in his writings. He says: "Could the father have foreseen the future greatness of his son? But what was it that the father thought? It has been made known to us. While he looked upon the son so much desired, this was the thought: 'If that boy is permitted to grow up, I will give him lessons in thinking.' As he thought and determined, so he acted. An old man in Meissen, who had forgotten the son, when he heard of his fame, said, smilingly, 'Many a time have I taken a walk with his father, and ever at the certain hour he would say: 'I must go home now, I have to give a lesson to my son Samuel, a lesson in

---

*Elwert's Nachrichten von dem Leben und schriften jeztlebender teutscher Aerzte. Hildesheim. 1799.

thinking; that boy must learn to think.' "* And the childhood habit followed him through his lifetime. It must have been a very earnest desire for knowledge, of which Hahnemann so modestly speaks in his story, that would prompt the great men of the little German village to urge the unwilling father to grant the means of education to his studious son; there must have been something vastly superior about the boy, when the village teachers were desirous of imparting to him knowledge without payment. Imagine the delicate and slender boy of twelve with his earnest and pure face, teaching the rudiments of the Greek language to the other children, or talking enthusiastically about the "old writers," while his good master, the rector, "listened attentively and lovingly" to him. During the days of his boyhood, Hahnemann was in the habit of taking frequent rambles over the hills of his native town, and during this time, he also formed an herbarium of the plants of his beloved Saxony.† It is also related, that in his father's house he was accustomed to study at night, long after the rest of the household were in bed, by means of a lamp fashioned from clay, so that the light was concealed. Albrecht says regarding this circumstance, in a note to his Life of Hahnemann:‡ "His father, says a reliable witness, tried to prevent him from becoming deeply interested in reading and study, and probably may often have wished to frighten him from his books. The boy would endeavor to hide, and would flee with his beloved books to the remotest nooks of the house. The light there was not always sufficient, for we are told that he made for himself a lamp out of clay, with which to study in these nooks, because he feared that his father might miss a light, and subsequently put a stop to his cherished occupation." His studies while at Meissen, included Latin, Greek, Hebrew, and history, physics and botany. His favorite study was medical science.

When he left the princely school of Afra he presented a thesis, written in Latin, upon the " Wonderful Construction of the Human Hand."

During his student life at Meissen he did not enjoy very

---

*Programme of Centennial Celebration of Hahnemann's Birthday, Phila., 1855.

†Dudgeon's Biography of Hahnemann, London, 1851.

‡Albrecht's Hahnemann's Leben und Wirken, p. 11.

robust health, and was much favored by his teachers. It was at
Easter, 1775, that with his patrimony of twenty thalers and
with letters from his teachers to the professors at the University
of Leipsic, he set out for that city. Regarding Hahnemann's
going to Leipsic, Albrecht says:* "A more accurate account
comes from a well-informed source who says: 'His father at first
put him in a grocery store at Leipsic. So he was to become
a merchant. But tending the store, however pleasant it might
have been, was to the intellectual lad something dreadful and
unendurable. He stayed but a very short time. He left his
employer without any foolish reasons, merely following the inner
impulse to a higher calling, and returned to his parents, although
dreading to meet his father. His mother, fearing the anger of
his father, kept him hidden for several days, until she had succeeded in softening his father's heart, and reconciling him to
the wish of his son. With such difficulties Hahnemann was
compelled to make his own way at the University at Leipzig."
A youth of twenty, born and educated in a German village, yet
with knowledge of several languages, with but twenty thalers
with which to face the future, and yet with an indomitable determination to succeed.

CHAPTER V.

LIFE AT LEIPSIC AND VIENNA.

He began his student life in Leipsic by attending lectures
during the day and devoting his nights to translations from the
English into the German; he taught also German and French.
His lectures in medicine were free, although it is likely that his
numerous literary occupations prevented him from attending
them regularly. In the meantime he was carefully saving his
money, and preparing to go at the end of the two years to
Vienna, where the advantages for medical study were much
greater. The small sum that he had saved was stolen from him,
and it is to this that he alludes as a "malicious trick" in his
autobiography. But it is evident that he forgave, as he never
disclosed the names of the guilty parties, and says that "repentance demands forgiveness."

*Albrecht's Leben und Wirken, p. 13.

During the sojourn at Leipsic he translated the following books, all from the English: "John Stedtmann's Physiological Essays," "Nugent on Hydrophobia," "Falconer on the Waters of Bath," in two volumes; "Ball's Modern Practice of Physic," in two volumes; this in addition to the study of medicine and teaching.

In a Leipsic Homœopathic journal of 1865 was published a Latin poem composed by Hahnemann soon after his arrival at Leipsic. It is addressed to the distinguished philologist, Professor Zeune, and bears date September 20, 1775, and must have been composed in his twentieth year. It is as follows:

*" M. Joanni Carolo Zeunio
Professori recens creato
Vota faciunt
tres ejus auditorum
Mich. Christ. Justus Eschenbach
Johannes Fridericus Eschenbach
Christianus Fridericus Samuel Hahnemann, *Autor*.

Quid cessas hillari Pieridum choro
Misceri, Philyrae docta cohors? Age!
Celebrate modis hancce diem bonam.
Digni Calliope diem

Alumni; titulos qui debitos diu
Jam tandem senior (nobilis o pudor!)
Admittit, Capitum nostrae Academiae
Non ignobilium Decus.

Penna Fama, volans usque agit integra
Te Zeuni! Pietas cujus et ingeni
Dotes perpoliunt perpoliereque
Nostrum nive animum rudem.

Tu recludens opes et Latiae bonus
Et Grajae, juvenum languida melleo
Minervae recreans munere pectora,
Formas et Patriae et Deo.

A. D. XX Septembris, MDCCLXXV : Lepsiae.
Ex officina Buttneria."

Not so bad for a village youth of twenty years!
But the knowledge of medicine that he was able to obtain in

Leipsic was not so extensive as he desired, and his thoughts turned towards the great medical school at Vienna; and in the spring of 1777 he departed for that place. It must have been soon after his arrival that he was robbed, or in some manner defrauded of his savings, so that for nine months he was compelled to live on the small sum of sixty-eight florins.

In one quarter of Vienna, known as the Leopoldstadt, there was a very extensive hospital conducted by the Brothers of Charity, and in this Hahnemann received instruction under the guidance of the celebrated doctor, Von Quarin. Freiherr Von Quarin was body physician to Maria Theresa and the Emperor Joseph, he filled six times the post of rector of the University of Vienna.* In fact, Von Quarin was so impressed by the ability of his student that he made him his especial *protege*, taking him to visit private patients, a thing he had never before done. Throughout his life Hahnemann spoke of Dr. Von Quarin with great friendship, and credited to his influence the fact that he had been able to gratify his ambition and become a physician.

At Vienna he did no translating, but devoted himself entirely to acquiring the principles of medicine, and to his studies in the hospital.

But his little hoard at last gave out, and he was reluctantly compelled to tell his benefactor of his inability to continue his studies. As he so quaintly expresses it: "My last crumbs of comfort were just about to vanish." Nine months of the delightful student-life had exhausted all his means. Then Von Quarin came to his aid and secured for him the position of family physician and librarian to the Baron von Bruckenthal, who was the Governor of Siebenburgen and who lived in the city of Hermanstadt.

CHAPTER VI.

LIFE AT HERMANSTADT—GRADUATION AT ERLANGEN—RETURN TO SAXONY—DESSAU.

It must have been about the close of the year 1777 that Hahnemann went to Hermanstadt. Here he was far away from everything that could distract his mind from study. He passed the greater portion of his time in the valuable library of his patron.

*Ameke, p. 58.

He gained some knowledge of numismatics, and classified and arranged the "matchless collection of ancient coins" that he found there. He carefully catalogued Baron Bruckenthal's immense library of books and rare manuscripts. It was during the quiet, scholarly days, in the secluded library at Hermanstadt, that he acquired that extensive and diverse knowledge of ancient literature, and of occult sciences, of which he afterwards proved himself to be a master, and with which he astonished the scientific world.

He learned also several languages, and must have given much time to philology. When he left Hermanstadt, at the age of twenty-two years, he was master of Greek, Latin, English, Italian, Hebrew, Syriac, Arabic, Spanish, German, and some smattering of Chaldaic. It is said that when he wished to understand anything in a language with which he was not familiar he at once commenced the systematic study of that language. Here he was unwittingly preparing himself for his great future.

He remained in this hospitable haven for one year and nine months, when he was able to gratify his desire to obtain the degree of physician.

In the spring of 1779 he bade a reluctant good-by to his good friend, the Baron, and to the delights of his library, and departed for the University of Erlangen. Here he attended the lectures of Delius, Isenflamm, Wendt and Schreber. He expresses himself greatly indebted to Schreber for instruction in botany.*

He had been nearly ready to graduate, when his poverty compelled him to leave Vienna, and after listening for a few months to the lectures of the above mentioned professors, he presented himself for graduation. He chose Erlangen for his place of graduation because the fees were less than at Leipsic.

He defended his thesis successfully, on the 10th of August, 1779, receiving his degree as doctor of medicine. The subject of this thesis was, "A Consideration of the Etiology and Therapeutics of Spasmodic Affections." It was published at Erlangen in 1779, as a quarto of twenty pages.

After Hahnemann had obtained his medical degree his first

---

*It has been said by one of Hahnemann's detractors that he received the degree at Erlangen "in absentia." This is not true; he attended this University and was present at his graduation.

thought was for the hills of his beloved Saxony, and thither he at once journeyed.

He located in the little town of Hettstadt, on the river Whipper, situated nine miles from Eisleben, the capital of Mansfield county, and devoted to copper mining. The place was very small, and the young doctor had but little to do professionally, and remained but nine months, going thence in the spring of 1781 to Dessau. Hahnemann says in his autobiography that he left Hettstadt in the spring time (Fruhling) of 1781, after a stay of nine months. He graduated in August, 1779, and there is no account of his whereabouts from August, 1779, to the time of his arrival at Hettstadt, which must have been in the summer of 1780. It is known that Hahnemann at this period of his life practiced medicine for a time in several towns of Lower Hungary. On page 114, vol. 2 of the translation of Cullen's Materia Medica, Hahnemann, in a foot note, speaking of the Intermittents of marshy countries, says: "Cullen is wrong; he seems to have been unacquainted with the stubborn intermittents of hot, fenny countries. I observed such in Lower ·Hungary, more particularly in the fortified places of that country, which owe their impregnability to the extensive marshes around them. I saw such in Carlstadt, Raab, Gomorrn, Temeswar, Hermanstadt." May it not be probable that the missing year was spent in these places? Dr. J. C. Burnett in "Hahnemann as a Man and as a Physician," London, 1881, page 22, thinks the sojourn in Hungary was previous to graduation, and that he did not remain for a year and nine months at Hermanstadt, but Hahnemann distinctly says that he did remain there for that length of time At Dessau, on the Mulda, Hahnemann met more congenial society, and also succeeded in gaining some practice. Here he first turned his attention to chemistry, of which he was destined to become one of the most skillful exponents, and of whose skill that greatest of chemists, Berzelius, afterwards said: "That man would have made a great chemist, had he not turned out a great quack." He was also accustomed to take long geological walks; he visited the mines in the vicinity and learned much about practical mining and smelting, that he afterwards used in his writings on these subjects. As he so naively says: "I thus filled up the yet quite large dormer windows of my mind." He became a regular visitor at the laboratory of the apothecary Haseler, where he was enabled to perfect himself in practical pharmacy and chemistry. And here he met his future wife.

CHAPTER VII.

MARRIAGE—LIFE AT GOMMERN—UNCERTAINTY—FIRST ORIGINAL WORK.

Apothecary Haseler succeeded apothecary Kuchler in business at Dessau, and he also married his widow, who was blessed with a young and charming daughter; and the young doctor and chemist discovered in her the beloved "Elise" of many long and trial-filled years. Hahnemann's term of endearment for his wife was the name Elise, and it frequently occurs in his letters to her. But our young genius was poor, and in order that he might soon marry, he obtained the position of parish doctor at Gommern, removing to that place in the latter part of 1781. Gommern is a small town, only a few miles from Magdeburg, and Hahnemann was the first physician who had ever been settled there. Hahnemann was married to Miss Kuchler in the latter part of 1782. The registry of St. John's church in Dessau contains the following entry :* "On the 1st of December, 1782, Mr. Samuel Hahnemann, Dr. Med., Electoral Saxon parish doctor in Gommern, twenty-eight years old, eldest legitimate son of Mr. Christian Gottfried Hahnemann, artistic painter in the porcelain manufactory of Meissen, and of his wife, Johanna Christiana, was married to spinster Johanna Henrietta Leopoldina Kuchler, nineteen years old, only legitimate daughter of the late Godfried Henry Kuchler, and of his wife, Martha Sophia, in St. John's Church here."

He settled at once in Gommern and commenced the practice of his position. He had just been appointed to it at the time of his marriage. He also resumed his literary work.

At the end of 1783 or the first of 1784 the eldest child, Henrietta, was born.

It was while living at Gommern that Hahnemann translated, from the French, the chemist Demachy's Art of Manufacturing Chemical Products.† Demachy was one of the first chemists of

*British Journal Homœopathy. Vol. 36, p. 259.
†See Ameke's History of Homœopathy, p. 8.   ‡Salt of Amber.

the day, and the French Academy had published his book in order that the people of France might learn the various processes of the manufacture of chemical productions heretofore for the most part kept carefully as trade secrets by the manufacturers, especially by the Dutch. Hahnemann, by his translations into the German, rendered a like service to his fellow-countrymen. About the time he completed his translation a new one was issued by the chemist Struve, of Berne, with additions. Hahnemann added Struve's additions or comments to his own translation, at the same time making copious and original notes on them. Examination of the notes in this book reveals the marvellous chemical knowledge of the young translator. He quotes exhaustively from many authors, in many cases corrects mistakes. He cites ten authors on the preparation of the antimonials, quotes works on lead, quicksilver, camphor, succinic acid,‡ borax. Where Demachy remarks that he knows no work on carbonification of turf, Hahnemann mentions six. Demachy quotes a French analyist without giving his name, but Hahnemann gives not only the author's name, but also the name of his book. Demachy mentions a celebrated German physician. Hahnemann gives his name, his book, and the particular passage in question. On every page his notes appear. He gives new directions for making retorts; is well acquainted with the manufacture of chemicals in the different countries; corrects the mistakes of Demachy regarding the use of alum in Russia, Sweden, Germany, Italy, Sicily and Smyrna. He understands the use of pit coal in England and in the Province of Saarbruck. He introduces many original chemical improvements and tests. Crell, in his *Annalen*, the chemical journal of that day, says: "We can affirm that no more complete treatise exists on the subject of the manufacture of chemicals than this work." This valuable book, in two volumes, was published in 1784, in Leipsic. In 1785 he published, also at Leipsic, a translation of Demachy's Art of Distilling Liquor; also in two volumes. Westrumb, writing in Crell's *Annalen*, in 1792, thus speaks of this book: "Few manufacturers have listened to my suggestions to arrange their retorts as Demachy and Hahnemann describe. Distillers should entirely reject the old distillery apparatus and should use the French arrangement, clearly described by Hahnemann."

While living at Gommern he also published some medical essays in the second volume of Kreb's Journal, and several translations from the English and Latin in Weygand's Journal. Also an original book on the treatment of scrofulous sores, published at Leipsic, in 1784.

This was his first original medical work. Even at this early period Hahnemann was not quite satisfied with the methods of medical practice. He says in this book: "This much is true, and it may make us more modest, that almost all our knowledge of the curative powers of simple and natural as well as artificial substances is mainly derived from the rude and automatic procedures of the common people, and that the wise physician often draws conclusions from the effects of the so-called domestic remedies which are of inestimable importance to him." The book was largely the result of his experience in Transylvania, and he quite frankly says that his patients would probably have done better without him.* At this time, when very little attention was paid to hygiene, Hahnemann devoted considerable space to it. He recommends exercise and open air, the benefit of a change of climate and of the seashore, the value of cold water as a remedial agent. In speaking of the treatment of a caries of one of the metatarsal bones he, after giving the dressing he used, says: "I scraped the carious bone clean out, and removed all the dead part, dressed it with alcohol and watched the result." This book was received with much praise by the profession.†

CHAPTER VIII.

DISSATISFACTION WITH MODE OF PRACTICE—LETTER TO HUFE-
LAND—HUFELAND ON HOMŒOPATHY—MEDICAL
ANARCHY OF THE TIME.

Hahnemann remained at Gommern for two years and nine months. During this time his practice was not large nor did he seem to make much effort to increase it, preferring to devote himself to his translations and studies. His position as parish doctor, with his translations, supported him and his increasing family. But he was a sincere man and was greatly dissatisfied

* Dudgeon's "Life of Hahnemann," 1854.
† Ameke. "History of Homœopathy," p. 59.

with the vague and unsatisfactory medical knowledge of the day. Perhaps in no better way can his feelings on the subject be described than by presenting a letter written to Hufeland regarding this period. This letter is published in Lesser Writings under the title: "Letter to a Physician of High Standing on the Great Necessity of a Regeneration in Medicine."* "It was agony for me to walk always in darkness, with no other light than that which could be derived from books, when I had to heal the sick, and to prescribe, according to such or such an hypothesis concerning diseases, substances which owed their place in the Materia Medica to an arbitrary decision. I could not conscientiously treat the unknown morbid conditions of my suffering brethren by these unknown medicines, which being very active substances, may (unless applied with the most rigorous exactness, which the physician can not exercise, because their peculiar effects have not yet been examined) so easily occasion death, or produce new affections and chronic maladies, often more difficult to remove than the original disease. To become thus the murderer or the tormentor of my brethren was to me an idea so frightful and overwhelming, that soon after my marriage, I renounced the practice of medicine, that I might no longer incur the risk of doing injury, and I engaged exclusively in chemistry, and in literary occupations. But I became a father, serious diseases threatened my beloved children, my flesh and blood. My scruples redoubled when I saw that I could afford them no certain relief." He continues in telling Hufeland his feelings regarding the uncertainty of medical practice, and says that he felt sure that God must have ordained some certain method of healing the sick. The Rev. Thos. Everest, in a letter to Dr. Rose Cormack, says:†

"After passing through the usual studies with great credit to himself he took his degree and began to practice as a medical man. It soon struck me, he said to me, that I was called upon to admit in the practice of medicine a great deal that was not proved. If I was called to attend a patient I was to collect his symptoms, and next to infer from these symptoms that a certain internal condition of the organs existed, and then to select such

*Brit. Jour. Hom., Vol. 1, p. 105. Lesser Writings, New York. Allg. Anzeiger, July 14, 1808.
†Russell's "Homœopathy in 1851," p. 305.

a remedy as the medical authorities asserted would be useful under such circumstances. But it is very evident that the argument is most inconclusive and that room was thus left for many serious errors, and so I determined to investigate the whole matter for myself from the very beginning."

Hufeland, whom Hahnemann calls the Nestor of Medicine, was always a friend to Hahnemann. He allowed him to publish his new opinions in his Medical Journal. When, in 1826 and in 1830, Hufeland himself wrote an essay on Homœopathy, which he published in his journal, he was honest and fair to Hahnemann in his deductions. He says:* "I was first induced to notice Homœopathy, because I deemed it undignified to treat the new system with ridicule and contempt. Besides I had a long time esteemed the author for his earlier productions, and for his sterling contributions to the science of medicine; and I had also observed the names of several respectable men, who, in no way blinded by prejudice, had recognized the facts of the science as true. I need only enumerate President Von Wolf, of Warsaw; Medical Councillor Rau, of Giessen, and Medical Councillor Widmann, of Munich. I then made several successful experiments with Homœopathic medicine, which necessarily still further excited my attention to the subject, and favourably convinced me that Homœopathia could not be thrown aside with contempt, but was worthy of a rigid investigation."

Hufeland then in a dispassionate and careful manner discusses the question at length; predicts the gradual amalgamation of the more liberal members of the two schools; and says in closing, that: "The peculiar and important problem for Homœopathy is to search for and find new specific medicines."

"At this period," says Rapou,† "there was a complete anarchy in the domain of therapeutics. Theories Hippocratico-vitalistic, Galenic, Mathematical, Chemical, Humoral, Electro-Galvanic, formed an inextricable tissue of variable opinions. Hahnemann had abstained from a search for therapeutical indications in this mass of hazardous theories. He had adopted a simple medication, partly expectant, that corresponded more fully with his ideal of the art of healing.

---

*British Journal Homœopathy. Vol. 16, p. 179.

†Histoire de la doctrine medicale Homeopathique, Paris, 1847. Vol. 2, p. 295.

CHAPTER IX.

GOMMERN—LIFE AT DRESDEN—LITERARY WORK—THE WINE
TEST—SLUMBER SONG.

Hahnemann now used only the remedies called "specifics,"
whose effects were in a measure known. Their physiological
action was, however, but little understood. The schools were
not in accord. One school would prescribe for a given disease a
drug that another would unreservedly repudiate. It was known
that a certain drug in a certain case would produce a certain
effect. But the combination of drugs in vogue prevented this
property from being perfectly ascertained. His dissatisfaction
increased. He looked to the medical knowledge of the day for
a reliable method of curing his patients, and met nothing but
doubt and disappointment.*

One can readily understand that to Hahnemann, the translator, the philologist, accustomed to the arbitrary rules govern-
ing language, this laxity and confusion in the laws of medicine
must have been a continual source of annoyance.

Let it be borne in mind that he was a thoroughly well-posted
physician, skilled both in theory and practice, better read in the
various notions of the medical books of the time than most of his
fellows. Besides, his position as "Stadtphysikus" was an influential one.† In Germany the pharmaceutical chemists are
under the control and supervision of a medical officer called the
"Stadtphysikus," who must necessarily be a well-posted medical
man. He visits the chemists' shops and drug stores of his
neighborhood at stated intervals to inspect the drugs. The fact
of his holding this position is proof enough of his ability as a
physician.

He was also a surgeon; his treatment of necrosis by scraping
the bone proves that. He was a prominent physician of the
time, and yet we find him honestly saying, so little confidence
had he in the prevailing methods, that most of his patients
would have done as well without his aid.

The inconsistencies and fallacies of the day fell so far below
his ideal of a possible healing art that he was loath to continue
in practice. He had dear ones depending upon his labors, and

*Hom. World, Vol. X., p. 132. †Burnett's "Ecce Medicus," p. 133.

his position as health officer gave him a certain means of support, and on the other hand, he was a conscientious man, and remembered the teachings of his good father, never to accept anything in science until it had been proven to be true by investigation. After some time of doubt his honesty won the battle, and he resolved to investigate for himself; to discover if God had not indeed given some certain law by means of which the diseases of mankind could be cured with certainty.

Although his heart was absorbed in the desire to do good, and his love for medical science was very great, his ideas of right prevented him from continuing longer in practice.

Consequently he resigned his position at Gommern, in the autumn of 1784. He, in his autobiography, says that he located at Gommern towards the close of the year 1781, and that he remained there for two and three quarter years, marrying soon after entering upon his duties as town doctor. The parish register of Dessau gives December, 1782, as the time of his marriage; Albrecht also mentions 1782, as the bridal year. According to this, Hahnemann must have been at Gommern for some months before his wedding occurred. Living two years and nine months at Gommern, he must have departed for Dresden in the fall of 1784.

It has been asserted that Hahnemann was compelled to relinquish at this time the practice of medicine, because he was unable to earn a living. This, however, is not true. He had the important position of town physician, with its certain income; he had also other practice until he absolutely refused to treat those who had long been his patients, and besides this his translations brought him in a further sum. Had he wished he could have remained in Gommern, for means for his ample living were assured. According to the statements made by his contemporaries and by himself, he resigned his position, and left Gommern simply because he had become disgusted with the errors and uncertainties of the prevalent methods of medical practice, and wished earnestly to seek for some better method. He reduced himself and his family to want for conscience sake.*

Despite the perplexities of his professional life, Hahnemann enjoyed a happy home life; he had his young wife and his little Henrietta to gladden his heart. That he was a tender and

---

* "Ecce Medicus," p. 40.

affectionate father, is well shown by the following slumber
song, or lullaby, which he composed for his baby, while living
at Gommern.   It may thus be translated, and still retain all the
sweetness and force of the original German :

> Sleep daughter, gently !
> The yellow bird chirps in the wood;
> Lightly it jumps o'er the ice and the snow,
> And quietly sleeps on bare branches—so,
> Gently sleep.*

As has been stated, Hahnemann located at Dresden in the
autumn of 1784; he remained in that city until the time of
Michaelmas (last of September), 1789.   Dudgeon says that the
latter portion of this time, he passed in the village of Lockowitz,
near Dresden.†

The change from the dead and alive Gommern, whose inhabitants never before had a doctor and did not wish for one, to magnificent Dresden, the home of the arts and sciences, must have
been, to our scholar, very delightful,   Dresden, at this period,
was a fortified city, the residence of the Elector of Saxony, and
contained many handsome buildings, among which were the
Elector's palace; the great cathedral; the gallery of paintings,
rich in the masterpieces of Correggio; the Academy of Archi-
tecture, Sculpture and Painting; and many fine private mansions.

There was also a Japanese palace, which was a vast museum
of valuable articles of *virtu*, among its treasures being a collection of foreign and Saxon china and porcelain.   The first and
second stories of this palace were devoted to the Electoral
Library, that had been made up of several smaller collections
and at the time of which we write contained some 140,000 volumes.   This library was one of the richest in Germany in historical and antiquarian works.

Dresden, with its wealth and culture, with its massive bridge
spanning the swift-flowing Elbe and uniting the old and new
town—princely Dresden, gave to Hahnemann ample opportunity for the life of scholarly delights that he had so greatly
desired.

He did not practice medicine, but devoted himself to his translations from the French, English and Italian.   He also pursued
with renewed zeal the study of his favorite chemistry.   He be-

---

*"Biographisches Denkmal," p. 111.   †"Biography of Hahnemann,"
1854, p. 21.

came a very great friend of the town physician, one Dr. Wagner, who gave him valuable assistance in the study of medical jurisprudence, introduced him to the hospital, and, on account of his own illness, obtained magisterial consent to his appointment to the charge of the town hospitals for a year, placing all the infirmaries under his charge. It must be remembered that the Hahnemann who was chosen to take the place for the time of the highest medical officer in that country was no unknown young physician. He was well known to the world of medicine and of science; his chemical researches and his masterly translations of scientific books had also spread his fame beyond his own country.

He also formed the friendship of the celebrated philologist, John Christopher Adelung, the superintendent of the Electoral Library. There was much similarity of thought between these distinguished scholars. But a short time before Adelung had resigned a position of honor at Erfurt for opinion's sake, as Hahnemann had for a like reason just done at Gommern.* Like Hahnemann, Adelung was a man of great industry; he possessed a vast knowledge of languages, had composed much, and was a close student, devoting himself, it is said, for fourteen hours daily to study. To show the extent of his learning it may be mentioned that he was the compiler of a book in five large volumes, Berlin, 1806–17, which is a history of all the known languages and dialects of the world, with an account of all the books printed in or relating to them; it is known as the "Mithridates" of Adelung.

The use of this extensive library, which his friend Adelung granted freely to Hahnemann, was of great benefit in his studies. Dassdorf, the librarian, also became his friend and greatly assisted him. During this delightful literary life Hahnemann met the author and experimentalist Blumenbach, and the brilliant but ill-fated chemist Lavoisier, who in the reign of terror at Paris became a victim to the guillotine.

Happy in the congenial company of these talented men, at home in the quietness of the great library, with all his desires for knowledge gratified, the four years of Dresden life passed very speedily.

His son Frederick was born in Dresden, in 1786; and his second daughter, Wilhelmina.

---

* "Biography of Hahneman," *Hom. World*, Vol. 10. p. 134.

Here he made the following important translations:

In 1787, Demachy's "Art of Manufacturing Vinegar," from the French; in this giving many original notes and an original appendix. The same year he made another French translation, on the "Detection of the Purity and Adulteration of Drugs," by J. B. Van den Sande. Van den Sande was an apothecary at Brussels, who had in 1784, published a book with the above title.

Hahnemann, in translating it into the German so added to, and amended it that the main part really was his work. All Hahnemann's directions are as usual complete and careful. His tests for drugs are concise and correct. He introduces many new discoveries and suggestions for the detection of adulteration. He shows also earnest efforts to determine the limits of the activity of substances and their solubility. In all his suggestions he is exceedingly accurate. He complains of the untrustworthiness of pharmaceutical preparations "which no conscientious doctor could prescribe," and asks, "on what can a doctor rely?" He imparts many important chemical discoveries. It is in this publication that he first gives his celebrated wine test. Wine was often sweetened by the addition of sugar of lead which caused colics, emaciation and death. The Wirtemberg wine test, in use at this time, was very uncertain; and by it iron and lead could not be distinguished. After exhaustively discussing the subject, he presents the following: "Acidulated sulphureted hydrogen water precipitates arsenic, lead, antimony, silver, mercury, copper, tin and bismuth, present in a suspected fluid. By the addition of the acid, metals of the iron group to be tested remain in solution."

This is Hahnemann's wine test, and is to-day used in the laboratory of the chemist as a test for metals. With this he detected lead in a solution of the proportion of 1 to 30,000. This test was greatly praised by the chemical and scientific journals of the day. Trommsdorff's *Journal of Pharmacy* stated that ignorance of Hahnemann's Wine Test was damning evidence of the incompetence of many apothecaries.[*]

In 1789 he translated the "History of the Lives of Abelard and Heloise" from the English of Sir Joseph Barrington. This translation was mentioned by the critics as being correct and fluent, and of value to romantic history.

[*] "Ameke," pp. 21-29.

CHAPTER X.

LIFE AT DRESDEN—ORIGINAL WRITINGS—CHEMICAL DISCOVER-
IES—SOLUBLE MERCURY—DEPARTURE FOR LEIPSIC.

Hahnemann, during his stay at Dresden, published also the following original books. In 1786, a masterly work on "Poisoning by Arsenic: Its Treatment and Judicial Investigation." This book marked a new era in the analysis and best modes of detection of arsenical poisoning. This he calls his firstling, and dedicates it "To the Majesty of the good Kaizer Joseph."

In it he devotes space to discussion of the limit of the activity of the *Arsenic*. He opposes the unregulated sale of *Arsenic* "fever powders," and advances plans for the prescription of poisons, that have since been adopted. He suggests that there be a locked room for poisons in the drug store; that only the proprietor or some responsible representative should have the key; that record should be kept in a book of the name and address of each purchaser, who should also sign this record, which should be open to the inspection of a Board of Examiners, yearly. In his patient research he quotes 861 passages from 389 different authors and books, in different languages and belonging to different ages, and gives accurately both volume and page.*

By means of Hahnemann's book new and better modes of analyzing *Arsenic* were introduced into medical jurisprudence. It received praise from the leading scientists of the day.

Hahnemann's opinion in regard to the medicine of the time is fully shown by the following statement published in the preface of this book:

"A number of causes—I dare not to count them up—have for centuries been dragging down the dignity of that divine science of practical medicine, and have converted it into a miserable grabbing after bread, a mere cloaking of symptoms, a degrading prescription trade, a very God-forgotten handiwork, so that the real physicians are hopelessly jumbled together with a heap of befrilled medicine mongers. How seldom is it possible for a straightforward man by means of his great knowledge of the sciences, and by his talents to raise himself above the crowd of

* Ameke, p. 17.

medicasters, and to throw such a pure, bright sheen upon the Healing Art at whose altar he ministers that it becomes impossible even for the common herd to mistake a glorious, benign evening star for mere vapoury skyfall. How seldom is such a phenomenon seen, and hence how difficult it is to obtain for a purified science of medicine a renewal of her musty letters of nobility."*

At this time he was greatly devoted to chemistry, and contributed, during the years 1787–88–89, the following important essays to Crell's *Annals of Chemistry*. This journal was the first to be devoted to chemistry in Germany, and Hahnemann was a contributor from 1787 to 1794. "On the Difficulty of Preparing Soda from Potash and Kitchen Salt." At this time soda prepared by means of the methods known, cost nine shillings a pound. Hahnemann by means of potash and by crystallization at different temperatures obtained it from salt much cheaper. "On the Influence of Certain Gases in the Fermentation of Wine." The method for the rapid manufacture of vinegar, discovered in 1833, and at this time in use, was to let alcohol rapidly run over chips of beech wood. In this essay Hahnemann announces his discovery that the influence of the oxygen of the air will rapidly produce the desired result. He tried the effect of three gases on wine. He prepared three bottles, each containing four ounces of wine, In one he placed oxygen gas; in another, nitrogen; in the other, carbonic acid. He sealed them, kept them for two months at the same temperature, shaking each thirty times a day. Upon examination, he found that the wine in the oxygen bottle had become strong vinegar. "On the Wine Test for Iron and Lead," "On Bile and Gall Stones." In this he exposed the fresh bile from a man who had been shot while in health, to the effect of certain salts, in order to test their value in liver diseases. "Essay on a New Agent in the Prevention of Putrefaction." He found that lunar caustic is an antiseptic in a solution of 1 to 1000, and observed antiseptic effects from a solution of 1 to 100,000. "Unsuccessful Experiments," "Letter to Crell on Baryta," "Discovery of a New Constituent in Plumbago," "Observations on the Astringent Principles of Plants."

We come now to another important treatise, the "Exact Mode

*J. C. Burnett's "Ecce Medicus," p. 33. London, 1881.

of Preparing the Soluble Mercury, 1789." Chemists had for a
long time been searching for a preparation of *Mercury* less
corrosive than the sublimate, muriate or sulphate, then in use.
Hahnemann, by the use of nitric acid and iron, at last obtained
the desired result.   Gren, who had previously attacked Hahnemann on his test for metals, said of this: "The problem of Herr
Macques to obtain a preparation of *Mercury* which is at once
very soluble in the acids present in the body, and yet free from
corrosive properties, is fully solved by Herr Hahnemann's *Mercurius solubilis.*"   This preparation has been greatly praised by
chemists and physicians.

  "Instructions Concerning Venereal Diseases, Together with a
New Mercurial Preparation."   In this he gives instructions concerning the use of *Mercury*, and treats of its effects on the body,.
known as "mercurial fever."   This book was written at Lockowitz, near Dresden, in 1788, and was published at Leipsic, in
1789.   He also published several other papers about this time
on the subject of *Mercury* and its relation to syphilis.

  But the insatiable thirst for extended knowledge still impelled
Hahnemann, and in the latter part of September, 1789, he removed to Leipsic "in order to be nearer to the fountain of science."

  It is well to consider the next words of his autobiography very
carefully: "Here I quietly witness the Providence which Destiny assigns to each of my days, the number of which lies in her
hand."   Only ten years before he had received his degree as
physician, and during that time had become so dissatisfied with
medical methods that he preferred to devote all his time to literary life, continuing in the meantime his chemical labors and investigations.   In this time he had discovered very many valuable
facts in chemistry, had translated several scientific books into the
German, and had given to the world a number of essays on important subjects.   It is interesting in this connection to note the effect.
of the life of the man during these ten years upon his future.   It
would seem that the days passed in the library of Baron Bruckenthal, the practice in Hungary, the hours of doubt and uncertainty
in sleepy Gommern, the delightful intercourse in scholarly Dresden, all became means to develop and equip Hahnemann for the
brilliant discoveries that he was soon destined to make.   The
translation concerning the adulteration of drugs led him to doubt

the good faith of the pharmacists, and his knowledge gained while inspector of drugs, of their substitutions and fraudulent practices probably went far in the future to favor his desire to prepare and dispense his own medicines. And the hours of painstaking necessary in translating were the means of giving his mind the needful exactness for the future mathematical law of healing God was to allow him to discover. How little did he yet understand the "Providence that Destiny was to assign to his days !" The long years of persecution; the quiet of the garden of Kœthen; the luxury of life in the gayest city in the world; and the peaceful end with the knowledge that he "had not lived in vain !"

CHAPTER XI.

BELOVED LEIPSIC—CULLEN'S MATERIA MEDICA—FIRST EXPERIMENTS WITH PERUVIAN BARK—FIRST PROVINGS UPON THE HEALTHY.

Once more established in his beloved Leipsic, he resumed his translations. In 1790 he published a translation from the English: "Ryan on Diseases of the Lungs," and the same year, from the Italian: "Fabbroni on the Art of Making Wine on Rational Principles," adding, as was his custom, many notes. Crell's *Annalen* says:* "Well merited applause this work has received. Besides the fact that this translation is faithful and successful, Herr Hahnemann has added precious notes which expand and elucidate Fabbroni's principles; he has thus enhanced the value of the work."

We now come to the translation of a very important book, from which must be dated the discovery of the Law of the Similars, Cullen's "Materia Medica." It has been asked why Hahnemann at this time *happened* to translate this particular book, and it has been asserted that he used it as a blind to foist on the world his particular theories. It is not probable that when he commenced upon "Cullen" Hahnemann had any particular medical theories, but only a growing disgust for the medical fallacies of the day. This is clearly evidenced by his writings at that time. It is not to be wondered at that he should translate the work at that time. He was translating for money, for the booksellers

*Ameke, page 40.

and publishers of Leipsic, and it is not likely that he selected the books which he was to translate.

Dr. Cullen was an authority on the subject of the Materia Medica of his day, an experienced lecturer, a talented chemist, and a brilliant and popular teacher in Edinburgh. Naturally the Germans wished to learn of his new and peculiar theories regarding disease, as well as to obtain the use of his Materia Medica, that at this time was a standard work.*

Hahnemann was the most accomplished translator of medical works of the time, and what more natural than that the task should be given to him. Cullen published the first edition of this book, in London, in 1773. Another edition was issued in 1789, in two volumes, and it was this edition that Hahnemann used in his translation. In this book, Volume II., Cullen devotes about twenty pages to *Cortex Peruvianis* (Peruvian Bark), giving its therapeutical uses in the treatment of intermittent and remittent fevers, advises its use to prevent the chill, and gives minute directions for the safest period of the disease in which to use it. Hahnemann was impressed with the use of this drug, with which he as a physician had before been familiar. Something in the manner in which Cullen wrote decided Hahnemann to experiment with it upon himself and to see what effect it would have upon a person in perfect health. The result of this experiment will be given in Hahnemann's own words. In the translation of William Cullen's "Materia Medica," Leipsic, Schweikert, 1790, page 108 of Volume II., appears the following foot note by Hahnemann: "By combining the strongest bitters and the strongest astringents, one can obtain a compound which, in small doses, possesses much more of both these properties than the bark, and yet no specific for fever will ever come of such a compound. This the author (Cullen) ought to have accounted for. This will, perhaps, not so easily be discovered for explaining to us their action, in the absence of the *Cinchona* principle."

"Substances which excite a kind of fever, as very strong coffee, pepper, *Aconite*, *Ignatia*, *Arsenic*, extinguish the types of the fever. I took by way of experiment, twice a day, four drachms of good *China*. My feet, finger ends, etc., at first became cold; I grew languid and drowsy; then my heart began to palpitate, and my pulse grew hard and small; intolerable anxiety, trem-

---

*Cullen died in 1790.

bling (but without cold rigor), prostration throughout all my limbs; then pulsation in my head, redness of my cheeks, thirst, and, in short, all these symptoms, which are ordinarily characteristic of intermittent fever, made their appearance, one after the other, yet without the peculiar chilly, shivering rigor."

"Briefly, even those symptoms which are of regular occurrence and especially characteristic—as the stupidity of mind, the kind of rigidity in all the limbs, but, above all the numb, disagreeable sensation, which seems to have its seat in the periosteum, over every bone in the body—all these make their appearance. This paroxysm lasted two or three hours each time, and recurred *if I repeated this dose, not otherwise;* I discontinued it, and was in good health."* The next note, occurring but a few pages beyond, in the German translation, is as follows:

" Had he (Cullen) found traces in bark of a power to excite an artificial antagonistic fever, he certainly would not have persisted so obstinately in his mode of explanation."

Further on Cullen says: † "Although I would not rigourously insist on the employment of a single dose near to the time of accession, yet I am strongly of opinion, that the nearer the exhibition is brought to that time, it will be the more certainly effectual. To explain this not commonly understood; we must remark, that the effects of the bark on the human body are not very durable. I have had opportunities of observing that a considerable quantity of bark given, was not sufficient to prevent a relapse in a few days after." Hahnemann makes the following foot note about this: " How comes it that the effects of bark are so short lived, as is indeed the case, if it be not true that bark, besides the astringent and tonic bitter propensities ascribed to it by writers, especially by the author, possesses another power, (that of exciting fever of a peculiar kind)?" ‡

A very graphic description of these experiments of Hahnemann is given in "Samuel Hahnemann, a Biographical Study,"‖ as follows: "To judge of the physiological effect of bark he took several doses as prescribed by the profession for ague. The re-

*Brit. Jour. Hom., Vol. 24, p. 207. Ameke, p. 103.

†Cullen's "Treatise of the Materia Medica. Edinburgh, 1789 Vol. 2, p. 64.

‡ Brit. Jour. Hom., Vol. 24, p. 215.

‖ Hom. World, Vol. 10, p. 234. 1875.

sult was that in his previously healthy system there occurred
decided paroxysms resembling those of ague.   The experiment
had carried him farther than he anticipated.   It had taught him
not only the exact physiological effects of bark; it had shown
him that those effects were apparently the same as the symptoms
of the disease it was given with undeniable success to cure.
Does Bark, then, he asked, produce the same symptoms as it
removes?   Does it alike produce and cure Ague?   It is called a
Specific.*   Is the Specific curing power of drugs founded on
such a principle?   Do they all uniformly excite a counterfeit
disease to that which they remedy?   Drug after drug, specific
after specific was tested on himself and on healthy friends with
one unvarying result—each remedy of recognized specific power
excited a spurious disease resembling that for which it was considered specific.   But many more symptoms than those diag-
nostic of any one disease resulted from almost every medicine,
and aroused a hope in the experimenter's mind of specifically
treating a greater number of diseases than had ever been so
treated before.   Besides discovering many valuable medicinal
phenomena undreamt of, he verified his discoveries and observations by ransacking the volumes of recorded experiments on
Materia Medica and the whole history of poisoning.   The effect
of his investigations was not, therefore, a blind leap from one
false theory to another which might be equally fallacious and
more mischievous than the former one.   Six years were expended in proving drugs and verifying his principle before proclaiming it to the world."

Regarding these first experiments in proving drugs on the
healthy, Everest says: † "Inasmuch as the action of the same
substance varied according to the age, sex, and idiosyncrasy of
the subject to whom it was administered, it was not considered
sufficient to experiment on a few individuals.   His own family
were all pressed into the service, and each substance was tried
in various doses on many different persons, under every possible
variety of circumstance, and beneath the immediate inspection of
Hahnemann himself."

----

* Well known to physicians at that time.

† "Popular View of Homœopathy," p. 85. New York, 1842.

CHAPTER XII.

POVERTY—CONTINUED LITERARY LABORS—POWERS OF PERUVIAN
BARK—FAITH IN GOD'S GOODNESS.

Hahnemann at this time, 1790, was poor; he had a growing
family, and nothing to depend upon but his translations, to
which, and to his chemical researches, he devoted all his time.
The Rev. Mr. Everest, who was a personal friend of Hahnemann during the latter years of his life, and who certainly knew
from his own lips somewhat of his earlier years, says:* "It was
in the midst of poverty, in one little room which contained his
whole family, in a corner, separated from the rest of them by a
curtain, under every discouragement, and with a hungry family
to maintain by hard drudgery, in the intervals of his own investigations, that he set himself to his task.   It may, perhaps,
give a better idea of the man himself, if I mention, that when
I once asked him why he smoked he replied: 'Oh, it's an idle
habit, contracted when I had to sit up every other night, in
order to get bread for my children, while I was pursuing my own
investigations by day.' I then learned on farther inquiry, that
having resigned his practice as a medical man, he was compelled
to earn a living by translating for the booksellers, and had, to
enable him to continue his investigations, adopted the plan of
sitting up the whole of every other night."
Thus it may be seen that Hahnemann was greatly in earnest
to thus follow his new theory, and endeavor to find some better
and surer method of healing the sick than was at that time
known. Certainly his self-denying life is sufficient answer to
the half lies of his detractors, ancient and modern. It was the
effort of a single-minded and pure-hearted man to discover the
truth in the manner that his father had long before taught
him in this maxim: "Never take anything for granted, nor
receive anything in any science as a truth, until you have investigated it for yourself."
During the year 1791, Hahnemann received honors from two
important societies. He was elected a member of the Oekono-
mische Gesellschaft of Leipzig, and also Fellow of the Academy
of Sciences of Mayence.

*Russell's "Homœopathy in 1851," p. 305. Edinburgh and London, 1852.

His discoveries in chemistry, and his wonderful knowledge of medical subjects were attracting the attention of the scientific men of his time.

During the year, 1791, he translated Grigg's "Advice to the Female Sex;" Arthur Young's "Annals of Agriculture," in two volumes; Rigby's "Chemical Observations of Sugar;" Monro's "Medical and Pharmaceutical Chemistry," two volumes, from the English; and Metherie's "Essay on Pure Air," from the French. *Crell, in mentioning this new translation in the *Annalen*, says : "The translator is Dr. Hahnemann, a man who has rendered many services to science both by his own writings on chemistry, and by his excellent translations of important foreign works. His services have been already recognized, but deserve to be still more so."

He, also, during this year, wrote original articles for Crell's *Annalen* on "The Insolubility of Metals," and on the "Best Means of Preventing Salivation, and the Destructive Effects of Mercury."

Monro in his "Chemico-Pharmaceutical Materia Medica," also mentions the *Cortex Peruvianis*, devoting to it about twenty pages of the second volume, and Hahnemann again adds original notes as follows :

† Monro having said: "I have seen people who within a month have taken from eight to ten ounces of it (*Cortex Peruv.*) without the least good effect; but who on the other hand were cured when they took two ounces in a single day, and kept up this dose for two or three days successively."

To this Hahnemann made the following answer: " Nor is this quantity necessary. The patient is not overloaded, and an equally good result is attained in regular intermittent fever if, shortly before the expected attack, one or two good doses are administered; for instance, two hours and one hour before the approach of the paroxysm, from one and a half to two drachms in each dose of good bark in substance. All previous doses given long before the attack are of little or no avail in checking it. Should the first attack not appear, then let the same treatment be followed with respect to the second, and reduce the dose to half at the time the third may be expected."

*Ameke, p. 40,
† *Brit. Jour. Hom.*, Vol. 24, p. 218.

"If, as Cullen and others suppose, the anti-pyretic power of bark proceeded from its tonic properties, it would be more to be depended on to cure intermittent fever in the first mode of exhibition than in the second, since the system must be certainly more strengthened by taking ten ounces in a month than by taking one or two ounces in five or six doses immediately before the attack; but this is not the case. If, however, my opinion, more circumstantially worked out in the remarks on Cullen's 'Materia Medica,' be admitted, 'that the bark, besides its tonic property, overrules and subdues intermittent fever by exciting a fever, peculiar to itself, and of short duration,' then it will not be difficult to solve this paradox. All other substances which excite antagonistic irritability and artificial fever, check intermittent fever, if administered shortly before the attack, as specifically as bark, only they are not so certain in their operation. Of this kind are *Ipecacuanha*, taken dry, *Ignatia*, *Arsenic*, Pepper, Wine, and Brandy, a concentrated infusion of several ounces of burnt coffee with lemon juice, and so on, none of which belong in the least to tonic remedies. The first (*Ipecacuanha*) is even useful in cases where bark has been already tried in vain, or with injury to the patient. Besides, there are medicines much more bitter and astringent than bark, for instance, the powder of gall apples mixed with gentian root, and still the bark is preferred for checking intermittent fever; indeed, all bitter plants excite, in large doses, some artificial fever, however small, and thus occasionally drive away intermittent fever by themselves. I have stated my opinion on this subject and would add that this power to excite a peculiar fever appears the more probable from the well known fact that, in common with everything which stimulates the action of the heart and arteries, it increases the heat, even in the mildest attacks, if administered during the hot stage itself, especially where fulness of blood predominates."

The next remark on the bark disease can be found in the "Organon." There is also a note in the third volume of the 1825 edition of the *Materia Medica Pura* regarding the fever-exciting power of *Cinchona*.

It may be mentioned that Hahnemann was not the first to translate "Cullen's Materia Medica" into German. In 1781, Dr. Geo. W. Chr. Consbruch made the translation: It was pub-

lished in Leipzig by Weygand. A second edition was issued in
1790.*

So much has been written about this discovery of the intermittent fever producing powers of *Quinine*, and so many mis-
representations made of Hahnemann's position in the matter that
it has been deemed wise to make these quotations at length.
"Hahnemann never said that bark could produce intermittent
fever in a healthy person, but that the artificial, antagonistic fever
produced by bark is attended with symptoms similar to those
which appear in the intermittent fever."†

In Hahnemann's proving of *China* the names of twenty-one
of his pupils are mentioned as provers.‡

Hahnemann was not the first to try drugs on the healthy organism. Anton Stoerck, on June 23, 1760, rubbed fresh *Stram-
ony* on his hands to see if, as the botanists said, it would inebri-
ate him.‖ It did not, and he then rubbed some in a mortar, and,
sleeping in the same room, got a headache. He then made an
extract, placing it on his tongue. He wished to know if the
drug could be safely used as a remedy. Stoerck says that if
Stramonium disturbs the senses and produces mental derangement in persons who are healthy, it might very easily be administered to maniacs for the purpose of restoring the senses by
effecting a change of ideas. Crumpe, an Irish physician, tried
drugs on the healthy, and published a book in London on the
effects of *Opium*, in 1793, three years after the first experiments
of Hahnemann. Hahnemann refers in the "Organon" to the
Danish surgeon, Stahl, who says: "I am convinced that diseases
are subdued by agents which produce a similar affection."§

Haller, of the University of Gottingen, wrote:¶ "In the first

---

*Dr. Wilhelm Cullen's, Professors der medizinischen Praxis in Edin-
burg Materia Medica, oder Lehre von den Rahrungs-und Arzneymitteln.
Nach dem neuen und vom Verfasser allein fur acht enerkannten Original.
Zweite Auflage. Aus dem Englischen mit nothigen Zusassen herausgegeben von G. W. C. Consbruch, Doktor der Arzneywissenschaft in Bielefeld
in Westphalen. Mit Chursachsischer Freiheit. Leipzig: Weygand. 1890.
80 pp. 609.

†*Brit. Jour. Hom.*, Vol. 24, p. 218.

‡*Brit. Jour. Hom.*, Vol. 24, p. 232.

‖ "Ecce Medicus," pp. 91–4.

§ "Organon," New York, 4th ed., p. 91.

¶ *Monthly Hom. Review*, Vol. 10, p. 584.

place the remedy is to be tried upon the healthy body, without any foreign substance mixed with it; a small dose is to be taken; attention is to be directed to every effort produced by it on the pulse, the temperature, the respiration, the secretions."

The first portion of the "Organon" is devoted by Hahnemann to citations from medical writers in whose experiments the law of the similars is clearly forshadowed. Several *almost* reached the practical deductions from this law. Hahnemann alone possessed the necessary medical and chemical knowledge to follow out and develop the vague ideas of his medical fathers. The years of study in the vast libraries were beginning to bear fruit. The law was there, had been from the first; the mind to grasp that law was needed. Hahnemann always modestly said that his discovery was God's gift to him for the benefit of mankind.

During the year 1792 Hahnemann published an article in Crell's *Annalen* on the "Preparation of Glauber's Salts," and also on the "Art of Wine Testing." He also wrote the first part of the "Friend to Health." This consists of a series of short essays on hygienic subjects, and will well repay careful study at the present day. It may be found in the "Lesser Writings."

He did not now practice medicine; his translations gave him but a meagre support; he had a growing family, and some time, probably in the year 1791, poverty compelled him to remove from Leipsic to the little village of Stotteritz. Burnett says of this time: *"He there clad himself in the garb of the very poor, wore clogs of wood, and helped his wife in the heavy work of the house, and kneaded his bread with his own hands."

His children fell sick; the future looked very dark to the honest seeker after truth. He had lost faith in medicine. Of this time he writes: †"Where shall I look for aid, sure aid? sighed the disconsolate father on hearing the moaning of his dear, inexpressibly dear sick children. The darkness of night and the dreariness of a desert all around me; no prospect of relief for my oppressed paternal heart."

*"Ecce Medicus," p 43.
†Letter to Hufeland, "Lesser Writings," New York, p. 513.

CHAPTER XIII.

FURTHER EXPERIMENTS—INSANITY OF KLOCKENBRING—ASYLUM AT GEORGENTHAL—GENTLE METHODS WITH THE INSANE.

It is to be remembered that during the two years following the translation of Cullen, Hahnemann continued to experiment upon himself and on his family and certain of his friends with different substances. But he had not as yet tested the truth of his new principle on the sick. The insanity of Klockenbring gave him this opportunity.

In 1792 he went to Georgenthal, in the Principality of Gotha, to take charge of an asylum for the insane and to treat Herr Klockenbring. There are several different accounts of this period of his life. Hartmann says: * "The opportunity for confirming his opinion was soon afforded, especially in the hospital for the insane at Georgenthal. This institution had been erected by Duke Ernst of Gotha, and was situated in one of the most beautiful portions of the Principality of Gotha, at the foot of the Thuringian Forest, three leagues distant from Gotha, the capital city. He was appointed manager by the Duke, and opened the institution in the beginning of August, 1792. Here he cured, among others, the chancellor's private secretary, who had become insane."

There is some diversity of opinion as to whether this asylum was in operation before this time, or whether he was first called to the Duke as his private physician. It is most likely that it was not opened until the insanity of Klockenbring made it a necessity, and it also seems probable that he was the only patient treated there. Hahnemann himself says, in his description of this gentleman's case: "After having been for several years much occupied with diseases of the most tedious and desperate character in general, and of all sorts of venereal maladies, cachexies, hypochondriasis, and insanity in particular, with the assistance of the excellent reigning Duke, I established three years ago a convalescent asylum for patients afflicted with such disorders, in Georgenthal near Gotha."†

*Allgem. Hom. Zeitung, Vol. 26, p. 145.
†"Lesser Writings of Hahnemann," New York, p. 243.

In the *Monthly Homœopathic Review*, London, 1887, the following account of this important episode in Hahnemann's life is given:*

In the latter part of 1791 or the first part of 1792 a friend of Hahnemann, one R. Z. Becker, was the editor and proprietor of a paper called the *Reichanzeiger*, which was, while Hahnemann lived in Gotha, called *Der Anzeiger*, and was a newspaper used in discussions among physicians or in communicating the one with the other. It was afterwards called *Der Reichanzeiger*, and in 1806 was called *Der Allgemeine Anzeiger der Deutschen*. Hahnemann frequently wrote articles for its columns.

An article was published in this paper describing, at Hahnemann's suggestion, a model asylum for the treatment, by gentle methods, of the insane of the higher classes of society. The wife of F. A. Klockenbring, the Hanoverian Minister of Police, Secretary to the Chancellery of Hanover, saw this article and was by the editor referred to Hahnemann. For about five years Klockenbring had, from his severe labors and his fast life, developed a great eccentricity. In the winter of 1791–92 he became the subject of a lampoon by the German dramatist, Kotzebue, in which he was named "Bahrdt with the iron forehead." On account of this he became violently insane and had been treated by Dr. Wichmann, the Hanoverian Court Physician, whom Hahnemann calls "one of the greatest physicians of our age," for some time without benefit. Madame Klockenbring was so much impressed with this article and with an interview with Hahnemann that she desired him to take charge of the case of her husband. To this he consented, but as he had no place in which to treat this violent madman, and as no doubt the Duke of Gotha was also interested in the cure of so distinguished a man as much as was Hahnemann himself, the following arrangement was made: The Duke gave up to Hahnemann a wing of his hunting castle at Georgenthal, at the foot of the Thuringer Wald, nine miles from Gotha, and caused it to be fitted up as an asylum.

Hahnemann in his description of this case† speaks of the previous eccentricity of the patient, of its causes, and of the effect of the lampoon, acting upon a mind already shaken. In the

Monthly Hom. Review, London, Vol. 31, p. 544. (Dr. Dudgeon.) *Hom. World*, London, Vol. 10, p. 235.

†"Lesser Writings," New York, 1852, p. 244.

winter of 1791–2 the most fearful madness developed itself. He
was brought to the asylum toward the end of June, 1792, in a very
melancholy state accompanied by strong keepers. His face was
covered with large spots, was dirty, and imbecile in expression.
Day and night he raved. He was afflicted with strange halluci-
nations, imagining himself in many positions. Would recite in
Greek, recited, in the actual words of the Hebrew text, a Bible
story to his keeper. His quotations from various languages
were exact. He lived on terms of amity with emperors and
queens. He destroyed his clothing and bedding, took his piano
to pieces to discover the complementary tone of harmony, wrote
at one time a prescription for his own cure that seemed adapted
to the treatment of insanity—in fact, exhibited the most perfect
forms of excitable mania.

Hahnemann remarks that for two weeks he watched him carefully before giving him any medicine. At the period of which we
write the usual treatment of all forms of insanity was by violence,
by chains, abuse, whipping and dungeons. Ameke says: "Physicians treated excitable and refractory maniacal patients like wild
animals, corporal chastisement and nauseating medicines were
ordinary means used. Furious maniacs were strapped down on
a horizontal board which could be quickly turned on an axis to
a vertical position, or put in a so-called rotating chair. 'It is
shameful to confess,' says Westphal, in 1880, 'what a short time
has elapsed since the insane were shown to the Sunday visitors
of hospitals and workhouses as a sort of sport, and teased in
order to amuse the visitors.'"

Hahnemann did not countenance such cruelty and used only
the mildest of methods in his treatment of the insane. He said:
"I never allow an insane person to be punished either by blows
or any other kind of corporal chastisement, because there is no
punishment where there is no responsibility, and because these
sufferers deserve only pity and are always rendered worse by such
rough treatment and never improved."

Dudgeon in his biography of Hahnemann says: *"May we
not then justly claim for Hahnemann the honor of being the
first who advocated and practiced the moral treatment of the
insane? At all events he may divide the honor with Pinel, for
we find that towards the end of this same year, 1792, when

*Dudgeon's Lectures on Homœopathy, 1852.

Hahnemann was applying his principle of moral treatment to practice, Pinel made his first experiment of unchaining the maniacs of the Bicetre.'' (At Paris.)

Klockenbring, as the result of his treatment, returned to Hanover *cured* in March, 1793. For this cure Hahnemann received a fee of 1,000 thalers, about $750, in addition to the expenses of the board of the patient. There is no record of any other patients in this asylum. H. A. O. Reichards in his autobiography says:* ''On asking the witty Judge of Georgenthal, W. H. Jacobs, how many mad people Hahnemann had at that time in his asylum, he dryly answered, one, and that's himself.''

In *Hufeland's Journal*, Vol. 2, p. 313, appears the following note: ''An account of Hahnemann's treatment of the insanity of Klockenbring is published in the *Teutsch Monatschrift* for February, 1796.''

CHAPTER XIV.

MOLSCHLEBEN—LETTERS TO A PATIENT--PYRMONT—WOLFEN-BUTTEL—KONIGSLUTTER.

In a little book, published about 1887, at Tubingen, by Dr. Bernhard Schuchardt of Gotha, are published a series of letters written by Hahnemann, between the years 1793 to 1805 to a patient, and by means of their dates his whereabouts during this time is quite exactly determined. A part of these letters were published in the *Monthly Homœopathic Review* for September, 1887. They are of interest, as by them can be traced the gradual changes in his prescribing from the ordinary methods of the day to the more careful prescriptions of later years. This book and story were made the subject of Dr. Dudgeon's Hahnemann Oration, delivered at the opening of the London Homœopathic Medical School, October 3, 1887.†

Hahnemann left Georgenthal about the middle of May, 1793, going from there to Molschleben, a small village near Gotha. Here he again devoted himself entirely to his literary pursuits. He continued work on the second part of the ''Friend to Health,'' and composed the first part of the '' Pharmaceutical Lexicon,'' or

*'' *Monthly Hom. Review*,'' Vol. 31, p. 544.
†'' Idem,'' Vol. 31, p 719.

"Apothecaries' Dictionary," as it was also called. Ameke says:
The subjects are arranged alphabetically, and it treats of everything which could be of use to the apothecary in his work. The
necessary utensils are carefully described. Each article shows
how well Hahnemann understood the subject. He often describes new apparatus invented by himself; the apothecary's
business of making up prescriptions and his laboratory work
are accurately and clearly explained. He gives many directions
which have now become legal enactments. He mentions the
rules for the sale of poisons, gives the most minute directions for
the care and preparation of drugs, gives the botanical description
of remedies, their time of flowering and rules for their collection, and refers to much literature upon this subject. He quotes
from more than one hundred works of botanists and zoologists.
He recommends the preparation of tinctures from fresh plants,
and describes the medicinal uses of many drugs. This work appeared in numbers. It received the praise of all the scientific
physicians of the day, and became the standard work on pharmacy.

And yet it may be well to remember that this consummate
chemist, botanist, and practical pharmacist, who had been a regular pharmaceutical examiner, who was competent to write an
exhaustive work upon these subjects, and who was, without
doubt, the most qualified man of his time for such a task, was not,
at a little later period, considered by the physicians of Leipsic
a proper person to prepare and dispense his own medicines.

The most skillful chemist of his time forbidden to dispense
drugs! And yet it is to be presumed that at the same time the
excuse of these doctors was that the *people must be protected from
irregular practitioners, as is in very isolated cases the argument at
the present day!* At this time the following cure was made by
Hahnemann:

"While living in the village of Molschleben, 'where my children enjoyed perfect health,' there were many children affected
with so-called milk crust, and to an unusual degree. As Hahnemann thought the disease could be communicated, he endeavored
to prevent intercourse between his own and the infected children
belonging to the village. One of the boys gained access to
them. 'I saw him playing in close contact to them. I sent
him away, but the infection had already taken place. The

complaint began in the first child kissed, and then spread to the other three children.' "*

" I poured warm water over dry *Hepar sulphuris* (powdered oyster shells mixed with equal parts of *Sulphur*, and kept for ten minutes at a white heat), and thus made a weak solution. I painted the faces of the two who had the eruption worst with this every hour for two consecutive days.   After the first application the complaint was arrested and gradually got well."

Hahnemann's letters continue to be addressed from Molschleben until October 19, 1794, when he writes: "Pyrmont, where I think I shall remain."

This place is situated in Westphalia, and was celebrated at that time for its extensive mineral springs, utilized for bathing and drinking.   He remained there but a short time, going thence in 1795, to Wolfenbuttel, a large fortified place on the river Ocker, five miles from Brunswick, and the same year, 1795, again removing to Konigslutter, a small town ten miles from Brunswick, and in the principality of Wolfenbuttel. There he remained until 1799, when he went to Hamburg.

At Konigslutter, he wrote the second part of the "Friend to Health," and finished the "Pharmaceutical Lexicon."   He also wrote articles on the Wirtemburg and Hahnemann Wine Test; on the Preparation of Cassel Yellow; on Crusta lactea; Description of Klockenbring during his insanity; on the Pulverization of Ignatia Beans; and several other articles.   He translated from the French, Rousseau on the Education of Infants, under the title of "Handbook for Mothers;" from the English, the "New Edinburgh Dispensatory" in two volumes; and "Taplin's Veterinary Medicine."   The translation of the Dispensatory called forth from the chemists of Germany unstinted praise.   As was his custom, he enriched it with copious notes.†

CHAPTER XV.

FIRST ESSAY ON THE CURATIVE POWER OF DRUGS—"HUFELAND'S JOURNAL."—ENMITY OF KONIGSLUTTER PHYSICIANS.

It was during his residence at Konigslutter, in 1796, that Hahnemann first communicated to the world by means of the

*Ameke, page 73.   †Ameke, page 41.

public print his new discovery in medicine. In 1795 Hufeland, renowned in all Germany, began to publish in Jena, a medical journal called, *Journal der practischen Arzneykunde und Wundarzneykunst.* Hahnemann and Hufeland were personal friends; Hufeland was at the time professor of physics at Jena. Hahnemann is quoted in the first volume; his cure of Klockenbring is mentioned in the second volume. In this journal, volume two, parts three and four, (1796), Hahnemann published the article entitled: "Essay on a New Principle for Ascertaining the Curative Powers of Drugs."* In this he reviews the condition of medicine at that time; argues that chemistry is not the proper exponent of the curative action of drugs; that the experimentation on animals with poisons is of little use since many plants deadly to man are innocuous to animals; that the true method of experimentation with drugs is by testing them on the healthy body; says that the so-called specifics in common use are but the result of empirical practice, that the pure action of each drug should be obtained on the human body by itself.

He presents his theory in the following words: "Every powerful medicinal substance produces in the human body a kind of peculiar disease; the more powerful the medicine, the more peculiar, marked and violent the disease. We should imitate nature which sometimes cures a chronic disease by superadding another, and employ in the (especially chronic) disease we wish to cure that medicine which is able to produce another very similar artificial disease, and the former will be cured; similia similibus."

Hahnemann very carefully argues the question of the new law; he adduces many results of poisonings by drugs, gives his experience in the uses of medicines prescribed according to the law of similars, and records the symptoms that certain medicines produced on himself and others. He brings example for every assertion and discusses the matter in a calm and convincing manner.

This essay can be found in the various editions of the "Lesser Writings" of Hahnemann. To quote: "It displays to full advantage the exceeding gentleness of Hahnemann's temper, the respect he entertained for the opinions of his professional brethren, the modesty of the estimation in which he held his own,

* "Lesser Writings," New York, 1852, p. 249.

and the philosophical and comprehensive grasp of his mind. Its tone was calm and impartial, its language clear and accurate, its reasoning convincing, its arguments forcible, and its asser-tions moderate. It bears no sign of prejudice, much less of acrimony. We think its scientific mastery of a question con-fessedly among the most vexed in medicine, the best answer to those who glibly charge its author with charlatanry and igno-rance. Let them answer Hahnemann's arguments, which they have never done, before they abuse himself." *

It was the first essay by Hahnemann that appeared in *Hufe-land's Journal*. After this he was a frequent contributor until 1808, the last article being about a prophylactic for scarlet fever. In 1797 he published a cure of a case of colicodynia after the usual means of cure had failed, by means of a medicine pro-ducing very similar morbid symptoms. (*Veratrum album.*)

His next article was: "Are the Obstacles to Certainty and Simplicity in Practical Medicine Insurmountable?" In it he argues in favor of simple, careful methods. He says: † "Why should we complain that our science is obscure and intricate when we ourselves are the producers of this obscurity and in-tricacy? Formerly I was infected with this fever; the schools had infected me. The virus clung more obstinately to me be-fore it came to a critical expulsion than ever did the virus of any other mental disease. Are we in earnest with our art?

"Then let us make a brotherly compact, and all agree to give but one single simple remedy at a time for every single dis-ease, without making much alteration in the mode of life of our patients, and then let us use our eyes to see what effect this or that medicine has, how it does good or how it fails. Is not this as simple a way of getting over the difficulty as that of Colum-bus with the egg?"

At this time .Hahnemann was habitually depending on the single remedy, and says in this essay that it has been a long time since he has given more than one remedy at one time. He also prescribed according to the law of similars. He was in the habit of preparing and dispensing his own medicines independent of the apothecaries. By all his writings at this time he endeavored to induce his professional brethren to try the plan of simple reme-

* *Hom. World*, Vol. X., p. 334.
† "Lesser Writings," New York, 1852, p. 320.

dies given according to a precise law. But it was in vain, they became jealous of his success, for he was now engaged in active practice.

"And the physicians of Konigslutter incited the apothecaries to bring an action against him for interfering with them in dispensing his own medicines. He appealed to the letter of the law regulating the business of the apothecary, and argued that they had the sole privilege of compounding medicines, but that any man, especially any medical man, had a right to either give or sell uncompounded drugs, which were the only things he employed, and which he also administered gratuitously. But it was in vain, and Hahnemann, a past master of pharmaceutical art, was forbidden to dispense his simple medicines." *

And now he must again think of leaving his home and finding a new one where he could practice his methods and experiment in peace.

In a letter written to a patient, and dated March 14, 1799, he says:†

"To-day I make you my confidant. Kindly give the enclosed letter as soon as you can to the Minister Von Frankenberg, if he is still alive, but if Zigesar is in his place give it to him, but before doing so have the goodness to write the name of the present First Minister in Latin characters on the envelope in the blank space. I was not quite sure if Frankenberg is still living, otherwise I would have written his name myself. I am applying in this letter for Dr. Buchner's post with the Duke, and would like to return to Gotha in that capacity, for I have always preferred Gotha to Brunswick. But it is impossible for me to have an excuse for changing my abode unless I get an appointment of this sort.

"But do not let anyone know a word about all this, in order that no intrigues may be set on foot, as would certainly happen. But how will you manage to get this letter at once and with certainty into Frankenberg's hands? As it is, the news of Buchner's death reached me a week later than it ought, so I must now lose no time. Forgive me for the trouble I am putting you to, and with best wishes I remain

"Your most devoted servant,

"DR. HAHNEMANN."

*Dudgeon's Biography, 1852.
†*Monthly Hom. Review*, Vol. 31, p. 617.

The Dr. Buchner whom he mentions was the former physician in ordinary to the Duke, and had died a month before this. It can plainly be understood that Hahnemann thought that could he become physician to the Duke of Gotha he would be in a great measure freed from the persecution of the jealous physicians and apothecaries. But this appointment he failed to procure.

CHAPTER XVI.

LETTER TO PATIENT ON CHEERFUL METHODS OF LIFE.

The next letter to his patient, who was a tailor in Gotha and died at the age of ninety-two, is so filled with advice that must be of benefit to every one in this age of haste that it is given here in full:*

" *My Dear Mr. X——:*

"It is true that I am going to Hamburg, but that need not trouble you. If you do not grudge the few groschen a letter will cost you can still have my advice when I am there. Merely write my name, and Hamburg beneath it, and your letter so addressed will find me.

"For the present I must say that you are on the fair road to health, and the chief sources of your malady cut off. One source still remains, and it is the cause of your last relapse. Man (the delicate human machine) is not constituted for overwork, he can not overwork his powers or faculties with impunity. If he does so from ambition, love of gain, or other praiseworthy or blameworthy motive, he sets himself in opposition to the order of nature, and his body suffers injury or destruction. All the more if his body is already in a weakened condition; what you cannot accomplish in a week you can do in two weeks. If your customers will not wait they cannot fairly expect that you will for their sakes make yourself ill and work yourself to the grave, leaving your wife a widow and your children orphans. It is not only the greater bodily exertion that injures you, it is even more the attendant strain on the mind, and the overwrought mind in its turn affects the body injuriously. If you do not

Monthly Hom. Review, Vol. 31, p. 617. *N. E. Med. Gazette*, March, 1887.

assume an attitude of cool indifference, adopting the principle of living first for yourself and only secondly for others, then there is small chance of your recovery. When you are in your grave men will still be clothed, perhaps not as tastefully, but still tolerably well.

"If you are a philosopher you may become healthy, you may attain to old age. If anything annoys you give no heed to it; if anything is too much for you have nothing to do with it; if any one seeks to drive you go slowly and laugh at the fools who wish to make you unhappy. What you can do comfortably that do; what you cannot do don't bother yourself about.

"Our temporal circumstances are not improved by overpressure at work. You must spend proportionately more in your domestic affairs, and so nothing is gained. Economy, limitation of superfluities (of which the hard worker has often very few) place us in a position to live with greater comfort—that is to say, more rationally, more intelligently, more in accordance with nature, more cheerfully, more quietly, more healthily. Thus we shall act more commendably, more wisely, more prudently, than by working in breathless hurry, with our nerves constantly overstrung, to the destruction of the most precious treasure of life, calmly happy spirits and good health.

"Be you more prudent, consider yourself first, let everything else be of only secondary importance for you. And should they venture to assert that you are in honor bound to do more than is good for your mental and physical powers, even then do not, for ·God's sake, allow yourself to be driven to do what is contrary to your own welfare. Remain deaf to the bribery of praise, remain cold and pursue your own course slowly and quietly like a wise and sensible man. To enjoy with tranquil mind and body, that is what man is in the world for, and only to do as much work as will procure him the means of enjoyment—certainly not to excoriate and wear himself out with work.

"The everlasting pushing and striving of blinded mortals in order to gain so and so much, to secure some honor or other, to do a service to this or that great personage—this is generally fatal to our welfare, this is a common cause of young people ageing and dying before their time.

"The calm, cold-blooded man, who lets things softly glide, attains his object also, lives more tranquilly and healthily, and

attains a good old age.   And this leisurely man sometimes
lights upon a lucky idea, the fruit of serious original thought,
which shall give a much more profitable impetus to his temporal
affairs than can ever be gained by the overwrought man who can
never find time to collect his thoughts.

"In order to win the race, quickness is not all that is required.
Strive to obtain a little indifference, coolness and calmness, then
you will be what I wish you to be.   Then you will see marvellous things; you will see how healthy you will become by following my advice.   Then shall your blood course through your
blood vessels calmly and sedately, without effort and without
heat.   No horrible dreams disturb the sleep of him who lies
down to rest without highly strung nerves.   The man who is
free from care wakes in the morning without anxiety about the
multifarious occupations of the day.   What does he care?   The
happiness of life concerns him more than anything else.   With
fresh vigor he sets about his moderate work, and at his meals
nothing, no ebullitions of blood, no cares, no solicitude of mind
hinders him from relishing what the beneficent Preserver of Life
sets before him.   And so one day follows another in quiet succession, until the final day of advanced age brings him to the
termination of a well spent life, and he serenely reposes in another world as he has calmly lived in this one.

"Is not that more rational, more sensible?   Let restless, self-
destroying men act as irrationally, as injuriously towards themselves as they please; let them be fools.   But be you wiser!   Do
not let me preach this wisdom of life in vain.   I mean well to
you.

"Farewell, follow my advice, and when all goes well with you,
remember

"DR. S. HAHNEMANN.

"P. S.—Should you be reduced to your last sixpence, be still
cheerful and happy.   Providence watches over us, and a lucky
chance makes all right again.   How much do we need in order
to live, to restore our powers by food and drink, to shield ourselves from cold and heat?   Little more than good courage;
when we have that the minor essentials we can find without
much trouble.   The wise man needs but little.   Strength that
is husbanded needs not to be renovated by medicine."

CHAPTER XVII.

EPIDEMIC OF SCARLATINA—DEPARTURE FROM KONIGSLUTTER—
ACCIDENT ON THE JOURNEY—COMPLAINT TO THE PUB-
LIC—BELLADONNA IN SCARLATINA—ALTONA-
MEDICAL LIBERALITY OF THE NINE-
TEENTH CENTURY.

During the summer of 1799, the last year of his sojourn in Konigslutter, an epidemic of scarlet fever occurred, during which Hahnemann discovered the great value of *Belladonna* as a prophylactic against this serious disease. Hahnemann says: *"At first smallpox came from the vicinity of Helmstadt to Konigslutter, spreading slowly around; the eruption was small, warty looking, and it was accompanied with serious atonic symptoms. In the village it came from scarlet fever was prevalent at the time, and, mixed up with the latter, the smallpox made its appearance in Konigslutter. About the middle of the year the smallpox ceased almost entirely, and the scarlet fever then commenced to appear more frequently and alone. This epidemic was exceedingly contagious; it extended through families. If a single child was affected by it, not one of its brothers and sisters remained exempt, nor did it fail to affect other children who came close to the patients or to things that had come in contact with their exhalations."

Hahnemann was very successful both in the prevention and treatment of this terrible scourge, but at this time did not reveal the name of the remedy he used. No doubt this may have further embittered the physicians against him. Despite the wishes of his numerous patients, who were grateful for his skill, the unjust opposition of the jealous doctors was too powerful for him, and he had to again resume his wanderings.

Burnett says: †"The vulnerable point with Hahnemann was this: At Konigslutter he gave his own medicines to his patients, though gratuitously. The physicians of Konigslutter became jealous of his rising fame, and they incited the apothecaries against him, and these brought an action at law against Hahnemann for dispensing his own medicines, and thus encroaching

---

*"Lesser Writings," New York, p. 370.
†"Ecce. Medicus," p. 131.

upon their rights. It was decided against him; he was forbidden to give his own medicines, and this, of course, rendered his further stay impossible."

He could not remain in Konigslutter, and in the autumn of 1799, with his family, he departed from the ungrateful city.

Dudgeon says:* "He purchased a large carriage or wagon, in which he packed all his property and family, and with a heavy heart bade adieu to Konigslutter, where fortune had at length begun to smile upon him, and where he found leisure and opportunity to prosecute his interesting discoveries. Many of the inhabitants, whose health he had been instrumental in restoring, or whose lives he had even saved by the discoveries of his genius during that fatal epidemic of scarlet fever, accompanied him some distance on the road to Hamburg, whither he had resolved to proceed, and at length, with a blessing for his services, and a sigh for his hard lot, they bade him God speed. And thus he journeyed on with all his earthly possessions, and with all his family beside him. But a dreadful accident befell the melancholy cortege. Descending a precipitous part of the road the wagon was overturned, the driver thrown from his seat, his infant son so injured that he died shortly afterwards, and the leg of one of his daughters was fractured. He himself was considerably bruised, and his property much damaged by falling into a stream that ran at the bottom of the road. With the assistance of some peasants they were conveyed to the nearest village (Muhlhausen), where he was forced to remain upwards of six weeks on his daughter's account, at an expense that greatly lightened his not very well filled purse."

It would seem that after the accident Hahnemann settled first in Altona, as he dates a letter from that place on November 9th, 1799, while the letters dated from Hamburg occur in the year 1800.

Kleinert, in his "History of Homœopathy," says he resided first at Altona. That he was here annoyed by people fond of gratuitous advice is evidenced by the following letter that he caused twice to be inserted in the *Reichanzeiger* and for which he had to pay one thaler and eight groschen.

---

*Biography of Hahnemann, 1852.

"COMPLAINT AND RESOLVE."*

"*Dear Public!* It will scarcely be credited that there are people who seem to think that I am merely a private gentleman with plenty of time on my hands, whom they may pester with letters, many of which have not the postage paid, and are consequently a tax on my purse, containing requests for professional advice, to comply with which would demand much mental labor and occupy precious time, while it never occurs to these inconsiderate correspondents to send any remuneration for the time and trouble I would have to expend on answers by which they would benefit.

" In consequence of the ever-increasing importunity of these persons, I am compelled to announce:

" 1. That henceforward I shall refuse to take in any letters which are not postpaid, let them come from whom they may.

" 2. That after reading through even paid letters from distant patients and others seeking advice, I will send them back unless they are accompanied by a sufficient fee (at least a Friedrich d'or) in a cheque or in actual money, unless the poverty of the writer is so great that I could not withhold my advice without sinning against humanity.

" 3. If lottery tickets are sent me I shall return them all without exception; but I shall make the post office pay for all the expenses of remission, and the senders will get them back charged with this payment.

"SAMUEL HAHNEMANN, Doctor of Medicine."

" *Altona, by Hamburg, November 9, 1799.*"

This announcement, compelling patients to pay for consultation by letter, being against the usual custom of the time, aroused a very great amount of adverse criticism, and gave the doctors another opportunity for cavilling against their successful rival.

His stay at Altona was short, and about the beginning of the year 1800 he removed to Hamburg.

The epidemic of scarlatina still claimed numerous victims, and Hahnemann's success at Konigslutter in the prevention and treatment had been so great that the name of the remedy there used was demanded.

He now published a letter in the *Reichanzeiger Journal* for

Monthly Hom. Review, Vol. 31, p. 622.

May 12, 1800 (Gotha), in which he stated that he was about to issue a pamphlet giving a complete history of the Konigslutter epidemic, with an account of his treatment, and the name and method of preparation of his prophylactic and remedy. But, he also stated, that before he could publish this he must have 300 subscribers at one Friedrich d'or each, pledged to take the work, to each of whom he would give a quantity of the remedy with full directions for its proper use.

He added, in the way of excuse, that he deserved something both from the public and from the Government for his most important discovery.

This statement gained for him very few subscribers, but a vast amount of abuse and calumny. He was accused of seeking to obtain money under false pretenses. The physicians declared that the substance he employed was a violent poison that would profoundly affect the health, and that he dare not announce its name.

Hahnemann justified his course by saying that he wished the trial to be made by a medicine prepared carefully by his own hands, and not in the careless manner in which drugs were so often prepared; that he had no intention of keeping the truth from the profession, but considered himself entitled to some honorarium. This refutation he published in December, 1800.

Again, in the *Allgemeiner Anzeiger* for February 7, 1801 (No. 32), he published the following article addressed to the physicians of Germany:

"Considerations Upon the Liberality of the Medical Fraternity at the Commencement of the Nineteenth Century."*

He reviewed the professional jealousy of physicians; cited examples of the abuse that had in the past fallen on discoverers, such as Wichmann, Hufeland, Tode, Sommering; recalled the attacks on himself after his chemical discoveries regarding *Mercury;* the constant abuse of his New Principle of Healing.

"Now," he says, "once more, at the end of the century that has just expired, my zeal for the welfare of mankind misled me to announce a prophylactic remedy for one of the most destructive of children's diseases, scarlet fever. Scarcely a fourth part of the number I might have expected subscribed for it. This lukewarm interest shown for such an important affair discouraged

*"Lesser Writings," New York, 1852, p. 365.

me, and I arranged that the subscribers should receive a portion
of the medicine itself, in order to satisfy them, in case my book
on the subject should not be published. The subscribers consisted chiefly of physicians who had epidemics of scarlet fever
in their neighborhood. At least thirty of these, whom I begged
by letter to testify to the truth and to publish the result, *be it
what it might*, in the *Reichsanzeiger*, made no reply.''

Certainly not fair to Hahnemann after he had given the medicine, and had only asked, as he always did, for but a fair trial.
And with the fact before us, that *Belladonna* is by all now recognized as a valuable preventive of scarlet fever, it becomes still
more certain that this action on the part of the physicians did
indeed arise from bigotry and envy, as Hahnemann declared.

He continues in argumentative form regarding the use of
Mercury and of the *Belladonna*, and its value in scarlet fever,
expostulates against the prejudice of one Dr. Jani, who at first
published articles in favor and then against this remedy, and
declares that the common object which physicians must attain can only be gained by unity, mutual intercommunication
and brotherly friendship. And lastly, these words: ''Physicians
of Germany, be brothers, be fair, be just !''

When we consider the fact that heretofore Hahnemann had
always been willing to freely impart any and all of his discoveries to his brethren; when in every book he had translated he
had freely given of the treasure of his memory and of his invention; when we remember that just as soon as he became satisfied
of its truth he announced to the world the discovery of the new
law of similia; when we read his essay on that subject, with its
wealth of careful advice and argument, we certainly cannot for
one moment think that he withheld the name of the *Belladonna*
from any sordid motive of concealing from the world a useful
remedy.

Is it not more probable that by this plan he wished to ensure
for his prophylactic fair treatment? He had but just been driven
from Konigslutter, where he had done so much good with this
same medicine; he had been compelled to give up his practice,
to lose his child by an accident incident to his moving. He was
poor. He wished some recompense as a discoverer. He wished
unbiased treatment.

So very much has been written about Hahnemann as the dispenser of secret remedies, meaning this fact of the *Belladonna*, that before judging him it is but just to examine carefully all the circumstances of the case. This is the only time when he did not at once freely give to the world every discovery that he made. And judging the past and the future of the man, is it not fairer to decide that he hid the name of this remedy for some good and sufficient purpose, perhaps thinking that were the subscribers compelled to pay for the knowledge they would give it more careful consideration.

The article on "Liberality" was the last that he wrote in a spirit of conciliation. After that he viewed his detractors with disfavor and contempt. From this time he steadily and in a dignified way followed his medical researches and discoveries, and responded but very seldom to tne attacks of the doctors.

He did not wait for his three hundred subscribers, but in 1801 published the secret of the discovery of the prophylactic properties of *Belladonna* in scarlet fever in a small pamphlet printed at Gotha. It was called: "Cure and Prevention of Scarlet Fever." * In the preface he says that had he compiled a large book on scarlet fever he would have gotten, through the usual channels of publication, as much of an honorarium as from the subscribers of the pamphlet. But as he wished to interest the many, he adopted the more popular form of the small book. He gives a history of the epidemic of smallpox reaching Konigslutter, the scarlet fever mixing with it; the final disappearance of the smallpox and the spread of the scarlet fever.

The symptoms of the disease are carefully detailed, its great mortality, his treatment with small doses of *Opium* and *Ipecac*, and then under the heading: "Prevention against Scarlet Fever," he gives the particulars of his discovery of *Belladonna*.

He says: "The mother of a large family, at the commencement of July, 1799, when the fever was most prevalent and fatal, had got a new counterpane made up by a seamstress who, without the knowledge of the former, had in her small chamber a boy just recovering from scarlet fever. The mother received the counterpane and smelled it to be sure that it contained no bad odors. She then laid it on the sofa pillow, and took a nap the same afternoon on the same pillow. A week later she became

* "Lesser Writings," New York, 1852.

ill with the sore throat. Her daughter, ten years old, soon after manifested marked symptoms of scarlet fever." Hahnemann, judging from her symptoms, says: "My memory and my written collection of the peculiar effects of some medicines furnished me with no remedy so capable of producing a counterpart of the symptoms here present as *Belladonna*."

No guess work, only the application of the new law, and this valuable preventive was discovered.

He gave her the one four hundred and thirty-two thousandth part of a grain of *Belladonna*, with the result that in about twenty-four hours she became well. He next gave the remedy to other children, who did not take the disease although exposed.

He writes: "I reasoned thus, a remedy that is capable of quickly checking a disease in its onset, must be its best preventive; and the following occurrence strengthened me in the correctness of this conclusion: Some weeks previously three children of another family lay ill of a very bad scarlet fever; the eldest daughter alone, who, up to that period, had been taking *Belladonna* internally for an external affection on the joints of her fingers, to my great astonishment did not catch the fever, although during the prevalence of other epidemics she had always been the first to take them. This circumstance completely confirmed my idea. I now hesitated not to administer to the other five children of this numerous family this divine remedy, as a preservative, in very small doses, and, as the particular action of this plant does not last above three days, I repeated the dose every seventy-two hours, and they all remained perfectly well without the slightest symptoms throughout the whole course of the epidemic, and amid the most virulent scarlatina emanations from the sisters who lay ill with the disease."

He then gives preparations for preparing the remedy and prescribes the quantity to be used.

This publication did not silence his enemies. They ridiculed his minute doses of *Belladonna*, and laughed at its power to prevent the spread of scarlatina. Hahnemann, then, in *Hufeland's Journal*, Vol. 13, part 2, January, 1801, published another essay on "Small Doses of Medicine in General, and of Belladonna in Particular." In this he argues on the divisibility of medicine and its increase of power by subdivision, and supports his doses of *Belladonna* as previously given.

Afterwards many physicians bore testimony to the truth of this discovery.   Hufeland testified to its value as a prophylactic; articles appeared in his *Journal* regarding its virtues in May, 1812; November, 1824; November, 1825.   Hufeland himself wrote a work in 1825, entitled "The Prophylactic Power of Bella-donna," and in this he justly gives Hahnemann the credit of his discovery.   He also adduces a great deal of testimony to prove this assertion.*

Twenty years later, while Hahnemann resided in Leipsic, cer-tain of the physicians of that city recommended the use of *Bel-ladonna* as a prophylactic in scarlet fever, but *did not* mention the fact that Hahnemann had twenty years earlier discovered this.

CHAPTER XVIII.

CURIOUS PREFACE TO THESAURUS MEDICAMINUM—ALKALI PNEUM—MOLLEN—EILENBURG—MACHERN— DESSAU—TORGAU.

In the year 1800 Hahnemann translated from the English the "Thesaurus Medicaminum," which was a collection of medical prescriptions.

This translation was published anonymously, the notes by Hahnemann being signed " Y."

He, however, in a spirit of grim satire, wrote an original pre-face, in which he says: "I have translated the book entitled ' Thesaurus Medicaminum, a New Collection of Medical Prescrip-tions,' etc.   If, as the preface to the original informs me, even in London, medical frankness requires the ægis of anonymousness, in order to escape being chid; I need not say a word as to its ex-pediency for some time past in our own dear fatherland. * * * But how, it will be asked, did the writer of the notes, no friend to compound medicines, come to edit this work?   To which I answer, solely for that very reason.   I wished to show my country-men that the very best prescriptions have a hitch somewhere, are unnatural, contradictory and opposed to the object for which

---

*Hufeland in 1830 published an essay on Homœopathy which may be found in the "British Journal of Homœopathy;" vol. 16, p. 177.

they are designed. This is a truth that should be proclaimed from the housetops in our prescription-loving times."

He continues to argue against compound prescriptions and in favor of single remedies; says that two or more substances mingled do not have the same effect as given singly, and, in fact, condemns the use of the book itself.

In the notes he denounces the body of the work. In one case where five remedies are given in one prescription, he suggests including, also, the entire Materia Medica. He ridicules placing drugs antagonistic to each other in the same prescription, and advises a return to the simple methods of Hippocrates.

As he did no more translating at this time, it is very probable that his suggestions did not enhance the sale of the book, and that the bookseller for whom he worked was anything but satisfied with him.

In 1801 he published in *Hufeland's Journal* some observations on "Brown's Elements of Medicine," in which he again pleads against the use of so many drugs in one prescription, and earnestly recommends simpler methods of treatment.

With the exception of "Von Haller's Materia Medica," translated in 1806, this was the last of Hahnemann's translations.

A circumstance that happened while Hahnemann lived in Hamburg has been extensively used by his detractors to impeach his honesty. He announced the discovery of a new chemical salt that he called "*Alkali Pneum.*" It was offered for sale, but upon analysis it proved to be *Borax*.

According to the most reliable statements this must have been about the year 1800. Crell published an article about it in that year, and the result of its analysis was given in 1801. When he first discovered it is not known, probably some years earlier, when he was so deeply interested in chemical discovery.

This mistake his enemies have ever since been quoting as a proof that he not only sold secret remedies, but palmed off under a new name a well-known substance. The "*Alkali pneum*" and the *Belladonna* secret have been mentioned in every book that has been written against Hahnemann, and their number is many, in the last hundred years. In fact, it is impossible for the gentlemen who denounce him and his system to find any other circumstance of his long life with which, in the slightest manner, to assail his honesty. The facts of these two cases, to an unbiased person, do not show any swerving from the strict honor by which his entire life was guided and influenced.

Ameke says :* "The chemists of that day were seeking new substances.   Prof. Klaproth, one of the first chemists of the day, discovered a new substance, 'diamond spar ;' it was a mistake. Proust discovered '*sal mirabile perlatum*,' a salt of pearl, in the urine ; it was supposed to be a combination of *Soda* with a new acid (pearl acid); it was found to be the already known *Phosphate of Soda*.

"Van Ruprecht, a chemist, discovered *Borbonium* in baryta, *Parthenum* in chalk, *Austrum* in magnesia ; the sedative salt (*Boracic acid*) was supposed to have been reduced to a metal ; on examination these discoveries were found to be iron, probably derived from impure Hessian crucibles.

"*Borax* had long been an object of especial attention to chemists.   Prof. Fuchs wrote, in 1784, a monograph on it, with a historical account of the views as to its composition, which, in 1784, were still uncertain and contradictory.   He says in the preface: 'We know very little about borax, and are not yet agreed as to its composition, for one says it contains this substance and another that.'   Metherie gave the constituents of *Boracic acid* as atmospheric air, inflammable gas, caloric and water.

"In 1800, 'Crell's Annalen' published an article of four pages entitled, 'Pneumlaugensalz, endeckt von Herrn Dr. Samuel Hahnemann,' in which the latter describes the properties of a new kind of fixed alkali, called '*Alkali pneum*' from its property of swelling out to twenty times its size when heated to redness.   This article was copied into other journals.

"Hahnemann had worked zealously as an amateur in the field of chemistry for twenty years, and with the most valuable results for chemistry and for the welfare of mankind.   He never obtained any assistance from the State, or any other source, and was not even able to fit up a proper laboratory, such as the apothecaries possessed.   Disinterested love of research and of science had made him go to great expense for a laboratory, costly reagents, etc.   Thinking he had made a very valuable discovery, he handed over his *Alkali pneum* to an agent in Leipsic, who sold it for a Friedrichs d'or the ounce.

* "Ameke's History of Homœopathy," page 288.

"Professors Klaproth, Karsten and Hermbstadt analyzed the new alkali, and found that it was *Borax*. Instead of communicating their results to Hahnemann, who had given proofs enough, that he was striving after the same objects as themselves, and asking him for an explanation, they published their discovery in the *Jenaer Literatur Zeitung*, 1801, and called Hahnemann to account.

"Prof. Trommsdorff, who owned an apothecary shop, hastened to communicate this incident to a larger public in the *Reichanzeiger*, the name then borne by the *Allegemeine Anzeiger der Deutschen*, and called Hahnemann's proceeding 'unexampled impudence.' Crell lamented Hahnemann's 'great mistake.' "

Hahnemann at once explained the matter in several journals, among others in Prof. A. N. Scherer's *Journal der Chemie* (1801, p. 665).

He said: "I am incapable of willfully deceiving. I may, like other men, be unintentionally mistaken. I am in the same boat with Klaproth and his '*Diamond spar*,' and with Proust and his '*Pearl salt*.' I had before me some crude (probably Chinese) *Borax*, supplied by J. N. Nahrmann, of Hamburg. A solution of *Potash* dropped into a filtered ley of *Borax*, not yet crystallizable, precipitated a large floury saline sediment As authors assure us that pure *Borax* is rendered uncrystallizable by the addition of *Potash*, is it wonderful that I took the new precipitate for some new substance?"

Hahnemann devoted some space to the explanation of this mistake, and adds that he has refunded all the money he received from the sale of the substance.

Six years later he writes in the *Allg. Anzieger der Deutsch :* "If I once made an error in chemistry, for to err is human, I was the first to acknowledge it as soon as I was better informed." *

Dr. Rummel, in his oration at the unveiling of Hahnemann's statue at Leipsic, in 1852, mentions this story as follows: "The spirit of calumny raked up an incident that occurred in Hahnemann's past career, and repeatedly threw in his teeth a mistake he had committed long ago, although he had made the most honorable reparation for it. In former times he imagined he had discovered a new substance, namely, the *Alkali pneum*. It

---

* See Ameke, pages 288-92. Also *Brit. Jour. Hom.*, vol. 17, p. 110.

was afterwards found that he had made a mistake, and that it was *Borax*. As soon as he became aware of this, he unhesitatingly repaid the money he had received for it."

That Hahnemann maliciously offered the *Borax* for sale is in no manner probable; and yet his action has been called "an imposition upon the public." If he had known that this substance was really not new, would he have dared to so publish the discovery, even had he wished to defraud? There was nothing dishonorable about it, and in the state of chemistry at that time, it was only the mistake of one self-taught chemist, when all chemists were also guilty of mistakes.

Hahnemann remained at Hamburg until about the year 1802, when he went to the little town of Mollen, in the Duchy of Lauenburg, fourteen miles from Lubeck. Here the old longing for the fatherland took possession of the wanderer, and he journeyed to Eilenburg, in beloved Saxony. But he was not allowed to remain there ; the medical health officer, or physikus, of the place, drove him away, by his persecutions, in a very short time.

From thence he went to Machern, a small village about four leagues from Leipsic. He was very poor during this period of his life.

Dudgeon writes :* "This anecdote, related me by a member of Hahnemann's family, conveys some idea of the poverty they endured. During his residence at Machern, after toiling all day long at his task of translating works for the press, he frequently assisted his brave-hearted wife to wash the family clothes at night, and, as they were unable to purchase soap, they employed raw potatoes for this purpose. The quantity of bread he was enabled to earn by his literary labors for his numerous family was so small that in order to prevent grumbling, he used to weigh out to each an equal proportion. At this period one of his little daughters fell ill, and being unable to eat the portion of daily bread that fell to her share, she carefully put it away in a box, hoarding it up, childlike, till her appetite should return. Her sickness, however, increasing, she felt assured that she should never recover to enjoy her store; so she one day told her favorite little sister that she knew she was going to die— that she should never be able to eat any more, and solemnly

* "Biography of Hahnemann."

made over to her as a gift the accumulated fragments of hard, dried-up bread, from which she had anticipated such a feast had she recovered.''

From Machern Hahnemann went to Wittenberg, departing soon after for Dessau. Here he lived for two years. The exact time of his life in the above places is very uncertain. Hartmann, his pupil, frankly confesses that he does not know.

It is probable that Hahnemann left Hamburg the last of 1801 or the beginning of 1802. He could not have remained long in any one place. He was poor and persecuted, driven from town to town. He spent about two years at Dessau, and by the evidence of a letter written to the patient "X," he was settled at Torgau in June, 1805. This letter is dated Torgau, June 21, 1805.*

He gave up practice when he left Hamburg and did not resume it until he reached Torgau. During this time he devoted himself to his researches and writings. He resumed practice at Torgau, and continued it until the end of his life. Hartmann and Rapou mention 1806 as the year of his removal to Torgau, but by this letter it would seem to have been in 1805. He remained at Torgau until 1811, when he went to Leipsic.

As his essays in the medical journals only brought him opposition and obloquy from his confreres, Hahnemann ceased writing for them, and after this published his articles in the *Allgemeine Anzeiger der Deutschen*, a magazine of general literature and science.†

CHAPTER XIX.

ESSAY ON COFFEE—MEDICINE OF EXPERIENCE—DENIAL OF
FALSE REPORT ABOUT SCARLATINA—ÆSCULAPIUS
IN THE BALANCE.

Hartmann, in his "Life of Hahnemann," published in 1844, says:‡ "Notwithstanding a multiplicity of inquiry and research, it cannot be ascertained how long he resided at Eilenburg, nor is it even known how long he lived at Machern, a vil-

---

Monthly Hom. Review, Vol. 31, p. 621.
†"Dudgeon's Biography."
‡*Allg. Hom. Zeit.*, Vol. 26, p. 161. (April 29, 1844.)

lage situated four leagues from Leipsic and two from Wurtzen. We know, however, from definite sources that the following works were the products of his mental activity during his sojourn of about two years in Dessau, whither he had gone from Wittenberg, so as to devote more time to the elaboration of the homœopathic method of healing: "Coffee and Its Effects," published by Steinacker, Leipsic, 1803. "Æsculapius in the Balance," Leipsic, 1805. "Medicine of Experience," Wittig, Berlin, 1805 (a highly intellectual treatise appearing as the forerunner of his "Organon," published in 1810). Also, "Fragmenta de viribus medicamentorum, positivis sive in sano corpore humano observatis," 1805.

"He resided with the Medical Assessor named Hasler, who was at that time the owner of the apothecary shop, and he lived by himself and in his study, laying aside all medical practice, which he resumed when he went to Torgau in 1806, and again reminded the non-medical public of himself through brief articles published in the *Reichs Anzeiger.*"

One of these articles is as follows (No. 191, July 21, 1806):

"CENSURE OF AN UNFOUNDED REPORT."

"Five years ago a malicious report got into circulation among very young German physicians, and it has been revived in many books and at most of the medical schools, that I (Dr. Samuel Hahnemann) have promulgated an alleged means, or remedy, for preventing scarlet fever, and have thereby deceived the public, since experience has proved that *Belladonna* is no preservative against scarlet fever.

"Besides being so revolting to my feelings as such an audacious and, as will be shown, unfounded accusation, must be, because my character has been blameless during the whole of the thirty years of my literary and private life, to say nothing of my being a cosmopolite and benefactor of all mankind, I regret exceedingly that so large a number of my German fellow-citizens should circulate against me a false report, which might readily be considered by their posterity as a slander, coming from me as a citizen. However, I, myself, will call this revolting report only an error, and not a slander, because ignorance is the basis of it; and only an untruth intended to defame, and of the groundlessness of which the promulgator is convinced, can be called a slander.

"But this malicious and widely spread error rests upon what the non-partisan public, in whose estimable presence I have never knowingly asserted an untruth, will conclude from the following true, historical account of the matter.

"At the time that I made known the discovery that scarlet fever can be prevented with certainty by small doses of *Belladonna*, there had broken out (in the year 1800), at a great distance from me in Central Germany, a new epidemic, the malignant purple fever, against which physicians, just as if it were the old and real scarlet fever, did not hesitate to use my remedy, and for the most part with fruitless results. This was perfectly natural, since they used it against an entirely different disease. For the old true scarlet fever, with its bright, smooth, red blotches, has in its actual signs, scarcely a remote resemblance to this new disease, which has so mysteriously appeared in the West of Germany."

Hahnemann then continues in this article to explain the epidemic of the real scarlet fever, and to set himself aright regarding his position as to the prophylactic uses of *Belladonna*.

The essay against the use of coffee was written at a time when the Germans considered it a favorite beverage, especially the women, and the very poor people, as is tea with us to-day. It has been published in the "Lesser Writings," and in many medical journals, and translated into several languages.* He says that in order to enjoy a long and healthy life, man requires food and drinks containing nutritious, but not irritating, medicinal parts. He describes medicinal substances, and then says that coffee is a purely medicinal substance. He describes at length its injurious effects, recommends cocoa unspiced, in its place; but commends its medicinal virtues for chronic ailments that bear a great resemblance to its primary action.†

While living at Dessau, he published in the *Reichs Anzeiger* (No. 71, 1803) an essay on a "Remedy for Hydrophobia."‡

In 1805 he published an important pamphlet called "Æsculapius in the Balance," in which he reviews his own state of mind after he had become disgusted with the practice of the day. He shows the lack of certainty and progress in the art of medi-

---

* "Bradford's Bibliography," page 112.
† *Am. Jour. Hom.*, New York, June. 1835. *Hom. Exam.*, August, 1840.
‡ "Lesser Writings, p. 389."

cine, the ignorance of the physician in compounding, the fallacy of trusting to the druggist, who often sends a different prescription from the chemically impossible one ordered by the physician, or substitutes one drug for another; or again sends the erroneous compound as the doctor has written for it. He argues against the laws of the time, forbidding the preparing or dispensing of medicine by the physician. He says that the preparation should not be trusted to the apothecary who is not responsible, unless in rare cases, for the result, but that the physician should understand how, and be compelled, to prepare his own medicines so that he may know exactly what he is giving to his patient, and be certain that there has been no substitution nor mistake in the medicine given.

"I repeat," he says, "from the very nature of the thing, I repeat, the physician should be prohibited, under the severest penalties, from allowing any other person to prepare the medicines required for his patients; he should be required, under the severest penalties, to prepare them himself, so that he may be able to vouch for the result. But that it should be forbidden to the physician to prepare his own instruments for the saving of life—no human being could have fallen on such an idea *a priori.*"

It must be remembered that the man who thus argues is not a man ignorant of the art of the apothecary, but one who had but a short time before compiled and edited a very important book, giving in detail the principles and practice of pharmacy. And yet Hahnemann was forbidden to prepare or dispense his own medicines, and was driven from place to place because he attempted to do so. It is to be presumed that he really knew more about the business than most of the members of the Worshipful Company of the Apothecaries, who persecuted him.

He continues in this treatise as follows: "It would have been much more sensible to prohibit authoritatively, Titian, Guido Reni, Michael Angelo, Raphael, Correggio or Mengs from preparing their own instruments (their expressive, beautiful and durable colors), and have ordered them to purchase them in some shop indicated. By the purchased colors not prepared by themselves, their paintings, far from being the inimitable masterpieces they are, would have been ordinary daubs and mere market goods. And even had they all become mere common market

goods, the damage would not have been so great as if the life of
even the meanest slave (for he too is a man) should be endangered
by untrustworthy health instruments (medicines) purchased from.
and prepared by strangers.*

CHAPTER XX.

FIRST COLLECTION OF PROVINGS—THE LAST TRANSLATION—
MEDICINE OF EXPERIENCE—THE ORGANON—ATTACKS
UPON ITS TEACHINGS.

In 1805 Hahnemann published a very important book in two
parts, written in Latin. It was called "Fragmenta de viribus.
Medicamentorum positivis sive in sano corpore humano observatis."

Part I. contains the symptoms arranged carefully. Part II. is.
the Index, or Repertory. He gives the symptoms produced by
drugs on the healthy, and at the end of each remedy gives the
effects recorded by previous observers in cases of poisoning..
The remedies given are: *Aconitum napellus*; *Acris tinctura*
(Hahnemann's *Causticum*); *Arnica montana; Atropa belladonna;*
Laurus camphora; Lytta vesicatoria (Cantharis); Capsicum
annuum; Chamomilla matricaria; Cinchona officinalis et regia;
Cocculus menispermum; Copaifera balsamum; Cuprum vitriolatum,
Digitalis purpurea; Drosera rotundifolia; Hyoscyamus niger;
Ignatia amara; Ipecacuanha; Ledum palustre; Helleborus
niger; Daphne mezereum; Strychnos nux vomica l.; Papaver
somniferum (Opium); Anemone pratensis (Pulsatilla); Rheum;
Datura stramonium; Valeriana officinalis; Veratrum album.

It is the first collection ever made of provings of medicines
upon the healthy body, and contains the records of the symptoms.
produced in this manner upon Hahnemann and his fellow
provers.

In 1834 Dr. F. F. Quin, of England, edited this book and
published it, in one volume, in London.

The next year, 1806, Hahnemann translated the Materia
Medica of Albert von Haller, from the Latin. This was the
last book he translated.

---

*"Lesser Writings," New York, page 434.

The same year he published at Berlin a pamphlet entitled "The Medicine of Experience." This really was a forerunner of the "Organon" It contains arguments in favor of the new system. He speaks of the helplessness of infant man; of the powers that God has allowed to develop within him; of the great aid of nature in healing; he thinks that certainly a benevolent God must have intended mankind to discover some method of healing the sick that is definitely governed by law. He gives instruction in the proper manner to allow the patient to describe his disease, and propounds certain "Maxims of Experience." There are also instructions regarding the choice and administration of the proper remedy.

He next wrote an article for the *Reichs Anzeiger* on the "Objection to a Substitute for Quinine, and to all Succedanea." He published an article in *Hufeland's Journal* on the same subject.

During the years from 1805 to 1811, the time of his stay in Torgau, he published several articles in the *Reichs Anzeiger*. They may all be found in Dr. Dudgeon's valuable translation of the "Lesser Writings." •

In the *Allgemeine Anzeiger* for July 14, 1808, he published his "Letter to a Physician of High Standing on Reform in Medicine." Some parts of this have been quoted elsewhere.

The physician to whom this was addressed was his old and always true friend, Dr. Christian Wilhelm Hufeland. This letter is usually spoken of as the letter to Hufeland. In it he gives his own experience in the practice of medicine, the reasons that led him to cease from practice, his efforts to discover some more certain and reliable method than any known at that time. It is an analysis of his hopes and feelings. He declares that God must have designed that mankind should be blessed with some certain method of healing. This belief can be found in many of Hahnemann's writings; he always gave the praise to God, of whom he spoke reverently.

It was during his residence at Torgau that Hahnemann gave to the world his great book, "Organon der Rationellen Heilkunde," or "Organon of Rational Healing." It was published in Dresden, by Arnold, in 1810.

In the *Allgemeine Anzeiger* for June 7, 1810, had appeared a resumé of the forthcoming book, which was soon after published.

Hering says of the publication of the "Organon:"* "It required a grateful patient to print the 'Organon;' it was *nine years* before the first edition was sold. It is disgusting to state how it was received; it was, and it remains forever, an inexcusable meanness of the whole profession,"

This is considered the most important of all Hahnemann's books by the members of the Homœopathic profession, as in its pages he has fully explained his law of cure. It has been called the "Bible of Homœopathy." It contains a complete and exhaustive exposition of Hahnemann's discoveries, experiments, and opinions, concerning the healing of the sick.

The title page of the first edition bears the following motto from the poet Gellert:

> "The truth we mortals need
>   Us blest to make and keep,
> The All-wise slightly covered o'er,
>   But did not bury deep."

This motto is changed in the other editions to the words "Aude sapere;" and the title itself becomes: "Organon der Heilkunst."

He says in the preface: "The results of my convictions are set forth in this book. It remains to be seen, whether physicians, who mean to act honestly by their conscience and by their fellow creatures, will continue to stick to the pernicious tissue of conjectures and caprice, or can open their eyes to the salutary truth.

"I must warn the reader that indolence, love of ease and obstinacy preclude effective service at the altar of truth, and only freedom from prejudice and untiring zeal qualify for the most sacred of all human occupations, the practice of the true system of medicine.

"The physician who enters on his work in this spirit becomes directly assimilated to the Divine Creator of the world, whose human creatures he helps to preserve, and whose approval renders him thrice blessed."

The book consists of two parts: the introduction and the Organon proper. The introduction is first devoted to an analysis of the imperfect and erroneous method, distinguishing the old school of medicine. This he calls: "A mode of cure with

---

*The Organon, vol. 1, p. 245, Liverpool.

medical substances of unknown quality, compounded together, applied to diseases arbitrarily classified and arranged in reference to their materiality, called Allopathy."

The second part of the introduction is filled with examples from medical writings of cures unwittingly made by physicians in accordance with the law of the similars. These quotations are made from the writings of the ancients, from Hippocrates down through the great list of medical writers, with, as usual, careful references to each one.

It is as much a wonder of intimate research and acquaintance with the medical literature of the past, as is his essay on *Hellebore*.

He concludes: "Thus far the great truth has more than once been approached by physicians. But a transitory idea was all that presented itself to them; consequently the indispensable reform which ought to have taken place in the old school of therapeutics, to make room for the true curative method, and a system of medicine at once simple and certain, has, till the present day, not been effected."

The Organon proper is divided into paragraphs, each one of which contains one or more aphorisms in regard to the law of Homœopathy, and the way in which it should be practiced. He gives full and careful directions for preparing medicines homœopathically; states the proper size of the dose, expounds at length the doctrines of Homœopathy; explains why such small doses can, and do, cure quickly; gives full directions for proving: in fact it is a full exposition of the new law, as Hahnemann understood it.

To any one who wishes to become more familiar with the teachings of the "Organon" explained in a simple and plain manner, it may be stated that this can be found in an article by Dr. Samuel Lilianthal, published in the California *Homœopath*, for March, April, May and June, 1889, under the title: " A Catechism of Samuel Hahnemann's Organon," and which was also published in the *Homœopathic World*, for June and July, 1889, as "The Essence of Samuel Hahnemann's Organon." Its tenets may here be found in a nutshell.

The five editions of the Organon, that were published in Hahnemann's lifetime, differ somewhat from each other, the first edition is not as full as is the fifth, but the teaching is the same; that the duty of the physician is to cure the sick as easily and as speedily as possible.

It may be mentioned here that the Organon has been translated into English, French, Italian, Spanish, Hungarian, Dutch, Polish, Russian, Danish and Swedish.

The publication of this was the signal for the commencement of a violent warfare against Hahnemann. He had raised his hand against the traditions of many years; he had demonstrated to the minds of many, that the usual practice of medicine was founded on nothing but the greatest uncertainty and empiricism; he had shown up the fallacies and inconsistencies of the doctors, the mistakes and ignorance of many of the apothecaries.

In the place of all this doubt and confusion, he had clearly, and at length, proven that the system called by him that of the similars, or the positive method of healing, was really based upon a fixed and unalterable law; that homœopathic medicines really would cure in a quicker and more easy way than any hitherto discovered.

He was attacked in the medical journals of the day, books and pamphlets were fulminated against him and his strange doctrines. He was called a charlatan, a quack, an ignoramus. His minute doses were declared to be impossible. His tests of medicines were pronounced simply ridiculous.

Especially bitter in attack was one Dr. A. F. Hecker, of Berlin, whose articles were published in the *Annalen der gesammten Medicin*, Vol. 2. These reviews were so virulent that even Hahnemann's opponents condemned them. Hahnemann did not under his own name answer them, in fact he never stooped to reply to his numerous calumniators. His son, Frederick, however, published a Refutation, in a pamphlet in 1811.

The presumption is that Hahnemann himself and not the son wrote the Refutation to this bitter attack upon the "Organon."

In 1889 Dr. R. E. Dudgeon published in the *Homœopathic World* fifty-one letters written by Hahnemann, and extending from the years 1811 to 1842. The first letter is one to Arnold, the publisher of his books.* By it, it will be seen that Hahnemann was very desirous that the attack of Hecker upon the Organon should be answered. Dr. Dudgeon says in the introduction to this letter: "Accordingly a Refutation was prepared,

*Hom. World, London, Vols. 24, 25.

nominally by his son, but to those familiar with the father's writings, it is easy to see who guided the junior Hahnemann's hand. * * * * As Frederick Hahnemann was quite a young man when this masterly Refutation of Hecker was written, and had not yet graduated, it is extremely doubtful if he had much to do with this learned anti-critique beyond lending his name to it, and possibly writing it out to his father's dictation."*

The letter concerning the publication of this refutation is as follows:

" MY DEAR MR. ARNOLD:

" I wish you had read Hecker's abusive article against me; you would then think that the Refutation is only too moderate. You cannot wish that no reply should have been made by my son to those shameful accusations. In such cases every author should know best what answer he should make. You then returned the manuscript in order that some alterations should be made. (Who was it marked these passages? Was it you or was it Rober? If the latter, he must have already read the manuscript and considered the remainder faultless!) Look now— though the author did not consider it necessary, yet to please you he altered and modified those passages. You could not desire more, nor could you ask more. And when this is done, and yet your censor does not allow the manuscript to pass, it is not the author's fault that it is not printed, and that you should have made no preparations for printing it, as the censure was not justified.

" Moreover, no censor can refuse to allow the printing of a defensive work in which the assailant is repulsed with actual libels (which is not the case in this manuscript), for libels of private persons concern not the censor, but the author. If there are personal libels in the book, it is not the censor, nor yet the publisher, but only the author, who can be legally prosecuted. Consequently what Mr. Rober has written under the title is sham pretext for his refusal. The true reason can be nothing else than the rough truths told of the medical art in the work. If calumnies could prevent the printing of a book, then Hecker's abusive work would never have passed the censure. But we must take into consideration the underhand, backbiting, sneaking ways for which Dresden is distinguished.

*Hom. World, Vol. 24, p. 202.

"The truths of universal utility respecting the medical art contained in this book, and which constitute its chief value, would assuredly excite the opposition of the Leipsic professors, especially when they learn that its publication has been refused in Dresden. The plain truth it contains would only bring upon my son annoyances from his teachers, under whom he still must remain for a short time, and by whom he will soon have to pass the examination for his degree. As yet none of the professors have seen the manuscript, though they will hear of it.

"The best plan would be to have the manuscript printed in some small place where there does not exist any great prejudice in favor of the traditional medicine, out of which there is no salvation; where such (truthful) denials of its claims would not be thought so much of; or where the official doctor, if there is one, and he is inclined to be nasty, may be bribed to keep quiet with a few dollars.

"If you will adopt this plan, and assure me that copies of the book shall not be issued until my son has taken his degree, which he will do as soon as possible, then the manuscript of the Refutation is still at your service, and you shall then get the Materia Medica.

"If it had been secretly printed in Dresden, without the veto of the Holy Inquisition, then my son would have already got his degree before any particular notice had been taken of it in Leipsic.

"But now that so much fuss has been made about the thing in Leipsic, there is no other way to manage it but that which I have proposed. Nor can a single word of the manuscript be altered.

"It is incredible that charges of heresy and the spirit of persecution could prevail, even in matters of science, and exercise their despotism, but it is so, as we see in this case.

"But shall this miserable charge of heresy prevent the most salutary truths being said and printed? Freedom of action, and liberty of the press, must prevail when grand new truths shall be communicated to the world. What could Luther have done with his splendid ideas if he had not been able to get them printed? If he could not have sent his outspoken, plain truths hot from his heart to the press of his dear, courageous friend, the bookseller and publisher, Hans Luft, with all the hard words and abusive expressions he deemed useful for his object. Then everything was printed that was necessary, and it was only so, and in no other way, that the salutary Reformation could be effected. It is, of course, not necessary for me, like Luther, to abuse the Pope, and call him an ass in my writings, but I and my son must be able to say salutary truths in order to bring about the much-needed reform in medicine. Hans Luft was almost as indispensable an instrument of the Reformation as Luther himself.

"I, too, require for the good cause as warm, as hearty a friend of the truth for my publisher as Luft was for Luther.

"But if I experience such great resistance I cannot advance another step.

"It is just the same with the Materia Medica. If the enemies of truth are not either silenced or convinced and instructed by this refutation of Hecker, my Materia Medica cannot make any way. The public can never be brought to make any use of it if the malicious objections of Hecker and Company are not distinctly refuted. If Hecker and opponents of his stamp remain unrefuted, I cannot with honor go on with the educational works I am projecting, and even the Organon itself will cease to be respected. No one would believe the effect such mendacious representations have on the public.

"If the Refutation should not appear, it will be thought that these calumnies against myself and my Organon are unrefutable, and I would be, as it were, banished. No one would listen to what I said, even should I say the most salutary things. The prejudiced statements and miserable accusations of this more than spiteful man must be utterly smashed up, before I can go on with my educational work.

"This is the state of things. It is for you to determine whether you can interest yourself sufficiently in the truth and the good cause as to remain my publisher. See if you can realize my present wishes.*
                    "Yours sincerely,
"April 24, (1811.)   "DR. HAHNEMANN."

"I have just heard from Leipsic that pressure is to be put on my son to withdraw his Refutation. I beg Mr. Voigt to immediately write and tell Magister Schubert that the manuscript business is already settled, and that he should leave my son alone.''

Burnett says:* ''In all Hahnemann's checkered career nothing strikes me as showing more profound wisdom than his letting his adversaries alone in their vile abuse; he might have hurled back their slanders, and defended himself and his discovery with the eloquence of a Demosthenes; but, as Celsus remarks, 'Morbi non eloquentia sed remediis curantur ('Diseases are not cured by eloquence, but by remedies'), and so he plodded on at his 'Materia Medica,' on which much of his great glory must ever rest.''

The books and pamphlets written against Homœopathy at this time may be numbered by hundreds, and, in addition, the journals of the dominant school were filled with articles. One Simon even published a journal called the *Anti-Homöopathie Archiv.*, that extended through several volumes.

And Hahnemann, except in letters to his friends, and perhaps, in the above mentioned Refutation, replied to this hail of abuse by not one word. It reminds one of the old fable of the gnat which perched on the back of the ox and asked him if he hurt him much; and the good-natured ruminant answered that he did not know he was there.

But a fitting answer was given to the jealous horde in the year, 1811, when Hahnemann gave to the world the first volume of the "Materia Medica Pura." And during this period of abuse he also made many new converts to his mild and successful system of healing.

CHAPTER XXI.

REMOVAL TO LEIPSIC—LETTERS FROM SISTER CHARLOTTE—WISH
TO ESTABLISH A SCHOOL OF HOMŒOPATHY—DISSER-
TATION ON HELLEBORE—ALLOPATHIC PRAISE,
LECTURES COMMENCED.

In the early part of the year 1811 Hahnemann removed to the great medical city of Leipsic, in order to engage more actively in the propagation of his new system by means of didactic lectures.

What a marvelous variety of changes had compassed the life of this man since the time when he departed from the great city

---

*Ecce Medicus, p. 146, (See *Recorder*.)

a boy of twenty-two with the future all before him. Vienna, Hermanstadt, Erlangen, Dessau, Gommern, Dresden; the momentous discovery at Leipsic; Georgenthal, the Wander-years afterwards, and Torgau with its literary results, until now, with a name well-known in all Germany, with a new and superior system of medicine to his credit, he, a man of fifty-six years, and as he called himself—cosmopolite—once more turns towards the scene of his earlier student life.

Trial, sorrow, privation, malevolence, falsehood, all had followed him like shadows; yet had he gone patiently and manfully on in the path he had determined to follow. Now he returned to Leipsic to teach to others the truths that God had permitted him to discover; to disseminate a certain law of healing for the good of his fellow-men.

In this place two letters from his sister Charlotte may be of interest.

Charlotte was Hahnemann's favorite sister. For her first husband she married the Rev. A. B. Trinius, of Eisleben; after his death she wedded General Superintendent Dr. Muller, of Eisleben. The younger son of whom she speaks in the second letter, as seeing in the train of the Duchess Antoinette, of Wurtemberg, whose body physician he then was, was Hahnemann's favorite nephew, Trinius, and he was greatly distinguished as a botanist, physician and poet. Some further account of him may be found in the chapter concerning Hahnemann's family.

It is said of this lady: "Hahnemann's amiableness as a man is strikingly exemplified by the fact that he was dearly beloved, not only by his pupils but by his relatives, and the expressed opinion of the latter is extremely valuable in that connection; his eldest sister, the wife of the General Superintendent Muller, in Eisleben, deserves special mention. She possessed a most estimable character, and was extremely pious, learned and benevolent, and her ripe scholarship induced many young people to study more diligently. Hahnemann and his wife were her darlings. The following letters written at a very important period of her life permit a glimpse into the depths of her mind and heart:" *

"*My Dear Brother:* How much; O, how much, I should like to press thee and thine once more to my heart in this life! I

---

* "Biographisches Denkmal," p. 100.

would have traveled round the world to have done it; but, unfortunately, all thy news makes all, yes all, impossible. So then thou hast been right well, thou who hast been so mindful of me.

"Not a day passes that I do not offer a prayer for thee to God, who loves us all so much that in order to procure everlasting happiness for us, and to confirm his own attributes, He assumed the person of Jesus Christ for us all. Come all ye dear ones whom I would press to my heart at this solemn moment, and would greet with the greeting of love, come. We should permit no day to pass in which we do not pray for help from the Holy Spirit to enable us to be duly and truly thankful to the Father and His Eternal Son that He cares for us. How happy and well have I felt in the midst of my pains and griefs during the last thirty-four years; for thus long has it been that Jesus Christ has been my wisdom, righteousness, salvation and redemption.

"When you receive these lines I shall be on my way to where God called me, and where he caused manna to grow for me, a poor woman destitute of all property, and where I shall still use the faculties with which he has endowed me.

"My sons have just learned through me that I am going to Curland.

"Count von Lieven has written me an extremely kind letter, and has provided me with a pass and travelling expenses.

"When I shall have been in Senten for a little while I will send you a true account of my condition.

"May Leipzic be the scene of all the earthly happiness that it is possible for thee to enjoy in this world.

"Alas, my dear brother, I cannot tell thee all that my soul would express.

"Thy loving sister,

"CH. G. MULLER.

"Edersleben near Eisleben, June 18, 1811."

"SENTEN, October 17, 1811.

"My Dear Brother: I declare to thee that there passes scarcely a day that I do not think of thee, thy wife and children, and think of thee so justly with love, too. What it has cost not to see once more you all whom I would press to my heart from the

eldest to the youngest that knows how to love, can be better felt than described. I had a pleasant journey, which was without any important happenings; in fact, I was not seasick once during the twenty-four hours that we were crossing the Gulf of Curland.

"Three delightful stops, in Halle, Berlin, and Konigsberg, respectively—in all of which places there reside dear acquaintances of mine—added pleasure to the journey. How kindly and kinsmanlike I was received! I met Count and Countess von Lieven at the house of Herr von Sacken, the Countess's father. I rested there eight days, and then went on with the Count's family to Senten. If thou wouldst understand my position, it is that of a loving mother.

"I have now been here three months, and can bear testimony of two kinds: one kind is that what I teach the Countess is more like a pleasure than a burden; and the other, that no time is ever tedious here, for there are too many changes. I had formed a different opinion of Curland.

"Almost everything here betokens prosperity, and I had supposed that the inhabitants were poor and wretched.

"The weddings of the serfs, or bondmen, here cost one, two, and three hundred thalers; and whoever is not in good circumstances has himself to blame for it. Plenty prevails almost everywhere, and especially at the farmhouses. Breakfast at our house here consists of white and black bread, butter, cheese, pickled salmon and herring, a kind of sea fish called lamprey, sugared rum, liquor and orangeade. At the close of meals, however, there is no intoxication. Permit me to say that I am frugal, and in good health.

"I saw my eldest son for a few hours in the forenoon before I reached Frauenburg. He almost got on his knees and begged me to go live with him, and wished to share with me all that he had; but so long as I have my strength I will not eat the bread of my children. If I do not utterly mistake I may be buried here at the Lieven homestead.

"I saw my youngest son in the cortége of the Duchess of Wurtemberg, on its way from the sea baths to Witepsk, in Russia.

"It seems as if God had allotted me a resting place for the remainder of my life here in this dear family, where I might enjoy the most inspiring of all realities. Jesus Christ has made us unto wisdom, righteousness, salvation and redemption. My heart lives therein, and I am happy and of good cheer.

"Thy Sister,

"MULLER.

"She loves thee with her whole soul."

From the time of Hahnemann's settlement in Leipsic may be reckoned a new and important epoch in his life. Heretofore he had been driven from place to place, by the jealousy and bigotry of the physicians, and their allies, the apothecaries. He had endeavored by every possible means that an honest man could devise to persuade the doctors to try the new and simple system. He had, in his writings, placed the matter in a temperate way before the reading portion of the profession. He had carefully explained the path by which he reached certainty from the doubts of the old and imperfect methods of practice.

It had been all in vain, and now he gave up all thoughts of argument and of kindliness; persecution had made him bitter. From this time he became a most uncompromising foe to those who would not listen believingly to his doctrines.

He gave up the idea of modifying in the least degree the predetermined opinions of the older physicians. He turned to the students and the younger doctors who, as yet, were not so firmly fixed in prejudice, and who were willing to submit, with some degree of fairness, these new and startling theories of medicine to a reasonable test.

He soon collected from the students, congregated at Leipsic, a select coterie, to whom he commenced to teach his doctrines.

His first desire had been to establish a college with a Homœopathic hospital attached, but this he could not do, and therefore he resolved to deliver lectures upon the principles of his beloved Homœopathy.

Albrecht says: * "Hahnemann resolved to move to Leipsic to devote himself to instructing the pupils of the Medical Department of the University. When he asked for the privilege of delivering lectures, Rosenmuller, who was then the Dean of the Medical Faculty, told him that a doctor *extraneus*, although he is legally entitled to practice medicine, has not for that reason the privilege of delivering lectures, but that he must first gain

---

*Albrecht's "Leben und Wirken," p. 30.

such a privilege by the vindication of a dissertation with a respondent from the Medical Schools, and that he must pay to the Faculty a fee of fifty thalers. Then he becomes a member of the Faculty and may announce his lectures both in the catalogue of Lectors and by public posters."

In accordance with this regulation Hahnemann was now compelled to pay the usual fee, and to defend a thesis before the Faculty of Medicine.

In defending a thesis according to the law of the Universities of that day, the candidate was obliged to present it before a mixed body of scientists, and be prepared to defend it from criticisms and attacks that any one of his medical listeners might make against its truth.

On the 26th of June, 1812, Hahnemann presented a Latin thesis, entitled "A Medical Historical Dissertation on the Helleborism of the Ancients."*

His son Frederick acted as the respondent. The thesis was a marvel of research and erudition, concerning the white hellebore of the ancients, which he proved to be identical with the *Veratrum album* of the present.

He referred to many of the earlier writers, and in such a way as shows distinctly that he must have carefully studied their writings.

In order to have written this he must have read in their original language, the works of Avicenna from the Arabic, Galen, Pliny, Oribasius, Herodotus, Hippocrates, Ctesias the Coan, Theophrastus the Eresian, Haller, Scaliger, Dioscorides, Murray, Pallas, Vicat, Lucretius, Celsus, Jacquinus, Salmatius, Antyllus, Grassius, Muralto, Gesner, Bergius, Greding, Unter, Lorry, Reimann, Scholzius, Benevenius, Rodder, Lentilius, Strabo, Stephanus the Byzantine, Rufus, Ætius the Amideman, Rasarius, Archigenes, Aretæus of Cappadocia, Plistonicus, Diocles, Themison, Cælius Aurelianus, Alexander of Tralles, Paulus of Ægina, Johannes, Massarius, Petri Belloni, Pzusanius, Mnesitheus, Rufus the Ephesian, and many more.

The above medical writers are referred to in no superficial manner. Hahnemann must have read carefully each one of their writings, in order to quote them in the manner he does. In the Latin pamphlet published at the time, there are foot

*Published in Hahnemann' "Lesser Writings," New York, 1852, page 569.

notes on every page, and these references are very circum-
stantial, both in regard to the subject, and also concerning the
writer.*

He often corrects mistakes in the old writings, stating carefully wherein each one is wrong. Thus on page 603 he says:
"Pliny is, however, wrong in here stating Phocian Anticyra to
be an island for it was situated on the continent, half a mile
from the port. Pausanias has described its position." On page
613 he speaks of restoring a word in Sarrazin's text of Dioscorides, and says that he is fully borne out by Avicenna's
Arabic version. On page 615 he says: "Ætius is wrong in
saying that Johannes Actuarius was the first to allege that
Hellebore acts without difficulty."

Of Mesne he enters into particulars on page 594: "He
flourished in the reign of caliph Al Rashid, about the year 800,
a man of such celebrity that he was termed the evangelist of
physicians."

From all these writers he culls, and refers to the book and
passage in the writings of each in which any mention is made
of the *Hellebore*.

In order to do this their pages must have been all turned
over, and he must have read in Hebrew, Greek, Latin, Arabic,
Italian, French, English and German.

It is needless to say that no one attacked this wonder of
philological research. All his hearers were amazed. The Dean
of the Faculty publicly tendered his congratulations.

And yet, a few years later this master of medical learning was
hounded out of Leipsic by physicians who said he was not
capable of preparing his own medicines; they even burnt those
medicines, so great was their prejudice against the man!

Albrecht tells the following anecdote to illustrate the effect
that Hahnemann's scholarship had upon the physicians at the
time: †

"A Dr. Huck, of Lutzen, a small city near Leipzic, writes
thus to a friend in Penig: Dear Friend—Though I seldom talk
to any one about one of the greatest thinkers of all the centuries,
yet I gladly write to you about the man who, by evident proofs
of his great ability, has in a short time wholly won over to him-

---

*"Dissertatio Historico—Medica de Helleborismo veterum," Lipsiæ, 1812.
†"Leben und Wirken," p. 30.   "Biographisches Denkmal," p. 31.

self the unprejudiced portion of the medical as well as the non-medical learned men of Leipzic. To hear Hahnemann, the keenest and boldest investigator of nature, deliver a master-piece of his intellect and industry, was to me a truly beatific enjoyment. I returned home as if in a dream, and a wilderness seemed to surround me, as I was obliged to acknowledge to my-self, 'You are not worthy to loose the latchets of his shoes.'

"He will deliver a private lecture at Michaelmas. I shall be a student next year again, and if unforeseen circumstances do not prevent, will see what I can derive from this inconceivable source. If Hahnemann would stoop to act contrary to his noble character and play the hypocrite, like so many other (seemingly) great men, even the most renowned citizens of Leipzic would be obliged to lower their pretensions Most of his opponents were so candid and courteous as to acknowledge that they were wholly of his opinion, medically speaking, and they thought that any one in order to say anything would be obliged to dis-cuss the matter philologically. He covered himself with renown and remained victor.

"Had it not been a very unsuitable time to look for him on that day, I would have gone to him, and would have voluntarily and unconditionally betaken myself to his banner."

This letter is dated Lutzen, August 9, 1812. Albrecht adds in a note: "The physician, of whose letter this is an extract, as a token of his high regard for Hahnemann, christened his son Luther Reinhard Hahnemann."

Hartmann says of this period of his life:* "With the year 1811, when Hahnemann chose Leipsic as his place of residence, begins a new and very highly important era in his life. He doubtless moved to Leipsic to deliver lectures and thus to make accessible to the young medical students his new system of medi-cine, as he well realized that it would always remain a terra in-cognita to the physicians of the old school. For this purpose he became one of the Faculty through his disputation, and also wrote his 'Historico-Medical Dissertation on the Helleborism of the Ancients,' and publically vindicated the same on June 26, 1812, having selected as his respondent his son, Frederick Hahnemann, then a Baccalaureate of Medicine. There was at that time but one opinion concerning his intellectual and scholarly treatise,

*Allg. Hom. Zeit., Vol. 26, p. 180.

and Ludwig, then Dean of the Medical Faculty, publicly eulogized him for it."

In December, 1811, he had the following announcement inserted in the *Reichanzeiger:*

"MEDICAL INSTITUTE."

"I feel that my doctrine enunciated in the 'Organon of Rational Healing' aroused the highest expectations for the welfare of the sick, but by its very nature it is so new and striking, and not only opposes almost all medical dogmas and traditional observations, but also deviates from them as widely as heaven from earth, that it cannot so readily gain entrance among the otherwise educated physicians of my time, unless practical demonstration comes to its assistance.

"In order to effect this object among my contemporaries, and thus show them by the evidence of sight that the truth of this doctrine stands firmly upon an irrefutable basis in its whole extent, and that the Homœopathic method of healing, new as it is, is the only acceptable, the most consistent, the simplest, the surest and the most beneficent of all earthly ways of healing human disease, I have decided to open here in Leipzic, at the beginning of April, an Institute for Graduate Physicians.

"In this Institute I shall elucidate in every respect the entire Homœopathic system of healing as taught in the 'Organon,' and shall make a practical application of it with patients treated in their presence, and thus place my pupils in a condition to be able to practice this system in all cases themselves.

"A six months' course will be sufficient to enable any intelligent mind to grasp the principles of the Homœopathic law of cure."

Hahnemann thus announced his first course of lectures on the theory and principles of Homœopathy, and said that in them he would explain the principles of the "Organon." They were commenced in April, 1812.

He gave two lectures weekly, on Wednesday and Saturday afternoons, from 2 to 3 o'clock. These lectures were continued semi-annually during his entire stay at Leipsic, from 1812 to 1821.

As an example of Hahnemann's method of selecting the remedy the following letter addressed to Stapf, in 1813, may be interesting. It was first published by Dr. Hering, in the

Homœopathic News of Philadelphia, 1855, and then was copied into the *Zeitung* for June 25, 1855.*

Stapf consulted Hahnemann about his own child. At this time the first part only of the Materia Medica had been published. Stapf does not seem to have reported the symptoms very carefully, and he had mentioned as possible remedies, *Nux vomica, Chamomilla, Pulsatilla* and *China*. In the original letter Hahnemann, in mentioning the symptoms, calls them also by numbers.

"Notwithstanding that *Nux vomica* 795 produced perspiration standing on the forehead; 826, perspiration when moving; 830, in general, perspiration during sleep; *Chamomilla*, 826, perspiration especially about the head during sleep; *Pulsatilla*, perspiration during sleep, disappearing when awaking; *China*, perspiration when moving (crying), perspiration in the head especially (but also in the hair); there is more indication for *Pulsatilla* by the itching of the eyes, which *Pulsatilla* has, especially with redness in the external corner of the eye after rubbing, and with agglutination of them in the morning; if not, *Ignatia* would be preferable, which also cures itching and redness, but in the internal corners with agglutination in the morning, in case the child's disposition is very changeable, now too lively, and then peevishly crying, which *Ignatia* produces; and if there should be, at the same time, a great sensitiveness to the daylight when opening the eyes in the morning, which also is caused by *Ignatia*; or, in case of a mild disposition and a weeping mood in the evening, and a general aggravation of symptoms in the evening, *Pulsatilla*.

"The frequent awakening during the night indicates *Ignatia* more than *Pulsatilla*, the latter has more a late falling asleep. The itching of the nose has been observed mostly from *Nux vomica*. *Ignatia* and *Chamomilla* have both, the latter more—pain during micturition. *Pulsatilla* the most pain before urinating. The loud breathing has been observed of *China* and *Nux* —from the latter especially during sleep.

"As these remedies correspond much with each other (*China* excepted), and one corrects the faults and bad effects of the other (if only *Ignatia* does not follow *Nux*, or *Nux* is not given

Allg. Hom. Zeitung. Vol. 50, page 64. *Hom. News*, Phila., 1855, page 5.

immediately after *Ignatia* as they are not well suited to follow
one another, on account of their too great medical similarity),
you yourself can judge now, as to the succession in which you
may choose to employ *Ignatia, Pulsatilla, Nux vomica, Chamomilla,* if the first, or one of the others, should not alone prove
sufficient. To give *Chamomilla* there ought to be more thirst
at night than at present, and more irritability. *China* has little
or nothing for itself, and is therefore not to be chosen.''

Hahnemann's lectures were attended both by students and
physicians, old and young, nor were these confined to the members of the medical profession; others, as in the case of Baron
von Brunnow, who was a student of law, listened to the new
propaganda of this enthusiastic old man. The fame of his marvelous learning, the desire to understand something of the new
truth of medicine, and the wish, no doubt, to hear the man who
was making such wonderful cures, all were factors in attracting
many to his lectures.

We are indebted to Dr. Franz Hartmann, one of his pupils at
that time, for very much that we know concerning his life and
teaching in Leipsic. He says that had Hahnemann not been so
bitter in his abuse of the old school of medicine and its adherents, he would have attracted more real followers.

One can readily understand the reasons for this bitterness on
the part of this old man, for he was then nearly sixty years of
age; he had been driven from place to place, his statements
laughed at, his knowledge scorned, his efforts at conciliation met
with calumny and lies.

He had long before this time ceased to use his former methods
of temperate argument. He now exercised little patience for
the men who condemned his doctrines without investigation.

During this time he was working upon the ''Reine Arzneimittellehre,'' or ''Materia Medica Pura.'' The first volume was
published in Dresden by Arnold in 1811; the second and third
volumes in 1816–17; the fourth in 1818; the fifth in 1819; and
the sixth in 1821. A second edition was published by Arnold
(1822 to 1827).

The ''Materia Medica Pura'' consists of a record of the symptoms obtained from different medical substances proven upon the
healthy body by Hahnemann and his disciples. In the preface
to volume I. he says:

"I forbear writing a criticism of the existing systems and modes of preparation of remedial agents. Physicians imagine that they can judge of the remedial virtues of medicinal agents by their color, taste and smell; they suppose they can extract these virtues by distillation or sublimation in the shape of phlegma, ethereal oils, pungent acids and oils, volatile salts, or from the caput mortuum, they imagine they can extract alkalies and earths almost by the same processes, or agreeably to the modern method, they dissolve the soluble parts of those substances in different liquids, inspissate the extracts, or add many kinds of reagents for the purpose of extracting resin, gum, gluten, starch, wax and albumen, salts and earths, acids and alkaloids, or converting the substances into gases.

"In spite of all these violent transformations the medicinal substances never showed the remedial virtues which each of them possesses, the material extracts did not embody the curative power of the respective medicinal substances. That power cannot be presented in a tangible form but can only be recognized by its effects in the living organism.

"The day of the true knowledge of remedies and a true system of therapeutics will dawn when physicians shall abandon the ridiculous method of mixing together large portions of medicinal substances whose remedial virtues are only known speculatively or by vague praises, which is in fact *not to know them at all.*"

In the prefaces to the several volumes he mentions the fallacies of polypharmacy, the advantage of prescribing according to a simple and fixed law. He makes careful explanations of the experiments whose results are recorded, gives the order in which the symptoms of the drugs are classified and arranged, with explanations of certain obscure symptoms.

As a preface to volume IV. he publishes the essay : "How is it Possible That Small Homœopathic Doses Should Have Such great Power?"

In this he advances his theory that minute subdivision of a substance increases its power of medicinal action.

Under each remedy is first an introduction, giving its method of preparation and best limit of attenuation, with general remarks on its action on the system ; then follow the symptoms, classified according to the parts of the body.

In the German editions these symptoms are numbered. It was originally issued in six volumes, and contained the provings of fifty-four remedies.

In 1813 he published in the *Allgemeine Anzeiger*, for March, an article on "The Spirit of the Homœopathic Healing Law." This was a résumé of the truths regarding the effects of remedies prescribed in accordance with the Homœopathic law. It has been many times republished. It is to be particularly noticed, as it was the first essay on the subject of Homœopathy printed in the United States. It was translated into imperfect English by Dr. Hans Birch Gram, and published in New York city in 1825.

CHAPTER XXII.

CORRESPONDENCE WITH ROBBI—PROVING REMEDIES—HAHNE-
MANN TO STAPF, ON PROVING—HARTMANN'S STORY,
OF HAHNEMANN'S LIFE AT LEIPSIC—
HAHNEMANN'S STUDENTS.

Soon after Hahnemann commenced to lecture at Leipsic, one Dr. Robbi, a young Allopathic physician, succeeded in ingratiating himself in his favor by feigned respect and admiration for his genius. He afterwards became one of the foremost in ridiculing his system. Robbi's letter and Hahnemann's answer are both given in full, as illustrating the kindliness of Hahnemann towards the man whom even then he must have mistrusted. Dr. Robbi writes as follows:*

"*Noble and Honored Sir:* A year ago I heard you deliver your lectures on the 'Organon of Healing' with much pleasure, and how the scales fell from my eyes; much was clear to me, but there was much that was not clear, and therefore I had almost decided, along with my late friend, Mr. Hannemann, to investigate more thoroughly a system by which we might be able to attain to something more positive in medicine. My friend, H—— and I had incurred much enmity among our colleagues through our vindication of your method of healing, and especially that of Dr. N——.

"My friend, Hannemann, died, and his death took me back to

---

*"Biographisches Denkmal," p. 128.

practice in the hospital, and finally the derangement of my nervous system by a so-called typhus nosocomialis took me far from my beautiful goal. But, nevertheless, I studied your 'Organon.' I have now taken a degree, and have no longer to spend so much on the symbolical books of the *Ars conjecturalis*.

"I have taken the liberty to write to Prince Repnin, through his family physician, Dr. Bizzatti, who is my friend, about the public benefit that would be derived from introducing your method of healing, and I hope to receive more definite information about the matter in a few days.

"I should like very much to talk with you personally on some topics concerning your system. I have already gone twice to the lectures in your department and was not admitted, so that I suppose that my visit is not agreeable to you, and I must have recourse to writing.

"And, besides this, unfortunately, I have seen from one of your letters to Dr. Dienemann that you wholly misjudge me and already consider me to be sunk in the mire of the old school. I shall not cast aside my method of healing until I find a better one; and I shall by no means depend either on the prejudices of custom—that childish belief—and justify or defend what is nonsensical; only I must first have clearness, for then only am I successful.

"I have thought of translating your 'Organon' into English or Italian; but as I cannot previously have a personal talk with you about the matter, I think that it will scarcely be able to be done. There is no doubt that the publication of such a system of medicine would produce no insignificant revolution among the learned in England and Italy, since the unimportant system of the theory of contra-stimulation, which is nothing but a modification of Brown's theory of stimulation, has already taken root in the whole of Italy. I can send you an Italian treatise on this system, if it would be of interest to you, to make yourself acquainted with it.

"With profound esteem, I have the honor to be
"Your obedient servant,
"DR. HEINRICH ROBBI.

"P. S.—Of your works, I have only the 'Organon' and the defence of your system against Hecker's silly attack. I must procure for myself all the other books that you have written, and I therefore entreat you to furnish me with a complete list of the same.''

To this letter Hahnemann made the following dignified and kindly answer:

"*Dear Dr. Robbi:* Having taken your degree, you are now at liberty to think and act as you please—a desideratum of the greatest importance to every artisan. You are now free to go on in the old way, or to adopt the new one now pointed out.

"I am gratified to find that, though owing to my professional engagements, I was unable to converse with you at my residence, I am now able to communicate my meaning to you in another and more permanent manner, by writing. The tendency of my opinion is to warn you against the adoption of Homœopathy. Listen to me!

"When we pursue a practical career in life we usually have a threefold purpose: 1st. To make ourselves generally beloved by our mode of thinking and acting, to make no blunders, and to be corrupted by nobody. 2d. To arrange our business so as to transact it the most readily. 3d. To earn as much as possible by this business.

"You can reach no one of these three purposes so well through Homœopathy as through the way usually chosen. For you think, since one is tolerated among his colleagues if he wishes to do nothing that is new, and immediately pursues the same path as they do, that it commands respect not to raise yourself above them by introducing improvements, and not to cast suspicion upon the belief of your ancestors by any innovations.

"Then one is your 'dear colleague,' and it comes into the mind of no one of these colleagues to undermine your good name by defamation.

"If one is addicted to their way, to their belief—hallowed by time-honored opinions—in other words, does as they do, who should then calumniate, harm, and persecute you? How can it come into the mind of anyone who has a conscientious heart to do wrong to a brother of the same persuasion? By following this course you clearly see you secure good will of your colleagues, and you perceive that no one will then rob you of the esteem and confidence which you command among your patients. You remain without scruple a friend to their surrounding and in the most friendly understanding with them. Is this of no significance?

"On the other hand, I need not remind you of what the Homœopathist has to endure. Just recall what you have heard with your own ears, or have read here and there. Would you court such martyrdom? I do not advise you to do so.

"The second purpose, the readier transaction of business, you cannot reach as certainly as by the usual way. There are enough prescriptions of a prescribed form for all specified diseases, and if some disease has no name it is given a prescribed name, and there is applied to it the medical formula given to it by the learned man who wrote on that particular disease. Everything is at hand, and we have only to imitate, and if anyone censures or condemns the treatment he is referred to the book. Then he must hold his tongue! How easy it is to incorporate in one's memory a certain number of formulas which one need only to recall to mind at the bedside of the patient in order to jot down one thing or other on a slip of paper. This requires scarcely two minutes. The apothecary prepares the prescription for us, and what a convenience!

"And then only a few questions to ask the patient, to see his tongue and to feel his pulse, in order to know what is the ailment. In this way a dozen patients are prescribed for and got rid of in an incredibly short space of time; and then one can have to himself almost the whole day! By this method the apothecary remains favorably inclined to us; and who does not know how important and indispensable his favor is to the physician?

"How ill fares a Homœopathic physician! He must take the trouble to inquire about all the circumstances or conditions of the patient in order to be able to select a suitable remedy. This occasions a loss of time, at least at the first visit, and in this time the ordinary physician can prescribe for three times as many patients; and then he gives a very considerable number of glasses, jars and boxes. Sick people are accustomed to these, and they like to have many, and of different kinds; but, on the other hand, the little that the Homœopathist gives scarcely begets the confidence of the sick. It would be foolish to reply that the Homœopathic physician can have himself better paid, because notwithstanding the loss of time in questioning and meditating, yet he helps the patient in a shorter time than does the Allopath.

"And, besides all this, all the rest of the medical fraternity strive heartily and mightily to alienate their acquaintance from him. I well, too, know the might of the innumerable lashing tongues which can proscribe one Homœopathic physician. My worldly wisdom protects me from this vituperation, and it will so continue to do.

"And as regards the seemingly trifling matter of conscience which the Homœopathic physician awakens and develops by his precise delineation of disease, by his selection of the exactly suitable remedy, and by the conviction that he should conscientiously furnish the true remedy to the patient with his own hands and supply it, too, with the best talent at his command, he ought to strive to keep it pure.

"But in this respect the Allopathist has to render an account to no one. He thinks, though, that it cannot be so bad and sinful since there are so many others who do not do differently, and that if there is a future beyond the grave, and an accountability is to be rendered there, I too will remain where those many thousands of physician are; and he may even question whether there is a future, since so many jovial brethren say, 'Eat, drink and be merry, for there is no pleasure beyond the grave.' Though the conscience may sometimes permit itself to be set aside with the aid of a glass of wine, this cannot but be bad.

" In fact, whoever has led for a few years the jovial, unconcerned and easy-going life of the ordinary practitioner of medicine, will not long for a so-called conscientious, or at least painstaking, system of healing, such as is the Homœopathic. For what is more void of concern and more easy and comfortable than the usual method of healing?

"And the third purpose, earning a better livelihood, is wholly on the side of the ordinary physician. For we should bear in mind that he remains pretty nearly in the customary groove, or rut of practice, and does not stumble upon any innovation as regards his patients, and but little in respect to his colleagues and the apothecaries. And ought he ever to lack customers? The apothecary mostly refers patients to the physician who gives plenty of prescriptions, and the physicians do not advise against this, for the apothecary is of their way of thinking. And how many patients there are who get three or four prescriptions daily.

"The more of such prescriptions, the more there is doing, and the greater are the receipts of the apothecary. He, too, does not lack a good income; for the great quantity of prescriptions furnish it.

"If you wish to provide yourself as a matter of curiosity with what has been written by the man who at great personal sacrifice, has dared to contradict all that has been done to improve the status of medicine for many centuries, I respectfully refer you to the following few books:

"The 'Organon' describes the various diseases and the remedial virtues of medicines viewed from a new standpoint, and applied very differently from what has been done hitherto.

"The 'Fragmenta de viribus Medicamentorum positivis,' two volumes, published by Ambr. Barth, Leipsic, 1805, describes the few peculiar medicinal actions or effects that I have discovered, and without a knowledge of which I think that we cannot use a medicine properly and rationally in any ailment.

"The 'Pure Materia Medica' is a continuation of the 'Fragmenta,' though treating of only a small part of the medicines. The first volume of this was published in 1811 by Arnold, at Dresden, and by Bruder, at Leipsic. The publication of the second part has been delayed by the dilatoriness of the publisher.

"The title of the book which you request me to send you is 'Treasury of Medicine' (Arzneischatz), published by Wilhelm Fleischer, 1800. It contains some observations of mine.

"My contemporaries must resort to these few books, in order to make themselves familiar with Homœopathy; for I have not the time to tell to each personally what is requisite to become a Homœopathist.

"However, if I can be of assistance to you in understanding some phases of the subject, I will gladly give you audience any forenoon from 10:30 to 11 o'clock. My leisure time is very limited during the rest of the day.

                                        "S. HAHNEMANN."

What a quiet bit of meaning in Hahnemann's line concerning the Treasury of Medicine. "It contains some observations of mine." This is the book of medical prescriptions for which Hahnemann wrote that famous preface ridiculing and con-

demning the whole book. It certainly did contain some "observations !"

Robbi did not become a disciple. He entered the ranks of
Hahnemann's detractors. It would seem that he did not intend to honestly investigate, by the tenor of his letter.

Hahnemann's letter shows his opinion of Robbi; one reads
between its lines that he never was altogether his dupe, but
exercised a certain forbearance towards that young hypocrite.

Hahnemann now had a number of devoted disciples who
gladly and faithfully assisted him in testing the effects of drugs
upon their own healthy systems. This was a season of triumph
and happiness for the old reformer; he was busily engaged in
his favorite studies, and he also had the satisfaction of knowing
that at last he was educating others to aid him in disseminating
his new and beneficent law of medicine.

In connection with this epoch of proving, the following is an
extract from a letter written to Stapf in September, 1813:*

"You are right that the aggravation by any substance, or
symptoms which are present, most probably indicates that the
medicine has the power of exciting these symptoms of itself.
We must not, however, incorporate such symptoms in the list of
the positive effects of the medicine, at least not in writing.

"All we may do is to bear them in mind, so as to direct our
attention to them specially, should they occur for the first time
during the use of the medicine.

"When I propose any substance for proving, I will take care
that it is not one that is dangerous to the health, and so prepared that it will not affect you too violently; for we are not
entitled to do injury to ourselves. I send you along with this
some tincture of pure *Helleborus niger*, which I gathered myself.
Each drop contains one-twentieth grain of the root. Any day
when you are well, and have no very urgent business, and have
not eaten any medicinal substance (such as parsley) at dinner,
take one drop of this to eight ounces of water, and a scruple of
alcohol (to prevent its decomposition), shake it briskly, and take
an ounce of it while fasting; and so every hour and a half or
two hours another ounce, as long as you are not too severely
affected by what you take. But should severe symptoms set in,
which I am not afraid of, you may take some drops of tincture

*Stapf's "Neue Archivs.," vol. I. *Brit. Jour. Hom.*, vol. III., pp. 137-140.

of *Camphor* in an ounce of water, or more if necessary, and this will allay the symptoms.

"After all the effects of the *Hellebore* have subsided, I wish you to try the effects of *Camphor* alone (it is a divine remedy). About two grains dissolved in a scruple of alcohol, and shaken with eight ounces of water, taken four or six times a day, with similar precaution as the other.

"I thank you for the symptoms you sent me; many of them are very important. You must always strive to discover the exact expression for your sensations, and the changes in your sensations, as well as the conditions under which they are excited. My present scholars have a lighter task in this respect. Whenever they present me with such a list, I go through the symptoms along with them, and question them right and left, so as to complete from their recollection whatever requires to be more explicit, such as the time, conditions, etc., in which the changes were prescribed."

Stapf having suggested to Hahnemann the plan of inviting physicians to assist in proving medicines, he continues in the same letter as follows: "But all this you must do for yourself; you must go through the written prescription in order to find what has yet to be reported. In this respect yours is a harder task. From this strictness of mine for the promotion of the truth, you will perceive that your plan, although very well meant, is quite impracticable. Which of our everyday colleagues would undertake such laborious experiments? When he can tap upon his well-filled receipt-book and say: 'Thou art my comfort; never can I be in doubt what to prescribe when I have thee at hand. It may go with my patients as it likes; I am quite safe. These receipts of the learned masters, as long as I prescribe them, no person can find fault with me.'

"It would be in vain to attempt to elevate the views of such people. Even if we had an eternity to expend upon them, they never would resolve upon such careful experimentalism, since the common physician feels himself so comfortable without observing, in the easy following of others in quoting 'authority' for everything, in speculating and assuming.

"No, no, dismiss all such hopes. Such resolutions are not to be expected from such people. And what would the accomplishment of their attempt be, suppose they made an attempt

out of curiosity. Deceptions, imaginative stuff, or positive
falsehoods, with their irregular mode of life, their volatility and
their deficiency in the spirit of observation and integrity; may
God keep the pure doctrine from such dross.

"No, it is only the young whose heads are not deluged to
overflowing with a flood of everyday dogmas, and in whose
arteries there runs not yet the stream of medical prejudice; it is
only such young and candid natures, on whom truth and phil-
anthropy have got a hold, who are open to our simple doctrine
of medicine; it is only those who, impelled by their own natural
impulse (as I gladly observe in my pupils) to restore to the
light of day by their devotion to the truth, those treasures of
medicinal action—inestimable treasures which have been from of
old allowed to lie unknown in obscurity of self-complacent, false
reasoning ingenuity; and I think some of them have made considerable progress in the practice of observation, and so will the
good spread, but only where it finds suitable ground and soil.

"One word more: no encomiums of me; I altogether dislike
them, for I feel myself to be nothing more than an upright man
who merely does his duty. Let us express our regard for one
another only in simple words and conduct indicating mutual
respect."

It should be remembered that Hahnemann had previously
written in Hufeland's journal essays explaining his opinions,
and asking the aid of the profession in his plan for perfecting
the Materia Medica. Dudgeon says of this:* "Alas! for the
boasted zeal and earnestness of the medical profession, Hahnemann's appeal met with nothing but derision and contempt from
his colleagues. None, not one, saw the utility of putting himself to inconvenience for the purpose of ascertaining the powers
of the instruments he was hourly called upon to use in cases of
life and death. One and all were perfectly satisfied with the
traditional system they and their ancestors had practiced."

So, with his coterie of earnest students, Hahnemann quietly
continued to experiment with medicines, and to note their
effects upon each healthy person until a great book filled with
the provings was the glorious result; a book whose teaching
has since been the means of removing much suffering from
humanity.

---

* "Lectures on Homœopathy." 1854. Page 179.

The story of the life of Hahnemann and his students in Leip-sic has been told by one of them, Dr. Franz Hartmann.*

These events happened in 1814, and when Hartmann was eighteen years of age.

Hartmann says : "Hornburg was again my roommate; after three months' residence there he introduced me to the ac-quaintance of Hahnemann, and sought admission for me into the narrow circle of the friends of this great man. Whoever has seen Hahnemann, has personally made his acquaintance and has heard him speak, were it but once, with lofty en-thusiasm and transporting eloquence, of his important discovery in the domain of practical medicine, will surely think it by no means strange that a tyro in medicine should inwardly resolve to devote his whole life without reserve to him and his doctrine. I am confident that every one who knew Hahnemann at that time agrees with me, or surely does not blame my apparently extravagant praise of this venerable man endowed by nature with such a lofty intellect, if I set him by the side of the greatest intellects in the profession in our time, and even de-clare him to be the greatest of them all, since no physician has commenced such a gigantic work, and one so likely to endure the test of time, nor brought it to such a pitch of perfection that it may not only be compared with former medical systems, but is in many respects quite superior to them.

"This is readily admitted now, but even then, when I made Hahnemann's acquaintance, his fame was widespread, and he performed cures which bordered on the incredible, and which established his reputation more and more permanently. This was especially the case with those frequently recurring diseases from the undue use of medicines, the cure of which was the more easy to him, as he always made it a rule in his inquiry into the physiological effects of drugs to learn with accuracy the antidote of each one.

"I might have degenerated into a mere partisan if I had fol-lowed Hahnemann's advice to study nothing but his system, which had a firm and substantial basis, while in the old system nothing was reliable—a suggestion which he made to all his pupils, and which in many respects has been the occasion of

*Allgemeine Homoopathische Zeitung, vols. xxvi., xxxviii., xxxix.; Kleinert's "Geschichte der Homoopathie ;" Translations in Shipman's N. W. Jour. Hom , vol. iv., Med. Counsellor, vol. xi.

great mischief, and has proved unfortunate to many of his adherents.   I observed the surprise expressed by Hahnemann's
countenance when I asked him in return whether it would answer well merely to be examined in Homœopathy alone.   The
many evasions with which he used to avoid answering this
question quite convinced me of the danger and impracticability of
his advice, and the matter was never mentioned during the
course of my studies with him; indeed he seemed purposely to
avoid alluding to it in the presence of the other young men,
many of whom were studying with him at the same time, as if
he perceived how untenable was his position.

"He took pleasure in conversing with me on the sciences,
and was always most enthusiastic when on the subject of
Materia Medica and therapeutics.   I always took especial pains
to add fuel to the fire, partly because his fiery zeal was entertaining, and partly because I acquired thereby such a knowl-
adge of Homœopathy, and for many practical observations upon
Homœopathy I am indebted to these explosions.

"It was, moreover, particularly interesting to see Hahnemann, a small, thick-set man, constrained in his gait and bearing, with a bald head and a high, beautifully formed forehead;
as the blood at such times crowded up to his head the veins became turgid, the brow was flushed, his brilliant eyes sparkled,
and he was obliged to take off his little cap to admit the cool
air to his heated head.   It was usually only scientific subjects,
and among these his new doctrine especially which could excite
him to such a degree as this, and could inspire him with the
eloquence of an apostle.

"It was an elevating sight for his pupils, thus to see the
master in their midst; at such times everyone partook of his
enthusiasm, and resolved that in spite of every persecution, of
which we had already experienced enough, that he would pre-
severe and aid in the great work, for which Hahnemann himself offered the best opportunities, since he requested everyone
who was free from disease to engage in the proving of drugs.
Unlearned as we yet were in medicine, and still more unlearned
in the proper method of proving drugs, there was nothing left
for him but to teach us first, and to instruct us minutely in the
course we were to pursue, in every respect; this he did in a
few words, but in the clearest and most perceptible manner as
follows :

"The human body, when it has attained a development nearly complete, is the least exposed to sickness from transient influence, or from the deprivation of its accustomed food, because the powers of life existing in their integrity overpower any injurious effects from such causes before they can make any progress; hence, in case of young persons, a long preparatory course is not necessary before the proving of a drug; a resolute determination alone is requisite to avoid everything which may tend to disturb the process.

" During such a proving he absolutely forbade coffee, tea, wine, brandy and all other heating drinks, as well as spices, such as pepper, ginger, also strongly salted foods and acids. He did not forbid the use of the light white and brown Leipsic beer.

"He cautioned us against close and continued application to study or reading novels, as well as against many games which exercised not merely the imagination, but which required continued thought, such as hazard, cards, chess, or billiards, by which observation was disturbed and rendered untrustworthy. He was far from considering idleness as necessary, but advised moderate labor only, agreeable conversation, with walking in the open air, temperance in eating and drinking, early rising, for a bed he recommended a mattress with light covering."

CHAPTER XXIII.

HARTMANN'S STORY CONTINUED—METHODS OF PROVING—HAHNE-
MANN'S DOMESTIC LIFE—METHODS OF PRESCRIBING.

" The medicines which were to be proved he gave us himself; the vegetable in the form of essence or tincture—the others in the first or second trituration. He never concealed from us the names of the drugs which were to be proved, and his wish that we should in the future prepare all the remedies whose effects we had while students conscientiously tried, fully convinced us that in this respect he had never deceived us.

"Since he for the most part had previously proved the drugs upon himself and his family, he was sufficiently acquainted with their strength and properties to prescribe for each prover according to his individuality, the number of drops or grains with which he might commence, without experiencing any injurious effects. The dose to be taken was mixed with a great quantity of water, that it might come in contact with a greater surface than would be possible with an undiluted drug; it was taken early in the morning, fasting, and nothing was eaten for an hour. If no effect was experienced in three or four hours, a few more drops were to be taken; the dose might even be doubled, and the reckoning of time was to begin from the last dose; the same was the case where the drug was to be taken for the third time. If, upon the third repetition, no change was remarked, Hahnemann concluded that the organism was not susceptible to this agent, and did not require the prover to make any further experiments with it, but after several days gave him another drug to prove.

"In order to note down every symptom which presented itself, he required each one to carry a tablet and lead pencil with him, which had this advantage, that we could describe with precision the sensation (pain) which we experienced at the time, while this precision might be lost if these sensations were noted down at some subsequent period. Every symptom that presented itself must be given in its connection, even though the most heterogeneous symptoms were thus coupled together; but our directions were still more precise; after every symptom we must specify in brackets, the time of its occurrence, which time was reckoned from the last dose. It was only when one or two days had passed without the occurrence of any symptoms that Hahnemann supposed the action of the drug to be exhausted; he then allowed the system a time to rest before another proving was undertaken.

"He never took the symptoms which we gave him for true and faithful, but always reviewed them once with us, to be sure that we had used just the right expressions and signs, and had said neither too much nor too little. At first it often happened that there were errors enough, but these became fewer with every proving, and finally there were none at all. Peculiar care is needful to apprehend symptoms which do not make themselves so very prominent, for these are frequently the most important, the most peculiar and the most characteristic, of much greater significance than those which occur with violence. The former are most frequently elicited by the smaller and more delicate doses, while the latter owe their origin to the larger.

"I could get no symptoms after the second or third dose if not from the first. If after the first dose symptoms presented themselves even faintly, I could rely on more characteristic symptoms appearing every hour. Our old Provers' Union consisted of Stapf, Gross, Hornburg, Franz, Wislicenus, Teuthorn, Herrmann, Ruckert, Langhammer, and myself (Hartmann)."

These, the first pupils and adherents of Hahnemann, were bound very closely to the master. Hartmann gives a short sketch of the personality of each.* Franz, who had been cured by Hahnemann of a very serious disease, was older than the others, and was his assistant. He was a good botanist and collected plants for the master. When it was in Hahnemann's collection then no time was lost in preparing it as fast as possible for medicinal use. Both then labored with diligence, "no one was ashamed to perform the humblest labor, the chemical laboratory was a sanctum from which we were as difficult to drive as a fox from his burrow." Franz also arranged the symptoms of the provings, according to the schema of Hahnemann, copying them many times.†

Hartmann further says of this Provers' Union: "Their activity as drug provers began with *Causticum* and covered the entire period from the second to the sixth part of the Materia Medica Pura, without, however, ceasing with *Stannum.* But in other ways, a few years later, were they active factors in the development of Homœopathy, at first as medical practitioners successfully employed in every special field of labor; later as contributors to a literature which was now aiming to construct, then to combat opposition, and which finally sought to gain proselytes among professional men and among laymen."

Hartmann continues: "Hahnemann was an honorable man, and the peculiarities for which he was blamed were probably due to the unpleasant situations of his life, to the mistaking of his character, the unfounded and malicious calumnies and invectives, and his final withdrawal from all social intercourse.

"His only faults were mistrust and avarice, but so modified

---

*Biographical sketches of these men will be found in a future chapter.
†Shipman's *Northwestern Journal of Homœopathy,* vol. 32. *British Journal Homœopathy,* vol. 32, page 453. "Leben und Wirken," 1875. *All. Hom. Zeit.,* vols. 26, 38, 39. Kleinert's "Geschichte der Homoopathie," p. 88. *Med. Counsellor,* vol. 11, p. 238.

that only a long intercourse with him enabled them to be discovered.*

"In his domestic circle he displayed an amiability that charmed every one, as I with others of his favorite students had frequent opportunities for observing. There sat the silver-haired old man, with his high, arched, thoughtful brow, his bright, piercing eyes, and calm, searching countenance, in the midst of us, as among his children, who likewise participated in those evening entertainments. Here he showed plainly that the serious exterior which he exhibited in every day life, belonged only to his deep and constant search after the mark which he had fixed for himself, but was in no respect the mirror of his interior, the bright side of which so readily unfolded itself on suitable occasions in its fairest light, and the mirthful humour, the familiarity and openness, the wit that he displayed were alike engaging.

"How comfortable the master felt in the circle of his beloved and his friends, among whom he numbered not only his pupils but also the learned of other faculties, who did homage to his learning; how beneficial was the recreation which he then allowed himself after eight o'clock in the evening seated in his arm chair, with a glass of light Leipsic white beer. It was highly interesting at such times to see him become cheerful, as he related the procedure of the older physicians at the bed of sickness, when with an animated countenance he shoved the little cap to and fro upon his head, and puffed out clouds of tobacco smoke, which enveloped him like a fog; when he spoke of his deeply affecting life and related circumstances of it, his pipe often went out, and one of his daughters was then instantly required to light it again. He appeared displeased when in these hours his advice was sought in cases of disease. He was then either laconic, or called out to the patient in a friendly way, 'to-morrow on this subject.'

"His hours of audience were from 9 to 12 in the morning, and from 2 to 4 in the afternoon. No person was permitted to enter the hall who had not first passed the review, which function was performed every week alternately by one of his daughters,

---

*British Journal Homœopathy, vol. 8, page 548. "Caspari's Domestic Physician," edited by Hartmann. Leipsic, 1850. American edition. Philadelphia, 1852.

and for which she placed herself like a warder at a little window next the hall door.

"His apartment was usually filled with patients. He examined accurately, and wrote down in his journal himself all the symptoms of which the patient complained, even those apparently insignificant, to which he successively referred previous to furnishing the medicine required, and which was obtained from another room. After the clock had struck 12 in the morning and 4 in the afternoon no visit from any quarter was received. At 12 to the minute he was called to dinner, after which his attention was not easily called to anything else. At one time, in the warmth of conversation having twice disregarded the call, at the third more earnest one from his wife, he smilingly observed, 'This time I shall get a gloomy look.' This expression several times heard from him convinced me that this great man, who had so much influence over others, had to be placed under a guardian in his own house, which, however, he willingly endured, and granted to his wife this slight triumph, since she watched with the greatest attention and punctuality all his peculiarities, sought to gratify them, permitted him to want for nothing, and also undertook alone the bringing up of his children, so that they might not disturb him in his numerous engagements.

"After the expiration of the time allotted to giving advice in the afternoon, it was the daily custom of himself and family, in all weathers, to take an hour's ramble through the city, where he walked arm in arm with his wife in the van, and several paces behind them came his three daughters, also arm in arm; sometimes a more extended jaunt to Schleuzig, little Kuchengarden or Gohlis was undertaken.

" He sometimes invited us to supper; the food was temptingly savory, and instead of the usual white beer a good wine was served. Hahnemann was on these occasions the happiest of men, and joined with the rest in the most mischievous mirth, without, however, violating the dignity of his station or in any respect making of himself a target for wit.

"About 11 o'clock we took our leave of Hahnemann and banqueted long after on the recollection of those delightful evenings."

It may be mentioned here that Hahnemann's residence in

Leipsic was in the Burgstrasse, in a house known as the "Goldenen Fahne."

The year of 1813 was one of triumph to Hahnemann. The contagious typhus fever, the typhus of the camps, prevailed throughout the length of Germany. Hahnemann attended cases of this terrible disease with a success that silenced his critics, and proved the superiority of the new method and of the truth of his principle. This malady was introduced by the French in the retreat from Russia. Out of the great number treated by Hahnemann he lost but two—an old man, and another who died from neglect in his diet.

In January, 1814, he published in the *Allgemeine Anzeiger* an article on the "Treatment of the Typhus or Hospital Fever at Present Prevailing." In this he gives an account of his successes with *Bryonia* and *Rhus tox*.

In 1816 we find Hahnemann contrary to his usual customs, engaged in a battle of polemics with one Professor Dzondi, of Halle, in regard to the right treatment of burns. Dr. Dzondi had, in the *Anzeiger*, recommended the use of cold water, and Hahnemann mentions radiated heat and other warm applications. He published two articles on the subject.*

CHAPTER XXIV.

VON BRUNNOW'S STORY—HAHNEMANN'S APPEARANCE—MODE OF LIFE AT HIS HOUSE—PRINCE SCHWARTZENBERG.

At this period of his busy life Hahnemann did not leave his house to visit patients. His time was entirely devoted to his lectures, his studies, and his consultations at home. He, however, in fine weather took a daily promenade with his wife and children. Hartmann's narrative in the preceding chapter enables one to form a very distinct idea of his home life.

He attracted to him others than medical men, many of whom were greatly impressed with the old philosopher, and, too, became his followers.

---

*"Lesser Writings," New York. 1852.

The following interesting story was written by one of these, a young law student, the Baron von Brunnow:*

Ernst George von Brunnow was born at Dresden, April 6, 1796, and died there, May 5, 1845. He was of a noble Courland family. Ill health prevented him from devoting himself to philosophy and law, and he cultivated lighter literature. He became a convert to Hahnemann by whom he was greatly bene-fited in health. He translated the "Organon" into French; assisted in the Latin translation of the "Materia Medica Pura,' and was also the author of several novels.

He says: " It was on a clear spring day of the year 1816 that I, a young, newly-enrolled student of law, sauntered with some of my companions along the cheerful promenade of Leipsic. Among the teachers of the University were to be found at that time many notables, and not a few originals. Many a professor and master stalked gravely along in the old-fashioned dress of the former century, with peruque and bag, silk stockings, and buckles on his shoes, while the pampered sons of the landed gentry swag-gered about in hussar jackets and pantaloons ornamented with points, or in leather breeches, with high dragoon boots and clinking spurs.

" 'Tell me," said I to an older student than myself, who was walking with me, 'who is that old gentleman with so extra-ordinarily intelligent a countenance, who walks respectfully arm in arm with his somewhat corpulent spouse, and is followed by two pairs of rosy girls?'

" 'That is the celebrated Doctor Hahnemann with his wife and daughters. He takes a walk regularly every afternoon round the town with his wife and daughters,' was the reply.

" 'What,' rejoined I, 'is there about this Hahnemann that makes him celebrated ?'

. " 'Why he is the discoverer of the Homœopathic system of medicine, which is turning old medicine topsy turvy,' replied my acquaintance, who, like myself, was from Dresden and had also enlisted himself under the colors of Themis.

---

*"Ein blick auf Hahnemann und die Homoopathik, Leipzig: Teubner, 1844." (A glance at Hahnemann and Homœopathy.) Trans. into English by Norton, in 1845, in London. See also London *Hom. Times*, Vol. I., p. 688; Kirby's *Am. Jour. Hom.*, Vol. V., p. 157; Shipman's *N. W. Jour. Hom.*, Vol. I., p. 91; *Brit. Jour. Hom.*, Vol. III., p. 119.

"My curiosity was excited and I wished to know something more about him. My companion belonged to the enthusiastic admirers of Hahnemann who attended his lectures and gladly assisted in the proving of medicines. Everything he told me about this remarkable man excited my interest in the highest degree. From my childhood I had been delicate and a victim to physic, so that my confidence in medicine was very frail.

"Besides other grievances, I suffered especially from my eyes, which I required at that time most especially. Impelled by hope I read the 'Organon,' and was more and more taken with Homœopathy at every line.

"It was the first medical book I had had in my hand, so that it did not strike me at that time that doctrines which appeared so clear, supported by reasoning so consistent, might be yet too exclusive in their character and have their dark side. I was a zealous proselyte, and, like all neophytes, admitted no salvation beyond the pale of my own church I made the resolution of putting myself under Hahnemann's treatment.

"Hahnemann at that time was in his sixty-second year. Locks of silver white clustered round his high and thoughtful brow, from under which his animated eyes shone with piercing brilliancy. His whole countenance had a quiet, searching, grand expression; only rarely did a gleam of fine humor play over the deep earnestness, which told of the many sorrows and conflicts endured. His carriage was upright, his step firm, his motions as lively as those of a man of thirty. When he went out his dress was of the simplest; a dark coat, with short small clothes and stockings. But in his room at home he preferred the old household, gaily-figured, dressing gown, the yellow stockings and the black velvet cap.

"The long pipe was seldom out of his hand, and the smoking was the only infraction he allowed himself to commit upon his severe rules of regimen. His drink was water, milk, or white beer; his food of the most frugal sort. The whole of his domestic economy was as simple as his food and dress. Instead of a writing desk he used nothing but a large plain deal table, upon which there constantly lay three or four enormous folios, in which he had written the history of the cases of his patients, and which he used diligently to turn up and write in while conversing with them. For the examination of his patients was made with all the minuteness of which he has given an example in the 'Organon.'

"A very peculiar mode of life prevailed in Hahnemann's house. The members of his family, the patients and students of the University, lived and moved only in one idea, and that was Homœopathy; and for this each strove in his own way. The four grown-up daughters assisted their father in the preparation of his medicines, and gladly took part in the provings; and, still more, this was done by obliging students, whose names will be found carefully recorded in connection with their individual observations in the 'Materia Medica Pura.' That these experiments were not at all injurious to those engaged in them I can testify from personal observation.

"The patients enthusiastically celebrated the effects of Homœopathy, and devoted themselves as apostles to spread the fame of the new doctrine among unbelievers. All who adhered to Hahnemann were at that time the butt of ridicule or the objects of hatred. But so much the more did the Homœopathists hold together, like members of a persecuted sect, and hung with more exalted reverence and love upon their honored head.

"After the day had been spent in labor, Hahnemann was in the habit of recruiting himself from eight to ten o'clock by conversation with his circle of trusty friends. All his friends and scholars had then access to him, and were made welcome to partake of his Leipsic white beer and join him in a pipe of tobacco. In the middle of the whispering circle the old Æsculapius reclined in a comfortable arm chair, wrapped in the household dress we have described, with a long Turkish pipe in his hand, and narrated by turns amusing and serious stories of his storm-tossed life, while the smoke from his pipe diffused its clouds around him.

"Next to the natural sciences the condition of foreign nations formed a most favorite subject for conversation. Hahnemann had a special fondness for the Chinese, and for this reason, that among them the children were educated in the strictest obedience and respect for their parents, duties which in the civilized countries of Europe were becoming more and more neglected. Indeed the family of Hahnemann presented a pattern of the old German system of training children. The children displayed not only obedience, but the most hearty love towards their parents.

"Although living in luxurious and elegant Leipsic, yet the daughters of Hahnemann took no part in any public amusement; they were clad in the simplest fashion, and undertook most cheerfully the humblest household services. Hahnemann had but little satisfaction from his son, who led so foolish a life in the place where he was settled as to be obliged to leave it. His father never mentioned him.

"From his pupils Hahnemann exacted not only intelligence and diligence, but the strictest propriety of life. I know of one case in which he peremptorily closed the door against a young and talented medical student whom he discovered to be living with a person of loose character.

"With regard to religion, Hahnemann, who belonged to the Lutheran confession, held aloof from all dogmatic creeds. He was a pure Deist, but he was this with full conviction.

"'I cannot cease to praise and thank God when I contemplate his works,' he was accustomed to say.

"Strict as was the obedience Hahnemann demanded from his children, as a husband he was far from having the rule in his own hands. His tall and stout wife, who, as Agnes Frei did to the noble painter, Albrecht Durer, gave him many a bitter hour, exercised the most baneful influence upon him. It was she who cut him off from society and set him against his medical colleagues. It was she who often caused dissension between himself and his most faithful pupils if they did not treat the doctor's wife with the deepest respect. Notwithstanding this, Hahnemann was accustomed to call this scolding Xantippe, who took pleasure in raising a storm in the house, 'the noble companion of his professional life.'

"During my latter years at Leipsic Hahnemann's prospects were somewhat overclouded. His flourishing practice and numerous adherents had become too alarming to his adversaries not to prompt them to take such active measures for his suppression as lay within their power. The implement to effect this was, naturally enough, the laws against his dispensing his own medicines. The matter was brought before the courts of medical jurisprudence, and from them Hahnemann appealed, and the decision was delayed.

"At this time one of the heroes of the German war of liberation, the Austrian Field Marshal, Prince Schwartzenberg, had become affected, besides other complaints, with an apoplectic palsy of the right side, and for this he had tried the skill of all the most eminent physicians in vain.   Homœopathy alone had not yet been tried, and to enable him to get all the advantages of the new system he came to Leipsic, to place himself under Hahnemann's own eye.   The first consequence of this honorable tribute to Hahnemann was the suspension of the process the apothecaries had commenced against him.   Had Prince Schwartz-enberg recovered, then had Homœopathy enjoyed an immediate triumph in Saxony, and even in all Germany; but every art has its limits.   Hahnemann undertook the case as a desperate one on which he could try the effects of Homœopathy.   To the astonishment of all, the patient felt himself better from day to day; and he was seen driving about after a little time; but the powers of life had been too much weakened to permit of his recovery.

"The former malady returned, and the Field Marshal died in the same town into which, in the same month of the year 1813, he had entered as a conqueror.

"Although the post-mortem proved that no medical skill could by any possibility have been successful in the case, yet the issue of it was very injurious to Hahnemann.   The suspended process was immediately resumed, and it was decided that Hahnemann must give up dispensing his own medicines."

CHAPTER XXV.

HAHNEMANN'S OPINION OF ALLOPATHY—NEW PERSECUTIONS—
APPEAL TO THE COURTS—THE LEIPSIC APOTHECARIES—
TREATMENT OF FIELD MARSHAL SCHWARTZ-
ENBERG AND HIS DEATH.

Quite a good idea of the relations of Hahnemann with the Allopathic school may be obtained by the following extract from a letter written January 24, 1814, to his friend, Dr. Ernst Stapf: "I wish I could avoid reference to Homœopathy in all future anonymous writings so that we might get practitioners to make trials without their knowing all at once how the cures they thus make are effected. They would afterwards learn that to their confusion. For were they to know beforehand the *rationale* of the action of the remedies they would scorn to use them and refuse to make a trial of them, as was recently done by a certain Dr. Riedel, of Penig, now dead, poor man, who had much to do with the present epidemic of hospital fever, and sent many to their last home.

"When some one suggested to him a trial of my method, he exclaimed: 'I would die sooner than take Hahnemann's medicines,' just as if I had other medicines than the rest of my fellow-worms. He caught the fever and died. I was sorry for the poor, misguided man. We should feel compassion for those poor creatures. 'Father, forgive them, for they know not what they do.'"*

At another time Hahnemann thus mentions the Allopathic system: "The small amount of medical instruction which there is in the immense number of medical works consists in the cure, accidentally discovered, of two or three diseases produced by a miasm of a constant character, as autumnal, intermittent, marsh fever, venereal diseases, and cloth-worker's itch. To this may be added the accidental discovery of preservation from small-pox by vaccination. Now these three or four cures are effected only in virtue of the principle similia similibus. Medicine has nothing more of a positive character to offer us; since the time of Hippocrates the cure of all other diseases has remained unknown."†

The year 1819 proved to be one of great persecution to the Master. On December 16, 1819, the apothecaries of Leipsic presented to the city council a memorial in which they complained of their rights being encroached upon by Dr. Hahnemann's dispensing his own medicines. They still reserved the right to proceed at any time in the future against his students who were also dispensing their own medicines.

On the 9th of February, 1820, he appeared before the Court of Aldermen of Leipsic to answer the charge, and responded in an

Hom. World, Vol. XXIV., p. 208 ; *Med. Counselor*, Vol. VI., p. 139.
†Kirby's *American Journal of Hom.*, Vol. I., p. 8.

·essay, entitled:*   "Representation to a Person High in Authority."

It was a remonstrance addressed to the Chief Magistrate, and
in it he argues the question at length.   He says that the objections of the apothecaries to his dispensing of medicines are
not tenable; that his system of medicine has nothing in common
with the ordinary medical art; that the old system "makes use
·of complex mixtures of medicines, each containing several ingredients in considerable quantity," and which require much
time to compound as well as a skill in the preparation that the
physician does not always possess; that the right to dispense
medicines was by law conceded to the apothecary for these rea-
·sons; that wherever any royal decree occurred it referred to the
preparation of "compound medicinal formulas;" that the exclu-
·sive right of the druggist "is only to make up the mixtures
·ordered in prescriptions containing several medicinal ingredients,
and is not in the least degree interfered with by the new method
·of treatment called Homœopathy;"   that Homœopathy has no
·compound prescriptions for the apothecary, but gives "in
all cases of illness one single, simple medicinal substance in an
unmedicinal vehicle;" that it therefore does not compound nor
·dispense, and "that its practice cannot be included in the prohibition to dispense contained in the laws regarding medicine."
He then pleads in favor of the new system of practice; of the
impossibility of the apothecary being of use; that if the Leipsic
apothecary still persists in his demands it points to some secret
motive at work to throw obstacles in the way of the development of the new healing art.

At closing he says: "Finally, so far as my pupils are con-
·cerned, I am not in any way connected with them, and since
they are of different calibre I do not represent them.   I consider
no man my disciple who, next to an absolutely blameless and
thoroughly moral life, does not so practice the new art that the
remedy which he administers to his patient in a non-medicinal
vehicle (sugar of milk and diluted alcohol) contains so small a
dose of the medicinal substance that neither the senses nor
chemical analysis demonstrates the smallest amount of an absolutely harmful medicine or even the smallest amount of a

*"Lesser Writings." Kleinert's "Geschichte der Homoopathie," *Med.
Coun.*, Vol. XI., p. 347.

medicinal substance proper; this supposes a minuteness of doses
of medicine which absolutely does away with the necessity of
exercising anything like official supervision and care on the
part of the authorities.

"DR. SAMUEL HAHNEMANN,
"Member of several learned societies."
"*Leipsic, February 14, 1820.*"

The address was carefully and temperately arranged, but was
of no avail. He was soon after publicly notified at his own
dwelling "that he would be held to the penalty of twenty
thalers for the dispensation of each and every article of medicine to any person whomsoever, lest he should give occasion to
more severe measures."*

Nothing now seemed possible but that the old man again
should be compelled to make for himself and his family another
home. But just as he was looking about for some future
refuge from the persecutions of his enemies, a certain circumstance happened that for a time stopped the opposition. Of this
period Hartmann says:†

"In the year 1820 an event occurred of the greatest importance
to Homœopathy, the arrival of the Austrian Field Marshal von
Schwartzenberg, who came to Leipsic to be treated homœopathically, under the very eyes of Hahnemann himself. Dr.
Marenzeller, of Prague, a military surgeon, who had given some
attention to Homœopathy, was the cause of Schwartzenberg's
determination.

"Hahnemann had previously received a letter from the Marshal, asking him to visit Vienna, where he then resided, in
order to treat him. To this Hahnemann replied that his many
literary and scientific labors would not permit so long an absence from Leipsic, and that if he wished to consult him he
must visit Leipsic.

"It was a great triumph for Hahnemann to see this celebrated
man place himself under the Homœopathic treatment, but quite
as great was the jealousy which our adversaries, especially the
physicians of the old school, manifested in many ways against
Hahnemann and his new doctrine. The constant watch, or

---

*Hartmann's Life of Hahnemann.
†Experience and Observations of Homœopathy. *N. W. Jour. Hom.*,
Vol., IV., p. 203. Also *Allgem. Hom. Zeit.*, Vols. XXXVIII., XXXIX.

rather spying, of his patients, and, still more, of his students, was practiced after this with much more rigor, and the extreme malignity with which it was done excited the indignation even of those who were devoted to the old school. It was no scientific strife, but the furious cry of enraged fanaticism. A quiet spectator must have compared their senseless doings to the tarantula dance.

"All joined in an absolute war of extermination, and they were not ashamed to use the most reprehensible weapons. It was a time of the greatest depression and persecution of Homœopathy. It was easy to see that Hahnemann's doctrine would prove a thorn in the flesh to physicians of the old school, since it threatened grievously to compromise their pecuniary interests, for, although, as yet in its infancy, it had already shown itself superior to the old system in many incurable diseases.

"This doctrine was not to be met with calumny, and some other method must be adopted for its overthrow. This was found in accusations against the Homœopathists for dispensing their own medicines, which was, in Hahnemann's opinion, an indispensable requisite of the new doctrine.

"The medical treatment of Prince von Schwartzenberg put an end to these quarrels, as the Saxon government, out of regard to the exalted patient, checked these unjust persecutions by an exercise of its sovereign authority. But to ensure the destruction of Hahnemann, and since no time was to be lost, Hahnemann's pupils living at Leipsic, the most of whom were, as yet, without the *jus practicandi*, were watched with the greatest rigor, so that they might be attacked, should they attempt the treatment of the sick, with a double accusation—that of illegally practicing and of dispensing their own medicines, though all medical students were in the habit of treating patients.

"Dr. Clarus, then Professor of Clinical Medicine, was very active in this opposition. It was by his instigation, also, that in the year 1821 the Homœopathic medicines were taken from the residence of Hornburg and Franz, on the part of the Court of the University and the First Actuary, and by the aid of two beadles, and were burned in St. Paul's churchyard, a transaction which would have hardly found an excuse in the Dark Ages.

"It was Dr. Clarus who, in 1821, at the head of thirteen Leipsic physicians, attacked Hahnemann in the Leipsic *Journal*, to show that the prevalent purple rash, known as rother hund, was nothing else than scarlet fever and should be so treated."*

In a previous chapter may be found Hahnemann's refutation, published in 1806, of the report made by the physicians that *Belladonna* was useless in the treatment of scarlet fever, in which he says that they confounded this disease with the purpura miliaris, for which *Belladonna* was useless.

They had used *Belladonna* and then declared that it was of no value, when in fact they had used it not for scarlet fever, but for a different disease. In 1821, Hahnemann wrote a short account for the *Allgem. Anzeiger der Deutschen* of the proper treatment of the purpura miliaris. He says: "Almost all those, without exception, who are affected by the *red miliary fever* (falsely called scarlet fever) that is so often fatal, will not only be rescued from death, but also be cured in a few days, by *Aconite* given alternately with *Tincture of raw coffee.* * * * Besides this nothing should be done or given to the patient—no venesection, no leeches, no *Calomel*, no purgative, no cooling or diaphoretic medicine or herb-tea, no water compresses, no baths, no clysters, no gargles, no vesicatories, or sinapisms.

"The patients should be kept in a moderately warm room and allowed to adapt their bed coverings to their own feelings, and to drink whatever they like, warm or cold, only nothing acid during the action of *Aconite*.

"But even should these remedies be prepared and administered as directed, where is the practitioner who would refrain from giving something or another from his routine system, thus rendering the treatment nugatory?"†

In a note to Paragraph 38 of the fifth edition of the "Organon," he say: "The true scarlet fever of Sydenham has been very accurately described by Withering and Plenciz, and differs greatly from purpura, to which they often give the name of scarlet fever."

Again in a note to Paragraph 73, he says: "Subsequent to the year 1801, a purple miliary fever came from the west of Europe, which physicians have confounded with scarlet fever, although the signs of these two affections are entirely different,

---

Allgemeine Hom. Zeitung, Vol. XXVI., Nos. 14, 15. (Aus Hahnemann's Leben.)

†"Lesser Writings," New York, p. 695.

and *Aconite* is the curative and preservative remedy of the first, and *Belladonna* of the second."

Now Schwartzenberg, who thus became a patient of Hahnemann, was a very distinguished general. During the war of 1813 against Napoleon he had held a large command in the great army of the Russian, Austrian and Prussian allies. His command was estimated to consist of 200,000 men. After the three days' battle of Leipsic he had entered the city as a conqueror and hero. He had followed with the grand army to France at the head of three hundred thousand men, and in 1814, he was living in Paris as commander-in-chief of the allied armies. Such was the man, renowned all over Europe, who in despair sought Hahnemann's medical aid.*

Hartmann continues : " Prince Schwartzenberg lived on an estate, known as Milchinsel, outside the city. When Hahnemann visited him he always met the Prince's body physician, the Royal and Imperial Counsellor, Staff Surgeon, Dr. Von Sax, and the Royal and Imperial Regimental Surgeon, Dr. Marenzeller. The disease at first assumed a very favorable character, which had never been the case under any previous treatment. This was but temporary; his case soon assumed an acute form. From the first the case was an incurable one, however, and the patient died in an apoplectic attack on the 15th of October, 1820, after nearly six months' residence in Leipsic. Dr. Clarus conducted the post-mortem and published the result, with his private opinion of Homœopathy, in *Hufeland's Journal*, Vol. 51, part 4. Hahnemann was now derided on all sides. Yet he was so consciously proud of the knowledge that he had done his duty that, to show his respect for his patient, as well as to show how little he cared for the ridicule of the people, he accompanied the remains of the Prince to Leipsic on foot."†

Ameke says:‡ " Certainly the Field Marshal improved under Hahnemann's treatment; he was able to go out for regular walks. Dr. Joseph Elder von Sax, and other Allopaths, declared that Hahnemann neglected to employ ' powerful measures,' and that he was responsible for hastening the Prince's death. Some time before the fatal termination of the illness Hahnemann

---

* Peters' "Principles and Practice of Medicine," New York, 1859. p. 113.
† *Allgem. Hom. Zeitung*, Vol. XXVI., No. 14. (Auf Hahnemann's Leben.)
‡ Ameke's "History of Homœopathy," p. 186.

visited the patient, accompanied by Dr. Marenzeller, who had
been sent from Vienna, and found the Allopaths employed in
making a venesection.   After that he never visited the patient
again, as Dr. Argenti relates.   The report of the post-mortem
was signed by Clarus, Dr. von Sax, Dr. Samuel Hahnemann and
Prosector Dr. Aug. Carl Bock.''

CHAPTER XXVI.

PROSECUTION OF DR. FRANZ—HAHNEMANN'S WISH FOR PEACE—
LETTER TO DR. BILLIG—ACCUSATION AGAINST HART-
MANN—INVITATION TO COETHEN— LETTER
TO STAPF—REASONS FOR LEAVING
LEIPSIC—DR. A. J. HAYNEL.

" After this death the persecutions were redoubled.   Such of
the pupils of Hahnemann as held no license to practice were
especially exposed to the bigotry.   Dr. Franz was treating a
lady who was ill with the consumption, and she, wishing a
change of physicians, called Dr. Clarus.   He very violently assailed the treatment of Franz and proclaimed him responsible
for her death, although the case was incurable.   Dr. Franz
placed the matter in the hands of a lawyer and retired from
practice to his home at Plauen, where he was obliged to remain
for six months.   Although the charges were not substantiated,
yet he was obliged to pay costs.
    "Dr. Hornburg, on account of being a pupil of Hahnemann,
was twice rejected by the professors; was continually oppressed
in his endeavors to practice; underwent a trial for unlicensed
practice; was sentenced to two months' imprisonment; the grief
of this caused him to fall into a decline and he died soon after
of consumption.''
    In 1821 Hahnemann sent to the authorities of the State an-
other appeal regarding the personal dispensing of medicines
entitled: "The Homœopathic Physician is prevented by no existing Laws relating to Medicine from himself Administering
his Medicines to his Patients."*   Stapf first published this and

------

* "Lesser Writings."   New York.

the preceding address, in 1829, in his collection of the "Lesser Writings of Hahnemann."

In 1825, he published in the *Allgemeine Anzeiger* still another article on this subject: "How can Homœopathy be most Certainly Eradicated?"

Hahnemann was now sixty-six years of age and had been practicing medicine for forty-two years; the report of his wonderful cures attracted many from other countries to Leipsic, and all he wished was to be allowed to dispense the simple medicines that he himself made and to teach his benign methods. It was all in vain. The apothecaries were against him, and he must leave the old-time home where he had been a student, where he had lived in later years, and where he had taught for ten busy years the principles of the law of Homœopathy.

The Homœopathic practitioners, and even their medicines, were wonderfully obnoxious at this time to the Allopathic physicians and the apothecaries. And, much as at the present day, it was necessary to protect the innocent, the guileless public from innovators and teachers of strange doctrines, and the task then, as now, fell on the benevolent shoulders of the dominant school.

In 1851, Dr. Worthington Hooker, in one of the periodical fulminations for the destruction of Homœopathy that have appeared like locusts or cholera at certain dates, said, in relation to this opposition of the physicians and apothecaries to Hahnemann's dispensing his own medicines:* "It is strange that no one of his adherents could be found willing and competent to act as his apothecary."

Dr. Peters in his sketch of Hahnemann mentions this and says:† "Hooker very innocently asks why Hahnemann did not get one of his friends to act as his apothecary, not knowing that apothecaries in Germany are only allowed to follow their art by special license; that only a certain number of apothecaries are allowed to each town, district or population. A new one cannot get a license until the population increases to the required mark; that it is quite as difficult to establish a new apothecary shop in Germany as it is to admit a new State into our Union."

---

*"Homœopathy." Dr. Worthington Hooker, New York, 1851, p. 12.

†"Principles of Medicine," p. 115.

The following letter, written to Dr. Billig while Hahnemann was undecided what to do, well explains his wish for only some quiet place where he might be permitted to continue his researches in peace :

"LEIPSIC, 5th February, 1821.

"*Most Worshipful Obr., Esteemed Friend :*

"By the public proceedings directed against me by the Saxon medical men, you will have learned (I am sure with grief) how bitterly my method of treatment and its author are persecuted in this country. This persecution has now reached its climax, and I should be doing an injury to the beneficent art, and imperiling my own life, were I to remain longer here and not seek protection in some foreign country.

"Some propositions of this sort have been made to me from Prussia, but I should much prefer to find the protection I desire for the few remaining days I have to live (I am an old man of sixty-six) in the Altenburg country. In a country that is so mildly governed as Altenburg is, and where, moreover, I can still meet with true Masons, I think I may be most comfortably settled, especially as four and twenty years ago I enjoyed great distinction as physician to the dear old Duke Ernst, in Gotha and Georgenthal. I do not wish to go to the town of Altenburg itself, to be in the way of you, dearest friend, and of your colleagues.

"I only wish to be able to settle in some country town or market village, where the post may facilitate my connection with distant parts, and where I may not be annoyed by the pretensions of any apothecary, because, as you know, the pure practice of this art can only employ such minute weapons, such small doses of medicine, that no apothecary could supply them profitably, and, owing to the mode in which he has learnt and always carried on his business, he could not help viewing the whole affair as something ludicrous, and, consequently, turning the public and the patients into ridicule. For these and other reasons it would be impossible to derive any assistance from an apothecary in the practice of Homœopathy.

"I take this opportunity, my honored friend, of praying for such a reception in your country, and under your amiable protection, and I should do all in my power to prove to you my

gratitude and esteem.   I beg you to remember me most kindly
to our worthy Obr. Hofrath Dr. Pierer.

"You will oblige me greatly if you will be so good as to speak
of this matter to the President of Government, Von Trutschler, to
whom I have also applied.

"In the meantime accept a triple kiss from my esteem and
love, as from your true friend and Obr.*

"DR. S. HAHNEMANN."

Dudgeon says: "The letters Obr. found in this letter and
others written by Hahnemann probably refer to some title in free-
masonry."   From them, and the manner in which he writes, it
is likely that Hahnemann was a Mason.

Hartmann mentions his own treatment at this time.   He had
some time previously announced himself to the Dean of the
Medical Faculty, Counsellor Rosenmuller, Professor of Anatomy,
as a foreign candidate for a higher degree.   The Dean died soon
after, and he did not suppose a second announcement to the new
Dean was necessary.

He says: "I found myself engaged in a practice by no means
unprofitable, and with youthful presumption and carelessness
did not suppose that an obstacle could be laid in my way.   But
with all the caution which I exercised in my practice, the then
second surgeon at St. Jacob's Hospital, Dr. Kohlrusch, discovered that I attended one of his patients, and lost no time in
forwarding to the President of the Faculty a packet of my powders, and accusing me before this Court so bitterly opposed to
all Homœopathists.   I was summoned   before   Clarus, overwhelmed with reproaches and threatened with the severest punishment if I dared to practice again before the Counsellor
ordered my examination."

Hartmann fearing to pass an examination before the prejudiced Leipsic Faculty, after some difficulty in other places,
on account of the hostility of the physicians, finally passed successfully in Dresden.

Hahnemann had now no longer a wish to remain in the ungrateful city of Leipsic; in fact, without the privilege of practicing he could not remain.   In the meantime certain of his friends
and patients, influential citizens, had addressed a petition to the
King, and to the municipality of the city, for justice in behalf

---

* *Brit. Jour. Hom.*, Vol. xiv., p. 164.

of the persecuted physician. While this petition was yet unanswered, in the spring of 1821, his Highness, the Grand Duke Frederick, of Anhalt-Coethen, extended to Hahnemann an invitation to accept the post of private physician to himself, with free privileges of practice according to the feelings of his heart, within the limits of the Duchy. Hahnemann accepted with thankfulness this honorable and advantageous offer, and, without waiting to see the outcome of the petitions in his behalf, he went to Coethen.

Dr. Schwenke says that the reason why Hahnemann fixed upon Coethen as his residence, after the persecutions of the jealous physicians and apothecaries had driven him from Leipsic, was as follows :*

" The Ducal Chief Chamberlain, von Sternegk, it was to whom the credit must be awarded of having first directed the Duke's attention to Hahnemann. Von Sternegk had been cured by Homœopathy of a complicated disease that had defied all resources of Allopathic treatment, and he persuaded the Duke, who was a great sufferer, to consult Hahnemann, and try the new method of treatment. This trial succeeded beyond expectation and prepossessed the Duke in favor of Homœopathy, so that at von Sternegk's suggestion Hahnemann requested from the Duke permission to settle in Coethen, which was readily granted him."

In the circumstance in which Hahnemann was placed this permission, or invitation, of the Grand Duke Frederick was very opportune. He was at once appointed to a place of extreme honor as the Duke's physician in ordinary or private physician. He was given the privilege to practice according to the dictates of his own conscience; everything that he considered necessary to his new methods was granted to him. In a word, Coethen was offered to him and to his system as a free city, a favor never previously granted by any crowned head. With joy he accepted this permission, and left Leipsic early in May, 1821, never to return there to live. Many of his old pupils accompanied him for a distance upon the road to Coethen.

Hartmann says:† " I was not with them, having left Leipsic. Hahnemann took two of his pupils with him, Dr. Haynel and

*Brit. Jour. Hom., Vol. xxxvi., p. 379.
†N. W. Jour. Hom., Vol. iv., p. 210.

Dr. Mossdorf. The latter afterwards became his son-in-law, but was subsequently separated from him; the cause I never learned. Haynel, on the contrary, led the life of a true nomad; was at Berlin at the first invasion of the cholera; then in Merseberg; finally visited me in 1830, in Leipsic, where he provided himself with a large stock of Homœopathic medicines with the intention of going to North America."

Dr. Hering says:* "Dr. A. J. Haynel died at Dresden, August 28, 1877, æt. 81. He was an inmate of Hahnemann's family for more than ten years, and proved a number of remedies for him. About the year 1835 he came to America, and resided first at Reading, Pa., then at Philadelphia. In 1845 he lived at New York, and still later in Baltimore, from whence he returned to Europe several years previous to his death."

Dr. Gray says:† "At Baltimore, Dr. Haynel, an original pupil of Hahnemann, established the new method on a firm basis as early as 1838."

About this time a contemporary wrote as follows: "Dr. Samuel Hahnemann, the discoverer of the Homœopathic system, is about to leave Leipsic and to take up his residence at Coethen. His Highness, the Duke of Anhalt-Coethen, having been pleased to permit Dr. Hahnemann not only to reside there, but also to prepare and dispense his medicines without the interference of apothecaries, the Board of Health at Coethen set a praiseworthy example of impartiality and due regard to the progress of science.

"They did not consider it right to dispute the claim of the experienced philosopher to shelter and protection, nor of the renowned chemist and professor of pharmacy to the right of preparing and dispensing his medicines; the more so, as for a period of twenty years all apothecaries consulted his 'Pharmaceutical Dictionary.'

"As the system of Homœopathy is unavailing unless the medicines be prepared by the physician himself, many patients whose medical treatment has been interrupted by the expulsion of Hahnemann from Leipsic will now be enabled to gratify their feelings and follow their convictions, and the present liberal century is saved from the reproach of having suppressed

*N. Y. Hom. Times, Vol. v., p. 216.
†Trans. N. Y. State Hom. Med. Soc., 1863, p. 105.

one of the most remarkable discoveries that ever blessed mankind, of having consciously destroyed the soothing expectations of the suffering world."*

CHAPTER XXVII.

ACT GRANTING PERMISSION TO PRACTICE HOMŒOPATHY IN
COETHEN—PERMISSION GRANTED DR. MOSSDORF TO ACT
AS HAHNEMANN'S ASSISTANT—LETTER TO STAPF.

Albrecht in his biography of Hahnemann has divided his life into five epochs: The Lehrjahre or years of apprenticeship, the school days, extending from 1755 to 1792; the Prufungsjahre or trial-years, the wander-years from 1792 to 1811; the Kampfjahre or battle-years, the life of conflict in Leipsic from 1811 to 1821; the Meisterjahre or master-years, the quiet life at Coethen from 1821 to 1835; the Glanzjahre des Alters or splendid years of old age, the brilliant life in Paris and the peaceful end.

The story of the years of apprenticeship to knowledge, of the bitter days of wandering and adversity, has been told; we have seen Hahnemann surrounded by his pupils in Leipsic, teaching his important doctrines to the world; proving medicines and preparing their painstaking record for the Materia Medica Pura; we have seen jealousy and bigotry drive him forth from the great city.

Now, after these battle-years necessary to the future existence of his system of healing, we follow him to the calm and restful time at Coethen, during which he was the master and his students came from many parts to sit at his feet and learn.

The little town of Coethen in the principality of Anhalt was, in Hahnemann's time, the capital of one of those small but absolute kingdoms into which Germany was divided. It had its ruler, its own laws and customs, and the Grand Duke Ferdinand, Hahnemann's protector, was supreme in his own territory. Hence for the persecuted old reformer it became a veritable haven of rest, within whose borders he and his tenets were unmolested.

*Fischer's translation of Biographisches Denkmal, p. 45. (Biographical Monument to the Memory of Samuel Hahnemann. C. Fischer, M. D., London, 1852.)

Coethen is situated upon the little river Zittau and is twelve miles southwest from Dessau, about ten miles from Halle, and but a short journey from Leipsic. At the time of which we write it contained about 6000 inhabitants.

Dr. Peschier, of Geneva, who journeyed there upon a pilgrimage to Hahnemann in 1832, thus describes it:* "The route from Leipsic to Coethen is neither very interesting nor agreeable, though it is necessary for the driver to be familiar with it; my friend the Baron von Brunnow, who had set out with his sister, lost his way in a cross road and there wandered more than three hours before he discovered the right way.

"The little village of Coethen is not lacking in charms; it lies in a valley through which flows a little river, which gives freshness and beauty to the surrounding country. The streets are large and well laid out; the chateau of the reigning Duke, beyond its splendor, offers nothing remarkable; it is situated in a garden open to the public, where many varieties of rare flowers are cultivated with great care.

"The dowager Duchess Julie lives in a pretty house in the midst of gardens,† with a lake in which there are swans, and surrounded by all the pleasures of the country. It is situated near the gates of the town from which it is separated by a promenade and a grove. I have said *gates* of the town because Coethen was formerly a little fortress, and the same old walls, pierced with gates, still remain.

"The late Duke, having embraced the Roman Catholic faith, built a chapel adjoining his palace in which to worship according to his creed; in this there is a beautiful portal, with columns."

Rapou fils, also describes a visit made in the same year. He says:‡ "The railroad extending from Leipsic to Berlin crosses the Duchy of Anhalt-Coethen and its little capital, noted for the generous hospitality with which it received the chief of the new school. It is four years since my father and myself journeyed thither in the basket-work carriages of the Prussian post, over a miserable road, broken and muddy, towards the modest home of Hahnemann, which is to-day the principal point of convergence

---

Bibliotheque Homœopathique, Vol. i, p. 378.
†Her husband, Duke Ferdinand, Hahnemann's patron, had died in 1831.
‡"Histoire de la doctrine Homœopathique." Paris. 1847. Vol. ii, p. 287.

of the main railroads of northern Germany. In this borough, peaceful and rural, where the silver tinkling of the clock in the Ducal chateau wafts itself in chimes to the cattle coming from the pasture, the ardent reformer had found that salutary calm that he had lost after his great discovery.

"He lived there, entirely devoted to his art, afar from contradictions, and from the discussions that his doctrines had aroused throughout Germany. He was not, however, idle in his isolation. He carried on, with his partisans, a very extended correspondence, answered their objections, aroused the indifferent, admonished his disciples, and punished with reprobation those who transgressed his precepts."

The house in which Hahnemann lived from 1821 to 1835, the time of his sojourn in Coethen, is situated in the Wallstrasse and is now used as a Hahnemann museum. It is of two stories and stands upon the corner of the street. Approaching it one sees a sloping roof like the two sides of a square; in the middle of each side of this roof a quaint little dormer window appears, for all the world like a gigantic eyelid half open. The pavement before the house is of large and square slabs of stone.

Over the windows of the front of the house is a tablet on which is inscribed: "Here Samuel Hahnemann lived from 1821 to 1835."

In the rear of this house, in Hahnemann's time, there was a long and paved garden shut in by a grated door; at the end was an arbor covered with vines.

We now reach a very interesting period in the varied life of the venerable reformer. Previous to this he had never known freedom from persecution.

His discoveries had been hailed with ridicule by men who were infinitely beneath him in education and ability. He had been by such men persecuted and forced to make his life one of wandering and poverty.

He had patiently sought to induce his fellow-physicians to try the new system he had discovered. He had been such a prey to the pettiness of bigotry that his heart had become hardened. Here in this haven of quietness he was destined to pass many years, only leaving this to enter the last epoch of his long and tempest-tossed life in the luxurious, happy years at Paris.

Hahnemann lived a quiet and studious life at Coethen. Freed from the incessant irritation of the persecutions of his enemies, with nothing to distract his mind, allowed perfect freedom of opinion and action, he now devoted himself to his important studies. For some time he remained secluded from the world, seldom going out of his house except to visit the Grand Duke professionally. His other patients were obliged to go to him. He passed much of his time in the arbor in the garden at the back of the house. On every pleasant day he took a drive in his carriage into the neighboring country. It is related of him that one day a disciple was visiting him in this garden, and seeing its small and narrow space, in which at the time he took all his exercise, said: "How small this much talked of garden of yours is, Hofrath." Hahnemann responded: "Yes, it is narrow, but," pointing to the heavens, "of infinite height."

Among the State documents preserved in the Archives of the Duchy of Anhalt is the following:* "Acts relating to the permission graciously awarded to Dr. Hahnemann, of Leipsic, to settle in this capital, and as a Homœopathic physician to dispense his own medicines.

"We hereby announce to the Commissioners of the State Administration that we have graciously accorded to Dr. Hahnemann, upon his humble request, permission to settle here as a practicing physician, and to prepare the remedies required for his treatment, and hence the Sections 15, 17 and 18, of the Medical Regulations of 1811, have no application to him.

"In other respects Dr. Hahnemann is subject to all the rules and regulations of State and police, and to all the regulations of our Medical Direction, and our Commissioners of the State Administration will arrange all that is necessary, especially in regard to the Medical Direction.

"*Coethen, April 12, 1821.*"

Hahnemann was created Hofrath on May 13, 1822. The title Hofrath signifies Councillor to the Court. In a letter to Dr. Croserio, dated at Coethen, February 6, 1835, he signs his name Samuel Hahnemann, counseiller aulique. This is a French rendering of the same title. The term Hofrath is an

---

British Journal of Homœopathy, Vol. xxxvi., p. 260. Lutze's "Todtenfeier," p. 139.

honorary title given by princes to persons whom they wish to especially distinguish.

On June 1 the following decree was promulgated: "Hofrath Dr. Hahnemann, having practiced the Homœopathic method here for a year, and no case of death or accident from this method having come to my knowledge, I having, on the contrary, learned that many patients have been relieved and cured, I am confirmed that if Homœopathy is not more advantageous than Allopathy, it can at all events be considered as on a par with the latter. I therefore consider it my duty as a ruler to maintain it for suffering humanity, especially for my subjects, and as none of the physicians of the Dukedom has yet adopted the Homœopathic system, and owing to the great age of Hofrath Dr. Hahnemann, it is to be feared that his strength may not last very much longer, I have resolved to allow one of his most distinguished disciples, Dr. Theodore Mossdorf, a native of Dresden, to settle in this country as a practicing Homœopathic physician, and to prepare and dispense the remedies required in his treatment. On condition that Dr. Mossdorf is willing to render all assistance to Hofrath Dr. Hahnemann, he will not only receive a patent of naturalization, but also be admitted as my subject.

"Dr. Mossdorf will be exempt from the usual examination, seeing that Homœopathy is founded on quite different principles from Allopathy, and hence it would be improper to subject a disciple of Homœopathy to an Allopathic examination, just as it would be improper to ascertain the suitability of a Protestant candidate by making him be examined by a Catholic bishop. In other respects it is of course understood that Dr. Mossdorf has to submit to all other State and police laws and regulations and has to obey the orders of my Medical Directors, from which, however, like all my subjects, he can appeal to me. The Commissioner of the State administration has to do all that is required for carrying my resolution into effect, and to make it known to all whom it may concern."

Dr. Mossdorf afterwards married Hahnemann's youngest daughter Louise. He did not remain long at Coethen, as he and Hahnemann could not agree. He received from the Duke a yearly salary of sixty thalers for medical attendance on the Duke's servants.

After Hahnemann had been for six months quietly and happily living in Coethen, the petition to the Leipsic authorities in regard to the self dispensing of medicines was answered favorably. On November 30, 1821, a royal decree was promulgated, granting, to the Homœopathic physician, under certain conditions, the right to dispense. This was a formal recognition of the new method, and although life, now rendered possible in Leipsic, offered many advantages, Hahnemann preferred the exercise of the more perfect liberty in the practice of his art that had been so generously afforded him by the kind-hearted Duke at Coethen.

The Leipsic patients of Hahnemann, of whom there were many, consulted him still at Coethen, sending often by express for medicines to that town.

He soon became useful to his ducal protector, as is evidenced by the following letter dated March 9, 1824:* "Our most serene Duke, who was suffering from a severe nervous attack, is now out of danger, thanks to the successful exertions of Dr. Hahnemann, well known for his new method of curing. When the discoverer of Homœopathy took shelter in a country whose sovereign generously supports every attempt for the improvement of science, he scarcely foresaw that he was destined to save the life of his illustrious patron. Nor did our most gracious Duke imagine that such would be the case when he extended his protection to a noble and oppressed cause for the purpose of delivering it to the impartial judgment of posterity. Feelings of mutual gratitude cemented their union."

Duke Ferdinand and his wife, Julie, were always on the most cordial terms with their illustrious physician. The following letters written when he had been but two years at Coethen will illustrate this.†

" Coethen, January 29, 1823.

"*My Dear Hofrath Hahnemann:*

"While expressing to you my thanks for your medical help this year, and for the past two years, and assuring you of my complete satisfaction, I wish you to accept the enclosed trifle as

---

*Fischer's "Biographical Monument," p. 46.
†"Leben und Wirken," p. 111. Ameke's " History of Homœopathy,"
p. 155.

a slight recompense for your medicines and for your services. May heaven preserve you in good health for many years to the benefit of suffering humanity.

"FERDINAND, DUKE.

"My best thanks, my dear Hofrath, for your kind wishes for my birthday. I owe to your exertions one of the pleasantest gifts on entering on a new year, improved health. I hope to preserve this to your praise and credit.

"With sincere pleasure,
"Yours very affectionately,
"JULIE, DUCHESS OF ANHALT."

This kindness on the part of his princely patrons was continued during Hahnemann's whole sojourn at Coethen.

Four years after Hahnemann had removed to Coethen he wrote the following letter to his friend, Dr. Stapf. It throws some light upon his feelings during his persecutions in Leipsic, and his reasons for settling in Coethen.

"COETHEN, July 16, 1825.

"*Highly Esteemed Doctor:*

"To many of my disciples it must have seemed very suspicious when, four years ago, after receiving a similar summons from Dresden, I suddenly left the city and State and emigrated with all my family to this little principality at great expense and loss; but I knew well the inflexibility of the judges at whose ears stood my medical enemies. Remonstrances would avail naught, whatever the family doctor desires would take the form of a legal decision.

"But where is the prohibition of dispensing one's own remedies that applies to Homœopathy? To the apothecary is, by law, accorded the right that no one but himself shall dispense any medicament. But in no law relating to medical affairs is a simple remedy understood by the words medicament and medicine, but always and without exception a mixture of medicines to be compounded by the apothecary from a prescription, and prescriptions, in all the laws relating to medical affairs, always imply the mingling of several drugs in a mixture.

"Therefore the candidate for a degree must show in his examination that he has attended lectures on the art of prescribing and produce the certificates of the professor, or else he will not get the doctor's degree; for as Senner, in the preface to his 'Art of Prescribing,' expressly declares: 'A simple remedy ordered to be taken is not a prescription, that must contain several ingredients.' These mixtures and these prescriptions no one except the apothecary is permitted to make up, his privilege is only in respect to these. What medicinal authority can deny this? Who can hold a contrary opinion?

"A simple substance in a vehicle is not a medicine in the sense of the law relating to medical affairs, otherwise the apothecary would be practicing medicine on his own account when he, without let or hindrance, sells to every customer anise, sugar, peppermint drops and the like. He is not allowed to give, on his own account, medicines, medicaments, mixtures of drugs.

"Hence it follows that the apothecary's privilege refers only to the making up of the mixtures of drugs, but not to the giving of the simple substances of the Homœopath in a vehicle. If you can make any use of these remarks without mentioning my name, it will afford pleasure to

"Yours truly,
"SAM. HAHNEMANN."*

And again in another letter to Stapf, written October 17 of the same year, he says:† "The honest opinion expressed by the eminent lawyer Von Konen on my essay gave me pleasure. There was a point I did not allude to (and so he could not know the truth of the matter), and that was why it was absolutely necessary that Homœopaths should dispense their medicines. It is, however, connected with the circumstance that the Apothecaries' Guild has recently represented to the authorities that through their institution the safety of the public is best provided for, because thus only can a real control be exercised.

"Naturally the authorities desire above all things to secure such safety, and it redounds to their honor that they put this object before any other consideration. But control does not affect the apothecary in the least. The dishonest apothecary will take good care that at the annual or semi-annual inspection he will show the medical inspector fresh samples of the most expensive current articles, or small quantities of these things. But nobody sees what he has put in, or allowed to be put in, the Al-

*Hom. World, Vol. xxiv, p. 247.
†Hom. World, Vol. xxiv, p. 306.

lopathic mixtures of drugs, and the cleverest doctor cannot tell what is or is not in the made up compound powders, electuaries, mixtures, etc. Still less can a Homœopathic physician allow an apothecary to put a minute globule impregnated with an extremely diluted medicine into a powder of milk sugar.

"In his (the physician's) absence he cannot know for certain whether the apothecary has or has not done it, or if he has put in a globule moistened with some other medicine.

"He can never know this, or by subsequent examination of the powder convince himself on the subject, for the small globule cannot be found in the milk sugar powder, or if found, it is impossible to tell if it contains the medicine prescribed. Nay, more; if the physician has put it in himself, and has forgotten what it is, and has made no note of what medicine he put in, he cannot afterwards find out what is in it by examination of the powder.

"He must make up the powder himself, and make a note of it in writing. He cannot, without being quite uncertain about his treatment, allow it to be prepared by another. I request you to communicate this to Mr. Von Konen with my respectful compliments, as it is the simple truth. The quintillionth or decillionth of a grain of any medicine can never be pronounced dangerous by the apothecary, or be considered dangerous to life by the authorities.

"The Homœopathic physician's peculiar advantage consists in this, that he gives the right medicine in the smallest possible dose. No control is required here. In Allopathic practice the apothecary's intervention is almost indispensable, for how can the practitioner give the time required to make the mixture himself or see that the apothecary makes it?"

This law, by means of which Hahnemann was prevented from dispensing his medicines, and which was the cause of his leaving Leipsic, was an obsolete statute raked up for the purpose of suppressing Homœopathy. To, for a moment, suppose that Hahnemann was not the superior of the apothecaries and the doctors in the matter of preparing or dispensing medicines is to forget that for twenty years his Apothecary-Lexicon had been a standard work upon that very subject, in the hands of the same apothecaries. It was jealousy, nothing else, that banished Hahnemann from Leipsic.

CHAPTER XXVIII.

LITERARY WORK—EDITIONS OF THE "ORGANON"—FOUNDING
OF THE ARCHIV—PREFACES TO THE "MATERIA MEDICA PURA."

Hahnemann now devoted himself to literary work, especially
to the elaboration of that great monument to his genius, "The
Chronic Diseases." With the exception of a number of pamphlets and short articles, this is the only original work that he
published after this time. While living in Coethen he published
the 3d, 4th and 5th editions of the "Organon" and the 2d and
3d editions of the "Materia Medica Pura."

As has been mentioned, the first edition of the "Organon"
was published in 1810, while Hahnemann was living at Torgau.
It is not as large as the later editions, nor does it contain as
many notes.

Hahnemann first mentions the word Homœopathy in the
"Organon;" it is composed of two words from the Greek—
omoios, similar, and pathos, disease. He also used the word
Allopath to designate the members of the dominant school of
medicine.

The growth of the doctrines of Homœopathy can very plainly
be traced in the mind of its discoverer in the different editions.
In them all the arguments are consistent and any anomalies
are easily explainable. The third edition was issued in 1824;
the fourth in 1829; the fifth in 1833, all by Arnold of Dresden.

In 1824 Baron von Brunnow translated it into French. His
edition was published in Dresden. Of it Hahnemann says in the
preface to the third edition:* "A great help to the spread of
the good cause in foreign lands is won by the good French
translation of the last edition, recently brought out at great
sacrifice by that genuine philanthropist, my learned friend
Baron von Brunnow."

But five editions of the "Organon" were issued during the
lifetime of the master. He left the notes for a sixth edition
at his death, which as yet has never been published.

* Dudgeon's translation of the "Organon," 1893.

Dr. Arthur Lutze, in 1865, issued an unauthorized edition that was repudiated by the profession. An account of this and of the unpublished "Organon" is given in the chapter devoted to Madame Hahnemann.

In the *Allgemeine Anzeiger der Deutschen*, 1819, Hahnemann published a short article on "Uncharitableness Towards Suicides." He mentions the epidemic prevalence of suicide, maintains that it is a form of insanity and says:* "This most unnatural of all human purposes, this disorder of the mind that renders them weary of life, might always be with certainty cured if the medicinal powers of pure *gold* for the cure of this sad condition were known. The smallest dose of pulverized gold attenuated to the billionth degree, or the smallest part of a drop of an equally diluted solution of pure gold, which may be mixed in his drink without his knowledge, immediately and permanently removes this fearful state of the (body and) mind, and the unfortunate being is saved."

The Homœopathic practitioner knows that this advice is as true at the present day as when Hahnemann gave it.

In 1821 Dr. Ernst Stapf established at Leipsic a journal devoted to the spread of Homœopathy, which was issued three times a year. It was called "*Archiv fur die homoopathische Heilkunst*" (Archives for Homœopathic Healing). This was the first magazine ever published in the interests of Homœopathy. And now the followers of the Master had an organ in which to present their truths to the world. On the reverse of the title of each number, and facing the index, is the following quotation from Shakespeare's "Romeo and Juliet," act 1, scene 2:

> "Tut, man, one fire burns out another's burning;
> One pain is lessened by another's anguish;
> Turn giddy and be holp by backward turning;
> One desperate grief cures with another's languish.
> Take thou some new infection to the eye,
> And the rank poison of the old will die."

The initial number of this journal was issued in September, 1821. The first article was from the pen of Moritz Muller on "The Critical Examination of Homœopathy." Stapf published an essay upon Homœopathy, some cases, some aphorisms, a re-

† "Lesser Writings," New York, p. 695.

view of the sixth volume of the "Materia Medica Pura," and, in connection with Gross, certain provings of Platina.

At this time, besides the immediate pupils—the members of the first Provers' Union—there were a number of recent converts to Homœopathy who were in independent practice of that system.

Among them Gross was at Juterbogk; Moritz Muller and Carl Haubold were settled in Leipsic, as well as the veterinary surgeon Wilhelm Lux, who was to astonish the world with the remarkable nature of Isopathy.

Drs. C. F. Trinks and Paul Wolf were at Dresden. As early as 1819 Dr. Gossner had practiced Homœopathy in Oberholla-brun in Lower Austria and Dr. Mussek in Seefeld, a neighboring town. In Prague Dr. Marenzeller, military staff surgeon and attending physician to his Imperial Highness, the Archduke John, was becoming interested in the new system.

In Vienna, Veith was testing its virtues. Dr. Adam, who had met Hahnemann, was introducing it into Russia. In 1821 the Austrian Baron, Francis Koller, had carried the "Organon" to Naples, where a translation had been made under the auspices of the Royal Academy, and where, in 1822, Dr. George Necker, a pupil of Hahnemann, also settled and soon opened a dispensary for the poor.

In the meantime, in Coethen, Hahnemann was taking walks in his little garden, long drives into the surrounding country, writing letters to his many friends and followers, pondering over his new doctrines, and preparing for the press the second edition of the "Materia Medica Pura."

It does not seem that Hahnemann took any particular pains to assist his pupils before he left Leipsic or after he settled at Coethen. Kleinert says: * "That Homœopathy assumed defined shape and developed strength to live and to overcome obstacles is much more the result of their (the students and disciples) labors than that of Hahnemann. There is no doubt at all that at the beginning of the second decade of this century the tenacity of Hahnemann was commencing to yield to advancing years and that he had long ceased to enjoy the thickest of the battle. With his then strong inclination to dictate, and

---

* "Geschichte der Homoopathie," p. 107. *Med. Counsellor*, vol. xi, p. 270.

his more or less unwise tendency to isolate himself, there would have resulted a standstill or a retrograde movement which would have lasted for at least one generation if the tact, zeal and ability of these men had not made themselves felt everywhere.

"In spite of every species of adversity, not unfrequently proceeding from the master himself, they stood like beacon-lights of fidelity, and, when it became necessary, distinguished between the precious doctrine and its prophet, between the jewel itself and the setting.

"It is impossible to find a single statement in print, or an authenticated verbal statement, to show that Hahnemann, who was now blessed with a most profitable practice, ever spent upon his followers more than the spirit of his doctrine, although he well knew their great perplexities and fully understood their academic afflictions increased in proportion to their faithfulness to him. He left to their own fate two of his favorite disciples when they were on trial for illegally practicing, although in this case neither his position, living nor fortune, but only his honor, was involved. He well knew the schemes, plans, and doings of his opponents. We find his defense prepared by his pupils, in most cases they were not even indorsed or seconded by him, but, on the contrary, were received with contempt, suspicions and ridicule; he never took a hand in them!"

It would seem that Kleinert, and also Hartmann, thought that Hahnemann should have acted in a much different manner towards them. That his one aim was first and always the advancement of Homœopathy, no one who will carefully read his writings can deny. And that by allowing his followers to fight their battles for themselves he made them more bold, attracted the attention of the world more fully to the new system, and caused it to more quickly spread, is now seen to be true.

And, too, he naturally thought that his pupils were the proper persons to continue the fight that he had maintained singly for so many years.

Hahnemann took a great interest in the *Archiv der Heilkunst* from the first. In a letter to Stapf, written in 1826, he says:* "I still continue to read works on other scientific subjects, but nothing medical except your *Archiv.* I have not read even

Hom. World, vol. xxiv, p. 361.

Hufeland's Journal for years, and, in my present isolation and severance from well-informed physicians, I do not know where to get the loan of the number of *Hufeland's Journal* you refer me to. I am delighted to receive the important information that the leader of all writers of complicated prescriptions, and of the most material pathology of the ordinary stamp, has again bestowed a friendly glance on his antipode, who has in his writings indicated him as the champion of antiquated medical nonsense, and mentioned him alone by name (in the "Sources of the ordinary Materia Medica" at the beginning of the third volume of the "Materia Medica Pura").

"You would confer a favor on me if, when opportunity offers, you would make a short extract from his favorable judgment.

"I am pleased with Gross's refutation of the *Anti-Organon*. Gross, in my opinion, is growing more valiant. My only regret is that he has spent so much time and thought over that piece of sophistry.

"Believe me, all this senseless fighting against the manifest truth only exhausts the poor creatures, and does not stay its progress, and we would do well to allow such trashy, spiteful lucubrations to pass unnoticed; they will without aid sink into the abyss of oblivion and into their merited nothingness.

"I fear more the empirical contaminations of that society of half-Homœopaths about which you write, which they had sufficient prudence not to invite me to join, but of whose doings I have been pretty correctly informed by oral communications. I fear that inaccuracy and rashness will preside over their deliberations, and I would earnestly beg of you to do what you can to check and restrain them. For should our art once lose its attribute of the most conscientious exactness, which must happen if the *dii minorum gentium* seek to push themselves into notoriety by their so-called observations, then I tremble for the raising of our art out of the dust; then we shall lose all certainty, which is of great importance to us.

"Therefore, I beg you will keep out of your *Archiv* all superficial observations of pretended successful treatment. Admit only truthful, accurate, careful records of cases from the practice of accredited Homœopaths; these must be models of good Homœopathic art. In spite of all precautions, some of these

recorded cases of chronic maladies will incur suspicion that they
may not be permanent, when the eyes of medical men shall be
opened on the subject of the cure of chronic diseases by my
book, which, after ten years' labor, is not yet ready, but is
gradually approaching completion.

"Yours very truly,

"SAM. HAHNEMANN.
"Coethen, March 13, 1826."

And again:* "I thank you for the third number of the eighth
volume of your *Archiv.* It has pleased me very much, and I
can find nothing censurable in it. We must endeavor to maintain its old value, so that it shall remain unsurpassed in the estimation of the medical public. Gross, Rummel, and also
Aegidi and Hartmann have acquitted themselves well. I will
soon make a search to see if I have any presentable provings of
medicines."

In 1825 Hahnemann published in the *Allgemeine Anzeiger*
an answer to an article that had been published in the same
journal, entitled: "Information for the Truth Seeker in No.
165 of the *Allgemeine Anzeiger der Deutschen.*" This essay was
published in 1827 as an introduction to Volume VI. of the second
edition of the "Materia Medica Pura" under the title: † "How
can Small Doses of such very Attenuated Medicines as Homœopathy Employs still possess Great Power?"

In a preface to the fourth volume of the second edition of the
"Materia Medica Pura," 1825, was published an article: "Eine
Erinnerung," to which Dudgeon gives the title: "Contrast
of the Old and New Systems of Medicine." In this Hahnemann speaks of the fallacy of prescribing according to a nosological and capricious name for disease, and the ease of prescribing from a prescription pocket-book. He says: "But
how did the prescriptions for these names of diseases originate?
Were they communicated by some divine revelation? My dear
sir, they are either formulas prescribed by some celebrated
practitioner for some case or other of disease to which he has
arbitrarily given this nosological name, which formulas consist
of a variety of ingredients known to him no doubt by name,
that came into his head and were put by him into an elegant

Hom. World, vol. **xxv**, p. 113.
† "Lesser Writings," New York.

form by the aid of that important art which is called the *art of prescribing*, whereby the requirements of chemical skill and pharmaceutical observance were attended to, if not the welfare of the patient; one or several receipts of this kind for the given case, under the use of which the patient at least did not die, but, thanks to heaven and his good constitution!—gradually recovered.

"After three and twenty centuries of such criminal mode of procedure, now that the whole human race seems to be awaking in order powerfully to vindicate its rights, shall not the day begin to dawn for the deliverance of suffering humanity which has hitherto been racked with diseases, and in addition tortured with medicines administered without rhyme or reason, and without limit as to number and quantity, for phantoms of diseases, in conformity with the wildest notions of physicians proud of the antiquity of their sect?

"Shall the pernicious jugglery of routine treatment still continue to exist?

"Shall the entreaty of the patient to listen to the account of his sufferings, vainly resound through the air unheard by his brethren of mankind, without exciting the helpful attention of the human heart?"

Hahnemann then shows the simpler, more certain method of healing in accordance with the Homœopathic system, and in conclusion says: "Do old antiquated untruths become anything better—do they become truths—by reason of their hoary antiquity? Is not truth eternal, though it may have been discovered only an hour ago? Does the novelty of its discovery render it an untruth? Was there ever a discovery or a truth that was not at first novel?"

In the same volume (IV, second edition) is an article called "The Medical Observer." It shows the importance of the most careful observations of the patient on the part of the physician, with the proper means to be adopted to become a careful observer of disease. *

---

* "Lesser Writings," New York.

CHAPTER XXIX.

HAHNEMANN'S GREAT AND VARIED KNOWLEDGE — REIMARUS
FRAGMENTS—PAPER ON CHEMISTRY—ADVICE TO
STAPF—DEATH OF CASPARI.

Hahnemann was not a man of one idea; he was more or less conversant with many branches of knowledge, and was consulted upon many subjects besides that of medicine. He took a great interest in astronomy, and with his friend, the Court Chancellor Schwabe, who had an observatory on his own premises, Hahnemann was accustomed to hold long conversations. In his library among its other treasures was a large collection of maps, and he was well versed in geographical studies, of which he was very fond. He also was a naturalist; he was a student of ancient history. In addition to these pursuits, and to his large practice, he maintained a very extensive correspondence with his disciples and friends. And, too, there was seldom a day passed when he did not entertain and instruct some disciple who had journeyed from a distance to learn from the Master. At this time many who were weary of the old ways of medicine, went to this prophet of a new dispensation to be taught.

Let us from his own letters form some idea of the multiple pleasures and pursuits of this old man, then over seventy years of age.

Writing to his Fidus Achates, Stapf, in 1826, he says:* "The German translation from the Chinese of the writings of Confucius, by Schott, has given me great pleasure. I have endeavored in vain to procure the French translation by Deguignes. Now the first part of it has been published by Renger in Halle, and I will soon get it. There we read Divine wisdom without miracle-fables and without superstition. It is a remarkable sign of the times that Confucius can now be read by us. I myself will soon embrace, in the domain of blessed spirits, that benefactor of mankind who led us by the straight path to wisdom and to God six centuries and a half before the arch-visionary."

*Hom. World, Vol. xxiv, p. 363.

Again, to Dr. Stapf in 1827 he says:* "The work on entomology you kindly sent me is a beautiful book, and I think it
would be difficult to give a better explanation of the mysterious,
flight-like progression of spiders horizontally and upwards in the
air.   If this single branch of natural history (entomology) does
not show an infallible revelation of God's wisdom, power, and
goodness, in short, everything that should induce a well-dis-
posed man to do His will as conscience dictates; if true religion
is not to be learned from it, then I am spiritually blind.

"Now about Wild's book.   I beg him to inquire about the
price, in order that I may settle the business with all speed.   It
is without doubt a hitherto unknown fragment of the illustrious
Reimarus.   Nothing of it is known to us except the middle part
describing the passage of Moses through the Red Sea.   The Old
Testament is justly estimated there.

"What has become of the *Fragments* which we are told were
to have been published in 1817?   I beg Mr. Wild to get them
for me, even though I have to pay a good price for them.

"O God! that truthfulness and impartiality should be so
seldom met with, and that they should have to hide themselves
in the presence of the thoughtless swarm of worldlings who display their animal character to their last breath, and yet try to
sneak into everlasting happiness by a wrong road.

"Try and obtain for me, through Wild, all the *Fragments*,
whatever they may cost."

Again, in September, 1827 :† "The books on entomology are
excellent.   I thank you for sending them to me.   But they do
not solve the riddle respecting the spiders.   To judge from my
own experiments they appear to possess a power still unknown
to us to project themselves forward in the air—not on shot-out
threads!   In my experiments I made this impossible, and I saw
one, suspended by its thread from my finger, first hover in the
air in a horizontal position, then dart obliquely upwards, where
it disappeared from my sight."

The study of his old favorite, chemistry, was also continued.‡
In a letter to Stapf, of February 20, 1829, he says: "The
enclosed paper is not suited for the *Archiv* or for any other

---

*Hom. World, Vol. xxiv, p. 365.
† Hom. World, Vol. xxiv., p. 492.
‡ Hom. World, Vol. xxiv., p. 503.

medical periodical, as it is merely chemical. Moreover, it is not only anonymous (no one is to know that it is written by me; on account of the prejudice that the doctors and, along with them, the chemists, have for me and my doctrine, the chemical journalist would throw it aside), but it is also a chemical heresy. I beg therefore that you would get this little essay copied at my expense, so that it may not be lost, supposing the chemical journalist should be so·uncivil as to refuse to let it appear in his periodical, and should fail to send it back to me, but drop it into his waste basket or burn it for its heretical doctrines.''

The essay was probably upon the chemical properties or preparation of *Causticum*, called in the "Fragmenta" *Acris tinctura*.

The disposal of this paper on chemistry gave Hahnemann considerable trouble. In another letter dated July 14, 1829, he says, presumably of this same paper:* "Von Bock has just undertaken to travel to Halle in order to have it out with the professor of chemistry. This person has made no concealment of his resolution not to accept my article, as its views are opposed to the traditional teaching. That is just what I feared! What annoyance, what opposition to improvements must we not expect from the orthodox blockheads! But Von Bock pressed him so hard that he became ashamed of himself, and has given his word to get it printed at once; and he promised to send Von Bock a copy. If only he will keep his word, which time will soon show. I cannot publish the fourth part of my book, which contains *Causticum*, until this article appears." ·

And again on August 18, 1829, he says:† "Perhaps you have reason to be angry with Colonel von Bock. I know nothing about it. At all events he did me a great service in traveling at his own expense from here to Halle to see Professor Schweickert and Schweickert-Seidel, and when they scornfully refused to print my article, pressed them so hard that at length they had to promise to print it immediately and to send him a copy to Brunswick, *poste restante*, which they and the publishers did, with letters containing the condition that he should pay for the cost of printing (3 thalers) to the bookseller Vieweg in Brunswick, and send to them in Halle the receipt, otherwise the

---

* *Hom. World*, Vol. xxv., p. 21.
† *Hom. World*, Vol. xxv., p. 23. Annals Brit. Hom. Med. Society, Vol. iii., p. 161.

article could not be inserted in the *Jahrbuch der Physik und Chemie*, and so come before the public.

"I will leave you to judge of this behavior, as also of the preface these Halle people have prefixed to the little article, and for which, consequently, von Bock ·had also to pay.   They seem, in the preface to regard my article as an offense which requires to be apologized for, and with diplomatic punctiliousness, deny their responsibility for the printing of it; just as if my article contained verbal inaccuracies which should not be laid to the charge of the editors.   What gross insults and calumnies!

"I send the article to you now, but beg you to return it when you· have the opportunity.   But I fear they have pocketed the Colonel's three thalers and have not had the grace to insert the article in their periodical, whereby the whole object of it will be frustrated.

"I therefore beg of you as soon as Mr. Remler or you receive the number of this periodical with the appended article, to let me know immediately by letter, in order that I may make arrangements for the printing of the fourth part of the Chronic Diseases, but I will not touch a pen before this is done.   Good God! how tiresome and difficult and how beset with hindrances is the work of bringing the truth before the world, and of conquering prejudice!   If the good did not itself reward the doers by approbation from above and from the depths of the left breast, then it must assuredly remain undone.   * * *   I beg of you to keep it secret that I am the author of the Halle article, for if it is known, sentence of death would be immediately pronounced against it, and no one would put it to the proof."

In 1828 he requests Stapf to:*   "Ask Wild if he can procure for you the *old* edition of Lessing's "Contributions to Literature and Art," without hinting that the principal *Fragments* are contained in it.   I will willingly pay for it."

And in another letter also of 1828 he says to Stapf:†   "I am sorry that you should have so much trouble in procuring the *Fragments*.   Precisely that it is withheld from the view of mankind whence truth might beam into their eyes, and might divert

---

Hom. World, Vol. xxiv., p. 497.

†*Hom. World*, Vol. xxiv., p. 494.   Annals Brit. Hom. Society, Vol. ii., p. 149.

their vision to themselves and to the grand universe in whose constant presence they would be obliged to be perfectly good, for naught can deliver them from the hell of their conscience when, in the omnipresence of their supreme Benefactor, they forget the purpose of their being, and prefer the satisfaction of their animal lusts to His approbation.

"There cannot possibly be anything *in rerum natura* which can make the immoral happy (blessed). That is self-contradictory, and woe to the seducers who delude the immoral by holding out the assured prospect of attaining perfect felicity; they thereby only increase the number of human devils—they bring unspeakable, incalculable misery on mankind. The all-good Deity who animates the infinite universe, lives also in us, and, for our highest, inestimable dowry, gave us reason and a spark of holiness in our conscience—out of the fullness of His own morality—which we only need to keep kindled by constant watchfulness over our actions, in order that it may glow through our whole being, and thus be visible in all our transactions, that pure reason may with inexorable severity hold in subjugation our animal nature, so that the end of our existence here below may be profitably fulfilled, for which purpose the Deity has endowed us with sufficient strength.

"If you have an opportunity of informing dear Dr. Hering how highly I esteem him, please do so. He seems to be an excellent young man."

All the letters of this period written by Hahnemann show that despite his age he kept himself fully in touch with everything that was happening in the world of science and medicine. Dr. Stapf was his constant correspondent and confidant.

The following letter to Stapf is of great interest as illustrating this:*

"COETHEN, March 24, 1828.

"Dear Colleague:

"I thank you for sending me the *Notizen* (a charming paper) which I now return. The observations upon the movements of spiders through the air are not only the best I have ever read on the subject, but they agree perfectly with my own observations. He has, however, only made them on the very small species of spiders, which he calls *Æronautica*, but I myself have done

---

Idem., Vol. xxiv., p. 498. Annals Brit. Hom. Society, Vol. ii., p. 153.

so on the very much larger kind, *A. Diadema*. Great are the natural wonderful works of the Lord of creation, immeasurable His wisdom, power, and goodness !

"I hope, too, you will succeed in obtaining at Mohrenzoll's public sale of books the "Reimarus Fragments," which are incorruptible by superstition.*

"I thank you also for Caspari's book, and with your leave I will keep it for a short time, as also Rau's book which I have from you. May I keep it a little longer? Caspari's *Opusculum Posthumum, Beweis,* which Baumgartner has sent me, will have pleased you. It is a thoroughly good book of instruction for the laity as to the great advantage of Homœopathy over Allopathy. He seems in it to wish to withdraw his previous injurious observations about me. I had long ago forgiven him for those. But it would not be amiss to give an obituary notice of him in the *Archiv*, and to raise a sort of appreciative memorial to him, whereby we will do honor to ourselves. But this I will leave entirely to you, and do not wish to dictate.

"It seems to me that in Leipsic the Homœopathic world are at loggerheads among themselves, and are being ruined by cabals—evil passions destroy what, were it united by the beautiful art, should prosper and bear good fruit—

"'The seed of good grows out of the heart.—*Haller.*'

"The first number of the seventh volume, for which I thank you, is worthy of all honor. What Sch——t's† article wants in solidity he makes up for by his candor and honesty, and his confessions (he was for many years previously a zealous Allopath), weigh heavily in the scale of Homœopathy. He perceives the small value of Allopathy better than many old proselytes.

*The Reimarus mentioned in a previous letter was a distinguished German philologist and philosopher who had been a professor at Hamburg from 1727 to 1765, the time of his death. The "Fragmenta" which Hahnemann mentions, and which he wishes to obtain, were called "Wolfenbuttelsche Fragmenta eines ungenannten." They were published anonymously by Lessing in 1774 and were thought to be by him; but were really written by Reimarus. They consisted of a manifesto against the historical basis of Christianity and by their publication Lessing incurred the enmity of the church. Hahnemann's desire to see them shows how interested he was, although an old and very busy man, in all sorts of knowledge.

† Dr. Schweikert.

"It is to confer too much honor on such muddle-heads as Anton Frolig & Co. to condescend to refute their silly rubbish set forth in incomprehensible phraseology. I doubt if it were not better to pass over in silence such wretched stuff. It is so unintelligible and so unimportant that without that it would sink into deserved oblivion and be forgotten. The best of it is where the rascals confess (p. 142) that 'Homœopathy has spread to an unaccountable degree.' This confession is worth a great deal. We have no need to feel any further anxiety about the progress of the dear child in the wide world. The work has already been done for its proper outfit, and those brave men, Stapf, Gross, and some others, have helped to give the good child a sound and useful education, which will not fail to be acknowledged by our posterity.

"I have now had leisure to read your *Archiv* with great attention, and can accord to you both the highest praise. You have rendered *great* service to our beneficent art.

"But now endeavor to put your health (and that of your dear wife) into a better state. The extra medical serviceable for this purpose which I can advise you is the following: Not to undertake work beyond your physical powers, nor seek to get through it too quickly. It is for your advantage to combine the two dicta: *Expende quid valeant humeri, quid ferre recusent*, and *festina lente*. In this way you will accomplish your object better. Also anger and grief must be expelled from the bosom of a wise man, he must not allow them to enter, *æquam memento rebus in asperis servare mentum-moriture*. The wise man first provides for his own well-being so that he may be better able to contribute to that of others.

"As regards medical matters, the first thing to be attended to with regard to your dreadful cough is, does *Sulphur* suit your condition? If so, then, if for some time you have not taken any, I would advise you to take a small globule charged with *Tincture of sulphur* (*Spiritus vini sulphuratus*) and allow it to act for at least thirty days, this is to be followed by the alternate use of *Phosphorus* $\frac{1}{x}$ and *Sepia* $\frac{1}{x}$ (whichever is most suitable to be taken first), which is the best treatment for such a psoric cough.

"To be sure you have not got the second part of my book, but I shall soon have the proof sheets of both remedies, which I will send you, but only for a short time, as I often require them for my own use. You will get rid of your cough in this way.

"If what you write me about Austria is true, then I must say that Marenzeller is just the man for the situation. His extreme boldness and self-confidence are just what is needed, as also his indefatigable zeal, his iron endurance, and, when occasion demands, roughness and determination to administer a good box on the ear to anyone who comes across his path. All this sort of thing is, I repeat, required in such a nest of crazy allopaths as Vienna is, to bring into being and to conduct such an institution.*

"He will certainly not carry out the treatment with that extreme and requisite care which I exercise in selecting the medicines, but it is, at all events, a commencement.

"The acute outbreaks of psora such as the facial erysipelas of your dear wife, the acute isolated (not epidemic or sporadic) illnesses, pulmonary inflammations, and other similar inflammatory forms, are no doubt true explosions and outbursts of latent psora; but for these acute conditions the slowly acting antipsorics are not suitable, they require the other suitable non-antipsoric medicines for their cure in the meanwhile, after which the psora generally soon returns to its latent state, and after its eruption Vesuvius only continues to smoke a little.

"Yours very truly,

"SAMUEL HAHNEMANN."

Dr. Dudgeon, who translated the above letter, says in regard to Dr. Caspari, in a note:† "Caspari was actively engaged in practice and in literary works in Leipsic when, in the beginning of the year 1828, he was attacked with smallpox, which was then prevailing epidemically in that part of Germany. The attack was attended by delirium, and though carefully nursed by attached friends and colleagues, he contrived to get hold of a loaded gun which no one knew was in the room, with which he shot himself dead on February 15th. Hahnemann seems always to have disliked Caspari, probably because in the first work he wrote after his conversion to Homœopathy he blamed Hahnemann for having separated himself so completely from the old

---

* Trial of Homœopathy, by command of the Emperor, in the hospital, April, 1828. See "Hom. League Tract, No. 11." *Brit. Jour. Hom.*, Vol. xii., p. 320.

† *Hom. World*, Vol. xxiv., p. 497.

school, and set himself to try to amalgamate the two schools.
Caspari afterwards saw that this amalgamation was impossible,
and in his later works appears as a zealous and faithful follower
of Hahnemann.   But Hahnemann could apparently not forget
or forgive the opposition to his views contained in the earlier
work.''

In a former letter Hahnemann alludes to the death as follows:
"Though Caspari behaved in a very hostile manner to me, that
is very sad about him.''

Thus from the years 1827 to 1830 we find this man who had
lived his three score years and ten devoting himself not only to
his great work on the chronicity of disease, to watching carefully the growth of his favorite doctrines, to encouraging his
followers, but also taking an interest in all the new books, and
doings of the medical men.

Think of an old 'man of seventy-five years of age interesting
himself in the truth about the passage of the Red Sea, the habits
of spiders, and in preparing new books!   In the history of the
world they who have done this at an advanced age are the
world's great men, always.   Here was no sere and yellow leaf,
surely.

And, too, there was the home life, the evenings in which he
went into the parlor in intervals of his work and listened, while
his good and faithful wife played upon the ancient harpischord
in order to soothe the busy mind of the old Reformer.

CHAPTER XXX.

TOTAL DEMOLITION OF HOMŒOPATHY BY THE ALLOPATHIC PHY-
SICIANS—HAHNEMANN'S ANSWERS.

During all this time, from the appearance of the "Organon"
in 1810 to the celebration of the Jubilee of Graduation, in 1829,
a great many authors of the Allopathic school had been busy in
demolishing this new doctrine of Homœopathy, and in writing
Hahnemann down a fraud.

After Hecker had sought in a scurrilous and undignified
review to destroy the truths in the "Organon;" when other more
temperate pamphleteers had followed him; after Kranzfelder had

written his "Symbola;" after the apothecaries of Leipsic had
discussed in their domestic circles and in the beer shops of their
native town the question of Hahnemann being allowed to dispense his own medicines; when Meissner anonymously wrote the
"Works of Darkness in Homœopathy;" when Prof. Sachs of
Konigsberg had compared Hahnemann to the devil; when
Keiser had confidently prophesied for his system but an ephem-
eral existence; when Steiglitz dubbed it a "monstrous system;" when Heinroth, the editor of the *Anti-Organon*, a paper
expressly established to destroy this "great humbug," had
already "accompanied it to its death-bed;" when Simon, in the
"Anti-Homœopathic Archives," called Hahnemann "the same
unreliable ignoramus;" and Elias had condemned the whole
system, and had spoken of it as a most "useless thing;"
when the entire oligarchy of the Allopathic school had arisen
to defend the universal habit of bleeding and salivation, both of
which little pastimes Hahnemann had denounced; when Fischer,
of Dresden, had arrayed this "monstrous theory of Homœopathy
at the judgment-seat of common-sense;" when Anonyma,
despicable and snake-like, had everywhere ventured her venom;
when the inquisitors of the public press were preventing the
articles of the Homœopathic physician from appearing in print;
when Kovats in Pesth, called Homœopathy "a system of
juggling and of deception, quackery, foolish bungling, an occupation for idle cobblers," illustrating himself by a most ridiculous mythological fable about Hercules and the ubiquitous
serpent; when Wetzler had already written of "Homœopathy at
its last gasp;" when Bernstein, in Warsaw, had promised its
downfall; and Fischer had explained at length the reasons why
it could not possibly exist in Berlin, France and England; when
Sachs had settled the momentous question by declaring
"Homœopathy has never appeared and does not exist;" when
Steiglitz, the physician to the King of Hanover, advised the
members of the dominant school of medicine to "wait beside
the open grave of Homœopathy, as the corpse would soon appear;" when another noble and scientific person advised that
Homœopaths be burned as witches; when Puchelt, Jorg, Groh,
Sprengel, Widerkind, Mulisch, Stachelwroth and Schmidt, and
hosts of others were overwhelming Germany with polemical
pamphlets, journal-articles, and books, against poor old Hahne-

mann and his terrible doctrine;* behold what Hahnemann, the
old physician and philosopher, looking out upon his enemies
with eyes of three score years and ten, who was a physician
before his villifiers were born, and who had forgotten much
more than the most of them had ever learned, behold what he
said in a letter written to Stapf, from his refuge at peaceful
Coethen, on September 1, 1825:†

"Do not be uneasy that such a quantity of big guns are at
present being discharged at us; they never hit the mark; they
fall as light as feathers, and if we are true to ourselves they can
do no harm to us nor injure the good cause in the slightest, for
what is good remains good.

"All this scribbling is forgotten in six or twelve months.
The Homœopath tosses it contemptuously aside after reading it,
and feels only pity for the blinded zealots. The Allopaths
derive comfort from it in vain; their position is not improved by
it; and the public don't read it because they do not understand
the incomprehensible stuff; they only understand the abusive
expressions, which are no refutation.

"I do not know why we should fret or get angry about it.
What is true cannot be betrayed into untruth, even should a
privy councillor or an illustrious old professor write against it.
* * * I laugh at it all. In a short time it will all be forgotten, and the progress of our cause is not checked. All the
numerous opposition writings are merely the last shots of the
enemy into the air before the ship sinks to the bottom."

In another letter of the same year he says:‡ "The tissue of
theoretical subtleties contained in Heinroth's "Anti-Organon"
(thank God I do not read such rubbish) does little harm; the
readers will not understand it and will pass it by. But it cannot be easily refuted, for the person who undertakes this task
must first make the nonsense comprehensible to his reader
before he can refute it, and that is not worth the trouble.

"You are too much afraid of these libelous publications.
The enemy is merely firing off in the air his last ammunition,
and the truth remains unharmed, and gains over more accept-

---

* For titles of these books see Kleinert's "Geschichte der Homoopathie,"
p. 108. Trans. in Med. Counsellor, Vol. xi., p. 272.

†*Hom. World*, Vol. xxiv., p. 249. "Annals Brit. Hom. Society," Vol. i.,
p. 492. ‡The same, p. 252.

ance from people whose minds are unprejudiced.   And these are
the only persons of any consequence to us.   The truth which is
so opposed to the old rubbish could not be stated without exciting a violent reaction.   They are quite cognizant of the exist
ence of the well laid mine which will shatter their whole old
edifice, and they are naturally beside themselves with rage.
Their angry snorting and impotent gnashing of teeth can be
perceived far and near, but it will not help them.   I remain
quite well amid it all.''

In another letter to Dr. Stapf he says:

"*Esteemed Doctor :*

"Do you really believe these wretched fellows do any harm to
the good cause?   You are mistaken.   Their performances are
so bad, and bear their own condemnation on their face.   So I
have written Dr. Gross to request him to prevent any Homœopath taking the trouble to refute or answer them.   Still it
would not be amiss to say a few words to the public about
them.   I wish you would transcribe what I have written on
the enclosed leaf and send it to the editor of the *Anzeiger* for
insertion.

"This would, I know, be agreeable to the editor, who has
more than a dozen such hostile articles against the good cause
on his hands and does not know how to refuse them.   But at
my recommendation he would reject the most of them.

"I do not feel annoyed at the rubbish.   It has gone to such
lengths that it must now come to an end.   They scream themselves hoarse and lose their powers of speech.   The reading
public knows how to estimate their screaming, and despises the
rascals who among their neighbors pose as angels of light, as
friends of mankind, and as gentle lambs; but show by such invectives that they are raging wolves, and they must inevitably
sink low in the estimation of their neighbors.

"It is but natural that the thousands of such fellows who have
their corns trod on by the new doctrine, should find themselves
in the greatest straits, and should utter malicious exclamations,
but every rational person perceives from these cries how important the matter is in reference to which they behave so
extravagantly, and that they *cry out* because they wish to *cry
down* the better treatment which they are too lazy and too proud
to adopt.

"The stuff they write is too evidently dictated by passion and too full of errors and falsehoods to impose on the public and induce them to regard such bunglers as good judges of this important matter.

"The truth has already extended its rays too widely, and shines too brightly to admit of being eclipsed.*

"Yours very truly,

"Coethen, Nov. 14, 1825."   "SAM. HAHNEMANN.

And again in the same year he says:† "Remember how when Jenner's cowpox inoculation had been adopted far and near, quantities of disgraceful invectives were published against it in England—I once counted twenty such—now they are not to be found, probably the paper on which they were printed is now used to wrap up cheese in a grocer's shop.

"And look how limited are the applications of Jenner's discovery compared with those of Homœopathy. It puts to shame many thousands of the Allopaths, most of whom feel that they are all too narrow-minded and stupid to tread the new way with success. This makes many thousands malicious in the highest degree. They scatter broadcast, venom and bile, and seek to overwhelm it with sophistry, misrepresentation, and calumnies. But what does it matter? They injure themselves, not us. The truth continues to advance in silence, and sensible people think those who indulge in abuse are in the wrong."

Neither did Hahnemann have a very high opinion of the scholarship of certain of his detractors and critics. In the preface to Volume III. of the first edition of the "Materia Medica Pura" (1817) he published an article called: "Nota Bene for my Reviewers," in which he says: "I have read several false criticisms on the second part (vol.) of my 'Pure Materia Medica,' especially on the essay at the beginning of it, entitled 'Spirit of the Homœopathic Medical Doctrine.' What an immense amount of learning do not my critics display! I shall only allude to those who write and print 'homopathic' and 'homopathy' in place of Homœopathic and Homœopathy, thereby betraying that they are not aware of the immense differ-

---

* *Hom. World*, Vol. xxiv., p. 309. Annals Brit. Hom. Society, Vol. i., p. 495.

† *Hom. World*, Vol. xxiv., p. 311. Annals Brit. Hom. Society, Vol. i., p. 498.

ence betwixt ὁμὸν and ὅμοιον, but consider the two to be synony-
mous. Did they never hear a word about what the whole
world knows, how the infinite difference betwixt ὁμοούσιος and
ὁμοιούσιος once split the whole Christian church into two parts,
impossible to be re-united? Do they not understand enough
Greek to know that (alone and in combination) ομον means
common, identical, the same (e. g. εἰς ομον λέχος εἰςαναβάινοι—Iliad),
but that ομοιον only means similar, resembling the object, but never
reaching it in regard to nature and kind, never becoming identical
with it?

"The Homœopathic doctrine never pretended to cure a
disease by the same, the identical power by which the disease
was produced—this has been impressed upon the unreasonable
opponents often enough, but, as it seems, in vain; no! it only
cures in the mode most consonant to nature, by means of a
power never exactly corresponding to, never the same as the
cause of the disease, but by means of a medicine that possesses
the peculiar power of being able to produce a similar morbid
state.

"Cannot those persons feel the difference betwixt 'identical'
(the same) and 'similar?' Are they all 'homopathically'
laboring under the same malady of stupidity? Should not anyone who ventures to step forward as a reviewer of the 'Spirit of the
Homœopathic Medical Doctrine' have at least a rudimentary
idea of the meaning of the word Homœopathy?

"Perversions of words and sense, incomprehensible palaver,
which is meant to appear learned, abuse and theoretical sceptical
shakings of the head, instead of practical demonstrations of the
contrary, seem to me to be weapons of too absurd a character to
use against a fact such as Homœopathy is; they remind me of
the little figures which mischievous boys make with gunpowder
and set on fire in order to tease people, the things can only fizz
and splutter, but are not very effective, are, on the whole, very
miserable affairs.

"My respectable brethren on the opposition benches, I can
give you better advice about overthrowing, if possible, this doctrine which threatens to stifle your art, that is founded on mere
assumption, and to bring ruin upon all your therapeutic lumber.
Listen to me! . . . The doctrine appeals not only chiefly,
but solely to the verdict of experience—'repeat the experi-

ments,' it cries aloud, 'repeat them carefully and accurately and you will find the doctrine confirmed at every step '—and it does what no medical doctrine, no system of physic, no so called therapeutics ever did or could do, it *insists* upon being 'judged by the result.'

"Here, then, we have Homœopathy just where we wished to have it; here we can (come on, dear gentlemen, all will go on nicely) give it the death blow from this side!"

Hahnemann then challenges his adversaries to test the truth of his system according to his own rules laid down in the "Organon," using the same care as himself would, and then says: "If it does not give relief—speedy, mild and permanent relief—then, by a publication of the duly-attested history of the treatment according to the principles of the Homœopathic system strictly followed out, you will be able to give a public refutation of this doctrine which so seriously threatens the old darkness. But I pray you to beware of playing false in the matter."

He advises them "of the opposition benches" if they know any other way of "suppressing this accursed doctrine" to continue after the usual fashion. "Continue then to exalt the commonplace twaddle of your school to the very heavens with the most fulsome praise, and to pervert and ridicule with your evil mind what your ignorance does not pervert; continue to calumniate, to abuse, to revile—and the unprejudiced will be able plainly to comprehend on whose side truth lies.

"If you really wish to do as well as the practitioners of Homœopathy, imitate the Homœopathic practice rationally and honestly!

"If you do not wish this—well then, harp away—we will not prevent you—harp away on your comfortlesss path of blind and servile obedience in the dark midnight of fanciful systems, seduced hither and thither by the will-o'-the-wisps of your venerated authorities, who, when you really stand in need of aid leave you in the lurch—dazzle your sight and disappear.

"And if your unfortunate practice, from which that which you intended, wished and promised, does *not* occur, accumulates within you a store of spiteful bile, which seeks to dissipate itself in calumniating your betters—well then, continue to call the grapes up yonder, which party pride, confusion of intellect, weakness or indolence prevents your reaching, sour, and leave them to be gathered by more worthy persons."

This delightful bit of satire is dated Leipzig, February, 1817, and is signed "Dr. Samuel Hahnemann."*

CHAPTER XXXI.

PUBLIC TRIALS OF HOMŒOPATHY—HERING'S CONVERSION—
LETTERS TO HERING—ACCURACY OF HAHNEMANN—
HIS FAITH IN THE SPREAD OF HOMŒOPATHY.

Up to the year 1835 there were six public and formal trials, undertaken by order of governments, made of Homœopathic practice : 1. At Vienna, in 1828, conducted by Dr. Marenzeller. 2. At Tulzyn, Russia, in 1827. 3. At St. Petersburg, in 1829–30, by Dr. Hermann. 4. At Munich, in 1830–31, by Dr. Attomyr. 5. At Paris, in 1834, by Dr. Andral, Jr. 6. At Naples, in 1835, by order of the King, by a mixed commission in the hospital of La Trinite.

These were all made by Allopathic physicians and were not considered by members of the Homœopathic school as fairly conducted.

Dr. Tessier, in 1849–51, made tests at Hopital Ste. Marguerite, deciding in favor of the Homœopathic system. When he presented his report to the Paris Academy he aroused a storm of protest for his fairness in admitting that there was good in Homœopathy.†

It is worthy of mention that the Preface, "Nota Bene," quoted in the last chapter was the cause of Dr. Constantine Hering becoming interested in Homœopathy.‡ C. Baumgartner, the founder of a publishing house in Leipsic, wanted a book written against Homœopathy. This was about the time that Hahnemann was driven from Leipsic, and it was then supposed that such a book would quite finish the system.

---

*"Reine Arzneimittellehre," Vol. iii.   "Lesser Writings," New York.
†See *Hom. Examiner*, Vol. i., p. 20 (1840). Rosenstein's "Theory and Practice of Homœopathy," p. 267. *Brit. Jour. Hom.*, Vol ii., p. 49; Vol. xi., p. 133; Vol. xiv., p. 308.
‡*U. S. Med. and Surg. Jour.*, Vol. iii., p. 116.

Dr. J. H. Robbi, Hering's preceptor, was asked to write the book but refused and recommended his student, Hering, at that time twenty years of age. The contract was made and the book, written during the winter of 1821–22, was nearly completed, when, for the sake of making quotations, Hering was provided with Hahnemann's works. In the third volume of the "Materia Medica Pura" he discovered this "Nota Bene for My Critics." It induced him to make experiments.

The book was discontinued; Hering now endeavored to separate the true from the false that he yet thought must be in this new and peculiar system. Against the advice of friends, patrons, and teachers he continued his investigations. In two years he became convinced of the truth of Hahnemann's discovery. He now suffered persecutions, want, hunger, and was obliged to postpone his examination for his degree.

In 1825 a younger brother offered to loan him money, and while inquiring at which of Germany's thirty universities he could get his degree the cheapest, he saw some notes taken from the lectures of the celebrated pathologist, Schoenlein, of Wurzburg. He was so pleased that he took up his bundle and walked into Franconia to sit at the feet of Schoenlein.

He would not deny his allegiance to Hahnemann, and therefore was obliged to pass a most rigorous examination. He defended his thesis—"De Medicina Futura"—in which he acknowledged the Homœopathic doctrines, on March 23, 1826. He had been in correspondence with Hahnemann long before this time. The following letters, written to him by Hahnemann when he was yet a student of medicine,* show the kindly regard for the new convert, whom he had never seen. It may be not amiss to mention that, though Hahnemann and Hering were friends from this time until the death of the former, yet they never met. Hering almost at once after his graduation

---

*Some time previous to 1860, Dr. Hering sent to Dr. J. Rutherford Russell, of England, careful copies of thirty-five letters written by Hahnemann to himself and to Dr. Stapf. It was Dr. Russell's intention to publish a life of the master, and Dr. Hering thus assisted him. The life was not written, but Dr. Russell translated and published the letters in vols. i, ii, iii, iv of the "Annals and Transactions of the British Homœopathic Society, and of the London Homœopathic Hospital," 1860–66. He also used some of them in his "History and Heroes of Medicine." Dr. Dudgeon must have had access to these letters in 1889, as among the fifty-one

went to South America and from thence sailed for Philadelphia. Hering did not receive his degree as doctor of medicine from the University of Wurzburg until March 23, 1826, although he had for some years been a believer in the doctrines of Hahnemann. The letters are as follows:*

"*Dear Mr. Hering:*

" Your active zeal for the beneficent art delights me, and I believe that every one who desires to render valuable services to it must be animated by equal enthusiasm. The preparation you kindly sent me is, I perceive, pure iron in a form divested of solidity and the metallic character, modern chemists would probably call it *Hydrure de fer*. Dissolve a drachm of pure sulphate of iron in pure water, and precipitate it with *spiritus salis ammoniaci vinosus*, wash the sediment several times with pure water and dry it in blotting paper, and then see if you do not obtain the same iron powder. It is a fine discovery, and the Ostriz man deserves praise. It may be used with advantage.

" I regret that when your esteemed letter arrived the manuscript of the second edition of the second volume of my 'Materia Medica Pura' had already been sent to press; I was consequently unable to introduce the preparation of iron or to avail myself of your offer to make trials of it. But I intend ere long to take advantage of your kind offer for other substances. You make mention of your sister, is she with you in Leipsic? Do you also come from Oberlausitz? What led you to study medicine?

" I would like to become better acquainted with you, and I pray you to continue to be a right, genuine, good man, as it is impossible without virtue to be a true physician, a godlike helper of his fellow creatures in their distress.

" Yours very truly,

"SAMUEL HAHNEMANN."

"*Coethen, July 9, 1824.*"

And in December of the same year he writes: †

" *Dear Mr. Hering:*

" I have your letter of the 24th of November before me, an

letters of Hahnemann he translated and published in the *Homœopathic World*, the most of these thirty-five are to be found. The above letters to Hering are among the number.

* *Hom. World*, Vol. xxiv., p. 247. "Annals Brit. Hom. Society," Vol. ii., p. 242.

†"Annals of Brit. Hom. Society," Vol. i, p. 490.

earlier answer I was prevented from giving by the multitude of my occupations.

"As you wish to procure a master's degree in the old system of medicine next spring, I beg and counsel you not to allow your Homœopathic opinions to be known by the Allopathic physicians of Leipsic, least of all by that most implacable of all Allopaths, Clarus, if you do not wish to be grievously tormented at your examination or even rejected. * * *

"Yet, when you have got your degree, and have pitched upon the place of your future practice, then fear nothing more from the obstacles which the corporation of apothecaries will be able to put in your way. Some escape will open by which you will be able to put the good method into practice.

"I have confidence in you and am not afraid of being wrong in regarding you as one of the few of my followers, who, in a higher sense than the common (inspired only by desire of gain and reputation), will practice the divine art among your afflicted fellow-men under the eye of the Omnipresent, then, while you will not miss obtaining the so-called temporal gain, you will also secure the approval of your conscience, without which kingdoms cannot give happiness.

"If you wish to become a physician in this nobler sense (that is a pure benefactor of men), standing on earth a representative of God, our highest benefactor, and to be a right good man, then will you be one of the few, a truly happy, joyful man. This I wish and hope for you.

"Only he who is good can be sure of the support of God, without whom we can accomplish nothing, from whom everything comes which contributes to the cure of his beloved family of man.

"From your offer to make experiments with medicines upon yourself, assisted by your sister, I will make use when you are in a place and position to practice your art.

"Yours most obediently,

"SAM. HAHNEMANN."

"*Coethen. 31st of December, 1824.*"

Among the many visitors to Hahnemann at this busy period was Dr. F. F. Quin, of England, who, in 1826, went to Coethen for the purpose of studying Homœopathy under its founder. He had, as early as 1823, become interested in it. Dr. Quin returned to England in 1827, and at once commenced the practice of Homœopathy, having the honor of introducing it into that country.*

Exception has at times been taken by some members of the Homœopathic school to certain of the symptoms collected previously and at this time, and published in the "Materia Medica Pura" by Hahnemann.

Hahnemann's excessive carefulness in the matter of expressing his exact meaning is well illustrated in this letter to Gross, dated December 26, 1825:† "The terminology should be settled from the first. We will not make any change in what I decided respecting the difference betwixt *lancinans* and *pungens*. Beyer's *pressorie-pulsatorius* is certainly better Latin than *pressorio-pulsatorius*, and in future I wish that the first adjective of such composite terms should be changed into the adverbial form in the same way as *pressorie* instead of *pressorio*. When I find something better than my own I adopt it willingly. Kindly see this done.

"But not *pressorius* and *pulsatorius*, for that does not convey the idea of a sensation compounded of the two, but implies that it was sometimes pressure, sometimes throbbing; in short, both sensations singly side by side. This must not be used instead of *pressorio pulsatorius*."

Again, writing to Stapf, September 1, 1825, he says:‡ "One word more. In future volumes of the Latin translation of my 'Materia Medica' I hope you will be still more careful in the choice of symptoms, especially those taken from Allopathic sources. They were useful to me, as they served to gain for me the ear of the profession, showing as they did that other physicians had observed something similar, and that my observations should therefore not be doubted. But you do not require this in your epitome, it is not necessary to show this in your book.

"Yet another word. It is absolutely necessary that you give me the numbers of the symptoms in the original German text which you translate and condense, enclosed in brackets after each, thus, (220,221).‖ For how else can the reviser find them, or the for-

---

*"Annals Brit. Hom. Society," Vol. i., p. 5; also Appendix Report, ii.
† *Hom. World*, Vol. xxiv, p. 312.
‡*Hom. World*, Vol. xxiv., p. 250.
‖ He refers to the translation made by Stapf, Gross and Von Brunnow.

eigner who understands a little German look them up in the original in order to get further information about them? Do this, therefore, in your manuscript.

"Hartlaub's writings are well thought out and useful, and I think highly of them.

"Should you, in Naumburg, see a paper by me in the *Morgenblatt* on the refusal to allow Homœopaths to dispense their own medicines, let me know. I have exerted myself to procure for Homœopaths this, their inalienable right. He who allows the medicines to be made by another (the apothecary) is a poor creature, he can't do what he ought, he is no Homœopath.

"Yours very truly,
"SAM. HAHNEMANN."

"*Coethen, September 1, 1825.*"

Hahnemann felt no uncertainty as to the final fate of Homœopathy. Two years before the Preface, "Nota Bene," was written Stapf had expressed a wish that some distinguished Allopath should be converted to a belief in Homœopathy, to which Hahnemann made the following answer: "That you will find a great man who will come over to our side is, in the nature of things, impossible. If he be already a man of celebrity, as you represent him, he can have become so only by means of the gross empirical art which he contrived to support, after some new fashion, by compiling in manuals the thousand times ruminated trash of common medicine, or by hatching some unelaborated, unintelligible, fine-spun system, or by processes and fooleries of the ordinary sort, which he carried further than his colleagues, and raised himself above them only by telling greater and more audacious falsehoods than they. Such an one has long ago decided on the part he must play; he can worship only the false and sophistical system which raised him to his place of honor.

"Never would he be able to recog·ize from the wilderness of his multifarious knowledge the dignity of simple, humbling truth; and he would be on his guard, if some helps did not reach him, to take them as little as possible under his protection, inasmuch as they would expose the falsehood of all his former knowledge, by which he had become so great, and would leave nothing sound or entire about him, and destroy himself and his knowledge.

"He must tread under foot all his mock-consequence before he could even begin to be our disciple; and what would then remain of the great man who could raise us by his countenance, since his infallibility must be laid in the dust; and the halo of universal knowledge, for which he was indebted to his exalted station alone, must first be extinguished, by the study of a new truth, before he will become a worthy scholar of ours. How could he become our *protector* without first receiving the truth we teach, that is, without having first entered our school? And then must be thrown away all that rendered him great in the eyes of the world; and even to perform a moderate service in our cause he would stand in need of *our protection*, not we of *his*.

"Our art requires no political levers, no worldly decorations. At present it grows with slow progress amid the abundance of weeds which luxuriate about it; it grows unobserved, from an unlikely acorn into a little plant; soon may its head be seen overtopping the rank weedy herbage. Only wait—it is striking deep its roots in the earth; it is strengthening itself unperceived, but all the more certainly; and in its own time it will increase, till it becomes an oak of God, whose arms, unmoved by the wildest storm, stretch in all directions, that the suffering children of men may be revived under its beneficent shadow."[*]

This description of the so-called man of science applies very well to our own times and to the present scientific craze for germs, microbes, lymph-injections, bacilli and other short-lived "discoveries."

Dudgeon says:[†] "That Hahnemann felt, and felt deeply, the unjust calumnies and unceasing persecution to which he was subjected, we have ample evidence from various passages in his works, from the year 1800 upwards. Among the papers found at his death one bore the following inscription intended as an epitaph on his tomb, which reads like the last sigh of a martyr—'Liber Tandem Quiesco.'"

Hahnemann could not have been human had not this tempest of villification affected him. But that his firm faith in the future of Homœopathy was well founded is most powerfully illustrated by the colleges, hospitals, dispensaries and numberless followers of the school at the present day.

---

[*] Stapf's "Archiv.," Vol. xxi., pt. 2, p. 129. *Brit. Jour. Hom.*, Vol. iii., p. 197.

[†] "Biography of Hahnemann," p. 46.

CHAPTER XXXII.

THEORY OF CHRONIC DISEASES—LETTER TO BAUMGARTNER.

In the year 1828 Hahnemann published a most important book, entitled "Chronic Diseases, Their Nature and Homœopathic Treatment" It was issued in four volumes, three in 1828 and the fourth in 1830, by his old publisher, Arnold, of Dresden and Leipsic.

The first volume is dedicated "to Ernst, Baron von Brunnow, by his friend Samuel Hahnemann." In the preface to this volume he says: "If I did not know for what purpose I exist upon earth—to make myself as good as possible, and to improve things and men around me to the best of my ability, I should have to consider myself deficient in worldly wisdom for promulgating before my death an art, whose sole possessor I was, and which, being kept secret, might have become a source of permanently increasing profit to me."

In 1827, one year previous, he called his two eldest and best beloved disciples, Drs. Stapf and Gross, to Coethen, and told them about his great discovery of the origin of chronic diseases, and asked them to test in practice the action of certain remedies that he then designated by the name of antipsorics.

He had been slow, as he himself says, in imparting this secret to his pupils and followers. He had, however, as the following letter will show, made some confidants.

Hahnemann wished to establish a hospital, in order that chronic maladies could be treated in strict accordance with his own ideas. He had also endeavored to induce Duke Ferdinand to found this hospital at Coethen.

In the *Allgemeine Zeitung* for December 7, 1846, the following letter was published, preceded by these remarks by the editor:*

"We publish herewith for various reasons a letter written by Dr. Hahnemann to the deceased Consul General, Dr. Friedrich Gotthelf Baumgartner. It was among the documents left by the deceased, and was sent to us for publication by his son, Julius A. Baumgartner, City Counsellor. It seemed strange to

---

Allg. Hom. Zeitung, Vol. xxxii., p. 41 (Dec. 7, 1846); also *Neue Zeitschrift fur Hom. Klinik* (Hirschel), Vol. xvi., p. 105 (July 15, 1871).

us that Hahnemann, in his old age, should busy himself in founding a hospital, and should wish to assume the direction of it. It was some thing new to us that he could not make known his great discovery respecting the treatment of chronic diseases by his publications, but only by clinical instruction, which might be done if in accordance with his wish he should be permitted to have a hospital.

"It was well known to his old pupils that he left Leipsic unwillingly, and in this letter the reader finds the compelling reason. His mistrust of his pupils finds sufficient excuse in the many bitter disappointments which he persuaded himself that he had experienced to a much greater extent than any other person, an opinion that would naturally become more and more decisive with advancing age.

"We all know that he must have received a handsome royalty through his publications, yet we cannot blame him for estimating his communications at a far higher rate; but on the other hand, we must acknowledge that but few authors will be offered such a generous royalty, and that he won for himself through the publication of his teachings both an enormous throng of patients and well merited honors, which might easily make him forget the seeming ingratitude of his pupils. The following is the letter mentioned:

"*Right Honorable Doctor and Consul-General, Beloved Patron:*

"I regard it as a kind of providential foresight that you, a man of such high consideration and authority, should have the sagacity to try to help honor a healing art, which, because of its simplicity, verity and incredible efficacy, has been so maligned in a thousand ways, as well as often reviled and suppressed by the great fraternity of physicians, proud in their comfortable old practice.

"I have read your report to the City of Berlin, and I honor and revere you most sincerely for this great act of beneficence. May God bless you.

"I also thank you for the banquet which you have given in honor of my system of medicine, and I highly appreciate your public aknowledgment of the value of Homœopathy. It must have created quite a sensation among your friends.

"I heartily wish that the kingdom of Saxony had acted more fairly towards me, for a genuine Homœopathic physician who will practice his system exclusively and conscientiously can need no assistance other than in the preparation of his medicines, and can need no apothecary, which of itself would be a veritable blessing.

"In that case, too, I need not have left Leipsic, which is so dear to me, and been obliged to settle here at an expense to myself of more than two thousand thalers.

"I rejoice that you are so far on the way to recovery; I advise you to avoid, if possible, the least indisposition, and to relieve the nightly drying of the wound and the numbness of the large toe by such Homœopathic remedies as you see in the books.

"There will always remain some ailments uncured by Homœopathy, the remains of some deep-seated chronic disease. For the perfect healing of a large family of chronic diseases, not even all that I have written on Homœopathy is sufficient. But incredibly more is effected by it in these old diseases than by the medicines prescribed by the Allopaths. But, in Homœopathic writings as yet published, there is still lacking the great keystone which binds together all that has been thus far published, so that the healing of chronic diseases may be not only expedited, but also brought to the condition of complete recovery.

"To discover this still-lacking keystone and thus the means of entirely obliterating the ancient chronic diseases, I have striven night and day, for the last four years, and by thousands of trials and experiences as well as by uninterrupted meditation I have at last attained my object. Of this invaluable discovery, of which the worth to mankind exceeds all else that has ever been discovered by me, and without which all existent Homœopathy remains defective or imperfect, none of my pupils as yet know anything.

"It is still wholly my property. Therefore the worst chronic diseases which not only the physicians of the old school, but also the best among the Homœopaths, must leave unhealed, are still in the same condition; since, as said before, the Homœopathic system as till now promulgated by me, however much it can do, has not by a long way reached that perfect healing which has become possible only since this new discovery, the result of unspeakable efforts.

"But this knowledge, now finally attained, is of such kind

that I can impart it in a practical way to young students only by special inspection at the bedside in some clinical establishment. And in order that I might be able to do this before my death, I entreated our Duke to establish a hospital for the purpose.

"It appeared acceptable to him, but, notwithstanding his seeming willingness to establish one, I see plainly that nothing will come of it. We have as yet no public hospital in Coethen.

"Nothing will be done in the matter in this place, so far as I can see; and it would be much more agreeable to me to have such an establishment in a larger place.

"Since this knowledge cannot be communicated by written works, but men must hear, see, and be convinced for themselves, I shall, perhaps, have to take this treasure with me to the grave, and can merely appropriate it in my lifetime to my own needs in thus healing those invalids whom no one else can heal.

"This is but a slight advantage to be gained by me, who have so willingly communicated to the world everything prior to this discovery, and have received therefor but little thanks from my own pupils and from Allopathists, as well as persecution from public officials who have an eye to the benefit of apothecaries.

"I whisper in your ear this important confession, and I beg that you, who are my very dear friend, will impart it to no one in Leipsic. I may rest assured that you, whose heart is all aglow for the welfare of humanity, will make the very best use of it.

"A friend who esteems you most highly,
"Your humble servant,
"SAMUEL HAHNEMANN."

"*Coethen, January 10, 1823.*"

From the years 1816 to 1828 Hahnemann had been giving his thoughts to a new and startling doctrine regarding the origin and cure of diseases. There were certain diseases of long standing or chronic that did not respond properly to the Homœopathic remedies. For a time the small number of Homœopathic medicines known was the excuse given for this failure. Hahnemann says : *

"Hitherto the followers of Homœopathy were satisfied with

---

* The quotations in this chapter are from the MSS of an unpublished translation of "Die Chronischen Krankheiten," made by and in the possession of Dr. Augustus Korndoerfer, of Philadelphia.

this excuse, but the founder of Homœopathy never took advantage of it nor did he find comfort therein.   The yearly addition of proved powerful remedies did not advance the treatment
of chronic (non-venereal) diseases a single step, whereas the
acute if not fatal in character from the beginning were not only
markedly relieved by the correctly employed Homœopathic
remedy, but with the aid of our ever active life-sustaining force
promptly and thoroughly cured.

"Why should this vital force which, aided by the Homœopathic remedy is sufficient for the restoration of the integrity of
the organism, and for the accomplishment of perfect recovery
from the most virulent acute diseases, fail to afford any true or
lasting benefit in the various chronic diseases, even though
aided by the Homœopathic remedies, best indicated by the existing symptoms.   What prevents its action?

"In order to answer this most natural question, I was compelled to investigate the nature of these chronic diseases.

"Since the years 1816 and 1817 I have been occupied day
and night in efforts to discover the reason why the known
Homœopathic remedies did not affect a true cure of the above-
mentioned chronic diseases; and sought to secure a more accurate, and, if possible, a correct insight into the true nature of
these thousands of chronic diseases, which remained uncured
despite the uncontrovertible truth of the Homœopathic doctrine.
When behold ! the Giver of all good permitted me, after unceasing meditation, indefatigable research, careful observation and
the most accurate experiments to solve this sublime problem for
the benefit of mankind. "

And in a footnote he says: "During these years nought of
these efforts was made known to the world nor even to my own
disciples.   This was not owing to the ingratitude which I had
frequently experienced, for I heed neither the ingratitude nor
yet the persecutions which I encounter in my wearisome though
not joyless life-path.   No, I said nought thereof because it is
unwise, yea, even harmful to speak or write of things yet imma-
ture.   In the year 1827 I first made known the most important
features of my discoveries to two of my most worthy disciples,
not only for their benefit and that of their patients, but in addition that the whole of this knowledge might not be lost to the
world through my death, for having reached my 73d year it was

not improbable that I might be called into eternity before I could complete this book."

As early as 1816, in an "Essay on the Improper Treatment of the Venereal Disease," Hahnemann mentions the itch of wool manufacturers, and says:* "As soon as the itch vesicles have made their appearance this is a sign that the internal itch disease is already fully developed. The itch vesicles that now appear, are hence no mere local malady, but a proof of the completion of the internal disease."

This is much like the theory of chronic diseases propounded twelve years later.

Hahnemann found that the non-venereal chronic diseases, after being for a time removed by the Homœopathic remedies, often reappeared in a more or less modified form. He says of this:

"The constant repetition of the fact that the non-venereal chronic diseases, even after having been repeatedly relieved by the then known Homœopathic remedies, persistently reappeared in more or less modified form, yea, every year adding new symptoms, gave me the first intimation that the physician had not alone to contend with the phenomena which constituted the appreciable manifestations of disease, and that such phenomena were not to be regarded or treated as independent diseases. Had it been otherwise they would promptly and permanently have been cured by the Homœopathic remedies, which, however, was not the case.

"It was evident that the physician had to deal with a deep-seated primary evil, the great extent of which was made manifest by the new conditions which from time to time were developed.

"It was also evident that if he treated such conditions as separate and independent diseases, as hitherto taught, he dared not hope to so permanently cure them as to prevent their reappearance, either in their original form, or with new and more distressing symptoms; therefore, it became evident that the physician must know every symptom and condition of this obscure primary evil before he could hope to discover one or more fundamental remedies whose symptoms cover the totality of the symptoms of the primary affection, and through which he might compass the disease as a whole as well as its individual symptoms, thus radically curing and removing every portion thereof.

* "Lesser Writings," New York, p. 649.

"That, however, this primary affection must also be of a miasmatic chronic nature appeared to me quite evident, in that as soon as it had reached a certain height and development neither the most robust constitution nor yet the best regulated diet and mode of life proved sufficient to overcome it; nor did it ever cease of itself. On the contrary, its symptoms changed and became more serious from year to year to the end of life.

"This holds true of every chronic miasmatic disease, for instance syphilis, which, when the chancre has not been cured by its specific, *Mercury*, never becomes extinct of itself, but (despite the best mode of life and the most robust constitution) each year develops new and worse symptoms until the end of life.

"Thus far had I gone in my investigations and observations upon (non-venereal) chronic patients when I observed that the hindrance to the cure of these (seemingly independent) varied forms of disease by the best proved Homœopathic remedies in most cases lay in the fact of a pre-existent itch eruption. All the sufferings usually arose subsequent to such time. In those chronic patients who would not confess to such infection, or who through inattention had failed to observe it, or could not recollect the fact, careful inquiries usually disclosed the existence of vestiges of the itch (single itch vesicles, herpes, etc.), which from time to time gave unmistakable evidence of such pre-existent infection."

CHAPTER XXXIII.

CHRONIC DISEASES CONTINUED—PSORA A CAUSE OF DISEASE— THE ITCH THEORY—DR. RÁUE ON THE ITCH THEORY.

This latent taint in the system preventing the cure of certain diseases Hahnemann named *psora*. He considered it communicable from one person to another, and called it "a sort of internal itch." He further said that there were certain long-acting remedies that were peculiarly adapted to the eradication of this subtle poison from the system, and that until it was removed there could be no permanent return to health. To these remedies he gave the name of antipsorics. According to Hahnemann's theory there are three causes producing diseases of long standing, or chronic, and which can not be relieved by the *vis medicatrix naturæ*, or by the means used in curing acute diseases. To these causes he gave the names: Psora, Syphilis and Sycosis. These may exist alone or become combined in the system, and are characterized by certain groups of symptoms. A full elucidation of this doctrine may be found in Volume I. of the "Chronic Diseases."

It has been said that Hahnemann was the inventor of the "itch theory," so-called. This is not true, nor did he ever lay claim to be its discoverer. He says:* "Careful observations, comparisons and experiments during these latter years have taught me that these exceedingly varied sufferings of body and mind in the different patients are (provided they do not belong to the venereal diseases, syphilis or sycosis) but partial manifestations of this ancient chronic lepra and itch miasm; that is, they are but offspring of one and the same primitive evil, and though manifesting almost numberless symptoms, must be viewed as but parts of one and the same disease and treated accordingly.

"Psora is the oldest, most universal and most pernicious, yet, withal, the most misunderstood chronic miasmatic disease, which for thousands of years has disfigured and tortured mankind.

"In the thousands of years since it first visited mankind (the most ancient history of the oldest nations does not reach its origin) it has increased its manifestations to such a degree that its secondary symptoms can scarcely be numbered.

"The most ancient historical writings which we possess describe psora very fully. Several varieties thereof were described by Moses 3,400 years ago. At that time, however, and ever since, among the Israelites, psora appears to have affected more especially the external parts of the body.

"The same holds true among the early barbaric Greeks; later, in like manner, among the Arabians, and finally in the uncivilized Europe of the middle ages. It is not my object to detail the different names by which the various nations have designated the more or less severe forms of disease through which leprosy marred the external parts of the body (external symptoms of psora). Such names have no bearing upon the subject, as the essence of this miasmatic itch disease remains always the same.

---

*"Die chronischen Krankheiten, ihre eigenthumliche Natur und homoopathische Heilung." 1835. Vol. i., pp. 10–12. Dr. Korndoerfer's translation.

"In Europe during several centuries of the middle ages psora manifested itself in the form of a malignant erysipelas (St. Anthony's Fire). In the 13th century it again assumed the form of leprosy, brought by the returning Crusaders from the East. Leprosy was thus more than ever before spread through Europe (in the year 1226 there were in France about 2,000 leper-houses); nevertheless some alleviation of its horrible cutaneous symptoms was found through the means of cleanliness which the Crusaders also brought from the East; aids to cleanliness theretofore unknown in Europe, (cotton, linen) shirts, as well as the frequent use of warm baths. These means in conjunction with increasing education, better selected diet and improved mode of living succeeded in a couple of centuries in so diminishing the external hideousness of psora that towards the close of the 15th century it manifested itself only in the ordinary itch eruption."

Hahnemann then quotes from about a hundred Allopathic authorities who believed in the truth of this psoric or itch theory, and gives from their writings illustrations of cases of various chronic diseases resulting from suppressed eruptions.

Hahnemann undoubtedly uses the word itch to designate very many forms of skin disease. He says: "I call it psora with the view of giving it a general designation. I am persuaded that not only are the *majority of the innumerable skin diseases* which have been described and distinguished by Willan, but also almost all the pseudo-organizations, with few exceptions, merely the products of the multiform psora."

Hoffmann taught this theory before Hahnemann was born. Schoenlein, of Berlin, in a lecture said: *"It was remarkably impudent of Hahnemann to pretend that he was the first to point out the consequences of the itch. I have no doubt whatever about the existence of the consequences of the itch."

Dr. C. G. Raue, in a lecture delivered before the students of Hahnemann Medical College, of Philadelphia, said in relation to this subject: †"It seems, then, that the detection of the itch-insect by Bonomo in 1683 has, after all, nothing to do with Hahnemann's psora theory. This has its foundation deeper laid than the itch-insect will ever dig; and, as Hahnemann probably

---

*Henderson's "Homœopathy Fairly Represented," p. 169. Philadelphia, 1854. *Brit. Jour. Hom.*, Vol. ii, p. 316.

†*Med. Institute*, Philadelphia, December, 1886, p. 121.

knew of this little animal, it does not seem to have disturbed him much in his eleven years' work to find those grand remedies which we are still necessitated to employ against those deep seated, chronic ailments, the nature of which he designated by the term ' Psora,' 'that most ancient, most common, most ruinous and yet most misapprehended disease, of a chronic miasmatic nature, which has deformed and tortured mankind since thousands of years, and which, in the last centuries, has become the mother of the thousands of diverse chronic (or acute) complaints under which the civilized world now is suffering.'

" Does this sound as though it meant only the acarus itch? In order to be sure of it read the testimony of the hundreds of physicians, which Hahnemann quotes ('Chronic Diseases,' pp. 22-40) in order to show the pernicious effects which these physicians had observed in consequence of the suppression of all kinds of cutaneous eruptions. This oldest and commonest source of diseases had to have a name, and Psora was as good a name as Eczema, Impetigo, Prurigo, or any other. It is just as true to-day that a suppression of cutaneous eruptions of various kinds will be followed by disastrous consequences upon the general system, as it was when Hahnemann and others observed it ; and it is either ignorance or self-conceit that picks at a name without weighing its full meaning, or the vanity of scientific dudes who like to be seen among the fashionables."

CHAPTER XXXIV.

LETTERS TO STAPF ON THE "CHRONIC DISEASES."—VACCINATION-THEORY.

The following letter to Stapf, written just previous to the publication of the book on "Chronic Diseases," is of interest: *

"*Coethen, Sept. 6, 1827.*

" *Dear Doctor :*

" Your impatient vehemence is no doubt owing to your praiseworthy thirst for knowledge, but as regards its object it must be considered a slight mistake on your part. I have only written one clean transcript of the symptoms of the antipsorics, and it is

---

* *Hom. World*, Vol. xxiv, p. 490. "Annals Brit. Hom. Society," Vol. ii, p. 74.

in daily use; it is, therefore, impossible for me to communicate them to you.

"You cannot possibly be serious in expecting me to prescribe a treatment for the pathological names you mention. But if you will sometimes communicate to me the symptoms of disease, then if my limited time and my remaining vital powers will allow I shall be happy to advise you.

"I have cause to be thankful that you do not need to regard chronic diseases as paradoxes or inexplicable phenomena, the nature of which is hidden in impenetrable obscurity. You possess now the solution of the riddle why neither *Nux*, nor *Pulsatilla*, nor *Ignatia*, etc., will or can do good, while yet the Homœopathic principle is inexpugnable.

"You are now acquainted with the estimable remedies, you have them and can employ them, empirically at least, for you know even what doses to give them in. Just imagine what sacrifices it has cost me to carry out to the end this investigation for the benefit of yourself and the whole medical world. I cannot do more until my book appears, and it still demands an amount of work which is almost too much for my vital powers. Be reasonable, therefore, and do what you can with your antipsorics. Even after I had them I did not at first know what they would do. You may, whilst using them, make excellent observations on their peculiar effects and gain much knowledge respecting them, as also by the many splendid cures you may perform with them, as you have only six or eight medicines to choose from, and not from the whole Materia Medica.

"You and Gross are the only ones to whom I have revealed this matter. Just think what a start you have in advance of all the other physicians in the world. At least a year will elapse before the others get my book; they will then require more than half a year to recover from the fright and astonishment at the monstrous, unheard of thing, perhaps another half year before they believe it, at all events before they provide themselves with the medicines, and they will not be able to get them properly unless they prepare them themselves.

"Then it is doubtful whether they will accept the smallness of the doses, and wait the long time they ought to allow each dose to act. Hence, three years from this time must elapse before they are able to do anything useful with them.

"So please have patience with me and excuse me for not being able to put my book into your hands just yet, and try and do as much good as you can with what you know and have."

In the same letter, referring to the action of these remedies, he says: "Deafness and catarrh are such local affections that no medicines can be given with success for them until the general health has been perfectly restored by antipsorics."

Hahnemann, in a letter dated January 14, 1828, also to Stapf, mentions the fact that he is not of a psoric temperament. He says:

"*Dear Doctor :*

"I lately heard through Von Hayn that you had been laid up with sickness, and now I am glad to see again a letter in your handwriting. You also are, alas! psoric, and my book, the first small part of which will soon be published by Arnold, will, as soon as the second part (the antipsoric remedies) is printed and in your hands (I sent the MSS. to the printer in Berlin on the 12th of January), teach you how you can gradually expel this insidious dyscrasia from your body.

"I myself was never psoric, and hence, by comparing myself with psoric persons, could best demonstrate the difference. I ought to have done this in my book, but, alas! I either forgot to do so, or probably did not do it because I did not like to talk about myself."*

Hahnemann also mentions this fact about himself in the second edition of the "Chronic Diseases." It may be found as a note on page 57 of the German edition and on page 63 of the American translation.†

He says: "It was easier for me than for many hundred others to discover and discern the signs of psora, both those still slumbering and latent in the interior and those roused up out of the interior into serious chronic diseases, by careful comparison of the state of health of all affected with it with myself, because I, as is rarely the case, was never psoric, and hence, from my birth till now, when I am in my eightieth year, I have always remained completely exempt from all the ailments (great and small) described here and further on, though I am otherwise

---

Hom. World, Vol. xxiv., p. 493. "Annals British Hom. Society," Vol. ii., p. 149.

†"Hahnemann's Chronic Diseases." New York. Radde. 1845. P. 63.

very susceptible to acute epidemic diseases, and although I have undergone much mental labor and thousands of emotional mortifications."

Another letter to Stapf, dated February 23, 1828, also relates to the new psoric doctrine: *

" *Dear Colleague :*

"I was very sorry for you when I first heard from Dr. Rummel the sad account of the illness of your wife, and I now rejoice with you that it has yielded so happily and quickly to the true healing art.

"This was an example of the by no means rare explosions and sudden outbursts of the internal psora. These are always quite sudden illnesses, the cause of which (*causa occasionalis*): a chill, a fright, a vexation, &c., is often very insignificant. They only come singly. Therefore I consider all maladies that occur epidemically and sporadically as belonging to this class.

"Those single outbursts of the internal latent psora, which I have not sufficiently described in my book (which may easily happen in the first edition of a book), after their speedy defervescence or rapid cure by proper means, allow the previously latent psora to return to its latent state—as we often see in the case of poor people that a sudden inflammatory swelling in some part, a sore throat, an ophthalmia, an erysipelas, or other acute febrile disease (pleurisy, etc.), comes on in a threatening manner, but if it does not kill the patient, often subsides by the help of nature (frequently by the formation of an abscess), and then the stream that had overflowed its banks returns to its bed; *i. e.*, the psora again becomes latent, but with an increased disposition to repeat these or similar explosions.

"But among the well-to-do classes, who immediately resort to the Allopathic physician, such sudden illness generally goes on to the full development of the psora, and to a palpable progressive chronic disease.

"It ought not to cause astonishment that for such very acute outbursts of latent psora the antipsoric remedies are not suitable, therefore, that *spirit. vini sulphuratus* (or even *Graphites*, which is such an excellent Homœopathic remedy for erysipelas of the face) was not suitable in the face-erysipelas fever of your wife.

Hom. World, Vol. xxiv., p. 495. "Annals Brit. Hom. Society," Vol. ii., p. 151.

These remedies are appropriate for the slow, radical cure of the *causa prima* of the face-erysipelas. Now the unantipsoric remedies (like *Rhus tox.* in your case), which correspond to the present transient morbid picture, are the appropriate medicines; they can quickly quell the existing acute explosion, so that the condition calms down again into latent psora, to which these remedies have little or no affinity.

"To remove the tendency to such outbursts (dangerous sore throat, pneumonia, ophthalmia, typhus fever, erysipelas, etc.); that is, to effect a radical cure of the psora, requires the slow specific action of the antipsoric remedies—in the case of your wife, among other medicines, also *Graphites,* as you must give *Sulphur* soon again.

" If my discovery is well founded, as it certainly is, without any exception, I shall be curious to see what the adherents of the Allopathic school, who, up till now, have boasted of being sole proprietors of rationality in the medical art, and who asserted that they alone practiced and practice causal treatment (see Hufeland) will say—they must adduce *instar omnium,* their emetics in overloaded stomachs, which we do not envy them. With the exception of the employment of *Mercury* in syphilis, what causal treatment in the endless array of chronic diseases can they lay claim to, seeing that they do not know the cause?

"Von Gersdorff already suspected the heredity of psora, and I think I confuted him. Please to ask him for me to send you copies of the passages on the subject in my letters to him. He will be happy to do so. I do not quite remember what I wrote.

"I had hoped to have seen you and Gross this spring, but I regret the weather will prevent Gross coming. I must hope for another opportunity.

"Yours,

"SAM. HAHNEMANN."

In connection with the psora theory is the following opinion expressed by Hahnemann regarding vaccination. In writing to Dr. Schreeter, of Lemberg, on December 19, 1831, he says : *
"In order to provide the dear little Patty with the protective cow pox, the safest plan would certainly be to obtain the lymph direct from the cow; but if this cannot be done (children are also

---

*Stapf's "Archiv.," Vol. xxiii., pt. 3, p. 103. *Brit. Jour. Hom.,* Vol. vi., p. 415.

made more ill by it, than from the matter obtained from human beings), I would advise you to inoculate another child with the protective pox, and as soon as slight redness of the punctures shows it has taken, I would immediately for two successive days give *Sulphur* 1–30, and inoculate your child from the pock that it produced. As far as I have been able to ascertain, a child cannot communicate psora whilst under the action of *Sulphur*."

Dr. Schreeter in a note to this letter says that he has found this advice to be true and has acted upon it in vaccination with good results.

CHAPTER XXXV.

EXISTENCE OF THE ITCH-INSECT KNOWN TO HAHNEMANN.
LETTER ON BIRTHDAY TO STAPF.

Hahnemann's book on the cause and proper treatment of chronic diseases has been a source of much discussion and controversy among the members of the Homœopathic school, and of much ridicule from the members of the self-called rational, or Allopathic school. The book is readily to be procured. To an unbiased mind it is evident that the term itch was used to designate all sorts of diseases of the skin.

Again, it has been said that Hahnemann did not know that there was an *acarus scabei*, or itch-insect. The truth is, he did know all about it years before he propounded his theory of chronic disease.

Ameke says: *"Did Hahnemann know the existence of the itch-insect, and at what period did he become acquainted with it? In his translation of "Monro's Materia Medica," 1791, Hahnemann says in a foot-note (11, 49): 'If, in a recent case of itch, we make the patient wash himself several times daily with a saturated solution of sulphuretted hydrogen, and get his linen dipped in the same solution, the affection disappears in a few days and does not return except with reinfection. But would it not return if it was caused by acridity of the humors? I have often observed this, and agree with those who attribute the disease *to a living cause*. All insects (among which the itch-mite was at that time included) and worms are killed by sulphuretted hydrogen.'

*Ameke. "History of Homœopathy," p. 72.

"Further on in this work in another note (11, 441) he maintains that itch is a 'living eruption.'"

In a German daily newspaper, called *The Advertiser* (*Der Anzeiger, ein Tageblatt zum Behuf der Justiz, der Polizei und aller burgerlichen Gewerbe*), of July 30 and 31, 1792, appeared the following article, signed only by the initial "B:"*

"The itch itself does not consist of emanations or of congenital or acquired acridites, of a salt or acid character of the blood, but it is derived from small living insects or mites, which take up their abode in our bodies beneath the epidermis, grow there and increase largely, and by their irritation or their creeping about cause an itching; and owing to the afflux of humors thereby produced give rise to a multitude of vesicles, which, on being rubbed, or when the thin, watery fluid they contain has evaporated become covered with scabs. This is not an opinion adopted in order to get rid of a difficulty, but it is based on experience.

"August Hauptman, Bonomo, Schwiebe, and other trustworthy men, have frequently investigated the matter at various seasons of the year, in individuals of different ages and sexes, who have been laboring under itch, and have found these little animals in the skin itself, in the folds of the skin, but especially in the border surrounding the vesicles.

"They have extracted them, examined them under the microscope, made drawings of them, and observed how they lay their eggs, increase rapidly and enormously, and have found that they can live several days out of the human body."

The mode of infection is also described, and the use of *Sulphur* a teaspoonful morning and evening, as a cure.

Immediately after this is the following: "ADDENDUM," by Hahnemann: "The cause of itch given above is the only true one, the only one that is founded upon experience. These exceedingly small animals are a kind of mite. Wichmann has given a drawing of them; Dover, Legazi and others have observed them. Linnæus, however, thinks that the dry itch has a different variety of mite from that attending the moist itch.

"The itch attacks most readily and most virulently persons in whom the cutaneous transpiration is scanty or weakened, who lead a sedentary life; also delicate individuals, who have been

*Hirschel's *Hom. Klinik*, Sept. 1, 1863. *Brit. Jl. Hom.*, Vol. xxi, p. 670.

weakened by other diseases, such as fevers, etc., or by residence in impure air.

"The mode of treatment described above is also right and successful, except that the continued use of *Flowers of Sulphur* has a tendency to cause tenesmus and hemorrhoids. Only external anti-scabious remedies are required, and in very weakly subjects, internal, strengthening medicines, such as *China*, wine, steel filings.

"*Sulphur ointment* has the common but unfounded reputation of driving the itch back into the system. This prejudice will, however, be removed if instead of ointment we employ only a lotion, which eradicates the itch much more effectually and kills the small insects in the skin in a few days. Take half an ounce of (Hahnemann's) chalk-like *Liver of Sulphur*, in powder (every chemist knows how to prepare it with equal parts of oyster shells and *Sulphur* heated to redness), and the same quantity of *Cream of Tartar*, put both into a glass bottle, pour two pounds of cold water on them, and shake a few times. With the clear water that appears when the mixture settles the patient is to wash himself three times a day on all the spots affected with the itch.

"A recent case of itch under this treatment disappears without the least bad consequences in the course of six or seven days, a more severe case in fourteen days, and the most obstinate case in three weeks.

"This remedy has this advantage, that having a very penetrating odor the itch mites in the skin and clothes are killed by the mere exhalation from the parts washed, and then all danger of reinfection is avoided.

"In orphan asylums there is no remedy to be compared with it, because it protects beds, rooms and furniture, by its strong smell, from becoming a harbor for the itch-mites, and thus eradicates in a short time, in such houses, this pest, otherwise so difficult to be got rid of. This the *Sulphur ointment* can hardly effect. Cleanliness, fresh air and wholesome diet must be imperatively enjoined on the patient.

"DR. SAMUEL HAHNEMANN."

Volume I of the "Chronic Diseases" is devoted to the following essays: On the Nature of Chronic Diseases; on Sycosis; Syphilis; Psora. Directions are also given for the preparation of

Homœopathic medicines.   The remaining three volumes are devoted to the provings of the antipsoric remedies.

As has been stated, the first edition of the "Chronic Diseases" was published in 1828–30 in four volumes.

A second edition was issued from 1835–39, in five volumes, by Schaub, at Dusseldorf.   Only two German editions were ever published.   In 1832 the book was translated into French by Jourdan and published in Paris.   There were also two other French editions published.   Geddes M. Scott, of Glasgow, in 1842, published an English translation.   In 1849 it was published in Madrid in Spanish.   In 1846 an English translation was made by Dr. C J. Hempel, from the second edition, and published in five volumes by Radde, in New York.   A new translation is now (1894) being made by Rev. L. H. Tafel, under the auspices of Messrs. Boericke & Tafel.

On February 23, 1828, Hahnemann, in a letter to Stapf, complains of the delay of Arnold, his old publisher, in printing the book on chronic diseases, as follows:*

"It is a pity that the printing of this second part does not go on more quickly, in spite of my earnest request.   Besides the commencement (directions for preparing the antipsoric medicine) which Gross got from me, and will send to you, I have only as yet received three proof sheets from the printer."

Dr. Dudgeon says of this letter: "This does not seem to have been the only time Hahnemann had to complain of the dilatoriness of his publisher, for in a note to the first page of the preface to the second edition of the third part of his "Chronic Diseases," published in 1837, he complains that Arnold took two whole years to set up thirty-six sheets of the two first parts of the same edition.   He evidently lost patience with Arnold, or perhaps Arnold then failed, as we learn he did in one of the subsequent letters, for the subsequent parts of the 'Chronic Diseases' were published by Schaub, of Dusseldorf."

On his birthday Hahnemann writes to his old pupil Stapf the following kindly letter: †

" *Coethen, April 10, 1828.*

" *Dear Colleague :*

"I thank you for your well-meant, good wishes on the occa-

Hom. World, Vol. xxiv, p. 496.

†*Hom. World*, Vol. xxiv, p. 500.   "Annals Brit. Hom. Society," Vol. ii, p. 249.

sion of my seventy fourth birthday, and at the same time I this
day have a lively pleasure in the action and zealous help which
your unwearying enthusiasm has up till now contributed to the
development and establishment of the beneficent art, which I
can truly say was revealed to me by God, and I can acknowledge
it with emotion and thankfulness.

"I can with confidence affirm that you also share this beautiful self-consciousness, and that the sublime art itself will cheer
and render happy the days of the lives of yourself and your dear
family.

"Is there any greater happiness than in doing good?

"When, too, we leave this earth the great, the only, the infinite Being, who promotes the happiness of all creatures, will
direct us how to come nearer to His perfection and blessedness by
further acts of beneficence, and how to become more like Him
through all eternity.

"I must not write more to-day, but I hope to see you very
soon here, in the company of your two dear ones, and with the
most cordial greeting from my family, I am, yours very truly,

"SAMUEL HAHNEMANN."

CHAPTER XXXVI.

FIRST METHOD OF PREPARING HOMŒOPATHIC MEDICINE—FIRST
POCKET CASES—KORSAKOFF ON THE USE OF GLASS
VIALS—HAHNEMANN'S OPINION REGARDING
THE PRACTICE OF MEDICINE—LETTER
TO DR. EHRHARDT.

Up to the year 1821, Hahnemann had made his triturations
in porcelain mortars with sugar of milk, but the capsules for the
patient he filled with pulverized oyster shell, adding to it the
necessary amount of the trituration. At that time pure white
milk sugar was an expensive and rare article, for its chief source
of supply, Switzerland, made and exported only small amounts.
It became the first care of our people at Leipsic to secure it in
larger amounts and of better quality, for, like Hahnemann, they
were obliged to prepare all their medicines. The porcelain mortars used were soon replaced by better ones of marble. About

this time Hofrath Henecke, of Gotha, the editor of the *Reichan-zeiger*, and a good friend of Hahnemann, suggested Homœopathic family medicine cases.

At first there was also a scarcity of proper glassware for the very tiny vials.   Goose quills had been commonly used in private practice to contain the medicines.   Bohemia soon supplied its glass.   From the globules all starch was removed to prevent discoloration and crumbling, and they were made of different sizes.   As early as 1828, fine pocket cases were for sale, chiefly made by Lappe, an apothecary of Neudietendorf, of whom Hahnemann was in the habit of ordering several remedies. Christian Ernest Otto, of Roetha, near Leipsic, was the first to establish a regular Homœopathic pharmacy. *

In the *Archives of Homœopathic Medicine* for 1829, M. Korsakoff, a Russian gentleman, addressed a letter to Hahnemann in which he recommends the use of little tubes or vials, for holding the Homœopathic globules.   He suggests that the pills should be placed in the vial and two or three drops of the medicinal dilution be poured over them and that they then be shaken thoroughly.

Hahnemann in an answer published in the same journal, approves of this method, but advises that the pills be not shaken, but stirred with a glass pin until dried, adding that the evaporation will not effect the medicinal powers.   This answer can also be found in the "Lesser Writings."

Dudgeon says: "Korsakoff was the real original inventor of the high potencies." †

Hahnemann said that his experiments were of great value as illustrating the extreme divisibility to which the Homœopathic medicines could be brought, but advised some limit.   In a letter to Dr. Schreeter, dated September 13, 1829, he says : ‡   "There must be some limit to the thing, it cannot go on to infinity. By laying it down as a rule that all Homœopathic medicines be diluted and potentized up to thirty, we have a uniform mode of procedure in the treatment of all Homœopathists, and when

---

*Translated by Dr. H. R. Arndt from Kleinert's " Geschichte der Homöopathie," p. 155. *Med. Counselor*, Vol. xi., p. 312.

† Dudgeon's "Lectures on Homœopathy, " p. 351.   *Archiv fur die hom. Heilkunst*, Vol. viii, pt. 2, p. 161. "Lesser Writings," New York, p. 735.

‡ *British Journal of Homœopathy*, Vol. v., p. 398. Dudgeon's translation of "Organon," 1893, p. 303.

they describe a cure we can repeat it as they do, and we operate
with the same tools. ''

Dudgeon says that the introduction of sugar globules into
Homœopathic practice by Hahnemann dates from about the
year 1813, and refers to a note made by Hahnemann to paragraph 288 of the fifth edition of the "Organon," viz: * "A globule impregnated with the thirtieth potentized dilution and then
dried, retains for this purpose all its power undiminished for at
least eighteen or twenty years (my experience extends that
length of time,) even though the vial be opened a thousand
times during that period, if it be but protected from the heat
and sun's light. ''

Some notion of Hahnemann's ideas regarding the practice of
medicine at this period of his life may be obtained from the following letter to Dr. Schreeter: †

"*Coethen, June 19, 1826.*

"*Dear Colleague*:

"I thank you, your dear sister and your friends for your remembrance of my birthday. I see from that the interest you
take in me and in our good cause. I thank you also for your
news about yourself and your pleasing family affairs. I learned
from that your juvenile age, and can now easily understand how
it is that you have gone on so rapidly with the antipsoric treatment.

"Your want of success in the cases you have recorded is certainly owing to the rapid change of the remedies, the often unfitting dynamization and dilution and the too large doses.
Once you have spoilt matters with these three faults for about
four weeks, it is very difficult to set them right again. My advice is that you abide rigorously by the precepts contained in
my book on "Chronic Diseases;" and, if possible, go still further than I have done, in allowing a still longer period for the
antipsoric remedies to exhaust their action, in administering
still smaller doses than I have advised, and in dynamising all
antipsoric medicines up to 30. (You appear not to possess
them all yet.)

* Dudgeon's "Organon," p. 197.
† *British Journal of Homœopathy*, Vol. v, p. 397. Stapf's *Archiv*, Vol.
xxiii., pt. 2, p. 179.

"You should also, seeing that you can have no great need of money, living with your parents, make your visits to your patients rarer; keep up your dignity, and more frequently withdraw your attendance on patients who do not show sufficient confidence in you, if they do not show more respect for you and your art.

"You should never allow yourself to be dismissed, but whenever a patient does not do exactly as you desire, or ceases to talk in becoming terms, you should at once take leave of him; 'You don't act as I wish, but do so and so against my orders; employ whom you will, I will have nothing more to do with you;' and this do to one after another; to all who even speak of Homœopathy in a doubting tone, or do anything else unbecoming, be off at once. This would at first deprive you of a few patients who are of no importance, but in course of time, if you persist in your authoritative manner, you will be respected and sought after, and none will dare to use any liberties with you. It is better to be without patients, and devote yourself to study, keeping up your dignity, than to stand in such a relation with patients.

"The latter should thank God if you deign to accept them and treat them on your excellent system, and they must be content to be reproached by you for the senseless manner in which they had allowed themselves to be injured by the Allopaths, so that you could scarcely hope to effect a cure of such ruined constitutions. If any of your patients is not entirely submissive dismiss him summarily, even though by such conduct you should only retain two, or one single patient, or should be left without any. They would return by degrees, with more respect, submissiveness and humility, and more disposed to pay well.

"Do you not make the patient affected with chronic diseases, who can walk, come to your house? Who could submit to the degradation of visiting a patient who had gone out in the meantime and allowed you to come in vain? The chronic patients you must make visit you, even the highest among them; and if they won't come, let them stay away. You must take a higher standing. Rather suffer penury, which you are not likely to do, than abate one jot of your own dignity, or that of the art you practice." * * * * * *

In another letter written later in the same year, to one Dr.

Ehrhardt, of Merseberg, Hahnemann says: *"You are much too timid, much too obsequious to your patients, like the Allopaths, who are glad if they can only keep their patients as their clients. It should not be so. If you are perfectly conversant with your art you must command absolutely—not allow your patient to make conditions.

"He must obey you, not you him. To this end, in order that you may be perfectly free, you must limit your expenses at first, in order that you may not experience want, even though but few patients should seek your advice. You will be able to cure those few patients all the better and more certainly if you devote the necessary care to their cases, and you will have time for study. For we Homœopathists can not go too deep into our art.

"But if we have made ourselves masters of it, then may, then must we, indeed, comport ourselves with dignity. In order to spare our precious time and to keep up our dignity we must not pay visits to any patient with a chronic disease, were he even a prince, if he is able to come to us. We must only visit acute cases and such as are confined to bed. Those who are able to go about, but will not come to your house for advice, may stay away, it must not be otherwise. Anything like running after patients, as the Allopaths do, is degrading. You go to visit your patient, the servant maid tells you he is not at home, he is at the theatre, has gone out for a drive, etc. Pah! You must go on to a second or a third, like an Allopath or a beggar. Fie on it!

"Further, every time the patient comes to see you, you must make him pay you your fee for your trouble at once; it may be one or two shillings only from poor people, from rich ones as many crowns. If you make that arrangement and everyone knows of it, then your patient will always have his money with him; and if he does not come any more he may stay away. If, however, he have not got the money with him you may put off the consultation for an hour or two, so as to give him time to go and get it and bring you the remuneration for your trouble.

"Money gives courage, even though it be not a large sum; if I have got what is due in my pocket, then I feel that I am not working for nothing, that I am not dependent on every one's favor, and fearful lest I may not be paid. How does Mr. ———, the privy councillor pay you? I imagine the greater part of your fees is on credit, and hereafter when you remind him of payment, you will get no very kind looks, some reproaches, and probably no payment.

"Under such circumstances it is impossible to be in good spirits. After the treatment is over he will have forgotten all the trouble you have had with him. The world is ungrateful! Rich patients also should pay at each consultation immediately, or once a month; otherwise they might go away without paying. If you do not manage matters in this way, then you will be worse off than the most abject wretch. I said that you were timid. Running about paying visits takes away one's courage and makes one timid.

"From timidity, for fear you should lose him, you have given Mr. ——— far too much medicine, and that far too frequently, thereby you do not improve him, you make him worse, *you will never succeed in retaining this patient.* He cannot be restored quickly, he must have patience for years to come, and that he will not have, worried, tormented and rendered impatient, as he has been by Allopaths and apothecaries.

"It is to be supposed that Homœopathy can perform miracles, but it cannot do that, least of all where the patient is not quite a convert to our system, nor so conversant with it as to presume that beyond our art there is no cure for him.' Entirely unacquainted as this gentleman is with our art, he will be unable to withstand the persuasions of his Allopathic friends to give up, and to allow himself to be done to death in some bathing place by doctors of the old school.

"I tell you again you will not be able to prevent this. Even had he implicit confidence, which he has not, you would not be able to restore him in less than a year. So I advise you to get rid of him and not to take any more such difficult cases among persons of rank until you can assert your dignity and ensure obedience to your absolute commands, which must be unquestioningly obeyed. So the gentleman wants to make it a condition that he shall drink wine and coffee! For God's sake let him take himself off, he will do you no credit!

"All my patients of rank affected with chronic diseases must have read the 'Organon' and Bœnninghausen's 'Homœopathy,' otherwise I will not undertake their treatment.

"Yours sincerely,

"SAMUEL HAHNEMANN.

"*Coethen, August 24, 1829.*"

CHAPTER XXXVII.

FIFTIETH FEST-JUBILEE—LETTERS TO RUMMEL—HAHNEMANN'S
PORTRAITS.

The fiftieth anniversary of Hahnemann's graduation in medicine at the University of Erlangen was now approaching. For half a century he had been devoting his life and talents to the good of suffering humanity, and his followers in all parts of the world determined to celebrate in a proper manner this day of honor to the beneficent old man. For several months before his friends had been preparing this surprise. Contributions had been solicited, letters written to Homœopaths in other countries, and every effort made to fittingly commemorate the event.

Previous to this time there had been no very satisfactory pictures of Hahnemann. The editions of " The Organon " of 1819, 1824 and 1829 each contained a half length engraving, drawn by Junge and engraved by Stölzel, in which he is represented sitting with a pen in hand.

Callisen in his Lexicon* mentions these pictures, and a quarto lithograph by Fr. Jos. V. A. Broussais, in Froriep's *Notiz. aus der Natur und Heilkunst*, vol. iv., 1825, No. 12. (No. 78.) It is probable that there were no other pictures of the reformer.

While planning the Fest-Jubilee his friends wished a reliable portrait and medal of himself to present to him upon that occasion, and the difficulty was to get him to sit without letting him suspect the object. Dr. Rummel was intrusted with this task, and he succeeded in representing to him that the portraits hitherto published of him were incorrect and that some of his admirers wished greatly to have a portrait of him that would be a good likeness.

If the picture from which the former engraving had been taken was a good likeness (they knew it was not), a new engraving might be taken from it; but if it was not, he was told that funds for a new portrait had already been subscribed, and he was requested to give sittings to their artist. A similar story was invented in reference to the medal.

---

* " Medicinisches Schriftsteller-Lexicon." Copenhagen, 1831.

The celebrated portrait painter Schoppe was engaged for the painting, and a young medallist named Dietrich was requested to execute the medal.

The letters which follow are from Hahnemann to Rummel upon this subject, and are interesting exponents of Hahnemann's mind about the matter. Rummel published them in 1852 in the *Zeitung*, and they were translated into the *British Journal of Homœopathy.* *

"*Dear Colleague:*

" Your united desire to possess a counterfeit resemblance of my face which shall be a better likeness than the copper-plate and lithographic engravings that have hitherto appeared does honor to your partiality towards me, and cannot be otherwise than flattering to me, but it cannot be fulfilled by your proposition; what you miss in the copy is absent also in the painting, sufficient resemblance. I am not indeed as vain as Alexander, the conqueror of the world, *qui nec pingi, nisi ab Apelle, nec fingi volebat nisi a Praxitele*, but I have no desire to see another copy made of the unlike oil painting. For in that case the public would be made to believe that my face must be just as the second copy shall represent it to be.

"Should I live, and should some good portrait painter come in my way, I would get my likeness taken and that in a larger size than the last, as you desire; and if the engraver or lithographer would, before publishing his work, take a look at me himself, I believe a good likeness might be the result. But should this not happen, then let us leave things as they are, let me only be handed down to posterity in the spiritual features of the inner man which are not indistinctly portrayed in what I have written. My vanity does not go beyond this. It will be very agreeable to me to receive your visit, only I beg of you to let me know when you will come, some little time beforehand.

"The new number of the *Archiv*, is just what I could wish. Your reply to Wedekind and Hentschel is in what I consider an appropriate style, not so mild, and, if I may be allowed the expression, so humble and deferential as are some of the older criticisms in the *Archiv*, but you say in a manly way to *t*heir

---

Allg. Hom. Zeit., Vol. xliv., p. 3. (July 26, 1852.) *Brit. Jour. Hom.* Vol. xi., p. 62.

face and without sparing them what they ought to hear from the men who are assured of the goodness of their cause.

"Gross's commencement of the aggressive likewise gives me much pleasure; I have enjoyed it.

"No more to-day, as the post hour is come.

"Yours sincerely,

"SAM. HAHNEMANN."

"*Coethen, 19th Feb'y, 1829.*"

"COETHEN, 2d April, 1829.

"*Dear Colleague :*

"Young Dietrich has had two afternoon sittings for the purpose of modelling me, and the head seems to be getting very like. He is a clever and modest young man. You are such a good observer of yourself that you will pardon me for giving you some advice for the purpose of rendering your observations somewhat more certain and instructive.*

"I beg you will take these corrections in good part. He who can do much, of him will enough be expected.

"In that respect those are better off who can do little or nothing; with that you may console yourself. Have you still many epidemic diseases in your neighborhood? Does their treatment go on well? Intermittent fevers are also met with in this place, but I see but few of them. *Bellad.* and *Antim. crudem* 2 were sufficient.

"Yours sincerely,

"SAM. HAHNEMANN.

"You will oblige me if you will kindly send me when you have an opportunity about a drachm of *Regulus antimonii.* I must have the metal among my medicines, and am not content with the *Sulphuret* and *Tartrate of Antimony.*"

"COETHEN, 16th April, 1829.

"*Dear Colleague:*

"I thank you from my heart for your good and kindly meant wishes on the occurrence of the seventy-fifth anniversary of my birthday; may the Supreme Being preserve you also in good

---

*Here follows the citation of certain symptoms, with queries to make them more clear.

health for the benefit of our art and of your dear family. * * *
The first attacks of the intermittent fever that at present prevails
in your neighborhood, and throughout a great extent of the surrounding country, may certainly have a certain epidemic exciting
cause, may be of identical nature, and on their first appearance
the Homœopathic remedy adapted for the epidemic generally
will usually afford rapid and certain aid; but when after many
paroxysms they pass into the chronic state, it is certain that
psora soon begins in most cases to play the chief part, and
they then all pass into the psoric intermittent fever. That a
medical man engaged in active practice has not much time to
search about in the materia medica is very true. How useful
then will be a good alphabetical repertory once it is completed,
which it would be if my collaborators would but apply themselves diligently to the work.

"I know not if you have seen anything of my directions as to
how to proceed with this work. Some days since I sent such a
scheme to Dr. Schweikert, with instructions when he had made
himself familiar with it to communicate it on to Dr. Stapf, so
that the latter might then communicate it to you. Whether it
has got that length, whether Stapf has it yet I know not; but I
beg you, when you are acquainted with the idea, to devote a
portion of your leisure time to this generally useful work, and
to work up *Sulphur* upon octavo-sized sheets, written upon one
side only. I am very much obliged to you for the *Regulus
antimonii.*

"As regards the motto,* you are right in the main; I am
quite open to be informed of a better one. In place of the
former one I now send you one which you may perhaps think
more suitable, and I send another besides in order that you may
exercise a selection. Dietrich's bust every one says is a perfect
likeness. We cannot, however, reckon upon Schoppe. The
high synedrium of the Berlin Satraps, in whose sight the obscure
Coethen doctor has not yet found favour, would never forgive
him were he to degrade his art so low. I beg to be kindly
remembered to yourself and your wife.

"Yours most sincerely,

"SAMUEL HAHNEMANN."

---

* Refers to a motto which he had sent for his picture, but which Rumme
considered inappropriate.

"*Dear Colleague :*

"I thank you for having selected Schoppe. That eminent artist has been here for some days and has nearly finished my picture the size of life with hands, and has succeeded as completely as even you and my friends could wish. You will be delighted when you see it.

"And what shall I say of Dr. Schmit, of Vienna? His appearance here was highly prized by me; our art has much to expect from him. He was with me five evenings and afforded me rare pleasure, until Mr. Schoppe's business with me rendered it impossible for me to enjoy his society any longer.

"My bust by Mr. Dietrich, an excellent young artist, is finished and is *very* like, as Mr. Schoppe himself, who has seen it, confesses.

"Now I know that no wretched daub of me will be handed down to posterity, and I will also know that my friends will not allow my spiritual man to be transmitted to posterity in the caricature that calumnious enemies have sought to draw of me in their writings.

"I must beg you to inform Stapf of all this, and to thank him in my name for being so active as regards Count J.'s wishes. The letters he sent me to look at gave me much pleasure; I shall send them back to him by the earliest opportunity.

"Yours most sincerely,

"SAM. HAHNEMANN."

"*Coethen, 27th April, 1829.*"

Hahnemann during this spring and summer of 1829 was exceedingly busy. He was giving sittings to his two artists, working on the "Materia Medica," keeping up an extensive correspondence, all in addition to his large practice by mail and the time given to his numerous visitors.

In a letter to Stapf dated June 22, 1829, he says:* "I never read the *Allgemeiner Anzeiger*, because I have no time to do so. Even the political papers lie beside me several days before I can look at them. My time is much taken up, months fly past like days.

------

* *Hom. World*, Vol. xxv., p. 19; "Annals Brit. Hom. Society," Vol. ii., p. 156.

"As regards the publication of my 'Lesser Writings' I can confidently trust to your good judgment. I leave it entirely to you."

Hahnemann's fame had also extended to other countries, and many people were now becoming interested in the new law of cure.

Hahnemann mentions in a letter written in 1829 that Sir Walter Scott had requested a great patroness of literature, Baroness von Ende, to send him two copies of the fourth edition of the "Organon." Dudgeon, in a foot-note to this while wondering where Scott got his information about Homœopathy, says that nowhere does he find any mention of either the Baroness von Ende or Hahnemann in Lockhardt's "Life of Scott." *

In 1829 Hahnemann thus speaks of the tongue of calumny, and especially of schisms in the rank of his own school, in a letter to Stapf dated Coethen, February 20, 1829:† "Ingratitude recoils on those who practice it. We should have too much self-respect to get angry with it. We must judge of this attempt to injure us by our reason, we must not take it to heart if we are wise. Contemptible and detestable though this conduct seems to my reason, I do not vex myself about it because that would do me harm, and because, however much I might be annoyed, that would not alter the matter. It is a trial sent from above by the all-wise and all good Ruler, who guides everything for the best if we knew how to regard it as a good lesson, and to regulate our future course by it.

"He who, as regards vexations about injuries, etc., does not remain master of himself, does not treat them with indifference, but allows his mind to be embittered, poisoned by them, will not live long; he will so soon have to leave this world.

"And what an odious thing it is to be overcome by anger. Strive to keep far from you all sensitiveness in regard to such things so that nothing can deprive you of your composure, of your God-given mental tranquility, otherwise you will not be long on earth. Take warning! Learn this great beautiful lesson! It will do you good.

---

* *Hom. World*, Vol. xxv., 113. "Annals Brit. Hom. Society," Vol. ii., p. 242.

† *Hom. World*, Vol. xxiv., p. 502. "Annals Brit. Hom. Society," Vol. ii., p. 249.

" Do not allow your displeasure to find utterance, otherwise
the one may assert that there is schism amongst us, and that
would be injurious to the good cause. Feel your own value and
smile at this affair in the firm and well-founded conviction that
this alliance of these two gentlemen will not last long."*

CHAPTER XXXVIII.

CELEBRATION OF THE FIFTIETH FEST-JUBILEE AT COETHEN—
LETTER FROM HAHNEMANN CONCERNING IT—FOUNDA-
TION OF FIRST HOMŒOPATHIC SOCIETY.

On the 10th of August, 1829, the great Fest-Jubilee was celebrated.† It was fifty years since he graduated from the Medical
School of Erlangen.

All the town took on a gala dress. From everywhere the
friends and former pupils of the old Master gladly assembled to
do him honor. From all parts of Germany they came to crown
his head with garlands of laurel. They brought him many
presents. The Duke and Duchess gave him generous gifts. His
fellow-townsmen honored him. It was a red-letter day in the
history of Homœopathy.

Stapf, in his journal, gave the following account of this important meeting:‡

SAMUEL HAHNEMANN'S FIFTY-YEAR DOCTOR JUBILEE, HELD AT
COETHEN THE 10TH OF AUGUST, 1829.

Pleasing and noteworthy in more than one respect was this
day in the year-book of Homœopathic healing. The great
founder of the system has now finished half a century devoted
in a most successful, candid and zealous manner to the service
of humanity and science.

From the thorny fields of the past he now garners the fruits
of a fame-crowned present. That which he has so long strug-

---

*He refers to Hartlaub and Trinks.

†Schweikert's *Zeitung f. natur. d. Homoopathie*, October 12, 1831, Vol.
ii., p. 118. *Brit. Jour. Hom.*, Vol. xxx., p. 464. "Biographisches Denkmal,"
p. 62. *Allg. Hom. Zeitung*, Vol. xxvi., p. 233. Also in *Anhalt-Cothensche
Zeitung*, 1829, No. 63, 64. *Anhaltsche Magaz*, 1829, No. 34, 35. *National
Zeitung der Deutschen*, 1829, No. 67.

‡*Archiv f. d. hom. Heilkunst*, Vol. viii., part 2, p. 96.

gled to obtain now wreathes the sternly serene brow of the happy conqueror.

Around him who had been so long exiled, persecuted and insulted was now entwined the most gladsome recognition, heartfelt reverence, gratitude and love of a wide circle of friends, far and near, visible and invisible.

This festival had been planned on the year previously, and invitations had been sent to many of the friends of the cause in order to honor the man and the system. From far and near, from almost every country in Europe, even from far-off South America, came letters accompanied by handsome presents, with congratulations and good wishes.

So the festal day approached. On the evening before many friends had arrived from Berlin, Braunschweig, Dresden, Eisenach, Leipzig, Merseberg, and many other places far and near. From far-away Swiss-Basil came that old friend of Homœopathy, Dr. Siegrist.

Early on the morning of the 10th of August, at six o'clock, the matin-music of the old man's Jubilee was heard. At nine o'clock the enthusiastic assemblage of friends gathered in a room in his house.

On a table decorated like an altar, adorned with flowers and entwined with oak leaves, was placed the well-executed bust of Hahnemann. (This was the bust that was modelled by Dietrich, Jr., and was for sale for 4 thalers a copy.) On a side table stood a beautiful oil portrait of Hahnemann, with several lithographic copies taken from it.

Dr. Stapf now introduced the assembled friends to the grand old man and his family.

Dr. Regierungsrath Freiherr von Gersdorff, in a brief address of greeting and congratulation on this festal day, crowned his bust with fresh laurels.

Dr. Rummel then presented him, with hearty words, a splendidly written programme of the festival occasion.

Dr. Stapf gave him a jewel box lined with red velvet and containing a gold and a silver medal, on the face of which was a fine bust of Hahnemann in antique, with the words: "Samuel Hahnemann, born on the 10th of April, 1755, created a doctor at Erlangae on the 10th of August, 1779;" on the reverse the words: "Similia Similibus," and the inscription: "Medi-

cinæ Homœopathicæ auctori discipuli et amici d 10 Aug. 1829.''
Copies of this medal were sold, in silver, for a thaler and 12
groschens; in bronze, for one thaler. They were made by the
Leipzig coin engraver and artist Kruger.

Hofrath Dr. Muhlenbein, with a Latin address, presented a
document containing the signatures of all who had contributed
to this celebration.

Dr. Rummel presented him with an honorary diploma from
the University of Erlangen.

Dr. Stapf brought to the Master a copy of his recently published book, the collection of Hahnemann's Lesser Writings.*

Albrecht, of Dresden, delivered a very delightful poem on
the rise and merits of Homœopathy.

With deep emotion the venerable old man gave thanks to
God that he had been allowed to make so sublime a discovery,
and that he had been continued in bodily and mental vigor.
With deep feeling he thanked the friends present who had so
honored him on that day, thus made memorable in the annals of
Homœopathy.

From this meeting was formed the Central Homœopathic
Union of Germany.

The Duke and Duchess of Anhalt-Coethen sent a gold snuff
box having the letter ''F'' inlaid in brilliants, and a valuable
antique drinking cup, also writing the following letters of congratulation:†

'' HOFRATH HAHNEMANN.

Dear Doctor.—It affords me very great pleasure to be able to
congratulate you on this your 50th anniversary as a practising
physician. You have done so great and lasting a service
to mankind by the discovery and founding of the system of
Homœopathy now already extended to all parts of the world
that I gladly include myself among the number of those admirers who have assembled this day to bring you the tribute of
their gratitude.

'' As your Sovereign I feel myself doubly called upon to give
befitting recognition of your professional labors by means of
which you have done so much good to my country and myself.
Accept therefore my sincerest congratulations. I also send you

*'' Kleine Medicinische Schriften.''
†Stapf's *Archiv f. d. hom. Heilkunst,* Vol. viii.

the enclosed snuff-box with my initials set in diamonds, a present which you will please accept as a memorial of your festival
and as a slight token of my best wishes, and of the highest estimation in which I hold your services.

" Your faithful friend,

" DUKE FERDINAND.

" Coethen, August 10, 1829."

The good Duchess Julie sent her physician an antique drinking cup, and with it the following very kindly letter:

" HOFRATH HAHNEMANN.

" *Most Honored Sir*:   On this, your festival day, when so many
admirers of your highly meritorious services renew their acknowledgments of the same, I also shall not omit to tender you
my sincerest congratulations.   You have now reached the beautiful goal from which you can look back upon a long lapse of
years busily spent in useful labors, and can see now ripening the
most beautiful fruits of your many endeavors in the wide diffu-
sion of Homœopathy; this new system of medicine so advantageous to the welfare of mankind.

" May you yet experience for a very long time and with no
interruption this exalted joy, and be assured that I shall always
be a participant of it.   Accept also the enclosed souvenir as a
token of my gratitude, and with it the repeated assurance of my
high esteem and of my best wishes for your prosperity.

"Your faithful friend,

" DUCHESS JULIE.

"Coethen, Aug. 10, 1829."

A Society of Naturalists in the far east of Altenberg sent
him an honorary diploma of membership.

To him from that great scholar and ardent naturalist and propagator of Homœopathy, Dr. Constantin Hering, of Paramaribo,
in far off Surinam, there came a kindly letter.

After this festal friendly greeting the guests assembled in
the garden of Hahnemann's house and passed many hours in
social intercourse.

Later in the day a meeting was held in the assembly room
of the hotel, in which a banquet was spread.   It was at this
meeting decided to place the balance of the money remaining
after the expenses of the celebration were paid, in the hands of

Drs. Muhlenbein and Rummel, to be used as a nucleus for the establishment of a Homœopathic clinic at some suitable place to be hereafter decided upon. All pledged themselves to contribute to this.

Quite a considerable sum was realized for the forthcoming hospital, by the sale of Hahnemann's pictures. Hahnemann writing to Stapf on May 12, 1831, says: "The only object of my portrait is to provide funds for the Homœopathic Institute (*in spe*), so that the copies may be sold for its benefit, not for that of myself or my family."*

†A society was then formed under the name "Society for the Promotion and Development of Homœopathic Medicine." It was called later the Central Homœopathic Union, the name by which it is known to-day.

It was decided to hold the meeting of this Society on the 10th of August, annually, in future, as an act of honor to the Master. Dr. Moritz Muller was elected President, and Dr. Albrecht, Jr., of Dresden, Secretary.

At the conclusion of this meeting all sat down to a banquet, the company of physicians being augmented by many distinguished guests then staying at Coethen for Homœopathic treatment. Hahnemann could not take the head of the table, the chair was left unoccupied, no one deeming himself fit to occupy his place. Happiness and hilarity prevailed at the table. Toasts were drunk to the illustrious persons present.

Upon Hahnemann's invitation, all present resorted to his house in the evening and enjoyed the friendliness of his company.

During the year 1828 the Homœopathic physicians of Leipsic had held meetings. A small bi-mouthly paper, called *Praktische Mittheilungen der correspondenden Gesellschaft homoopathischer Aerzte*, was published. No. 1 commenced on January, 1828. It was devoted to reports of Homœopathic cures. Six numbers were issued during the year 1828.

It may not be amiss to mention that at a special invitation from Dr. Haubold, he, Drs. Franz, Hartmann and Hornburg held a meeting about the beginning of the year 1829, at Leipsic, for the purpose of discussing the doctrines of Homœopathy.‡ These

---

Hom. World, Vol. xxv., p. 258.
†*Brit. Jour. Hom.*, Vol. xxx., p. 464.
‡ Hartmann in *N. W. Jour. Hom.*, Vol. iv., p. 236.

meetings were continued monthly until the festival of the 10th of August.   The last one was held but a few days previously. In July Dr. Moritz Muller joined this little society, probably the first Homœopathic society in the world.

The thesis of Dr. Rummel at the Fest-Jubilee was delivered in Latin.   It was afterwards published in a quarto pamphlet at Merseberg; this pamphlet contains the names of those who contributed to this celebration.   Stapf also published in the *Archiv* (Vol. viii., pt. 2.) this thesis, Dr. Muhlenbein's address, the letters from the Duke and Duchess, Dr. Hering's letter from Surinam, and Dr. Albrecht's poem.

Rummel's thesis contains a biography of Hahnemann's life, a very complete bibliography of his writings, printed as foot-notes, the titles of many of the books of the time inimical to his system, the history of the discovery of the Law of Homœopathy and a number of deductions regarding its principles.

CHAPTER XXXIX.

LETTERS TO HERING, RUMMEL AND STAPF.

Albrecht says: "The foundation of the Homœopathic Society was confirmed by a diploma for every member now belonging to it or subsequently joining it.   This diploma is tastefully adorned with the well-known symbols of medical science—the rising sun in an oak wreath, Æsculapius and Hygeia being represented as standing near an altar, over which a good genius is drinking from a saucer; beneath it the motto, 'Similia Similibus,' and immediately under the three words, 'Non nisi digno' (for the deserving only), with the prayer Q. D. B. V.

"In the centre of the document are the following words: 'Societas medicorum homœopathicorum condita Anhaltin Cothenis die x mensis Augusti MDCCCXXIX virum—in sociorum—numerum cooptavit idque his litteris sigillo suo firmatis declaravit.'   Hahnemann was designated Perpetual President by his signature in lithography.   At the end of the diploma are the words: 'Concordia res parvæ crescunt.'"*

---

* "Biographical Monument to Hahnemann," Fischer's translation, p. 50. "Biographisches Denkmal," p. 64.

Hahnemann answered Hering's letter received on the fete day very soon, as follows:*

" COETHEN, 16th August, 1829.

"Dear Colleague:

"Your dear note was not the smallest gift which was made me upon the 10th of August. Oh, that I could only once before I leave this earth clasp you in my arms, to testify to you my joy at the unexampled zeal which you so efficiently bestow upon the restoration of the miserable, and the extension of the benefi- cent science with such high courage.

"I have succeeded in increasing the aids against that many- headed monster—psora, by the investigation of the action of *Kali, Causticum* (formerly called *tinct. acris sine Kali*), *Alumina, Conium maculatum* and purified salt—*Natrum muriaticum;* but unfortunately the fourth part of the 'Chronic Diseases' cannot yet be published, so as to enable me to communicate to you all the symptoms of those medicines in their completeness. I can only send you some of the medicines themselves.

"See how much you can begin with them; they are a great acquisition to the antipsoric materia medica. Accept the gift out of good-will. *Natrum muriaticum* will be of great use to your poor leprosy patient. Continue to prosecute your work as heretofore, until it be time to return again to Europe in good health, and hold dear,

" Your true friend,

" SAMUEL HAHNEMANN."

And a few days later Hahnemann writes to Dr. Rummel:†

" *Dear Colleague:*

"You have anticipated me, for I should first have thanked you for the inexpressible labour, trouble and devotion that you along with Stapf and the rest must have expended upon my fete in order to celebrate it in such a magnificent manner. I. especi- ally observed you to be so busy and zealous that I shall never forget it. It was a splendid festival, that astonished and greatly moved me.

---

* "Annals Brit. Hom. Society," Vol. ii., p. 159.
† *Brit. Jour. Hom.*, Vol. xi., p. 66.

"I beg you take upon yourself with *dulce decus columenque rerum* the management of the little endowment capital which is already a pretty good sum. A bountiful Providence seems to bestow a blessing on this honorable fund.

"A rich private merchant in L———, Mr. C. B. Sch———, a patient of mine, asked leave, when he heard about it, also to contribute something toward it. Has he done so? If not, I would suggest that you send to Dr. Franz a blank receipt from you without mentioning the sum, and the doctor will go to him and put him in mind of his promise, and if he gives a sum, as he certainly will do, it may be inserted in your receipt and then given to him. I think, indeed, it would be well to have prepared a number of such receipts (it would be best to have them printed), in order to be able to give the donors this small remembrance of our acknowledgments.

"When you have collected a couple of thousand thalers you will do well, if Muhlenbein approves, to invest it in Prussian bonds, which will produce an interest of 80 thalers a year. Do not be in too great a hurry with your work for the repertory; I am obliged to wait for others who have much more time to spare, and I must have everything collected together before I begin to arrange.

"Things are with me very much as they are with you. Besides my ordinary business, that constantly goes on, I have to write such a number of letters of thanks besides those I have already written, that I know not when I shall get time for anything.

"But I shall soon be clear of all that, for I am quite active, and then I shall expect you (say in a fortnight hence) and our Stapf, and I trust Gross also (and Franz?), on a long visit; for we have many things to say to one another.

"When you write to Stapf pray tell him, as he intended to write a complete account of the 10th of August, that on that day the Natural History Society of the Osterland sent me a diploma of Honorary Member, accompanied by a courteous letter. (Piener's name was among the signatures.)

"I regret to say that there was such a commotion the other day that I was unable to carry out my intention of having your ears mesmerized by Dr. Siegrist, who is said to possess great power that way. I have been thinking over the matter, and

consider it may be of great importance for you. We will say
more about it when we meet. I must conclude for to-day.

"Yours most sincerely,

"SAMUEL HAHNEMANN.

"*Coethen, 24th August, 1829.*"

Hahnemann was much gratified with the "Kleine Medicinische
Schriften," edited by Stapf, and presented upon his Jubilee Day.
In a letter dated September 28, 1829, he says: *

"*Dearest Friend:*

"You have rendered an immense service to me by your appropriate and necessary notes in the collection of my Lesser Medical Writings, published under your editorship; I may even be so
vain as to say that you have thereby rendered a service to the
world. † But I think you have almost given too high an estimate of me in your beautiful preface. In short, I am very much
beholden to you. Would you believe it? It is only within the
last few days that, owing to an accumulation of work, I have
been able, properly, to look through your well planned and well
executed laborious undertaking.

"I do not know how I am still able to get through such a
quantity of work. But what we do willingly only fatigues us
till bedtime. In the morning, thank God, there is a complete
return of strength.

"Your dear letter of the 6th of September gave me the pleasant expectation of seeing you soon here, and now your last letter,
containing an almost absolute refusal to pay me a visit, has proportionately disappointed me. Do not serve me so. How do you
know if next year, when the season is so far advanced that
traveling becomes possible, I shall still be alive! That cannot
be considered at all certain; and just consider for a moment how
much we have to talk over! * * * *

"The prohibition of the Homœopathic treatment of acute diseases in Russia is so abominable that it must be of the greatest
advantage to us. Every educated person sees that it is a con-

* *Hom. World*, Vol. xxv., p. 111. "Annals Brit. Hom. Society," Vol. ii.,
240.

†This letter is translated by Dr. Dudgeon, and in a note he says: "Hahnemann's Lesser Writings, collected and translated by myself, and published in one volume by Headland in 1851, contains many more of Hahnemann's writings than are included in the two volumes edited by Stapf."

trivance of the dominant Allopathic sect, in order to divert the attention of the public from the remarkable superiority of Homœopathy in the treatment of acute pleurisy.   But what would such a strabismic government do if a Homœopath were to cure a pneumonia or a pleurisy in a few hours?   Would it condemn the Homœopathic doctor to have his head cut off?   Hardly in our time, not even in Russia."

The Hahnemann who wrote this letter was then 75 years of age and so occupied with his work that for nearly two months after he had received Stapf's collection of his own writings he had not time to read the book!

And again we find him, not long after the Fest-Jubilee, expressing to Stapf the great happiness that the meeting had afforded him.   He says :*

"*Dear Colleagues*

"I can bear much joy and grief, but I was hardly able to stand the surprise of so many, and such strong proofs of the kindness and affection of my disciples and friends with which I was overwhelmed on the 10th of August.   Even now when I have regained my mental equilibrium and examine and reflect on all the tokens of cordial kindness with which I have been honored, I am lost in admiration over the handsome presents of tasteful and elegant design, and brought together with the best intention and with great labour.   I have not deserved them ; they are gifts of generosity, delicacy and excessive gratitude, whose value I fully appreciate.   May those who thought of giving me this pleasant surprise live long and prosper. * * *

"As I am sending a packet to-day, I may as well enclose a copy of our local newspaper, which contains an account of our festival.   I don't know where the editor got all his information, he did not get a particle from me."

---

* *Hom. World*, Vol. xxv, p. 22. "Annals Brit. Hom. Society," Vol. iii., p 160.

CHAPTER XL.

HAHNEMANN AND THE VIS MEDICATRIX NATURÆ.

It has been said that Hahnemann denied the healing power of nature.

There has been considerable doubt even upon the part of the Homœopathic school regarding this matter. At a meeting of the Central Homœopathic Society at Magdeburg, in 1830, its members passed a resolution declaring "that they did not agree with Hahnemann in rejecting the *vis medicatrix naturæ*."

Certain passages in the "Organon" have been quoted to prove that the Master repudiated the possibility of any inherent medical power in the body.

The opponents of the Homœopathic school have many times used this argument against the system.

The passage in the "Organon" mentioned above is as follows :*

"But the more modern adherents of the old school do not wish it to be supposed, that in their treatment they aim at the expulsion of material morbific substances. They allege that their multifarious evacuant processes are a mode of treatment by *derivation*, wherein they follow the example of nature which, in her efforts to assist the diseased organism, resolves fever by perspiration and diuresis, pleurisy by epistaxis, sweat and mucous expectoration—other diseases by vomiting, diarrhœa and bleeding from the anus, articular pains by suppurating ulcers on the legs, cynanche tonsillaris by salivation, etc., or removes them by metastases and abscesses which she develops in parts at a distance from the seat of the disease.

"Hence they thought the best thing to do was to imitate nature by also going to work in the treatment of most diseases in a circuitous manner like the diseased vital force when left to itself, and thus in an indirect manner, by means of stronger heterogeneous irritants applied to organs remote from the seat of disease, and totally dissimilar to the affected tissues, they produced

---

*Dudgeon's Translation of the "Organon," London, 1893, p. 16.

evacuations, and generally kept them up, in order to *draw*, as it were, the disease thither.

"This derivation, as it was called, was and continues to be one of the principal modes of treatment of the old school of medicine.

"In this imitation of the self-aiding operation of nature, as some call it, they endeavor to excite, by force, new symptoms in the tissues that are least diseased and best able to bear the medicinal disease, which should draw away the primary disease under the semblance of crises and under the form of excretions, in order to admit of a gradual lysis by the curative powers of nature.

(In a note.) "It is only the slighter acute diseases that tend, when the natural period of their course has expired, to terminate quietly in resolution, as it is called, with or without the employment of not very aggressive Allopathic remedies; the vital force having regained its powers then gradually substitutes the normal condition for the derangement of the health that has now ceased to exist.

"But in severe, acute and in chronic diseases which constitute by far the greater portion of all human ailments, crude nature and the old school are equally powerless; in these neither the vital force with its self-aiding faculty, nor Allopathy in imitation of it can effect a lysis, but at the most a mere temporary truce during which the enemy fortifies himself in order, sooner or later, to recommence the attack with still greater violence."

On page 19 of the same edition he says: "It is only by the destruction and sacrifice of a portion of the organism itself that unaided nature can save the patient in acute diseases, and if death do not ensue, restore, though only slowly and imperfectly, the harmony of life—health."

Hahnemann in other places alludes to "crude unaided nature," and mentions its limited powers.

Ameke says in relation to this:* "Hahnemann's enemies had cast upon him the reproach—Your method of treatment is a direct contradiction of our great teacher, Nature. Open your eyes! A rush of blood to the head, a congestive headache, is healed by nature by a wholesome bleeding from the nose. We copy nature and draw blood when congestion is present. You fly in nature's face and reject bleeding. In a case of ophthalmia you see an eruption make its appearance in the contiguous parts

---

*"History of Homœopathy," p. 296.

of the face, and the inflammation is thereby diminished. We follow this hint of nature and excite an artificial eruption or inflammation by means of blisters, moxas, cauteries, setons, etc. Have you never seen the original malady relieved by metastases? Have you never seen a skin eruption disappear on the supervention of diarrhœa? At variance with nature you try to fulfil her requirements.

"Hahnemann was often assailed with such reproaches by his earlier opponents, and the passage cited by later opponents from the fourth edition of the 'Organon' was an answer to these attacks, as is clearly shown by the text."

It certainly seems plain from his writings that he believed in the recuperative or healing power of nature. In the "Essay on a New Principle," 1796, he says:* "In acute diseases, which, if we remove the obstacles to recovery for but a few days, nature will herself generally conquer."

In 1797, he says in the "Obstacles to Certainty in Practical Medicine:" "I do not now allude to cures effected by dietetic rules alone, which, if simple, are not to be despised, and which are very serviceable in many cases. If it be necessary to make considerable changes in the diet and regimen, the ingenious physician will do well to mark what effect such changes will have on the disease before he prescribes the mildest medicine."†

In 1801 he says: "That kind nature and youth will, assisted by such an appropriate regimen (as food, pure air, &c.) and even by itself, cure diseases having far other producing causes than deficiency and excess of excitability, is a phenomenon daily witnessed by the unprejudiced observer."

Again:‡ "According to him (Brown) we must not trust anything to the powers of nature; we must never rest with our medicines; we must always either stimulate or debilitate. What a calumniation of nature, what a dangerous insinuation for the ordinary half-instructed practitioner, already too officious! What a ministration to his pride to be deemed the lord and master of nature!"

In the preface to the "Thesaurus," he says:|| "Nature acts according to eternal laws, without asking your leave; she loves

---

* "Lesser Writings," New York, p. 261.

† "Lesser Writings," New York, p. 312.

‡ Ameke's "History of Homœopathy," p. 298.

|| "Lesser Writings," New York, p. 350.

simplicity, and effects much with one remedy whilst you effect little with many. Seek to imitate nature."

In "Æsculapius in the Balance," 1805, he says:* "It were easy to run through a catalogue of similar acute diseases, and show that the restoration of persons who in the same disease were treated on wholly opposite principles could not be called cure, but a spontaneous recovery."

In 1808 he writes: "Do not the poor who take no medicine at all often recover much sooner from the same kind of disease than the well-to-do patient who has his shelves filled with large bottles of medicines?"

In "Allopathy," written in 1831, he says:† "If they call this an efficacious sort of method, how can they reconcile it with the fact that of all that die in a year, a sixth part of the whole number dies under them (the Allopaths) of inflammatory affections, as their own tables prove! Not one-twelfth of these would have died had they not fallen into such sanguinary hands, *had they been but left to nature*, and kept away from that old pernicious art."

Griesselich, who visited Hahnemann in 1832, says:‡ "Hahnemann has often been reproached for his contempt for the healing power of nature. I myself was led into this error by something in the "Organon." In conversing with Hahnemann I have never perceived anything tending to the denial of this healing power. It appears that the reformer must have given occasion to misunderstandings."

Hahnemann wrote a preface for a book published by a follower, one Dr. Kammerer, of Ulm, in 1834. In this book Dr. Kammerer frequently writes: "The healing power of nature often effects wonderful and rapid cures." "The severest illnesses often get rapidly well of themselves." "In chronic diseases the marvellous healing power of nature is seen." "Diseases are cured as rapidly, or more so, by the proper healing power of nature than by the best remedies."

Hahnemann endorsed everything in this book and thus concludes his preface: "Our dear Kammerer of Ulm, whose sensible treatise I have now great pleasure in introducing to the public."

---

* "Lesser Writings," New York, p. 412.
† "Lesser Writings," New York, p. 739.
‡ "Ameke's History of Homœopathy," p. 299.

From the above quotations it must be probable that Hahnemann *did* believe in the *vis medicatrix naturæ.** That he also believed it to be limited in power seems equally certain. But as he believed, as do his followers, that it had been granted to him through the goodness of God to discover the true law or plan by means of which disease can most surely be cured, and by means of which the *vis medicatrix*, or inherent power of nature, can be rendered best able to act, his statements in the " Organon " are not in any way contradictory. He said over and over, that in a crude limited way nature had power to throw off certain types of disease, but that in order to be able to act most successfully her power must be developed by her own law of healing—Homœopathy.

In the following letter to a patient, Hahnemann advises him to leave things to his active vital force :†

"Dear Baron :

"As your sister lives according to Homœopathic rule, the best thing you can do in a general way is to follow her example, and hence be as sparing as possible in the use of wine, coffee, Chinese and other teas; avoid altogether distilled spirits, punch, acids, spices, especially vanilla, cinnamon, cloves, and all kinds of perfumes and tooth powders. One of the most important rules for getting well is what Confucius called the golden mean, and described in an excellent book the aurea mediocritas, *rien de trop!* In this golden mean I would advise you to abide with respect to all allowed things. I would like you to walk every day in the open air, never to run, and only to ride or drive a little when necessary; to go to bed by ten o'clock ; not to read yourself asleep in bed; not to undertake any mental labor after eight o'clock in the evening; to take your supper before eight P. M., and then to eat but sparingly, and never of meat or eggs; to have frequently one or two friends about you, but to shun large parties; not to over-exert yourself in any way, and to coolly dismiss all disagreeable subjects like a wise man.

   *   *   *   *   *   *   *   *

"Arrange your time carefully, I pray you. Every hour

---

* A very interesting lecture on this subject by Dr. Leadam may be found in the *Brit. Jour. of Hom.*, Vol. xiii., p. 190.

†*Allg. Hom. Zeitung*, Vol. lxvii., p. 32. *Brit. Jour. Hom.*, Vol. xxi., p. 677. *Fliegende Blatter uber Homoopathie*, Aug. 10, 1863.

wasted; *i. e.*, not spent for our own or other's good, is an irremediable loss, which a delicate conscience can never forgive.

"Nothing is of more importance than to watch and restrain our physical inclinations, those of the imagination included. The animal part of us requires to be constantly supervised and to be unindulgently kept within bounds as much as our reason will allow; our constant victory in this direction can alone make us happy by an elevating consciousness of having done. our duty; we then feel that we rest in the friendship of the Only One.

"Would you like any other religion? There is no other. All else is miserable, degrading human invention, full of superstition, fraught with destruction to mankind.

"So then I would advise you to commence to live in a blessed manner—better late than never. And as your body is shattered by disease, take the small portion of medicine I trouble you with *uninterruptedly*, and write a *daily* account of what you experience while taking it.

"If you get a new symptom, I beg you will *underline* it, but nothing else in your report.

"You are to take every morning fasting one of these little powders moistened with a few drops of water, and drink nothing for an hour afterwards. Don't use any kind of baths; for the sake of cleanliness wash yourself rapidly down and dry yourself as rapidly, so that the whole operation shall only last a couple of minutes.

"If you can find a very good natured man among your people who has gained a reputation by his successful treatment of sprains and other injuries by manipulation, I would advise you to get him to give you, every other forenoon, a single pass, with both hands extended, slowly over the whole body, from the crown of the head along the arms (the hands the while resting on the knees), down to the tips of the toes, whilst you are seated in your ordinary clothing. Only you must not have on any silk garment. He must not press upon you as he is in the habit of doing. He should merely try with the whole power of his will to do you good.

"The spirit I ought to communicate to you by my treatment would evaporate if conveyed by a third party. We employ no doctor to go between us nor do we need one. Should you at any time feel more than usually indisposed, then remain for a few days quietly at home, living as abstinently as possible, and leave it to your active vital force to bring you round according to the organic laws, which will assuredly take place.

"Let us go to work as simply as possible, otherwise our efforts to restore your health, *jam aut nunquam*, will be fruitless. When you have taken No. 6 write me about yourself.

"Yours,   SAMUEL HAHNEMANN."

"*Coethen, Oct. 16, 1830.*"

"Have you really read the 'Organon?'"

CHAPTER XLI.

DEATH OF FRAU DR. HAHNEMANN—FAMILY LIFE DESCRIBED— LETTER TO STAPF ON THE SUBJECT OF THE LAST ILLNESS.

Hahnemann's wife died upon March 31, 1830. For forty-eight years she had been his faithful companion in all his wanderings, had shared his adversities, and in order that he might the more fully devote himself to his studies, had always taken upon her own shoulders the care of the family. She was, at the time of her decease, nearly sixty-seven years of age.

Authentic and interesting particulars of the last illness may be found in the following letter written by the bereaved old man to his lifelong friend, Stapf:*

"*Dear Friend and Colleague:*

"My cordial thanks for your kind wishes at the advent of my seventy-sixth year, and a reciprocity of many good wishes for the prosperity of yourself and your esteemed family at the hands of Him from whom all good things emanate to us in an unseen manner. In the moments that we can spare from our busy lives we should unceasingly thank the great Spirit from whom all blessings flow with our whole heart and all our undertakings worthy of Him, though in all eternity we can never thank Him too much for His goodness.

"Your welcome letter reached me when I was in the most extraordinary state in the world.

Hom. World, Vol. xxv., p. 209. "Annals Brit. Hom. Med. Society," Vol. ii., p. 355.

"My good wife, who for many years had been always very ailing, who three years ago had very nearly succumbed to an abscess of the liver that burst into the lungs, and who had always objected to take any medicine, trusting to her enormous vital powers, fell ill at the beginning of March, after taking a chill, when, as it seems, she was in a state of great mental irritation, with a very severe catarrh and cough, with much pain in various parts. The cough was attended by difficult expectoration, it increased and was accompanied by a well marked remittent fever, and she commenced to cough up pus, which was at first bloody and afterwards mixed with pure bile; then it became fetid, and at last extremely malodorous, just like an ulcer turning gangrenous.

"After great suffering, fever and pains, she at length (on the 31st of March, after midnight) gently fell asleep in our arms with the cheerfullest expression in the world, to wake up in eternity. The release was not to be regretted on her account.

"Several days before her decease a letter from Rummel gave me such an immense amount of vexation that I could speak to no one, and was unable to read or write a line. With difficulty I got out of bed several times a day to go to my dying wife (because she noticed my absence), but I took care not to show her that I was ill. *Staph.* and *Arsenic* several times in alternation set me right, so that I was recovering when she died.

"The worry caused to me by the pompous funeral (necessary in this place), the fetching hither of my two distant daughters, the division of the (considerable) maternal property, and in addition a relapse of my nervous fever which robbed me of all my strength for three or four days, and then the accumulation of unanswered patients' letters, the daily importunity of patients in this place, and so forth—while in this position, but thank God! quite recovered, I received your dear letter besides many others of felicitation. Is it a wonder that I could not answer you before to day?

"You have no doubt succeeded in keeping your good Mary Eylert alive, though the weather has been unfavourable. When you write me again (which I hope will be soon) tell me how she is now, and I will see if I cannot give you some friendly medical advice.

"If Yxkull will pay me a visit I hope you will accompany him.

You will find me as usual wrapped up in my mantle of God-given philosophy.

"Your true friend,
"SAM HAHNEMANN."

"*Coethen, April 24, 1830.*"

"Kindest regards from me and mine to your estimable family."

On the same morning in which Frau Dr. Hahnemann died Duchess Julie sent to her physician and dear friend the following kindly note of condolence: *

"I have learned with the greatest distress, my dear Hofrath, of the sad blow which has fallen on you this night. The news was all the greater shock to me since I had no suspicion of the illness of the departed.

"I beg you to be assured of my most hearty sympathy, and to grant my earnest request that, under this severe shock, you will not neglect your health, which is so necessary to the welfare of mankind.

.   "JULIE, DUCHESS OF ANHALT.

"*Coethen, March 31, 1830.*"

Eleven children were born to Frau Hahnemann, two sons and nine daughters. A complete record of them may be found in the chapter of this book devoted to Hahnemann's family.

A great deal has been written in regard to Frau Dr. Hahnemann's disposition. With the exception of Von Brunnow who, in one place, says that she exercised an arbitrary influence upon Hahnemann, all the people who have written of his domestic life from observation, agree that it was a happy one.

Albrecht says:† "Hahnemann was happiest in his family circle, and displayed here as nowhere else a most amiable disposition to mirth and cheerfulness. He joked with his children in the intervals which he could devote to them, sang cradle songs to the little ones, composed little verses for them, and used every opportunity to instruct them. Although at first he had but little, he spent all he could upon their education and culture. Hahnemann paid attention, too, to the education of his daughters. They were thoroughly instructed in all domestic and

---

* "Biographisches Denkmal," 1851.   "Leben und Wirken."   Ameke's "History of Homœopathy."   p. 155.

†"Albrecht's Leben und Wirken." Ameke's "History of Homœopathy," p. 159.

feminine duties by their mother. Their mother had, indeed, greater influence than their father over them while they remained at home. She was a remarkable woman, of an energetic character and educated above the ordinary standard. She was much beloved and respected by her husband and children. She also had a musical education and composed words to music written by herself. Hahnemann, too, was a great lover of music, and had a pleasant singing voice, but without knowing a note. He was fond of coming into the parlor when he took an interval of repose from his work, between nine and ten, and of getting his wife to play him something on the piano.''

Seminary Director Albrecht was familiar with the family of Hahnemann from 1821 to 1835, and certainly would have known were there any unpleasantness between the husband and the wife. Throughout his book, the ''Life and Works of Hahnemann,'' he constantly speaks of the accord existing between them.   .

Ameke says:* ''All the authors who describe Hahnemann's family life from their own experience agree in bearing witness to the cordial relations between Hahnemann and his children. They acknowledge the worth of his first wife, of whom Hahnemann always spoke with love and esteem.

''Even if she were, as Brunnow says, fond of power and imperious, and Brunnow's writings bear the stamp of truth, yet she must have possessed excellent qualities which were highly valued by her husband. Her energy was, no doubt, often a support to him in his stormy life. The region of romance was far from her, she lived in realities.''

CHAPTER XLII.

FRENCH BIOGRAPHY OF HAHNEMANN—TRUE PICTURES FROM THE LIFE OF FRAU HAHNEMANN.

†About the year 1862–3 a sketch of the life of Hahnemann was published in France in a book called '' Biographie Universalle, ancienne et moderne.'' In this book the biographer, after speaking of Hahnemann's conscientious sacrifices in giving up

* '' History of Homœopathy,'' p. 159.
† *Brit. Jour. Hom.*, Vol. xxiii., p. 661.

his practice after he decided that the medical methods in vogue
were wrong, says: "The miseries of his altered state were
increased tenfold by the bitter reproaches of his wife and daughters at his having sacrificed the realities of life for dreams and
chimeras."

The amiable charms of the second Madame Hahnemann were
placed in marked contrast to this picture.

In 1865 there was published in Berlin a book entitled "True
Pictures from the Life of the late Mrs. Johanna Henrietta Leopoldine Hahnemann, nee Kuchler, to serve to correct the unexampled perversion of history in the 'Biographie Universalle,
ancienne et moderne.'"*

The author of the "True Pictures" says: "It is a sad spec-
tacle when at the grave just closed of celebrated men the contention of parties is enkindled, and it is doubly sad when such
contentions are kept alive for decades by a malignant party.

"But when the flames of this contention even enter into the
sanctuary of a happy family life, so that its smoke envelops
beloved, dear forms, in order that other less noble forms may be
undeservedly transfigured, every true heart, every German
heart is outraged, and feels obliged to scatter this spurious glory,
and to win back their despoiled honor for those slandered noble
persons.

"Such a contention also arose at the grave of that celebrated
master of the healing art, Samuel Hahnemann. As is well
known, he died July 3, 1843, far from his loved ones, in Paris,
and in the same year still there appeared an article with respect
to him which was afterwards published anew in pamphlet form,
and in the most unpardonable manner attacked the first wife of
the Master, the noble Johanna Henrietta Leopoldine, *nee*

---

*"Treue Bilder aus dem Leben der verewigten Frau Hofrath Johanne
Henriette Leopoldine Hahnemann, geb. Kuchler, zur richtigen Geschichts-
verdrehung in der Biographie Universalle (Michaud) ancienne et moderne.
Paris, bie Madame C. Desplaces. Berlin, Ferd. Rob. Reichardt. 1865."
*This is a very rare pamphlet. The compiler sought vainly in
the book stores of Germany for a copy. It is due to the courtesy
of Drs. Puhlmann, of Leipzig, and Suss-Hahnemann, of London, that he is
able to give its contents. Both Drs. Puhlmann and Suss-Hahnemann
placed copies at his disposal. It is probable they are the only two copies
in existence. The translation was made by Rev. Mr. L. H. Tafel, of
Urbana, O.

Kuchler, in her relation to her celebrated husband and in her whole character. Since that time ever and anon, there have appeared at longer or shorter intervals repeated articles which were either inspired by the same party or blindly accepting those false allegations sought to cloud the image of this genuine German woman before the eyes of her native land, yea, of the whole of Europe.

"We shall not notice these, however, but shall only occupy ourselves with the latest fabrication of French journalism, with the article concerning S. Hahnemann in Michaud's 'Biographie Universalle, ancienne et moderne,' which will enable us most easily to find the source of all these false statements." * * *

"At page 29 we quote from this same Biography: 'On the 31st of March, 1830, Hahnemann lost his first wife, but then fame, plenty and peace had entered his house, and quite a while before her death she had had the leisure and opportunity to become freed from her prejudices as to the character and abilities of him with whom she had joined her fate.

"'In the year 1835 a French woman, Mademoiselle d'Hervilly, distinguished by her mental charms and excellences and an expert in knowledge unusual for her sex, came to Coethen in order to consult Hahnemann. She esteemed and admired him, and by this admiration the train was laid to a marriage which brought an uninterrupted happiness to the last years of the aged man. Hahnemann had always loved France, he possessed indeed very much of the French wit and spirit (beaucoup de l'esprit francais). He possessed above all things that flowing, clear, and at the same time decided and captivating style, which distinguishes his works, and which is one of the characteristic peculiarities of the French spirit, much more than the heavy, awkward German style. Hahnemann went to Paris, never again to leave it. Outside of the affections which drew him there he had been led to it by differences of view with respect to his teachings, which had arisen between him and some of his disciples. This contention was for him one of the most painful, and he was so much affected by it that he came to the determination to publish nothing more of the considerable amount of manuscript material he had in readiness.

"'The arrival of Hahnemann in Paris was announced in all the journals and was an event in the scientific world. Truth compels us to say that patients flocked to him in troops and that he soon had one of the most crowded clinics in Paris. His rich clientage did not prevent his devoting his treatment and counsel also to the poor without remuneration. Nevertheless, his opponents endeavored to cause him the same difficulties which had so disquieted his career in Germany, and we gladly give here an anecdote which does honor to Guizot. When Hahnemann settled in Paris Guizot was Minister of Public Instruction. Some persons crowded around him and went even so far as to claim an importance by pretending—no doubt without foundation—that they were members of the Academy, and they urged him to forbid the founder of Homœopathy to practice his art. 'Hahnemann is a scholar of great merit,' answered Guizot, 'science must be free for all. If Homœopathy is a chimera, or a system without any internal substance, it will fall of itself. But if it is an advance it will spread even despite our repressive measures, and this the Academy should wish above all others, for the Academy has the mission to forward science and to encourage its discoveries.'

"'Even to his last moment Hahnemann practiced his art without disturbance or obstruction, under the protection of French hospitality. He had finally entered into the harbor of his rest after a life tossed by many storms. Surrounded by the esteem of his adherents and disciples and encompassed by the intelligent love and affection of his wife, who not only comprehended him, but also participated in his labors and his studies; rich finally in the gain afforded him by his calling, he constantly to the last hour blessed the event that had brought him into our country. His vigorous age knew no bodily weakness nor mental debility, and he concluded his long career with a gentle death on the second of July, 1843, leaving Madame Hahnemann as the heiress of his teachings, precepts and observations which he had set down unremittingly in his numerous manuscripts. His teachings which he has left to science may be briefly summed up in a few comprehensive aphorisms: Diseases are healed by similar ones; i. e., through medicaments which in the healthy man produce the characteristic symptoms of the disorder to be combatted. The strength and the effectiveness of medicaments are only discovered by experiments with the pure matter on the healthy body; its purity; i. e., its unity is the indispensable

condition of its efficacy.   The motion which is communicated to
the medicines at their preparation gives them a force which is
multiplied through the division of their parts, whereby their
spiritual qualities are developed, and by the similarity of their
nature they can thus directly come to the aid of the suffering
organs.   The diseases with which men are afflicted are divided
into three great classes: the acute, the epidemic and the chronic
or psoric diseases.   But the same medicaments cannot be used
with each one of these three great classes of human diseases,
every disease is individual, the original element of disease modi-
fies itself according to the bodily constitution, according to
former processes in the body, and according to the mental and
physical state of the subject.

  " 'The Homœopath must therefore carefully search out the
various symptoms which constitute the morbid state of the
patient, and must seek out that medicament for its cure which
in the healthy body causes symptoms which are as nearly as
possible similar to those of the diseases to be treated.   The
Homœopathic medicaments are therefore in a certain degree individual like the accidents of disease.   Nature has richly supplied man in the plants, the metals, and in the apparently dead
matter, with the most effective and varied remedies, all that it
needs is to discover them; but this can only be done through
constant experimenting carried on for many years.   The Homœopathic Materia Medica contains the enumeration of a great
number of curative peculiarities and properties in the realm of
Nature, but it has still before it a whole series of observations
and discoveries immeasurable as Nature itself.

  " 'It is not our intention to pass judgment respecting the
merits of Hahnemann's teachings; we would also be utterly incompetent for such a work.   Our task must and does confine
itself to state and explain his method. But we would not fulfil our
duty as historians if we should not add that at this day his
method is practiced in the whole world; that it has numerous
and zealous apostles in France, the United States, and in all the
civilized countries of the Orient and Occident, and that it seems
to have won the supremacy in Germany through the importance
and excellence of its representatives.   If we still add, that it has
to a certain degree stood the test of time, and that we may con-
ceive the point of time to have come where it must draw on

itself the undivided attention and the serious investigation of
scientific bodies and of scientists who have made it their life's
work to alleviate the sufferings of humanity.

" 'A register giving the titles of the works either written or
translated by Hahnemann will still more contribute to give a
just idea of the extent of his labors and of his knowledge.'*

" Now the passages in this article to which we take exception
are the following:

" After Hahnemann's residence in Hettstadt, Dessau and Gommern has been mentioned, we read: 'He here on December 1,
1782, married Henriette Kuchler, the daughter of a druggist in
Dessau, by whom he had eleven children.'

" Shortly after this Hahnemann's grand intention, worthy of
a hero, to give up his practice until he should discover a new
curative method blessed for all mankind, instead of the old
method which he recognized as unsatisfactory, is introduced by
the words: ' He had already a practice of many years' standing,
a good reputation, he was married and the head of a numerous
family; to put the crown on his misfortune he was also exposed
to the reproaches of his wife and his daughters. This mother,
who was embittered on account of the privations laid upon his
family and who could not understand the sentiments which animated her husband, piled upon him bitter reproaches for having
bartered away his wealth for poverty, and for sacrificing the
reality of life for empty dreams and chimeras.'

" We would only here insist upon it that there is not a word
which would correspond with such views and reproaches; when
Hahnemann moved from Coethen to Paris he himself in a letter
to his neighbor, merchant Ulbricht, warmly commends both his
daughters to his care.

" How this picture contrasts with the brilliant portrait of the
second wife of the great man, Melanie d'Hervilly, in the same
article, which is found in this work that places on its title page
the proud name of ' Histoire.' 'She is distinguished by the
charms and excellencies of her mind and an extent of knowledge unusual for her sex. She esteemed and admired him (H)
and this admiration ended in a marriage which bestowed an uninterrupted happiness to the last years of the life of the aged

*(In the French article here follows a list of the works; this list is omitted
in the German book: "Treue Bilder.")

man. By her he finally found his haven of rest after a life so traversed by storms. Surrounded by the respect of his adherents and of his disciples, encompassed by the intelligent affection of a wife who not only understood but even took part in his labors and in his studies, etc.'

"Even the most impartial reader will here notice the intention, and smile. While the bond of the most lovely marriage and the happiness of possessing eleven excellent children is in the coolest manner merely mentioned, the trumpets sound at the approach of the charming French woman. While the reproach of unkindness, hardness and narrowness of mind is hurled at the most faithful companion of his life, Madame Melanie appears as the angel of peace, who fans tranquility to the old man weary from cares.

"A German who knows the sacred nature of German marriage and at the same time knows how corroded and corrupt marital relations are in our neighboring country, in the land of gallantry, and where the *esprit* gaps at us and disgusts us, a German will consider it a matter of deep interest to protect a German woman, the noble companion of one of its greatest men, from the insults of French perversions of history, now once for all.

"Let us then first of all see what these two wives were to this great husband. Johanne Leopoldine sacrificed to him her whole property when he, as already mentioned, formed the great souled resolution of withdrawing altogether into the sanctuary of his creative mind, in order to devise ways and means to relieve mankind from the bodily sufferings afflicting it, after he had recognized the existing methods though a thousand years old, still not only insufficient but as causing unceasing new corruptions. That the thoughtful housewife, the faithful mother often must have been full of anxiety when she considered what would become of her numerous family if Hahnemann should not satisfactorily solve the difficult problem—who would wonder at this? Who, rather, would not wonder if the German woman had not under such circumstances frequently looked anxiously into the future, instead of contenting herself, with French frivolity, with the joys of an evening.

"Melanie, as was found out later, was not rich when she came to Coethen, and ensnared the venerable old man in French style, with her bonds of love, and she finally, as it were, carried him away with a considerable part of his possessions, all of which the deceased wife had held together with wise economy; thus she transferred him out of the circle of a happy home into the brilliant salons of the French capital.

"Johanne H. L. watched with tender care over the domestic happiness, the tranquil peace of the great master, so that he only felt happy in his house, in his family, and seldom left them; a care and a loving activity which her faithful, noble daughters after her death undertook and exercised. Who has not read with heartfelt sympathy the passage in the 'Biography of Christian Friedrich Samuel Hahnemann,' Leipzig, 1851, page 103, which describes this state, to attest the authenticity of which the author could find numerous still living witnesses in Coethen.

"Melanie who, after her marriage with Hahnemann, led a most brilliant life (compare the description of the celebration of the 10th of August, 1836, in the *Frankfurter Journal*, No. 66), and who must have expended enormous sums which she made the old man of 80 years work for, by compelling him quite against his custom to establish a far extended clinic outside of his house (in Coethen he only visited his illustrious patron, the genial Duke Ferdinand), so that he daily drove about in the labyrinthine Paris to make calls on his patients. In a letter of the late Hahnemann, of April 17, 1842, to the Aulic Councillor, Dr. Lehmann, he wrote: 'Since I have been in Paris, no German physician has had any instruction from me, nor has anyone been allowed to visit patients in my name.' And in a former letter to Dr. Lehmann, he wrote: 'I have been able to restore some 1000 patients, and not one of them died, though it (the malignant grippe) has taken away many thousand men from the hands of others.'

"Was that the haven of rest, O noble old man, weary of laurels, into which your second wife, in her tender love, led you?

"How often there may you have wished yourself back in your quiet asylum, which even to this day is protected by the faithful hands of your children, like a sanctuary? How often, when the noise of the Italian opera sounded around you, did you long in your spirit to be back in your undefiled family room, where after your quiet activity and the blessed work of the day you were delighted with the happiness and the love of your dear ones!

"But the masterwork of the love of Melanie is the already cited testament of Hahnemann, which his grandson, the celebrated Dr. Suss-Hahnemann, in London, to the delight of all admirers of the family, has finally published in the before-mentioned journal.*

CHAPTER XLIII.

"TRUE PICTURES" CONTINUED.

Hahnemann's will is now quoted in full. It will be given later on in the present volume. The author of the "True Pictures," whose name is nowhere given, then continues in regard to this will as follows:

"Yes, noble spirit, this testament is not your work, you knew your loved ones too well to presuppose any such sentiments in them. As you yourself did good, as long as you were free, so your daughter and grandchildren have only done good as long as they lived, and those who are still alive are still doing good. And how could you have threatened the children of your Leopoldine, who faithfully shared with you storm and sunshine; how could you have threatened them, when you were compelled to always think gratefully of this noble wife, who not only gave you these children, but also gave them the heritage of her love for you.

"To the psychologist this authorship may be no secret, but sound common sense will see the secret wires at work which put in motion the powers which originated this testament.

" But we have not the duty of a psychologist but that of a historian before us, and shall now also walk in the historical pathway, although a German man and a German woman would be contented with this simple parallel for the formation of a sure judgment as to the character of the two wives of the great man.

"Let us then conduct the historical demonstration, in which we need not complain that, as a matter of course, we have only a few official documents with respect to the domestic circle of activity, of the noble housewife. For these few will suffice to free her memory from these slanders.

"The most important proof is given by Hahnemann himself,

*Brit. Jour. Hom., Vol. 22, p. 674.

in his autobiography (published in 'Chr. Fr. Sam. Hahnemann, Biographisches Denkmal,' Leipzig, 1851), which he wrote only for his own use, in his quiet privacy, and which was composed at the very time when he was involved in the most severe scientific and material conflicts, in the year 1791. The passages bearing on the subject are:

"'Yet I then (in Gommern) first began to enjoy somewhat more.fully the innocent joys of domestic life, together with the sweetness of employment, in the company of the companion of my life, whom I married immediately on entering on my office, namely, Henriette Kuchler, etc.'

"And, lastly, concerning his stay in Leipsic: 'Four daughters and one son, together with my wife, constitute the spice of my life.'

"Ernst von Brunnow, the author of the first French translation of Hahnemann's 'Organon of Medicine,' who had a long acquaintance with Hahnemann and his family, wrote, according to his own confession, free from all partisan spirit: 'Ein Blick auf Hahnemann und die Homoopathie.'

"In this work he says, on page 30: 'The family of Hahnemann really offered a model of the old German discipline of children. But not only obedience, but also really the most sincere love of the children towards their parents could be seen there. In the midst of the amusement-loving and elegant Leipsic his daughters took no part in any public amusement, went dressed simply, like the daughters of a mechanic, and attended to the most menial employments of the household with cheerfulness.'

"We further call particular attention to the fact that Hahnemann, in 1789, gave up his medical practice (see Argenti, above) and wrote down his acknowledgment, given above, on the 30th of August, 1791, thus just during the time (see Autobiography) when his wife and children are said to have set the crown on the misfortunes of the great thinker. How do you feel, Herr Biographer, as these facts are compared?

"What historian of even moderately honest intentions and scientific spirit can, after these testimonies, put any confidence in the communications of the ' Biographie Universalle?'

"And yet, let us bring some further documents from Hahnemann's own family. When Melanie had prepossessed the good father against the whole family, his daughter, Frau Dr. Louise

Mossdorf, *nee* Hahnemann, equally distinguished for her intelligence and her heart, wrote a letter to her father on November 10, 1834, which is in our possession in a well attested copy, and which contains a panegyric on her deceased mother that must move every impartial reader to tears.   It is as follows:

"'My ardently beloved father, do listen to me!

"'In recalling my blessed mother and her incomparable traits of character and her virtues, my heart breaks!   All the virtues of her mind and heart will make her ever memorable to you.

"'That the blessed departed for nearly forty-eight years clung to you with unchanging fidelity, brought up with you ten children, and this under the most crushing surroundings, roamed over a great part of the world with you, and, indeed, pursued by the most dreadful persecutions of the enemies of Homœopathy, of all kinds and in thousandfold distresses, want and care; that she always willingly and gladly sacrificed the last penny of her fortune as well as her most valuable jewelry, bedding, clothing, etc., in order to relieve you and the children from all want, and to drive away hunger and anxiety; that she in every condition gave you her faithful assistance comforted you and helped you to bear innumerable sufferings and pains; in the most deadly diseases offered you and the children her unswerving aid, and bore the most terrible persecutions with dignity; ever inspired the children with the greatest esteem due to you, and impressed upon them to consider what love and gratitude they owed to you; how she ever admonished the children to everything right and good and to every virtue.

"'We owe her never ending thanks, and once more loudly declare it!   Never ending thanks to her! All honor to her!   The most fervent love, affection and true reverence to the dear departed! Would that all wives and mothers might faithfully follow her example!

"'Fantastic and romantic notions she eschewed.   She lived only in the reality, till she at the end stretched out to us her dear hand with the most impressive maternal admonitions, and several times yet stretched out her faithful hand to you, which had assisted in guiding you happily through your life agitated by a thousand storms, and with tears clung to you with her loving, blessing gaze, and in consequence of her unexampled fidelity found it so hard to part from you.   What a touching

scene.   While we yet love on earth and have our complete consciousness, every thought of it must deeply move us and stir us
and can never, never be extinguished from our thankful heart,
if we belong to God and hope to be received into His fatherly
arms.

   " 'Written November 10, 1834, for a memorial of the dear
departed one.   " 'Louise.' "

   "According to this letter the departed one was quite the true
woman whom we have characterized above.   When on the centenary of Hahnemann's birthday, in the year 1855, his statue
was unveiled at Coethen, the daughters, grandchildren and
great-grandchildren dedicated a poem to the mother, which,
being composed by the daughter Louise, may here find a place.

   " 'For the celebration of the one hundredth birthday of
Samuel Hahnemann and the unveiling of his statue in the
garden of the Clinic of Sanitary Councillor, Dr. Lutze, on the
10th of April, 1855, the same festive day the remaining daughters, grandchildren and great-grandchildren sing humbly with
truly childlike love and affection to their mother and grand-
mother and great-grandmother, Johanne Henriette Leopoldine
Hahnemann, *nee* Kuchler, the following song:'*

   Here follows the song.

        *   *   *   *   *   *   *

   "So strong was the band of love with which Johanne had
enfolded her family that the children did not think it right to
celebrate the centenary of their father without proclaiming at
the same time to their mother, twenty-five years after her death,
these touching words of undying love.

   "We have numberless other proofs, but we do not use them
for fear that these family testimonials might be suspected of partiality, although we are so much convinced of their genuine
character that we would be glad to vouch for them with our
word."

-----

   *The music of this composition is placed as an appendix to the book,
"Treue Bilder," the full and complete score being written.

CHAPTER XLIV.

"TRUE PICTURES" CONCLUDED—ALBRECHT UPON THE MATTER
—HAHNEMANN'S LETTER TO ELISE.

"We will yet adduce another outside testimonial for the
happy family life of Hahnemann's first marriage, that of Dr.
Argenti, in Pesth, as we find it in Dr. Lutze's *Fliegende Blatter
ueber die Homoopathie*, Year 7, No. 20, p. 163. We there read:
'So four years passed in Dresden and its environs in a very
agreeable manner in the circle of his increasing family, for he
then already had four daughters and one son, who, together
with his wife, embellished his life.'

"Dr. Argenti rests as to this statement, evidently, and with
the highest scientific propriety, on the already adduced passages
of Hahnemann's autobiography.

"Just as important passages we might extract from the letters
of numerous young physicians (especially that of Dr. Hartlaub),
some of whom lived for a considerable time in Hahnemann's
house, and were here obliged to become acquainted with his
family life.

"They all praise the familiar, loving, harmonious life of his
family in the most indubitable terms; the beloved, honored lady
counsellor, the friendly, modest daughters. Especially we must
make mention of the lately deceased daughter, Charlotte, who
was distinguished for her kindly heart. She was the most constant assistant of her father in preparing and potentizing the
medicines; she had much perseverance, was extremely punctual
and conscientious, most resembled her father and was much
loved by him. She composed verses and drew very prettily,
and was especially useful in the housekeeping department.

"It is true, indeed, that a few of those physicians, and especially such as were largely aided in a material way by Hahnemann, afterwards sought to slander his family. But also this
contradiction is easily solved. For who of our readers does not
know how easily parasitical plants wind around a vigorous,
thrifty, proud tree, to waste in slothful idleness that which
genius in the wild storm of the contest and with manifold priva-

tions has gathered together. The child-like, pure spirit of Hahnemann, his (I am sorry to say, frequently abused) good nature, his mind ever pursuing the ideal, likely made him frequently forget that even the greatest genius cannot do without the firm soil of the solid earth so long as he lives here below with his own.

"We do not wish to introduce any individual case of this parasitical tribe, but shall only adduce an example of his liberal disposition in financial affairs. Hahnemann had offered a celebrated and rich publishing house in Leipsic the manuscript of a book about Allopathy, and he had entered into a contract securing him twenty thalers. Later on the publishing house complained of the bad times and he voluntarily reduced his demands to ten thalers. In a letter of July 16, 1831, the publisher accepted the present with the words: 'We accept your kindness in this present very depressed state of business and transmit to you enclosed ten thalers, Pruss. Cour.' And these ten thalers he at once donated to a charitable institution, while the same publishers afterwards printed abusive articles about Homœopathy in a journal appearing with their imprint.

"The arranging, penetrating mind of the first partner of his life, which instinctively separated the good from the evil (the enviable heritage of noble-minded women) no doubt always discovered such pretended admirers of her great husband and also made them harmless—*et hinc illae lachrimae!* On the other hand, the worthy Johanne H. L., like her daughters, showed her charity to innumerable worthy, deserving poor, as her admirers in Coethen will testify; and even thirty-four years after her death grateful friends visit the grave of the blessed departed.

"Her household always bore the impress of the well-to-do citizen, equally far removed from the foolish, extravagant luxury of the *haute volée* of Paris as from the meanness of the filthy avarice which would have been unworthy of the world-renowned founder of a new era in the field of medicine.

"We conclude our series of quotations from the beforementioned Biography of Hahnemann (Leipsic, 1851, its author a friend and admirer of Hahnemann of many years standing), with the following, concerning his family life: 'He had lived in a very happy marriage from which had sprung nine daughters and two sons. His wife (Johanne H. L.) had been, in the noblest and highest sense of the word, the treasure of his life. A whole souled woman, a whole-souled wife, housekeeper and mother, living only for her circle, resigning every worldly pleasure, she accompanied her husband through life with the most faithful affection. Lifted up by the pinions of her own spirit, she assisted in enabling him to soar up to the height of fame. Therefore he felt impelled, after having entered into the haven of external calm in Coethen, to say in his, happiest hour to the loving companion of his life: 'Yes, mother, that is true, how could I have helped succumbing to the manifold persecutions which passed over me, without your support? How could I have been able to pass with such courage and such strength through the storms of life which drove us through half the world if you had not so friendly stood at my side?'

"Such an (musical) enjoyment in his own house gave to his spirit the wished for relaxation, refreshed his heart and unveiled the depths of his heart. 'How would I have been able,' he exclaimed in such a moment, seizing the hand of his wife and looking into her eye with the fire of love: 'how would I have been able, my beloved, to have persevered in the many distressing relations of life without you; how could I have carried through my intention despite of all difficulties, how fight all my enemies with undiminished strength? If you remain by my side, I hope to gain the most complete victory and to raise up my system despite of all opponents, to be everywhere and alone acknowledged.'

"Impartiality is not a pleasant virtue, says a celebrated historian, just as it is not a pleasant duty to give sentence; it must almost always give with the one hand and take with the other. And yet we acknowledge that we have enjoyed exercising it in this case. For either this biographer of Hahnemann worked with a nonchalance inexcusable in so comprehensive a work, which carelessness did not even think it worth while to look through most important sources for this work, or he had his private interests, which are incompatible with the dignity of science.

"We are free to acknowledge that we are inclined to believe the latter, and to suppose that that treatise intends an apotheosis of Melanie at the expense of Hahnemann's own family. So that writer sought to find a motive for Hahnemann's leaving Coethen

in this, that his ungrateful fellow-citizens persecuted their benefactor.   He was insulted here, as he says, in a gross manner by
the mob.   Cries were uttered under his windows, and his window
panes were broken with stones, etc.   In the original we read:
'Il y fut outrage par la populace.   Des cris furent pousses sous
ses fenetres et ses vitres furent brisees a coup de pierres.'   Despite the remarkable success of his cures, he was none the less
the object of the manifestations mentioned by us and of the
grossest insults.   In the original we read: 'Ce succes remarqu-
able ne l'empecha pas d'etre en butte pendant huit ans aux
manifestations et aux outrages dont nous avons parle.'   Who
does not recognize the French author who sees before him the
'Canaille de Paris' with its 'a bas Guizot! Lampions! Lampions!'

    "The good people of Coethen are supposed to have been cap-
able of raising a tumult against a celebrated fellow-citizen who
is even at this day, after a separation of thirty years, loved and
honored by them; a tumult which we could only find in the
most ill-famed of the Faubourgs of Paris.   From eye-witnesses
and members of the family it is established to the contrary that
all these manifestations are to be reduced to the one fact, that
once a boy, who besides was regarded in the city as idiotic, made
a slip while playing with his cross bow on the street and shot
a pebble' into a window pane of Hahnemann's house.   'Sic
crescunt minimæ res,' etc., in the hands a French journalist!

    "If the 'Biographie' further relates that Hahnemann was in-
duced to his transfer to Paris by the differences of opinion as to
his teachings, which had developed between him and some of
his pupils, and that he was so affected by this most painful of
all disputes that he was considering the resolution not to publish
any more of the considerable amount of his writings which he
had prepared; this assertion is also refuted by the fact which
is well known to all German Homœopaths of that time, that
Hahnemann in the year 1835 at the parting banquet which he
gave to his disciples in the Hotel de Pologne in Leipsic, offered
to leave to them the royalty of the last book he had written in
Germany for a memorial, and that his disciples, though they did
not need it, promised to receive it thankfully as a loving legacy
of their master.

    "Why, finally, the 'Biographie' does not, with a word,

mention his funeral, unworthy of a great man, and also by this invites the reproach of a particular tendency, will best appear from the passage of the above printed article from Meyer's *Homoopathische Zeitung.*

"We would only, finally, request the reader to carefully compare the sketch in 'Michaud's Biographie universalle ancienne et moderne' with the testament of Hahnemann. Even the reader, who is least influenced by prejudice, will not fail to notice a certain relation of affinity between the two documents, and he will not then consider our supposition as to the tendency of the former to be frivolous.

"But thou, noble Johanne Henriette Leopoldine, slumber quietly under the wreaths of love and reverence with which thy husband, thy children and thy friends have so richly decked thy grave; yes, and still adore it to this day. Thy spirit, now raised above the tumultuous conflicts of this lowly life on earth, enjoys gladly the reunion with the beloved husband and the children who have followed thee in those higher regions, while here below, in the remembrance of a grateful posterity, a second immortality is found for thee.

"Whilst thou above walk in the light of the eternal truth, shades of falsehood, malignity and ignorance often yet cloud thy image; but the truth will finally conquer also here, and will glorify and protect thy memory for all times!"

It needs no printed name to the above vindication of the memory of Frau Hahnemann to indicate that the pamphlet was the work of one of Hahnemann's daughters. It has been given just as it was published. That Frau Hahnemann was a good wife and mother, faithful amid trials and always loyal, all evidence decides.*

Albrecht, the author of the "Biographisches Denkmal," says that in order to understand Hahnemann's character one must realize fully his relations to his family and friends. He then illustrates his kindly feeling towards his wife by quoting the following letter, written to her upon their wedding day. He uses the familiar name of endearment, *Elise*, as was often his custom. "He usually called her Elise, because he was very fond of that name."†

---

*A portrait of Frau Hahnemann was published in Dr. Puhlmann's *Leipziger Populaire Zeitschrift fur Homoopathie,* July 1, 1893.

†"Biographisches Denkmal," p. 110.

"On the day of my union with my beloved Johanne Henriette Leopoldine Kuchlerin (born at Dessau, December 1, 1763).

"Elise!

"What solemn stillness is in the world around me!

"Presentiments of higher feelings pulse gently through all the nerves of my expanding senses. Never did the sun rise more solemnly for me, never flowed the warm blood more uniformly in my veins, never did my heart beat more harmoniously and significantly than to-day, when it beats for thee, Elise, for thee!

"Feel here, how warm, how sincere! It beats not thus in the bosom of the effeminate or unfeeling! Here, faithful friend, shalt thou rest!

"Here shalt thou await whatever blessings may flow softly over thee from my hand! Here mayest thou listen to the grateful sharer of thy virtues as he tells thee of the world and ensures to thy virtue the reward ever bestowed upon the good, as experience has so often proved; here thou mayest enliven thy mournful hours, and wisely confirm the wavering heart on which thou reposest so trustfully.

"There, take forever the hand which will with joy smooth the roughness of thy pilgrimage! Take the heart which never ruined the innocent, never refused consolation, and sometimes—rejoice to think of it—has done good, which, in a word, is proud to have selected thee.

"If you deem it of any value, take it. I praise thee not, I only know thee; admire thee not, only love thee; and, willst thou believe me? so calmly, so judiciously, that I am satisfied that after many years, if possible, that I shall feel still more for thee, if at least the closest of all happy ties can be enduringly interwoven by Providence.

"Let us then, Elise, entwined in each other's love, seize the happy moments and string them as pearls on our common thread of life, regardless that an irresistible something may rend our God-like cord, revenging the greater happiness, should this fail, in the pleasant memory of bygone enjoyments.

"Darling! I go to encounter the battles, the weary burden of life! but I shall also encounter thy animated, innocent embraces, the encouragement of thy example, the trustful nature of thy full heart which beats for me. Would that I had a thousand times greater strength to imitate thy diligence, unswervingly to follow the example of thy virtues, to respond with fuller power to all thou dost for me and to all thou feelest for me. Dearest friend, be happy!

"The soaring power of all my youthful nerves filled with the spirit of life, as well as the cooling warmth of the blood which soon will become chilled in my dying heart, belong to thee, Elise, to thee!"

After the death of Frau Hahnemann the household was conducted by the two daughters, and the domestic life went on in the usual quiet, scholarly fashion. Albrecht says:* "He was the same stately, vigorous old man, whose regular manner of life went on as in the lifetime of his wife."

CHAPTER XLV.

CURE OF DR. AEGIDI.

It was during the year 1830 that Hahnemann made a wonderful cure, which conclusively proved that his new doctrine regarding the cause and cure of chronic diseases was correct. His distinguished patient was one Dr. Julius Aegidi, a prominent Allopathic physician and army surgeon. As a result he became a believer in Homœopathy, which method he practised until his death.[†]

In a Leipsic Homœopathic journal Dr. Aegidi published an article giving his reasons for examining and believing in Homœopathy, as follows:[‡]

"In the autumn of 1830 I was thrown from a vehicle, severely injured my shoulder and also took a violent cold. By local bloodletting and the usual antiphlogistic treatment the most distressing of my symptoms were removed in the course of a few days; still a paralytic heaviness of the arm remained, and in the course of a few weeks very severe periodical pains set in, which shot from the shoulder to the elbow; and gradually I lost the

---

* "Leben und Wirken," p. 73.

† Dr. Aegidi died at Freienwalde, Germany, on May 11, 1874, in his 79th year.

‡ *Hom. Examiner*, Vol. ii., June, 1841. *Northwest Jour. Hom.*, Vol. ii., p. 142. *Allg. Hom. Zeit.*, Vol. vii.

use of the arm more and more, while the sensation of palsy and heaviness increased daily; every, even the slightest, pressure upon the diseased part, caused the most insupportable pains; the suffering limb commenced to waste away, while the shoulder and elbow joints began to swell.

"After exhausting my own medical knowledge, I placed myself under the care of several of my most worthy colleagues; but after the lapse of a year the above mentioned symptoms still continued, with even more than their former severity; all motion of the arm was suspended; the shoulder hung one inch and a half lower than the sound one; the anterior surface of the shoulder joint and the articular surfaces of the elbow joint were much enlarged; the elbow stood about four inches off from the body, and every attempt to approximate it to the side occasioned the most intense pains; the left shoulder blade was drawn strongly outwards and to one side; the coracoid process was situated about half an inch below the collar bone; the supraspinatus muscle had diminished perceptibly in size.

"The pains, which were increased to an insupportable degree by the slightest external pressure, were always very intensely aggravated at night, so that any rest and sleep was out of the question. My whole body, but the affected side in particular, became much emaciated; the emaciation even extended to the left half of the face. My pulse was slow; skin pale; I suffered much from coldness of the whole body, and my digestion was much impaired. On account of an hereditary predisposition to gout, anti-arthritic treatment was now instituted by my medical advisers, and two large issues were opened, one upon the arm, the other upon the shoulder blade.

"After the continued use of these means for about four months, without any improvement, the issues were allowed to dry up, and two setons were inserted in their places. As no essential improvement took place in the course of several months, the actual cautery was applied to the shoulder joint; and in consequence I enjoyed comparative freedom from pain for about one month, during which period of time I also recovered the use of my arm in some measure, and even began to flatter myself with the hope of a perfect restoration.

"But my joy did not last long; for when the burnt places began to heal slight returns of my former pains set in and con-

centrated themselves about the elbow joint, which began to
swell, while the shoulder joint diminished in size in the same
ratio; so that in the course of several months the elbow joint
had become the seat of the same disease that had formerly
affected the shoulder joint. To complete my misery, enlargements of other bones, viz.: the clavicles, the sacrum, etc., took
place and rendered every position that I assumed in bed
extremely painful. In utter despair of any relief from the use
of Allopathic remedies I desisted entirely from all medical treatment, and my condition grew worse from day to day.

"At length I concluded to consult Hahnemann. I wrote him
a statement of my case, and begged for advice and assistance.
He answered me, among other remarks: 'Your disease is of far
older date than you have any idea of. You must have had the
itch at some time, or some other eruptive disease which was im-
properly cured. Your disease is constitutional, and however
scientifically the issues, setons, and the hot irons may have been
applied, their action, of course, could only be local. You thought
if free suppuration could be brought about, your shoulder would
be cured and your whole body would remain fresh and sound.
But how miserably were all your hopes disappointed—how rapidly
did your disease extend itself. How foolish are such gross ideas
of disease, and what cruelty attends their application in the attempt to cure disease. But a ray of truth must soon penetrate
into this Egyptian darkness; the dawn of better things ap-
proaches.'

"No words can express my astonishment at the positiveness
with which Hahnemann asserted that I must have been afflicted
with some eruptive disease which had been suppressed, but not
cured. Five years before, while I was officiating as assistant
surgeon in the Berlin Hospital, I had pricked my finger with a
lancet with which I had just opened an abscess in the person
of a patient who was at the time affected with the itch. I
thought nothing about it at the time, but on the following day
a small pustule formed on the finger and occasioned an intense
itching and burning. I applied caustic to it, and a small sore
remained for several days, to which I applied an ointment.

"About this time I received an appointment as an army
surgeon and traveled by mail to join my division; but on the
second day of my journey the wound in my finger became in-

flamed, and not only my hand, but the whole arm, as far as the
shoulder joint, became so swollen and painful that I was obliged
to discontinue my journey.   Rest and warm fomentations soon
relieved me, but several months elapsed before I succeeded in
healing the wound on my finger.   Soon after it had entirely
healed, I was attacked with acute rheumatism on my left shoulder,
that lasted for several weeks, but I did not dream that there was
any connection between it and my former affection of the hand.
With the exception of transient twinges and darts of pain about
the shoulder joint, I had considered myself perfectly well up to
the time that I was thrown from my vehicle.

"Convinced that Hahnemann had formed a correct opinion
of my case, I commenced taking the powders he had sent me,
and indulged in the highest hopes of a speedy recovery.   But
my patience was destined to be sorely tried; I had received
nine powders, of which one was to be taken every fifth day.
During the course of the first week several new symptoms arose,
but no amelioration of my suffering took place.   Soon after,
however, a slight improvement commenced and gradually prog-
ressed until towards the end of the fifth week, when I could
lift my arm with comparative ease, and could bend and extend
my elbow; the swelling of the joint had disappeared entirely and
all pain had left me; and from that time to the present (eight
years) I have never had the slightest return of my former complaint.

"After so brilliant a confirmation in my own person of the
value of Homœopathy, I applied myself with zeal to the study
and practice of it, and have been abundantly rewarded in frequently witnessing the most rapid and permanent cures of the
most dangerous and deep-rooted diseases."

Dr. Dudgeon, in speaking of Aegidi, says:* "Dr. Aegidi, of
Freienwalde on the Oder, though an ardent disciple of Hahnemann, went very near to ruin the system.   He began to make
experiments along with Bœnninghausen, of Munster, in 1832,
with respect to the administration of mixtures of Homœopathic
medicines, and Hahnemann was so taken with the idea that he
proposed inserting a paragraph in the fifth edition of the
'Organon' (1833), recommending such mixtures.   He was,
however, induced not to do this by the protests of the Central

*Hom. World, Vol. xxv., p. 113.

Society of Homœopathic Physicians, and Aegidi, himself becoming convinced of the dangers of such a practice, joined in per- . suading Hahnemann to abandon his project. Lutze, of Coethen, as is well known, published an edition of the 'Organon' in 1865, with the suppressed paragraph recommending medicinal mixtures."

The matter will be more fully mentioned in the chapter on the rival Organons.

After Aegidi's conversion he became physician, through Hahnemann's recommendation, to the Princess Frederika of Prussia. Hahnemann mentions him thus to Stapf:* "Enclosed I return you Aegidi's letter. I felt it incumbent on me to communicate it to the Princess, and I did well, for the Prince has already found a vacant post of regimental surgeon in a hussar regiment, and has begged the General Staff Surgeon von Wiebel to appoint Dr. Aegidi to the post. This I have already announced to Dr. Aegidi. I am happy to have been able to procure this good fortune for the excellent Aegidi, and in addition to the pay attached to the post, he can freely and frankly practice Homœopathy in a populous town under the protection of the ruler of the land, and may even prepare his own medicines and dispense them unhindered to all his patients. If this is not a real piece of Homœopathic good luck, then I don't know what is. I have also received for him the patronage of the Princess, which he will retain, though at the same time I remain her chief physician." (Dated February 3, 1831.)

In a letter dated May 12, 1831, he continues:† "If you mention in the *Archiv* the good fortune that has befallen Cammerer, do not forget to set forth, as a pendant to this, that Dr. Aegidi has been summoned from Tilsit to assume the post of Homœopathic physician-in-ordinary to the Princess Frederika of Prussia in Dusseldorf, with a salary of six hundred thalers per annum, traveling expenses, free post, and a written permission from the authorities to enable him to prepare and dispense his Homœopathic medicines, and that he has already entered upon his duties. Aegidi has now gone to fetch his family.

"He writes me word on his way thither from Berlin that Bœnninghausen, during his absence, will attend to the Princess'

---

*Hom. World, Vol. xxv., p. 254.

† Hom. World, Vol. xxv., p. 258.

health, and that he has converted to Homœopathy an eminent
Allopathic physician in Alberfeld, Dr. Regenstecher—a very
remarkable story. He winds up with this true remark: 'The
greatest Allopathic thinkers, it they only possess hearts and
heads, will by and by become the most zealous adherents to the
truth.' "

CHAPTER XLVI.

REPORT OF CASES BY HAHNEMANN—ESSAY ON PHTHISIS—PITCH-
PLASTER RECOMMENDED BY HAHNEMANN.

The first part of the third edition of the "Materia Medica
Pura" was published by Arnold, of Leipsic, in 1830. A curious
omission is mentioned by Hahnemann in a letter to Stapf, dated
February 15, 1830:* "It is a pity that in the new third edition
of the first volume of the 'Materia Medica Pura,' which is now
being printed, I have forgotten to mention in the prefatory note
to Nux vomica that even in persons of mild disposition a want
of resolution (hesitancy) makes the patient a suitable subject for
the employment of Nux vomica if it is indicated by the other
symptoms. I beg you to communicate this to others."

The second volume of this edition appeared in 1833. In the
preface the reports of two cases treated by Hahnemann in 1815
may be found. These cases had appeared in the first edition of
1816, but much explanatory matter is printed in this edition that
did not appear in the two earlier editions. In this preface he
gives his reasons for his decided aversion to publishing cases.
Hahnemann never published but these two cases. He says:†

"The request of many of my half-converted friends to give
them specimens of my cures is difficult to do and of little use
when done. Each case of disease that is cured shows how that
particular case has been treated. The prosecution of the cure
rests always on the same principles which are already known.
In such case they cannot well be shown in the concrete, nor can
they, by the mention of a few cures, become more distinct than
by the exhibition of the principle."

* *Hom. World*, Vol. xxv., p. 115.
† "Reine Arzneimittellehre," 1833, Vol. ii.

These cases were published as a preface to the second volume of the "Materia Medica Pura," third edition, 1833. They may be found in Dudgeon's edition of the Materia Medica, also in the Lesser Writings and in the *British Journal of Homœopathy.** They were also published in Hempel's edition of the Materia Medica.

Two cases were communicated by Hahnemann, from his note-book, to Bœnninghausen, in 1843, and were by him published in Stapf's *Neues Archiv*, vol. 1, 1844. They also may be found in the Lesser Writings. With these exceptions, Hahnemann did not give to his followers any account of his cures. As an illustration of his reasons may be cited the story of the cure of Dr. Fleischmann, of Vienna.† He had for a long time been suffering with the rheumatic gout and had tried many remedies. In despair he wrote, stating his symptoms, to Hahnemann. Hahnemann returned for answer a package of powders with directions. Improvement followed, and soon after the receipt of more powders, complete cure. Fleischmann wrote asking what had cured him. Hahnemann replied: "No; read the 'Materia Medica Pura,' and you will find out. If the medicines were suited to any other case they would be found characterized there; if not, it is not necessary for you to know more."

Dr. Fleischmann did study the Materia Medica and, impressed with that great book, finally became one of the most distinguished Homœopathic physicians in Germany.

Only the first and second volumes of this third edition of the "Materia Medica Pura" were ever published. Hering once, in scoring some of the fault-finders, said:‡ "We never got the third edition of any of the other four volumes because the anti-Hahnemannians, by their boasting and their braying, brought it into such a discredit that the second edition of the 'Chronic Diseases,' 1837 to 1839, became like the most of the Materia Medica, waste paper."

Hering says that in the first and second editions of the Materia Medica Hahnemann kept his own symptoms separately from those of his fellow-provers. But in the 'Chronic diseases' and in the third edition of the Materia Medica he allowed his own

---

* *Hom. Times*, London, Vol. i., p. 9. *Brit. Jour. Hom.*, Vol. i., p. 178.
† *Brit. Jour. Hom.*, Vol. i., p. 178. Vol. xxxi., p. 386.
‡ *N. Am. Jour. Hom.*, Vol. xxii., p. 102.

symptoms with those of his provers, and such as were obtained from books of the old school, to be brought into one arrangement.

. The "Materia Medica Pura" was translated into Italian by Dr. Romani and published in Naples in 1825–28; in 1826 it was translated into Latin by Drs. Stapf, Gross and Von Brunnow, and published by Arnold at Leipsic. Dr. Bigel translated it into French in 1828; and Dr. Jourdan issued another French translation in 1834 at Paris; in 1877 Dr. Leon Simon again made a translation into the French. Dr. Hempel, in 1846, made a translation which was published by Radde, of New York. In England, in 1880, it was translated by Dr. Dudgeon and issued in London by the Homœopathic Publishing Co. in two volumes. In 1873 Dr. Dadea rendered it into Italian, publishing it in parts in Turin, Italy.*

In an article published in Stapf's *Archiv.*, Dr. Moritz Muller had already pointed out the existence of two factions in the ranks of the Homœopaths, whom he called the purists and the liberals. But the most cordial relations yet existed between them.

The Central Homœpathic Union, founded at Coethen in 1829, met on August 10, 1830, at Leipsic. Everything passed off pleasantly and there was no lack of friendly feeling on the part of all present.

Hahnemann sent by the hand of Stapf an essay upon the treatment of chronic local diseases and particularly of phthisis, accompanied by the following letter:†

"COETHEN, Aug. 5, 1830.

"Dear Friend and Colleague :

"Enclosed is the communication which I would like to make to the meeting of the 10th of August. Let the sheet be slowly read aloud, and if you are going to give a report of the Congress in the *Archiv*, and include in the report this sheet as having been read before the Congress, you are at liberty to do so.

"If after it has been read, and after other business, you should communicate to the meeting the enclosed anonymous article as though it was by some other person, you would do

* See Bibliography at end of this book.

† *Hom World*, Vol. xxv., p. 210. "Annals Brit. Hom. Society," Vol. iii., p. 254.

well. There are probably some among you who will understand
its meaning and act accordingly. But to be serious, the
Homœopathic physician must eventually resolve that he shall
no longer give sham medicines, but only the active remedy
when and where it is necessary. In this way he will evade all
so called prohibitory laws against dispensing our own medicines,
and no criminal law court will be able to say a word.

"Yours very truly,

"SAM. HAHNEMANN."

"Bear in mind that any one who undertakes the treatment of
a chronic disease must always have the Allopathic prescriptions
previously used before him; so that in his treatment he may
avoid giving those medicines which the Allopath has already
given before in large doses; e. g., *Sulphur*, when *Sulphur* has
previously been given to excess; *Natrium* when much Selters-
water has already been drunk, and *Murias magnesia*, when the
patient has already taken too many sea baths."

As this essay contains a recommendation for the use of an
external application, and as it has been quite freely mentioned
on this account, it is given here.

The whole essay was published in Stapf's *Archiv.** It is
not published in the "Lesser Writings."

After speaking of the psoric theory and of the relation between internal and skin diseases, he recommends the use of a
plaster under the following conditions:

"Now in order to diminish the morbid projection of the psoric
affection upon the smaller and nobler organs, and to procure for
this effort of the vital force to keep the internal dyscrasia in
abeyance a more extensive surface on which it may expend its
virulence, we must apply to the back something that shall at
once check the cutaneous transpiration and at the same time be
slightly irritant.

"This may be accomplished by means of a plaster composed
of six parts of Burgundy pitch to one of turpentine mixed together over a charcoal fire, spread upon soft chamois leather,
and applied warm by a uniform close pressure to the skin. It
usually happens that a fine rash accompanied by considerable
itching is soon produced thereby on the surface of the back.

Brit. Jour. Hom., Vol. xi., p. 34. Stapf's *Archiv fur die hom. Heilkunst*, Vol. ix., part 3, p. 72.

"If in the course of time the itching should become excessive, the plaster may be removed for a few days but then again applied and continued. When this artificially produced psoric affection of a large extent of skin is in full operation, we shall observe a great diminution in the morbid state of the small, noble organ, and the local disease will thereby be rendered more curable by the internal antipsoric medicine." This was sent to Stapf in the letter of August 5, 1830.

He afterwards, in the fifth edition of the "Organon," 1833, retracted this advice in the following words:* "Homœopathy is a perfectly simple system of medicine, remaining always fixed in its principles as in its practice, which, like the doctrine whereon it is based, if rightly apprehended, will be found to be so exclusive (and only in that way serviceable) that as the doctrine must be accepted in its purity so it must be purely practiced, and all backward straying to the pernicious routine of the old school (whose opposite it is as day to night) is totally inadmissible, otherwise it ceases to deserve the honorable name of Homœopathy.

"I am, therefore, sorry that I once gave the advice, savoring of Allopathy, to apply to the back in psoric diseases a resinous plaster to cause itching, and to employ the finest electrical sparks in paralytic affections. For as both these appliances have seldom proved of service, and have furnished the mongrel Homœopathists with an excuse for their Allopathic transgressions, I am grieved I should ever have proposed them, and *I hereby solemnly retract them*—for this reason also, that, since then, our Homœopathic system has advanced so near to perfection that they are *now no longer* required."

---

*Dudgeon's translation of the "Organon," London, 1893. Preface to 5th Edition.

CHAPTER XLVII.

RIGHT OF THE PHYSICIAN TO BE WELL PAID—"ALLOPATHY"— CENSORSHIP OF THE PRESS.

On the 19th of May, 1831, Hahnemann writes to Rummel as follows in regard to the right of the physician to speedy and generous payment for his services:*

"*Dear Friend and Colleague:* Your kind visit on the 10th of April must, on account of its shortness, be regarded more as a compliment to me than as a full visit. Ah, how much we might and would have said to one another had we not been disturbed by strangers and had you not been obliged to return so soon. In order to make up for this there is nothing for it but that I must have the pleasure of seeing you again soon, for a longer visit, and I will let you fix your own time, for any time will be agreeable to me.

"Doubtless such a title as that of medical counselor has now this advantage, that it enables the physician to obtain better fees; and it is particularly useful to the Homœopath, as it serves to humiliate the enemies of his art; but even were it not so, it is advisable for the plain Homœopathic doctor to attach so much value to his infinitely better mode of treatment that even without any title he should demand larger fees; at all events he should make patients affected with chronic diseases pay (beforehand) a monthly honorarium, and take from poorer persons at each consultation (and dispensing of medicines) some payment (were it only a few pence, he should take payment at each visit— *accipe dum dolet*).

"In this way only is it possible for the medical man never to go unremunerated, and it keeps him in good humor when he gets ready money for his trouble. Even these small fees, if they are paid at every visit and never neglected, accumulate unobservedly to a considerable sum, and the patient who pays every time scarcely misses them from his purse, because he only parts with them gradually; and when he is cured or leaves off before he

---

Brit. Jour. Hom., Vol. xi., p. 68.   *Allg. hom. Zeit.*, Vol. xliv., p. 19.

ought to, we are done with him; he has no claim on us nor we on him, and he takes leave of us, if not with contentment and gratitude, at all events without unwillingness, the sums he has gradually parted with are forgotten by him, and the doctor has what was justly his, and the money collects in the doctor's purse without any regret on the part of the patient.

"On the other hand, how disagreeable is it for the physician who has to send in his account at the last when the patient has quite forgotten his gradual recovery and the great trouble the doctor has had, *ut fieri solet*.

"Since I have commenced my successful mode of treatment, I have never sent in a demand after the treatment was over, but always done as above stated. Whenever the payment at each visit of the poorer classes, and. the monthly payments of the richer ones, shall be generally introduced, and patients not know any other method of payment, then every one will bring his money with him as a matter of course, or will send it every month by the post, and then business will go on without grumbling.

"If the doctor himself is a good economist he may, if he is a skillful Homœopathist, be able to earn and lay by something.

"When Gross was here last I put him up to this plan, and he cannot think enough of the good effect it has had on his practice during the last half year; he has become quite another man.

"I could convince you of all this much more effectually by word of mouth. He who does not know how to take payment for the assistance he dispenses is unable to form a proper estimation of himself and of his art.

"In his last letter written a few days ago Stapf denies having got from you the article, 'On Natural Labor.' This *varians lectio* no doubt is owing to the circumstance that he had for-. gotten to read it and seeks to excuse himself. I should like to have it again, for others wish to see it. If you are writing to him beg him to mention in the *Archiv* with especial commendation the exemption of the Brunswick Homœopathists from the necessity of prescribing from the apothecary's shop—as he told Gross of Juterbogk—in order to induce others to follow this example. Farewell till we meet again, which I trust will be soon, and believe me,   .

"Yours most sincerely,

"SAM. HAHNEMANN."

In the earlier part of 1831 Hahnemann wrote a pamphlet entitled: "Allopathy; A Word of Warning to all Sick Persons."* It was published in Leipsic, by Baumgartner. This was an arraignment of the prejudiced and irrational methods of the Allopathic school. The compiler of this has an original letter of Hahnemann's written regarding the publication of this pamphlet, and which plainly shows the jealous spirit with which Hahnemann was watched by the Allopathic authorities at that time. It is as follows:

"*Most Honorable, the Privy Counselor and Favorer!*"

" I accept the conditions offered me by your bookstore without reserve, and only beg for the last correction if I can possibly get it.

"But as this book reveals to the ordinary physicians extremely unwelcome truths, I take the liberty to ask your personal especial protection for it, that the printing may not be hindered by the Allopathic physicians. Therefore I put the MSS. in your hands first, and do not address it simply to your bookstore."

"Your obedient,

"SAM. HAHNEMANN."

"*Coethen, 19th June, 1831.*"

In this essay Hahnemann caricatures and turns the Allopathic system into ridicule. He says in regard to the plan of putting from two to a dozen medicines in one prescription: "According to that old, so-called art of medicine, so repugnant to common sense, there should be more than two, at least three, different things in an artistical prescription; apparently, in order that the physician who prescribes *lege artis* from the use of such prescriptions for diseases may be deprived of all chance of ascertaining which of the different ingredients was useful or which did harm, and may also never see or be taught by experience what particular effects each of the several ingredients of the prescription, each simple medicinal substance therein, produces on the human health in order to be able to employ it with certainty in diseases!"

"*This, therefore, is an art the professors of which have and wish to have no knowledge of all their tools !* Among the very meanest

---

* Lesser Writings, New York, p. 736.

of arts there does not exist one such as this. The medical art of the old school alone gives an unheard of example of the kind!

"And yet these gentlemen boast so loudly, notwithstanding their incredible irrationality, of being the only rational physicians.

"Of this stamp, dear sick people, are all the ordinary physicians. Of such alone do the medical authorities of all civilized lands consist. These alone sit on the medical judgment seat and condemn all that is better, which, whatever advantage it may be of to mankind, is opposed to their antiquated system!

"These alone are the superintendents and directors of the countless hospitals and infirmaries filled with hundreds and thousands of patients pining in vain for health! Of such alone are the body physicians of princes and ministers of state! Of such only are the ordinary professors of medicine in all universities!

"With such routine practitioners alone, of great and small degree, do our towns swarm; from the celebrities who use up two pairs of horses daily in swift-rolling gilded chariots in order to pay visits of a couple of minutes' duration to sixty, eighty or more patients down to the crowd of low practitioners who, in worn out clothes, must exert their legs to pester their patients with frequent visits and numerous prescriptions."

The whole essay is a rare example of delightful satire.

At this time there was a censorship of the press, and the Allopathic physicians used every means to prevent the publication of Homœopathic literature. Hahnemann was, as may be seen by the above letter, obliged to use great caution in printing his books and pamphlets.

As a sample of this unfair and bigoted censorship it may be stated that in 1831 an Allopathic physician in Coethen published in the *Cothener Zeitung*, the village paper, a bitter attack upon Hahnemann and his treatment of the cholera. When Hahnemann, desiring to respond, sent an article to the same paper it was refused because the censor of the press was a personal friend of the Allopathic doctor. Hahnemann then published his defence in Magdeburg.

Hahnemann sent his treatment of cholera to the *Preussische Staats Zeitung*, but the Berlin censor would not permit it to be inserted. Dr. Kiesselbach, of Hanau, wished an account of the

Homœopathic treatment of croup to be published in a Kassel paper, but this was vetoed by the censor.   In Raab, in Hungary, while the cholera was raging, certain of the people who had heard of the Homœopathic success in the disease wished to insert a notice in the paper asking Homœopathic physicians to go there, but it was not permitted.*   Every effort possible was made to keep the facts of Homœopathy from the people.

CHAPTER XLVIII.

CHOLERA IN 1831–32—HAHNEMANN'S OPINION OF BLEEDING—HOMŒOPATHIC TREATMENT OF CHOLERA.

In 1831 the cholera appeared in Russia, coming over the border the latter part of July.   Of course the medical profession were busy inventing new remedies for the scourge.   Among those recommended were *Aurum muriaticum*, oxygen gas, charcoal, *Quinine*.   Ameke says :†   Then there were the absorbents "to absorb the poison out of the primæ viæ;" "the absorbents are coming into favor."   People read with terror that "in the corpses of those who died of cholera vessels gorged with blood were to be found in the right ventricle of the heart and the vena cava, also in the lungs, liver, etc."   We say they read "with terror," for where blood was thus found congested in the corpses, on scientific principles the patients must be bled during life.   But "Science" could surely hardly go as far as to bleed in cases of cholera.

Doubt did not last long on this point, for soon after the notices from Russia appeared we read: "A vein is at once and without delay to be opened and as much blood taken from the patient as seems suitable to his condition."   This remedy was useful in nearly all cases.   *Calomel* and *Opium* were to be given.   In another article blood-letting, leeches, cupping, mustard plasters were recommended.   Emetics were mentioned.   One Dr. Meyer suggested that as *Belladonna* was prophylactic for scarlet fever it might also be for cholera.

Among other articles recommended were prohibition from

---

* Ameke's "History of Homœopathy," p. 251.
† Ameke's "History of Homœopathy," p. 235.

anything to drink; the use of *Zinc, Bismuth, Musk* with *Camphor, Ipecacuanha, Valerian, Sal volatile, Hartshorn, Natron carbon, Menth., Piperit., Arnica, Colombo, Cascarilla* with *Naphtha*, and *Opium, Tinct. Aromatica, Calam., Arom.*, cold douches, leeches, emetics and *Cinchona*.

Then followed a pamphlet war upon the various pathological fancies advocated by the professors and the doctors. More than three hundred pamphlets and some books were written upon the subject, and in the most of them the free, continued and persistent practice of venesection was advocated. It was bleed, bleed, open a vein freely; bleed, leech, ad nauseam. This was a period of very scientific insanity. In the meantime the poor victims persisted in dying.

One of the Leipsic Faculty of Medicine, a Dr. Moritz Hasper, in *Hufeland's Journal* for September, 1831, said that small bleedings were of no use, that "a large opening must be made in a vein in order that the blood may flow out in a free stream, if the patient is to be freely relieved." "Bleed freely" is repeated at least ten times in this truly scientific pamphlet. Leeches, bleeding, even the application of a red hot iron to the stomach is recommended.*

As early as the year 1784, Hahnemann in the "Guide to the Cure of Old Sores," denounced blood-letting. In the translation of Cullen in 1790, he attacks the habit of bleeding.

Early in 1792, the Emperor Leopold of Austria, who had reigned since 1790, and who by his love for peace had greatly endeared himself to his subjects, unexpectedly died. Hahnemann at that time lived in Gotha, where the newspaper *Der Anzeiger* was published. The editor, Dr. Becker, as has been stated, was an acquaintance of Hahnemann. In this paper, Nos. 137, 138, (1792,) appeared an account of the post mortem upon the Emperor, in which it was stated that a "semi-purulent exudation of about a pound weight was found in the left pleura.

In the *Anzeiger* for March 31, 1792, Hahnemann thus criticises the treatment of this great man. He says: "The report states 'his physician, Lagusius, observed high fever and swelling of the abdomen early on February 28,' he combatted the malady by venesection, and as this produced no amelioration, three more venesections were performed without relief. Science

---

*Ameke's "History of Homœopathy," p. 239.

must ask why a second venesection was ordered when the first had produced no amelioration? How could he order a third, and, good heavens, how a fourth! when there had been no amelioration after the preceding ones? How could he tap the vital fluid four times in twenty-four hours, always without relief, from a debilitated man who had been worn out by anxiety of mind and long-continued diarrhœa? Science is aghast!''*

Hahnemann continues: "The clinical record of the physician in ordinary, Lagusius, says: 'The monarch was on the 28th of February attacked with rheumatic fever (what symptoms of a rheumatic character had he?) and a chest affection (which of the numerous chest affections, very few of which are able to stand bleeding; let us note that he does not say it was pleurisy, which he would have done to excuse the copious venesections if he had been convinced that it was this affection), and we immediately tried to mitigate the violence of the malady by bleeding and other needful remedies (Germany, Europe, has a right to ask, which?).

"On the 29th the fever increased (after the bleeding! and yet), three more venesections were effected, whereupon some (other reports say distinctly *no*) improvement followed, but the ensuing night was very restless and weakened the monarch (just think! it was the night and not the four bleedings which so weakened the monarch, and Herr Lagusius was able to assert this positively), who on the 1st of March began to vomit with violent retching and threw up all he took (nevertheless his doctors left him so that no one was present at his death, and indeed after this one of them pronounced him out of danger). At 3:30 in the afternoon he expired, while vomiting, in presence of the empress."

This violent attack resulted in a discussion upon the case among the German physicians, in which the course of Hahnemann was very generally condemned.

After this time Hahnemann protested in his writings against bloodletting, which practice was still continued. He was even denounced as a murderer because he denied his patients the "benefits" of bleeding.

His attitude also lost him the friendship of several of his professional friends. In 1809 he says:† "The principal manœuvre of

---

* Ameke's "History of Homœopathy," p. 88.
† "Lesser Writings," New York, p. 537.

the humoral school consisted in the evacuation of bad blood (bleeding mania) and in the expulsion of the impure fluids by the mouth and anus. How? Did they pretend to let out the impure blood only? What magician's wand could separate, as through a sieve, the depraved from the good blood within the blood vessels, so that only the bad could be drawn off and the good remain? What head is so rudely organized as to believe that they could effect this? Sufficient for them that streams of blood were spilt—of that vital fluid for which even Moses showed so much respect, and that justly. The more refined humoralists, in addition to the impurities in the blood, alleged, besides, the existence of a pretended, almost universal, plethora, as an excuse for their frightful, merciless bloodlettings; they also gave out that these acted derivatively, depressed the tone, and ascribed many other subtle scientific effects to them.''

All his life he continued the bitter enemy to bleeding, and whatever may be presented to the contrary, it is most certainly due to his influence that bleeding is abolished in the ranks of the medical profession.

Of course Hahnemann opposed this method of bloodletting in the cholera.

The Homœopathic physicians began to treat this terrible cholera according to the principles of their system. Dr. Petersen, of Pensa, treated from July 9th to 30th 68 cases, of whom 14 died. He used *Ipecac* 20th, *Chamomilla* and *Arsenicum* 30th dilution. Dr. Arnold, of Russia, was also successful. Dr. Schubert, of Leipsic, in 1830 recommended *Veratrum, Ipecac, Arsenic, Chamomilla.* Dr. Preu, of Nuremberg, spoke of *Arsenic* and *Veratrum.*

Dr. Bakody, a Homœopathist of Raab, in Hungary, was much more successful than the Allopaths. Of 1501 patients treated Allopathically 640 died. Dr. Bakody treated 154 cases of real cholera and lost but six cases.*

The inhabitants wished to appeal through the papers for more Homœopathic physicians. The Protomedicus of Hungary, Dr. Lenhoscek, did not think this appeal suitable for publication, and, as censor, refused to permit its publication in the newspapers! After the epidemic was over Bakody told a colleague, Dr. Ant. Schmit, of the treatment and its results, and he, against

---

* Ameke, p. 249. *Brit. Jour. Hom.,* Vol. i., p. 58.

Dr. Bakody's wish, sent an article to the *Allgemeine Anzeiger* on the subject. The county physicus, Dr. Joseph v. Balogh, and the town physicus, Dr. Ant. Karpff, replied, stating in words of most insolent denunciation that Dr. Bakody basely lied, calling him all sorts of pretty names. Bakody produced in answer 112 legally attested certificates relating to the 154 cholera patients he had treated, of whom but six died. And his witnesses were from the most reliable and influential citizens of the town.*

Dr. Seider, in Russia, treated 109 Homœopathically and lost but twenty-three. Of ninety-three treated Allopathically, sixty-nine died. The percentage in Vienna of deaths was: Allopathic, thirty-one per cent.; Homœopathic, only eight.†

Letters and reports came from every quarter to Coethen with the glad message: "Homœopathy has triumphed over the cholera." Thomas Count Nadasdy presented a full report (17th September, 1831) from Daka, in Hungary, beginning with these words: "When the cholera broke out in Daka no medical aid could be obtained from Papa, on account of the prevalence of cholera at that place; being unwilling to see my subjects die without making an effort to save them I tried the experiment of curing the disease with spirits of camphor, recommended by Dr. Hahnemann, and by the blessing of Providence my efforts were crowned with perfect success. Of 161 cholera patients at Daka, to whom spirits of camphor were administered, only fourteen died; namely, eight who solicited assistance in the last stage of the disease, and seven who, by improper living after three or four relapses, could not be saved. This statement can be proved by more than seventy sworn witnesses."‡

In Asterwettingen, near Magdeburg, out of 800 inhabitants eighty were attacked. Without a physician, they treated each other with *Camphor* and cold water, according to Hahnemann's instructions, and sixty of the patients recovered.

There was no propounding of ridiculous scientific (?) pathology, no recommending of marvellous compounds on the part of the Homœopaths.

Independently the one of the other, judging by the symptoms of the disease and their knowledge of the action of medicines

* Ameke, p. 256.
† *Brit. Jour. Hom.*, Vol. i., p. 58.
‡ Fischer. Trans., "Biographisches Denkmal," p. 56.

upon the well, the four or five medicines each thought about and used were the same. The principle that Hahnemann taught was proven and found not wanting. His followers, knowing the drugs that would produce similar symptoms to those of the cholera, applied those drugs when the cholera came with success. It was not guesswork; just the application of a law! *Arsenic, Veratrum, Ipecac, Camphor, Cuprum*—the same remedies that have since also proven themselves in other cholera epidemics when given in accord with this law.

CHAPTER XLIX.

HAHNEMANN'S ADVICE FOR TREATMENT OF CHOLERA.

The cholera advent seemed to restore Hahnemann to the freshness and vigor of life of a young man. It was with wonderful acuteness that he described the symptoms and phenomena of this disease. His marvellous knowledge of the effects of drugs on the human body enabled him to determine according to the Homœopathic principle those that would be of service in this terrible scourge.

This is the more remarkable, as at this time he had never had an opportunity of personally examining any actual cases.

In this connection the following story well illustrates this knowledge of his materia medica:[*] "A gentleman consulted him about one of his family, suffering from very severe illness, with certain very marked symptoms. Hahnemann heard him to the end; 'the patient is suffering from a medicinal disease,' and he named the drug. The gentleman was certain that the patient was not so suffering, and had made no use of that drug. But Hahnemann was right, as was proved upon inquiry."

Hahnemann soon began to take an active part in advising his disciples. He published articles in the papers, and issued pamphlets. The following letter, written to Dr. Stapf, December 27, 1830, well shows his feelings upon the Allopathic treatment of the epidemic. He says:[†]

---

[*] *Hom. Times*, London, Vol. ii., p. 335.

[†] *Hom. World*, Vol. xxv., p. 212. "Annals Brit. Hom. Society," Vol. iii., p. 254.

"It certainly looks ill that the many indubitable reports in the papers about the marvelous curative powers of Homœopathy (and of *Veratrum*) in cholera have not yet reached the ears of Nicholas in particular, but it can hardly be doubted that they will eventually do so. The great, infinitely good Spirit who cares for the fate of every mite will also with mighty hand silently bring about the establishment of that great affair which is so intimately connected with the well being of sick mankind hitherto so neglected, though it may not be perceived how all is ordained.

"Traditional medicine and surgery is a much too shamefully cruel business. Just read, for example, how Hasper, Kreuzing of Leipsic's nephew, in the face of the Homœopathists, teaches how to mistreat cholera and make it fatal with bloodletting to 30 ounces, quantities of leeches, and *Calomel* to the extent of three or four drachms, on a false theory and after the example, as he says, of *the best physicians in the world—the English*. Is that not enough to rouse the anger of the Homœopathists? I would that Attomyr were the man to raise his voice against the Allopathic murderers, for the reviews of Allopathic pamphlets as they have hitherto appeared in your *Archiv*, written in a mild, deferential, gentle manner, do not appear to me calculated to stir up the deaf, infamous rogues. The cautious, timid comments of our Homœopathic reviewers are of no use; they have no more effect on them than so many flea bites. Can anything worse befall us than that we should be deprived of all our civil and natural rights if we were to proclaim aloud their injustice, give them literary blows, and make war to the knife on the murderous gang?

"They must be taught to fear our assaults, which should give the death blow to their false art. They must be made to tremble before us, otherwise we shall make no way and our immense superiority will never be acknowledged; we shall never gain any honor, nor induce the public to regard them with well-merited horror and disgust.

"I entreat our fellow-workers to bestir themselves and do their utmost to demonstrate the superiority of our divine art by stout resistance and attack, and to expose the miserable nakedness of these destroyers of mankind. If I were thirty years younger I would undertake to do this unaided, and none would escape my death-dealing blows; they would no longer write in their wretched journals; they would be reduced to silence. But now I may fairly expect that I might relinquish this duty to my vigorous disciples. But I see that I am mistaken. But now I am near the completion of my seventy-sixth year, I can no longer wield the controversial club; I have, at least I think I have, with great labor built up my art on irrefragable pillars.

"But to drive the rascally, conceited rogues out of the temple of Æsculapius with scorpion-whips—nothing else will do—is a task which ought not to be imposed on me.

"Would to God some man would arise among us with head, heart and mighty arm who would devote his life to this second urgently needful work as I have mine to the first, the foundation of Homœopathy!"

Again, writing to Stapf, in a letter dated August 5, 1831, Hahnemann says:* "Preu of Nurnberg pleases me much. I thank you for sending me his essay.† As long as the Allopaths represented to us (without giving any trustworthy picture of the disease) that cholera is a compound of vomiting and purging, so long we poor Homœopaths at a distance had to regard *Veratrum* and *Arsenic* as the specific remedies for it. But the faithful description by a Homœopath has taught us that its character is quite different. It is a tonic, spasmodic diathesis of all the systems, spheres and tissues of the organism, which only towards the end of life passes into convulsions and paralysis, and then there follows watery vomiting and diarrhœa, and that only in some cases; nothing of the sort is to be seen in most cases, but only rapid death.

"Such being the case neither *Veratrum* nor *Arsenic* can be of much use. Schreter writes me from Lemberg, where he arrived on the 15th of July, that he was able to do some, but not much, good with *Veratrum*, and when it did no good then *Camphor* was successful (when he wrote he had just received my essay on *Camphor*).

"Two days ago I was told by an eye witness from Prague that when the cholera raged in Odessa, some months since,

---

* *Hom. World*, Vol. xxv., p. 417; "Annals Brit. Hom. Society," Vol. iii., p. 71.

†"What Have We to Fear From Cholera Morbus?" He recommends Arsenic in this.

and the doctors were unable to do anything serviceable, they only rubbed the patients with *Camphor*, which restored them to health; he himself had assisted to rub nine of the cases, and all the nine recovered.   Do we need any further testimony.

"My pamphlet,* which you are familiar with, has been refused insertion in the public papers by the medical authorities of Vienna and Berlin.   In Berlin a bookseller is about to print it with Stuber's preface.   I have sent to Stuber (as he has written a great deal about the malicious comments upon the large doses of *Camphor*) the enclosed explanation to be added to his preface, which I beg you to read aloud at the meeting on the tenth of August in place of my usual communication.

"I have been asked by a Leipsic publisher for an enlargement of this essay.†   It will appear in a few days, published by Gluck.   I did it not long ago.   The price he will sell it at will be a groschen.   I have put in it everything useful for the public to know, but I have left out the scientific matter.

The pamphlet which Hahnemann mentions in the above letter was entitled "Cure and Prevention of the Asiatic Cholera."   It was originally published in the *Archiv der hom. Heilkunst*, vol. xi., part 1, page 122.   It was dated "Coethen, Sept. 10, 1831," and is signed "Dr. Samuel Hahnemann, Hofrath."   It may also be found translated in the Lesser Writings.

In this he recommends *Camphor* as the principal remedy, but says it must be used in the first stage and as a household remedy before there is time to summon a physician and while awaiting his arrival.   He says: "In the first stage, accordingly, the patient must get as often as possible (at least every five minutes) a drop of *Camphor* (made with one ounce of *Camphor* to twelve of alcohol) on a lump of sugar or in a spoonful of water.   Some spirit of *Camphor* must be taken in the hollow of the hand and rubbed into the skin of the arms, legs and chest of the patient; . he must also get a clyster of half a pint of warm water mingled with two full teaspoonfuls of spirit of *Camphor*, and from time to time some *Camphor* may be allowed to evaporate on a hot iron so that if the mouth should be closed by trismus, and he can swallow nothing, he may draw in enough of *Camphor* vapor with the breath."

---

* "Cure and Prevention of Asiatic Cholera."

† "Appeal to Thinking Philanthropists Respecting the Mode of Propagation of Asiatic Cholera."   See "Lesser Writings."

It will be seen that he gives the *Camphor* in quite large doses, and because he was criticised for it he wrote an explanation, of which he speaks in the previous letter as there enclosing to Stapf. Stapf published this in the *Archiv*, vol. xi., part 1, p. 100. Hahnemann says that the reason he gave *Camphor* in large doses *is that the effect* to be produced is an Allopathic and not a Homœopathic one. A palliative action must be at once produced or the patient will die before the Homœopathic medicine has time to act.

Dr. Bœnninghausen, in September, 1831, published at Munster this article in a small pamphlet, and with it another letter addressed to him by Hahnemann and dated September 18, 1831. He also makes some original suggestions. This is really another edition of the Hahnemann pamphlet. He says in the preface:

"The account given in No. 210 of the Westphalian *Mercury* about the remedy discovered by Dr. Hahnemann for Asiatic Cholera, was copied from No. 235 of the Prussian *States Gazette*, because I had not at hand then the Gotha *German General Advertiser*, which, under date of 20th August, contains the ungarbled essay of this indefatigable investigator.

"I have just received an original essay of the date of September 10, and, therefore, I presume still more complete, and accompanying it was a letter from the Hofrath himself. Said letter was dated September 18th, and it contained much additional valuable information respecting this frightful disease. So I deem it my duty to publish both of them.

"C. v. BŒNNINGHAUSEN."

"*Munster, Sept. 23, 1831.*"

Hahnemann's article was also published in the form of a tract and freely distributed in Vienna, Hungary, Berlin, Magdeburg, and other places where the cholera was active.

Hahnemann in a letter addressed to Dr. Schreter in Lemburg, thus speaks of the cholera:*

"COETHEN, 19TH DEC., 1831.

"*Dear Colleague:*

"I have had no opportunity of treating fully developed cholera myself, but have often, by advice and directions, been enabled

---

Brit. Jour. Hom., Vol. vi., p. 413; also *Hom. Times*, London, Vol. i., p. 84; Kirby's *Am. Jour. Hom.*, Vol. iii., p. 87; Stapf's *Archiv*, 1848, Vol. iii., part 3.

to stifle it in the bud. At least 30,000 copies of my directions have been circulated among the inhabitants of Vienna, Hungary, Berlin and Magdeburg, and many thousands have been saved, when each, the instant he was attacked with cholera, had administered to him by his friend a drop of spirit of *Camphor* every five minutes, and was well washed over head, neck and chest with a solution of *Camphor* (1 to 12) by means of the hand, and in less than an hour he was quite well, without secondary sufferings, as if nothing had happened to him.

" By this means as I said, according to the accounts I have received, many thousands have been saved in secret without the knowledge of a physician or of the neighbors in the house. Now, as by my experience, *Camphor* vapor is the only trustworthy means of annihilating the probable animated miasma of cholera. it is easy to understand how the cholera was so rapidly extinguished by its means in Vienna, Berlin and Magdeburg. This extinction of cholera in the first quarter of an hour by *Camphor* is available only in the acute attacks of cholera, and as I have said only in the first hour in which the aid of a physician cannot be obtained, and the disease is still in its stage of tonic cramp; when, however, this, as is soon the case, passes into the stage of relaxation and of clonic cramps, then the Homœopathic physician can still do good, though with difficulty enough, with *Veratrum*, *Cuprum*, etc.

" Much more troublesome are those (not acute) gradual diseases which arise from cholerine (as Father Veith, in Vienna, calls these insidious cases), when the inhabitants of a town, owing to the widely diffused and hence more diluted miasmatic vapor (the focus of which are the dead bodies of those who die under Allopathic treatment), get only a few symptoms of the cholera, which pass off in the case of robust individuals, but in weak persons turn gradually into vomiting, but principally into painless but very debilitating diarrhœas, with much flatulence, and which (if not well treated) end in tetanic convulsions, delirium, and death. In these insidiously occurring affections the employment of *Camphor* is inadmissible; it would only hasten the patient's death. *Phosphoric acid*, as Father Veith found, has proved specific in these colloquative diarrhœas accompanied with rumbling in the bowels, which exhaust the vital powers; and I, too, have found it the same in patients affected in this way in Magdeburg.

"When the cholera actually attacks, if those seized by it should be immediately treated by their friends with *Camphor* spirit, there would then be no fully developed cholera; or such cases would at least be much more rare, and still more rare fatal cases; and hence also no spreading of the miasmatic vapor through the town, consequently also no cholerine, nor any of that lingering kind of cholera, which I consider the most dangerous of all.

"As regards the controversy upon the contagiousness of cholera, I beg you will read at your leisure my little pamphlet, entitled: 'Appeal to Philanthropists Respecting the Mode in Which Cholera is Infectious, With an Appendix by Anthony Schmit,' published by Charles Berger; and thereafter Schnitzer's 'Cholera Contagiosa,' Breslau." * * *

In a letter to Stapf, September 23, 1831, he says:* "I have already sent Schweikert two different articles on the treatment of cholera; he has not answered me, and I don't know if they have been printed. I have also offered him the situation, and he has not given me any answer upon that subject. Has the man whom I considered my friend anything against me?

"Many thanks to your Provincial Counselor for having inserted my paper in the local newspaper, and still more thanks to you for having got him to print and distribute separate impressions of it. Schmit has had some thousand copies of it made in writing (it is not allowed to be printed in Austria because I am the author) and widely circulated. The indefatigable man! If Attomyr should refuse the appointment to England I will offer it to Schmit.

"I am afraid lest our letters containing medicine should be cut through and fumigated, and thereby spoiled. We might employ thin glass tubes, such as you once sent me with *Iodine*, filled with the larger sort of globule, so that they lie one above the other, and not side by side.

"The glass *tubes* might be inserted into a quill corked up and placed at the side of the letter, with directions to take the topmost globule first, and so on. By this plan the globules would escape the fumigation.   *   *   *   *

"Our Rummel has also issued a paper of directions for the

---

* *Hom. World*, Vol. xxv., p. 419. "Annals Brit. Hom. Med. Society," Vol. ii., p. 356.

treatment of cholera, in which he recommends *Cuprum* and *Camphor*. It is only Homœopaths that can act thus. The remedies recommended by the blind Allopaths, everyone advising a different medicine, are almost uncountable. One of the last is a stomach plaster, which is much bepuffed and distributed by the Duke of Bernburg. A just Providence has sent cholera to serve as a sort of pillory for the Allopaths, in which the uncertain and pitiful character of their treatment is exposed; then all the world can see their nakedness.   *   *   *

"What do you say to this, that Schmit assures me of, namely, that Metternich has taken globules of *Cuprum* as a prophylactic, and that his wife is partial to Homœopathy? And here is another piece of important intelligence communicated to me by another friend from Prague. Father Veith, of Vienna (a practical friend of Homœopathy), when the cholera broke out in Vienna cured several persons who were suffering from cholera with *Camphor* according to my directions (he was previously doctor of medicine and director of the Veterinary College in Vienna). He is preaching in the Cathedral of St. Stephen, and he preached a sermon before the Imperial Court in this church on 'The Cholera in the Light of Providence,' in which he says (the sermon is now printed): 'It is a remarkable provision of Providence that in the same part of the earth which was the birthplace of cholera its most powerful remedy (*Camphor*) is also to be found.' Everyone, says my correspondent, was delighted and in ecstasies at this.

"Dr. Schmidt, of Konigsberg, writes that though he had had no opportunities of seeing and treating cases of cholera he had to treat a boy who had been suffering for twenty-four hours from cholera and was extremely ill with vomiting and purging, and yet he cured him with *Camphor*, given according to my method (spirits of *Camphor* diluted with hot water). First the diarrhœa and finally the vomiting yielded. The people there, he says, firmly believe (and rightly too, alas!) that the doctors administer poisons. Do you think the anecdote about Father Veith suitable for the *Allg. Anz. d. Deutschen?*

"I enclose a cutting from the *Journal des Debats* which will do for the *Archiv* or Schweikert's periodical, or the *Allg. Anz. d. Deutschen*. When you are done with it, please return it to me. What about the *Edinburgh Review?*

"Yours truly,

"SAM. HAHNEMANN."

Dudgeon, in a note to this long letter, says: "Doubtless Hahnemann had just heard of the article on his system that was published in the *Edinburgh Review* of January, 1830."

CHAPTER L.

DR. QUIN'S ATTACK OF CHOLERA—LEGAL HINDRANCES TO HOMŒOPATHY.

This same year of 1831 Dr. F. F. Quin, who had first introduced Homœopathy into England, was in Moravia, where he had gone to study the cholera. He, with Dr. Gerstel and two surgeons, had charge of all the cholera cases in the town of Tischnowitz and the neighboring villages. Quin wrote to Hahnemann that while he was sitting at dinner he had been attacked with cholera without warning, and that he had been relieved by *Camphor*. To which Hahnemann replied as follows:

"I am much obliged to you for the details of your researches upon the nature of cholera and of the appropriate Homœopathic treatment. You are right in the opinion you express, and it is one borne out by my own observations, that the worst form of cholera is presented by cases of degenerated cholerine. I have already heard from Dr. Gerstel of your attack of the epidemic, and your cure by *Camphor*. I congratulate you on your restoration, and I render thanks to Almighty God for having preserved you to give aid to the unfortunate victims who so sadly require your assistance. Your success in the treatment of cholera is more remarkable from your ignorance of the Moravian language.

"May the gracious God conduct you safely to your own home, and bless your efforts to instruct your countrymen in the art of healing in conformity with the laws of nature.

"Your sincere and affectionate friend,

"SAMUEL HAHNEMANN.

"*Coethen, 4th February, 1831.*"

So great was the success in Tischnowitz that the Chief Magistrate sent to Dr. Quin this address:*

"At the time of Dr. Quin's arrival here for the purpose of

* "History and Heroes of the Art of Medicine," J. Rutherford Russell, London, 1861, p. 426.

observing the epidemic of cholera it had reached its greatest malignancy in the villages that surround the town and castle; this was shown, not only by the numbers who fell ill, but by the shortness of the interval between the commencement of the attack and its fatal termination—often only a few hours. It happened that at the time Dr. Gerstel and surgeons Hanush and Linhart were all three confined to bed by illness.

"Although you yourself, upon your arrival, were attacked with cholera, you nevertheless, during your convalescence, with the most humane zeal, undertook the treatment of those ill with cholera during the period when Dr. Gerstel was obliged to keep his bed, and this you did with such success that not one patient died.*

" The authorities feel themselves under the obligation to make their respectful acknowledgments to you for the assistance you afforded, with such generous humanity, to the inhabitants of this district.

" ERNST DIEBLE, *Chief Magistrate.*

"*Tischnowitz, November 30, 1831.*"

M. Dieble also sent a table with the above letter as follows: Out of 6.671 inhabitants 680 had the cholera ; of these 331 were under Allopathic treatment and 102 of them died ; 278 were treated Homœopathically and only 27 of them died ; of 71 treated with *Camphor* alone only 11 died.

In a letter to Dr. Gerstel, dated December 18, 1831, Hahnemann says:† "You have also found *Phosphorus* useful in the stage of collapse of the cholera and half infection (cholerine), as was first pointed out by Father Veith in Vienna; yet he soon found reason to prefer *Phosphoric acid* (even by frequently smelling of the drug) in those weakening diarrhœas, with much rumbling in the bowels, that occur in the cholerine (a disease brought on by semi-infections, caused by the diluted miasm in the air, in the greater part of the inhabitants of infected towns), so that in such cases I would give the *Phosphoric acid* the preference over *Phosphorus.* Mr. Fischer's experience and testing of *Carbo vegetab.* in the appropriate severe cases is very valuable."

The Rev. Father Veith, the doctor-priest, incumbent of the Cathedral of St. Stephen in Vienna and chaplain to the court,

---

† Three died the day after the report was signed.

†*Brit. Jour. Hom.,* Vol. xv., p. 335.

was very successful while acting as a physician in this cholera
epidemic. He was very enthusiastic in the results of the
Homœopathic medication. He says: "It is a method more
speedy than any I have previously tried." Dudgeon says that
out of 125 patients treated Homœopathically, he lost but three.*

The story of the first Homœopathic treatment of cholera, in
the epidemic of 1831 is carefully and exhaustively told in
"Homœopathic Treatment and Prevention of Asiatic Cholera,"
by R. E. Dudgeon, M.D., London, 1847.

Rapou, in speaking of this epoch of cholera, says:† This
epidemic of cholera, which was for Homœopathy so great a
triumph, also contributed to modify certain assertions of
Hahnemann in regard to the administration and repetition of
remedies.

At this time Hahnemann addressed a letter dated November
7, 1831, through the columns of the *Allgemeine Anzeiger*, to the
King Frederick William of Prussia, begging him in the name of
humanity to test his system in this fatal disease.

He was unsuccessful. It was during this same year of 1831
that the Prussian Government forbade the Homœopaths
dispensing their own medicines This prohibition lasted for
twelve years; then an examination of candidates was ordered,
with the curious proviso that any one who had previously dispensed Homœopathic medicines should forever lose the privilege
of being examined for the right of dispensing.

The right to dispense was the great drawback to the practice
of the new Homœopathy in all Germany at this time; although
a lawyer, one C. A. Tittmann, had in 1829 published a book
upon the police laws of the state in which he defended the right
of the Homœopath to dispense his own medicines.‡

In Russia, into which Homœopathy had been introduced by
Dr. Adam in 1823, a trial of the new system was made, in a
military hospital, in 1829. In 1831, although the Emperor
Nicholas was said to be favorable to Homœopathy and even had
a case of Homœopathic medicines, the opposition was very
great. In the cholera trials Hermann wrote that he had to give

---

* Albrecht's "Leben und Wirken." *Brit. Jour. Hom.*, Vol. i., p. 59;
Vol. vi., p. 414.

† "Histoire de la doctrine Homœopathique," Vol. ii., p. 307.

‡ "Die Homœopathie in staatspolizeirechtl Hinsicht." Meissen. 1829.

up the treatment of cholera patients in the hospital, as only the dying were sent to him by the Allopathic authorities.

About this time laws were enacted as follows: The Central pharmacies in St. Petersburg and Moscow could supply other pharmacies and physicians with Homœopathic medicines, but only in preparations not lower than the first dilution or trituration. Physicians could only prescribe by written prescription except in urgent cases or when no pharmacy existed in the place; in the latter case the physician was compelled to write on a printed blank, with a special stamp, the date, name of remedy given, its dose, the name and social position of the patient, the chief symptoms of the disease, and the name of the physician. When the doctor gave from his own case he must duplicate the package; one being for the patient's use, the other being sealed and endorsed by the physician with the name of the patient, date, etc., and the doctor's signature. In case the patient died this package, kept with the seal unbroken, enabled the authorities to determine if death was the result of the medicines.

Dr. J. Rutherford Russell says of this epoch, that the adherents of Hahnemann's system, in order to avoid the prohibition against compounding medicines acted as follows: "When they gave advice to the patients who sought their aid they made a free gift of the medicine. Even this, however, would not do, for on the 13th of June, 1832, an order to the following effect was published at Darmstadt: 'There is no permission granted to the Homœopathic physicians to dispense their own medicines. The law can make no difference between Homœopathic and other physicians; both must alike prescribe out of the apothecaries' shop.' Dr. Weber, physician to the Prince of Solms-Lich, was fined thirty. dollars for administering medicine gratuitously to his patients."*

The matter was afterwards brought before the Baden Landtag and it was granted to physicians to dispense their drugs gratuitously.

When Dr. Quin returned to England, in 1832, he attracted the notice of the College of Physicians, who ordered him to appear for examination and licensure; he took no notice of the order and a second letter was sent to him. To this he answered that he meant no disrespect by not answering the first letter and ac-

---

*"History and Heroes of Medicine," p. 440.

knowledged both epistles, saying nothing about any examination. This seemed to satisfy that body, for no further attempt was made to examine or license him.

In 1829 Dr. Trinks, of Dresden, was subjected to a criminal process on account of the death of a patient, after being under his treatment for four days with the typhoid fever. He was condemned to pay one-third of the costs. The same year an action was brought against Trinks, Wolf, Lehmann and Helwig for not bleeding a patient who had inflammation of the lungs and who died. Trinks and Wolf, who had not seen the patient, were acquitted; Lehmann, who saw the case once and reported on it to Trinks without prescribing, was condemned to six months' imprisonment at hard labor, and Helwig, who saw the case once and prescribed *Aconite* and *Bryonia*, was sentenced to four weeks' imprisonment. This sentence was enforced against Helwig; Lehmann was finally acquitted.*

In 1831 Hornburg, one of Hahnemann's disciples, was arrested for the treatment of a case of pleurisy, which did not die under his treatment, but under that of Dr. Clarus. After the matter had continued for two years Hornburg was sentenced to two months' imprisonment. He died soon after this sentence.

CHAPTER LI.

LETTERS TO SCHWEIKERT.

The following letters addressed by Hahnemann to Dr. Benjamin Schweikert† were published in the *Allgemeine homoopathische Zeitung* for July 2, 1891, (Vol. cxxii., p. 193).‡ They were preceded by the following letter:

"The undersigned is in possession of a large number of letters of Hahnemann to his father, but not all of these are suitable for publication. He will present them to the Homœopathic Hospi-

---

*Hom. League Tract, No. 6.

† George Augustus Benjamin Schweikert was born at Zerbst, September 25, 1774. He died at Breslau, December 15, 1845.

‡ The compiler is indebted for the translation of the above letters to Prof. Louis H. Tafel, Professor of Languages at Urbana University, Urbana, Ohio. They are literal translations from the original German, and show quite well Hahnemann's peculiar habit of extending his sentences.

tal at Leipsic, so that they may be preserved for posterity in the room which has been specially furnished for keeping the relics of Hahnemann. He will also add to this present a lithograph of the second wife of Hahnemann, Melanie, *nee* d'Hervilly-Gohier. When the Hahnemann monument in Leipsic was unveiled, original letters of Hahnemann were sold at a ducat (about two dollars).

"DR. JOHANNES SCHWEIKERT,

"*Medical Director in Breslau.*"

Although of different dates, the letters are given together. They well show the state of Hahnemann's feelings towards Schweikert at that time.

"*Highly Honored Doctor:*

"From time to time I have heard of the progress which you have made with so much success in Homœopathy, and I have rejoiced over your honest endeavor to receive, wherever you found it, the truth, without prejudice, even at the sacrifice of a whole world full of old long-practised doctrines of the old school. I, myself, was at first in a similar position with you, having been instructed in their universities in the old system of medicine and its many statutes, and having remained for many years in this practice I know well how much self-denial it requires to leave the old train of ideas, to suppress it, and to wipe out, so to say, from the whole memory all the apparatus of ideas required by study, in order to give ingress, free ingress, on the soil thus laboriously cleared to the truth, without which we cannot bring true aid to suffering men, to our brethren.

"I say, I can very well put myself in your place; with what trouble and with what exertions you must have striven so as to become in your advanced years fully a Homœopathic physician.

"Besides the great trouble demanded, it requires just as much honorableness, love of mankind and self-denial, all of which I am glad to find united in you.

"You give others a worthy example to pattern after, and I, who never pretend, feel it my duty to declare this to you. Your consciousness of doing right will be your best reward.

"The book you kindly forwarded to me as the beginning of a treatise for the easier discovery of the symptoms of the medi-

cines proved heretofore,* meets with my full approval, and I
would exhort you to faithfully persist in your course, without
any regard to the labors of others, who, with the same intent, follow another path, and not to be deterred from it by this apparent
competition: Duo cum faciunt idem, non est idem. (When two
men do the same, it is not the same.)

"I believe your work will retain the pre-eminence. Reason
demands something systematic; you present the subject to be
treated in a systematic manner. But the alphabetical arrangement is an additional desideratum and assists in finding what we
want as no other system can do.

"Remain true to this system without alteration, if I may
advise you.

"As to your question, I have not stated everywhere, as it
ought to have been, that in preparing tinctures 100 drops of the
best alcohol, about 80 per cent., should be taken for five grains
of powder. But I would ask you to take this for granted in all
cases of this kind, since twenty-fold weight would produce quite
a different result, which cannot be my desire.

"As to the beer, which would not interfere with our fine doses
of Homœopathic medicine, I prefer the light beer brewed
from wheat malt which has not been dried or parched;
when this beer is prepared, as is often and usually done, without
the addition of any intoxicating vegetable product. If it is thus
prepared without any addition, like the so-called wheat beer in
Thuringia and Arnstadt, it is, indeed, to be preferred to all
others, only it cannot be preserved without passing over into
a strong vinous fermentation with violent foaming, and then
soon into acetic fermentation. A middle course is pursued by
the brewers of *Gose* (light beer) in Goslar, in the Duchy of Anhalt, as in Sondersleben, Glauzig and Wendorf. They also take
air-malt of wheat for brewing, but they add a small amount of
the decoction of hops, which is hardly, or not at all, tasted in
drinking it. This keeps better, and our nature gradually, so
easily and so fully accustoms itself to the small quantity of hops
that it eventually produces no difference in the effect of Homœo-

---

*The book which Hahnemann here mentions and which is spoken of in
several of the following letters as the "Materialien," was the "Materialien
zum Gebrauche fur homoopath, heilende Aerzte. Leipzig: Brockhaus.
1826-30." It was issued in parts, a volume being published yearly. Four
volumes were issued.

pathic doses of medicines. The light beer of Kirchberg, however, and other similar light beers, have an intoxicating, injurious ingredient in them. Even brown beer, which in itself I can not recommend, if it only contains hops and no other bitter herb or intoxicating growth, but only hops in limited quantity, may yet, in default of a better, be permitted if the patient was before used to it, whereby it becomes pretty much indifferent. If the patient can get no good light beer, let him get malt extract made of wheat, or lacking this, malt extract made of barley; let him dry it hard and cut it into dice-shaped pieces; let these be crushed into a coarse powder, pour boiling water over it, twenty-three times the weight of the malt, cover it and let it draw out. This strained decoction should then be preserved in bottles for future use. This gives us quite a harmless drink, which after being kept up for a few days becomes somewhat spirituous and is lightly nourishing.

"If I should be able to get to see and to speak to you once before my end it would give me joy.

"Yours devotedly,

"S. HAHNEMANN.

"Coethen, November 24, 1826."

"Dear Doctor:

"You gave me much joy with your dedication. I quite recognize its value, and only wish for the opportunity to show you my gratitude for the same.

"Also in this part of your 'Materialien,' for the transmission of which I give you my best thanks, I again realize the convenience for finding everything in it, which is afforded by the alphabetical order adopted by you. Your painstaking care is unmistakable. If it is possible for you to grant me very soon the honor of your personal acquaintance you will give great pleasure to

"Your most devoted,

"S. HAHNEMANN.

"Coethen, August 17, 1827."

"Dear Colleague:

"With many thanks I acknowledge to you the receipt of the third part of your 'Materialien,' collected by you with so much trouble and industry, with which you kindly present me. They will not fail of their intended use with Homœopathic physicians.

"It cannot be denied that the alphabetical arrangement affords a great facility in finding what you desire, and when there are a great number of subjects it is an indispensable help.

"I know what service was rendered to me in my formerly as yet small practice by the second part of my "Fragmenta de viribus medicamentorum positivis." Leipsic: Barth, 1805, namely, by the Latin Index.

"If you have this Index in your possession, you will readily concede this. Such a small vocabulary does not indeed seem to have any learned appearance, nor to deserve much esteem, but it only seems so, even as many a thing in the world seems to be of quite a different nature than it is in fact and reality.

"Let such a Criticaster nosotolus only try to produce something similar. Incredible efforts as well as judgment are required to turn the phrases so that the leading word offers itself to the alphabetical arrangement, and when this word occurs frequently so to arrange that the symptoms containing the same may also through the secondary ideas follow each other, divided into subdivision in alphabetical order. It is, therefore, a work full of skill, which, on account of the facility afforded for finding what is wanted, deserves the greatest esteem.

"I have on this account concluded to prepare in German, with the help of good friends, and to publish as soon as possible, such a general register like the above-mentioned Latin Index, to contain the symptoms of the antipsoric medicines, which will now very soon be published. I know that this great multitude of symptoms will only become useful to the Homœopathic physician when he can quickly find every idea and expression that he is in search of.

"I prepared such a vocabulary for my own practical use twelve years ago with respect to the medicines then already proved. This is a large folio volume which I shall show you when you will do me the honor of paying me a visit. I cannot tell you what great service this book has rendered me; it has been really indispensable for me to save valuable time which would have been required for finding out the facts from the text.

"Should this undertaking please you on examination, and

should you be willing to become a co-laborer in this scheme, it would be very agreeable to me. I should take care to provide a fitting stipend.

"In the meanwhile I beg you to think kindly of me.

"Your devoted,

"S. HAHNEMANN.

"*Coethen, April 5, 1828.*"

"*My Dear Colleague:*

"Only lately I became certain that H——b's handiwork is only a systematic presentation after the fashion of his former work, for Arnold has now accepted the publication of my alphabetical repertory.

"On this account I could not answer your friendly letter before this. Our work requires more headwork and more thought, but then it is also just what we should wish it to be, immensely facilitating the finding of all the states of health and disease and presenting quickly to the investigator all the particular ideas worth knowing, which often lie hidden in the symptoms.

"Let us use all care to make it most perfect. I therefore take the liberty of communicating to you in the enclosed leaflet my idea of how it may be best arranged, so that you may then send it to our friend Stapf, in order that he may hand it to Dr. Rummel. For on account of my being so fully occupied it is impossible for me to read it to each one separately. If it will not give you too much trouble I would ask to revise the part kindly forwarded to me, which I herewith return to you, according to my direction, and to go on in the same way with the remaining symptoms of *Phosphorus.*

"I have pressed out the juice of *Rad. cyclamen Europ.* during the winter, and also the herb of *Helleborus niger* when it commenced to bloom in January, and the juice of both of them will be at your service when you shall do me the honor to pay me a visit.

"In Warsaw, Dr. Bigel has received from Grand Duke Constantine 500 sons of soldiers for Homœopathic treatment, and Dr. Cosmo de Horatiis, in Naples, has received from his king the transfer of a large Homœopathic clinic. Thus things are progressing in foreign parts.

"And even to the Russian army operating against Turkey, Dr. Hermann, of Petersburg, has been sent by Grand Duke Michael, to treat the hospital patients Homœopathically. And we in Germany, how far are we behind them! We have no powerful patron, and even the originator of the art must be glad to practise his beneficent art in a little foreign place, without being publicly authorized, while he is in exile and denied the privilege of administering his own medicines, and the next thing is that his bones, now growing old, will be buried in a foreign land. O tempora! O mores!

"All is in vain that the good Tittmann and Albrecht have written. Hahnemann is forbidden, according to the edict, to prescribe anything in Saxony but the apothecary's mixtures, and his native land remains closed to him.

"If we had a Homœopathic clinic it would be easy to study out *Lactuca virosa*, which would surely prove beneficent, and also many other treasures of nature. God grant that I may soon be able to see and to talk with you here, sound and in good health. Preserve to me your love. This is written at the entrance of my seventy-fifth year, April 10, 1829.

"Your most devoted,

"SAM. HAHNEMANN."

CHAPTER LII.

LETTERS TO SCHWEIKERT, CONTINUED—HAHNEMANN'S OPINION
OF SPINAL BRACES.

"*My Dear Friend and Colleague:*

"Ever since I have been able to think, Saxony has advanced in all good things at a snail's pace, and its constitution will only be able with great trouble to make a commencement in improvement, for all the limbs of this State are fast asleep. Only what is old and fixed by custom seems best to it, and whatever is at present customary, however bad and corroded with rust it may be.

"Therefore the good members of our Legislature have not been able to do anything effective for us, as I always have foretold. Still it was rather strange that no one was bright enough to exclude Heinroth from the consultation, though he already before had taken part against our art as in his sophistical Anti-Organon. It was very wrong of the President that he admitted this spiritual adversary to the consultation. Your Grossman has shown himself to advantage in this business. Although I did not find a sample of the highly recommended steel pens in your letter, I confide in your recommendation, and would ask you at once to send me three dozen for a dollar, if I had a note for that amount at hand.

"I have finished my whole elaboration of this second edition of the "Chronic Diseases," and have a stack of documents lying before me which our good friend Isensee* has written and collected of impressive transactions with Arnold, whom we have not been able to induce to send me a few proof sheets of the first part, so that I might be able to see whether he has really commenced the work or not. (The wicked —— behind his back— you know him—bewitches him, and makes him grow numb as from a rattlesnake, only to torment me to death.)†

"I kept Mr. Jahr for eight months to assist me in this work, an expense of more than five hundred thalers, and nevertheless, I have not seen one proof sheet! No demonstrable beginning of the printing of the work! Also the good notary Albrecht we have called to our aid, but all in vain. Neither will he return the first part, thus preventing me from applying to another publisher. The boy behind his back is not worth the gallows!

"You will regret with me that I cannot put the money derived from the reprint of the first two parts to some useful purposes, we have to thank the bad boy for that!

"Enclosed find twenty-eight gulden from Prague and a short list of the donors. I would send you far more from the hands of Bœnninghausen, if he had only received your part of the 'Jahrbucher;' he writes me that in that case there would be no lack of contributions. This good man is now placed in a favorable position by the powers above, whereby he gains more leisure for our art.

"Don't listen to others! Give us in the 'Jahrbucher' only

---

* Isensee was his solicitor and lived at Coethen.

† Hahnemann seems to refer to Trinks. In a letter to Stapf written in 1836 he says: "The inimical spirit of Trinks has been very evident. It must have been by his devilish interference that Arnold let my manuscript lie so long unprinted."

successful cures. Remain strong and in good health, and give
my greetings to your Anna, also to Haubold, Wahle, Lux and
whoever else is worth greeting, from,

"Your,

"SAMUEL HAHNEMANN.

"*Coethen, Nov. 25, 1830.*"

Hering said of Arnold, the publisher of so many of Hahnemann's books: * "Subsequently (to the publication of the
'Fragmenta') owing to the increase in the number of remedies
the difficulty of reference increased to such a degree as to lead
Hahnemann to prepare an elaborate index, in which symptoms
pertaining to each organ, locality, sensation, functional change,
condition and modality, as well as each combination of symptoms
could be found and compared.

"Aided by this bulky 'Index', Hahnemann succeeded in curing a young man who had for years been tortured with most horrible pains, the result of old school medication. This young
man subsequently became the head of the publishing house of
Arnold, in Dresden, and out of gratitude he offered to print the
'Organon' in 1810; this was followed by the first volume of
the 'Materia Medica Pura' in 1811. Eleven years were required to sell the edition of the first volume of the 'Materia
Medica.'"

The next letter in this interesting series is as follows:

"*Dear Friend and Colleague:*

"After having become better acquainted with your journal,†
I beg you not to let it fall again at any price or for any reason.
I foresee that you will forward through it the development of
our art infinitely more than could be done through all other
Homœopathic writings, mine not excepted. Think what a good
work you are doing, what great service you are thereby rendering to humanity. Your inventive genius will yet discover ways
and means to continue this journal in an instructive manner, and
as it daily increases its list of subscribers, the publisher must
come and increase your stipend (still more in the future), so that

---

* Trans. World's Hom. Convention. 1876. Vol. 1, p. 1094.

† The journal to which Hahnemann alludes was the *Zeitung der natur-
gesetzlichen Heilkunst fur Freunde und Feind der Homoopathie.* It was
issued weekly as a small quarto, and was a popular and family sheet. It
was commenced in July, 1830.

you will finally have a satisfactory income. Think of me. It would also be advisable to request one and another Homœopath by letter to furnish news from his part of the country.

"Did Stapf, as I requested, give you the news for publication that Dr. Aegidi, of Ilsit, has accepted the call as Homœopathic physician in ordinary to her royal highness, Princess Fredericka of Prussia, in Dusseldorf, with a yearly salary of 600 thalers, traveling expenses, and the written official permission to prescribe his own medicines, and that he has entered on his office?

"A reader of your journal reports not having found in it this good news. Herewith I communicate to you, in addition, the following for publication:

"St. Petersburg.—A very zealous Homœopath, Dr. Zimmerman, formerly having a position in the hospital at Oranienbaum, who is now at Zarskoe-Selo (three miles from Petersburg) physician to a newly established Institute for the care of soldiers' boys, 400 in number, accepted this position only on condition that he be allowed to treat the patients Homœopathically.

"They have there even children with nurses, and also boys up to ten years of age. The Institute is under the charge of the Empress, who is interested in it. This Homœopathic treatment was not only granted by the authorities, but a sum of money for procuring a Homœopathic pharmacy was also granted him. Tu ne cede malis sed contra audacior ito! (Do not give way to the wicked, but boldly meet them!)

"All will come better if we only persevere. That is what I did, and God has at last blessed me, after all my trouble and affliction.

"I anticipate with pleasure your visit after the celebration of the 10th of August. "Your devoted,

"Sam. Hahnemann.

"*Coethen, July 2, 1831.*

"P. S.—For the twenty-one year old patient so dreadfully injured by *Iodine*, whom I consider almost a desperate case and poisoned, I advise to use yet *Phosphorus* and *Natrum muriaticum* alternately."

———

"*Dear Friend and Colleague:*

"I rejoice in your operations. What Dr. Lehmann writes I confirm; as to the rest, more orally, as I wish. Or—— wrote to me himself, how rudely he treated you, and I gave him a good lecture.

"He is as yet too rough; necessity will have to polish him. You are right in leaving him severely alone. For Lehmstaedt I advise to alternate with *Platina*, *Hepar* and *Toxicodendron*, leaving each medicine to act fourteen days.

"Hoping to see you soon,   Your

"SAM. HAHNEMANN.

"*Coethen, March 17, 1834.*"

It is of interest to know Hahnemann's opinion of braces and machines in the treatment of spinal diseases, and it may be learned by the following letter, written to Dr. Loewe of Prague:*

"As regards the girl with the crooked spine I would never recommend machines, which, as far as I know of them, are very far from attaining their object, but, on the contrary, do much more harm than good; and as, moreover, the disease that lies at the root of the softening of the bones, causing the curvature, is purely a psoric one, you will find it best to give first, tinct. *Sulph.*, one, two or three globules; then *Calcarea;* then *Phos. acid;* then *Baryta* and *Phosphorus*, and *Silicea*.

"At the same time the patient should walk out in the open air, and should use gymnastic exercises of the cross bar daily, several times, by hanging from it with both hands and swinging to and fro several minutes at a time. You will, of course, also order that coffee, tea, and vegetable acids should be avoided. Stroking the crooked parts with mesmerizing hands has often been of use alone, and we should at least use it as an auxiliary means.

"Farewell, and remember yours,

"S. HAHNEMANN.

"*Coethen, 23d Sept., 1831.*"

Hahneman also in a letter to Stapf, dated June 22, 1829, says in regard to spinal diseases: †"I have improved and even cured several cases of curvature of the spine by antipsoric remedies (*e. g. Calc.*) without the aid of a machine. A respectable unmarried lady, of about forty years of age, who was very deformed, while taking antipsoric medicines for periodical head-

Brit. Jour. Hom., Vol. xv., p. 336.
†*Hom. World*, Vol. xxv., p. 18.

ache and some miliary eruption became two inches taller, so that I scarcely recognized her when I saw her a year afterwards."

Again to Stapf he says:* "I am delighted with the effect of *Sulphur* on your little Mary, which is as striking as it is beneficial. Without using any machine I have cured a number of deformities of the bones with antipsorics. The healing power of God with which He has endowed the antipsoric remedies given to us has no need of such painful appliances. Simple mechanical means may certainly prove of use. Thus I saw a very deformed lady, forty-eight years of age, who, after a nearly completed antipsoric treatment for persistent headache, felt an urgent desire to stretch herself frequently. In order to do this she often hung and swung herself by an elevated cross beam; in a short time she became three inches taller and straighter, so that I was amazed and hardly recognized her when I saw her a year afterwards. That must obviate the necessity of employing the machines of Heine and others." This letter was written in 1826.

CHAPTER LIII.

DEATH OF DUKE FERDINAND—HAHNEMANN'S LETTER TO DUKE HENRY—LETTER TO AEGIDI.

Hahnemann's good protector, the Duke Ferdinand, died in 1831. From his first acquaintance with his friend and doctor he had treated him with uninterrupted kindness. After his death the medical authorities of the State, the Allopathic physicians, got the ear of Duke Henry, the brother and successor of Ferdinand, and sought to prejudice him against Hahnemann.†

Hahnemann and Dr. Mossdorf did not agree well, and Mossdorf finally left Coethen, leaving Hahnemann without any assistant.

Hahnemann addressed the following letter to the Duke Henry on August 6, 1832:

"*Most Serene and Gracious Lord:*

"For some years I availed myself of the permission most graciously accorded by your lamented brother, my never to be

---

Hom. World, Vol. xxiv., p. 362.
† *Brit. Iour. Hom.*, Vol. xxxvi., p. 262.

slightly honored patron, to associate with myself a Homœopathic medical assistant independent of the Allopathic medical
authorities, whom I would still have retained had his moral
conduct been only tolerable.

"Now I am compelled, by my great age and the afflux of
patients from far and near that overtaxes my powers, to select
another successor and assistant, and my choice has fallen on Dr.
Lehmann, of Leitzkau, a man who has for several years enjoyed
a good repute as an Allopathic physician, and a person of quiet
and steady character, who has now embraced Homœopathy
from conviction, and displays such an active zeal for his health-
promoting art, that he gives hopes of being able, with my aid,
to do some excellent service therein.

"I have considered it my duty to announce my choice to your
Serene Highness as your most obedient servant,

"SAMUEL HAHNEMANN."

The jealous medical authorities of the State obtained the ear
of the Duke and endeavored to persuade him not to grant to Dr.
Lehmann the same privilege that Dr. Mossdorf had enjoyed.
He was allowed to go to Coethen as the assistant of Hahnemann,
but could not take patients independently of him, and was subject to the control of the Allopathic authorities.

Therefore Hahnemann, on the 3d of December, 1832, addressed
the following remonstrance to Duke Henry:

"*Most Serene Duke, Most Gracious Lord:*

"I beg to offer my most humble thanks to your Serene Highness for your gracious permission to choose Dr. Lehmann as my
medical assistant. Dr. Lehmann, who was already versed in
the Homœopathic doctrine, has by zeal, under my guidance, in
a short time attained such proficiency in it that I can already
reckon him one of my good disciples.

"He has already procured me some relief in my excessive
labors.

"But the afflux of patients given over as incurable by your
Allopathic physicians to the Homœopathic system, from far and
near, increases daily, so convinced are the public that real and
permanent cure is only to be obtained from the new system of
medicine.

"I therefore make bold once more to beg your Serene Highness, humbly, but confidentially, that you would generously

please to accord to Dr. Lehmann, in order that he may be able to give me his aid in full efficiency, the same independent position towards me as was enjoyed by Dr. Mossdorf, my former medical assistant, by the grace of the unforgetable Duke Ferdinand, your lamented brother.

"Only thus can I have in Dr. Lehmann a true and lasting aid and support, and on my decease your Serene Highness will have in your capital a true Homœopathic physician trained under my guidance, whereas otherwise he will soon return to his own country to practice as a Homœopathic physician in Magdeburg, and I in my advanced age will be again left alone, and will be compelled to turn away more than half of the patients who flock to be cured.

"Your Serene Highness's most obedient,

"SAMUEL HAHNEMANN."

Duke Henry, without consulting the medical authorities, granted this favor. He issued a decree dated January 14, 1833, as follows:

"We grant permission to Dr. Lehmann to settle here as a practicing Homœopathic physician for the purpose of assisting Hofrath Dr. Hahnemann, and as such to prepare the medicines he requires for his treatment. In other respects, Dr. Lehmann is subject to all State and police laws and regulations.

"HENRY."

Hahnemann soon after published in Schweikert's journal the following letter upon the subject of self-dispensing:*

"THE DISPENSING OF HOMŒOPATHIC REMEDIES EXEMPT FROM THE OLD APOTHECARIES' PRIVILEGE.

"In contradistinction to what was published in the *Prussian States Gazette* on April 17 of this year (1833), whereby out of courtesy to an old-time apothecaries' privilege, the dispensing of their own medicines is again refused to Homœopathic physicians, it is a pleasure to make known to our age the disposition of a noble hearted sovereign, Duke Henry of Anhalt-Coethen, who, upon self-acquired conviction of the infinite superiority of Homœopathic remedies to the old physic, of his own accord and in unison with the previous good sense of his deceased brother Ferdinand, granted full permission to Dr. Hahnemann to prepare his own medicines himself, and thus to lend a helping hand

---

* *Zeit. der hom. Heilkunst,* Vol. vii., p. 188.

to his patients, in a rescript executed in his own handwriting, on the 14th of this January (1833), and has now conferred upon Dr. Lehmann also the same right to heal unhindered his patients with Homœopathic remedies prepared by himself—a privilege which has been attended with blessed results to sick people.

"SAMUEL HAHNEMANN.

"Coethen, April 26, 1833."

After Hahnemann had left Coethen in 1835 the apothecaries of the Principality presented a petition signed by all of them asking that not only Hofrath Lehmann should be deprived of the right to prepare and dispense his own medicines, but that the right should be denied to all other Homœopathic physicians who might settle in Coethen.

The Duke rejected this and confirmed Dr. Lehmann in his privilege. Lehmann remained for many years in Coethen, where he died on January 9, 1865, aged 77 years.

Hahnemann was in the habit of sending to him from Paris for his medicines, and he supplied him with them until the time of his death.*

The following letter to Dr. Aegidi is of interest as showing Hahnemann's opinion at this period of his life in regard to the repetition of the Homœopathic dose, especially of the antipsoric remedies :†

"First about your good Princess. In October 1829 she sent me the heavy package of your prescriptions up to that time, from which I have made the enclosed extract. From this I see that she had already abused baths with *Hepar Sulphuris* and precipitated *Sulphur*. From a great fear, warned by experience, I avoided entirely giving her the like. Nevertheless, my later observations have taught me that even after being abused it may after two or three years be used with great profit and without harm in our preparations of the same.

"Now since *Sulphur* as prepared by us and in our doses remains the most excellent of all the antipsoric remedies which therefore cannot help advancing her in her cure, I herewith send you nine little powders; in these, in No. 1, 4, 6 and 9, is one little pellet of Tct. *Sulphur*, x.

"Wolf, in Dresden, has in the *Archiv* called attention to the

---

* *Brit. Jour. Hom.*, Vol. viii., p. 555.

†*Allg. hom. Zeitung*, Vol. lxviii., p. 16.

fact, but I perceived it already before that in very old psoric ailments *Sulphur* in one dose is not sufficient, and I therefore effect
far more in the worst cases by giving in the commencement
several doses, especially with patients who have already been
much spoiled by many wrong remedies, if only they have not
lately received *Sulphur*; we, as it were, penetrate by means of
this remedy through the diatheses of the diseases caused by
medicines, so as to surely affect the vital force with the necessary
healing *Sulphur* disease.

"I was led to this through the perverse Allopathic practice,
by means of which these gentlemen through daily (often through
several daily) doses of one and the same medicine, within
a few weeks produce with certainty a long-enduring, medicine
sickness (though they do this to the destruction of their patients
not only when the medicine was considerable and unhomœo-
pathic; since through these means used in so long a repetition
and largeness of dose, the vital force is only suppressed and rendered incapable for any beneficial healing action). *Sed abusus
non tollit usum.*

"I drew from this the instruction that likely several repeti-
tions of the dose of a Homœopathic remedy within a short
period may be required to effect thereby gradually such a degree
of medical transformation of the vital force as may be necessary
for the production of a reaction of the vital force sufficient to
cure a severe chronic disease. Experience also taught me that
this repeated giving of the smallest dose is in practice immeasur-
ably preferable to any merely single prescription of this dose.
Three or four days in succession (*e. g.*, 1' 2' 3' Tct. *Sulph.*, x)
such a smallest dose has surely already done me good service
with persons not too excitable, but with very sensitive persons
that order is more effective in which I herewith send you the
Sulphur for the Princess, who will therefore take on each one of
the nine mornings one moistened powder, moistened without
drinking anything within one-half hour afterwards. Still it will
be best if this is not done shortly before an expected monthly.
I hope very much from this medicine.

"I would beg you to communicate something of what I have
said to our excellent Homœopathic friend, von Bœnninghausen.

"You have given me as much pleasure by the rest of your
news concerning the progress of our art, both in your practice

and in the better opinion of the public with respect to it, as if you had made me a great present. For the welfare of suffering humanity is very dear to my heart. Of the enclosed two steel engravings, one is intended for you and the second for the good Princess.

"Schmit's well-written pamphlet is also intended for you. The enclosed little sealed packet I would request you to be so kind as to transmit to our dear R. R. v. B. The letter of the worthy v. Lotzbeck has given me pleasure. God grant you great good fortune is the wish of

"Your friend,

"S. HAHNEMANN.

" *Coethen, Jan. 6th, 1832.*"

CHAPTER LIV.

LIFE AT COETHEN—DR. PESCHIER'S VISIT—HOMŒOPATHY IN AMERICA—LETTER TO TRINIUS—WANTED, A HOMŒOPATHIST.

Rapou says: "From 1829 to 1832 were three very happy years in the life of Hahnemann; honored by the friendship and protection of a generous Prince, glorying in a reputation more than European, chief of a school whose pupils were zealous and respected. His practice was very large.

" Dr. Mossdorf had at first been his assistant, but in 1832 he engaged Counsellor Lehmann to assist him. Just when Dr. Mossdorf left Coethen is uncertain, but it is probable that he had, in 1832, been gone for several years when Hahnemann asked to be allowed to engage Dr. Lehmann as assistant.

" Many of his believers from Europe and other countries visited Coethen, the Mecca of Homœopathy."

Hull says: *"A trait of character especially manifested at this period of Hahnemann's career commands our deepest respect, his charitable treatment of the poor, medically and pecuniarily. The poor of the district of Coethen were especially the beneficiaries of his medical skill and attainments, although the incessant applications of the influential and wealthy were more than sufficient to engross his entire time. The unwearied at-

*Hom. Examiner, Vol. ii., p. 8.

tentions bestowed by him upon an infant, in particular, elicited the ardent eulogium of the distinguished Peschier, who took advantage of the opportunity to record the habits of practice adopted by Hahnemann."

There is an idea that Hahnemann borrowed his doctrines from Paracelsus. He himself did *not think he did*, as is seen from the following extract from a letter to Stapf, dated May 5, 1831: *"What do you say about Professor Schultz's work on the homeobiotic medicine of Theophrastus Paracelsus, which has been published in Berlin† (and of which there is full notice in the *Vossische Zeitung*, No. 92)? According to him I borrowed my system from this man's writings (incomprehensible gibberish), but did not rightly understand the matter and made a bungle of it. Th. Paracelsus, he tells us, understood it much better.

"No one hitherto has attempted to attack Homœopathy from this side—that alone was wanting."

From a literary point of view the year of 1832 was exceedingly important to Homœopathy.

To this year belongs the establishment of another Homœopathic paper, the *Allgemeine homoopathische Zeitung*, a weekly journal of Homœopathy. It began on July 1, 1832. The editors were Drs. G. W. Gross, of Juterbogh; F. Hartmann, of Leipsic, and F. Rummel, of Magdeburg. The journal is still published, and has always been one of the most important in the history of Homœopathy.

In 1832 Arnold published a new edition of von Brunnow's French translation of the "Organon." Arnold in a note says that this edition, made from the fourth German edition, was all ready to be published in 1830, but that political troubles and the slight gain of Homœopathy in France prevented its issue. Brunnow's preface is dated Dresden, April 30, 1830.

In this same year of 1832 another French translation was made by Dr. A. J. L. Jourdan, and issued by Bailliere in Paris.

Arnold mentions this edition in his note, and says he is innocent of its merits, but refers the reader to a letter from Hahnemann, printed on the same page:

Hom. World, Vol. xxv., p. 256.
†The full title is: "The Homeobiotic Medicine of Theophrastus Paracelsus contrasted with the Medicine of the Ancients, and the Source of Homœopathy. C. H. Schultz, Berlin, 1831."

"I declare that my friend M. de Brunnow has perfectly rendered the text of my ' Organon,' and that this French translation is the only one which I regard as authentic.

"SAMUEL HAHNEMANN.

"*Coethen, 10th March, 1832.*"

This book also contains a sketch of Hahnemann's life and a general exposition of the principles of Homœopathy by von Brunnow.

Dr. Jourdan published a French edition of the " Chronic Diseases," in 1832, in Paris. The same year Dr. Bigel issued an edition at Lyons, also in French.

Bœnninghausen, at Munster, published his celebrated repertory in 1832.

In 1832–37 a translation of the " Chronic Diseases " was made into Italian by Dr. Belluomini, and published in four volumes, in Teramo, Italy.

Dr. C. G. Peschier, of Geneva, of whom Hull writes, became interested in Homœopathy in 1832. * He attended the meeting of the Central Union at Leipsic, in August of that year, and afterwards visited Hahnemann at Coethen. An account of the meeting of the society and also of the visit to Hahnemann was furnished by him in two letters published in the *Bibliotheque Homœopathique*, Vol. I. 1833. This was the first Homœopathic periodical published in the French language, and Dr. Peschier afterwards became its editor.

Dr. Peschier was at Coethen about the middle of August, 1832, and remained there for some time, learning the new medical doctrine at the home and from the lips of its discoverer.

The following is a free translation of the letter describing this visit. † "After the meeting at Leipsic, many of the visiting physicians went to Coethen to pay their respects to Hahnemann.

"The hour on which I could meet the venerable Hahnemann arrived, and already one of the many patients of the great man coming from his office informed me that Hahnemann knew of my arrival and was very anxious to see me. Upon these flattering words I at once prepared to wait upon him, when a message came saying that he would be detained for an hour by

---

*Biography in *Brit. Jour. Hom.*, Vol. xii., p. 166.
†*Bibliotheque Homœopathique*, Vol. i., p. 378.

patients. The hour passed slowly. I presented myself at last, and the old man hastened to me and pressed me in his arms, calling me his son, his dear son; on my part I addressed him as my father, and kissed with respect the honorable hand that had written so much for the good of humanity.

"Time passed rapidly and already we were conversing as two friends; I told him how I had learned of his new system and of my success in its practical application, and he explained to me his opinions on the chronicity of diseases, on the method of their attack and the difficulty in curing them, also that certain so-called incurable affections ought not to be so regarded by the Homœopath.

" I said to him that I had not been able to follow the precept never to repeat the same remedy, and that I had not been able to discover the evil in doing so; to which he answered that experience had caused him to modify his system on that point and that he now agreed to the repetition of doses, and that he had made it the subject of the first part of the recent work by Dr. Bœnninghausen, entitled 'Alphabetical and Systematic Repertory of the Action of Antipsoric Remedies.'

" Already the physicians of Leipsic have said that the repetition of the dose is necessary in the treatment of chronic diseases.

"But he insisted upon small quantity, and understanding always the subtlety and divisibility of Homœopathic medicines, he said to me that it is often the case that it is sufficient to smell of the bottle containing the medicament.

" This subtlety is a thing very well assured, and, as is well known, persons are often restored by olfaction of certain substances from faintings and vertigoes; until the use of the smelling bottle has become a habit of society.

" After this Hahnemann instructed me in regard to the action of certain 'polychrest' substances combining the action of prompt and decisive remedies and those of antipsorics, that have a very long and continued action.

" He confirmed me in the opinion that had already been formed by experience, that antipsorics, properly applied, are speedily successful in the cure of maladies, a long time after the special affection for which they ought to be prescribed has disappeared; in this case they cause to disappear a host of symptoms considered in the face of the more grave ones unimportant;

and a strong and endurable state of health then succeeds the
habitual malaise, while there is a slight reappearance of the
malady for which the physician had been consulted.

"This long and interesting conversation was prolonged during a supper amicably offered and sumptuously served by the
two daughters of Hahnemann, who rivaled each other in politeness and attention to the friends of their respected father.

"After this evening conference had been prolonged late into
the night, I requested another for the morning, which was affectionately accorded. At the hotel where I was staying, it was
customary to hear many times during the day the tramping of
horses at the arrival and departure of the strangers who attended
from all parts on account of the great reputation and successful
practice of Hahnemann. This hotel at this time had a majority
of its chambers occupied by those persons who had come from
distances to consult the oracle of Homœopathy; for example, I
noticed among others a Dane, a Courlander, a Hungarian, a
Russian and a Silesian.

"But to return to Hahnemann: at the end of the day I had
found him occupied in a consultation on an infant of a poor
woman, for the poor were the same to him as those who had
riches; it taught me his manner of proceeding.

"Hahnemann writes punctually the totality of symptoms, or
entire group of sufferings of the patient, including all constitutional ailments previously manifested in his own person or of
any hereditary taints characteristic of his progenitors. On the
completion of his record, the symptoms of the disease are most
carefully arranged to correspond with the indications of the drug
he deems most appropriate to the case; but in reaching this conclusion he neither confides in his memory nor relies solely upon
his long experience, but has constantly before him the 'Materia
Medica' and Ruckert's 'Repertory,' from whence he culls every
remedy the emergency of the case demands.

"As he pursues this course towards every patient we can
readily perceive how completely and incessantly his time must
be occupied by the history of his consultations.

"The register of his consultations, every day increasing in
magnitude, forms at this moment a stupendous medical encyclopædia. We have seen upon one of the shelves of Hahnemann's
library thirty-six quarto volumes of at least 500 pages each,

entirely written by his own hand; and to those who are curious
as to the penmanship of the venerable octogenarian, who has
never used spectacles, we can testify to writing as fine and beautiful as the mignonne of Didot.

"But this is only a part of the daily occupation of this great
man; medical correspondence holds an important place in the
occupation of his time, and this is truly immense.

"The collection of his received letters, which are subsequently
arranged into volumes, forms no trifling compilation; and the
repertory alone of his letters, containing the names of his correspondents and the dates of their missives, is an enormous
volume, in folio, which is kept under the superintendence of
Miss Hahnemann.

"All this work absorbed the time of our common master,
who regretted that he had no more to devote to the development
of the science; so that he had asked as an assistant Dr. Lehmann,
who would probably continue the treatment commenced and
only render an account of the results to Hahnemann ; I have had
the pleasure to take tea with this doctor, who merits at the same
time the confidence of the Master and of the public.

"The father of Homœopathy possesses at Coethen a rather
small house that probably he finds large enough, and which is
joined to a very small garden entirely enclosed and screened
from sight; I state this circumstance, because this same en-
closure, which is just twenty-five foot paces long, is his one and
only promenade, in which he never puts off his dressing gown
and his slippers; there are for him neither fetes nor Sundays ;
his patients do not permit him to distinguish that day from
others.

"Hahnemann never pays any visits, the people of Coethen
and their neighbors, who have recourse to his advice, send to
him an account of the condition of their maladies and he sends
to them that which is necessary ; I know certain people of Leipsic who have sought counsel from him for their relatives and
themselves, sending over the eight leagues that separate the
two villages, twice daily, an express, in acute diseases.

"It may be permitted me to state that one of the persons of
whom I have spoken, M. the Counsellor de Freygang, consul
general of Russia at Leipsic, is one of the most amiable, best
educated men whom I have ever known, which made his reception in respect to myself all the more amiable and obliging.

"His respect for Hahnemann is without limit; and it is, they say, to his zeal and affection that the latter owes the protection of the Duke d'Anhalt Coethen, whom M. de Freygang made imperfectly understand the glory that would redound upon his name, so that he gave an honorable asylum to the useful savant that his merit demanded from the persecution of Leipsic. This anecdote, I have never heard from himself, he is too modest to permit others to understand his services.

"During many days, I passed five and six hours of the evening and night with Hahnemann, conversing with him upon his doctrine and his practice, while his amiable daughters lavished their cares and attentions in providing refreshments, a collation, a supper, which testified to their abundance and to their delicacy of pleasing by means of which this distinguished family extended its hospitality to a guest come from so far.

"One night this politeness had for its main object another Swiss, Doctor Huber, of the Canton of Zurich, who had come to Coethen solely to pay his respects to Hahnemann; the meeting of two Helvetians, natives of the two extreme points of their country is worthy of remembrance; M. Huber had not assisted in the Leipsic fete, and only remained at Coethen a day.

"One other night, I had for messmate M. the Russian Counsellor Wraski, who had translated the 'Organon' into Russian, and who, after a sojourn of some months in Germany, from whence he was carrying a complete pharmacy, proposed to practice Homœopathy at home, upon his countrymen and neighbors. Without doubt he has rendered them great services.

"I will here mention that the 'Organon' has already been translated into five languages. I have seen copies of each one of these translations upon Hahnemann's table, that is completely covered with offerings of books, of brochures and Homœopathic journals.

"It is without doubt homage due to the inventor of this science, but in the present name of the author of each work it is a homage inutile, because Hahnemann has not the time to read a single page of the writings of others, and also to record the practical observations which he has made so precious. *   *   *

"I told him of the success I had obtained in the use of spirits of *Sulphur* in many chronic maladies, and particularly in

phthisis pulmonalis, in the 12th potency; he seemed both surprised and satisfied and asked me to make it the object of a
small memoir for general use. I observed to him that I had con-
formed to that idea so simple, and so rich in consequence, contained in the first volume of the 'Chronic Diseases', which asserts
that lasting diseases of the lungs do not exist without psoric
antecedents.

"This thought struck him as it has myself, and I have no
doubt that experience will always justify it.

"After a stay in Coethen of about a week I feared to
abuse the kindness of my venerable master, and expose his com-
plaisance to too great a trial by my multiplied questions; I,
therefore, thought of leaving him.

"At the last moment, which occurred at his home at night,
there was a repetition of the expressions of respect and esteem
which had accompanied my arrival. I quitted him with a deeper
knowledge, and more impressed with veneration than ever, and
firmly decided to use every effort of zeal and study to progress in
scientific attainments, grateful for the honor of so long having
enjoyed his fatherly friendship."

Peschier then gives an account of the books upon Hahnemann's table and of their authors, of the progress of Homœopathy and of the coming meeting of the German Society.

In a letter to Dr. Stapf, written May 19, 1832, Hahnemann
thus mentions Homœopathy in America:* "Nowhere are
Homœopaths better off than in North America. There only is
freedom. The day before yesterday a merchant called on me,
who was very well informed about and a proficient in the practice of Homœopathy. He told me of the great progress of our
art in that country, principally through the labors of Dr. Ihm
there, and two others, in Bethlehem and Nazareth (two Moravian
colonies), of whom I only remember the name of one, Dr.
Freitag."

In 1829 Hahnemann's favorite nephew, Dr. Trinius, a short
sketch of whose life is given in the chapter on Hahnemann's
family, wrote to him requesting him to recommend a suitable
Homœopathic physician for the Princess Mary of Wirtemberg.
She had been under Trinius' care in St. Petersburg, where he
was physician to the Czar. About this time she had married
the Duke of Saxe Coburg-Gotha and removed to Coburg.

*Hom. World, Vol. xxv., p. 503.

Trinius accompanied her, but was obliged to return to Russia. Hahnemann freely states his opinions in regard to the position in the following letter:*

"*My Dear Nephew:*

"Your commission shows your confidence in me, and that is what I wished to deserve. Still, as you cannot be aware how inevitable and intolerable are the hindrances, calumnies and persecutions which a true Homœopathic physician in Germany has to encounter in every place where he settles as an unprotected stranger, so to advise any Homœopathist to take such a step *un-supported* were to induce him to court misfortune. Under such circumstances Allopathic intrigues have perfectly free scope, under the pretence of ancient legal right to display their well-known malice against the medical innovator who gives his medicines to his patients; and they are supported by the judges whose medical attendants they are. 'What,' they say, 'does the horrid fellow want here? He is not authorized either by the State or by the municipal medical authorities, nor can he be, as he is an accursed Homœopath. We have the power to pervert and twist the old laws regulating medical practice (though they only have to do with the compounding of Allopathic mixtures by the apothecaries) so that they shall compel the Homœopath to get all his simple medicines prepared and dispensed to patients by the apothecaries, though they do not understand how to prepare them. In order to crush the hateful Homœopathy, which would interfere with their usurious profits, the apothecaries would be only too willing to put no or a wrong medicine in the powders, and as the dose is so minute, the deception would never be discovered. But a Homœopath, left to the mercy of the apothecaries and not allowed to give his own remedies to his patients, is reduced to impotence, just like a painter deprived of permission to prepare his colors, and even worse. And if he succeeded in surmounting this difficulty, we could always get up a criminal process against him in the event of the death of one of his patients, because he had not adopted the treatment of our old school. By our artful persecution of his patients, and by the dissemination of calumnies against his art, he would be so pest-

---

Hom. World, Vol. **xxvi.**, p. 151. *Brit. Jour. Hom.*, Vol. **xxiii.**, p. 151. Vol. **xxx.**, p. 293. *Zeit. f. hom. Klinik.*, Vol. **xiii.**, p. 118.

ered and disheartened that, with the loss of his money and health, he would take himself off and relieve us of his odious presence, which is exactly what we, the dominant medical guild, desire with all our hearts.'

" Many such sad experiences have been undergone, so that no true Homœopath who can make a moderate income in his own locality would be so foolish as to subject himself to such a palpable disadvantage.

" Without a special license from a reigning sovereign, authorizing him to exercise his beneficent art, and prepare and dispense his own medicines unhindered by the medical authorities, no worthy Homœopath chosen by me will or can consent to set up in Coburg, and even then not before his subsistence is assured by an annual allowance subscribed for by a sufficient number of families; for the Allopaths, without exception, will seek to keep the public away from him by the most dreadful calumnies, so that even the very poorest will hardly dare to cross his threshold, as I know by experience.

" But if the ruler of the country appoints him physician in ordinary, and gives him the license above alluded to, he will still have to undergo the serious attacks of Allopathic intrigue; but he has assured means of existence, which every true physician should possess.

" I can only recommend and persuade a good Homœopath to accept this post provided he is appointed physician to the Duke with a salary for life, and is granted a license authorizing him to practice freely—unhindered by the medical authorities—in the capital and surrounding country, with medicines prepared by himself.

" If you feel disposed to see once more your loving uncle before his exit from this earthly stage, then do not hesitate to come a little out of your way for his sake. Trusting that you will do this, I am your affectionate uncle,

"SAMUEL HAHNEMANN.

" *Coethen, September 17, 1832.*"

The following week Hahnemann advertised in the *Zeitung* for a physician, as follows:*

" A physician wanted. I am seeking for a physician to go to

Allg. hom. Zeitung, Vol. l., p. 72 (Oct. 11, 1832).

a neighboring city on an assured salary of 900 thalers per annum. He must be one who has taken a degree and is legally qualified to practice in the Prussian States, and who can show himself to be a Homœopathic practitioner capable of being my assistant. But only one who is sure of his capability in Homœopathic practice can correspond with me post free.

"SAMUEL HAHNEMANN, *Hofrath.*

"*Coethen, 26 September, 1832.*"

CHAPTER LV.

DR. GRIESSELICH'S VISIT TO COETHEN—LETTER TO DR. GERSTEL.

Griesselich also visited Hahnemann in 1832 and thus speaks of him :* "Hahnemann at the age of seventy-seven showed in every action all the fire of a young man. No trace of old age could be detected in his physical appearance, except the white locks surrounding his temples, and the bald crown, which is covered with a velvet cap. Small, and sturdy in form, Hahnemann is lively and brisk; every movement is full of life. His eyes reveal his inquiring spirit; they flash with the fire of youth. His features are sharp and animated. As old age seems to have left few traces on his body, so it is with his mind. His language is fiery and fluent; often it becomes vehement as a stream of lava against the enemies and opponents, not of himself personally, for that he never alluded to, but of the great truths to the testing of which he had summoned his colleagues for many decades. His memory seems to be unaffected; after long interludes and side conversation he continues where he left off.

"When he becomes heated in conversation, which often happens, whether about friend or foe, or on scientific subjects, his words flow forth uninterruptedly, his whole manner becomes extremely animated and an expression appears on his countenance which the visitor admires in silence. Perspiration covers his lofty brow; his cap is removed; even his long pipe—his trusty companion—goes out and must be relighted by the taper that is

* "Skizzen aus der Mappe eines reisende Homoopathen." Karlsruhe. Groos. 1832. Also trans. in Ameke's "History of Homoeopathy," p. 161. *Zeit. hom. Heilkunst,* Schweikert, Vol. ix., p. 364. (Dec. 6, 1834.)

at hand and kept burning all day.   But the white beer must not
be forgotten.   The venerable old man had so accustomed himself
to this sweet drink that it always stood in a large covered glass
on his table; at his meals, too, he takes this drink, which is unknown in South Germany.   He does not drink wine; his mode
of life is very simple, abstemious and patriarchal.''

Although in 1832, when the following letter was written, Hahnemann was very happy and prosperous, yet it plainly shows
that the first years of his stay in Coethen were embittered by the
medical hierarchy of Anhalt.   It is addressed to Dr. Gerstel.*

"*Dear Colleague:*

"I have read with great pleasure what Dr. Gross wrote to me
on the report sent by you, and am surprised that the authorities
have given you such good (so true) testimonials, and I beg you
to make them known in several widely circulated newspapers.
You cannot believe how much good is done by a well deserved
vote of thanks, and how much you stimulate other authorities to
render similar services to the cause of Homœopathy.   Hitherto,
the Homœopathists could bring forward nothing but bitter complaints about the injustice and neglect that were shown them.

"And however pardonable such complaints and accusations
might be, still they, nevertheless, made a bad impression on the
public, and by no means tended to raise Homœopathy in its estimation.   I have therefore never openly made a grievance of
the bitter and cruel enmities which were shown to me during the
first five or six years of my residence here.   *For I would far
rather be envied than pitied.*   Yet I would, if possible, avoid the
former.

"It is only within the last few years that I have been able so
to win over and convince, of the superiority of our art, the public,
which for years had been prejudiced and hounded on against me
by Allopaths, apothecaries and surgeons, that now even this
same public are so much the more angry with the doctors and
apothecaries, and prefer me so much above all others, that I am
quite at a loss how to take in all the patients; I am, as it were,
carried off my feet.   So I thought things had happened for the
best, and my opinion is you have no need to be afraid of the ill-
will of your colleague in Moravia, for in your country the frightful impediment to Homœopathic practice, *i. e.*, the prohibition

* *Brit. Jour. Hom.*, Vol. xv., p. 336.   *Prager Monatscrift*, Vol. v., p. 32.

to dispense our own medicines, is, as you assure me, done away with. This impediment still exists in almost all other countries and renders Homœopathy almost impracticable here except to me alone, as I have a letter of permission from the Sovereign of the Land. That the doctors in Brunn could hunt out Mr. Fischer, who was certainly a very capable man, arose from the circumstance that he had no diploma; and in this respect they can do nothing against you.

"The public in Brunn is already favorably disposed towards Homœopathy, and, therefore, I would not counsel you against establishing yourself there. From the Prague bills of mortality, which I have consulted diligently, it appeared to be plainly shown that you cannot have had your hands free to act there, otherwise the rate of mortality would have been more favorable, and a number of patients would have been rescued from death by your aid. It would please me to receive further good news from you.

"Your devoted,

"SAM. HAHNEMANN."

" *Coethen, 12th February, 1832.*"

Rapou *pere* visited Hahnemann in 1833, and afterwards addressed the Lyons Society of Medicine upon the subject. He says:* "I was unable, upon seeing Hahnemann, to restrain from the feeling of veneration that this man of genius and science impressed upon me. His white hair, his grave air and stern mien tempered by very affable manners; his high forehead, his look vivacious and piercing and the hidden irony of his smile revealing well the profound thought, ripened by experience, and the merciless criticism that has so bitterly assailed the vain and pretentious doctrines of the schools.

"The first conference that I had with him was the day after my arrival, and continued from four till ten o'clock. He had closed the door, constantly besieged by a throng of sick people, so that I might the more benefit by the time which he gave to me. We spoke of the great spread of the new method in all the countries near Germany, and of its already important position in Austria, where its introduction had to encounter almost innumerable obstacles.

---

* "Histoire de la Doctrine Medicale Homœopathique," Paris. 1847. Vol. ii., p. 288.

"I spoke of my knowledge of Homœopathy, and requested information regarding the better methods to be acquired to give it value and permit me to entirely renounce the ordinary medical practice.

"He thought a moment, and after having passed in review the principles expounded in the "Organon" he proposed to me a plan of study that I have the happiness of at present following. It consists in a combination of clinical and pathogenetic researches to determine the choice of the remedy by characteristic indications.   *   *   *

"The next day Hahnemann gave me an interview at the same hour, and showed me some volumes of his immense correspondence. Among other letters were those of Dr. Mauro, of Naples, who at the age of 60 had issued the result of his study of Homœopathy in a book ; of the celebrated Kiesselbach, of Hanau ; of Paubel, from Gotha; of the Counsellor Klein, all of whom at an advanced age are studying with zeal the new doctrine. But that which interested me the most was a letter from Dr. Biett, in which he asked Hahnemann for light upon his method, and besought him to send him a collection of properly prepared remedies in which he had confidence."

In the eighth number of the *Allgemeine homoopathische Zeitung*, published September 30, 1832, Dr. Hartmann published a list of physicians who were known to be practicing Homœopathy; this list embraces 226 names, among whom are "Hering, of Surinam; Wesselhoeft, of Pennsylvania; Bute, of Bethlehem, in Pennsylvania; Haynel, of Baltimore, in North America."

From 1830 to 1835 the quiet little village of Coethen became the school house of Homœopathy.

The most liberal of the physicians and many laymen had heard with interest of the new and mild method of healing, and a great many of them journeyed to the home of the old master to sit at his feet.

In fact the history of the introduction of Homœopathy into several countries commences with the visit of some physician or layman to the old sage, Hahnemann, in the vine covered arbor of the little garden at Coethen.

Thus about 1830 Benitua Iriarte, a rich merchant of Cadiz, with his friend Villalba, went to Coethen and soon after introduced Homœopathy into Spain.*

---

*Rapou's "Histoire de la doct. med. Homœopathique," Vol. i, p. 175.

Dr. F. F. Quin visited Hahnemann in 1821, and in 1827 carried the new doctrine to England.

Dr. Adam met Hahnemann in 1823, and soon after introduced Homœopathy into Russia, commencing its practice in St. Petersburg. Dr. Adam was also one of the provers of the "Materia Medica Pura." At this period Hahnemann's time was greatly occupied in receiving his distinguished visitors from all parts of the world.

CHAPTER LVI.

HISTORY OF LEIPSIC HOMŒOPATHIC HOSPITAL—LETTERS TO MULLER.

As has previously been stated, the Fiftieth Fest-Jubilee was the origin of the German Homœopathic Central Union, which since that date had met yearly on the 10th of August.* The first meeting was held in Leipsic in 1830. Dr. Moritz Muller was President. Everything was harmonious, and the rules of the Society were for the first time drafted. The meeting of 1831, under the Presidency of Dr. Stapf, occurred at Naumburg. Hartmann says that this meeting was largely attended on account of the interest in the cholera then prevailing and the hope that Hahnemann would send some communication regarding its treatment. In 1832 it met at Leipsic. Dr. Schweikert was President. It was held in the evening, and after the address and the scientific papers Dr. Schweikert, Sr., made a proposition to establish, with the funds then on hand, a Homœopathic hospital at Leipsic. He had already interested Hahnemann in the project. The capital from the Coethen celebration had now by contributions reached the sum of 4000 thalers. It was unanimously decided to use this money to establish a Homœopathic hospital and medical school at Leipsic.

Dr. Schweikert was especially enthusiastic regarding the project, and even volunteered to take charge of the new hospital without remuneration, and to remove from Grimma to Leipsic for the purpose. Dr. Moritz Muller was elected director of the

---

* *Allg. hom. Zeit.*, Vol. xxvi. *Brit. Jour. Hom.*, Vol. xxx., p. 464. *N. W. Jour. Hom.*, Vol. iv, p. 275. *Schweikert's Jour.*, Sept. 1, 1830.

hospital for the ensuing year, and with energy and with great influence he commenced to labor for its successful opening.

Dr. Muller was a notable man.. Born August 1, 1784, at Olebitz, near Wittenberg, he attended the Gymnasium at Torgau from the age of eleven to seventeen, when he entered the University of Wittenberg. It was there that he first met Schweikert, who became a Homœopathist through his influence. Dr. Muller went to Leipsic in his twenty-first year, and soon was appointed first Clinical Lecturer and Under Surgeon in Jacob's Hospital. Three years later he took entire charge of the hospital.

He received his degree as doctor in 1810. In 1813, when Napoleon's army was fleeing from Russia, and when the camp-typhus prevailed in Europe, so that dwellings, school houses and churches were utilized as hospitals, Muller had charge of one.

Hartmann says of him:* "I remember one day in the year 1819 Muller sent his secretary to me with the request that I would lend him my 'Organon' to look through; I gave it to him, shaking my head, with the remark that a star of such magnitude in the Allopathic firmament would scarcely come to have a right representation of Homœopathy. Nevertheless, as often happens in this life, I deceived myself; the power of truth soon became manifest in Muller's clear and unprejudiced mind, and he became a complete convert."

Dr. Muller always held an important place among the early followers of Hahnemann. He had a very extensive practice, and was greatly respected.

He had a presentiment that he would die of cholera; upon its approach he used extra care in his food. Hartmann says: "On the 22d of September he visited me early, in good spirits; the next day I heard that he had been seized with diarrhœa, but that he was cheerful, and merely keeping his bed by way of precaution; on the 24th instant, at half past 5 A. M., vomiting set in, accompanied by icy coldness and a pulseless state, yet he complained but little of pain; already in the afternoon all hope of his recovery was over, and at six o'clock P. M. he sunk to rest." This was on September 24th, 1848, at Leipsic.

Hahnemann seemed at this time to be greatly pleased with

* *Brit. Jour. Hom.*, Vol. viii., p. 268.

Muller's zeal, and in September, 1832, he wrote him the following kindly letters:*

"*Dear Colleague:*

"A press of patients has made it impossible until now to consider duly my obligations and return you my best thanks for
your plain summary of the Festival on the 11th of August. I
cannot sufficiently assure you how much I am interested in the
whole affair. and particularly in the organization of the Union.
In the allotment of medical diplomas to Homœopathic students
who distinguish themselves I consider it a good plan to make
special mention of those who do the best and are the best pupils,
and thus encourage them to become true disciples of the art of
healing. This seems to me so much the more necessary since
there are still many who palm themselves off as Homœopathists;
but, influenced by the old doctrine which they were obliged to
learn, still use this and that Allopathic remedy in their practice,
a custom which is wholly inconsistent with true Homœopathy,
just as those who worship the true God, occasionally offer sacrifices to Baal, while every one who understands precisely what our
healing art can accomplish never has any need to let a drop of
blood, nor to resort to emetics or laxatives, or even a single
stimulating remedy other than Homœopathic.

"I have needed nothing of the kind for the past thirty years,
and yet have healed with the best results. Therefore, wherever
you can eradicate from the minds of our pupils false notions, occasioned either by misunderstanding of our merciful art or by
the old Allopathic practice, do so by all means; and I request
you, dear associate, to say to them that there is no conceivable
case of disease where the old practice is still necessary and, indeed, where it is not harmful, that cannot be treated better
Homœopathically. Let them tread in my footsteps, which, ever
since I have demonstrated the better way, have never been
soiled by the filth of the old-time practice.

"I wish most heartily, as I have already stated in my answer
to the letter of our friend Haubold, who as Secretary of the
Central Union desired my signature, that we may soon be so
fortunate as to establish, under Royal sanction, a hospital containing two or three instructors and Homœopathic practitioners,

* "Zur Geschichte der Homoopathie," Von Dr. Moritz Muller, Leipzig,
1837, p. 30.

where the pure system of Homœopathy can be shown in the treatment of all kinds of patients, and where it can be demonstrated how successfully they can be brought to convalescence in every case of disease without having to resort in the least to those old quack mal-treatments of the sick. Only by opening a hospital thus conducted will we be able to triumph over the old practice and to say: 'Come here and look, and be confounded!'

"With usual esteem, yours,

"SAMUEL HAHNEMANN."

"*Coethen, 24 September, 1832.*"

LETTER II.

" *Dear Colleague:*

"It is strange that the Munich speculation, the establishment of a Homœopathic hospital, with the aid of our capital of 3000 thalers, has kindled in you the heroic resolution to found with so small a beginning as 3000, thalers an Institution similar to the present large Orphan Asylum founded by Francke at Halle, with scarcely any money in his pocket.

"And it is still more wonderful that you had the heart to ask authorization and assistance from the Saxon Government, whose servitude under the petticoat administration of the hostile Dresden Board of Health you know so well. It was a great present from the opposite party, and I am astonished that you did not prohibit it. I would not have imagined that you would permit it. Yet *audaces fortuna juvat!* On the contrary, your City Council has shown itself more praiseworthy, especially if you procure for the establishment the rights of religious institutions.

"I am very much astonished also at the small price for which you have purchased a house with so much room. In a word, I see in the whole proceeding the remarkable Providence of God in enabling us to procure for our healing art an indispensable need, and to show publicly and in a matter-of-fact way that art to friends and foes and prove its superiority to the old practice. The first planning will require the greatest pains. We must try to avoid obvious mistakes. As soon as you shall have but three beds containing invalids you will have an effective beginning of the Institute, and friends and well-wishers will be sympathetically summoned through Homœopathic papers;

through the *Allg. Anzeig. der Deutschlands*, the *Augsburg Allgem. Zeitung*, through the *Genfer homoopathische Journal*, and thus through all literary channels to rear by your benevolence a Medical Institute as it will be called in its very infancy. I wish a sketch of this from your energetic pen.

"And, if I do not mistake, rich blessings of praise will soon follow in streams; and having printed a few of them they can be disseminated in behalf of our glorious cause. I would like to send you a couple, of about a hundred pages each, myself.

"I conclude with best wishes,

"Yours most devotedly,

"S. HAHNEMANN."

Coethen, 28th Sept. 1832."

Hartmann says that everything up to this time was satisfactory, and that a favorable issue seemed certain. But from some cause, on the 13th day of October, 1832, Schweikert declined the post of director that he had previously wished to take without pay and that he had previously told Dr. Muller that Hahnemann wished him (Schweikert) to assume.

Hahnemann now seemed to turn against Dr. Muller. Dr. Gustave Puhlman, in his history of Homœopathy in Germany, says:*

"The Central Society from which Samuel Hahnemann had withdrawn some years before was reorganized on a broad and democratic basis, and it was decided to admit into membership any physician who showed some interest in the cause, even if he did not practice Homœopathy exclusively.

"Hahnemann expressed his disapproval of this movement to some friends, and when the society elected Moritz Müller as director instead of Schweikert, the progressive tendencies of the former having excited his displeasure, he feared that his method would not be strictly carried out according to his intentions."

Dr Fischer, of Weingarten, says:† The tendency of the Central Society to think for themselves, which was prominently displayed at the meeting in 1832, excited the displeasure of Hahnemann, who, moreover, fancied he saw a dangerous rival in Moritz Muller, the director chosen for the next year.

---

*"Trans. World's Hom. Convention." 1876, Vol. ii., p. 23.

†*Brit. Jour Hom.* Vol. **xxx**, p. 465.

CHAPTER LVII.

MULLER'S ACCOUNT OF THE HOSPITAL—LETTER TO THE HALF-
HOMŒOPATHISTS OF LEIPSIC.

Dr. Muller says:‡ "Closely connected with the hospital project was the eventual organization, so long contemplated by
myself and others, of the General Homœopathic Society. I believe this was also embraced in the proposition by Schweikert,
who was then one of the directors of the "Central." Schweikert
and the local society at Leipsic appointed me to elaborate the
necessary plans. I discharged this duty, and after presenting
several plans and making the changes which it seemed best to
make, there was had the sanction of the local society and the resolution to submit the matter to the Central.

"Two or three days before the meeting of the Central Society
the resident members of the Leipsic Society, acting upon the
suggesting of Franz, concluded to vote for Schweikert as director
for the ensuing year, thus to facilitate the carrying out of the
hospital project. A General Convention took place on August
10th. It sanctioned the Constitution and By-Laws (in which, at
the suggestion of the General Convention, several changes were
still made, so that it did not pass into the hands of the printer
until November 10th) and the founding of an hospital at Leipsic.
In accordance with the by-laws, the board of directors (for the
ensuing year) of the General Convention were authorized to superintend the starting of the hospital and to select among the
leading physicians one or more as its medical staff. The nomination to this position was left to the resident directors of the
society upon the special motion of the Convention itself or of the
board of directors.

"The constitution itself was democratic, aiming to peacefully unite both factions. Every friend of Homœopathy became
a member by giving proof in some way of his interest in its
welfare. Every physician who was a member had a right to
vote on medical questions. Of exclusive Homœopathic practice,
as little was said as heretofore. It had never occurred to the

‡"Zur Geschichte der Homoopathie." Leipzig, Reclam, 1837. *Med.
Counsellor*, Vol. xi., p. 497.

writer of the Constitution and By-Laws that Hahnemann expected to embrace in this Society only those physicians who were exclusively Homœopathic. Had not Hahnemann, three years previously, at the organization of the General Homœopathic Convention, refused his co-operation in any shape? And had not all who later called themselves his 'pure' disciples sanctioned the draft without raising an objection, and voted to make it a law?

"The law-making power was vested wholly in the General Convention. At the election of directors held at the General Convention the desire of the members of the Leipsic Society to secure Schweikert's election to the presidency miscarried. The majority of votes called me to the presidency, while I am sure that the members of the Leipsic Society had voted for Schweikert. Had this result been anticipated, and had I been requested to decline this election in case it should fall upon me, I should have done so, just as I cheerfully pledged myself to vote for Schweikert. My acceptance implied no breach of faith, and it did not at that time appear to me an obstacle in the way of starting an hospital if the physician selected for the hospital superintendency was not also the president of the Society.

"The other members of the Board of Directors were Schweikert, Stapf, Gross, Rummel, Muhlenbein, Hartlandson, Raehl, Wolf, Trinks, and of the Leipsic physicians, Hartmann, Haubold, Franz and Schubert.

"As president of the Society, I secured within four weeks the permission of the Government of Saxony to erect a Homœopathic hospital out of private funds, certain promises from the city government, and soon after, and with the efficient help of Haubold, an appropriative building and the necessary furniture.

"On October 27, seventy-eight days after the tenth of August, in order to insure the opening of the hospital with the new year, I was able to call together the resident directors in order to formally nominate the candidates for the hospital positions, and then to have the full board select from them a superintendent. I proposed Schweikert as the man for the position, and the others present, Hartmann, Haubold and Franz, coincided with me. I appointed the opening of the ballots and the result of the election for November 10th. After we had risen to adjourn, it occurred to Haubold, at that time Schweikert's most intimate friend, to propose me as a candidate, the others concurring.

"Since it was a well-known fact that the Leipsic physicians for three months had been a unit in advocating the election of Schweikert; since the other members of the board had for two months known and concurred in this fact, since we were only going through a certain legal formality, the proposition seemed to me a mere courtesy, and at the same time a matter of satisfaction to Hahnemann who had asked me to become a candidate, and from whom I had exacted the promise that he would not nominate me for the medical superintendency of the hospital.

"And since Schweikert had particularly expressed a wish for my aid in teaching, securing my pledge to that effect, I had no hesitancy to allow this last proposition to be spread upon the minutes, with the qualifications on my part that I would not accept the position and consider the matter a mere formality. I did all this, not knowing what had just taken place at Coethen, and wholly unconscious that I was suspected of an itching for the hospital superintendency.

"Under each copy of the proceedings which was sent to distant members, Stapf, Gross, Wolf, Trinks, Rummel, Muhlenbein, Hartland and Roehl, to elect the superintendent, I wrote with my own hand that I would not accept the position and that Schweikert was the only man for it. Since it was not to be assumed that Schweikert would vote for himself, and since I did not know that he considered me his rival, this postscript, so far as I know, was not added to the copy sent to Schweikert.

"Two days before this Haubold had privately communicated to me Schweikert's secret wish that the president of the Society might allow him as hospital superintendent the yearly salary of two hundred thalers. In the first flush of enthusiasm Schweikert had offered to assume the management of the hospital without any remuneration; with equal enthusiasm, the General Convention had voted on August 10th that the hospital physicians should act without salary. (No one knew the expenses of the Institution, and it was thought that the funds on hand would not be sufficient for a year.)

"I here showed my lack of knowledge of the world and of men, as well as of executive ability, by refusing this request on the plea that I had no authority to grant it. I had then as yet failed to realize that Schweikert had lost his desire to act without salary, and that the resolution to employ unsalaried officials would sooner or later be reconsidered as wholly impracticable.

"The majority of distant members of the board had already sent me their vote, and I could already calculate that Schweikert's election would be unanimous, when there appeared unexpectedly, on the morning of November 3d, in the *Leipziger Tageblatt* (daily journal), a letter from Hahnemann, dated October 23d, in which those Homœopathic physicians of Leipsic, who did not exclusively practice Homœopathy (Muller, Hartmann, Haubold), without being mentioned by name, were denounced as silly confounders of Homœopathy and Allopathy, as immoral scum of humanity, who aimed to become teachers in the new hospital and thus to imperil the new doctrine."

The following is the letter of which Dr Muller speaks, and which without warning was published in the *Tageblatt* for November 3d, 1832, falling like a bomb upon the minds of the followers of the stern, old man:

"A WORD TO THE HALF HOMŒOPATHISTS OF LEIPSIC."

" I have heard for a long time and with displeasure that some in Leipsic who pretend to be Homœopathists allow their patients to choose whether they shall be treated Homœopathically or Allopathically; whether it is that they are not as yet thoroughly grounded in the true spirit of the new doctrine, or that they lack due benevolence to their species, or that, contrary to their better convictions, they scruple not to dishonor their profession for the sake of sordid gain, let them not require that I should recognize them as my true disciples.

"It is remarkable, and a striking indication of the power of improvement of the new system, that in no place where this system has even moderately flourished are there such Homœopathic-Allopathic mongrels to be found, it grieves me to say it, as in Leipsic, which has hitherto been so dear to me.

"Blood letting, the application of leeches and Spanish flies, the use of fontanels and setons, mustard plasters and medicated bags, frictions with salves and aromatic spirits, emetics, purgatives, various sorts of warm baths, destructive doses of *Calomel* and *Quinine, Opium* and *Musk*, these, and other quackeries, in connection with the use of Homœopathic remedies, are sufficient to identify these crypto-Homœopathists seeking to gain public favor as a lion is known by his claws; *let such be avoided, for they regard neither the welfare of the patient nor the honor of the profession, the name of which they usurp for the purpose of gain.*

"They rear their heads in the cradle of Homœopathic doctrine, as they delight to call Leipsic ; in the cradle of the Homœopathic doctrine, where its founder was first recognized as a teacher ! depart from me, ye vile medical changelings!

"Either be honorable, as Allopathists of the old fraternity, ignorant as yet of anything better, or as pure Homœopathists, for the welfare of our suffering brotherhood of mankind. *But so long as ye wear your double masks, so long shall ye be the most contemptible hybrids of all who style themselves physicians, and the most pernicious.*

"Once more, and for the last time, I exhort you to quit this *disingenuous* course and set a better example, and one worthy of imitation to those abroad.

"But he who from this day forward hesitates to follow this faithful advice, to prove himself in word and deed a Homœopathist, let him never come again to Cœthen while I behold the light of day, for he may look for no friendly reception.

"But if ye will continue in this deceitful and dishonorable course, do ye alone bear the disgrace.

"Now when an Institution is about to be founded for the fair and practical demonstration of the unsurpassable efficacy of the simple, true, pure Homœopathic practice upon the sick, before the eyes of the whole world, now the matter becomes infinitely more serious. Hence I consider it my duty to raise my voice aloud, lest these scandalous abuses should impart in this prospective college and hospital a disreputable character to the system.

"Hence I most solemnly protest against the employment of such a reprobate bastard Homœopathist, whether as a teacher or a medical attendant.

"Let no one of this description enter upon the sacred offices of our divine art in this hospital ; no one of this description.

,,Should any false doctrines be taught under the honorable name of Homœopathy, or should the patients be treated otherwise than purely Homœopathically with any imitation of Allopathic practices, I solemnly declare to you that I will raise my voice to its utmost, and will, by means of the public press, warn a world already weary of deceit against such treachery and shameful degeneracy which deserves to be branded and avoided.

"To-day my paternal voice sounds through this journal within the precincts of Leipsic, hoping for your improvement.*

                                        "SAMUEL HAHNEMANN."

"*Coethen, Oct. 23, 1832.*"

Of course this very severe letter was the cause of much ill feeling in the Homœopathic ranks.

Hahnemann next withdrew the use of his name from the diploma issued to members by the Central Homœopathic Society. It should be remembered that Hahnemann, at the meeting of 1829, had been designated as its perpetual president, his signature being lithographed with the other permanent parts of the diploma.

CHAPTER LVIII.

DISCUSSION IN THE DAILY PAPERS—INTOLERANCE OF HAHNE-
MANN—LETTER FROM HAHNEMANN TO HERING.
HAHNEMANN TO STAPF.

On the 4th of November, 1832, Hahnemann wrote to one Dr. N—— as follows: "After fresh and numerous proofs of how many persons have announced themselves as Homœopaths, who in reality are mere sciolists, and intermix Allopathic nonsense of every kind with their practice, thus grossly calumniating that noble art; after mature consideration I resolved no longer to lend the sanction of my name, though merely lithographed, for the purpose of legitimatizing any Homœopathic pretender, with whose scientific attainments and qualifications for Homœopathic practice I am not perfectly acquainted. I therefore, with all form and solemnity, withdrew my name."

The society responded in the *Tageblatt* of Nov. 13, 1832, thus: "He, Hahnemann, could withdraw his name if he were prepared to pay the expenses of paper, printing, &c., of the diplomas on hand."†

The Leipsic Homœopathic Union replied to this "Letter to the

---

*Muller's "Geschichte der Homoopathie," p. 27. *Med. Counsellor*, Vol. ., p. 530. *Shipman's N. W. Jour. Hom.*, Vol. iv., p. 281. Kleinert's Geschichte der Homoopathie."

† Fischer's translation of "Biographisches Denkmal," p. 58.

Half-Homœopathists " in the same journal for November 8th as follows: " The Leipsic Local Union of Homœopathic Physicians declares, in reference to an article contained in the *Leipsic Daily Journal* of November 3d, that it recognizes no absolute authority in science. However much all the members of the Local Union prize Homœopathy, yet this must ever remain without dispute, that every scientific physician must in the practice of the healing art be guided entirely by his own convictions. .

" Science, as the offspring of untrammelled reason, can never be established by anathemas !

" Leipsic, November 5th, 1832. Der Leipz., Local Verein Homoop. Aerzte."

Muller continues in a note: " The individual signatures were not printed; they were Franz, Hornburg, Haubold, Hartmann, Lux, Guttmann, Drescher, Apelt, Langhammer, Wahle, and myself. If, as I am not now sure, Hartlaub, Jr., failed to sign, it escaped attention. Schubert had never taken part in our Local Society, the majority of whom, although without proof, suspected him of having influenced Hahnemann's course. He maintained in the daily papers a war of words against the society, and withdrew from the Board of Directors prior to November 10."

There can be no doubt from the statements published then and later by the actors in this matter that Hahnemann really did injure the welfare of the hospital before it was opened. That his object was to preserve at all hazards the tenets of the Homœopathic law as he himself interpreted it seems certain. The very fact of his persecutions throughout the long years of his life no doubt rendered him more bitter at this time. This spirit of intolerance grew upon him as he grew older. It was but the natural result of the opposition he had encountered.

A writer in the *British Journal of Homœopathy* says:* "That Hahnemann became in latter years bitter, sarcastic, intolerant, and dogmatic is true. but that at first he was just the opposite of all this, modest, conciliating, diffident, is equally true. The treatment of his colleagues brought all this about.

"We shall then (remembering the years of persecution) cease to marvel at Hahnemann's bitterness, and shall then understand how it was that he insisted on his disciples renouncing all connections with that school of traditional medicine, whose profess-

*Brit. Jour. Hom, Vol. xvii., p. 116.

ors had treated him as a pariah and trampled him under their feet.''

Besides, here for the first time an Institution was to be opened for a public demonstration of the truths of Homœopathy, and it is natural that Hahnemann, with the eyes of all Europe looking to see the result, should wish that nothing but the most perfect adaptation of his own careful methods should be allowed within its walls.

Albrecht says of this characteristic: ''His intolerance for those who differed from him latterly attained to such a height that he used to say, ' He who does not walk on exactly the same line with me, who diverges, if it be but the breadth of a straw, to the right or to the left, is an apostate and a traitor, and with him I will have nothing to do.' ''

'' Dr. Gross, who was one of his most industrious disciples and enjoying his most perfect intimacy, having lost a child, wrote in the sorrow of a bereaved parent to Hahnemann, and said that his loss had taught him that Homœopathy did not suffice in every case ; this gave great offense to Hahnemann who never forgave Gross for this remark and never restored him to his favor.'' *

In a letter to Stapf, written in 1829, he speaks in very severe terms of Trinks and Hartlaub, saying :† ''Their conduct, I plainly perceive, since it affects me also, is egotistical, arrogant, offensive, ungrateful, deceitful, and is calculated to vex us.''

Dudgeon says he can find no reason for this bitterness on the part of Hahnemann.

In a letter written in 1833 to Dr. Constantine Hering, Hahnemann throws some light upon his side of the hospital question. ‡

''To Dr. Hering, President of the Hahnemannian Society of Philadelphia:

''*Dear Good Hering:*

''Good luck to you, in the land of liberty where you can do all that is good without let or hindrance! There you are in your element! I have no design to stimulate you on behalf of our beneficent art; that would be pouring oil on the fire. You should rather be restrained so that you may not injure yourself,

---

*Dudgeon's Biography of Hahnemann.

†*Hom. World*, Vol. xxiv., p. 502.

‡*Hom. World*, Vol. xxv., p. 505. Annals Brit. Hom. Society, 1864. Vol. iii., p. 162.

and you should take great care of your health, which is precious to all true friends of Homœopathy. When you see Kopp's book and the *Allgemeine homoopathische Zeitung* it will pain you to read with what insolent dogmatism they have begun to vaunt a mixture of Allopathic bed practice with a superficial sort of Homœopathy as something vastly superior to pure Homœopathy, and to denounce this as imperfect and insufficient for curing disease.

"In Leipsic, Moritz Muller was the head of this sect, and almost all the members of the Homœopathic Society there (which strove to constitute itself the Central Society over all German societies) took part in this deviation.

"On two successive years I warned them privately in a fatherly but energetic manner, but they would still carry on their disorderly practices; and they would have conducted their proposed Homœopathic hospital in this abominabie manner had I not denounced them in the *Leipziger Tageblatt* of the 3d of November. Then they cried out that I wished to interfere with their honest work, and that I was wrong to fear that they would practice otherwise than purely Homœopathically in the hospital, that it was self-evident that they would only act quite faithfully there.

"But you need only read M. Muller's declaration in *Archiv* xiii, part 1, p. 104 (which Stapf ought not to have allowed to appear without a note refuting his statements), and also what appeared in the *Jahrbucher der Homoopathischen Heil-und Lehr-anstalt*, 1833, pp. 19 and 25, in order to perceive distinctly that it was confessedly M. Muller's plan to practice Allopathically there which would certainly have been a public scandal and would have thrown suspicion and been an outrage on our art had I not launched my thunderbolt at them on the 3d of November.

"Then came forward in their defense a certain Dr. Kretschmar, whom I soon settled. He was followed by M. Muller and Rummel, who impudently and publicly contended that, according to their experience, venesection, leeches, &c., were absolutely necessary in order to effect cures. I might have answered (but I did not) that their want of Homœopathic knowledge could not be the measure whereby the power of pure Homœopathy could be judged; seeing that they left uncured, or sent to their graves, many whom true Homœopathy could have cured.

"The whole of the Leipsic Society sided with Muller and

threatened me with open enmity. But I suffered them to parade their false doctrines, which they call eclecticism, in the *Allgem. hom. Zeitung*, whereby they create a public scandal and incur the contempt of my true disciples. That was enough for me. However, in the fifth edition of the ' Organon ' I have characterized their conduct as it deserved. But this scandal has caused me a great deal of vexation. On the 10th of August I had with me here upwards of twenty of my best disciples from all parts (our Boenninghausen was among the number), and all agreed that the true Homœopathist, besides administering a single Homœopathic medicine carefully selected for the accurately ascertained morbid state, should eschew all palliatives and all that might weaken the patient, all stimulation by so-called tonics, and all external painful applications. May God strengthen them in their beneficent labors.

" I beg for your continued friendship and love.

"Yours truly,

"SAM. HAHNEMANN."

"Coethen, Sept. 13, 1833."

Vol. 1 of the *Allg. hom. Zeitung* contains this controversy. Kretschmar wrote an article in answer to Hahnemann's "Half-Homœopathist" epistle. Rummel, Muller and Trinks also took his side. Hahnemann wrote another letter and insisted that it be published without a word of change in the *Zeitung*. It appeared in Vol. ii., No. 1.

He said : * "The pure science of Homœopathy is entirely lost, if essays of the character of Dr. Kretschmar's, in number 22 of the *Allg. hom. Zeitung*, are admitted. The pernicious error of treating Homœopathic patients by Allopathic means are there clearly taught. No true Homœopath can peruse a paper contaminated by such flagrant errors. I consider it ominous that Kretschmar's essay has been admitted into the *Journal* by the editors. It is an indication that those gentlemen secretly countenance the errors it contains."

Dr. Kretschmar favored a union of the Allopathic and Homœopathic Schools which Hahnemann, of course, opposed.

In a letter to Stapf, dated May 19, 1832, Hahnemann gives a rather emphatic opinion of the conduct of the *Zeitung*, as fol-

---

* Fischer, Trans. "Biographisches Denkmal," p. 59.

lows:* "What you tell me about the *Allgemeine homoopathische Zeitung* surprises me, as no one has written to me one word upon the subject. So Hartmann is to be one of the editors! Is Saul also among the prophets?

"How can we trust such a weak-kneed fellow who would like to Allopathize us, and would teach the laity to treat mere names of diseases. Our art requires much too minute accuracy in its practice for such as him; he would greatly prefer to cure (or rather kill) all his patients with mercury; he behaves like a sham Homœopathic quack, and engrafts on our art the infamy of popularization—this fellow, who is more hurtful to us than all our enemies, is to be one of the editors—the mouthing braggart! What do I live to see? Let every honorable man withdraw from association with this presumptuous babbler.

"If you continue to be a strict editor of the *Archiv*, and *from this time forth* print nothing wrong in it, you will maintain your periodical in honor; *Videatur* my *Hints and Warnings*, which I beg you to print exactly as written."

Dudgeon, who translated this letter, says in a note: "Apparently boycotting is not altogether such a modern invention as we are accustomed to think it. Hahnemann's remonstrance was ineffectual, however, and Hartmann did better than was expected, and lived and died highly respected by all his Homœopathic colleagues. I can find no trace of these *Hints and Warnings* in the *Archiv*, they were probably too strong even for the faithful Stapf."

Puhlman says:† "The protest of Hahnemann had fallen into fertile soil with many of his followers, and although they could not find any fault with the management of Muller, which was strictly according to the rules of Homœopathy, they suspected Hartmann, who had written a Homœopathic Therapeutics, and by means of which he had incurred Hahnemann's disapprobation. They desired that Hornburg, one of Hahnemann's oldest pupils, who had not yet graduated, should be appointed in place of Hartmann. This Muller refused to do. The result was that Hahnemann repeatedly declared in the Leipsic paper (the *Zeitung*) that he took no interest in the Institution under such impure management, and two parties were formed, one supporting Muller, the other Hahnemann."

---

* *Hom. World*, Vol. xxv., p. 504.
†"Trans. World's Hom. Convention," Vol. ii., p. 24.

The numbers of the *Zeitung* of that date are filled with the letters arising from this controversy. Muller afterwards wrote a pamphlet in which he gave a history of the whole matter.

CHAPTER LIX.

PURCHASE OF THE HOSPITAL—THE OPENING—INSTALLATION OF
DR. SCHWEIKERT—HAHNEMANN'S LETTER—FICKEL.

In the meantime, immediately after the meeting of the 10th of August, 1832, the directors endeavored to find suitable premises for the hospital, but no rentable building adapted to the purpose could be obtained. Later on a house was found in one of the healthiest parts of the city, the so called Peter's Portion near the outermost Sandgate, No. 1, Glockenstrasse.* The owner, who had just built it, had planned it for eleven small families. This house was purchased for 3525 thalers, which in the opinion of experts was cheap, since the seller obligated himself to make at his own expense, within six weeks (which he did), the alterations required to fit it for a hospital. In these alterations every two rooms were changed into one, and a larger kitchen and laundry made. Two thousand thalers were also allowed to remain on mortgage at four per cent. interest, the balance was to be paid on New Year's, 1833.

This house had a free exposure on three sides; on the east it was built up to the next house. but on the south it formed the front of the street, on the west it was contiguous to a large garden and on the north was bordered by little gardens belonging to its grounds. The street was quite wide, and beyond the hospital, extending obliquely, was a large open space around which, near the outer gate, there had been recently laid out a multitude of cheerful gardens. The garden attached to the house contained some fruit trees, but for the most part was laid out in beautiful walks and parterres so that the convalescent patients enjoyed their exercise amidst beautiful surroundings. A wall covered with grapevines separated this garden from the public gardens. The house was of three stories, and had a capacity for

* "Jahrbucher der Homoopathischen Heil–und Lehranstalt in Leipzig." Erstes Heft. 1833. pp. 2, 197, 201.

twenty-four beds, twelve for men and twelve for women. On the ground floor there was a wide door in the middle with a room on either side, where the pharmacy, library and other offices were situated.

This Institution was formally opened with appropriate ceremonies, on January 22, 1833. Dr. Moritz Muller was installed as director, or chief, without any salary; Drs. Franz Hartmann and Haubold, assistants; Dr. E. Seidel was surgeon.

The name under which it was known was: "Homoopathischen Heil-und Lehranstalt zu Leipzig." During the first year it received only the poor gratuitously. Dr. Muller remained in charge the first half-year and delivered lectures upon Homœopathy which were published in the *Allgemeine Zeitung*.

A very complete account of this opening may be found in Stapf's *Archiv* in an article entitled: "Opening of the CLINICUM HOMOOPATHICUM."[*]

Rapou says: "I assisted with my father at the opening of this hospital in January, 1833. Drs. Muller, Hartmann and Haubold were the officers, the first, physician in chief, the two others assistants. A daily dispensary was annexed to the clinic, and all the Homœopaths of Leipsic united in giving time and labor to this undertaking. This zeal promised very brilliant results, and all the brothers of our cause in Germany awaited the outcome of the experiment."[†]

Three months after the opening of the hospital a pamphlet of 200 pages was published bearing the title: "Jahrbucher der Homoopathischen Heil-und Lehranstalt zu Leipzig. Herausgegeben von den Inspectoren derselben. Leipzig. Schumann. 1833."

The preface is signed by Drs. Muller, Hartmann, Haubold, Inspectors. It contains a history of the hospital from the meeting of 1829, an account of the opening, a report of the work and plans and descriptions of the building. A second part was issued on June 30 of the same year, the third part appeared September 30th signed by Moritz Muller; these were issued in one volume.

A year book of the hospital was also published in 1840 by Dr. Seidel, the physician then in charge.

In the *Allgemeine hom. Zeitung* for 1833 may be found notices

[*]*Archiv fur die hom. Heilkunst*, Vol. xii., pt. 3, p. 167.
[†]"Histoire de la Doctrine Medicale Homeopathique." Vol. ii., p. 144.

of the coming meeting of the Central Union on August 10th, called at Leipsic.

Hahnemann had in the meantime sent out notices in May of the same year calling on physicians not to meet at Leipsic, but at Coethen.

On August 10th meetings were held at both places. The followers of Hahnemann assembled at Coethen, while a few, having entreated Dr. Muller to preside, met at Leipsic, according to the original intention and appointment.

The members of the Leipsic meeting, regretting the differences of opinion and rupture, sent a deputation to Hahnemann at Coethen in order to show respect to him, and to make peace if possible. * He refused all overtures until they had consented to subscribe to certain maxims propounded by himself, and called by him the fundamental doctrines of Homœopathy. † A truce was however declared.

The more liberal of the physicians retired from the direction of the Central Society and of the hospital, and Hahnemann now had matters entirely his own way. He assumed entire control of the hospital.

In order to end the quarrel, Dr. Muller resigned on November 1, 1833, and Dr. Benjamin Schweikert, Sr., was installed as director, with a salary of 400 thalers. ‡

On November 9, 1833, the following article appeared in Schweikert's own journal: ||

"INSTALLATION OF DR. SCHWEIKERT AS DIRECTOR OF THE LEIPSIC HOMŒOPATHIC INSTITUTE AND HOSPITAL."

"Since Dr. Moritz Muller has resigned from the directorship of the Homœopathic Hospital in Leipsic, to whom, as well as to Drs. Haubold and Hartmann, public thanks are hereby duly tendered for the troublesome erection and first management of so highly important an Institution, I, Samuel Hahnemann, so long as I remain the overseer and counsellor for the advancement of Homœopathy in general, and of our purely Homœopathic Public Hospital in particular, shall be delighted that Dr. Schweikert, distinguished both by his pen and his practice as a

---

* Stapf's *Archiv*, Vol. xiii , part 3, p. 134.
† Muller's "Geschichte der Homoopathie."
‡ Stapf's *Archiv*, Vol. xiv., part 1, p. 131.
|| *Zeit. der hom. Heilkunst*, Vol. vii., p. 297.

true and renowned Homœopathist, has concluded at the sacrifice of many of his former benevolent enterprises, out of pure love for our healing, and out of zeal for the welfare of mankind, to settle in Leipsic and assume henceforth the management and direction of this Homœopathic Institute and Hospital.

"And to lend my approval thereof in a distinguished manner publicly on that day, I have requested my friend and colleague, Dr. Gottfried Lehmann, to go to Leipsic, so that he, as my representative, may convey my best wishes to Dr. Schweikert and may install him solemnly in this Institute, in order that he may appear as the director of said Institute, and as the physician and teacher of the Homœopathic healing art for the welfare of mankind. And may God grant him good health !

"At the same time I call upon all friends and admirers of Homœopathy far and near, especially those who are already indebted to this healing art for their deliverance from disease and restoration to health, as well as all those genuine Homœopathic physicians hereby solicited, to send in a yearly contribution for the support of this thus promising hospital to the treasurer of the same (Dr. E. G. Franz, in Leipsic), since the State does not assume its support, so that this Institute representing to the eyes and ears of the whole world the superior merits of Homœopathy, already supported by the contributions of benevolent citizens, may steadily rise, grow and flourish. I myself, so near the end of my career, can at the present time lay upon the altar of humanity a contribution of only twenty louis d'or for the Institute.

SAMUEL HAHNEMANN."

"*Coethen, October 31, 1833.*"

This letter from the master is followed in the *Journal* by the following comments: "This wish of the noble founder of Homœopathy was solemnly performed by the deputed Dr. Lehmann. On the first of November, 1833, at 10 o'clock A. M., in the presence of Homœopathic physicians and a few other friends of Homœopathy, this person installed Dr. Schweikert as the new director of the Homœopathic Hospital, publicly read the above mentioned letter of Dr. Hahnemann in the conference room of the same, and Dr. Schweikert feelingly and gladly extended his hand as a promise to care for the welfare of the hospital with all his ability according to the true meaning of the great Hahnemann.

"Therefore there was held the first clinical talk by the new director as well as the treatment of patients in the general clinic. With the best wishes for the future prosperity of this important Institution and with the most hopeful expectations, to which on the one hand the lively interest which Dr. Hahnemann himself now takes in the welfare of the Institute, and on the other the good will and sacrifices of Dr. Schweikert entitle it, the assemblage dispersed."

But the fact that a salary was attached to the directorship caused further trouble. One Dr. Fickel, incited by this salary and wishing to obtain the position of director at the hospital, published a small book containing fictitious symptoms of certain medicines and cures made with them according to the Homœopathic method. He succeeded in ingratiating himself with the hospital authorities and was appointed director. Dr. Noack soon after exposed the worthlessness and fraud of these pretended physiological provings, and he was removed from his position. He now, in revenge, wrote a book entitled: "Direct Proof of the Nullity of Homœopathy."

Dudgeon says: "This respectable individual is great authority with the Allopathic writers against Homœopathy in this country (England). His career is too well known in Germany to allow him to be used there with equal effect."* The last information Dudgeon had of this pseudo-Homœopath, was that he was imprisoned for swindling.

Dr. William Henderson says of this Dr. Fickel: "He was convicted of gross deceit during his professed attachment to Homœopathy, and to revenge himself on his Homœopathic castigators, he published a book, 'Die Nichtigkeit der Homoopathie.' He was not long afterwards in jail for swindling."

Fickel had, however, been for some time engaged in fabricating pathogeneses of drugs, and had, under various pseudonyms, published several books.†

When the hospital was started a subsidy from the Government had been asked; this however, had never been granted, and the Institution was entirely maintained by private contri-

---

* Dudgeon's Life of Hahnemann. *Brit. Jour. Hom.*, Vol. xxx., p. 467.

† See Rapou's "Histoire de la Doctrine Medicale Homœopathique." Vol. ii., p. 150. It is the intention of the compiler of this book to publish in the future in connection with a History of the First Provers, a more complete account of this rascal.

butions. The particular transactions to which it had been exposed made the citizens of Leipsic chary of giving it support.

CHAPTER LX.

ILLNESS OF HAHNEMANN—CELEBRATION OF 1833—LETTER TO
STRAUBE—AMERICAN DIPLOMA.

It must be remembered that the Hahnemann who was at that time leading such a busy and honored life was nearly seventy-eight years of age, when most men are in their slippered dotage. But his mind was as strong as in the days of his storm-swept past, and with the exception of occasional attacks of bronchial catarrh, he seems to have enjoyed splendid health. For some years he had been a sufferer from this catarrh, which seems to have been asthmatic, and which was eventually the cause of his death.

About this time he had an attack, of which he thus writes in a letter to Bœnninghausen, dated April 28, 1833:[*] "I kept myself very calm, yet the annoyance I received from X—— may have contributed to bring upon me the suffocative catarrh that for seven days before and fourteen days after the 10th of April (birthday) threatened to choke me with instantaneous attacks of intolerable itching in the glottis that would have caused spasmodic cough had it not deprived me of breath altogether; irritation of the fauces with the finger, so as to cause sickness, was the only thing that restored the breathing, and that but slowly; there were, besides other severe symptoms, very great shortness of breath, without constriction of the chest, total loss of appetite for food and drink, disgust at tobacco, bruised feeling and weariness of all the limbs, constant drowsiness, inability to do the least work, presentiment of death, etc. The whole neighborhood proved their great affection for me by sending so frequently to enquire how I was that I felt quite ashamed. It is only within these four days that I have felt myself out of danger; I obtained relief by two olfactions of *Coffea cr.* x, first, and then of *Calcarea; Ambra* too was of use. And so the great Protector of all

---

[*] *Brit. Jour. Hom.*, Vol. vii., p. 498. "Lesser Writings of Hahnemann," New York, 1852, p. 776.

that is true and good will grant me as much more life upon this earth as seemeth good to His wisdom."

Every anniversary after 1829 was distinguished by some mark of appreciation on the part of the disciples and friends of Hahnemann. On August 10, 1833, he received a cup with this inscription: "To Dr. Samuel Hahnemann at Coethen, a gift of friendship from his devoted admirer, Dr. Friedrich Gauwerky, of Soest in Westphalia, August 10, 1833." It also had the following Greek inscription: "*Askleipioi Archegetei*."

There was a very important celebration of this day at Coethen by the Society of Homœopathic Physicians. Albrecht, the author of "Biographisches Denkmal," says: "Strangers from far and near had assembled for that purpose at the hotel at Coethen, and Hahnemann received in due form a deputation which had been appointed to fetch him in a carriage. He enjoyed a hearty welcome. The chairman, Dr. Schweikert, director of the Homœopathic Hospital at Leipsic, commenced the discussion. The great physician greeted the assembled company in the most cordial and inviting manner, and solicited all present to contribute information respecting the progress of Homœopathy. The reports read on this occasion formed the subject of an intensely interesting and learned discussion.

"In the banquet room, which was adorned with the bust of Hahnemann, the company joined several friends of the new system from Coethen at a cheerful dinner. After the toast, proposed by the chairman, to his highness, the Duke of Coethen, and responded to enthusiastically, three songs, adapted to the occasion, were sung and received with great applause, reminding the guests of their happy academical career.

"On the 11th of August the scientific discussions were resumed. The great master delivered several admirable speeches, glowing and eloquent, and astonished all who heard him. The strangers who still remained, and several friends from Coethen, were invited on that day by Hahnemann to a splendid banquet. During these two days there prevailed the profoundest feeling of sincere love and regard for the great discoverer, and the deepest conviction was manifested by all, of the high character of the new system."

It was during a speech made at this meeting that Hahnemann publicly "expressed his gratitude to the Dukes Ferdinand

and Henry for the kind reception, protection and shelter they had afforded to him, the exile, and to his new doctrine. He expressed his particular thanks to the latter for inviting Dr. Lehmann, his first pupil, to settle at Coethen."*

Despite the occasional illness of the venerable master, he still continued his interest in life. He was devoted to the welfare of the hospital, he continued to practice, to write to his many friends and disciples, and to interest himself in his scholarly home-life.

The following letter written to Mr. Straube, shows us that the old man loved his faithful daughters.

This letter is written to Mr. Straube the father. The son, Adolph, had a short time before modelled Hahnemann's bust in wax. An advertisement appeared in the *Allgemeine hom. Zeitung*, Vol. ii., p. 40, in which these medallions were offered for sale.

"*Dear Mr. Straube:*

"For your complaints of which you notified me January 21 I herewith enclose you six small powders, of which you take one every week, in the morning, before breakfast, and with No. 1, 3, 5 you smell once with both nostrils into enclosed quill, without losing the small ball out of it.

"I have an old letter of your dear son in my possession; extraordinary work prevented me as yet from answering it, especially as his health condition didn't appear urgent, but these several months his health condition might have altered, so that my directions suited to those older ones might not be proper now. Therefore I beg of you with my best greeting to induce him to write how he is now feeling, after which I will send him whatever may be serviceable. Could he send me eight more pieces of iron casts of my bas reliefs (my likeness) the size next to the smallest, about this size. †

"I would like to please my daughter with them. Do not forget your daily necessary walks, and remember in love,

"Your obedient,
"S. HAHNEMANN."

"*Coethen, 2 Feb., 1833.*"

During this same eventful year of 1833 Hahnemann was

---

* Fischer's trans. "Biographisches Denkmal," p. 125.

† Represented in the letter by a circle the size of a twenty-five cent piece.

honored by a diploma from an Allopathic society in far-off North America.

On November, 1832, on the recommendation of Dr. John F. Gray, a prominent physician of New York city, and a member of the Society, the "Medical Society of the City and County of New York" named Hahnemann an honorary member of their body, and presented him with a Latin diploma.* The minutes of the society show that at a regular meeting held on September 10, 1832, "S. Hahnemann was nominated by Dr. Gray as an honorary member." At a meeting held November 12, 1832, "Dr. James W. Anderson, of the Island of Cuba, and Samuel F. Hahnemann, M. D., were elected honorary members."

Dr. Gray, in a letter dated April 6, 1833, notified Hahnemann of the honor, and with it sent the diploma, of which the following is a copy:

"SOCIETAS MEDICA CIVITATIS NOVI EBORACI ATQUE COMITATUS, OMNIBUS HAS LITERAS PERLECTURIS, SALUTEM.

"Virum Probum et Ornatissimum SAMUELEM C. F. HAHNEMANN, Auctorem Homœopathiæ, quem fama promit scientiarum medicinæ et chirurgiæ cultorem, liberalium honoribus artium provectum, placuit nobis Præsidi cæterisque Sociis hujusce Comitatus Concil. Med. Facultatis, Socium constituere Honorarium; atque auctoritatem ei donare privilegia et immunitates ad nostras Medicæ Facultatissquæ pertinent, ubique terrarum dextra et honore amplectendum.

In quorum fidem hæ literæ pro Emerito Socio Doctore Hahnemann manibus sigiloque Archiatrum munitæ lubentissime mandantur. Medicis Aedibus Novi Eboraci, Ao. 1833.

"DANIEL L. PEIXOTTE, M. D.,
Præses.

"FRANCIS N. WALSH, M. D., *Scriba.*
SAMUEL AKERLY, *Facultatis Scriba.*"
(L. S.)

To this honor Hahnemann replied to Dr. Gray as follows:

*"Minutes of Medical Society of County of New York, from 1808 to 1878." Dr. Purdy, editor. New York. 1879. Also, *Hom. Leader*, New York, July, 1883.

"*Dear Colleague :*

" You have afforded me great pleasure by this honorable token in recognition of my endeavor to introduce into the world a mild and true way of healing the sick instead of the hitherto pernicious method of cure; and I feel especially honored by the fellowship of those men of North America who are a pattern to our Europe. These North Americans, actuated by a pure zeal for human welfare, renounce the old-time and prevailing method of cure, which needs but little consideration; and on the other hand, like genuine friends of humanity, they prefer the new and as yet bitterly persecuted Homœopathic treatment, which requires far more care and thought if rightly practiced. May our all-benevolent heavenly Father, who sent us this healing art, bless your honorable body. I subscribe myself with love,

" Yours most devotedly,
"SAMUEL HAHNEMANN."

"*Coethen, 17th July, 1833.*"

The society that thus honored him was composed of the leading Allopathic physicians of New York City.

In Schweikert's *Zeitung* for September 28, 1833, Dr. Lehmann states these circumstances in a letter. Following this is Dr. Gray's letter to Hahnemann, Hahnemann's answer and a copy of the diploma, all printed both in German and in English.* .

That this action on the part of the Society in electing Hahnemann a member was *not* taken in haste is well proven by the fact that between the meeting of Hahnemann's nomination and that of his election two stated meetings, a regular and special, were held. Hahnemann continued a member until 1843, when his honorary diploma of membership was withdrawn, *one week after his death !* In the minutes of the meeting of July 10, 1843, it is recorded that: "On motion of Dr. Jas. R. Manley it was then *Resolved*, That the resolution of the Society of November 12, 1832, conferring honorary membership of the Society on Samuel F. Hahnemann, of Germany, be, and the same is hereby rescinded; carried, ayes 28, nays 2." The opposing two were Drs. B. F. Joslin, Sr., and B. F. Bowers, neither of whom were at that time Homœopaths, but only fair-minded men and physicians. As is known, Hahnemann died in Paris on July 2,

*Zeitung fur hom. Heilkunst, Vol. vii., p. 201. Also in Everest's "Popular View of Homœopathy," New York, 1842, p. 135.

1843, about one week before this action, although, of course, the society could not have known of his death at the time.

The year 1833 is notable for the founding of the first Homœopathic Society in the United States. In the same number of Schweikert's *Zeitung* is a letter dated Philadelphia, May 13, 1833, addressed to Dr. Hahnemann, announcing the formation of the society "for the purpose of giving extension to Homœopathic medicine," the forwarding a copy of the constitution and the proceedings, and asking if he would accept a diploma from the society and grant them permission to place his name at the head of their list of members. This letter was signed by Constantine Hering, president, and William Geisse, treasurer. Dr. Chas. F. Matlack, the secretary, added a postscript, wishing the Master years of health and happiness. In the next number of the *Zeitung* the constitution of the Society appeared, both in German and English.

CHAPTER LXI.

CONDITION OF HOMŒOPATHY IN 1834—LETTER AND DIPLOMA
FROM THE GALLICAN SOCIETY—HAHNEMANN VISITS THE
LEIPSIC HOSPITAL—DENUNCIATION OF HOUSEHOLD
ADVISER—SIXTH MEETING OF CENTRAL UNION.
LAST FESTAL DAY IN GERMANY—LAST AP-
PEAL FOR THE HOSPITAL.

The year 1834 opened favorably for Homœopathy throughout the world. Quite a coterie of faithful men in America were following the path of Hahnemann. The new system had gained a foothold in New York, in Philadelphia and in the surrounding country. A Homœopathic journal had been started in Philadelphia. Russia had granted to Dr. Herrmann the right to practice in every part of the kingdom. In Naples trials were being made in the military hospital with good results.

In Karlsruhe a Homœopathic journal called the *Hygea* was established, of which Greisselich became the principal editor. The *Allgemeine Zeitung* was in a flourishing condition. The *Archiv* was still published by Stapf.

Several Homœopathic societies had been formed in different countries. Homœopathic books were being published. The previous year Mr. Charles H. Devrient had rendered the "Organon" from the fourth German edition into English; this was edited by Dr. Samuel Stratten, who did not practice Homœopathy and only understood it theoretically, and was published at Dublin, Ireland.

As early as 1830 the "Organon" was rendered into Hungarian, and before this date Bernardo Guaranta had given it to the Italians.

It is estimated that at this time the number of Homœopathic physicians in Germany, exclusive of Switzerland and Austria, was eighty-eight.

A Homœopathic society was in 1834 founded in Paris; Dr. Leon Simon and Dr. Curie had also founded the *Journal de la Medicine Homœopathique.*

In 1830 Dr. Des Guidi returned from Naples to Lyons, introducing Homœopathy into France, while in 1834 there were quite a number of practitioners of the system and several Homœopathic books had also been issued from the French press.

In May, 1834, the Gallican Homœopathic Society, a national society established since 1832, sent Hahnemann an honorary diploma, in reply to which he wrote the following letter :*

"COETHEN, 6 February, 1835.

"To THE GALLICAN HOMŒOPATHIC SOCIETY.

"*Gentlemen and Honorable Brothers :* I have at this late day received your letter of the 12th of May, 1834. I am profoundly affected by the sentiments that you have so kindly expressed towards me and which you have in such a delicate manner shown through your honorable secretary. I accept with pleasure the title of honorary member transmitted to me by the diploma and by your letter, and beg of you to accept my sincere thanks for your graceful attention. Our beneficent art progresses in France as you tell me, and other reports confirm this. The society recently established at Paris and which has named me its president of honor gives a happy proof. I love France and her noble people, so great, so generous, so disposed to reform abuses by adopting new and better ways ; this predilection

* *Bibliotheque Homœopathique,* 1835, Vol. v., p. 61. *Hom. Exam.,* Vol. ii., p. 10.

has been increased in my heart by my marriage with a noble French lady worthy of her country. May God, of whom I am but the instrument, bless the efforts of all of you who labor with me in the medical reformation so necessary for the good of men. Blind as many still remain, let us do them a service despite themselves, they will be grateful sometime, because our principle is, like the light, one of the grandest truths of nature.

"I commend myself to your remembrance and friendship.

"May good luck attend you,

"SAMUEL HAHNEMANN."

Hahnemann continued during all this time his interest in the Leipsic Hospital. In June, 1834, he visited Leipsic and assisted at a celebration held at that Institution.

Schweikert's *Journal* gives the following account:* "The 17th of this month (June) was established by the Homœopathic Union as a day of celebration for the Homœopathic Hospital founded in this city and maintained by private effort and charitable contributions, and the day was made thus important just because during the forenoon of it the hospital was inspected by the Honorable Dr. Hahnemann, the venerable President of the Union. He had arrived there for that purpose the day before, accompanied by his three daughters and by Dr. Lehmann, Herr Isensee, Councilor of Justice, Herr Rhost, Superior Bailiff, and their wives, and Dr. Jahr, of Gotha.

"The resident Homœopathic physicians whom he had invited to meet him in the evening of that day to confer about certain new regulations for promoting the further success of the hospital celebrated his arrival with a serenade in front of the windows of the Hotel de Pologne, where he was stopping, and at the conclusion of it the assembled multitude burst forth in a shout of applause. He, not having visited Leipsic for thirteen years, was greatly surprised at such a demonstration of welcome, and several of the friends surrounding him exclaimed: 'Vox populi, vox Dei— the voice of the people is the voice of God.'

"The hospital was splendidly decorated for the reception of Hahnemann, and he was enthusiastically welcomed with befitting ceremony by an address in Latin by its director, Dr. Schweikert. This address (which is one of the grandest tributes ever paid to the distinguished services of a great public benefactor in the

Zeitung der homoopath. Heilkunst, June 28, 1834.

annals of history.—Ed.) was delivered in the conference room, in which was assembled a highly respectable company of ladies and gentlemen, as well as nearly all the Homœopathic physicians of the city.

"The venerable man, then in his seventy-ninth year, responded in German and expressed his thanks, as well as his perfect satisfaction with the Institution and with its director. He made a donation to the endowment fund as well as presents to the staff of nurses, and then visited the rooms of the patients, where he appeared much pleased with the deportment of the occupants. He dined in his rooms with many of his admiring guests, and after enjoying a delightful afternoon in the little 'Swiss Hut of the Rosenthal' he spent a few hours with the guests in instructing and entertaining converse. His time did not permit him to tarry any longer in Leipsic, and he left it early the following morning (the 18th) accompanied with many hearty wishes that he might have a long and happy life."

Rather a peculiar circumstance occurred in July of 1834, which will quite plainly show Hahnemann's opinion upon domestic hand-books. This year his daughter Eleonore, wife of Dr. Wolff, published a small book entitled "Homœopathic Household Adviser." Hahnemann inserted the following note in the *Allg. hom. Zeitung* for August 11, 1834:*

"EXPLANATION.—The book, 'Homœopathic Adviser,' under the name of my daughter Eleonore, wedded to Dr. Wolff, and who has never had anything to do with this method of healing, has been published without my knowledge and in opposition to my wish. Of course, I am well aware how misleading and injurious such incomplete, superficial and doubtful prescriptions can and must become to the general public. I, therefore, publicly avow myself to be in nowise connected with the said publication and I challenge everybody (see *Magdeburg Gazette*, No. 156,) to point out to me any secret remedy that I would not have communicated to the world.

"DR. SAMUEL HAHNEMANN, *Hofrath.*
"*Coethen, July 10, 1834.*"

Hahnemann plainly refers to the episode of the *Belladonna.*

An extended criticism of this book had appeared in the *Zeitung* for July 28, 1834, by Dr. Alphons Noack. It is likely that

Allg. hom. Zeit., Vol. v., p. 31.

the criticism induced Hahnemann to repudiate this " Rathgeber
fur das Haus, von Eleonore Wolff, geb. Hahnemann."

The sixth meeting of the Central Union was held at Coethen,
on August 10, 1834,* under the presidency of Hahnemann, who
now assumed the supreme power. His personal friends only
were present, and Dr. Lehmann, Hahnemann's assistant, moved
the dissolution of the Central Society and the formation of a
Saxon Provincial Society. Dr. Schweikert having applied to
Hahnemann to use his influence in raising money to continue
the Leipsic Hospital, and Hahnemann having asked for donations,
the money was all sent to him and he assumed entire control of
its destinies, forbidding the Central Union to interfere, though
the hospital was really their own property.†

He raised Schweikert's salary from 400 to 800 thalers,and he
assumed entire management, spending the money without giving any account.

Hahnemann declared Lehmann director of Homœopathy, and
Schweikert and Seidel resigned. None of the Leipsic physicians
would become director and the fate of the Institution was in
doubt. Before the 10th of August, 1835, Hahnemann had left
Germany, and the Central Society again assumed control of the
hospital.‡

This meeting on the 10th of August, 1834, was the last time
Hahnemann was destined to greet his disciples in his native land.
That in the affair of the hospital he had been arbitrary is quite
sure, but may not his action be justified when we remember that
with him his method of healing was a religion, and that his opposition was not so much to the individual as to the principle at
stake. Hahnemann feared that his cause would be weakened
were anything but pure Homœopathy to be taught in this first
hospital.

Albrecht says of this period: "The 10th of August, 1834, was
the last Festal day he celebrated in Germany. We pause now at
a mile stone and reflect upon the life of Hahnemann. He had
much of prosperity in his married life, in which nine daughters
and two sons were given him. His spouse was of a generous
and proud spirit, and was the treasure of his married life. A

---

*Stapf's *Archiv*, Vol. xiv., part 3, p. 92.

†*Brit. Jour. Hom.*, Vol. xxx., p. 466.

‡ " Trans. World's Hom. Convention," 1876, Vol. ii., p. 26.

worthy housewife, a faithful partner, hostess and mother, and throughout her life renouncing pleasure, she had journeyed through the world his faithful helpmate. Elated by the aspirations of her own soul she had considered him capable of passing forward to the height of renown. So that after he had reached the haven of rest at Coethen he was often impelled in his brighter hours to say to the dear life partner: 'Yes, little mother, it is true, how many and varied the persecutions I would have had without thee, persecutions which would have overwhelmed me; how could I have been able with such courage and strength to endure the storms of life, which drove us over half the world, if thou hadst not stood so faithfully and lovingly by my side.'*

"One would hear similar utterances when Hahnemann left his work early in the evening, often between nine and ten o'clock. He would then come into the sitting room, sit down by his wife and ask her to play something on the piano. 'How would I have been able,' he would exclaim in such moments, grasping the hand of his wife, and looking fondly in her eyes with the ardor of the love of youth, 'how would I have been able, I repeat, without thee, beloved,† to persevere in so many relations of life that were liable to fail; how, without thee, to achieve my undertaking in spite of all difficulties and to conquer, with unimpaired strength, all my enemies? If thou remainest by my side I trust to obtain the most complete victory.' But death dissolved the happy bond."

That Hahnemann was interested in the welfare of the Leipsic Homœopathic Hospital until the very time of his departure for Paris is well demonstrated by the following letter:

"AN APPEAL TO ALL HOMŒOPATHIC PHYSICIANS"

"Ever since it has been in existence, and especially in the last few years, the Leipsic Homœopathic Hospital has accomplished much that is good and gratifying through the exemplary regulations which its internal management has received at the hands of its present director, the well-known, truly practical Homœopathic physician, Dr. Schweikert, as well as through the unwearied activity with which he directs the whole Institution. It will be seen from the forthcoming annals of the Institute how much need there is of the most active and powerful support of

---

*"Hahnemann's Leben und Wirken." Albrecht. Leipsic. 1875. P. 72.
†The German word used here is Geliebte.

Homœopathic physicians and beneficent friends of humanity if it is to be permanent and produce further good for science and mankind. Since the number of beds is now twenty-one, and the whole cost of the yearly support, according to a superficial estimate, amounts to 3,000 thalers, and in addition to this the patients themselves may possibly amount to about 1,300, in accordance with the regulation now in vogue, the Institute can only be permanent if an additional 2,000 thalers is raised annually by contributions. And, apart from this, the slight capital ought not to be exhausted. This is very easily done if every Homœopathic physician, as many have already agreed to do, obligates himself to contribute a definite yearly amount, according to his ability (although at present only in five years), and if each of them makes an effort to induce other beneficent friends to make contributions and collects them and sends the sum total every year, not later than the 10th of August, to the Steward, the bookseller Schumann, through either the bookseller or the Provincial Society in his neighborhood. To such assistance and effort I urgently invite all worthy Homœopathic practitioners and friends of humanity who have at heart the promotion of our only true healing art, by means of the exemplary Homœopathic Hospital in Leipsic, in which everyone can be convinced with his own eyes of the unsurpassability of this art of healing.

"SAMUEL HAHNEMANN.*

"*Coethen, 8th May, 1835.*"

After Hahnemann went to Paris the Central Society becoming free from his domination the members became more united ; the government subsidy asked for the hospital was as yet withheld, but it managed to struggle on until, in 1836, a small yearly subsidy was allowed from the Saxon Government. In 1839 it had in a measure regained its usefulness ; the Leipsic physicians assumed the management and there was a sufficiency of patients. But there was not sufficient funds and it was decided to gain them by mortgaging the hospital property. The government subsidy was continued and the Institution continued, until in June, 1841, the money being almost gone and a foreclosure of the mortgage imminent, it was changed into a dispensary.†

In 1837, after all the trouble was over, Dr. Moritz Muller, in

---

* *Allg. hom. Zeit.*, June 29, 1835, (Vol. vi., p. 366.)
† *Brit. Jour. Hom.*, Vol. xxx., p. 466.

a pamphlet entitled the "History of Homœopathy"* gave an account of the growth of the Homœopathic system, the Fest-Jubilee of 1829, the meeting of 1830, the establishment of the hospital, the difficulties in regard to its progress; in fact, gave a complete analysis of the whole transaction.

The German physicians all unite in saying that Hahnemann by his spirit of domination greatly hindered the growth of the Homœopathic system at that time in Germany. But it cannot be denied that this spirit arose from a fear that the law of the similars, as Hahnemann understood it, would lose credit in the hands of men who might use it in connection with the old manner of prescribing. And this fully explains the seemingly extreme course that Hahnemann took previous to his departure from Germany.

Before Hahnemann left Germany he had the satisfaction of seeing the right granted in the Duchy of Saxe-Meiningen, by the Grand Duke Bernhard, to Homœopathic physicians to practice Homœopathy and to dispense Homœopathic medicines. This grant is dated October 21, 1834.†

CHAPTER LXII.

MLLE. D'HERVILLY—SECOND MARRIAGE—ROMANTIC STORIES
ABOUT THE BRIDE.

We now reach a romantic episode in the life of this wonderful man. At the age of eighty he married a wife of thirty-five.

After the death of the wife of his youth he had continued to live very quietly in the house at Coethen, well taken care of by his daughters, devoting his time to his large practice and to the delights of his medical researches.

In the latter part of the year 1834 Mlle. Melanie d'Hervilly Gohier, adopted daughter of Louis Jerome Gohier, Minister of Justice and President of the Executive Directory of the French Republic in the time of the 18th Brumaire (1799), having heard of Hahnemann's skill as a physician, came to Coethen in order

---

* "Zur Geschichte der Homoopathie." Leipzig. Reclam. 1837.
† *Hom. Exam.*, Vol. ii., p. 72.

to benefit by it. Mlle. Gohier was a French artist of some note, of a good family and possessed of an independent fortune, who was making a tour through Germany at this time. What her complaint was does not seem to be very clearly shown. It has been stated that it was some pulmonary trouble, and again that it was the lady's mother and not herself who was ill.

However, they became interested mutually, and she was so impressed with the vast treasures of Hahnemann's mind and he was so well pleased with her attainments that he asked her to share her life with him.

Hartmann says:* "The high estimation in which they held each other favored and realized this wish; no motive of self-interest led to this bond, for his wife sprang from a good and rich family and had the independent disposal of her wealth."

So, on the 28th of January, 1835, they were married in Coethen. His wedding journey was to Leipsic.

Albrecht says:† "As a bridegroom he traveled to Leipsic, accompanied by his bride and daughters. Here he gave, in the Hotel de Pologne, a festive farewell banquet to his pupils, and indulged in converse with them regarding the new system of medicine."

Homoeopathy had in the meanwhile gained a footing in Paris, as in many other places. During the winter of 1834–5 Dr. Leon Simon, *pere*, had delivered a course of lectures on the principles of Homoeopathy. These lectures were published under the title: "Lecons de Medicine Homoeopathique. Paris. Bailliere. 1835." The first lecture of the course was delivered on January 26, 1835, in the Royal Athenaeum.

In 1834 there was organized a Homoeopathic Society in Paris called the "Institute Homoeopathique."

The same year the *Journal de la Medicine Homoeopathique*, under the editorship of Drs. Leon Simon, *pere*, and Curie, *pere*, was organized. Dr. Jourdan, in 1834, commenced to publish the *Archives de la Medicine Homoeopathique*.

Among the honors that Hahnemann received at this time was one from the new Homoeopathic College, in far-off Pennsylvania, in the United States. He was, on his birthday, April 10th, 1835, elected Honorary Member of the Board of Directors of the North

*Hartmann's "Life of Hahnemann" (Caspari's Domestic). *Allg. hom. Zeit.*, Vol. xxvi., p. 245 (Hartmann's "Leben ").

†Albrecht's "Leben und Wirken," p. 74.

American Academy of Homœopathy, at Allentown, Pa. His wife received a little later an honorary diploma from the same Institution.*

In the year 1835 the Homœopathic physicians of Paris, through the Gallican Homœopathic Medical Society, requested from the Minister of Public Instruction of France permission to establish Homœopathic dispensaries and a hospital in Paris. This request was by the minister referred to the French Academy of Medicine. Hahnemann, seeing this fact in the French *Moniteur*, addressed the minister in a letter dated Coethen, Feburary 13, 1835, asking him to consult the Homœopathic society for information. Among other things he says:† "The welfare of humanity interests me too intensely to allow me to remain silent before a question of such importance. All the systems of medicines hitherto invented regard diseases as capable of being displaced materially by violent means which weaken the vital force with bloodletting and evacuations of all sorts. Homœopathy, on the contrary, acting dynamically on the vital spirits, destroys diseases in a gentle, imperceptible and durable manner. Hence it is not merely an ingenious invention, a skillful combination that produces results more or less beneficial in its application, but it is a principle of eternal nature, the only one able to restore to man his lost health."

It may be stated that the petition was not granted by the French authorities. This letter, written in the next month after marriage, indicates that the old man was already looking toward Paris and becoming interested in the future of Homœopathy in that city.

Madame Hahnemann wished to return to Paris, and Hahnemann does not seem to have made any objection to leaving his own country. This plan must have been decided upon soon after marriage, if not before, as Albrecht speaks of a farewell dinner to the pupils at Leipsic.

A great many diverse accounts of this period in the life of Hahnemann have been published. It is stated that when Mlle. Gohier first visited Coethen she was dressed in male attire. This is probably true. The friends of Madame Hahnemann admit this. The fact is excused by the argument that it was not un-

---

* "Trans. World's Hom. Convention," 1876, Vol. ii., p. 784.

† *Brit. Jour. Hom.*, Vol. xxxviii., p 64.

common at that time.   From the year 1824 it was a sort of fashion among women to dress in male costume.   Sue, the novelist,
says that in 1824 it was estimated that not less than 2000 women
were in the habit of wearing trousers in Paris.   It was by no
means considered as any proof of lack of good character, nor
has anyone, for one moment, ever doubted that Mlle. d'Hervilly
was a pure minded lady.   M. Sanches, a French gentleman, in
a letter to the editor of the *British Journal of Homœopathy*, in
1878, soon after Madame Hahnemann's death, says:*   "Mlle.
Marie Melanie d'Hervilly only changed her feminine garments
for male attire when she was an artist and when she went alone
into the country to sketch some beautiful views and landscapes.
The wearing of the male attire by lady and girl artists when they
go to set up their easel in solitary places in order to pursue their
artistic studies is not only a recognized habit in France, it is in a
manner obligatory on them."

It is said that the great French artist, Rosa Bonheur, never
dressed in any other manner while on her sketching excursions.

Another story is told as follows:†   "Mlle. Gohier arrived at
Coethen in the evening dressed in male attire and stopped for
the night at the Central Hotel.   As it was late when she arrived no particular attention was paid to the young stranger at
that time and she retired to her room.   The barber attached to
the hotel, as was there the custom, in the morning presented
himself to inquire if the gentleman wished to be shaved, and was
greatly astonished on entering the bed room to find instead of the
young Frenchman he expected an elegant lady lacing her stays."

In an article in the *Homœopathic World*, August 1, 1878,
written by a "Relative of the Family," it is stated that:
"Hahnemann's name and fame had already obtained a world-
wide reputation when he lost his first wife, who had been a real
treasure to him. . It all at once struck the fancy of a young
French woman to woo the distinguished widower, if possible to
marry him and bring him to Paris where she would be sure to
realize a fortune, if the kind fates would only favor her plans.
She, therefore, set out in the year of 1835 on the tedious journey from Paris to Coethen, and arrived one evening dressed in
male attire.   Great was the astonishment in the morning at the
hotel to find the young Frenchman of the evening transformed

---

* *Brit. Jour. Hom.*, Vol. xxxvii., p. 99.
†*Brit. Jour. Hom.*, Vol. xxxvii., p. 102.

into a well-dressed and good-looking woman. She at once made minute inquiries about the habits of our master, and having obtained sufficient information she went straight to Hahnemann's residence for the purpose, as she alleged, of consulting him about herself."

After the death of Madame Hahnemann, in 1878, the circumstances of his life were discussed at some length in the British and French Homœopathic journals. It is, however, generally admitted that whatever the manner of the first meeting Hahnemann's second wife made the last years of his life very happy.

Albrecht thus writes concerning Mlle. d'Hervilly Gohier:[*] "We purposely limit ourselves to the very little that we have in manuscript about Melanie. Melanie, who was a second Marchioness Dudevant[†] in intellectual ability, had learned riding and swimming, and was passionately fond of these physical accomplishments. She possessed all kinds of guns and knew how to handle them in genuine sportsmanlike manner. She had been at the school of painting and had visited the dissecting room. On a visit to the Paris Bourse one day she learned that Hahnemann had been appointed president of the Medical Faculty of New York. Then she immediately said to herself: 'Where the man lives I must go, I must investigate this.' This is her own language. Following her own inclination, she went most of the time in male attire. Hahnemann, who had strong moral views, could not approve of such conduct and opposed it. But how was he to help it? After their marriage they travelled as father and son from Coethen to Paris. She was wont to say, 'I prefer going about with men, for no sensible word can be addressed to a woman.' As a matter of curiosity, we find room for the following particulars:

"The father of Hahnemann's second wife was a painter from Saxony, who was blind and destitute. Hahnemann took him to his home and cared for him. Her mother was severely afflicted with the gout. She had a brother who was a merchant in New York."

---

[*] "Ein Biographisches Denkmal," Leipzig, 1851, p. 114.
[†] The real name of the novelist whose nom de plume was George Sand.

CHAPTER LXIII.

After Hahnemann's marriage certain of the German newspapers notably one published in Coethen, made him the butt of a species of small wit. This paper had before refused an article by Hahnemann, in refutation of an essay against his treatment of cholera, that had appeared in its columns, simply because the Allopathic censor of the press disliked Hahnemann.

Some of the statements are given below. The last letter is from the lawyer Isensee, who, as he was Hahnemann's own attorney, may be depended upon to know the truth. Ameke (p. 287) also mentions the ring, worth 500 thalers. and some other of these false statements.

"HAHNEMANN'S SECOND MARRIAGE."*

"Who has not heard that our still vigorous, eighty years old Dr. Hahnemann was married again on January 18, 1835? (Albrecht names the date of marriage as the 28th of January.—ED.) The reason for marrying again at so advanced an age has been given by himself many times, and several newspapers have heralded the matter; but no one has hit the nail on the head.

"And there has been no lack of mockers and evil prophesiers, who have made fun of the old man and his flame, as they call her. And if only the witty remarks are taken into account they have been 'downright bad,' as we are accustomed to say, since the editor of the ——— is certainly not the last and the least. But, whether the facts related by him are true or false, it is of no concern to the venerable man, for only the little village community laughs at them. This writer says, in No. 22 of his paper for 1835: 'The renowned father of Homœopathy, Dr. Hahnemann, in Coethen, in order to show the world how his system of medicine is glorified by the act, was married again the 18th of last January, in the eightieth year of his age. His wife is a young Catholic woman, the daughter of a nobleman in Paris. The *young* old man is still in the prime of his vigor and challenges all Allopaths, 'Imitate me, if you can.' Besides other

---

* *Volksblatter fur hom. Heilverfahren.* Wahrhold, Vol. i., p. 150.

costly things, the old bridegroom presented to his young bride, when she came to consult him, as an invalid, dressed in men's clothes, a ring worth 500 thalers, and bequeathed to her 40,000 thalers; but to his children only 30,000 Homœopathic thalers. It is common rumor that certain Allopaths are inclined to practice Homœopathy.'

" The writer says later, in No. 37 of his paper: 'We see that not merely German Homœopathy, like Dr. Hahnemann, can bequeath to wife and children properties worth hundreds of thousands, but also French Allopathy. The renowned surgeon, Dupuytran, who has just died in Paris, has left his daughters seven millions francs.'

" Again, in No. 43: 'Dr. Hahnemann, the father of Homœopathy, has gone on a visit to Paris with his young French bride, and his daughters are obliged to keep house all alone for the first time.'

" Lastly, in No. 53: 'People of discriminating minds wish to know whether the journey of Dr. Hahnemann to Paris is merely a Homœopathic preference. The young French woman whom Hahnemann married soon hastened to Paris after the wedding. In order to cure the matrimonial ill the experienced Homœopath, in accordance with the fundamental principle of his school, has made a practical application of similia similibus (like to like) and has also hastened to Paris.'

" In order to stop the circulation of such untrue reports and worthless witticisms, a well-known lawyer of Coethen prepared this document-scourge and lashed therewith the mouths of the noisy blatants, as follows :

" ' PUBLIC DECLARATION OF THE TRUTH.' "

" 'The reports about the marriage of Dr. Samuel Hahnemann, in Coethen, to Miss Marie Melanie d'Hervilly Gohier, of Paris, published in our village *Gazette*, and in some Berlin newspapers, are wholly lies and are the most infamous slanders, with the sole exception that such a wedding did take place. It cannot but be agreeable to the better class of people to learn the truth; and I, who drew up the marriage contract or settlement between the married couple and between Dr. Hahnemann and the children of his first wife, and have the most exact knowledge of the circumstances, believe this declaration to be due both to the highly esteemed couple and to the public.

" ' The marriage has on neither side any ambiguous subordinate purpose whatever. The old man, grown grey in incessant activity, and persecuted and aggrieved by all of his more intimate acquaintance, soon experienced in his conversation with Mlle. d'Hervilly, who had come to him as an invalid to be treated, a higher enjoyment of life than he had previously surmised, and this rare enjoyment elicited a profound desire to end in quiet and cheerfulness the last days of his stormy life, in cordial union with the creator of this higher felicity.

" ' She, the spouse, of a highly respectable and wealthy family; thirty-five years old; possessed of considerable unincumbered property of her own; cultured in art and science, being a clever painter and poet; but, which is more important, highly honored by the most renowned and greatly esteemed persons of her native land; sincerely beloved as a friend, and esteemed and honored by all her acquaintances without exception; she, this woman, who had determined to devote herself to painting and scientific acquirements, and to marry no one, was noble-minded enough to neglect her beloved country, her family ties and artistic studies in France and Italy, as a sacrifice to the wish of an old man, who highly deserved such a sacrifice in order to render cheerful the evening of his troublous life.

" ' Only two conditions, or stipulations, both of them purely unselfish and delicate in character, were involved in the assent to this marriage:

" ' 1. That she should receive no portion whatever of the whole property of Hahnemann, either during their lifetime or at his death, but that all of it should go to his children and grandchildren without the slightest abatement.

" ' 2. And that Hahnemann should immediately apportion his property among said children and grandchildren.

" ' The first condition is fully carried out in the marriage contract drawn up by me; and, as respects the second, I induced Doctor and Madame Hahnemann to assent to an arrangement whereby 48,000 thalers of Hahnemann's property should be immediately apportioned among his children and grandchildren, and be placed in the Government Bank, in their names, to draw interest; but that Hahnemann should receive the revenue during his lifetime of about 15,000 thalers still remaining to him, inclusive of his land lots; and, finally, that his children and grandchildren (after his death) should receive this reserve, together with *any residue that he may yet earn*. I have this entire document respecting Dr. Hahnemann and his children and grandchildren in my safe, and administered the entire estate.

"'Madame Hahnemann, except a very plain gold marriage ring, received nothing whatever, no goods or household effects, and not a penny in money, of Hahnemann's property.

"'These are facts, which directly and indirectly refute the circulated lies, and expose the liar himself to the just judgment of the world.

"'I conclude this declaration by informing the public that the generous-hearted and noble-minded wife of Hahnemann has gloriously attained her object, and finds in the unmistakable happiness of her husband her own, as well as ample reward for many a sacrifice.

"'ISENSEE,
"'*Justice of Peace.*

"'*Coethen, March 11, 1835.*'"

It is an open secret that the daughters of Hahnemann were very jealous of the second wife, and that they sought in every way to cause her trouble. After Hahnemann by will left his second fortune to Madame Melanie there was rupture complete between them. Hahnemann does not seem to have been unjust to his daughters, inasmuch as he gave them a very large fortune before he left Germany. Had he not then a perfect right to give to his French wife the fortune that she had assisted him to earn? It is certain that she made his last years happy. The only thing that can be adduced against her is that she buried Hahnemann almost like a pauper; that she refused to give up the manuscript books that Hahnemann had willed to his daughter and that she exacted an exorbitant price for the sale of the unpublished writings left at his death. These writings are yet held by Madame Hahnemann's heir, Madame Bœnninghausen, who refuses them to the profession.

CHAPTER LXIV.

DR. PUHLMANN'S ACCOUNT OF HAHNEMANN'S DAUGHTERS.

An article was published in the *Populaire Zeitschrift*, of Leipsic, for July 1, 1893, entitled :* "The Semi-Centenary Memorial of the Death of Dr. Samuel Hahnemann, July 2, 1893." In this the author, Dr. Puhlmann, makes plain several points heretofore uncertain. He evidently knows whereof he writes. After a short account of the burial he gives a biography of the master, a fac simile of a letter, portraits of himself and his first wife and ends the very entertaining sketch in the following manner: "Glowing accounts of Hahnemann's material prosperity in Paris had naturally reached the ears of his children, though he never spoke about the matter in his letters to them ; and his children might therefore have hoped that they would some day receive a second inheritance from Paris. So their disappointment was the more bitter after his death.

In an indisputable will Samuel Hahnemann had named his second wife his sole heir, and in this will he expressly says that his children had already received their due inheritance in his settling upon them the property which he had acquired up to 1835 ; so that people cannot now impute to him a want of love for them on account of this act of gratitude to the second partner of his life.

"The contentions of the Hahnemann family on account of this will have lasted for many years, and Frau Melanie Hahnemann probably insisted upon maintaining her rights because the children and their friends seemingly attacked her only and meddled with nothing else. In fact she did not give to the children her deceased husband's journals, which he had left behind in Coethen, with the express understanding that they were to be given to his children after his death.

"For the sake of preserving peace in the Hahnemann family, the writer of this article prevented this matter from coming to a sensational scandal until thirty years afterwards.

"The Seminary Director, Franz Albrecht, of Coethen, had

Leipziger Populaire Zeitschrift fur Homoopathie. Leipsic, July 1, 1893.
Dr. Willmar Schwabe.

published in 1851 a biography of Samuel Hahnemann.* The material for this biography had been given to him, a long-time neighbor of the Hahnemanns, by the deceased's daughters, Frau Dr. Louise Mossdorf and Charlotte Hahnemann. Albrecht, after giving up the seminary, removed to Leipsic and settled near the publisher of this *Gazette*, so as to expedite the publication of a new and enlarged edition of this biography, which appeared in 1875 under the title ' Dr. Samuel Hahnemann's des Begrunders der Homoopathie Leben und Wirken. Leipzig. Schwabe. 1875.'

"Director Albrecht announced that Hahnemann's daughter, Frau Dr. Mossdorf, was very much interested in the publication of this new edition; and, if published, she offered to buy for cash five hundred copies. Her offer was accepted and the printing was begun. But the printing had to be interrupted; for it was found that Director Albrecht, at the instigation of Frau Mossdorf, had made intercalations in the former edition; and these insertions had turned the book into a sort of pamphlet against Hahnemann's widow, who was still living. There were inserted in the book numerous attacks upon the widow, Madame d'Hervilly Hahnemann, and also various private letters not meant for publication; and so the work might be seized by order of the aggrieved party, and thus both author and publisher might get into litigation.

"Director Albrecht was aware of this dilemma, but thought that Madame Mossdorf would not be likely to buy five hundred copies, if the inserted matter were omitted. Five signatures of the book had already been printed, and so I decided to have a personal interview with the lady about the matter, for I was acquainted with her and I believed that she would listen to any reasonable remonstrances.

"I had been at the Hahnemann residence during the lifetime of her sister (before 1863) and had been received with unusual courtesy. The two ladies showed me, with the greatest pleasure, all the mementoes of their deceased father. On my departure I even received from them a small glass cylinder that had belonged to the deceased, some leaves from the arbor in the small garden, where he spent so many of his leisure hours, and a goose quill pen, with which he had once written. This quill-pen had no

---

* " Christian Friedrich Samuel Hahnemann. Ein biographisches Denkmal." Leipzig. Hinrichs'che Buchhandlung. 1851.

slit in the nib, and I could then readily understand how Hahnemann had been able to write in so small and distinct a hand on the rough paper then in current use, and on which we could not thus write with our steel pens.

"Had I specially requested it they would certainly have given me also a tobacco pipe which had belonged to the deceased. But I dared not ask it, considering the several mementoes they had proffered me already.

"After the first ludicrous impression made upon me by the profuse manifestations of civility shown by the ladies had been superseded by a graver demeanor on my part, the devil tempted me to elicit from them the same courtesies again, by making profound bows to them and giving them assurance of the high esteem in which I held them; and every time, to my great delight, these were followed on their part by courtesies so low that one might have thought the two ladies would sink into the earth. They were both dressed in mourning, and they repeated these profound courtesies at every bow and complimentary phrase from me, till I was at length really embarrassed, for I was constrained to preserve a grave demeanor and dared not laugh.

"Charlotte Hahnemann had died before I called on Madame Mossdorf to have this personal interview respecting the objectionable matter in the forthcoming book. She received me at her residence in Coethen in the presence of a servant maid. As I entered the house I had explained to this servant the object of my visit and she must have told her mistress. After the formalities of greeting were over, which were profound bows on my part and still more profound courtesies on hers, I endeavored to make her understand that so censurable a work could not be published, even though she believed herself to be in the right and all that was in the Albrecht manuscript should be true; and I said to her that most unpleasant relations might arise, both for author and publisher, if such a work were published.

"But she was not to be persuaded in the matter, and she advanced every reason and argument at her command to justify her purpose. I heard from her lips things much worse than were in the Albrecht manuscript. I had to leave without having accomplished the object of my visit, and my bow at departure was not even returned by her by even the merest courtesy. The portions of manuscript already in type, containing expressions of feminine grudge that she had nursed for many a year, were laid aside and left out of the book.

"For this reason the lady renounced the fulfilment of a wish that she had harbored for a generation, in a letter written to Director Albrecht, with the sharpest expressions of ill humor she had ever uttered, and in a more effusive way, too, with the single exception of a long-winded dedication that she had once furnished to a book.

"She has now been dead for a long time, and Frau Melanie Hahnemann has departed this life, as well as all the other persons named in this article. Whatever of the suppressed portions of the Albrecht manuscript could be made public without wounding the feeling of reverence for the great founder of Homœopathy, the curious reader will find interwoven in this article.

"And, as was stated at the beginning, this article was meant to be not a portraiture of the importance of Hahnemann to the mere science of Homœopathy, but of his life and works viewed from a purely human standpoint as a great benefactor to the human race.

"And yet reflections on his two marriages, and especially upon the latter portion of his life in Paris, were not to be dispensed with because many erroneous views were formerly current respecting this matter in Homœopathic circles. We know for certain that his second wife took him to her native land, rendered more beautiful the evening of his life and assisted him in every way in the most confiding and loving manner, till the hour of his death ; whilst, had she been heartless, she would have left him to himself or else in the hands of nurses. So Jahr related of her that when Hahnemann in his last days had violent paroxysms of pain in his breast she used to console him and cheer him up and say to him that Providence owed him a remission of his sufferings."

CHAPTER LXV.

HAHNEMANN'S WILL.

In so far as one may judge at this late day regarding the matter, it seems to be very probable that Mlle. Hervilly Gohier did not marry Hahnemann from interested motives. She had money in her own right, she was of an excellent family. Doubtless, she possessed the eccentricities so usual to genius, and understanding this, much becomes plain in her actions. That she was disinterested may be inferred by the fact that she insisted upon Hahnemann making a will before his departure from Germany and giving all he then possessed to his children, although this was afterwards used as an argument in favor of her cupidity. The following is a copy of this document:

HAHNEMANN'S WILL.

"In the name of God. Amen. Although on the 16th September, 1834, I made my will and duly deposited it with the Ducal Government, and although likewise for the purpose of avoiding every kind of dispute with regard to my property among the members of my family and wishing to live the last days of my life in undisturbed peace and quiet, I divided on the 17th February last nearly the whole of my fortune amongst the children ; yet after careful consideration, finding that those very dispositions (which in some respects contradict themselves) might engender mistakes and misunderstandings, and also in consequence of my contemplated journey to Paris, from whence it is quite impossible to say when, if ever, I shall return again, my views and intentions have become altered on some points; therefore I herewith cancel and annul my first will and place in its stead this present will which contains all my wishes regarding my property and other matters.

"1. Before all I commend my immortal soul to the grace and mercy of God, in the steadfast belief that this most high and potent Guide of my destinies will allow it to participate in His heavenly glory.

"My mortal remains shall be left to my dearly beloved wife, who alone is to choose the place of interment and the kind of funeral according to her choice, unfettered by anyone; but should one of my children or grandchildren dare to interfere with her directions, he is forthwith to be punished by losing one-half his whole inheritance.

"2. My whole property, consisting of £9,000 cash, two houses in the *Wallstrasse* in this town, some articles of virtu and furniture, is to be divided in equal parts, but subject to certain conditions hereafter to be mentioned among the members of my family, as well as all the children who may arise from my present marriage.

"3. As mentioned above, on the 17th February I disposed of nearly the whole of my property by a deed of gift to my children, giving each of them the sum of £900, subject to certain conditions specially stated in the aforesaid document. This deed of gift is to remain for the present in power so far as this will of mine does not alter it, but I declare herewith most emphatically that with the view not to bind myself by it, this deed has not been submitted to my children for their approval, and therefore has no binding character on both parties, but contains only my own dispositions of my property, an arrangement which I have made solely for the purpose of affording my children during my lifetime some assistance. It is, therefore, not irrevocable, but can at any time, according to my judgment, be altered or cancelled.

"4. Should my son Frederick be incontestably found to have died before me, then his daughter is to be placed in his stead, and should she have died childless previous to my decease, then her portion, as well as that of any others who may have died without issue before my demise is to fall back into the general estate.

"5. I leave as a special legacy to my two youngest daughters, Charlotte and Louise, for their joint use, my house, 270 *Wallstrasse* in this town, free of all debts and mortgages, so that they may take possession of it immediately after my death. Likewise I bequeath to my daughter Amalie, as a reward for her constant filial affection and devotion, my house, 269 *Wallstrasse*, in this city, for her sole and absolute use, free from any charge, except allowing her sister Eleonora, should she be a widow and willing to live in Coethen, the use of a room in the said house or the sum of twenty thalers instead, according to the choice of the legatee.

"6. The golden snuff-box with the letter F in brilliants, which the late Duke Ferdinand presented to me, I hereby bequeath to my absent son Frederick, should he be still alive, otherwise his daughter is to receive it, like the other portions of her father's inheritance. All the other valuable articles and moveables belonging to me have already, for the most part, been divided among my children during my lifetime by a special deed of gift. The lists containing those articles which each of my heirs has received, or is to receive, are all signed with my name, and are marked, respectively, A, B, C, D, F, G, H, and are annexed to this will. ·

"7. With regard to the house which I bequeathed to my two youngest daughters I have particularly to state, that should one of them die before me the other one is at once to take possession of it. If both are alive at the time of my death they are at liberty to dispose of all their legacies according to their own free will.

"8. All those articles of my property which have not been mentioned or disposed of, either in this will or in the annexed lists, belong to the general estate and are to be divided equally among my heirs; but all the other properties, which·I take with me to Paris, do not belong to the general estate and will be disposed of hereafter.

"9. The presents and dowries which some of my children have received during my lifetime are not to be brought to account.

"10. All notes written and signed by my own hand, with my name, which may be found after my death among my papers, disposing of articles, or assigning legacies or other properties to friends of mine, are to be considered as codicils to this will and are equally binding on my heirs.

"11. I trust that all my heirs will acknowledge in these arrangements my paternal affection, as it will greatly contribute to my comfort during the last days of my life. But should any of my family, contrary to all expectation, not be satisfied with this my last will, and begin an action at law about it, he is to lose at once one-half of his whole inheritance.

"12. On the eve of my departure to Paris, where, far away from the country in which I had to suffer so much, I probably shall remain, and where I hope to find with my beloved wife that peace and happiness for which my desired marriage will be a sufficient guarantee, I declare that I have divided nearly the whole of my property among my children solely on the particular wish and desire of my wife, which is a proof of her noble disinterestedness; to her my children owe it that they have received nearly all my own fortune, which I have acquired with so much labor and exertion, but which I never could quietly enjoy. I have only reserved for myself the small sum of £2,000, and shall take, on the particular wish of my wife, only my linen, wearing apparel, library, medicines, and a few valuable articles, as watch and signet ring, with me to Paris.

"I am now in my eighty-first year, and naturally desire at last to rest and to give up all medical practice, which is at present too burdensome to me.

"I, therefore, disclaim all intention of augmenting my fortune and renounce all further gain, which, after having amply provided for my family, I am not in need of. Deeply impressed with gratitude to my wife for all the happiness she has conferred upon me, and by inducing me to distribute my property amongst my children (thus securing them an independent existence), for the happiness and comfort she has bestowed upon them I now consider it my sacred duty to take care that the future peace and happiness of this most amiable wife is secured. To guard her against any unjust claims which might be made by members of my numerous family, a proceeding which would only show a culpable malice or sordid avarice, I order that she is to keep, without any exception, all articles which I take with me to Paris; I forbid that seals be put on her house when I die, or that inventories be taken, or any description be demanded; in short, I desire that my wife be left forever undisturbed by my family, who have no claim whatever on her, but who should rather bless her for her noble disinterestedness. But if there should be one found among my children so unworthy as to dare to disturb my beloved wife in the least, he is to lose forthwith one half of his whole inheritance; and if all my heirs be disobedient and refractory, and jointly should, contrary to my orders, molest their stepmother in any way whatever, then one and all are to lose the half of their inheritance. In such a case I request the Ducal Government to apply these fines, according to their choice, for some charitable purpose.

"13. Should my present wife bear me any children, then this

child or children, as a matter of course, have the same claims on my property as the children of my first marriage. Lastly, I request my Government to take care that this my present will be faithfully executed.

"Given under my hand and seal.

"CHRISTIAN FRIEDRICH SAMUEL HAHNEMANN.

"*Coethen, 2 June, 1835.*"

The lists marked A, B. C, D, F, G, H, contain the enumeration of the movable and fixed property. In list G he gave to his youngest daughter Louise the books containing the cases of all his patients, carefully written in his own hand. When Hahnemann had been in Paris but a short time, having gone into active practice in the meanwhile, he felt the need of these books and asked Louise for them as a loan, promising solemnly that they should be returned to her immediately after his death.

Although applications were made to Madame Hahneman after that event for their return, she refused to surrender them.*

CHAPTER LXVI.

DEPARTURE FOR PARIS—LETTER BY DR. PESCHIER—PERMISSION
TO PRACTICE GRANTED—HONORS FROM GALLICAN HOM-
ŒOPATHIC SOCIETY—ADDRESS OF HAHNEMANN.
KRETZSCHMAR ON A UNION OF HOMŒOPATHY
AND ALLOPATHY—HAHNEMANN'S
ANSWER.

And now, his property divided, his children provided for, once more this old wanderer takes up his household gods. Albrecht says :†

"Early on the first day of Whitsuntide, 1835, he departed from Coethen with his bride. His children and grandchildren accompanied him by extra post as far as Halle. He dined at the *Crown Prince* there, and then immediately resumed his journey. The leave taking of his relatives was so affecting that even strangers, who happened to be spectators, were moved

---

* *Brit Jour. Hom.*, Vol. xxii., p. 674. *Am. Hom. Review*, Vol. v., p. 476. *Allg. hom. Zeitung*, Vol. lxix., p. 100.

†Albrecht's "Leben und Wirken," p. 74.

with the profoundest emotion. His daughters returned to
Coethen with the tears coursing down their cheeks incessantly.
Alas! they had lost the one whom they had called their father
with genuine childish affection, and honored as their benefactor
with implicit obedience, and had cherished as their idol with
most self-sacrificing devotion. He had lived in the *Wallstrasse*
in Coethen for fourteen years, in a house of his own with a
garden attached, and his youngest daughter now occupies this
dwelling."

The following note may be found in the *Allgemeine hom.
Zeitung* for July 13, 1835: "Dr. S. Hahnemann on the 14th of
June last departed for Paris."

In this place an extract from a letter written to Stapf six years
before, in 1829, may be interesting:* "I thank you most cordially for your kind invitation to come to Naumburg. I must
take it as already having been done. I cannot now travel a mile
from home, if I am to live a year longer. I must observe
punctually my regular mode of life, and dare not swerve from it
a single hair's breadth. Travelling has therefore become impossible for me; I cannot visit even my married children, cannot
even get the length of Leipzic. So forgive me that I must refuse
your invitation."

But the charming invalid and artist from Paris made him forget his old age.

It has been said that Hahnemann was compelled to leave
Coethen secretly on account of the great affection in which he
was held by the inhabitants, who did not wish him to leave them
and sought to restrain him by force. This is all false; many of
his fellow-townsmen accompanied him for a short distance on his
road. † Hahnemann and his bride travelled toward Paris as
father and son, the lady again assuming her masculine attire.‡
They reached Paris the last of June or the first week in July,
and at once settled in a house situated near the Garden of the
Luxembourg. || He did not reside long in this comparatively
small house, but soon removed to a larger and more elegant
mansion at No. 1 Rue de Milan.

Hom. World, Vol. xxiv., p. 502.
† "Leben und Wirken," p. 74.
‡ *Brit. Jour. Hom.*, Vol. xxxvi., p. 301.
|| *Brit. Jour. Hom.*, Vol. xxii., p. 678.

In a letter dated Paris, July 13, 1835,* Dr. Peschier says:
"Thanks to God, our venerable Master Hahnemann has arrived safe and sound. * * * I remember my former introduction in the country, when he received me in a manner so
affecting, so paternal; I know not how to describe the feelings
of pleasure and of respect that conference produced. How much
soul and goodness his countenance expressed. He seems happy
in his determination to come to France; his marriage has in all
ways proven a happy one; his young wife is prodigal in the most
intelligent, assiduous and tender attention to his wants. How
is it possible to spread unworthy calumny about such a noble
character. He thus replied to an Allopath who had approached
him filled with spleen: 'Sir, I am come to Paris to rest myself
and to see what I will do next.'

"He has decided to remain here to labor for Homœopathy.
He wishes to found a dispensary by voluntary subscription for
those natives of France who desire the Homœopathic treatment.
If each Homœopathic physician would interest himself no doubt
the necessary amount could be raised. The Homœopathic Society
of Paris paid Hahnemann an honorary visit. He afterwards
addressed them. He recommends the study of the German
language in order that they may the better understand the principles of our science, and may trace to their sources the experiments regarding the therapeutic employment of remedies."

     *   *   *   *   *   *   *   *

Peschier also mentions his love for France and his wish to
spread Homœopathy there as the reason for his arrival; of his
painstaking in prescribing; of his trust and faith in God and his
desire to worthily employ his talents to further his method of
healing; he mentions Hahnemann's announcement to the French
physicians that he would devote two hours one day in the week
to answering all the questions that they might wish to ask him
about Homœopathy.

Madame Hahnemann at once set about obtaining for her husband the right to practice in Paris, and through her influence
with M. Guizot, the Minister at that time, she soon succeeded.
Albrecht says:† "The *General Gazette of Prussia* publishes the
following report, October 12, 1835: "By a Royal edict of August

---

* " Bibliotheque Homœopathique," Vol. v., p. 320.

† Albrecht's " Leben and Wirken," p. 77.

21,* permission to practice medicine is given to Dr. Hahnemann, who has resided in Paris for several months."

Le Temps, of Paris, contains the following article in relation to the report: "At last the Homœopathists have to a certain extent won their process. After permission was denied them to dispense their own medicines, as well as to open a special clinic, they have brought their old Master to Paris; and in doing this the wishes of Madame Hahnemann, herself, have been of admirable service. He allowed himself to be patiently led by his wife, and exchanged Coethen for Paris.

"Hahnemann has found some zealous pupils in Paris; and others from the Provinces and from England have hastened hither to see, admire and honor their Master. This man has already presided at one public convention and now a second is announced, at which the patriarch can be seen very conveniently. In order to practice his healing art in Paris Hahnemann needed permission from the Government. This has now been courteously granted to him through the intercession of M. Guizot. No one need wonder at this, for Dr. Hahnemann is as good a *doctrinaire* as M. Guizot. Hahnemann's doctrine consists in prescribing to his patients medicaments in as small doses as the Mininisterial *doctrinaire* dispenses freedom to the country. It is said to be difficult to gain access to Dr. Hahnemann, and that he is accessible only through his wife. It is also said that he sells his advice very dear, asking ten louis d'or for each consultation. It is obvious that opposing forces are in contact with each other in this healing method also."

On the 15th, 16th, 17th of September, 1835, there was a meeting of the Gallican Homœopathic Society for the purpose of extending to Hahnemann a welcome to Paris, and to show the great esteem in which he was held.† On the 15th a deputation waited upon Hahnemann and his wife and invited them to be present at a public reunion of the society.

Hahnemann, who had been elected honorary president, was introduced, and took his place upon the platform. M. Simon then read Hahnemann's opening address, which was as follows:

"I am come into France for the propagation of Homœopathy, and I am most happy to meet so many of you.

---

* In "The British and Foreign Medical Directory" by George Atkin, 1853, this date is given as August 31.

† *Hygea,* Vol. iii., p 277, 379.

"In the name of all Homœopaths, I thank the Government of France for the liberty it has accorded to our meetings and our work. I hope to increase the numbers of those who will prove the excellence of our art, and who then will grant us the means to practice it successfully for the greater benefit of humanity.

"In a document which I will shortly prepare, I will speak to the public concerning Homœopathy, that malevolence and errors have prevented them from perfectly understanding. I will speak of what a Homœopathist must be and what powers he must exercise in the practice of an art so beneficent.

"I will only acknowledge as disciples those who practice pure Homœopathy, and give medicine absolutely free from the powerful mixtures employed by the old school of medicine. In the name of my long-continued experience, I affirm that the public will not give its trust until the zealous disciples of my doctrine who hear entirely renounce that medical homicide.

"My long and successful practice, attested by my records, which I offer in evidence, prove that pure Homœopathy practiced by those who have studied deeply and who exactly understand it, suffices alone for all the wants of suffering humanity.

"I thank the Gallican Society for their labors. I see with great pleasure among its members industrious and zealous men who will continue that which they have so happily commenced.

"I am deeply affected by the proofs of attachment which I have received from all the members composing it. I will unite with the zeal which animates them and I will second their efforts for the propagation of our divine art; because age which has never diminished its march, has not chilled my heart, nor enfeebled my mind, and Homœopathy will always be to me an adoration.

"As to the Society of Paris, if it has hitherto, with some exceptions which I shall be pleased to understand, been slow to wish for a more profound instruction in our art, it is without doubt on account of the newness of the appearance of Homœopathy in Paris. In exhorting the members of that society to an indispensable redoublement of study, I will observe to them, and to you also, that to them who practice the art of saving life, to neglect to understand is a crime.

"Surely am I convinced that this reproach cannot longer be

advanced; because, animated as you all are with the love of humanity, you will neglect nothing to attain the end that we propose for ourselves, and which you will certainly obtain if, as I deeply wish, you remain united in heart and principles.

"And you, studious young Frenchmen, that the old errors may no longer encompass you, and that your search after truth may be no longer difficult, come to me, for I will impart to you that truth much sought for, that divine revelation of a principle of eternal nature. It is to existing facts that I appeal to convince you; but these facts do not expect to acquire except by means of conscientious study, and success will be complete and assured; then, like myself, you will bless Providence for the immense benefaction that it has permitted to descend upon earth by my humble interposition, for I have been nothing but a feeble instrument of that Majesty before which all should humiliate themselves."*

This address was greeted with much enthusiasm. Afterwards Dr. Pierre Dufresne delivered the presidential address, and the the regular business of the society was transacted.

The "Societe Gallicane" was organized in 1832; it was a National Society and held meetings in different cities. The first two sessions were held in Geneva, the third at Lyons, the last, in 1835, at Paris. No more meetings were held. Hahnemann's title of President d'Houneure then bestowed was continued during his life, and always when he was present at a meeting he took the chair. After his death this title was conferred on Dr. Quin of England.†

After the session on September 17 was ended a banquet, at which all the members of the society were present, was given, and which Hahnemann honored with his own presence. Among the toasts given was the following: "To the speedy union of Allopaths and Homœopaths." "A l'union prochaine des Allopathes et des Homeopathes, a la justice que les premiers ne tarderont pas a rendre a nos efforts constans par activer les progres de l'art de guerir." (*Bibl. Hom.*, Vol. vi., p. 25.)

About this time Dr. Kretzschmar, a Homœopathic physician, published in a French Homœopathic journal an article entitled:

---

* *Bibliotheque Homœopathique*, Paris, 1835, Vol. vi., p. 29. *Allgemeine hom. Zeitung*, Vol. viii., p. 178.

† "Annals of Brit. Hom. Society," Vol. i., Report 2.

"Is an alliance possible between Homœopathy and Allopathy?"*

In this he maintained that under certain circumstances it was wise and even necessary to use auxiliaries such as leeches, sinapisms, and even bleeding, in connection with the Homœopathic remedies. He says: "Is this Allopathizing? No, it is having recourse to palliatives in cases of necessity. Borrowing from the old school some harmless palliatives is not Allopathizing; and whilst considering such borrowing useful and necessary I have no hesitation in affirming that *there is no alliance possible between Allopathy and Homœopathy.*"

Hahnemann, in the *Bibliotheque Homœopathique* of the same year (1835), answered the article, and as this answer very distinctly states his opinion at this time on the subject of palliatives and accessory treatment, it is here given in full.†

"I invite all my true disciples to publish their opinions on the article of Dr. Kretzschmar, and I shall set them an example.

"The employment of mixtures of medicines, an association, the inconvenience of which is felt even by persons unconnected with the profession, is not the only motive which should make us reject Allopathy, seeing that it feels no hesitation in oppressing life, oftentimes irreparably, by means of a single medicine, for instance *Calomel.*

"It also deserves this fate, in consequence of the other processes by which it exhausts the strength and the humors of the diseased body, by means either of blood letting, of sudorifics, hot baths, emetics and purgatives or painful processes, as cauteries, vesicatories, sinapisms, acupuncture, moxa, etc., processes which all debilitate beyond belief the vital force, the energy of which, combined with the action of a well-selected remedy, can alone effect a cure.

"Homœopathy alone knows and teaches that the cure is to be effected only by means of the entire force still existing in the patient, when a medicine perfectly Hofnœopathic to the present case of disease, and administered in the proper dose, causes this force to exert its curative activity.

"One of the most inestimable advantages of Homœopathy is to husband as much as possible this vital force, which is indis-

---

* *Archives de la Medicine Homœopathique*, Paris, 1835, Vol. ii., p. 177.

† "Etudes de Medicine Homœopathique," Hartung, Paris, 1850, p. 266. *Hom Times*, London, Vol. i., p. 249.

pensable to the cure in the course of treatment. It is this which places it above all the Allopathic methods. It alone then avoids all those means ruinous to life, which are never necessary and constantly adverse to the end aimed.

"That Homœopathist must know very little of his profession, he must be very incapable of selecting remedies and of employing them properly, not to know, without thus mismanaging his patients, how to cure them in a manner infinitely more sure, more prompt and more perfect than the most noted physicians of the old school.

"For the last forty years I have not let one drop of blood, nor applied rubefacients or vesicatories, nor practiced cauterization nor acupuncture. I have never exhausted my patients' strength by hot baths; I have never abstracted from them their best vital juices by sudorifics; I have never had occasion to scour out their body and ruin their digestive organs by emetics and purgatives; and yet I have cured with so much success, even under the eyes of my enemies, who would not have failed to show up the least false step, that public confidence brings me patients of all classes, from the nearest as well as the most remote countries.

"My conscience is clear; it bears testimony to me that I have sought the good of suffering humanity; that I have always done and taught what appeared to me to be best, and that I have never had recourse to Allopathic processes, to indulge my patients and not to drive them from me; I love my fellow-creatures too well and the repose of my conscience to act so.

"Those who will imitate me, as I act on the verge of the grave, will be able, like me, to await with calm confidence the moment of reposing their head in the bosom of the earth, to yield up their soul to a God whose omnipotence must make the wicked man tremble in his heart."

CHAPTER LXVII.

Hahnemann now not only saw patients at his home but made regular professional visits, a thing he had not done for some years in Coethen.

His life was one of very great activity. From the cloister-like stillness of the quiet house in Coethen, where he only went out to visit his royal patient, to the din and excitement of a fashionable practice in the gayest city in the world. What a change! And not alone his practice; every year of his life in Paris had its red-letter day, in which the old scholar was honored by his disciples.

His birthday, the anniversary of his graduation so many years ago in the fatherland—in fact, any day that could serve as an excuse for testifying to the universal reverence in which he was held. His ante rooms were constantly crowded with people. He was visited by his disciples from distant parts of the world. He did not write any more books after he came to Paris; he revised and published the second edition of the "Chronic Diseases," and, it is said, revised and prepared the manuscript for a sixth edition of the "Organon," which has as yet never been published.

But he had already fully explained his discovery and plainly laid down rules for its successful practice. It seems fitting that in the last brilliant years of the Paris life the Master should enjoy somewhat of that luxury that had before been denied him. If, as Hahnemann says in his will, he came to Paris to rest and not to practice, then was fate too powerful for him; for never before had his practice been so large. This fact has been urged against the disinterestedness of Madame Hahnemann; that she knew could she but get the old man to Paris she could make of him a gold producer, and that this promise of rest she never desired nor intended to fulfill.

Might it not, however, be nearer the truth, that after Hahnemann had been for a short time in Paris, had appreciated the eagerness with which people desired his services, and had rather tired of a life of comparative idleness, that it was by his own wish that he again entered active practice? Is it not, when we look at the whole previous life of the man, more probable that he really was happier in leading the gay and active life he did in Paris than if he had indeed sat down to the slippered ease of old age.

Soon after his establishment Dr. Peschier published the following article in volume six of the *Bibliotheque Homœopathique* for 1835:

"The Master has finally reached Paris, but he has not come like many distinguished men of the past and present to make a display or advance the celebrity of his name. Hahnemann, conducted by his French spouse, of the noblest French and Parisian, has come to the capital to obtain rest from his immense practical labors and to live as inconspicuously as possible, and to quietly conclude a scientific production written by himself in French and destined to present his doctrine in a light best adapted to the genius and spirit of the French people. Homœopathy, as a medical doctrine, has been for a number of years the object of numerous attacks; the Homœopathists themselves have discussed the theory of its author, have rejected certain peculiarities, and have substituted different ideas. Hahnemann has not yet taken the trouble to answer these different critics, and has allowed their objections to accumulate; it is now presumed that he will discuss these cavillings and will dedicate his energies to the creation of a work in which he will arrange his reflections anew, and will present an argumentative array of testimony perfectly ample to silence unjust or incompetent criticism.

"I have stated that Hahnemann desired to remain inconspicuous; in confirmation it is true that he took such precautions that his most faithful Parisian disciples, those who would have esteemed it the highest pleasure to have welcomed him, were ignorant of his arrival for a fortnight or more.

"He selected a residence out of the way; he made no visits; he even denied himself his wonted and necessary exercise, but a renown like his own traverses distance and penetrates walls. In brief time his dwelling has become known, and at this moment his portal, as in Germany, is besieged by the multitudes who esteem health as the first of human blessings.

"But a faithful guardian watches over him night and day, his wife, who will not allow the precious moments and days to be scattered and wasted for the interest of individuals; consultations are not indistinctly allowed, and in the audiences that are demanded Hahnemann well knows what is due the scientific world, and the time required for labor of his head and his pen must not be given to private consultations.

"We are glad to be able to say that the illustrious old man enjoys the happiness very rarely granted to men and especially to savants, in that he relishes the many delights and gifts of life at an age that is usually only marked by infirmities and privations. Hahnemann is in full possession of his senses, and his intellectual faculties were never clearer at any time in his life; his health, perfect in all points, is a most convincing proof of the benefits of the Homœopathic regimen followed by him; at eighty years of age he possesses all the bodily vigor desirable, and does not feel the slightest discomfort. He is the object of the greatest solicitude and attention from his new wife, and we do not hesitate to say regarding this lady that it is a veritable adoration filling her whole life. Hahnemann is for her more than man, she worships him; we cannot express this sentiment by any other expression; she consecrates to him every moment of her life; she never leaves him; she is his shadow; she has become his *alter ego*. Gifted in a very great degree, speaking fluently many languages, among them German, she formerly occupied herself with poetry, she paints in oil with rare talent (she has executed a portrait of the great man bearing the most exact resemblance),* she now applies all the force of her mind to the study of Homœopathy, and possessed of a most excellent memory she is able to narrate promptly to the learned physician the symptoms recorded in the Materia Medica corresponding to the diseases. She has become capable of tabulating morbid symptoms with great exactitude; in the same manner that she has become the hand of Hahnemann has she also become his head.

"Knowing all this, one can readily understand this admirable woman. She receives the respect of all the Homœopaths. On one formal occasion when they were received by the master she extended her regards to all the enthusiastic disciples, the adorers,

---

*An engraving from this was published in Dudgeon's translation of the "Organon," London, 1847.

so to speak, she regards them all as friends. It is difficult to describe the grace with which she did the honors at a fete given to Hahnemann by the Homœopaths residing in Paris. Hahnemann received his friends with great courtesy, and she had a kindly word of welcome for every one. * * * Hahnemann will not return to Coethen." *

During the year 1835, among other distinguished patients, Hahnemann treated and cured the Lord Paget, Marquis of Anglesey, of facial neuralgia. The account appeared in the *New York Albion* in 1848. Dr. John T. Temple published it in his Homœopathic journal and says:† "To ascertain the accuracy of this account we applied to Dr. Hull, editor of the *Homœopathic Examiner*, who, while in England, acquired a personal knowledge of the fact, and he has obligingly favored me with the following memorandum:

"'It cannot fail to give unfeigned pleasure to learn that the Marquis of Anglesey has fully recovered from the dreadful tic-douloureux with which he has for so many years been afflicted. The malady appeared soon after this gallant nobleman submitted to amputation of the leg, which was shattered in the battle of Waterloo, and assumed after a few years the most aggravated form of prosopalgia Fothergilii, affecting the right side of the face. The cure was effected by the celebrated author of Homœopathy, Hahnemann. The Marquis applied to this venerable physician in 1835, at the instigation of his medical attendant, Dr. Dunsford, of London, after having tried the ordinary methods under the ablest masters in Europe for sixteen years. The paroxysms for a long time previous to the application of the Homœopathic method had recurred at intervals of from six to ten minutes only, night and day, and had reduced the brave old nobleman to a mere wreck of his former self. The Marquis has had no relapse whatever since the cure, which occupied a few months, and has enjoyed uninterrupted health for nearly five years, having wholly recovered his flesh, strength and constitutional vigor.'"

Dr. Wm. Tod Helmuth also alludes to this wonderful cure.‡

---

* *Bibliotheque Homœopathique*, 1836, Vol. vi , p. 118. *Hygea.*, Vol. iii., p. 392.

† *Southwestern Hom. Journal and Review*, St. Louis, 1848, Vol. i., p. 81.

‡ *N. Am. Jour. Hom.*, Vol. xix., p. 534.

Stœqueler, in his "Life of the Duke of Wellington," says: "The gallant Anglesey precedes the Life Guards, a cannon shot takes off his leg." He afterwards became Lord Lieutenant of Ireland.

The year 1836 was memorable by reason of the presentation by the French Homœopathic physicians of a medal to Hahnemann. In the *Allgemeine Zeitung*, Vol. ix., appears the following:* "The French Homœopathic physicians have honored Hahnemann and expressed their pleasure at his settling among them by presenting him with a medal on which is his bust. This they did in deputation, waiting upon him for the purpose." This item or account appears in a letter written to the German journal, dated Paris, July 15, 1836.

Albrecht says: " Among the almost innumerable proofs that Hahnemann and his wife, who most zealously aided him in his medicinal and medical endeavors, quite to as great an extent as he had been accustomed to have it done by his daughter, succeeded perfectly in subduing and captivating the hearts of the French people, it is to be mentioned that the Homœopathic physicians living in France had a medal struck containing Hahnemann's bust, in order to honor him and to thank him for settling in their Fatherland. This medal was presented to him by a deputation about the middle of 1836.

"In France, also, the 10th of August was also celebrated as a holiday by the adherents, friends and reverers of Homœopathy. The springs of enthusiasm welled up more and more copiously on these occasions.

"Two French poems, which were veritable masterpieces of their kind, demonstrated clearly that the enthusiasm reached a singularly high pitch.

"Only upon Napoleon have we read odes, which breathe equal heartiness and truthfulness of feeling and warmth of ardor."

Hahnemann still remembered Germany, and in a letter to Stapf, from Paris, in 1836, again alludes to the hospital controversy of 1833:† "Many thanks for sending me the first volume of your 'Contributions to the Pure Materia Medica.' I value them highly; and also for the third part of the fifteenth volume

* *Allg. hom. Zeit.*, Vol. ix., p. 112 (August 1, 1836).
† Albrecht's "Leben und Wirken," p. 78.
‡*Hom. World*, Vol. xxvi., p. 116.

of your *Archiv*, which gives promise of a reaction against the sansculottism of the superlatively clever perverters of our experience-proved Homœopathy. I never cared to engage in polemics. If I once broke my resolution (when I attempted in vain to set Dr. Kretzschmar right), I am determined never to do so again.

"My disciples will perform this duty instead of me, if they have any regard for the propagation of our divine art and for their own honor. No defensive article is needed for me. I only beg the shameless, ignorant assailants of the present day to bear in mind the *experimentium corucis*, that they should prove their own qualifications to speak on the subject of Homœopathy by their deeds—real quick, frequent cases of serious diseases. Mere arguing, contemptuous utterances and fault finding with the better method and arrogant presumption are no qualifications. I trust that the best of my followers will put them to shame and by degrees overcome them.

"Your additions to Anacardium, etc., which you kindly communicated to me, have been utilized by me for, and incorporated into, the second edition of the 'Chronic Diseases,' as you no doubt have seen in the second part of that edition.

"In respect to that also the inimical spirit of Trinks has been very evident. It must have been by his devilish interference that Arnold let my manuscript lie so long unprinted. It was only after an innumerable quantity of worrying letters and threats of legal prosecution that, after two whole years, I got him to go to press; but he only printed the first two parts (altogether thirty-six sheets).

"Then Arnold became bankrupt; he could not continue the publication, and Trinks's devilish object, to hinder the appearance of the work, was attained. However, it will soon see the light through another publisher. I believe it will be a profitable undertaking.

"I live here with my dear wife, healthy, happy and honored, and shall be always delighted to hear good news of the well-being of yourself and amiable family.

"Your friend,

"SAM. HAHNEMANN.

"*Paris, November 14, 1836.*

"I return you the Allentown *Correspondenzblatt* with thanks.

There I have zealous, pure followers. Soon they will surpass Germany.

"If our Gross has not put his name along with the rest to the Magdeburg declaration of the 10th of August, then you may remember me kindly to him."

The second edition of the "Chronic Diseases," Vols. I. and II. was published in 1835, by Schaub, at Dusseldorf ; the third volume in 1837; the fourth in 1838; the fifth in 1839. But two editions were ever published in the German.

CHAPTER LXVIII.

DR. DETWILLER'S VISIT TO HAHNEMANN—HAHNEMANN TO DR. HERING.

In 1836 Dr. Henry Detwiller visited Hahnemann in order to interest him in the welfare of the then newly opened Allentown Academy of Medicine.

He held several interviews with him and a reception was held at Hahnemann's house in regard to the matter, but nothing was done to aid the Institution.*

At a banquet tendered the Homœopathic Medical Society of Pennsylvania, at Easton, September 8, 1880, the venerable Dr. Henry Detwiller, then eighty-five years of age, made the following after dinner speech concerning his visit to Hahnemann : †

"Now past forty-four years I sailed to Europe, entrusted my practice to the care of Dr. N. Wohlfart, a Homœopath, and my family in the charge of my brother, then in the village of Hellertown, twelve miles from here.   My main object was to interview Dr. S. Hahnemann in Paris, Professor Schoenlein in Zurich, and Professor Werber in Freyburg, in the interest of the Allentown Academy of the Homœopathic Healing Art.

"Dr. Hahnemann and lady received me with marked kindness, and he was very much surprised at our enterprise in establishing an Institute to teach Homœopathy, more so when I told him that Dr. C. Hering was the pivot of the enterprise.   I

---

* " Trans. World's Hom. Convention," 1876, Vol. ii., p. 783.

† The compiler is indebted to Dr. J. C. Guernsey for the use of the original manuscript in Dr. Detwiller's handwriting, of which the above is a copy.

solicited his advice if it were probable to obtain material aid amongst the friends in Europe in subscribing stock, to which he answered that he would take the matter in due consideration, and held forth the hope to do something till my next visit.

"On my next visit, in October, 1836, he stated his inability to obtain, or to give himself, pecuniary aid, but he would send us his life-size marble statue then just in course of sculpture by the famous sculptor David, in Paris. He kept his word, but by shipwreck the statue was lost. On my departure he implored God's blessing to our enterprise, and madame, with a parting kiss, joined with the imploration that the good work begun might prosper and spread like the Christian religion all over the world. The result you all know."

Among the very interesting collection of Hahnemann's letters, translated by the indefatigable Dr. R. E. Dudgeon, is one written to our own Dr. Hering soon after the arrival of the Master in Paris:*

"To Dr. Hering.

"*Truest and most Zealous Propagator of our Art!*—An adverse fate has apparently caused to be lost and not allowed to reach you my two letters to you; the first, thanking you for electing me honorary president of the Hahnemann Society of Philadelphia, and for sending me a diploma; the second, giving a detailed account of my disagreeable relations with the German Homœopaths. The first was sent by the Prussian Post Office in Hamburg, the second by the Homœopath in Bremerlehe. I am now very much nearer to you on account of the sure and regular communication from this place through Havre.

"I am in Paris, and may settle here. My incomparable second wife, a model of science, art, industry, with the noblest heart and intellect, and filled with unspeakable love for myself, from her youth honored and valued by the most highly esteemed people here, Marie Melanie d'Hervilly, makes what remains to me of life a heaven upon earth, since the 18th January, 1835, in Coethen, and since the 25th June, 1835, in Paris. She is already so skillful in our divine healing art, and such a zealous student of it, that she has already effected a number of splendid cures of the most difficult chronic diseases among the poor. All this has

---

* *Hom. World*, Vol. xxvi., p. 74. "Annals Brit. Hom. Society," Vol. iv. p. 172.

made me at heart ten years younger, and for forty years I have not enjoyed such unalloyed health as since then. My Melanie anticipates all my wishes and needs, without waiting for a hint from me—she is an angel in human form!

"I have met here a number of so-called Homœopaths; they indeed confidently call themselves so, but are and continue to be mostly charlatans. But among the others in the provinces, of whom there is a considerable number, there are many good ones. The better Homœopathic school at Geneva wanted to persuade me to endeavor to convert those here by means of stirring appeals and controversial writings. But I never had any inclination for that sort of thing, and never shall have. I chose to act in another way. I cured, which of course they couldn't do, a number of very highly distinguished persons of the most serious diseases, which not only gained me immense renown (which is very remarkable in so short a time in this immense city), but which also put a stop to the persecution of the influential half-Homœopaths here who pursued me with scorn and calumny, and stirred up the honest converts to study our art in a genuine and thorough manner. Every Monday evening I invite the better sort to assemble in my beautiful drawing-room adorned with the finest collection of pictures, and I hold friendly converse with them on the most important points on which they need instruction, for I now speak French pretty fluently—which it was rather difficult for me to learn at my advanced age. All this shocked and silenced the Royal Academy of Medicine, who, before I came here, had pronounced a sentence of excommunication against Homœopathy in a decree intended as an answer to a letter addressed to them by M. Guizot, the Minister of Public Instruction, in which he asks them whether hospitals and schools for Homœopathy should not be instituted. This ancient body, composed of so-called committees of Allopaths, will eventually cut but a sorry figure in the history of medicine. They are almost without exception the most barbarous bleeders and leech-appliers. They do, teach, and know nothing else. Broussais' false teaching has for the last twenty years turned them into shameless murderers; whilst Broussais himself is now beginning to repudiate his own doctrine and to incline to Homœopathy. In establishing his frightful blood-letting method he completely destroyed the whole system of drug-prescribing, so that the apothecaries here have a wretched part to play. The 1,300 French Allopaths here give their patients, instead of medicine, nothing but a solution of gum Arabic, called *eau de gomme*, and subject them to a starvation diet. This will eventually prove very advantageous to Homœopathy.

"The Griesselich schism, which has already spread extensively in Germany, has taken root here too. Everything that can prostitute the practice of the most difficult of all human arts, encourage caprice, avarice, and laziness, and destroy love for one's fellow-creatures, is attributable to this false doctrine. Such a wicked perversion of our holy doctrine was unavoidable among the baser sort of men; it is full of attractions for them.

"But the day will come when a discerning posterity shall regard it with contempt—*parturiunt montes nascetur ridiculus mus*—the boasted effect, the real cure of serious diseases, does not take place. Hence I have never troubled myself about it. Bragging, boasting, promising grand things may for a while excite attention and gain adherents in many of the so-called arts (as formerly in the art of making gold), but in the healing art all this avails nought; here *cures* must be made. The public rightly demands *facta*, and that is just what Griesselichism cannot give.

"I have made some improvements in the technicalities of our art, which I will now *first* communicate to you. Before Aegidi's suggestion I was in the habit of giving the globule or globules dissolved in water, so that the patient might take them or it in divided portions. Now, as my medicines are very powerful, I dissolve seldom more than one globule in 7, 15, 20, 30 table-spoonfuls of water, and, because the patient has no distilled water (which, besides, after a few days becomes spoilt and ferments), I employ spring or river water for this purpose, mixed with 1-15th or 1-20th part of spirits of wine, or I put three or four small pieces of hard wood charcoal into the solution. This mixture, of which the patient affected with a chronic malady takes a tablespoonful every day or every other day, or 1, 2 or 3 teaspoonfuls, is to be shaken in the bottle five or six times every time a dose is taken, in order to change the degree of dynamization each time. The effect of this is that the vital force of the patient assimilates the remedy more kindly. When the patient has taken all the mixture, and the same medicine seems still to be required, I never repeat it in the same potency, but always in another, generally a lower potency.* Thus, for instance, I have often been able to administer *Sulphur* daily for months at a time with the most astonishingly good effects. And so also all other well-indicated medicines, as long as they continued to do good. But as there are some maladies which require more energetic action than can be obtained by internal administration or by olfaction—*e. g.*, remains of apparently cured cutaneous disease, unattended by morbid sensations, or old malignant affections of another kind, either external or internal—I use the same medicinal solution, which was prepared for internal administration and which proved most useful when so given, for external friction on a considerable surface of the skin *where it appears to be most healthy*. A half or a whole tablespoonful at a time is to be rubbed on an apparently healthy arm, leg or thigh by the patient himself or by a friendly powerful person, until the wetted hand becomes dry. It is inconceivable how much more one can do by this method. But this medicinal fluid must also be succussed five or six times before each application.

"So much for this time. Probably you yourself have already adopted this plan in the case of old, obstinate diseases.

"I do not know or learn much in my present circumstances, as I have very little time left for reading.

"I am very pleased to hear about your fine Institution, your Homœopathic Academy in Allentown. Already you beat everything we can show in Europe in that way. Your *Correspondenz-Blätter*, nine of which you have kindly sent me, are very practical, and written in an excellent spirit. But be very careful that your colleagues write good German. Aphoristic brevity has its limits; it will not do to leave out the necessary articles nor yet the prepositions. That the Academy is German in its origin and should so remain is a patriotic arrangement and is of advantage to the art, for it came from heaven on German soil and may reckon on getting further additions from thence, when the unseemly follies which at present deform it, and which have

---

* [Hahnemann here means by *lower*, a *less* (not as formerly a *more*) diluted preparation, as we find on reference to his latest directions for repeating the medicine in the third part of the second edition of his *Chronic Diseases*, published the following year. Indeed, the directions given in this letter are a mere abridgment of what he says in that part of the work referred to. A translation of these final technical changes in Hahnemann's practice will be found in Dudgeon's edition of the *Organon*, p. 295, note.]

their origin in impudence, ignorance, vanity and laziness, shall be exposed in all their nakedness and emptiness.

"I thank you for the *Rhus vernix* and *Cistus canadensis* you sent me. I will endeavor to prove them. *But I would more particularly request you to send me the third trituration of Lachesis and Crotalus*, for the knowledge of which we are indebted to America and to you. How much have we not to thank you for besides!

"It is a great grief to me that I cannot get the remaining third and fourth parts of the second edition of my *Chronic Diseases* published. Arnold (probably instigated by Trinks) made me wait two long years for the first two parts; and then he could go no further, being impoverished by his own fault, and so he gave up the further publication. Must I, in the 82d year of my age, go begging for a publisher? Ludwig Schumann refused it on account of want of means. I doubt if Köhler, in Leipsic, will accept it. I have a large amount of valuable emendations and additions in manuscript. I trust you will get a capable man for your hospital, who, when he visits his patients, will collect the students around him, and dictate the examination of the patients to a clerk in their presence, and the changes observed at subsequent visits, and give a lecture of an hour or two upon them. Do not make post-mortem examinations of the bodies of Allopathic patients in order to obtain pathological preparations from them, for they can only furnish the results of medicinal mistreatments. The autopsies of persons who have died of natural diseases with hardly any medical interference can alone be instructive. The time of the students should not be wasted with anatomical subtleties, nor should botany or chemistry be carried too far. *Sit modus in rebus!* Schönlein's views—which, as I gather from your *Blätter*, are excellent—might, as you think so highly of them (I am not acquainted with them), be advantageously taught in your Academy. Do not fear any rival English institute; there are as yet no English translations of the chief works. To what works, then, could they refer their students?

"I have, I am sorry to say, received no letter from you except your first one. Our good God will *certainly* bless your great undertaking. *I know Him!*

"May you continue to enjoy the best of health, for the advantage of mankind, and may your dear family also prosper! I and

my beloved wife send you our kindest regards, and I beg to be
remembered to all your fellow-workers.

"SAMUEL HAHNEMANN.

"Paris, Rue de Milan, October 3, 1836."

It has been said that Dr. Hering never saw Hahnemann.
This is not true. It is well known that Hering in the year 1820
was at Leipsic engaged in study. Dr. C. G. Raue says that he
has often heard Hering speak of seeing Hahnemann with his wife
and daughters upon the promenade at Leipsic, his favorite walk.
But, as Hering at this time was an Allopathic student, he never
spoke to Hahnemann, and although they were always friends
they never actually met.

CHAPTER LXIX.

LIFE IN PARIS—STORY TOLD BY A FORMER PATIENT OF HAHNE-
MANN—CORRESPONDENCE BETWEEN DR. BALOGH
AND THE HAHNEMANNS.

The following account of Hahnemann appeared in the *Allgemeine hom. Zeitung* for November 20, 1837:*

"DR. SAMUEL HAHNEMANN IN PARIS."

"Under this heading in the *German General Gazette* of
Friday, October 6th, 1837, a writer who signs himself 'Bn'
gives to Homœopathic physicians a very welcome account of
this distinguished man, to whom we are indebted for so much
that is great and important in the practice of medicine. The
editor deems it a duty to impart to the readers everything having reference to Hahnemann, so much the more because they
even then receive in Germany so little information about the
founder of Homœopathy; and he therefore believes that he com-
mits no mistake in admitting into the *Gazette* information about
him which has already been published but has not been noticed
by all its readers.

"Hahnemann lives at No. 1 Rue de Milan. The place is
beautiful and the surroundings agreeable, just as he always
liked them to be. His external appearance has remained almost

---

Allg. hom. Zeitung, Vol. xii., p. 120 (Nov. 20, 1837). *Volksblatter fur
hom. Heilverfahren.* Wahrhold. Vol. iii., p. 202.

the same as formerly, neither Paris nor old age having left any perceptible impress upon him; and it is to be presumed that his mental and bodily activity will be maintained at its unusual strength and vitality for an uncommonly long period.

"It may be difficult to decide whether his audience of office patients is as large as some assert, who regret that his advanced age must succumb to impracticable exertions, or whether we may believe a less enthusiastic portion of the people, who maintain that he has a select circle of patients and from among the higher ranks; but this much is certain that the ante-room to his office is always filled and that a newcomer has to wait for hours until it is his turn to be admitted.

"Hahnemann never curtails that thorough examination of the patient so earnestly recommended by himself, and each one thus takes up more time than is the case in the offices of other physicians. It is noticeable that he now also visits patients in the city. He formerly was but little inclined to make such vis· itations. A regard for his health, which might be slightly endangered by constant sitting, ought to have determined him to take such exercise.

"The magnitude of this recognition on the part of the public is not real, however, if it depends on an estimation of its scientific standpoint in general, and of its relations to the Homœopathic medical public in particular. It is relatively of the greatest importance for the contending and disputing parties and tendencies respectively in Homœopathy that the author does not seem at all disposed to lend an open ear to the additional facts and instructions proffered to him, with more or less discretion, or for a long period, by the adherents of his doctrines. He knows how to cling resolutely to the truth, not only of his generally received fundamental tenets, but also to the rejection of the old pathology, and especially nosology (a characteristic feature of the Hahnemannian practice); in a word, he will know how to protect against the common methods of treating disease, and especially against every beginning in accordance with the old school.

"This is not the place, nor is it my design, to criticise the different parties in Homœopathy, and therefore we must pass over the importance of the reasons which make him the greatest scientific reformer known to history. But it may be permitted to state here that the question is far from being settled by the common so-called scientific arguments of which Homœopathic literature begins to receive a superabundance and also that in the eager but not therefore unscientific pursuit of Hahnemannic tenets the way is opened to a research not as yet anticipated, and absolutely incalculable in its results. Unfortunately this party has now but one representative of importance in Hahnemann himself, though Bœnninghausen may possibly be added to the number. (If the laity in medicine are to be counted among the representatives of this party, then there are many more of them.—ED.) At all events this small number of professionals is to be deplored, and can be explained only by the defective discernment of physicians with respect to the vast importance of the matter, and by the very great difficulty in the practice of this profession. (May not these be the real reasons?—ED.)

"Hahnemann's eager zeal for his cause and strenuous opposition to his enemies are still the same as formerly. * * *

"The continuation of Hahnemann's 'Chronic Diseases' furnishes a proof of his enduring activity in the aim which he has so long pursued. (Third volume, second edition.) This work is carefully executed in his own hand-writing and with minute industry. A mere glance at the volume (third) last published will suffice to convince one of the careful and thoroughly systematic elaboration of the material and of the critical aim.

"It would be an important loss to mankind, although many seem to be unwilling to acknowledge it, if Hahnemann should be prevented from completing this highly important work, a second revised edition of which is now in course of publication.

"The completion of a plan already promising to be successful would be of the greatest consequence to Hahnemann's doctrine. This plan is the erection in Paris of a vast hospital which is to be under his supervision and direction, and to have its physicians appointed by himself.

"Herein would be found the opportunity to verify on a large scale what is isolatedly reported from so many directions about the brilliant results of Homœopathy. Whatever might be the result, science could only be won over by such an enterprise, and every physician seeking the truth, of whatever school he may be, must heartily wish the speedy promotion of this plan. —BN."

The following is an account of his treatment of a patient in 1837:

Under the title of "A Reminiscence of Hahnemann," an account is given in the *Medical Advance*, for April, 1893, of the presentation of a patient of Hahnemann to the students of the Hering Medical College of Chicago, February 23, 1893. The name of this gentleman is John B. Young, of Clinton, Iowa. He was taken from Paisley in Scotland to Paris, and was placed under Hahnemann's care when he was twelve years of age.

He had previously been ill for two years, and had been given up by his physicians, when a charitable lady took him to Paris by short stages.

"You went from London to Paris?"

"Yes, I went from London to Paris."

"When you arrived in Paris, did you go to see Hahnemann, or did Hahnemann come to see you?"

"He came to see me the second day after my arrival, and gave me an examination that lasted about an hour and a half."

"Did he strip you?"

"Yes, I had to go to bed. He went over me more thoroughly than I have ever been gone over before or since."

"Dr. Allen. 'And still it is said that Hahnemann was a symptomatologist and usually prescribed for symptoms; and rarely made a physical examination.'"

"Mr. Young. He would make me count one, two, three, etc., up to one hundred, and put an instrument to my chest and did the same to my back, and he did more thumping of my chest than I ever had before." * * * * *

"He said he *knew* that I had come to him in time and he could cure me."

"Did he give you very much medicine?"

"Not a very great deal. I think I had medicine about four times a day at first, including what I got at night."

"What was your impression of Hahnemann?"

"The first impression made on my mind when I saw him was that his face had a luminous expression. He looked more to me, as I would call it, a divine man—there was divinity about his appearance. He was a good man undoubtedly, and I was informed that he often when he gave his medicine said to his patients that he was but the instrument, that he did the best he could and then they must look to God for the blessing."

"At that time were there many patients visiting Hahnemann at his office, and what was the size of his office?"

"He had a very large room, and when I was there he had some two hours that he met 'counsel patients.' There were generally sixty or more patients at any time in his office when I was there."

"Were there any foreigners at that time who came to Hahnemann?"

"Oh, many of them. I became acquainted with quite a number of his patients.. I had been there quite a while and there were patients there from America, and Germany, and Russia, and a number from my own country, and they were there from all parts of the world, and there were a great many who expressed themselves to me in this way, that they had not gone to Hahnemann until they were in the last stage of the disease and had been given up by their regular physician. Hahnemann got them when, like me, they were pretty nearly gone, so that it looked to me more like a place where miracles were being performed than any place in which I have ever been, and numbers he brought from death into health."

"He finally cured you?"

"Yes, I came home strong."

"How long were you under his care?"

"About nine months. There is one thing I would like to tell about him. Of course I was indebted to Miss Sterling for being taken to Paris and placed under his care, and just before she left Paris she wanted to settle with Dr. Hahnemann, and of course under ordinary circumstances it would have been a large bill she would have had to pay. Hahnemann refused to make a bill, and when she insisted he said: 'Madam, do you think you have more benevolence than I have? Do you suppose that you should have had all the trouble and anxiety and expense of bringing him from Paisley and that I should then charge anything.' He says, 'No.'"

"I suppose he received a present that was worth more than the bill. That was the disposition of the woman. Mrs. Hahnemann, the young wife, was there to assist. It was in 1837. I was put on diet, a special diet for morning and evening. I had babies' food; that is, bread and milk and sugar. The bread was cut up in small pieces and boiled milk poured over it with sugar and allowed to stand a while and soak soft, and I had that for my morning and evening meals. All stimulants were forbidden. He gave the orders for my meals. I do not know that I should reveal his private affairs, but I was going to say that Hahnemann was an inveterate smoker. I have seen his young wife fill his pipe for him many times."

The following communication appeared in Dr. Wahrhold's *Volksblatter* for 1838:*

"DR. SAMUEL HAHNEMANN IN PARIS."

"Dr. Paul Balogh, a Homœopathic physician of Pesth, sends to the *Allgemeine Anzeiger der Deutschen* of February 5, 1838, a communication concerning that remarkable man (the Hofrath Hahnemann), for which all disciples of the great Master will be very thankful. Dr. Balogh says: 'It was in the year 1825, when I was attending the Universities of Germany, that I was so fortunate as to make the acquaintance, among other distinguished Germans, of Dr. Hahnemann at Coethen. I found him to be an upright and amiable old man, who gave me many interesting ideas and eminently practical instruction in the new doctrine. His friendly manner and profound scientific knowledge made me esteem him highly and attached me strongly to his person. After I returned home I became more closely allied to the practice of Homœopathy, and have remained faithful to the new doctrine in all its purity, and I rejoice in its most praiseworthy results.

"'With this great reformer, whose friendship cheered and consoled me on my thorny pathway, I kept up a correspondence until he married Melanie d'Hervilly and exchanged his ungrateful Fatherland for Paris. The year prior to this, when Dr. Moscovich concluded to make the tour of France, England and Germany, he also wished to make the acquaintance of this celebrated man, whose doctrine had interested him. This was my motive for giving to this doctor letters of introduction to both Dr. Hahnemann and his worthy wife. As the letters which I received throw some light upon Dr. Hahnemann's life at that time, I hope that their publication will interest his friends. The following are the letters:'

* *Volksblatter fur hom. Heilverfahren mit Bezug auf Wasserheilkunde,* Leipzig, 1838, Vol. iv., p. 118.

"'Paris, August 6, 1837.

"'Rue de Milan, 1.

"'*Dear Sir:* Accept my sincere thanks for the very kind letter which you were so good as to write to me. The sentiments expressed by you so well in a language foreign to your own, but which you write like a native, have really touched my heart. I feel poignant grief at not knowing personally so distinguished a man, and one so full of zeal for our good cause, the cause of humanity; but there is left me the hope that you will pay us a visit, as did Dr. Moscovich, for whose acquaintance we are indebted to you. I do not say, as did the poor Poles: 'It is too high to God, and too far to France.' God is always near those who are right, and France is accessible to all courageous men who love science; and have not I, though a woman. traversed Europe in order to fetch Hahnemann to Paris? Rest assured that the most thoughtful and tender cares are bestowed incessantly upon him. He is as fresh and ruddy as a rose and as blithesome as a young bird; indeed, one might truthfully say that since he has been with me he becomes every year one year younger. May God give him health here with us! I send you herewith a medal which represents him perfectly. It was designed by one of our most distinguished artists.

"'May you be happy and prosperous, Sir, and preserve your friendship for us! Good health and good luck to you!

"'Melanie Hahnemann.'

"'*To Dr. Paul Balogh, Homœopathic Physician at Pesth :*

"'*Dear Friend:* Your friendly remembrance of me has given me great pleasure. I send you my best love, and wish you and your faithful wife every comfort of life.

"'Your true friend,

"'Samuel Hahnemann.'

"The letter of Madame Hahnemann shows a noble spirit, and attests both the amiable personal character of the writer and the matrimonial happiness of her venerable husband. It indicates besides a warmth of zeal for the great discovery of her husband. She has made it the task of her life to make more beautiful the evening of the stormy life of one who formerly saved her own life, by the beneficent balsam of true fidelity, loving care, tender regard and delicate attention. She really seems to have perfectly comprehended the great and grand art, the problem of which the greatest minds try to solve, of preserving the waning spirit of life in youthful vigor, and of warding off all the happenings which cripple the power of old age.

"With the letter came the beautiful large medal of Hahnemann, which was designed by the famous artist David. The medal is a most lifelike representation of the celebrated man. After seeing so many bad copies of his countenance, it affords me unbounded joy to possess a good one at last, through the kindness of his noble wife. It brings his face vividly to my mind after an absence of twelve years. As respects the features of the venerable man, they are the most unanswerable witnesses of the fresh vigor which animates the members of his body. These firm, pure, beautiful, youthful features scarcely permit us to believe that they are those of a man eighty-two years old. What the distinguished naturalist said about style—that the style is the man—might to some extent be applied to a person's handwriting. His extremely neat, firm and charming chirography corresponds perfectly to a pure and clear doctrine resting on a firm basis.

"According to the statement of Dr. Moscovich, Dr. Hahnemann lives very pleasantly in Paris and enjoys the high esteem of all classes of people. Only very few persons are fortunate enough to see him face to face since his noble wife takes good care to keep away all who might in any degree annoy him or might overtax his powers in office consultations.

"And he very seldom goes into the city to visit the sick. During Dr. Moscovich's visit to Paris, Baron Rothschild was the only person whom he thus visited. For this reason more sick throng his dwelling, but the greater portion receive medical advice only from his highly cultured and intelligent wife. We may expect many interesting accounts about him from Dr. Moscovich, since he often had the opportunity to come into close contact with him.

"PAUL BALOGH, M. D."

CHAPTER LXX.

In the same journal Dr. Hennicke, Counsellor of Legation and editor of the *Allgemeine Anzeiger der Deutschen*, writes as follows: "The publication of the following letter which the undersigned received from Dr. Hahnemann, will doubtless not be unwelcome to his many friends and relations, since it gives definite information about the happy domestic relations and professional activity of the most praiseworthy man in the history of science. It is a psychological phenomena that a youthful spirit still animates this Nestor among physicians, now in his eighty-fourth year, and that his handwriting still exhibits the same neatness and beauty as in the prime of youth. The undersigned can judge of this matter for he has been in friendly relations and correspondence with Dr. Hahnemann for forty-three years.

"'Dr. J. Fr. H. (Hennicke.)

"'*Dear Friend:* Your kindly interest in me and whatever befalls me since I have been here, which is expressed by your previous letter to me under date of 3d of November, had warmed again my old gratitude to you How greatly indebted to you is the new true art of healing, which you have disseminated so effectively by voice and pen.

"'So you wish to hear something about me and my doings since I have been here? I am more cheerful and contented here under the unwearied and unexampled care of my incomparable Melanie than I was during my last years at Coethen. She cures gratuitously every day under my supervision a great number of poor people. Such supervision is now almost unnecessary, since she makes great progress every day through her own study of our system of healing. Her cures of the worst diseases, which may be called natural, these poor people being too impecunious to get themselves botched as do the well-to-do and the rich by the pernicious method of healing, often amazed everybody, and even myself. I did not wish to write anything for France, or what is almost the same thing for Paris, in order to make our healing art better known to a praiseworthy land of freedom, a land where one can do whatever is good without being hindered and without being punished for it. Far too much has already been written about a system which the unbelieving ignoramus lets be perverted.

"'No, I wished, by repeated cures of the worst kinds of uncured sick persons, to thoroughly convince the public of the infinite superiority of our healing art to any other that can be named; a task which it would seem could not be performed in a city of more than a million of inhabitants. But God be praised! this task has already been partially performed. Our system is getting to be respectable in the estimation of the Parisian public on account of its unprecedentedly favorable results.

"'More I could not desire, and yet, on account of these successes my persistence in the cure of proscribed cases is at the same time the jest of all those who, before my arrival, palmed themselves off, both in Paris and in the Provinces, as Homœopathic physicians, because more and more enthusiastic, and I have been urged on to the more zealous study of this most abstruse and most beneficent of all human arts.

"'Every Monday morning from eight to eleven and a half o'clock there assemble in my quite unpretentious hotel a number of the best Homœopathic physicians of the city for the purpose of exchanging views on Homœopathic matters; and even transient Homœopathic physicians and friends of our system participate in this voluntary union.

"'The news thus imparted from Rome, Munich and North America is partially new to me and very agreeable.

"'May God continue to keep you and yours in as great prosperity as you could desire, and keep unchanged your love to me, a love which I shall never neglect to repay with that of equal ardor.

"'Yours sincerely,

"'SAMUEL HAHNEMANN.

"'*Paris, 16th December, 1837.*

"'*Rue de Milan, No. 1.*"

"'Dr. Plaubel sends a friendly message.'"

Dr. Hennicke was a lifelong friend of Hahnemann, and his influential paper greatly aided in the spread of Homœopathy. The Allopaths called the editor the Sancho Panza of the Don Quixote, Hahnemann.

Dr. Hennicke writing of Hahnemann in 1825 says in his paper: "The editor had in 1792 the honor of making the acquaintance of this man distinguished by his rare acumen, his powers of observation, his clear judgment, as well as by his originality of character, uprightness and simplicity." And again in 1833: "Two cures which Hahnemann successfully accomplished in the year 1792 in Gotha and Georgenthal, and which excited general admiration, together with the opinion of him held by a doctor who died here (Dr. Buddeus), first directed my attention to Hahnemann, filled me with the greatest esteem for him and were the origin of our friendly relations and of our subsequent uninterrupted correspondence."*

Hahnemann, in a letter to Stapf dated Dec. 22, 1825, in speaking of this same Hennicke, says:† "It is a good thing that the memorial of the Society of Homœopathic Physicians against the redoubtable Messrs. Schnaubert and Mombert has appeared in the *Anz. d. D.* before the door was closed.

"In the meantime the editor wrote me a letter, which did great credit to his heart, in which he regretted the admission of the lucubrations of these gentlemen,‡ and begged my pardon. I replied that I was quite indifferent to such calumnies, that they did not disturb my equanimity for one moment, and that he need not give himself any anxiety on my account, and he was welcome to publish all and anything however extravagant; but that his paper was only defiled by the trash, which I very much regretted, and if it went on thus it would become so distasteful that honest people would cease to read it. His concern should be for his own interests not for my feelings.

"This made an impression on him—so that he did not allow any more copies, even of those two articles against Homœopathy, to be thrown off, and announced that for the future he refused to admit anything that did not contain novel scientific views and proved facts. Read what he says in No. 323. So this theatre for the display of such venomous diatribes is closed forever. That is another victory over the black demons.

"Away, then, with your pusillanimous fears! Such things cannot do the slightest harm to the good cause   Patients who

---

*"Ameke," pp. 161, 283.

† *Hom. World*, Vol. xxiv., p. 311.

‡ The Allopathic physicians. He said he had to admit two out of the large number of hostile articles, to be impartial.

allow themselves to be misled by them are to be pitied, but if they cause one to turn his back on us, they bring over to our side in their stead three other more reasonable ones who have the good sense to be guided by experience."

In 1838 the eighty-third birthday was chosen for a grand celebration. The following account originally published in the *Hygea* is of interest:*

" My friend C. called on me a few days ago and offered to conduct me to a festival which was to be held in honor of a celebrated German.

" When we had arrived at the Chausse d'Antin he told me at last, ' we go to Dr. Hahnemann: to-day is the celebration of his eighty-third birthday; you will here have an opportunity of correcting your opinion respecting the actual state of Homœopathy in Paris.' ' The Rue de Milan, where Hahnemann resides, was filled, as is usual at great soirees, to the right and left with private carriages and hackney coaches. The Father of Homœopathy, observed my friend, has, as you perceive, a splendid residence; we passed through a gate and court-yard to a hotel surrounded by a garden, occupied by Hahnemann alone; from here we entered a large salon on the first floor, already crowded by the *beau monde* of Paris, in the middle of which stood a marble bust, ornamented with a golden laurel crown and with wreaths of the flowers of cicuta, belladonna and digitalis. This, said C., is the bust of Hahnemann, and with this golden crown of laurel it has been ornamented to-day, in celebration of his birthday, by his grateful disciples and friends.

" On both ends of the crown hanging over the shoulders were engraved distinguished names from all countries of Europe and America. The bust is the work of David, who, himself a zealous adherent of Homœopathy, was present at this festival. While I conversed with David about Boerne, whom he designated with emotion as his dear friend, Hahnemann, in the full vigor of health, looking more like sixty-three than like eighty-three years of age, entered the saloon upon the arm of his lady, also much distinguished for her high intellectual powers, and warmly

---

* *Miscellanies on Homœopathy*, 1838, p. 17. *Hom. Exam.*, Vol. iii., p. 345. *Homœopathist*, Dio Lewis, Dec. 1, 1850. *Hygea*, Vol. viii., part 5, p. 461. Albrecht's "Leben und Wirken," p. 78. *Archives de la Med. Homœopathique*, March, 1838.

welcomed his guests. One of the first Homœopathic physicians
of Paris, Dr. Leon Simon, now took the noble old gentleman by
the hand and conducted him in front of the bust crowned
with garlands, proclaiming to him, in an animated speech,
Immortality. He was followed by French and Italian poets
with poems written for the occasion; after which German musical virtuosi, like Kalkbrenner, Panofka, Hate, delighted the
company with their performances. On our return C. said:
'You have seen how many Americans, Englishmen and Italians
attended the festival and what class of Frenchmen believe in
Homœopathy. Hahnemann realizes annually from his practice
alone not less than 200,000 francs. You know now where he
resides; do me the favor and call to-morrow morning at his
house, and you will see how it stands with the faith in Hahnemann and his art.' Arriving the following morning in Hahnemann's hotel I found the court-yard and stairs filled with poor
persons, whom Hahnemann treats gratis, and in the ante-
chambers I counted no less than fifteen persons."

Though this was a birthday celebration, and this should have
been on April 10, yet the account in the *Hygea* is given as
occurring on the 19th of February.

Soon after this Hahnemann wrote to his old friend Stapf, in
the Fatherland, as follows:*

"*Dear Friend:* Your genial letter, which the Polish doctor
brought me, gave me much pleasure, as I received from it a confirmation of my comforting conjecture, that there is still in Germany a small body of true Homœopaths (among whom I never
forget to reckon you and Gross) who are not led away by that
vulgar, bragging joker and impudent sansculotte, Griesselich,
and his crew. But in truth I do not apprehend that these
wretches, with all their abusive talk, will make any impression
on the rising generation of doctors. They will soon learn from
their own experience that no good can come of such distorted
travesties of my doctrine, and will remain all the more immova-
bly devoted to the true healing art.

"Honest Germany! I had credited it with greater powers of
judgment and discrimination. At all events, these heresies
have met with no response in France, England or Italy.

"I found that France was, and is still, very weak in our art.

* *Hom. World*, Vol. xxvi., p. 117.

But there are more true followers and capable, zealous disciples in the provinces than in the capital. (Be so good as not to make publicly known my sentiments about the Homœopaths in the capital.)

"During the last half year an ardent zeal for Homœopathy has been aroused among the young graduates by the number of cures effected by myself and my dear wife; for she has cured the most serious diseases of a much larger number of the poor than I have of the rich. From fifteen to twenty daily crowd the ante-room and even the stairs of our little house, which is occupied by us only.

"The astonishment caused by these cures excites the interest of the intelligent youths, whose feeling for suffering fellow-creatures has not yet been extinguished by the practice of Allopathy. What I found among the older so-called Homœopaths here was very much the same as the bastards of this sort in Saxony. What I desire to live to see in Paris is not yet there, but is still in the future, for there are hardly four or five really good ones among the Homœopathic practitioners.

"But a good Homœopath has to fight a hard battle with the many prejudices of the public who think nothing of any system of medicine or of any doctor who does not bleed, apply leeches, stick on fly blisters, insert setons, prescribe tisanes, etc.

"Of late years great obstacles have been thrown in the way of foreign medical men obtaining leave to practice here by the Royal Academy of Medicine, probably in order to prevent the introduction of Homœopathy. Moreover, everything here is four or five times dearer than elsewhere. The rent of my house is six thousand francs per annum, and my carriage (without which a medical practice cannot be carried on) costs me nine thousand francs.

"In England our art makes greater progress than in Paris; the cures I have performed on Englishmen who have left their country to be under my treatment may have had something to do with this.

"I live here highly respected, partly no doubt because my wife is a Frenchwoman of good family and has a large circle of distinguished friends; and I enjoy better health and spirits than for the past twenty years. Many Germans who knew me formerly tell me I look many years younger, for which I have expressly to thank my loving warden, my dear Melanie, who joins me in kind remembrances to you and your amiable family.

"Farewell! and be assured of the unalterable friendship of your devoted,

"SAMUEL HAHNEMANN.

"*Paris, April 20, 1838, Rue de Milan, No. 1.*"

"You would oblige me if when opportunity offers you would send me the first part of the sixteenth volume of your immortal *Archiv*. My copy has got lost. I thank you for the two other parts. I also thank you very much for Lachesis and Crotalus, though Dr. Andrew has not yet delivered them to me. You would oblige me very much if you would send me Hering's book on Serpent Poison."*

CHAPTER LXXI.

HELEN BERKLEY—MRS. MOWATT'S VISIT TO HAHNEMANN.

In 1839 the celebrated actress, Mrs. Anna Cora Mowatt, while visiting Paris, called upon Hahnemann. An account is given in her book "Autobiography of an Actress."† Upon her return to America, Mrs. Mowatt, in 1840, wrote a series of articles concerning the celebrated persons that she had met in Europe, under the nom de plume of "Helen Berkley," and among others one about Hahnemann and Madame Hahnemann. This was copied into the Homœopathic journals of the time and has been several times published in pamphlet form.

It is given here in full. As the account in the Autobiography is but short and is essentially the same as in the following sketch, it is here omitted. We quote:

In 1839, Dr. Hahnemann was residing in Paris near the Garden of the Luxembourg. During the winter of that year, desiring to consult him in behalf of an invalid friend, I made him my first visit. That I might obtain an audience as early as

---

* "Wirkungen des schlangengiftes zum arztlichen gebrauche vergleichend zesammengestallt durch Constantin Hering, Allentaun, Pa., A. und W. Blumer, 1837."

† "Autobiography of an Actress." By Anna Cora Mowatt. Boston. Ticknor. 1854.

possible, I entered the carriage which was to transport me to his residence at a quarter past nine o'clock in the morning. After about half an hour's ride, finding that the coachman stopped his horses without dismounting, I inquired if we had reached our destination. No, madame, it is not our turn yet. We must wait a little while. See, there is Dr. Hahnemann's house, he replied, pointing to a palace-like mansion at some distance. This mansion was surrounded by a massive stone wall with an iron gate in the centre. Impatient at the delay, I leaned out of the window and beheld a long line of carriages in front of us driving one by one through the gate, and out again, as fast as their occupants alighted. This was vexatious, I had taken such especial pains to be early, and all to no purpose. Behind us stretched a line of coaches lengthening every minute, and already quite as formidable as the one in front. I had unconsciously taken my station in the midst of a procession slowly advancing to pay homage to this modern Æsculapius. I already knew something of Hahnemann's celebrity ; but my opinion of his skill was marvellously fortified as I stared behind me and before me, and then at the empty carriages driving away around me.

In about twenty minutes the carriage in which I sat wondering and waiting, during that time having moved a few paces forward every minute, at last drove briskly through the iron gate, around the spacious court, and deposited me, to my great satisfaction, at the front entrance of Hahnemann's magnificent dwelling. Three or four liveried domestics assembled in a large hall received the visitors as they alighted, and conducted them to the foot of the wide staircase. At the head of the first flight they were received by a couple more of these bedizened gentlemen, who ushered them into an elegant saloon, sumptuously furnished and opening into a number of less spacious apartments.

The saloon was occupied by fashionably dressed ladies and gentlemen, children with their nurses, and here and there an invalid reposing on a velvet couch or embroidered ottoman. The unexpected throng, the noisy hum of whispering voices, the laughter of sportive children, and the absence of vacant seats were somewhat confusing. I entered at the same moment with a lady who, with her nurse and child, had alighted from her carriage immediately before myself. Probably noticing my bewildered air, and observing that I was a stranger, she very courteously turned to me and said in French: "We shall be able to find seats in some other room; permit me to show you the way." I thanked her gratefully and followed her. After passing through a suite of thronged apartments, she led the way to a tasteful little boudoir, which was only occupied by one or two persons. I knew the lady who had so kindly acted as my conductress was a person of rank, for I had noticed the coat of arms on the panels of her coach, and remarked that her attendants were clothed in livery. But to meet with civility from strangers is of so common an occurrence that her graciousness awakened in me no surprise.

I afterwards learned that she was the Countess de R., a young Italian, who had married a French count of some importance in the *beau monde*.

We had hardly seated ourselves in the quiet little boudoir when a valet entered and politely demanded our cards. They were presented and he placed them in the order received, amongst a large number in his hand. It was obvious that we should be obliged to wait an indefinite period, and I soon commenced amusing myself by examining the fine paintings with which the walls were lavishly decorated, the pieces of sculpture, the costly vases scattered about the apartments, and a number of curious medals heaped upon a centre table. The sculpture, vases, medals, and even some of the paintings had been presented to Hahnemann as memorials of the esteem and gratitude of his patients. Every room contained several marble busts of Hahnemann himself, some much larger than life, some as large, and some smaller. These also had been presented to him on different occasions as tokens of respect.

I was standing before a most lifelike portrait of the great doctor, lost in admiration of its masterly execution, when the young Countess, who had retained her seat while I wandered around the room, joined me and said: "Do you know who painted that picture?"

"No," I replied, "but although I am not a judge of art, I should almost venture to say that it was the work of a master's hand."

"Undoubtedly it is a master-piece of workmanship. It was executed, however, by Madame Hahnemann."

"Madame Hahnemann! is it possible. Is Hahnemann married then?"

"To be sure, and so happily that to become acquainted with his domestic history is of itself almost enough to induce one to venture upon matrimony."

"I am delighted to hear it. I knew nothing of him except as a skillful physician, and a man of extraordinary genius."

"His private history is equally interesting, and quite as remarkable as his public."

"Have you known him a great while? How old is he? How long has he been married?" questioned I, anxious to obtain all the information in my power.

"I have been acquainted with his wife and himself several years. He is about eighty-four years old. He was married to his present wife in his eightieth year."

"Indeed. Was he a widower then? Is his second wife young or as old as himself?"

"She is about forty-five years his junior, and she still retains much of the vivacity and freshness of youth."

"What induced her to marry him?"

"Veneration for his talents, esteem for his virtues, affection for himself, mingled, perhaps, with a spice of gratitude for his services to herself. You are a stranger to her and will laugh if I say she adores him, but the term is not too strong to convey an idea of the truth."

"Pray tell me something of her history. I am deeply interested."

"With pleasure. Hahnemann is the father of the most united, prosperous and the happiest family I ever beheld. He had been for many years a widower when he was called in to attend Mlle. d'Hervilly, who was pronounced by her physicians to be in the last stages of consumption. He was residing at the time at Coethen. Marie Melanie d'Hervilly Gohier, then his patient and now his wife, is descended from a noble French family of immense wealth. She had suffered a number of years with a pulmonary affection and disease of the heart. The most eminent physicians in Europe had fruitlessly endeavored to benefit her. After passing the winter in Italy, whither she had been sent in the hope that a mild climate might effect what medicine had failed to accomplish, she returned to Germany in a state which her physicians declared beyond the reach of medical aid. She is a woman of remarkable strength of mind and most comprehensive intellect. The fame of Hahnemann's wonderful cures had reached her, but she was unacquainted with his reasons for his peculiar mode of practice. Though so debilitated by protracted suffering that she was unable to make the slightest physical exertion, she examined his system for herself and then determined upon consulting him. He became deeply interested in her case, and in an incredibly short time her sufferings were relieved, her cough subdued, and her disease of the heart assumed a different and more agreeable shape.''

"And she married him out of gratitude?"

"By no means; she was charmed with his genius, his character, his manners, everything about him; and conceived an affection for him perhaps deeper and truer than the passion which we generally call love."

"Which he reciprocated?"

"Now you question me too closely; I cannot answer on which side the attachment first sprung. Nor do I know any reason why it should not have originated in the doctor himself. Madame Hahnemann is a woman of the most brilliant talents; her information is extensive, her mind highly cultivated, and she is proficient in almost every elegant accomplishment you can name. Combine these attractions with that of a prepossessing person, and you will not find it easy to imagine a man insensible to her charms."

"How do Hahnemann's children like the idea of a stepmother?"

"She is tenderly beloved by them all. Her delicacy and generosity towards them are worthy of mention. Hahnemann had amassed a large fortune, which she refused even during his lifetime to share with him. She was determined to give no room for the supposition that she could have been influenced by interested motives in forming this union. She stipulated before her marriage that she should ever be excluded from any participation in the avails of Hahnemann's estate; and induced him to settle the bulk of his fortune on the children of his first wife, merely reserving for himself an annuity sufficient for his personal expenses."

"How, then, was she provided for?"

"She was already independent as to fortune."

"Madame Hahnemann must undoubtedly be a very talented woman, if this painting is hers," said I, resuming my examination of the fine portrait which had first attracted my attention.

"Not only that one, but several others in the larger apartments," replied Madame de R. "Some of her paintings have been even admired in the galleries of the Louvre. Thus · her name is classed with those of the most distinguished French artists. She is a poetess, too, and her works have won a truly flattering approbation from the public."

"A poetess. Where will her qualifications end?"

"I almost believe they have no end. She is mistress of five or six languages, which she both writes and speaks with ease and fluency."

"She appears to be worthy, indeed, of being the wife of Hahnemann."

"He thinks so, I assure you. He would not now find it so easy to dispense with her services."

"Is he infirm, then?"

"Not in the least. He has always enjoyed excellent health. His sight and hearing are unimpaired. His activity is remarkable. Even yet there are an elasticity in his movements and sprightliness in his manners which make you feel that something of youth has been left to him even in age. He would never remind you of the fable of the frog, whose discerning patients cried: 'Physician, cure thyself.'"

"Perhaps that is quite as remarkable as anything you have told me about him; medical men generally look as though they needed, but feared to try, the effects of their own medicines. Since he is so active, I suppose it would be possible to induce him to visit a patient."

"I do not think that could be easily accomplished. In a case of great peril, perhaps you might obtain the services of his wife."

"His wife? Why surely—"

At that moment our conversation was interrupted by the entrance of a lady. She was attired in a simple demi toilette and wore no bonnet; I therefore concluded she was not a guest. The instant she entered, the delicate-looking child my new acquaintance had been caressing upon her knee, sprang to the ground and greeted the lady with expressions of the most affectionate joy. She was an elegant-looking woman, with a finely rounded form, somewhat above the medium height. Her face could not be called beautiful or pretty, but the term handsome might be applied to it with great justice. Her forehead was full and high, and her hair thrown back in a manner which perfectly displayed its expansive proportions. Those luxuriant tresses of a bright, flaxen hue were partly gathered in a heavy knot at the back of her head and partly fell in long ringlets behind her ears. Her complexion was of that clear but tintless description which so strongly resembles alabaster. There was a thoughtful expression in her large blue eyes, which, but for the benignant smile on her lips, would have given a solemn aspect to her countenance.

CHAPTER LXXII.

HELEN BERKLEY'S STORY CONTINUED.

She exchanged a few words with Madame de R., kissed the child with much tenderness, and addressed several other persons present. While she was conversing, the child still retained her hand, following her about and pressing close to her side, with its little, pale, affectionate face upturned at every pause, as though earnestly soliciting a caress. In a few minutes she retired.

I turned to Madame de R. and inquired: "Is that Madame Hahnemann?"

"Yes; is she not a fine-looking woman?"

"Undoubtedly. And from her appearance alone I can well imagine her endowed with many of the attributes you have described her as possessing. Your little son seems very much attached to her."

"Poor little fellow. He has good cause to be so. He had suffered from his birth with a scrofulous affection which baffled the skill of the best medical men in Paris. They gave me no hope of his recovery, and he is my only child. At three years old he was unable to walk or even stand alone. It was then that Hahnemann arrived in Paris, and I immediately called upon him. It was impossible to bring the child here without risking his life, and Hahnemann attends to no patients out of the house. Madame Hahnemann told me, however, not to be uneasy, as she would herself take charge of the boy. She visited him regularly twice a day, watched him with the anxious tenderness of a mother, and prescribed for him in a manner which proved the extent of her judgment and skill. In a few months the child recovered. He has never had a positive return of the disease, but he remains exceedingly delicate. I bring him to see his good friend and physician every few weeks for the sake of learning her opinion of his health and consulting her concerning his management."

"Do you mean that Madame Hahnemann prescribes for him on her own responsibility?"

"I do. She is almost as thoroughly acquainted with medicine as her husband. She became his pupil with the view of assisting him when age might weaken his faculties. She now attends to all his patients, as you will find directly, merely consulting him in cases of great difficulty."

"That is being a helpmate indeed. But are the patients always willing to trust her?"

"Assuredly; she has too incontestably proved her skill not to be trusted. Hahnemann is no longer able to endure the fatigue of attending to the multiplicity of cases crowded upon him. Madame Hahnemann is universally confided in, respected and beloved, especially by the poor."

"I can well believe it. Is Hahnemann assisted by any of his children in the same manner as by his wife?"

"Not exactly in the same manner, but still he is assisted by them. One of his daughters, and a fine, intelligent girl she is, has the sole superintendence of an enormous folio, containing the names of all his correspondents and the dates of their letters; also of several other folios, containing the letters themselves, arranged in alphabetical order. His other children are of service to him in various ways. To assist him is their chief delight. As I told you before, I never beheld a more united family."

"Miss Hahnemann's services alone must spare the doctor a vast deal of trouble."

"Yes, but still every moment of his time is employed. He is the most systematic man imaginable. In his library you will find thirty-six quarto volumes, his register of consultation, written entirely by himself. Apropos, his hand writing is really worth seeing. What do you think of a man eighty-four years of age who writes a hand firm as a man's ought to be, fine enough to be a woman's, and elegant enough to be traced on copper plate, and this without spectacles?''

"Think? Why, I think I have wondered at what you have told me as long as I could wonder, and now I can only come to the conclusion that Hahnemann and his wife should be ranked among the curiosities of Paris, and that the sight seeing stranger has not beheld all the marvels until he has seen them.''

Our conversation was interrupted by a valet, who announced that Monsieur le Docteur was at leisure and would see Madame la Contesse.

She bade me good morning, saying: "It will be your turn next, I shall not keep you waiting long.''

I hope not, thought I, as a glance at the clock informed me that it was somewhat more than three hours since I first entered the house.

A few moments after Madame de R. left me I was startled by hearing the same valet distinctly pronounce my name, somewhat Frenchified, and announce that Monsieur le Docteur was ready to receive me. I was too much surprised to do anything but stare, until I remembered that I had placed my card in his hand some three hours before. I arose and followed him. He led the way through the same apartments I had traversed on entering. The doctor's reception chamber was situated at the further end of the suite. Throwing open a door he loudly announced me and retired.

I stood in the presence of Monsieur le Docteur and Madame Hahnemann. The chamber I now entered was more simply decorated than any I had visited. In the centre of the room stood a long table; at its head a slightly elevated platform held a plain looking desk covered with books. In front of the desk sat Madame Hahnemann with a blank volume open before her and a gold pen in her hand. Hahnemann was reclining in a comfortable arm chair on one side of the table. They rose to receive me, and I presented Madame Hahnemann a letter from Herr Dr. Hirschfeldt, of Bremen, an eminent physician, who had formerly been a pupil of Hahnemann's.

While Madame Hahnemann was glancing through the letter I

had an opportunity of taking a survey of Hahnemann's person, for he had not yet resumed his seat. His slender and diminutive form was enveloped in a flowered dressing gown of rich materials, and too comfortable in appearance to be of other than of Parisian make. The crown of his large, beautifully proportioned head was covered by a skull cap of black velvet. From beneath it strayed a few thin snowy locks, which clustered about his noble forehead, and spoke of the advanced age which the lingering freshness of his florid complexion seemed to deny. His eyes were dark, deep set, glittering and full of animation.

As he greeted me he removed from his mouth a long painted pipe, the bowl of which nearly reached to his knees. But after the first salutation it was instantly resumed; as I was apprized by the volumes of blue smoke which began to curl about his head as though to veil it from my injudicious scrutiny.

Madame Hahnemann gracefully expressed her gratification at the perusal of the letter, read a few lines of it to her husband in an under tone, and made several courteous remarks to me; while the doctor bowed without again removing his long pipe. It was evident that he did not immediately recognize Dr. Hirschfeldt's name; and he was too much accustomed to receive letters of introduction to pay any attention to their contents.

Madame Hahnemann placed herself at the desk, with the doctor on her right hand and myself on her left. I stated the principal object of my visit, attempting to direct my conversation to Hahnemann, rather than to his wife. But I soon found that this was not *salon en regle*. Madame Hahnemann invariably replied, asking a multiplicity of questions, and noting the minutest symptoms of the case as fast as my answers were given. Several times she referred to her husband, who merely replied with his pipe between his teeth, "Yes, my child," or "Good, my child, good." And these were the only words that I as yet had heard him utter. After sometime spent in this manner, Madame Hahnemann accidentally asked: "Where was your friend first attacked?"

"In Germany," I replied.

Hahnemann had been listening attentively, although he had not spoken. The instant I uttered these words his whole countenance brightened as though a sunbeam had suddenly fallen across it, and he exclaimed in an animated tone: "Have you been in Germany? You speak German, don't you?'' The conversation had hitherto been carried on in French, but the ready ''Certainly'' with which I answered his question apparently gave him unfeigned pleasure.

He immediately commenced a conversation in his native tongue, inquiring how I was pleased with Germany, what I thought of the inhabitants, their customs, whether I found the language difficult, how I was impressed with the scenery, and continuing an enthusiastic strain of eulogium upon his beloved country for some time. Then he asked from whom was my letter. When I pronounced the name of Dr. Hirschfeldt, which he had listened to so coldly before, he expressed the deepest interest in his welfare, and spoke of him with mingled affection and esteem.

I was too much delighted with the doctor's animated and feeling remarks to change the topic. Yet I felt that he had lost sight, and was fast inducing me to do the same, of the primary object of my visit. Madame Hahnemann, however, though she smiled and joined in the conversation, had not forgotten the host of good people who were taking lessons of patience in the ante-chambers. She finally put an end to the discourse by a gentle admonition to her husband, warning him that he must not fatigue himself before the hours devoted to business were half spent.

Turning to me, she apologized for the interruption, saying that they received their friends in the evening and would be happy to see me, then immediately resumed the subject of my friend's indisposition.

After a few more inquiries, I received some medicine from her hands, with especial directions concerning the manner in which it was to be used. She also presented me with a paper on which the different kinds of food, vegetables, seasoning and odors which counteract the effects of Homœopathic remedies were enumerated. After cordially shaking hands with the kind old man and his talented and exemplary wife, I bade them good morning. One of the domestics in attendance conducted me down stairs and handed me into the carriage; and I drove home, passing along a file of coaches stretching from Hahnemann's door rather farther than I could venture to mention and expect to be believed.

The favorable impression I had received on my first interview with Doctor and Madame Hahnemann was subsequently strengthened and confirmed.

Hahnemann expressed the same enthusiasm as before at the mention of his own country, and on hearing that I was an American made many inquiries about our young land, and especially concerning the progress of Homœopathy. I could not, however, give him much information which he had not previously received from other lips.

Hahnemann amongst his innumerable estimable qualities, possesses that of the most indefatigable industry. The pains which he takes in studying and examining a case are almost incredible. He records with precision the minutest symptoms of every patient, all constitutional ailments, hereditary taints and numerous other particulars; never trusting his memory, and only prescribing after a deliberation often tedious, though always necessary. To the poor he has always shown untiring benevolence.

Certain hours of the day are set apart for the reception of persons unable to offer compensation. They are attended with equal care, their symptoms recorded, and their diseases prescribed for with the same precision which is bestowed upon the *haute noblesse* of the land. It frequently occurs that Hahnemann is so fatigued with his morning duties, that patients who apply for advice in the afternoon are placed under the sole superintendence of Madame Hahnemann. But they seem to consider this gifted couple one in skill, as they are indeed one in heart.

Hahnemann appears to take pleasure in confessing to the world his affection, almost veneration, for his wife. Shortly after his marriage in a reply to the Gallican Homœopathic Society of Paris, who had made him their honorary president, the following paragraph occurs: "I love France and her noble people, so great, so generous, so disposed to rectify an abuse by the adoption of a new and efficient reform. This predilection has been augmented in my heart by my marriage with one of the noble daughters of France, in every respect worthy of her country."*

---

*"Sketch of Hahnemann and his wife, from the portfolio of one who knew them." New York. Radde. 1850.

CHAPTER LXXIII.

A CURE BY HAHNEMANN—HIS PREFACE TO ARSENICUM—SIX-
TIETH ANNIVERSARY OF GRADUATION—RULES OF FRENCH
HOMŒOPATHIC COLLEGE—HOMŒOPATHY IN PARIS.

The following letter, signed "A Lover of Hahnemann," was
published in the *Homœopathic Times* for February 7, 1852:*

"Thirteen years ago I was given up by the Allopathic doctors
for consumption. A goodly number of them had pronounced me
incurable. At this period a benevolent lady sent from Paris an
invitation for me to visit her in that city, in order that I might
get the advice of the immortal Hahnemann. At first the doctor
then attending me sent word that I was too weakly to undertake the journey, but the lady persisted and he yielded.

"In a month after I was examined and sounded by Hahnemann, who smiled as he stroked my head and said: 'I am glad
you have come to me in time, I shall cure you.' Now I had
been examined by more than twenty eminent Allopathists (Sir
James Clark being one of them), all of whom thought me beyond
human skill; but the old, bald-headed, persecuted Hahnemann,
the great medical benefactor of mankind, after an hour's examination of my lungs, said: 'I shall cure you.' After being under
his treatment for eight months, I returned to Scotland completely cured.

"I may mention that the good old man (for whose good doing
to me and to mankind I have often felt grateful to God) refused
to take a single farthing for his advice and medicine, although
he knew that the lady who took so much interest in me was in
opulent circumstances."

It was in the year 1839 that Hahnemann made his last contribution to the "Materia Medica," the preface to the provings of
Arsenicum. He says:†

"The mentioning of *Arsenic* calls up powerful recollections in
my soul.

Hom. Times, London, Vol. iii., p. 416.

It is likely that this letter was written by Mr. Young, whose cure is narrated at length in a previous chapter.

† Hahnemann's "Chronic Diseases," New York, Vol. v., p. 361.

"In creating the iron the All Merciful permitted his children to transform it, at their choice, either into the murderous dagger or the blessed plowshare, and to use it either for their destruction or preservation. How much more happy mankind would be if they used God's gifts only for the purpose of accomplishing the good. It is his will that we should do this, and for this end we have been created.

"It is not the fault of Him who loves us all that we abuse powerful medicinal agents, administering them either in too powerful doses or in cases for which they are not suitable, being merely guided by the caprice of miserable authorities, and without having taken the trouble to investigate the inherent virtues of the drug, and to make our selection depend upon the knowledge thus obtained.

"If one is found willing to make that investigation in a conscientious manner, those pretended authorities overwhelm him with their wrath as the enemy of their comfort, and permit themselves the most ignoble and malicious calumnies. * * * I hear it said one-tenth of a grain (of *Arsenic*) is the smallest weight used in practice. Who could prescribe less without making himself ridiculous.

"Indeed, one-tenth of a grain sometimes endangers life, and giving less should be contrary to rule. Is not this deriding common sense?

"Have the rules of practice been established for irrational slaves or for men endowed with rationality and free will? Who or what prevents them from giving a smaller dose when a larger one would prove dangerous? Obstinacy? Dogmatism? or what other fetter of the mind?

"'Yes,' say they, '*Arsenic* would still be hurtful even if we used only one-hundredth or one-thousandth of a grain. *Arsenic*, even when used in a very small quantity, is nevertheless a virulent poison; we proclaim this *ex authoritate.*'

"Supposing you have hit the truth, it must likewise be true that by diminishing the dose gradually we must finally arrive at a quantity which has nothing of the danger of your orthodox dose of one tenth of a grain.

"'Such a dose would be something new altogether. What sort of a dose would that be?'

"Novelty is indeed a heinous crime in the eyes of the orthodox doctors, infatuated with the drugs of their school, and whose minds have lost all their independence in the tyranny of hoary rules.

"What miserable law, or what anything else, can prevent the physician, who ought to be a scholar, a thinking and free man, from attenuating a dose by reducing its quantity?

"Why should he not give 1-100.000 or one-millionth of a grain, if experience teaches him that one-thousandth of a grain is too strong? And if he should discover by experience that even 1-100.000 of a grain is still too powerful, why should he not reduce the dose to one millionth or one-billionth?

"And even if this dose should be too powerful, why not descend to one-quadrillionth or lower.

"But here my opponents, suffocating as it were in the bog of hoary prejudice, will exclaim: 'Ha! ha! ha! that is nothing!'

"Why not? Does a substance that has been divided ever so minutely lose any of its original properties? Even if divided, as it were, to an endless extent, does not something of the original substance remain? What sound mind should contradict this?

"And if something of the original substance remains, why should not that something have some effect? What that effect is cannot be decided speculatively, but has to be learned by experience. Experience alone can decide whether this small portion is too feeble to relieve the disease for which it is suitable."

Here, in his eighty-fourth year, as a parting word to his followers, we find this grand old scholar reiterating his oft told saying: "Try, only try and do not condemn without trying." And one can readily see that his one idea is to find the very smallest possible quantity with which to make the cure. It always was his aim.

On August 10th, 1839, Hahnemann celebrated the sixtieth anniversary of his graduation at Erlangen. The day was observed with appropriate festivities. The following account may be found in Stapf's *Archiv*:*

"PARIS, August 18, 1839.—A few days ago the sixtieth anniversary of Hahnemann's doctorate was celebrated in his hotel in

---

Archiv f. d. hom. Heilkunst, Vol. xvii., part 3. *Allg. hom. Zeit.*, Vol. xvi., p. 95.

Milan street. The venerable man, still active and vigorous, although in his eighty-fourth year, was congratulated by almost all the nations of Europe, partly by letter, but mostly by representatives. Poems were recited in almost all the European languages. The German muse was the only one lacking; and Dr. Jahr, editor of the widely circulated "Repertory," was the only German physician of that time who saved his country's honor by reciting an old poem.

"It will be difficult for posterity to comprehend this indifference of Germany to one of her sons, a benefactor who will be the honor and pride of the German name thousands of years hence. To us this is easily explainable. There are so many great men in the little cities of Germany, men who have such immensely great reforms in proportion to their little code of medical practice, and such ponderous volumes in contrast with the little "Organon," that it is not to be wondered at that the little man in Milan street should thrive in forgetfulness. It is otherwise in other countries. Thither the names of these German country, village and city celebrities have not yet found their way; only the name of the founder of Homœopathy is known to the people. His name is in all mouths and each new year, which the active old man adds to the great number of the old ones, since it illustrates anew the truth and efficacy of his doctrine, is celebrated as a new triumph. To all appearance Hahnemann will reach the age of one hundred years. He looks as yet like a man of sixty; and what is more, his mind has still all the strength of its maturity. He still practices, thinks and writes just as he did a half century ago; in fact, he possibly does still more of each and does it better. But why, if the German youth forget their master, does not German poetry at least remember him? Has a German poet never been sick? Or does the German poetry of pain feel itself in kinship with the painfulness of Allopathy? The German science of music, however, has made glorious this beautiful eventide of Hahnemann's life. It has abundantly supplied what the art of poetry omitted. The celebrated Clara Wieck, a country woman of Hahnemann's, enraptured the company of celebrities with the most beautiful strains of music; and a young German dilettante intoned her famous voice in praise of the man whose triumph they were celebrating. The renowned violoncellist, Max Bohrer, fittingly

closed the musical performances. We think that Clara Wieck
will next season dominate the musical throne of Paris, in spite
of the presence of the first pianists of Europe; indeed, the
Russian and English nobility are vieing with each other to
secure her for the year of 1840.''

This article continues with a history of the growth of Homœopathy in Sicily, Italy, France, England and North America.
As one would expect, three or four lines only are devoted to the
latter place.

Croserio mentions this sixtieth fete day as follows:* ''On the
tenth of August last we celebrated in Dr. Hahnemann's hotel,
Milan street, No. 1, the sixtieth anniversary of his acquiring the
degree of doctor of medicine. Almost all European nations had
sent their representatives to congratulate the illustrious old gentleman, who, notwithstanding his eighty-four years, is endowed
with perfect health. Poems in his praise were read in almost
every European language.''

One of the odes delivered on this occasion was by the young
physician, Dr. J. B. Mure. It was published in pamphlet form
and also in his book: ''Doctrine de l'Ecole de Rio de Janeiro et
Pathogenesie Bresilienne. Paris, 1849.''

In a letter dated Paris, October 20, 1839, Dr. Croserio writes
to Dr. Neidhard as follows:† ''Under the name 'Institut de la
Medicine Homeopathique' we have erected and shall open in a
few weeks in the Rue de la Harpe, No. 93, in the immediate
neighborhood of the School of Medicine, a large institution for
the following purposes:

'' 1. To teach students the theory and practice of Homœopathy, by public lectures.

''2. To spread the benefit of Homœopathy among the lower
classes of the capital, by giving consultations gratis to those who
will personally apply for them.

''3. To give advice in writing to those patients in the country
and in the provinces of France, who, having no Homœopathic
physicians near themselves, apply for it.

''4. To prepare Homœopathic medicines according to the
method of Dr. Mure.

* *Hom. Exam.*, Vol. i., p. 103.
† *Hom. Exam.*, Vol. i., pp. 104, 346.

"5. To translate into the French language practical works on Homœopathy.

"6. To publish, under the title of "Le Propagateur de l'Homœopathie," a monthly periodical, by which all new Homœopathic works and periodicals will be reviewed, etc.

"7. To procure for those Homœopathic physicians and other individuals in the provinces, or in foreign countries, who would apply for them, Homœopathic books, instruments, medicines and practical advice in particular cases.

"8. To open *a cabinet de lecture* where students, physicians, may read or borrow all Homœopathic books and periodicals, published in France or other countries.

"9. To consult strangers who come to Paris, either for studying Homœopathy, or for taking general information on the state of Homœopathy, or for buying Homœopathic medicines, books, etc.

"10. To serve as a central point for Homœopaths of all nations, and to nominate correspondents for that purpose in all foreign countries.

"For the present I can inform you that Dr. Jahr will teach Materia Medica Pura, and the German as the Homœopathic language; Dr. Mure, Pharmacology and Mnemonics applied to the Materia Medica; and that I have accepted the Homœopathic clinic."

In another letter, dated July 1, 1840, Dr. Croserio writes:

"Two Homœopathic institutions have been established in this city during the past year, one in the Rue de la Harpe, the other in the Rue Gil-le-Cœur. Both are situated near the School of Medicine, and in both, courses of public lectures are delivered on Homœopathy and the Materia Medica, and public consultations have been organized, which are frequented daily by sixty to one hundred invalids from the laboring classes of society."

At this time there were also two well-appointed Homœopathic pharmacies in Paris. The first one was opened by Henri Petroz. In 1833 he began to prepare medicines and put up the prescriptions of a few physicians and in 1837 he opened his pharmacy.*

* "Trans. World's Hom. Convention," 1876, p. 154.

CHAPTER LXXIV.

PLEASANT HOME LIFE—CORRESPONDENCE WITH HIS DAUGHTERS.

Albrecht in speaking of the pleasant relations of the daughters with the household at Paris writes as follows:* "The following family letters furnish us the best proof that Hahnemann, although he found himself impelled to be in Paris, in many ways a different person from what he had previously been at Coethen, had remained just the same in his affection for his daughters left behind in Germany. It is as if he considered it his duty to recompense them in some measure for their separation from him by more frequent proofs of his remembrance and enduring affection.

"Hahnemann does not, indeed, discuss public affairs with his daughters, very seldom mentions the system of medicine founded by himself, and does not expatiate in an exchange of weighty ideas and opinions; nay, he is, in these letters, entirely a father, nothing but a father, a father who enshrines the existence of his children in the inmost depths of his heart, concerns himself about all their affairs, sympathizes intensely in all their sorrows and afflictions, counsels and consoles and encourages them, directs them to come soon to Paris to see him, if they complain about his absence, and then gives them some errand or commission to perform, requests them to send him a greeting in a letter. In the postscript, and with the accustomed superscription, there is always the never-forgotten message, 'a greeting from Melanie.'

"Festal and triumphant tones resound quite often in these pastoral symphonies. But let each read for himself what pleases him from these letters, which have been selected from a large collection of similar import. We follow the chronological order, deviating from it only in the first letter.

"This letter, belonging apparently to the year 1839, at which time Hahnemann was already shining as a star of the first magnitude in the heaven of erudition in Paris, transfers us to the sisterly circle of Hahnemann, his daughters, and serves in some measure as a commentary on their opposite dispositions. A

---

* "Biograph. Denkmal," p. 116.

sister in Paris, writing to her sisters at Coethen, describes in vivid, but plain language, an important festal event in the life of their beloved father, and promises to tell them still more of all the almost indescribable splendors of the celebration when she comes, 'right soon, to see them.' The gentle and tender breath of childlike love breathes in every word and wafts it caressingly to the heart of the reader. Her father and his wife read the sisterly letter before it is mailed to Germany, and both add to it an independent postscript in a brief note of their own. Moreover, the letter contains so many and various interesting particulars that the attention becomes enlisted more and more closely. This is this three part letter:

"'*Dear Sisters Louise and Lottie:*

"'It affords me unspeakable joy to write you also something about our beautiful festival. First of all, mother and father (who are perfectly well and cheerful), received a very handsome silver and gold cup on the upper part of which is inscribed, *Sante*, and on the lower, *Zum 60th Doctorat*. Thus began the day which was replete with pleasure and joy; then came one of the greatest violoncellists in Europe, named Bohrer, who fairly surfeited us with the sweets of music during the whole day until evening; then the whole company assembled, a vast throng of ladies and gentlemen, who brought beautiful flowers and recited admirable poems. After this we had the most delightful music; the celebrated Clara Wieck, who is now singing here in Paris, gave us the pleasure of her brilliant musical talent.

"'She and the violoncellist charmed us so much that we were perfectly entranced. The vast saloon where we were was splendidly adorned with beautiful oil paintings, which mother had arranged tastefully and illuminated brilliantly. More than one hundred wax lights were burning.

"'Among the company was a young physician from Lyons, named Mure, who had composed a capital poem in praise of father. He declaimed it, too, so grandly, that it thrilled my inmost soul. There were several more who recited very beautiful poems. In short we had a splendid time. The festivities lasted till about three o'clock in the morning. And you, as well as every friend, would have imagined yourself in love with the entertainment, but you especially, dear sisters, because your dutiful letters had made a delightful impression upon our dear parents, for which they thank you most heartily. Mother does this particularly, and thanks you for your affectionate letter in which you expressed that pretty wish. You dear little Wiesy, you ask whether the stockings sent to father will answer? To be sure they will; they fit very well, and you may knit the rest just like them. Father sends you many thanks for your great pains and skill.

" 'I am glad to hear that good Mrs. Lehmann is so well and also dear old Mrs. Schrœder. I send them both my heartiest greetings. I read with sincere regret that Lottie is ill. May God, our only Deliverer, help her! I send herewith a couple of flowers for you, so that you also may have a token of the celebration. They are at the same time a souvenir of dear father's 60th doctorate. In September I shall set out to come to you, and hope to find you all very well and in the best of cheer.

" 'This will be my last letter before starting. You need have no anxiety for I shall be delayed somewhat on the way, as you already know, because I cannot yet drag one foot after the other on account of my rheumatism. Adieu! May you continue very well meanwhile. Give my love to all our dear friends. In spirit you are already embraced by your loving sister,

" 'AMALIE LIEBE, GEB. HAHNEMANN.'

" ' *Dear Children:*

" 'I thank you for the sincere wishes you sent to greet my 10th of August festival. I have accomplished them, thanks to our merciful Heavenly Father; and along with my Melanie, have kept your remembrance thereby in sincerest affection.

" 'Your devoted father,

"S. HAHNEMANN.

" 'My compliments and thanks to Councillor Lehmann. I shall write to him next.

" ' *Dear Lottie and Louise:*

" ' I received your letter with great pleasure and I thank you for your kind wishes. I duly received your previous letter also, The expression of your friendship will always be very dear to me. I wish you good health and much happiness.

" 'MELANIE HAHNEMANN.'

"The grateful daughters do not forget to acknowledge to their far-away father their participation in the celebration of his birthway and in the jubilee of his doctorate. Nor does the father forget to acknowledge to his daughters his joy at their manifestation of such dutifulness.

———

" *'Dear Children:*

"'Your hearty congratulations to my festivals of 10th of April and of 10th of August are enshrined in my heart, and I send you many and profoundest thanks. May God grant you good health and enable you to live all your days in cheerful contentment. My dear Melanie, too, wishes you all the good things of life that are to be enjoyed.

"'Your devoted father,
"'S. HAHNEMANN.

" *'April 27, 1839.*

"'I hereby return thanks to Councillor Lehmann for the medicines. My dear Melanie and I both send our warmest greetings to him, his devoted wife and lovely daughters.'"

———

" *'Dear Children:*

"'Accept my thanks for your kind wishes respecting my last 10th of August festivities. I know that your intentions are the kindliest toward both Melanie and myself. Morover, live a cheerful and happy life like good children, and continue to love us as dearly as we love you.

" 'Your loving father,
"'SAMUEL HAHNEMANN.

" *'Paris, Octo. 6, 1839.'* "

———

"The two following somewhat expressive letters were written with a similar motive;

" *'Dear Daughters:*

"'It is my ardent wish that your indisposition, of which I am informed by your letter to *Malchen*,* may have become changed again to lasting health; for I desire very much to have the satisfaction of thinking that you are well. I thank you heartily for your kind wishes both at the beginning of the year and on my birthday. I know that you meant both from the depths of your hearts; and this is and will always be to me a cherished recollection. Strive to make yourselves as happy as possible in this brief earthly life, which is the school in which we fit ourselves for eternity; and if you earnestly wish to do so, it will not be

*Meaning Amalie.

difficult to accomplish. Continue steadfast my good daughters,
I love you. You devoted father,

"'SAMUEL HAHNEMANN.

" '*Paris, April 17, 1838.*

" ''My dear Melanie has wrested ever so much time from her
many and varied household duties so as to get my picture ready
to send to you (and Lehmann). Every one here thinks it bears
a striking resemblance to the original. Melanie, too, writes to
you in the German language, since she can then generally enable
you to comprehend what she means.' "

" '*Dear Children:*

" ''We express to you our sincerest thanks for your kind wishes
as well as for the little songs set to music, which ought to cheer
our leisure hours, which are so rare, and should remind us of
yourselves.

" ''Take courage! Your wish to visit Paris can soon be gratified,
for they are making progress with the railways everywhere in
Germany; and they are already beginning to extend the railway
as far as Frankfort on the Main, and so in France as far as the
Rhine. Therefore be tranquil, and live in good hope, just as we
do. You have still a great many advantages over many thousands
of people, no lack of anything whatever, for the support of life,
and withal a good name in the estimation of everybody, and good
friends. And then, too, we love you. What more do you lack
to make you contented? Therefore, thank God, our Preserver,
who never forsakes us, and lead a tranquil and contented life.
The Almighty demands nothing more from you, dear children.
I remain,

" 'Your loving father,

" 'SAMUEL HAHNEMANN.

" ' *Paris, June 10th.*

" ' I received with pleasure grandfather's seal and presented
it to my dear wife, who will have a similar one made for Louise.
" ' *Dear Children:*

" 'I wish you the greatest happiness.

" ' MELANIE HAHNEMANN.' "

" Here is a letter from the memorable year of 1840. We perceive from it that Hahnemann lived entirely shut off from public

events, heard the rumor of war and revolution only behind closed shutters, and stood majestically alone and out of the reach of the tumult of the present generation of mortals. He says in this letter: 'You have no need to be concerned about the disquietude in Paris, for this will become far greater in time than it is at present. We live close by a *barriere;* and in our walled city there is never any disquietude. If there should be an uprising, we shall go quickly to friends in the country; but this is by no means to be feared.'"

In this very interesting series of letters, that show fully the good feeling between the old doctor, in Paris, and his lonely daughters in the little town in Germany, now appears the last which Hahnemann wrote to his daughters. Albrecht writes: "It is not without such an emotion, as we ever willingly consecrate to the shades of the ever memorable man, that we take up the last letter which Hahnemann sent to his beloved daughters prior to his death. This letter is characterized by that tenderness of feeling which the mother is accustomed to manifest unconsciously and involuntarily, by reason of undisguised separation from her son. We still derive consolation from this letter. It shows thet Hahnemann suffered but a short time previous to his death.

"'*Dear Children:*

"'We have received your letters so full of kind wishes, and we wish you also all the possible good to which health specially belongs.

"'Keep in good health. We are now in the midst of winter. I enjoy my life as much as business permits me, and shall go today, as I did last Thursday, to the Italian Opera until midnight in company with my dear Melanie and Father d'Hervilly.

"'The little book is precious to me. I thank you for the great trouble that it must have cost you to procure it. I can use it, although it is not the one I meant—the one which the Torgau doctor (I think his name is Lehmann) had written anonymously at the time, and in which the wonderful cures of Grabe are named. It was printed at Torgau, and not at Zerbst, as was the one sent to me. This doctor must still have some of them remaining. Perhaps, if he is still living, he will sell you one. Give him my compliments. Then the Coethen publisher has no more copies of the weekly paper published at that time, in which he speaks of Grabe?

"'But I should be sorry if it should give you too much trouble. Please write to me what expense you have incurred in the matter.

"'Ask Dr. Lehmann, in my name, for one or two grains of the third trituration of *Mercurius solubilis*, which was not in the box sent to me.

"'My dear Melanie sends you much love along with mine. She wishes to know whether Louise has received father's ring through *Malchen*, to whom it was sent from Weimer to Dresden. May you live in health, comfort and contentment, dear children!

"'Your loving father,

"'SAMUEL HAHNEMANN.

"'*Paris, January 5, 1843.*'"

Dr. Lehmann, so long his faithful assistant at Coethen, remained always his dear friend. He prepared his medicines up to his death, Hahnemann sending to Coethen for them. At Hahnemann's request he had his bust taken. It is written: *"The bust of these two great men should, like the originals, stand together. So Hahnemann directed."

Dr. Lehmann died at Coethen on January 9, 1865, aged 77 years.†

CHAPTER LXXV.

EIGHTY FIFTH BIRTHDAY—CURE OF THE CHILD OF LEGOUVE.

The birthday of 1840 was celebrated in the usual delightful manner.

The following letter appeared in the Leipsic *General Gazette* on April 19, 1840, as correspondence from Paris, regarding the celebration of Hahnemann's eighty-fifth birthday:

"‡Paris, April 12, 1840. Day before yesterday Hahnemann celebrated his eighty-fifth birthday. The elite of the German residents and many celebrated Frenchmen had assembled in his saloons in the evening to congratulate the aged Commander-in-Chief of our Homœopathic Phalanx. which is increasing every

*Fischer's Trans. "Biog. Denkmal," p. 94.
†*Allg. hom. Zeit.*, Vol. lxx., p. 40.
‡*Allg. hom. Zeit.*, Vol. xvii., p. 287.

day. And it was delightful and inspiring to see with what cordiality these congratulations were given and received.

"One often heard the heart of some one who had been delivered from disease express itself to its deliverer with sincerest thankfulness.

"The old reformer of medicine, with his lofty brow and kindly smiling face, was the most life-like exemplar of his system of healing; for there surely are but few persons eighty-five years of age who are so active and busy as he, and who, in his profession, do the honors in many a crowded saloon long after midnight. Art and science had combined to celebrate his birthday worthily. It was plainly perceptible that the Germans played the chief role in this celebration. In an ante-room, just beneath, there was a new statue of Hahnemann, sculptured by Woltreck of Dessau. It is a masterpiece in conception and execution. He is represented sitting upon a rock and clothed in a plainly but beautifully draped mantle open at the breast; and the details and incidents are so conceived that they satisfy and compose the eye without fixing it, and thus divert it from the main design to the beautiful and expressive head, which combines benevolence and intellectuality. The whole work does honor to the artist and will transmit to posterity the life like image of its original.

"The celebration began with musical entertainments These are now everywhere about as much alike as one egg is to another.

*	*	*	*	*	*	*	*	*

"After the musical part poems were recited and speeches were delivered.

"I might again have received some 'ennobling ideas, as from the music, from these speeches and poems, but they were only prepared for the occasion, and yet, as such, they were not without worth, and at all events did not fail to make their impression. Suffice it to be said that the celebration was a consummate affair and was in every way worthy of the distinguished man in whose honor it was given. If Madame Hahnemann, as a French woman, is to blame because the discoverer of the new healing principle lives to-day in Paris, she has thereby made infinitely more interesting the last days of a brave battler for a cause that in many respects may surely be called holy, and has doubled and even increased ten-fold his renown. The brilliant and select company that yesterday thronged around Hahnemann, and which could scarcely have been found anywhere in Germany, is a proof of this opinion. And then the number of his pupils and also his very lucrative consultations are increasing in Paris every day. Seldom has an aged man seen his last days made so beautiful, and it may well be said, too, that not many have deserved to be thus esteemed and honored by mankind.''

Dr. Croserio, in a letter to Dr. Neidhard in 1840,* thus mentions Hahnemann: ''Invalids from the highest classes of society are constanty flocking to the cabinet of Hahnemann; and notwithstanding the heat of the season, which drives all our aristocratic families into the country, his saloon is always full, and the patient is frequently compelled to await his turn from five to six hours before he can reach the sanctuary of Æsculapius. His weekly receptions—every Monday—are frequented by physicians and gentlemen of the first distinction from different sections of Europe. Hungary, Italy, Germany, England and the Iberian peninsula, furnish visitors to this great man; some attracted by the desire of acquiring valuable instruction from his long experience, others instigated by the laudable curiosity of enjoying the sight of a man celebrated in their respective countries, and all retire with hearts of grateful emotion, which the affectionate gentleness of his entire deportment ever inspires, and with minds charged with admiration for the vast erudition and profound knowledge of the venerable Reformist.''

The following is an account of a wonderful cure made by our old doctor. Its authenticity has been questioned, but it has been thought advisable to include it in this history.

It is the cure of the child of the French poet, Legouve, and was printed in *Le Temps* and was also published in the *Homœopathic World* for June, 1887. The editor says of it: ''We publish for the entertainment rather than for the instruction of our readers a translation of an article on Hahnemann. We need not inform our readers that, in this article, the Hahnemann described is almost purely mythical, being founded on the fact that an illustrious person of that name did once reside in Paris.''

In a letter addressed to the editor of the *Homœopathic Times* (English) in 1850,† the Rev. Mr. Everest mentions the ''most marvellous cure of the child of M. Legouve, the well-known

* *Hom. Exam.*, Vol. i., p. 346.
†*London Homœopathic Times*, Vol. i , p. 565.

French poet." Whether the present account be true or false, it
is probable that Hahnemann did really cure the child, else Mr.
Everest would not mention it as a fact. The story is as follows:

"My daughter, aged four years, was dying; our medical man,
a physician, of the Hotel Dieu, Dr. R———, had told one of our
friends in the morning that she was irrevocably lost. Her
mother and I were watching, perhaps for the last time, beside
her cradle; Schœlcher and Goubaux were watching along with us,
and in the room there was also a young man in evening dress,
whom we had only known three hours previously, one of M. In-
gres' most distinguished pupils, Amaury Duval.

"We wished to have a souvenir of the dear little creature
whose fate we already bewailed, and Amaury, at the earnest request of Schœlcher, who had gone to fetch him in the midst of
a ball, consented to come and make this sad portrait. When the
dear and charming artist (he was then twenty-nine years old)
came overcome with emotion in the midst of our distress we had
no idea, nor had he, that a few hours later he would do us the
greatest service we had ever experienced, and that we should be
indebted to him for something more valuable than the likeness
of our child, to wit, her life.

"He placed at the foot of the cradle, on a high piece of furniture, a lamp, whose light fell on the child's face. Her eyes were
already closed, her body was motionless, her dishevelled hair
hung about her forehead, and the pillow on which her head lay
was not whiter than her cheeks and her little hand; but infancy
has such a charm of its own that the near approach of death
seemed only to lend an additional grace to her face.

"Amaury spent the night in drawing her, and he had, poor
fellow, to wipe his eyes very frequently in order to prevent his
tears from falling on his paper.

"By morning the portrait was finished; under the stimulus
of emotion he had produced a masterpiece. When about to
leave us, in the midst of our thanks and our sorrow, he all at
once said: 'As your medical man declares your child's case
hopeless, why do you not make a trial of the new medical system
which is making such a noise in Paris; why do you not send for
Hahnemann?' 'He is right,' cried Goubaux, 'Hahnemann
is a near neighbor of mine. He lives in the Rue de Milan, opposite to my institution. I do not know him, but that is no

matter; I will go and bring him to you.' He went, he found twenty patients in the waiting room. The servant informed him he must wait and take his turn.

" 'Wait,' cried Goubaux, 'My friend's daughter is dying, the doctor must come with me at once.' 'But, sir'—exclaimed the servant. 'I know I am the last. What does that matter? The last shall be first, says the Evangelist.' Then turning to the patients, 'Is that not so, ladies? Won't you oblige me by letting me go up before you?' And without waiting for a reply, he walked straight up to the door of the doctor's study, opened it, and burst in in the middle of a consultation. 'Doctor,' he said, addressing Hahnemann, 'I know I am acting contrary to your rules, but you must leave all and come with me. It is for a charming little girl, four years old, who will die if you do not come. You cannot let her die. That's impossible.' And the irresistible charm of his manner prevailed, as it always does, and one hour afterwards Hahnemann and his wife came with him into our little patient's room.

" In the midst of all the troubles that distracted my poor head, racked by pain and want of sleep, I thought I saw one of the queer people of Hoffman's fairy tales enter the room. Short in stature but stout, and with a firm step, he advanced, wrapped in a fur great coat and supported by a thick gold-headed cane. He was about eighty years of age; his head of admirable shape; his hair white and silky, brushed back and carefully curled round his neck; his eyes were dark blue in the centre, with a whitish circle around the pupils; his mouth imperious; the lower lip projecting; his nose aquiline.

"When he entered he walked straight up to the cradle, threw a piercing glance at the child, asked for particulars about her disease, never taking his eyes off the patient. Then his cheeks became flushed, the veins of his forehead swelled, and he exclaimed in an angry voice: ' Throw out of the window all those drugs and bottles I see there! Carry this cradle out of this room. Change the sheets and the pillows, and give her as much water to drink as she likes. They have put a panful of hot coals in her inside. We must first extinguish the fire and then we will see what can be done.'

"We hinted that this change of temperature and of linen might be dangerous to her. 'What is killing her,' he replied impatiently, 'is this atmosphere and these drugs. Get her into the drawing room, I will come again in the evening. And mind you give her water! water! water!'

"He came again that evening; he came again the next day and began to give his medicines, and each time he only said: 'Another day gained!'

"On the tenth day dangerous symptoms suddenly developed themselves. Her knees became cold. He came at eight o'clock in the evening and remained for a quarter of an hour beside the bed, apparently a prey to great anxiety. At last, after consultation with his wife, who always accompanied him, he gave us a medicine with the remark, 'Give her this and notice if between this and one o'clock the pulse gets stronger.'

"At eleven o'clock, while feeling her wrist, I fancied I perceived a slight modification of the pulse. I called to my wife; I called to Goubaux and Schœlcher.

"And now see us all feeling the pulse one after the other, looking at the watch, counting the beats, not daring to affirm anything, not daring to rejoice, until, at the expiration of a few minutes, we all four embraced each other, the pulse was certainly stronger. About midnight Chretian Uhran came in. He came towards me, and in an accent of profound conviction, said, 'Dear M. Legouve, your daughter is saved.'

"'She is certainly a little better,' I replied still desponding, 'but between that and being cured—.' 'I tell you she is saved,' and going to the cradle he kissed the child on her forehead and took his departure. Eight days after this the patient was convalescent.   *   *   *   *   *   *   *

"The powerful structure of Hahnemann's face, his square jaw; the almost incessant palpitation of his nostrils; the quivering of the corners of his mouth, depressed by age; everything in him expressed conviction, passion, authority. His language, like his appearance, was original. 'Why,' I one day asked him, 'why do you prescribe, even for these in health, the continual use of water?' 'When one is strong or active, of what use are crutches of wine?' At another time I heard him make use of this expression, which sounds so strange if taken in a literal sense, but which is so profound if properly understood. 'There are no such things as diseases; there are only patients.' His religious faith was as genuine as his medical faith. Of this I had two striking instances.

One day in spring I called on him and said, 'Oh, M. Hahnemann, how fine it is to-day.' 'It is always fine,' he replied with a calm and serious voice. Like Marcus Aurelius, he lived in the midst of genial harmony.

"When my daughter was cured, I showed him Amaury Duval's delicious drawing. He gazed long and admiringly at this portrait, which represented the resuscitated girl as she was when he first saw her, when she seemed so near death. He then asked me to give him a pen, and he wrote beneath it:

"'Dieu l'a benie et l'a sauvee.'

"'SAMUEL HAHNEMANN.'

"His portrait would not be complete unless I added that of his wife. She never left him. In his reception room she sat beside his desk at a little table, where she worked like him and for him. She was present at all the consultations whatever might be the patient's sex or disease. She wrote down all the symptoms of the disease, gave her advice to Hahnemann in German and made up his medicines. If he paid any professional visits, which he only did in exceptional cases, she always accompanied him. It is a curious circumstance that Hahnemann was the third old man to whom she had become attached.

"She commenced with painting, then changed to literature and finished with medicine. At twenty-five or thirty years of age, M'lle. d'Hervilly (that was her maiden name), pretty, tall, elegant, with a fresh complexion, her face surrounded with little blonde curls, and her small blue eyes as piercing as black ones, became the companion of a celebrated pupil of David, M.L——. In marrying the painter she married painting, and she might have signed more than one of his pictures, as she subsequently signed the prescriptions of Hahnemann.

"When M. L—— died, she turned to poetry in the person of a septuagenarian poet, for the further she went the older she liked them. This was M. A——. She now devoted herself to making verses with the same ardor with which she had set about painting big historical pictures, and A having died in his turn, septuagenarians no longer contented her. She married the octogenarian Hahnemann! She now became as revolutionary in medicine as she had been classical in painting and poetry. Her devotion to Homœopathy went the length of fanaticism. One day when I was complaining in her presence of the dishonesty of one of our servants whom we had been obliged to turn away, 'Why did you not let us know that sooner?' she replied, 'we have medicines for that.' Let me add that she was a person of rare intelligence and that she had wonderful skill as a sick nurse. No one knew better than she did how to devise all sorts of expedients for the comfort of poor patients. In her was combined the pious zeal of a sister of charity and the delicate resources of a woman of the world. The care she took of Hahnemann was admirable.

"He died as such a man ought to die. Up to the age of eighty-four he remained a most eloquent proof of the excellence of his doctrine. He had no infirmity, not the slightest sign of failure of intelligence or of memory. His regimen was simple, but without any affectation of rigour. He never drank either pure water or pure wine. A few spoonfuls of champagne in a jug of water was his only drink, and in place of bread he ate every day a small sponge cake. 'My old teeth,' he said, 'find that easier to chew.' In summer he walked every fine evening from the Arc de Triomphe, and stopped at Tortoni's to eat an ice." *   *   *   *   *   *   *

CHAPTER LXXVI.

EPIC POEM ON HOMŒOPATHY—DR. HULL'S VISIT TO HAHNEMANN
—LETTER TO DR. SCHREETER—EIGHTY-SIXTH BIRTHDAY.

In 1840, one "Guancialis" wrote an epic poem in praise of Hahnemann.

It was published in Naples, and contained eight books of Latin hexameters. It gives a history of the discovery of the law of similia and of its introduction into the different lands of the earth. A review may be found in the *British Journal of Homœopathy*, Vol. 4. p. 424.

Dr. A. G. Hull visited Hahnemann in Paris, in 1840, and thus writes of it: "Furnished with letters from Dr. Hering, of Philadelphia, and Dr. Quin, of London, I found a welcome access to our venerable master. At this period Hahnemann occupied a spacious mansion in the vicinity of the Luxembourg Gardens. Ushered by an attendant into the grand saloon at a

moment when he was engaged with a patient in his adjoining
study, I had an opportunity of individualizing the appointments
of this noble apartment. Its walls were hung with varied and
choice paintings in oil, many of them the productions of his accomplished wife. Vases, busts and medals—donatives from
those whose gratitude his cures have evoked—were disposed in
tasteful arrangement, and his centre table was laden with the
productions of German, French and other tongues, presentation
copies. Introduced into the library or study, I had for the first
time the inexpressible gratification of beholding the face and
grasping the hand of the great Reformist of our century. I felt
myself in the presence of a mighty intellect, once compelled to
struggle with keen adversity, to contend with the persecution
and cupidity of his rivals, and in banishment to depend upon
the protective shelter of a noble stranger, now independently
situated in the heart of Europe, and proudly eminent in the admiration of literati, philosophers, noblemen and crowned heads.
Hahnemann, who is now approaching his 90th year, recalls in
his venerable appearance the ideal of a Seneca or Plato, an
Aristotle or Socrates. Attached to the usages of his study, he
was, as is his general habit, attired in a morning gown, his
silvered locks flowing on either side of his head from beneath a
small and close German cap, after the fashion of a German
University student. His capacious head of the finest Saxon
mould, presented a full broad face, expressive of a noble benevolence and high intelligence. I had anticipated many exhibi-
tions of the progress of age in the physical condition of
Hahnemann. But his firmness of figure, activity of movement
and unimpaired sight and hearing are characteristic of the
perfect health he enjoys, and form no slight or inconclusive
commentary upon the excellence of the Homœopathic regimen
he has so scrupulously and so long observed. His mental
faculties seem also in the judgment of all who have known him
long to retain the vigor of former days; and if I may be allowed
to judge by the masterly criticisms and powerful arguments I
have heard fall from his lips, the apostle of modern Germany
has not succumbed to the ordinary ravages of time, but in manhood and strength of intellect is in his green old age, 'Lord of
the lion heart and eagle eye.'* I shall ever bear in mind the

* *Hom. Exam.*, Vol. II, p. 12.

cordial greeting and warmth of welcome with which the great master received his American disciple. Immediately at ease, I engaged in a conversation, the recollection of which will continue to cheer me in the struggle that is now pending on this side of the Atlantic. Hahnemann having relinquished visiting the sick for many years, his practice is to a great extent consulting, and is exclusively confined to his office; so that the sickness which commands his attentions and prescriptions, is of a chronic character. This experience is not to be estimated as inconsiderable as the revenue of Hahnemann from this form of practice exceeds 200,000 francs per anuum. Hahnemann made earnest inquiries as to the condition and prospects of Homœopathy in America.

"From among the physicians of America he especially designated Dr. Hering, of Philadelphia, his personal and long tried friend and former companion, and Dr. Gray, of New York, who some time before had communicated to him the pleasing intelligence of one of the highest concessions and compliments that could be paid to his worth by his Allopathic opponents in the United States, that of honorary membership in the Medical Society of New York." (The same society afterwards decided to reclaim this empty honor and so did.—B—D).

"He spoke of Dr. Hering in the most affectionate terms, and expatiated freely upon his merits, attainments and perseverence in the humane cause he has espoused. He considers Dr. Hering one of his most efficient disciples; to which decision all will respond who are acquainted with the devotion of this early pioneer, who fearlessly faced the yellow fever and exposed his system by patient experiments to the deadly influence of the venomous reptiles of Surinam. I bore with me from the hands of Madame Hahnemann a superb medallion of her husband, modelled by the celebrated sculptor David, as a souvenir to this estimable man and undeviating Homœopathist. Hahnemann felt quite interested in the course of education adopted by American Homœopathists, and in his rejoinders gives a direct denial to the calumnious circulation charged upon him ,that medical instruction was not vitally essential to successful practice. In answer to inquiry on this point, I stated that our regularly recognized Homœopaths were qualified by their diplomas from the legal institutions of our country in the departments of anatomy, physiology, surgery, midwifery, materia medica, chemistry, botany and Allopathic medicine; *i. e.*, were "regular physicians" before they commenced the study of Homœopathy, which accomplished, rendered them alone competent to judge between the merits of the two systems—to avoid the dangers of Allopathy and to appreciate the demonstrable advantages of Homœopathy.

"Hahnemann 'rejoiced that his American disciples pursued the only true and creditable course for maintaining the exalted dignity and sacred duty that belongs to the physician.' He further inquired if his American adherents had acquired their knowledge of his system in the German language. I replied that I had made it my duty to do so, and hoped that no Homœopathist among my countrymen would with the present limited works in the English language consider himself a competent practitioner until he had studied well the fountain from whence the system flowed.

"The memory of that moment is before me and I shall not soon forget the suddenly illuminated countenance of that good old man. His eyes flashed, his form expanded, and with the vehemence of one intensely interested in the cause of his heart and life he spoke deeply eloquent.

"'The toil of my early Homœopathic life and the labors of my German associates are principally confined to the language that gave them birth. To accumulate these treasures my disciples united with me in the midst of contempt and persecutions, in self-denials and life-periling experiments. Is it possible, then, that any man who professes to be a Homœopathist and to love his species will not take the comparatively trifling trouble of acquiring this important preliminary to a correct acquisition of this great boon to the sick? No; it cannot be! Their solemn obligations to diseased and dying humanity, to confer the benefits of medicine in the very best possible manner, should appeal to their consciences as they expect to be judged hereafter.'"

"The time for farewell having arrived, I acquainted the venerable sage and his most excellent wife of my intention and offered my grateful acknowledgments for their civilities. The old man, seemingly as a patriarch of old, arose, and embracing me most affectionately with both hands, gave me a parting benediction, which like 'a pillar of cloud by day and pillar of fire by night shall guide my feet' in the trackless field of contention the enemies of Homœopathy are creating.

" 'Farewell, my son! Persevere as you have commenced, and you will rejoice in the gratitude of your beneficiaries. Go to your native land, where the spirit of your Constitution spurns the tyranny of opinion, and propagate the truths I have so long and so successfully inculcated. Your efforts, guided by these truths, will acquire for you a brilliant triumph. God bless you, my son! Farewell!'"*

In a letter to Dr. Schreeter Hahnemann thus expresses himself regarding his life in Paris,†

"PARIS, 13th August, 1840.

"*Esteemed Friend and Colleague:*

" I know not when, in the course of my long life, I have been better or happier than in Paris, in the loved society of my dear Melanie, who cares for naught in the world more than for me. I also begin gradually to find that my professional labors are creating in the great Metropolis more than mere attention, a high respect for our divine healing art. All patients who are not bedridden, whatever their rank, visit me every day (Sundays excepted) in my study. To those only who are confined to bed I drive from eight to ten in the evening. Two or three times a week I go with my wife to a theatre or concert."

The following letter was written to some one in America in 1841—Dudgeon says probably to one of Hering's German collaborators in the Allentown Academy:‡

"*Dear Friend :*

"How are you and your two dear boys? I hope I may receive a very good account of you. I would also like to know if you have become familiar with our difficult, no doubt, but very efficacious Homœopathic practice?

" I and my dear wife, both together, cure a very great number of patients. She alone, at a later period of the day, cures very many poor patients, often to my astonishment. We receive patients of all ranks, even the highest, in our consulting room,

---

* *Hom. Examiner*, Vol. i., p. 241. (July, 1840).

† *Brit. Jour. Hom.*, Vol. vi., p. 416. Stapf's *Archiv*, Vol. xxiii., pt. 3, p. 107.

‡ *Hom. World*, Vol. xxvi., p. 119.

and I pay visits along with her, in my carriage, only to patients who are obliged to keep their beds, generally in the evening till midnight. I have consultations at my house only from ten in the morning until four in the afternoon. We are regularly besieged by patients, even in summer, when so many families live in the country.

"There has been a great accession of nominal Homœopaths since I came here (six years ago), but there are very few good, true, pure ones. There may be some good ones in the country towns.

"If I have been rightly informed, your Academy in Allentown grants diplomas to good Homœopaths. If that is so, you would confer a favor on me if you would send one to my dear wife, Marie Melanie Hahnemann, *nee* d'Hervilly, for she is better acquainted with Homœopathy, theoretically and practically, than any of my followers, and lives, I may say, for our art.

"The two little cameos which the dear clergyman, Mr. Bayer, is taking to you will give you a good idea of my head; the copper-plate engraving is, on the whole, also very like, only the artist has taken me in an unfortunate moment, when I was probably vexed by the bad behavior of the bastard Homœopaths in Germany; there is no trace in it of the kind-heartedness which is usually seen on my countenance.

"God keep you in good health and prosperity.

"Your quite devoted,

"SAMUEL HAHNEMANN.

"*Paris, March 28, 1841.*

"Write to me by post (that is the best way) to Paris, Rue de Milan—Clichy, No. 1."

In the *Allgemeine Zeitung* may be found a short account of the eighty-sixth birthday celebration. It is as follows:*

"Another acknowledgment of his distinguished services was recently given in Paris to Dr. Samuel Hahnemann on his eighty-sixth birthday. The city council of his native city, Meissen, unanimously conferred upon him the honor of citizenship, the mayor of the city engrossing the diploma which was presented to him at the jubilee on the 10th of April by his excellency, the Saxon ambassador at Paris. How much this mark of attention rejoiced and honored the aged man is plainly to be inferred from his official reply to the city council of Meissen.

Allg. hom. Zeitung, Vol. xx., p. 112. (July 5, 1841).

"May the great renovator of medicine receive many more such tokens of honor in his old age. They would afford him the best assurance of his rational and unceasing strife for the truth."

Dr. Croserio, in a letter addressed to Dr. Neidhard, of Philadelphia, and dated Paris, September 25, 1841, mentions this circumstance as follows:* "The burgomasters of the city of Meissen have bestowed the title of honorary citizenship on Hahnemann, and have had the delicacy to present the diploma to him through the minister of Saxony, on the 10th of April, his birthday. This spontaneous act of the principal association of a city in favor of the founder of doctrines which they consider beneficial to humanity, living twelve hundred miles apart from them, and all these acts of other bodies, are the best proofs of the consideration and esteem in which Homoeopathy is held throughout the country."

The 10th of August, 1841, was also celebrated as usual. Croserio says:† "You will doubtless be glad to learn that our venerable master enjoys excellent health, notwithstanding his great age. His body and mind preserve all the activity and energy of middle age. He is going to publish the sixth edition of his 'Organon,' revised, in French, and written entirely by his own hand, in the intervals taken from his occupations with the immense circle of patients by whom he is continually surrounded. The 10th of August we celebrated at his own house the sixty-second anniversary of his doctorate. The guests were numerous and animated with pleasure at seeing this man thus recompensed in his old age for his immense labors in the cause of humanity. The illustrious host also visibly rejoiced in seeing himself surrounded by his attached friends, his numerous patients and disciples; for his heart is open like a child's to every mark of friendship and affection. Drs. Calandra, of Palermo, and Sommers, of Berlin, read, each of them, a copy of verses in their mother tongue on a subject of great interest to the company; for these reunions have a peculiar character of cosmopolitanism, which is met with nowhere else. The language of the country is the one least spoken, and I had the pleasure of conversing in Spanish, Italian, English and German.

---

* *Hom. Exam.*, Vol. iii., p 61.
† Letter to Dr. Neidhard, *Hom. Exam.*, Vol. iii., p. 59.

This is a centre where all nations unite in brotherhood, in sentiments of veneration for the illustrious founder of Homœopathy,
and in reciprocal testimonies to the superiority of this doctrine
over all others which have preceded it, being for the most part
living proofs of that power to which they owe their health, and
many of them their lives.''

What more potent answer to the great little men of the present
day, who just about so often inform us what an old ignoramus
Hahnemann was, than to invite them to picture to themselves
this scene of his declining years. The old man, with his
fine intellectual face, his white hair curling on either side of his
lofty brow, his manner filled with the enthusiasm and unrest of
genius, surrounded by learned men of half a dozen countries,
able to speak to each in his mother tongue. Imagine this
brilliant assembly, met to do honor to the most brilliant of them
all. Here a sentence in English, there a soft Italian phrase,
then some witty sentence in the diction of his fatherland, anon a
Spanish question, again a witty French bon mot—Hahnemann
answering each in its own tongue. The while Madame Hahnemann, the hostess, charming in her easy grace, giving to all a
worthy welcome, and honoring the dear old man, her medical
Master and her beloved husband. And this in the brightest city
in the world.

It is quite time that the medical and other critics and detractors of Hahnemann fit glasses of truth to their myopic and astig-
matic eyes, and let Hahnemann alone.

As has been seen all of the birthdays of Hahnemann were
utilized to honor him. His life at Paris was one long fete.

CHAPTER LXXVII.

HAHNEMANN'S MODESTY CONCERNING AN HONORARY TABLET
—LAST ILLNESS AND DEATH.

In 1841 two of Hahnemann's admirers, Mr. William Leaf, of
London, and Mr. Franz Arles-Dufour, of Lyons, France, wished
to place an inscription in the house at Meissen in which Hahnemann was born. The following is a copy of the Latin inscrip-

tion that was prepared by these gentlemen together with a letter from Hahnemann written in French concerning it:*

"Chr. Fr. Samueli Hahnemann, *conditori*[x] Medicinæ vera celeberrimo immortali artis medendi Homœopathicæ auctori ijusque primo professori, ægrorum præsidio firmissimo summo saxonum decori. Hoc patria domo monumentum Guilielmus Leaf, Londinensis, grati piique cultores posuerunt anno MDCCCXLII."

[x]Antimdo *Emendatori.*

In the original as sent to Hahnemann the word *emendatori* was used instead of *conditori.* As will be seen by the letter this was not pleasing to Hahnemann. The original of the following letter is written in French, and as usual with Hahnemann's writing is so fine and exact as to resemble copper plate:

"PARIS, Dec. 11, 1841.

"Dear Doctor and Friend:

"I have received all your amiable letters, for which I thank you most heartily, also for your good friendship which I herewith reciprocate. Dr. Schubert, of Leipsic, has written me that Mr. Leaf and Mr. Arles-Dufour intend to place an inscription on the house in which I was born at Meissen. He sends me a copy of it so that I may correct anything that I should judge improper.

"While I appreciate the smallness of my personal value I must claim in the name of Homœopathy that the entirely false expression of *emendatori* be changed into that of *conditori. One must break every alliance with untruth.* Mr. Schubert writes me to address this correction to you in order to lay it properly before Mr. Leaf, which I herewith do; embracing you,

"I wish you good health and success,

"SAMUEL HAHNEMANN."

Dr. Black, of England, in an address before the British Homœopathic Congress, held in 1872, said:† "I knew Hahnemann a year before his death, but age had told on his frame and his intellect; it left untouched his enthusiasm and his desire to work. When he bade me good-bye, embracing me, he said: 'Work, work, and the good God will bless thee.' "

---

*The compiler is indebted to the courtesy of Dr. J. H. McClelland, of Pittsburgh, Pa., for the above inscription and letter. Dr. McClelland owns the original letter by Hahnemann.

† *Med. Investigator,* Vol. ix., p. 558.

It may be mentioned here that Hahnemann was, during his life in Paris, visited by several prominent Allopathic physicians.

Dr. Valentine Mott, of New York, the celebrated surgeon, visited him, and after his return thus spoke: "Hahnemann is one of the most accomplished and scientific physicians of the present age."*

But the days of celebrations, fetes and interviews with great men, with which his life in Paris had been filled, were now about to cease. He, who ten years before in Germany had spoken of himself as on the verge of the grave, was now a very aged man.

We have nearly reached the end of the story of this magnificent life. From privation, trial, calumny; from the peace of Coethen; from the distinguished honors of Paris; let us turn to a death calm and dignified, worthy in every way of the life.

For the previous ten years Hahnemann had been every spring a sufferer from that disease of the very old, bronchial catarrh. In April, 1843, he was again taken with this disease and became at once seriously ill. He as usual prescribed for himself, and when he became too weak to do this recommended the remedies that his wife and Dr. Chatran should use. Patiently he suffered the severe paroxysms of difficult breathing peculiar to his disease, evincing to the last that benign spirit of devoutness to God that had characterized his whole life. The end came early in the morning of Sunday, July 2, 1843.

Jahr, writing to the *Allgemeine Zeitung*,† two days later, says:‡

"HAHNEMANN IS DEAD!"

"About the 15th of April he was taken ill with the malady that usually attacked him in the spring, a bronchial catarrh, and

---

* "Trans. N. Y. State Hom. Med. Soc.," Vol. i., p. 119 (1863).

† *Allg. hom. Zeitung*, Vol. xxiv., p. 257 (July 10, 1843). Ameke, p. 166. *Leben und Wirken*, p. 80.

‡ Rather a singular error occurred in the letter written by Jahr to the editor of the *Allegemeine homoopathische Zeitung* announcing Hahnemann's death. Instead of writing July he wrote June at the beginning of the letter. In Dr. Hering's copy of the *Zeitung* the letter is dated *Juni 4*, but Dr. Hering in his characteristic blue pencil mark has crossed this and written *Juli*. From the *Zeitung* this error was copied into the Albrecht books, Ameke gives it as June 4, Fischer in his translation from Albrecht gives July 4, and this date is correct. Hahnemann certainly died on July 2d, at five in the morning, and Jahr sent the first news to Germany, writing two days later, on July 4th.

it took such hold of him that his wife admitted no one. The report was spread several times that he was dead; this, however, was contradicted. I had been intending to call myself when I received a note from Madame Hahnemann begging me to come that same day. I went at once and was admitted to Hahnemann's bedroom. Here, think of the sight, instead of seeing Hahnemann, the dear, friendly old man, smile his greeting, I found his wife stretched, in tears, on the bed and him lying cold and stiff by her side, having passed five hours before into that life where there is no strife, no sickness and no death. Yes, dear friends, our venerable Father Hahnemann has finished his course; a chest affection has, after a six weeks' illness, liberated his spirit from its weary frame.

"His mental powers remained unimpaired up to the last moment, and although his voice became more and more unintelligible yet his broken words testified to the continued clearness of his mind and to the calm with which he anticipated his approaching end. At the very commencement of his illness he told those about him that this would be his last, as his frame was worn out. At first he treated himself, and till a short time before his death he expressed his opinions relative to the remedies recommended by his wife and a certain Dr. Chatran. He only really suffered just at the end from increasing oppression on the chest. When after one such attack his wife said: 'Providence surely owes you exemption from all suffering, as you have relieved so many others and have suffered so many hardships in your arduous life;' he answered: 'Why should I expect exemption from suffering? Everyone in this world works according to the gifts and powers which he has received from Providence, and *more or less* are words used only before the judgment seat of man, not before that of Providence. Providence owes me nothing. I owe it much. Yes, everything.'

"Profound grief for this great loss is felt here by all his followers. All shed tears of gratitude and affection for him. But the loss of those who have had the happiness of enjoying the friendship and affection of this great man can only be estimated by those who have known him in his domestic circle, and especially during his last years. He, himself, when not persecuted by others, was not only a good, but a simple-hearted and benevolent man, who was never happier than when among friends to whom he could unreservedly open his heart. Well, he has nobly fought through and gloriously completed his difficult and often painful course. Sit ei terra levis!''

Dr. Hull announced his death in the *Homœopathic Examiner* for September, 1843,* as follows: ''This impressive event took place on the second of July, after a protracted bronchial catarrh. The disease began on the twelfth of April, two days after he had celebrated his eighty seventh birthday in excellent health and spirits. Hahnemann had for twenty years suffered from attacks of this disease in the spring of the year. He had ever, as in this instance, prescribed for himself. This last attack set in with a serious diarrhœa, which exhausted him very much. In the early stages of the sickness he announced to his friends the opinion that he could not survive it. 'The earthly frame is worn out' was his expression. He seems to have suffered but slightly till a short time (probably a few days only) before his decease, when a dyspnœa came on in paroxysms increasing in severity until the final one, which lasted thirteen hours and terminated in suffocation.'' Croserio writing to Dr. Hull, says:

''How much equanimity, patience and imperturbable goodness he exhibited! Though he had a distinct presentiment of his approaching end, yet he never permitted an expression to escape him which could alarm his wife; he calmly made his final arrangements, and embraced each of his friends with tenderness, such as belonged to a final adieu, but with steady equanimity. Hahnemann expired at 5 A. M. Two hours afterwards I visited his sacred remains. The face expressed an ineffable calm. Death could not detract the least from the angelic goodness which belonged to the expression of his features.''

It is said that the widow of Hahnemann applied for and received permission to retain his body for twenty days beyond the usual time of interment. The body was embalmed by Ganal.†

It does not seem that many people saw Hahnemann during his last illness. Jahr expressed himself to that effect, implying that his best friends were excluded from the sick chamber.

Dr. Suss-Hahnemann, in a letter to the editor of the *British Journal of Homœopathy*, May 30, 1865, says:‡ ''Unfortunately

---

* *Hom. Exam.*, Vol. iii., p. 257 (Sept., 1843).

† *Hom. Exam.*, Vol. iii., p. 258.

‡ *Brit. Jour. Hom.*, Vol. xxiii., p. 423.

I was only present at the very last dying moments of my grand-father, not even on the eve of his death, although my late mother and I had arrived in Paris already a whole week previous to this sad event taking place. In spite of our most earnest entreaties, in spite of Hahnemann's own wish to see once more his favorite daughter, Madame Hahnemann resolutely and sternly refused us an interview with our dying parent, when he would have been still able to speak to us and to bless us.''

Hahnemann's death was a great grief to the many friends of the new system of medicine. It was generally noticed in the journals of both medical schools.

The following account appeared in the *British Journal of Homœopathy:**

"DEATH OF HAHNEMANN."

"It is our painful duty to announce the death of our venerable Master, an event quite unexpected by those who on his last birthday, three months before, were witnesses of the mental and bodily vigor of which he then gave proof.

"Samuel Hahnemann died in his eighty-ninth year at his house in the Rue de Milan, Paris, at five o'clock on the morning of Sunday, 2d July, after an illness of six weeks.

"His remains are for the present laid in Madame Hahnemann's family vault at Montmartre, but will probably, ere long, be transferred to Germany.

"His illness commenced with a bilious diarrhœa, succeeded by an intermittent fever, which greatly reduced his strength. It first assumed a tertian, then a quotidian type; he rallied surprisingly, however, and was deemed convalescent, when bronchitis senilis supervened, under which he sunk in three days. He retained his faculties entire to the last, and shortly before he expired dictated a short and simple epitaph.†

"He bade adieu to his wife and friends, commended himself to God, and died.

"Shortly before his death, while suffering from difficulty of breathing, his wife said to him: 'Providence owes you a mitigation of your sufferings, since, in your life, you have alleviated the sufferings of so many, and yourself endured so much.' 'Me,' replied the dying sage, 'why then me? Each man here below

---

* *Brit. Jour. Hom.*, Vol. i., p. 415 (Oct., 1843.
† Non inutilis vixi. (I have not lived in vain).

works as God gives him strength, and meets with a greater or less reward at the judgment seat of man; but he can claim no reward at the judgment seat of God. God owes me nothing, but I owe God much, yea all.' These are memorable words, spoken in death-bed sincerity.

"Hahnemann is dead, but his mighty truth cannot die; so that while we turn sadder and wiser from the deathbed of our great Master, who, when living, taught us how to live, and now has taught us how to die, if we would have him still to guide our way, we must seek his spirit, and may it prove a bond of sacred union in the work he has so nobly done; and while we prosecute this we shall have the proud gratification that we are completing his labors and erecting his monument."

In the same number of the *British Journal* appears the following: "Though he had been ill for many weeks before, few of those around him anticipated that his demise was near at hand; but he himself seemed to have expected it, as some months before he said to a friend, 'It is perhaps time that I quit this earth, but I leave it all and always in the hands of my God. My head is full of truth for the good of mankind, and I have no wish to live but in so far as I can serve my fellowmen.'

"His intellect remained quite unclouded to the last, and but a few moments before his death he uttered some epithet of endearment to his wife, and pressed the hand of his favorite servant, who was supporting him in his arms."

Albrecht writes: "How deeply it grieved us when on the 10th day of July, 1843, and therefore just one month before a convention of Homœopathic physicians was to be held in Dresden under the direction of Dr. Trinks, President of the Board of Health, we read the following communication: 'Homœopathy has suffered a great loss. Its founder, Samuel Hahnemann, the Nestor of German physicians, died yesterday morning at five o'clock in his eighty-eighth year. The sorrow on account of his death is extraordinarily great, and his funeral may be one of the largest ever solemnized in Paris.'"

CHAPTER LXXVIII.

BURIAL OF HAHNEMANN—MEETINGS OF RESPECT—TRANS-
LATIONS OF RUMMEL'S POEM.

It was the wish of the many friends and disciples of Hahnemann living in Paris to honor and show him respect by attending his funeral. But he had none. The time of his burial was
kept a secret. The following account appeared in the *British
Journal of Homœopathy :**

"Though her union with the illustrious Founder of Homœopathy had been so profitable to Madame Hahnemann, her gratitude towards him did not assume the form of wasting any of the
money he had earned on ostentatious funeral obsequies. Probably she thought that as expensive *pompes funebres* would not
profit the dead, she might as well practice a strict economy in
the matter of his burial. Many of Hahnemann's friends in Paris
were desirous of testifying their respect for him by attending his
body to the grave, but this wish his widow disappointed by
keeping the time of his funeral a profound secret. Early one
morning a common hearse drove into the courtyard of the mansion in the Faubourg St. Honore, the coffin was put into it, and
the hearse was speedily driven off to the Montmartre Cemetery,
followed on foot by the bereaved widow; by Hahnemann's
daughter, Madame Liebe, and her son; and a young doctor
named Lethiere. These were the only mourners. The body
was consigned to an old vault without any ceremony, religious
or otherwise, and to this day, we understand, there is no tombstone or inscription to distinguish his obscure grave, so it would
now be difficult, if not impossible, to discover the last resting-
place of the great man."

Dr. Puhlmann, in the *Leipziger Populaire Zeitschrift fur
Homoopathie*, July 1, 1893, says: "As early as six o'clock, in the
morning in gloom and rain, on July 11, 1843, a funeral procession moved through the streets of Paris to the Cemetery of Montmartre. Only a few persons walked behind the hearse, which
bore, encased in a plain coffin, the worthy remains of a man who

---

* *Brit. Jour. Hom.*, Vol. xxxvi., p. 301.

had begun fifty years before to reform radically the system of healing—a German physician whose corpse was to be interred in a foreign land—Dr. Samuel Hahnemann.

"For many years the aged physician had suffered every spring from bronchial catarrh, but had always completely recovered again; so that the customary return of this disease, which attacked him again about the middle of April, 1843, had no special significance. But it was to be his last sickness. The aged man grew weaker and weaker. And sometimes, when paroxysms of suffocation or choking set in, they occasioned much anxiety. But the dying embers of the fire of life in the venerable founder of Homœopathy always rekindled; and although he predicted his own death, his family would not believe that his end was so near. Hence his death, so soon following on the second of July, was quite unexpected to them. His widow could scarcely realize her great loss; and, in her bewilderment, omitted to send notice of his funeral to relatives and friends.

"But she went to the proper magistrate to get permission to have his remains embalmed, so that their entombment might be delayed as long as possible. She obtained the permission, and Ganal, the most celebrated embalmer of his day, discharged with great skill the duties assigned to him. Then, for the first time, she issued notices of the funeral, and relatives and friends thus knew of the actual decease of the great man, whom the daily press during the few months preceding had repeatedly reported to be dead.

"The hour of the funeral services, however, was not stated in the notices. The many tokens of love and sympathy, which are sent to the house of mourning in the form of crosses and palm leaves, would have put the sorrowing widow in a frame of mind in which she would no longer have had control of her thoughts, wishes and purposes; and hence the entombment of the body on that morning early, without the many admirers of the deceased having any knowledge of it. Instead of an imposing funeral procession, as the world-renowned physician had deserved, there were in the procession only the sorrowing widow, the deceased's daughter, Madame Suss, and her son, who had hastened hither from London, the Homœopathic physician, Dr. Lethiere, and the servants of the household.

"A monumental stone with the inscription: 'Chretian Frederic Samuel Hahnemann,' on the left side of Section 16 of Montmartre Cemetery, marks the spot where the deceased was laid in his eternal resting place. This resting-place, as well as those of many other celebrated men buried in Montmartre, as, for instance, that of the poet Heinrich Heine, belongs to those historic sepulchres that are kept in repair at the expense of the government, when relatives no longer care for their departed."

Concerning this funeral, Albrecht writes: "In order to show that it is a matter of no consequence to us to place in a favorable light an event interwoven with the catastrophe of Hahnemann's life-drama, or to work it up in any partisan sense and erect thereon a showy structure of artistic finish, and in order to remain entirely free of prejudice also, we will give here a manuscript report of the interment of Hahnemann's earthly remains. Of course Melanie plays a very conspicuous part in the obsequies. Hahnemann's body was embalmed, laid in an exceedingly plain wooden coffin, lined with zinc, and placed in a vault, in which Melanie had already buried two friends. All the coffins are visible through a grated door. At the hour that Hahnemann was buried the rain poured down in torrents. The funeral cortege was very small (einfach), consisting only of Melanie, daughter Amalie, Dr. Suss, Uncle Leopold Suss and the servants of the household."

He further says that the funeral occurred on the rainy morning of August 11, 1843, and continues as follows: "No splendid monument is required for Hahnemann. Over his tomb, like the angel with the leaf of eternal peace, lingers the heaven-born consciousness of a life devoted to duty, science, art, the welfare of mankind and the service of God. By the side of this angel stands another, the certainty that nothing really good, really beneficial, can ever perish, but defies death and the grave, continuing in everlasting activity, and thus identifying itself with the highest order of things and the government of the universe. A third angel hovers there, revealing to our gaze the name of Hahnemann, and the significant words '*Non inutilis vixi*'* are graven there as with a sunbeam."

The following account of the burial may be found in the *Hom-*

* I have not lived in vain. Hahnemann wrote these words as a suitable inscription for his own monument on July 28, 1839.

œopathic World: * "Madame Hahnemann buried her husband with less decency and less regard than that which is shown to the poorest of our sorrowing poor. Many were the applications and requests of his admirers and disciples to be allowed to attend his funeral, but all to no purpose. The day and hour of the funeral were kept a perfect secret. Early one morning in July, 1843, a common hearse drew up in the courtyard of Hahnemann's mansion, the coffin was quickly lifted into it, and as quickly as the hearse had entered the courtyard so it drove away again. His wife, his daughter, his grandson and a young Dr. Lethiere were the only mourners who followed the hearse—on foot—to the neighboring cemetery of Montmartre.

"There Hahnemann's coffin was pushed in a most unseemly manner into an old vault, where two coffins had already been previously placed by Madame Hahnemann. There was no funeral ceremony whatever, no funeral rites, no blessing on the distinguished dead."

Dr. Suss Hahnemann, who was the grandson present, says of this funeral:† "The ostentatious affection which the wife displayed towards her husband whilst alive soon vanished after his death. The immortal Founder of Homœopathy was buried like the poorest of the poor; his funeral taking place as early in the morning as six o'clock, under a pelting rain, a common hearse bearing the remains of the great man to his last rest, only his wife, his widowed daughter, my late mother, myself, and Dr. Lethiere being the mourners who followed. The coffin was deposited, and is still at the present moment, in an old vault, where his *devoted* wife had already deposited the remains of two aged *friends*, so that Hahnemann's wish to have on his tombstone the words written, 'Non inutilis vixi,' remains in abeyance."

After the death of Madame Hahnemann, in 1878, the most of the above statements were printed. In the obituary of that lady, printed in the *British Journal of Homœopathy* for July, 1878, the account of Hahnemann's obscure interment is given. In the January number, 1879, of the same *Journal* is published an answer from one M. Sanches, who signs himself a man of letters

---

Hom. World, Vol. xiii., p. 349.
† *Brit. Jour. Hom.*, Vol. xxii., p. 679.

attached to the Prefecture of the Seine.* He advances excuses for Madame Hahnemann's course. He excuses the visit to Coethen in masculine garments; says that Madame Hahnemann was not influenced by avarice, and that after her husband's death she continued to treat patients, but gratuitously; that the obscure funeral was at Hahnemann's own wish; and the reason why his grave was not distinguished by some sign was that she feared the malicious attacks upon it of jealous physicians. However, it thus happened, and, so far as the compiler has been able to discover, Hahnemann still rests in the unknown grave in the old cemetery on the hill of Montmartre, in Paris.

The New York Homœopathic Physicians' Society called a special meeting on the 10th of August, immediately after the news of Hahnemann's death had been received, and Dr. Gray was selected to pronounce, at a future occasion, a eulogy upon the illustrious man. It was decided to hold this meeting on the 10th of April of the following year. The New York Homœopathic Society, of which William Cullen Bryant was the President, also assembled in order to co-operate with the Physicians' Society. A letter of condolence was sent to Madame Hahnemann, dated New York, August 9th, 1843.†

In Philadelphia a printed circular was sent about for signatures. It read as follows:

"*To Melanie D'Hervilly, Widow of S. Hahnemann, and to His Children and Grandchildren :*

"Fully sensible that to you who stood nearest to the venerable Hahnemann, the sorrow occasioned by his decease must be the severest, we desire to send a word of condolence from this far land. You will receive this expression of our sympathy as a token also that he still lives—still lives not only in the world to which he is gone, but here also, where he was and where we yet are. He lives in the great principles which he asserted, he lives in the thankful regards of the great multitude whom he has relieved. He lives, for he is still ministering to human infirmities, still alleviating human suffering; and he will live so long as the healing art continues to be a blessing to the world."

Dr. Hering, in speaking of the death of Dr. Hahnemann, said:

---

*Brit. Jour. Hom., Vol. xxxvii., p. 98.
† Hom. Exam., Vol. iii., p. 319.

"When at last the fatal hour had struck for the sublime old man who had preserved his vigor almost to his last moments, then it was that the heart of his consort who had made his last years the brightest of his life was on the point of breaking. Many of us seeing those who are dearest to us engaged in the death struggle would exclaim, why shouldst thou suffer so much ! So too exclaimed Hahnemann's consort. 'Why shouldst thou who hast, alleviated so much suffering, suffer in thy last hour? This is unjust, Providence should have allotted to thee a painless death.' Then he raised his voice as he had often done when he exhorted his disciples to hold fast to the great principle of Homœopathy. 'Why should I have been thus distinguished? Each of us should here attend to the duties which God has imposed upon him. Although men may distinguish more or less, yet no one has any merit. God owes nothing to me, I to Him all.' With these words he took leave of the world, of his friends, and his foes."

The calmness and resignation with which Hahnemann viewed death is well expressed by words written by him in a letter to his dear friend and pupil, Stapf, in 1816:* "We want but a little space of the completion of our course. Already does the last hour, the last minute, of my passage to the Father of purity and virtue stand vividly before my eyes, in which, with my cold finger, I shall point, almost imperceptibly, upward; and then comes the last moment. Pleasant, joyful, grateful is that hour to the man who has striven to enable himself to meet it worthily."

At a festival held on the 10th of August, 1843, in Dresden, at which the minds of those present turned on Hahnemann, Dr. Rummel delivered the following poem in his memory:†

AN HAHNEMANN.

(Geb. d. 10 April, 1755 zu Meissen, gest. d. 2 Juli 1843 zu Paris.)
Zum 10 August, 1843.

Du willst schon schlafen, müder Wahrheitspfleger?
Des neuen Lichtes Strahlen röthen kaum
Der alten Nächte tiefsten Wolkensaum
Und Deine Freunde schleichen träg' und träger.
Steh' auf, als Vaterlands vertrieb'ner Kläger,

---

*Brit. Jour. Hom., Vol. iii., p. 139.
†Allg. hom. Zeitung, Vol. xxv., p. 7. "Leben und Wirken," p. 83.

Und donn're aus dem selbstzufried'nen Traum
Sie auf von der Gewohnheit liebem Flaum,
Dass se erwachen munterer und reger.
Tritt zu den Feinden mit der Zornesmiene,
Mit der Du: " Menschenmörder " riesst, heran,
Ein Hamletsgeist, ein Schrecken selbst für Kühne,
Zerstore ihren Dunkel, ihren Wahn.
Dann erst reich' Deine kalte Hand zu Sühne
Und schlafe, wie Du jetzt zu früh gethan."

In the same paper for April 1, 1844, appeared the following:
" We have received an imitation in French, published on the
10th of last August, of the German poem, by Rummel, on the
death of Hahnemann, and we give it a place in our *Gazette* the
more gladly because it may be known to but a few of our readers,
and because it is from the pen of the widow of the deceased.

" A HAHNEMANN."

" LE 10 AOUT, 1843."

 " Tu veux dormir deja, toi de la verite
  Vieux tuteur fatigue ! la nouvelle clarte
  Dore a peine les bords du tenebreux nuage,
  Fils trompeur de l'antique nuit;
  Et desunis, tes amis sans courage,
  Se trainent lachement et suivent au passage
  L'habitude qui les conduit.
  Toi dont l'exil accuse la Patrie !
  Tonne sur eux, des feux de ton genie
  Brule leurs coeurs ! bientot regeneres,
  Qu'ils triomphent partout sous tes lauriers sacres.
  Puis de faux dieux, destructeur intrepide,
  Aux prophetes menteurs va crier: Homicide !
  Aux rayons de l'astre sauveur
  Que l'effroi les poursuive et le remord vengeur !
  A la raison convertis leur folie;
  Qu'ils adorent enfin la sainte verite,
  Lors seulement tends une main amie,
  Bienfaiteur des Humains, O toi ! pere d'Higie,
  Savoure l'immortalite."

"Par Madame Hahnemann, Imitation libre des Vers allemands, publies a
Dresde, par M. le dr Rummel."

Which freely translated is as follows:

" To HAHNEMANN, AUGUST 10, 1843."

" Sleep gently wrappeth thee now in her fold,
 Thee, truth's grandest teacher, weary and old,
 A new light just gilds the edge of the cloud
 That, born of old night, appals like a shroud.

Disunited, thy friends halt on the way;
In old paths of habit, faint-hearted, stray.
Thou, whose exile shames thy own fatherland,
Thunder above them ! burn their hearts where they stand
With thy fire of soul ! till, wakened, they find
In thy sacred laurels new triumphs twined.
Then to the false gods, destroyer, well tried,
To prophets of lies then cry—homicide !
May the brilliant light of thy guardian star,
A fear and remorse, pursue them afar !
Hold outward thy friendly hand as of yore;
From folly to reason turn them once more,
That at last the holy truth they adore.
Benefactor of men, O, thou father of health !
Art well dowered at last with Immortality's wealth !

CHAPTER LXXIX.

PERSONALITY—LESSONS FROM HIS LIFE—BIRTHPLACE—PER-SONAL TRAITS—EXAMINATION OF A STUDENT.

Such was the life of a great benefactor to mankind. Born in
the middle of a century whose influence shaped our own; a century prodigal in great men; in the year when Frederick, destined to be called *The Great*, was masquerading among the art
galleries of Holland; wandering in boyhood on the fair hills of
Meissen when all Europe was engaged in the Seven Years' War
and Saxony was crushed by iron heels; going forth the young
scholar to Academic Leipsic just when that unfortunate monarch,
Louis XVI., was ascending the guillotine-shadowed throne of
France; when George the Third was king and America was only a
colony of England; when Rousseau was yet writing of the Rights
of Man; when cynical Voltaire was mentor to Prussian Frederick.

A man in his prime, he was patiently searching for nature's
law of cure when the world was appalled by the Reign of Terror;
when the little sous-lieutenant of artillery, Bonaparte, saw with
indignant eyes the *sans culottes* of Paris, drunk with blood, be-
siege the dissolute court of Marie Antoinette; when noble Mirabeau
yet lived; when Marat and Robespierre led in France the Devil's
Dance of Death.

He was of the time of the Boston tea party and the declara-

tion on the State House steps of Philadelphia; of the day of
Washington and Lafayette. He saw Napoleon build an empire
on the ashes of a revolution; saw him march across the lands
of Germany; saw Austerlitz; saw the dismal retreat from Moscow, and acted there as good physician to the sick and suffering
army of 1813. He listened to the echoes of Waterloo—the story of
St. Helena. He left Germany for brilliant Paris when Bis-
marck was a student of twenty; he, the recluse, the scholar, the
thinker, became in his old age the fashionable physician in the
gayest city in the world.

He lived through the changes of a world's century; saw his
system of healing rise from contempt to honor; knew hardship;
died in luxury in the world's capital.

Scholar whom scholars honored and respected. Physician
whom physicians feared. Philologist with whom philologists
dreaded to dispute. Chemist who taught chemists. Philosopher
whom adversity nor honor had power to change.

HAHNEMANN, one of the figures standing out boldly from the
canvas of that great century on which are painted the exploits of
many remarkable men.

Jean Paul Richter, "the only one," who was in Leipsic at the
same time that Hahnemann was, and most probably knew him
personally, thus speaks of him:* "Hahnemann, this extraordinary, double brain (Doppelkopf) of philosophy and erudition,
whose system must eventually lead to the ruin of the common
recipe-crammed brains, but which as yet has been little accepted
by practitioners, and is more detested than examined."

That this man was a scholar, a thinker, was of indomitable
will, was respected, is not to be denied. He was a careful man,
painstaking, methodical. In his experiments, exhaustive. That
he in a great measure changed in character during the last years
of his life is true. From being very liberal he became opinion-
ated, unyielding. From the time of his persecution at Leipzig
he seems to have put aside all liberality and to have become
miserly in disposition and unyielding in character. That he
was hardly liberal enough for his German colleagues his history
well shows. That he injured the spread of Homœopathy in
Germany by his treatment of his disciples regarding the Leipsic
hospital is certain. And yet to the end of his life in his home

* Rutherford Russell's "History and Heroes of Medicine," p. 418.

relations he was always the same good, tender, kindly philosopher and husband and father as before the calumny of the outer
world had embittered him.   But had he not ample excuse for
his firmness and reluctance to relent from his one and unwavering platform of conduct?

His poverty influenced his life.   His lessons in thinking were
never forgotten; the lamp of clay taught its lesson.   Poor,
obliged to translate through the long night hours, he in that
translation, and the study necessary, laid the foundations for the
marvelous knowledge that he afterwards exhibited.   And through
it all may be seen that unwavering faith in the goodness of God
who must have endowed mankind with some sure method of
healing.   Hahnemann believed that his discovery was a gift to
him from God in trust for the benefit of his fellow-man.

The house in Meissen in which Hahnemann was born is still
standing (1893).   It is situated at the corner of the Hahnemann
Place and the Newmarket.*   It was formerly known as the
Eckhouse, at the upper end of the Meatway and close by the
Newmarket, No. 459 of the new Brandkataster.   With the exception of a few needful repairs, it is to-day as when Hahnemann
was born.   It is a plain, old-fashioned building of three stories
with a steep apexed roof, and towers high above the surrounding buildings.†   A lamp, looking like a Philadelphia street lamp,
is suspended from the angle of the house front.   The house front
looks upon the Hahnemann Place, and near the corner are two
large windows with wooden shutters, and between them a double
door.

Over the front window, between the first and second story, a
sign is fixed against the wall, bearing in large letters the legend,
"Restaurant Hahnemann."   Beside this sign, and directly over
the door, a niche in the wall holds a bust of Hahnemann, while
on the other side of the bust is an iron tablet, set in the wall,
bearing the following inscription: "Chr. Fr. Samuel Hahnemann, the Founder of Homœopathy, was born here the 11th of
April, 1755."   Further down this side of the old house is still
another door, and over this there is a sign reading: "Schmied-
ewerkstatt, A. Schone."   Beyond this are two shuttered windows

---

*Hundertjährigen Geburtstage Samuel Hahnemann's, Dessau, 1855, p.
25.

† Villers' *International Homœopathic Annual*, Leipzig, 1891.

of a room on the ground floor, and within that room Hahnemann was born.

Hahnemann was an abstemious man. His only habit of self-indulgence was his pipe. The Rev. Mr. Everest once asked him why he smoked and he replied:* "Oh, it's an idle habit contracted when I had to sit up every other night in order to get bread for my children, while I was pursuing my own investigations by day." This habit continued until the end of his life.

He possessed only simple ways, disliking all ostentation. In a letter to Stapf, dated December 17, 1816, he says:† "No more enconiums of me; I altogether dislike them, for I feel myself to be nothing more than an upright man who merely does his duty. Let us express our regard for one another only in simple words and conduct indicating mutual respect."

"Hahnemann's handwriting was small and neat but firm, and he preferred to write on small-sized paper, as appears from his letters and notes. He took pains to write every letter distinctly and he wrote a beautiful hand. He was very particular in his forms of expression, and often we find in one line two or three corrections. Up to his latest years he read and wrote without spectacles."‡

Hull says: "The Register of his Consultations, every day increasing in magnitude, forms at this moment a stupendous medical encyclopædia.

"We have seen upon one of the shelves of Hahnemann's library thirty-six quarto volumes of at least five hundred pages each, entirely written by his own hand; and to those who are curious as to the penmanship of the venerable octogenarian, who has never used spectacles, we can testify to writing as fine and beautiful as the *mignonne* of Didot.||

Dudgeon writes:§ "We may form some idea of Hahnemann's immense industry when we consider that he proved about ninety different medicines, that he wrote upwards of seventy original works on chemistry and medicine, some of which were in several thick volumes, and translated about twenty-four works from the

---

* "Hom. in 1851," London, p. 306.
† *Brit. Jour. Hom.*, Vol. iii., p. 141.
‡ Ameke's "History of Homœopathy," p. 164.
|| *Hom. Examiner*, Vol. ii., p. 8. Hull's "Life of Hahnemann."
§ "Biography of Hahnemann."

English, French, Italian and Latin, on chemistry, medicine, agriculture and general literature, many of which were in more than one volume.''

He ever had an exalted opinion of the dignity of the medical profession. In alluding to his discovery of the prophylactic for scarlet fever, he said: ''The furtherance of every means, be it ever so small, that can save human life, that can bring health and security (a God of love invented this blessed and most wondrous of arts!) should be a sacred object to the true physician; chance or the labor of the physician has discovered this one.''

Again, in writing of the duties of the nurse and the physician in the time of pestilence:* ''They are two persons ordained by God, and placed, like Uriah in the battle, in the thickest of the fight—forlorn hopes, quite close to the advancing enemy, without any hours of relief from their irksome guard—two very much misunderstood beings, who sacrifice themselves at hard-earned wages for the public weal, and, in order to obtain a civic crown, brave the life-destroying, poisoned atmosphere, deafened by the cries of agony and the groans of death.''

The following is a letter written by Hahnemann which gives his idea of what should constitute an examination in Homœopathy:

''*Dear Mr. Steinestel:* I have much pleasure in making your acquaintance, and agreeably to your desire I put to you some questions, from your answers to which I shall be able to judge of your capability to practice Homœopathically and to cure patients of all sorts.

''1. What course does the true physician pursue in order to obtain a knowledge of what is morbid, consequently what he has to cure in the patient?

''2. Why does a name of a disease not suffice to instruct the physician as to what he has to do in order to cure the patient? For example, why should he not at once give Cinchona bark when the patient says he has got fever (as the Allopath does)?

''3. How does the true physician learn what each medicine is useful for, and consequently in what morbid states it can be serviceable and curative?

''4. Why does the true physician view with horror the pre-

---

* Dudgeon's ''Hahnemann,'' 1852.

scribing of several medicinal substances mingled together in one prescription for a disease?

"5. Why does it shock the true physician to see blood drawn from any patient, whether by venesection or blood-sucking leeches,* or cupping-glasses?

"6. Why is it an abomination for the true physician to see Opium given by the Allopath for all sorts of pains, for diarrhœa, or for sleeplessness?

"7. Why does the Homœopathist prepare gold, plumbago, lycopodium-pollen, culinary salt, etc., by triturating them for hours with a non-medical substance, such as sugar of milk, and by shaking a small dissolved portion of them with water and alcohol, which is termed dynamizing?

"8. Why must the true physician not give his patients medicine for a single symptom (for a single morbid sensation)?

"9. When the true physician has given the patient a small dose of a medicine selected by reason of similarity of the most characteristic symptoms of the disease, that is to say, capable of itself producing similar symptoms in the healthy individual, with good results (as might naturally be expected), when ought he to administer another dose of medicine? How does he then perceive what medicine he ought to give?

" 10. Why can the Homœopathic medicines never be dispensed by the apothecary without injury to the public?

"When you shall have replied to these questions in writing I shall be able to judge if you are a true Homœopathic practitioner.

"Hail to the king who cherishes only wholesome truth, and who with a vigorous hand overthrows many *injurious time-honored customs;* such an one is the viceregent on earth of the all-bountiful and all-wise Godhead!"†

---

*Blutsaugende Egel.

†*Brit. Jour. Hom.*, Vol. x., p. 167.

CHAPTER LXXX.

While—because he was driven from one town to another for a time in his life—Hahnemann was poor, yet he divided a fortune on leaving Germany.

It is estimated that during the eight years which he passed at Paris he amassed a fortune of 4,000,000 francs.*

That Hahnemann rigidly followed the law of similia as it is laid down in the "Organon" is very certain. There are some questions, however, regarding his modes of practice that have been in much dispute. The principal points are: Size of the dose. Did he or did he not alternate remedies? Did he use auxiliaries? The question will be discussed in a separate chapter.

That Hahnemann was perfectly satisfied and happy in gay Paris during the last years of his life is the testimony of every one who knew him at that time. He himself said as much. Ameke writes that he kept up a constant and affectionate correspondence with his family in Germany, who also visited him in Paris.†

It has been said that during his residence in Paris he was not permitted to receive the visits of his colleagues. That he had but little intercourse with medical men.‡ "Their visits, if not absolutely denied, were studiously discouraged, and his medical converse was almost limited to non-medical gobemouches, who eagerly swallowed as Gospel everything he said and encouraged him in the path of authorizing."

In an article published in an English Homœopathic journal in 1878,‖ by "A Relative of the Family," the following statements are made:

"Patients who could not pay the regular physician's fee never saw Hahnemann, but only his *partner*, Madame Hahnemann,

---

* *Brit. Jour. Hom.*, Vol. xxii., p. 678.
† Ameke's "History of Homœopathy," p. 166.
‡ *Brit. Jour. Hom.*, Vol. xxiii., p. 664.
‖ *Hom. World*, Vol. xiii., p. 348.

who managed also to break her husband of his favorite habit of smoking, as his fashionable patients did not approve of a doctor whose consulting room gave more evidence of bird's eye than of eau de cologne. Hahnemann, when living in Germany, used to smoke from morning till night, but when in Paris, his wife said, *Il faut changer tout cela*, and all was changed. She gradually limited him to only one pipe a day, which he had to smoke in a small corrider of his great mansion. Only those who know the effects of this comforting weed will be able to understand the great denial Hahnemann imposed upon himself in his eightieth year, when he reduced his allowance to one pipe a day, so that there should be no obstacle to his amassing a princely fortune for his wife, a sweet, unselfish creature, who never parted with a penny to any member of his family.''

The English Homœopathic journals, who chronicled the death of Madame Hahnemann, almost invariably spoke in the same manner of her. It is the duty of the historian to relate facts, not to criticise. It would seem, however, from certain accounts of the life of the old physician in Paris, that this statement about the tobacco is somewhat overdrawn. Mrs. Mowatt (Helen Berkley) particularly mentions the long painted pipe, the bowl of which reached nearly to his knees, that he only removed from his mouth long enough to welcome that lady to his presence. Others also write of his smoking constantly. And in regard to the aid refused by Madame Hahnemann to the German relatives, it may be that she thought that when her husband had divided a fortune with his children before leaving Germany, he had fulfilled his duty in the matter.

Albrecht, however, also says, that his manner of life was greatly changed at Paris, and that he was in a great measure compelled to give up the loved tobacco.

It has also been questioned whether Hahnemann's second marriage was a benefit to Homœopathy. Probably its principles became better known in Paris than had the old man remained at Coethen. Be that as it may, he was happy there, and as he had already given a lifetime, longer than that usually granted, to the good of mankind, and had carefully set down in his wonderful books the tenets of his law of healing, it must be admitted that he was hardly to be blamed if during the few last years of his life he consulted his own satisfaction and pleasure even at the expense of his fellow-men.

Albrecht says:* "The friend of Hahnemann wishes to know and understand in what manner the master lived. Not in his hotel in Paris is it described, but it can be found in his old residence at Coethen.

"The house that Hahnemann occupied in Coethen from 1821 to 1835, yes, even the library in which he wrote his world renowned work, from the devotion of his youngest daughter Frau Dr. Louise Mossdorf, is unchanged.

"It stands in the Wallstrasse, bright and beautiful, where from the east and from the west the rays of light converge and mingle.

"To the right of the street door are to be found three great windows with dark green shutters, to the left from the repaired side are two windows. The first story has a stairway with black balusters, with large round windows, the spacious hall is lighted by one large window, and a corrider extends the length of the house. The living room on the right hand and the study on the left contain many precious mementoes of the departed. The window of the dwelling-room has a high estrade. In the niche and window-frame bloom potted plants, opposite to the life-size, half-length portrait of Hahnemann painted in oil by the artist Schopenhauer. On the secretary stands, under a high glass case, a gilt Æsculapius, the same that the admirers of the great man had presented at the Doctor-Jubilee, and a portrait-bust modeled by Steinhauser. The principal wall is adorned by the miniature pictures of different members of the Hahnemann family taken before the time of the photograph. At the window stands the ancient harpsichord by whose means Hahnemann had passed so many pleasant evenings with his family. Behind the parlor may be found a small sleeping cabinet, whence one reaches a small conservatory.

"Opposite to this the kitchen is situated. The study is in the same condition as at the time of Hahnemann's departure for Paris. There still stands his writing-desk with writing materials, pens, etc., a table clock for which he had great fondness, and which he would wind up and regulate daily, and the old mended furniture. Here one sees the fan of white ivory, the wedding present from Hahnemann's father to the bride of his son, painted with his own hand. It pictures the master visiting

---

* "Leben und Wirken," p. 84.

his first patient, sitting by the bedside giving him medicine from a spoon, while the expectant wife, recovered, is sitting on the other side of the family circle.   It is a fascinating little example of his genre painting, and bears a striking resemblance to the original.

"Hahnemann's favorite spot was the little garden back of the yard which was paved with slabs and was shut in by a grated door surrounded by an arbor.   The garden was well tended, and walks divided the small beds, which were encircled with box bush; and at the farthest end stood the lower arbor, which was covered with thick foliage in summer and entwined with ivy, and was the place where the previously mentioned bust was modeled, and where the intellectual master gladly and assiduously toiled during the greater portion of the year, often remained for hours in the morning, received his patients, ate his breakfast, etc.

"At the present time, only his daughter Louise, the widow of Dr. Mossdorf, occupies the house in companionship with a faithful servant.   One of the most active and energetic of the sisters, Madame Suss, the mother of a Homœopathic physician who settled in London, died in Coethen, and was buried in the city cemetery.

"After Dr. Hahnemann went to Paris, there remained, besides Madame Mossdorf, an elder sister, Charlotte, who helped to take care of the small household, and guarded the remembrance of her beloved father as something sacred, until she died in the spring of 1863, after a short but severe illness.

"Hahnemann's routine of daily work was very strictly regulated.   The great and learned man arose at 6 o'clock in summer and at 7 in the winter, drank a few cups of warm milk, lighted his pipe, and then went to promenade in his garden.   So far as the season of the year permitted it he ate some fruit about 10 o'clock in the forenoon.   He went to dinner at 12 o'clock, and usually ate very strong beef tea, roasted beef, mutton, or venison of every kind, roasted larks, chickens or doves, and similar food. He was very fond of roast veal and pork, and a dish in order to be to his taste must be very sweet.   He did not wish to know of any vegetables besides new beans, cabbage and spinach, and he gladly used cake instead of bread.   At table he drank some good wine when he had guests; but his daily drink was sweetened gose, a kind of mild beer. After eating, he slept an hour on the sofa, then attended to his patients again until 7 o'clock, at which time he had supper, which in winter consisted of warm milk, and in summer of gose (small beer) and bread.

"After supper he promenaded for awhile in his garden both in summer and in winter. His companion in these recreative walks was usually a little pet dog, which also kept close by his side when he sat at table.

"After the walk he spent an hour in the sitting-room, and then went into his office, where he wrote at his books until 11, 12 or 1 o'clock, or busied himself with other work.

"When a boy Hahnemann wore a queue, short trousers, and shoes with buckles; and as a physican he always wore in the house a dark velvet cap, a black silk necktie and vest, a cassimere dressing-gown and long trousers. In summer, cotton stockings and light wadded slippers, and in winter woolen stockings and fur boots. When on the street he would be seen with a round hat and overcoat. Only on holidays did he dress in frock coat and long trousers, silk stockings and shoes. In winter he wore a beaver hat, fur coat and black sealskin boots. People very seldom saw him with silk pocket handkerchief and gloves.

"He burnt in his room only a tallow light, which he often made use of to light his pipe, for he smoked a great deal. If he had befouled his pipe and laid it aside, it would be again cleaned out and refilled. He was really interested in only one game, that of chess; and he was passionately fond of this, though, for lack of time, he very seldom played.

"He never slept in a room warmed by artificial means. Plainness and love of order were expressed not only in his handwriting, but also in the accounts which he kept as a physician. He wrote in a very small and neat, but plain hand, upon small-sized sheets, was very choice in expression, and therefore often made corrections; he read and wrote until an advanced age without spectacles.

"His mental energy was conspicuous, even in the common events of his everyday life.

"When traveling in Transylvania he encountered a lady of high rank at an hotel; the landlady, in providing dinner for her guests, neglected the fire, and in a short time the whole house was in a blaze.

"Everyone thought of his own safety, no one attending to the lady, whose apartments were in the upper story. Hahnemann, thinking of her safety, rushed through the midst of the flames, returned with the rescued lady, and also saved her heavy trunk. Being satisfied of her safety, he immediately entered the stage and drove away.

"When he resided in the country at Lobkowitz, near Dresden, a dreadful fire broke out. Everyone was at a loss what to do. 'Will you follow my advice?' enquired Hahnemann, of those who knew him. 'Willingly, willingly,' they replied. He now gave instructions, and, although a father of four children, encountered all risks; the fire was very soon extinguished."*

Hahnemann seems to have thoroughly understood the ingratitude of patients and the difficulty of getting money from them after the cure had occurred. He gives in 1826 the following excellent advice to his friend and pupil, Dr. Ernst Stapf:† "See that you get paid every month, and do not trust to running accounts to be paid afterwards by an ungrateful world; for then you will be cheated! *Accipe dum dolet.* During many, many years I have never found one who has shown himself grateful after being cured. But when they have paid you every month, they cannot demand repayment; but we have got it, and have done them no harm. Their ingratitude can then do us no harm. I beg you to let Gross, also, read this."

"Only in discussions did he indulge in strong and vigorous language; and this was done that the truth might have its whole weight of effect.

"While in Leipsic he had already planned a register of symptoms, that had soon grown to two folio volumes. They subsequently appeared unsatisfactory to him and he rewrote them in a new order and with improvements. He prepared at Coethen two new folio volumes and did it with the most scrupulous exactness. Unfortunately these, which would have been an invaluable possession for science, were taken along with him to Paris, and cannot be obtained, notwithstanding the fact that

---

* Fischer. Trans. of "Biographisches Denkmal," p. 92.
† *Hom. World,* Vol. xxiv., p. 362.

Hahnemann had bequeathed them to his youngest daughter, Madame Mossdorf, as her property, and had explicitly directed that these two folio volumes should be returned to the rightful possessor after his death. Madame Melanie Hahnemann says that said volumes were burnt up in the Paris revolution.

" But this assertion is very improbable, for the reason that she (Madame) had fled to Munich, to her son-in-law, five weeks before the Paris insurrection, and she doubtless took the precious legacy with her to her son-in-law, who was a Homœopathic physician there."

Dr. Schweikert, director of the Homœopathic hospital at Leipsic, asked him to present these volumes to that institution. He refused, saying: " I gave them to my youngest daughter, I cannot retract my promise."

" Hahnemann inherited from his parents the spirit of benevolence, and exercised it during his whole life. In his opinion it was sufficient to live for science, duty and the healing of his fellow-men.

" Hence he hastened to make his discoveries common property; and he did not wish to consider his laboriously prepared remedies as secrets or to sell them at a high price. He preferred to be poor with honor than to gain wealth through practice. To be sure he made the rich pay him well for advice and services, but only with the view not only of healing the poor gratuitously, but also with assisting them with money besides.

" His knowledge was marvellous. He was at home in all sciences, even in those which have no connection with medicine. Persons could get information from him about all matters, for though he had not pursued any one branch of science with special attention yet he had read extensively upon all of them. 'The man who is truly cultured,' he often said, 'must be well versed in all positive knowledge. He even should well understand astronomy.' A chart of the planetary system hung in his library, and he very gladly conversed about astronomical matters with his nephew, the Court Chancellor Schwabe, who had an astronomical observatory in his yard. He was a clever meteorologist and knew something of the science of the weather. But for this knowledge he was indebted to the hygrometer, the barometer and thermometer, upon which he was wont to cast his eye both in the house and in the garden. He was no less learned in

geography, and, therefore, in his library, which embraced scientific works of all kinds, there was an ample collection of maps.

"Magnetism and mesmerism, both intimately connected with
the study of medicine, were making progress. Hahnemann paid
special attention to them, and he occasionally applied both, in
attacks of sickness, with successful results. Until extreme old
age Hahnemann spent a great portion of his leisure time in
reading."

CHAPTER LXXXI.

RELATIONS TO HIS PATIENTS—MODE OF LIFE—HIS RELIGIOUS
VIEWS—VIGOR IN OLD AGE.

" Hahnemann's many translations prove that he was a master
in linguistics, or the science of new languages. But this fondness did not detract from his love for the old philology; he was
a complete philologist. He even understood somewhat of Chaldaic works. This explains to a great extent his intimate relationship with Prof. Adam Beyer. The two would often meet in
the evening and converse most animatedly about the syntactical
and higher critical subjects of Latin and Greek; and the Leipsic
professor listened with special attention to the critical acumen of
his medical friend in many a philological controversy. 'Officia
Ciceronis,' edited by Beyer, had an honorable place in his study.*

" His social relations with his patients were most exemplary,
for as a physician he was extremely humane and compassionate
towards those seeking help, and was always ready and willing
to make any sacrifice of time and effort. He kept an exact
register concerning his patients, punctually recorded therein with
his own hand the symptoms of their diseases, never put their
own words into their mouths when examining them with reference to their ailments, but earnestly entreated each one to
describe the symptoms. He would ask where the patient resided;
in what relations of life he lived; how he managed his house-

---

* This same Adam Beyer designed to render Hahnemann's books into
classical Latin, but he unfortunately died before he could accomplish this
task.

hold; how his kitchen was arranged; how, and how much he worked; how he disposed of his time, etc. The numberless letters from his patients, after being entered in a journal, were immediately pasted in covers, all of which bore upon labels the number, year and date. All these covers and numberless letters, all his journals and name registers, were taken with him to Paris.

"He earned very large sums every year through his extensive practice in the Capital of France. Unfortunately, he could no longer derive advantage from this income as respected his own person. He saw himself compelled, by his change of residence, to lead habits of life to which he was wholly unaccustomed and which were quite the reverse to those which have been previously described. He had to ride in a carriage very often, dared smoke but little tobacco, was necessitated to change his accustomed food and drinks for others, to go to bed much later than he had previously done, and to lie in bed very often until ten in the forenoon, so that he was compelled to dine and sup much later. The evening visit to the conservatoire, the Italian opera or the theatre was wholly against his custom and his own choice. We have the following memorandum in Hahnemann's own handwriting. He ordered his patients to observe a strict diet on account of the small doses and the great strength of the medicine. 'Avoid,' he said, 'spices, tubers and cabbage, acids, tea and coffee, spirituous and similar drinks.' He forbade all 'fumigation, perfumery, hair pomades, tooth powders and tinctures, mineral baths, warm footbaths, salves, plasters, poultices, blistering plasters, hairbands, leeches and cupping glasses.' He showed himself no less hostile to all 'bleeding, blistering with Spanish flies, burning, cutting, and all sudorifics, emetics and purgatives.' On the other hand, he advised 'plain and substantial food, pure beer, milk, buttermilk, cocoa, beef and mutton tea or soup, drinks of cold water, a walk or drive one or more hours daily, cleanliness and neatness, regularity in meals and hours of sleep, a moral life and a firm trust in God.'

"Although Hahnemann toiled from early morning until late at night in Coethen, yet he could not attend to all his practice himself, and employed Dr. Lehmann as an assistant. He esteemed this assistant more and more highly every year because the latter had the rare frankness to oppose his employer so often. Hahnemann well knew that we arrive at the truth by a due estimation of its contradiction."

Dudgeon says: "The portraits of Hahnemann all represent him with his hair elaborately curled. It would seem that he was in the habit of getting it curled as early as 1819. Mr. Cameron, who was much with Hahnemann during his residence in Paris, tells me that if he went to see him early in the morning, which he frequently did, he always found him with his hair up in curl papers."*

In religion Hahnemann was brought up a Lutheran. Hering said that it was Lessing's controversy with Gotze that formed Hahnemann's religious views for life. He was a Deist, everywhere in his writings may be found expressions indicating that he, in all matters, recognized God as the Supreme One, and that he viewed life as a vast field in which to do good according to the permission and wisdom of that God.

In a letter to his friend Stapf, dated April 15, 1827, he says:† "I acknowledge with sincere thankfulness the infinite mercy of the one great Giver of all good for having kept me hitherto in strength and cheerful spirits amidst all the assaults of my enemies; and I have no other wish here below than to lay before the world in a worthy manner the good which the Supreme Being permitted me to discover, I may say revealed to me, for the alleviation of the sufferings of mankind. Then I am willing to depart this life."

Hahnemann retained his vigor until the time of his death. Dr. Richard Hughes, in a lecture before the London School of Homœopathy in 1877, said of Hahnemann: "To make the Hahnemann of 1830-43 our guide is, I think, to commit ourselves to his senility." This called forth from Dr. H. V. Malan the following letter:‡ "I have looked over your lecture at the opening of the London School of Homœopathy, and, as a pupil of Hahnemann, the last living I believe, and having spent about a year and a half in 1841 and 1842 with him, and under his constant teaching in Paris, I wish to state that his intellectual powers there were not those of 'senility;' far from it! I have seen him make many remarkable cures, and heard him teach and speak with wonderful accuracy, learning and judgment, adorned with that deep modesty which was his remarkable attribute.

*Hom. World, Vol. xxvi., p. 449.
† Hom. World, Vol. xxiv., p. 365.
‡ "The Organon," Vol. i., p. 284.

"He never prescribed nor paid any visits to the patient's bed-side without taking notes of the case and consulting the Materia Medica; he never alternated medicines, no more than he ever mixed two together. ,

"I often saw him use very high dilutions, and one of his most remarkable cures was with one single dose of a very high one (Jenichen's, I believe), and I have frequently heard him say that the thirtieth was not to be fixed as the limit.

"As to his teaching, I never heard any equal to it; and having endeavored to follow it, as far as able, I have often expressed the thought that when we can do as well as he did, it will be time enough for us to try to do better. I may now sincerely add that in my thirty-five years' experience I have never yet done—or seen any one doing—as well as he did, nor have I had one occasion to find his teachings incorrect,

"Pray excuse these few words from one of his pupils,

"H. V. MALAN."

"*Montreux, December 18, 1877.*"

Did Hahnemann believe in hydropathy? Writing to Dr. Schreeter, August 13, 1840, he says:* "In all ages there have been some excessive panegyrists of cold water. The reasons why Priesnitz is so successful with gluttons and drunkards of many years' standing, and with patients ruined by effeminate habits, are not sufficiently attended to by the world and the medical profession; and the excellence of his scanty diet, his prohibition of coffee, tea, spices, his suitable forced walking in the open air not considered. To the cold water alone all the benefit obtained is attributed—thus are men led astray from want of judgment. Is it not plain that these old sinners who have originally good constitutions, but who are prevented from recovering by their balls, dissipations and other vices, are there compelled to live consistently with nature to their own advantage? Is this not the chief instrument of their restoration? And how many suffering from chronic disease, but not owing their complaints to an improper mode of living, has not Priesnitz ruined by the excessive use of cold water, whereby they have been deprived of their sight or hearing? A good, especially a Homœopathic physician, always knows when and in what cases to employ with advantage cold

Brit. Jour. Hom., Vol. vi., p. 416. Stapf's *Archiv.*, Vol. xxiii., pt. 3, p. 107.

water, without carrying it too far, and without doing any harm with it. Everything in its proper place! Cold water is merely a physical accessory means for the perfect establishment of patients cured by the appropriate medicinal agents."

CHAPTER LXXXII.

THE POSOLOGY OF HAHNEMANN.*

Previous to 1796, the period at which Hahnemann first gave to the world the discovery of the new law of healing, he used the ordinary remedies of the times, but even then, as we find by his writing he gave simple prescriptions. The awkward and often chemically ridiculous polypharmacy was objectionable to his fine and acutely trained understanding.

In 1789, in the "Treatise on Venereal Diseases," he says: "I have sometimes not had occasion to use more than one grain of soluble *Mercury* in all in order to cure moderate idiopathic venereal symptoms and commencing syphilis; yet I have met with cases in which sixty grains were necessary." For the time this was very minute dosage. It was the habit to give massive and repeated doses of *Mercury* until its effects were to be markedly seen on the system in salivation, swollen gums, glandular enlargements, bone pains, etc. Further on in this treatise he says:

"Not more than eight grains were required to eradicate a moderately severe syphilis, for a severe case twelve grains."

In Section 626: "I increased the quantity of the soluble *Mercury* very gradually from one fourth to one-third, one-half, three fourths, one, one and one-fourth grains, so that I could leave it off on the slightest appearance of salivation."

In 1793 we find him recommending his patient, the tailor, to apply petroleum to chilblains upon the fingers.†

---

*Data for this chapter is taken from Dr. Francis Black, on Posology, *Brit. Jour. Hom.*, Vol. xxix., p. 572; Hahnemann's Dosage, Dr. R. Hughes, *Brit. Jour. Hom.*, Vol. xxxvi., p. 114; Hahnemann's Doses, Dr. Roth, *Brit. Jour. Hom.*, Vol. xxx., p. 82; Griesselich on Medicinal Doses, *Quar. Jour. Hom.*, Boston, 1849, Vol. i., p. 165; Dudgeon's "Lectures on Homœopathy," Lecture xiv; Hahnemann's writings; Fincke, on High Potencies.

†*Monthly Hom. Review*, Vol. xxxi., p. 549.

The essay on the "Curative Power of Drugs" was the first published on the Homœopathic principle. In this he speaks of giving for dysentery *Arnica* root in powder. "I had to increase the dose daily, more often than is necessary with any other powerful medicine. A child of four years of age got at first four grains daily, then seven, eight and nine grains. Children of six or seven years of age could at first only bear six grains, afterwards twelve and fourteen grains were requisite. A child three-quarters of a year old, which had previously taken nothing, could at first bear but two grains (mixed with warm water) in an enema; latterly six grains were necessary."

He says that he took one grain of extract of *Æthusa cynapium* when distracted and mentally tired from literary work.

An infusion of ten grains of *Ledum palustre* was given to a child six years old.

Arsenic in one-sixth to one-tenth of a grain doses was recommended in periodical headache.

The landlord of a country inn had an asthmatic affection with loss of breath, constriction of the chest, suffocative attacks with suicidal thoughts: "The mania resembling that peculiar to *Veratrum*, the firm fibre of the patient, etc., induced me to prescribe three grains of it every morning, which he continued for four weeks, with the gradual cessation of his sufferings. His malady had lasted four years or more."

A woman of thirty-five with delirium and convulsions, after parturition, took one-half grain of *Veratrum* night and morning and was cured.

As early as 1797, in *Hufeland's Journal,* he says:* "May I confess it that for several years since I never administered anything else but one single remedy at a time and at once, and that I never have repeated it until the action of the former dose had expired? May I confess that I was successful in this manner, and that I have cured to the satisfaction of my patients, and that I have seen things which I could not have seen otherwise."

In 1797 he cured a case of colicodynia with a four-grain powder of *Veratrum album* daily; the patient having taken two in one day, suffered from medicinal aggravation. For asthma he gave five-grain doses of *Ipecac;* four grains, twice daily, of *Nux vomica.*

---

* "Lesser Writings," New York, p. 321.   "Fincke, on High Potencies," p. 106.

This same year of 1797 he mentions giving a girl of five years, who was poisoned by *Camphor*, four-drop doses of tincture of *Opium* until she had probably taken two grains of *Opium*. She recovered from the *Camphor* poisoning under this treatment.

For the leucophlegmatic cachexias of children he says that twelve grains of *Arnica* root can be taken with impunity.

In poisoning by *Cocculus* he gave fifteen grains of *Camphor*.

In an article on continued and remittent fevers, published in 1798, he says: "St. Ignatius' bean produced effects that were truly surprising. I gave it in large doses every twelve hours; to children from nine months to three years of age, from one-half to two-thirds of a grain; to those between four and six years, from one grain to one and one-half grains; to those between seven and twelve years, from two to three grains." To adults he gave eight grain doses. He says: "I accordingly gave *Opium* in the morning before the fit in the dose of one-fifth of a grain to an infant of five years, three-tenths of a grain to one of seven and another of eight years, seven twentieths to one of ten years. I took myself half a grain."

He gave *Camphor* in doses of fifteen to twenty grains daily, increasing them to doses of thirty and forty grains. He gave a child of twelve fifteen grains a day for a fortnight. *Ledum* he gave in doses of six or seven grains three times a day.

Cinchona bark was given in drachm and drachm and a-half doses.

Thus it may be seen that even after he had made and published his experiments with medicines he continued to use appreciable doses. But he used single remedies, and in the Essay on the Curative Power of Drugs he says, in speaking of the compound prescriptions to be found in the books of the old physicians:

"To me the strangest circumstance connected with these speculations upon the virtues of single drugs is, that in the days of these men, the habit that still obtains in medicine, of joining together several different medicines in one prescription, was carried to such an extent that I defy Œdipus himself to tell what was the exact action of a single ingredient of the hotch potch; the prescription of a single remedy at a time was in those days *almost* rarer than it is now-a-days. How was it possible in such a complicated practice to distinguish the powers of individual medicines?"

Now comes, in 1799, the treatment of the epidemic of scarlet fever, the discovery of *Belladonna*, and the sudden introduction of infinitesimal doses.

The paper upon the subject was not published until 1801, but he commenced this new treatment during the summer of 1799.

He recommends a paper moistened with tincture of *Opium* to be laid on the epigastrium of the child until it dries, in cases of convulsions. For internal use the *Opium* is prepared as follows: "The tincture is formed by adding one part of crude *Opium*, finely powdered, to twenty parts of crude *Alcohol*, letting it stand a week in a cool place, shaking it occasionally. For internal use I take a drop of this tincture and mix it intimately with five hundred drops of diluted *Alcohol*, shaking the whole well. Of this diluted tincture of *Opium* (which contains in every drop one five-millionth part of a grain of *Opium*) one drop given internally was amply sufficient in the case of a child four years of age, and two drops in that of a child of ten years to remove the above state. For younger children I mixed one drop of this with ten teaspoonfuls of water and gave them according to their age, one, two or more teaspoonfuls." He repeated the doses but seldom; every four or eight hours, or sometimes but twice during the entire fever. Larger doses, he says, cause medicinal aggravations.

For another stage of the scarlatina he says: "I gave, according to the age of the child, *Ipecacuanha*, either in substance in the dose of a tenth to half a grain in fine powder; or I employed the tincture, prepared by digesting in the cold for some days, one part of the powder with twenty parts of alcohol; of this one drop was mixed with one hundred drops of weak alcohol, and to the youngest children a drop of this last was given, but to the oldest ones ten drops were given as a dose."

Of *Belladonna* he gave a girl of ten years, who was sickening with scarlatina, a dose the one four hundred and thirty-two thousandth part of a grain of the extract, which he says is, according to later experience, rather too large a dose.

For a prophylactic Hahnemann says: "We dissolve a grain of this powder prepared from well-preserved *Belladonna* extract, evaporated at an ordinary temperature, in one hundred drops of common distilled water, by rubbing it up in a small mortar; we pour the thick solution into a one-ounce bottle, and rinse the mortar and the pestle with three hundred parts of diluted alcohol (five parts of water to one of spirit), and we then add this to the solution and render the union perfect by diligently shaking the liquid. We label the bottle *strong solution of Belladonna.* One drop of this is intimately mixed with three hundred drops of diluted alcohol by shaking it for a minute, and this is marked *medium solution of Belladonna.* Of this second mixture one drop is mixed with two hundred drops of the diluted alcohol, by shaking for a minute, and marked *weak solution of Belladonna;* and this is our prophylactic remedy for scarlet fever, each drop of which contains the twenty-four millionth part of a grain of the dry *Belladonna* juice.

"Of this weak solution of *Belladonna* we give to those not affected with scarlet fever, with the intention to make them *un-infectable by the disease*—to a child one year old two drops; to a younger child one drop; to one two years old, three; to one three years old, four; to a child four years old, according to the strength of his constitution, five to six; to a five year old child, from six to seven; to a six year old child, from seven to eight; to a seven year old child, from nine to ten; to an eight year old child, from eleven to thirteen; to a nine year old child, from fourteen to sixteen drops; and with each successive year, up to the twentieth, two drops more (from the twentieth to thirtieth, not above forty drops), a dose every seventy-two hours, well stirred with a teaspoon for a minute in any kind of drink, as long as the epidemic lasts, and four to five weeks thereafter.

"Half this dose given every three hours will often suppress the fever in its first germ."

Of the tincture of *Chamomilla,* for the after effects of the disease, a grain was to be dissolved in five hundred drops of water and mixed intimately with five hundred drops of alcohol. Of this solution one drop was mixed with eight hundred drops of diluted alcohol, and of this last diluted solution one drop (800,-oooth part of a grain of the inspissated juice) was given every day to a child a few years old, two drops to one of ten years of age.

By its use all tendency to ulceration of the skin was removed, and also the suffocating cough.

Hufeland having challenged Hahnemann to defend publicly these remarkable statements, he replied in *Hufeland's Journal:*

"You ask me what effect can the 100,000th part of a grain of *Belladonna* have? The word CAN is repugnant to me and apt to lead to misconception." He further says, that while a hard, dry pill of extract of *Belladonna* produces on a robust, perfectly healthy countryman no effect, yet he will be affected with the most violent and dangerous symptoms from one grain of the extract of *Belladonna*, if this grain be dissolved thoroughly in two pounds of water by rubbing, the mixture being made very intimate by shaking the fluid in a bottle for five minutes, and if he be made to take it by spoonfuls within six or eight hours."

"These two pounds will contain about ten thousand drops. If one of these drops be mixed with two thousand drops (six ounces) of water, mixed with a little alcohol, by being vigorously shaken, one teaspoonful of this mixture, given every two hours, will produce not much less violent symptoms in a strong man if he is ill. Such a dose contains the millionth part of a grain. A few teaspoonfuls of this mixture will, I assert, bring him to the brink of the grave if he was previously regularly ill, and if his disease was of such a description as *Belladonna* is suitable for."

Hahnemann gives no reasons for his sudden change from appreciable doses in 1798 to comparatively minute doses in 1799.

Dudgeon says, "that it was about this time that the persecutions of the apothecaries began, and it was probably a desire to evade their harassing annoyance that led Hahnemann to try, if on diminishing the dose to such an extent that it was beyond the ken of chemical or other research, the medicine still possessed the power of influencing the organism."

Undoubtedly he made experiments regarding this matter. In the answer to Hufeland he mentions the greater action of drugs when diffused in particles. As he, by experiments, discovered that medicines acted in minute doses even better than when administered in a crude form, he probably continued to reduce the size of the dose. He has many times said that it was his aim to cure as easily and pleasantly as possible. And he wished to give no more medicine than was absolutely necessary to complete the cure.

Again, in 1801, he writes: "I removed several paralyses by the use, during several weeks, of a very rarified *Belladonna* solution, where the whole cure did not require a full one hundred thousandth part of a grain of dried *Belladonna* juice, and some periodical nervous diseases, dispositions to furuncles, etc., required not quite one-millionth part for the whole cure."*

CHAPTER LXXXIII.

POSOLOGY CONTINUED.

The next that Hahnemann says on the dose is in the "Medicine of Experience," published in 1805, and in which he first announces the Homœopathic law. He says that if the remedy selected be the right one it will act in incredibly small doses. And again, if a small dose of diluted tincture of *Opium* is capable of removing sleepiness, the hundredth or even the thousandth part of the dose suffices as well.

In a paper published in 1808 he says that in certain bilious conditions "a single drop of the tincture of *Arnica* root will often remove, in the course of a couple of hours, all the fever, all the bilious taste, all the tormina."

In another article in the same year, for a fever then prevailing in Germany, he recommends *Nux vomica* in doses of the trillionth of a grain; *Arsenicum* in doses of a sextillionth. This would be in the ninth and eighteenth dilutions.

In the first edition of the "Organon," published in 1810, he still recommends the smallest possible dose. He says: "The smallest doses are equal to the disease." And again: "The dose must therefore be reduced to the smallest point capable of causing an aggravation of the symptoms, however slight; such is the standard of measurement and incontrovertible axiom of experience."

He does not mention the dynamization theory. The dose must be diminished to avoid aggravation. He uses the terms diminution, subdivision and attenuation. He does not give the limit of his method of dilution. He says, however, that a dose divided and taken at intervals will act better than if taken at once, and that the power of the medicine is increased by being intimately mixed with a larger amount of fluid.

---

* Fincke, on High Potencies, p. 108.

In the "Spirit of the Homœopathic Doctrine," published in 1813, he says: "The spiritual power of medicine does not accomplish its object by means of quantity, but by quality or dynamic firmness."

In the essay on hospital or typhus fever, in 1814, he recommends *Bryonia* and *Rhus tox*, each in the twelfth dilution; not by the centesimal scale, but in proportion of one drop to six drachms—equal to the fifteenth or sixteenth centesimal dilution. A single drop of each of these medicines is to be given for the dose. Neither must be used in a lower dilution nor in a larger dose. He gives sweet spirits of *Nitre*, one drop to an ounce of water, in teaspoonfuls, the whole to be taken within twenty-four hours.

In 1815 Hahnemann prescribed for a washerwoman a drop of the pure juice of the *Bryonia* root. This appears in one of his published cases. The same year he gave for dyspepsia, "half a drop of the quadrillionth of a strong drop of *Pulsatilla*."*

In a letter to Stapf, written in 1814, he says: "With this you will receive my strong tincture of *Rhus. tox.*, and the diluted tincture for use (the quadrillionth of a grain in each drop), also some tincture of *Bryonia* root (I have not now any of my strong one-twentieth tincture), strong and diluted (one sextillionth)."

In this same letter he says: "There are other States in which much good is done with the South pole of the magnet, but I will not describe them to you till I can do so by word of mouth."†

In the first volume of the "Materia Medica Pura," published in 1811, nothing is said of the doses of the medicines: But in the latter volumes the doses of nearly every medicine are given.

In volume two, published in 1816, he recommends *Causticum*, a drop of the original preparation. *Arsenicum* is to be given in the twelfth, eighteenth or thirtieth dilution.

Ferrum, the $\frac{1}{100}$, $\frac{1}{10000}$ or $\frac{1}{50000}$ of a grain is mentioned.

Ignatia is to be used in the ninth or twelfth potency.

Rheum, in acute affections in the ninth.

In the third volume, *China* is recommended in the twelfth dilution; *Asarum*, in the twelfth or fifteenth; *Ipecac*, in the third; *Scilla*, fifteenth or eighteenth; *Stramonium*, in the ninth; *Veratrum*, in the twelfth.

---

*"Lesser Writings," New York, p. 769. *Hom. Times*, London, Vol. i., p. 9.

†*Hom. World*, Vol. xxiv., p. 208,

In the fourth volume the directions are as follows: *Hyoscyamus* is to be used in the twelfth, fifteenth, eighteenth dilution; *Digitalis*, in the fifteenth; *Aurum*, the first and second triturations of gold leaf are suggested; *Guaiacum*, a drop of mother tincture; *Camphor*, drop doses of one part to eight; *Ledum*, in the fifteenth; *Ruta*, in the fifth decimal; *Sarsaparilla*, in drop doses of tincture; *Sulphur*, *Hepar sulphur* and *Argentum*, in grain doses of the second trituration.

The fifth volume of the "Materia Medica Pura" was published in 1819, and the recommendations were continued. *Euphrasia*, *Menyanthes* and *Sambucus*, the smallest part of a drop of the juice; *Cyclamen*, third dilution; *Calcarea acetica*, drop of the saturated solution; *Muriatic acid*, drop of the third decimal; *Thuja* is to be given in the thirtieth.

The second edition of the "Organon" was issued in this year; in it he refers to the "Materia Medica Pura" for the proper doses of the medicine.

In the same year, in an article on suicides, he recommends the sixth potency of pure gold.

The sixth volume of the "Materia Medica Pura" was issued in 1821. *Angustura* is to be given in the sixth; *Manganum acet.*, twenty-fourth; *Capsicum*, ninth; *Colocynth*, eighteenth, twenty-first; *Verbascum*, tincture; *Spongia*, for goitre the mother tincture, and for other uses the higher dilutions; *Drosera*, ninth; *Bismuth*, second trituration; *Stannum*, the sixth.

The first volume of the second edition of the "Materia Medica Pura" was published in 1822. Here we find recommended *Belladonna*, thirtieth; *Dulcamara*, twenty-fourth; *Cina*, ninth; *Cannabis*, tincture; *Cocculus*, twelfth; *Nux vomica*, thirtieth; *Opium*, sixth; *Moschus*, third; *Oleander*, sixth; *Mercurius sol.*, twelfth; *Aconite*, twenty-fourth; *Arnica*, sixth.

From this time to 1828, when the first three volumes of the "Chronic Diseases" appeared, there is but little change in the size of the dose. As may be seen, the dose differs in the different medicines, but it runs from the tincture to the thirtieth.

Hahnemann had now given to the world his psora theory, and now he greatly modified his former opinions in regard to the difference of medicinal doses and endeavored to adopt one uniform dilution for every medicine, the thirtieth. The dose must be but one globule not larger than a mustard seed soaked in this dilution.

Hahnemann in writing to Stapf, in 1826, says:* "For frequently recurring facial erysipelas *Sulphur* ♀♀♀ has proved serviceable. Stick to the lowest and smallest doses, and allow any one which is doing good to act sufficiently long until the old malady shows signs of recurring."

Dudgeon, in a note to one of these letters:† "Hahnemann originally termed those dilutions *low* which his adherents now denominate *high*. Hahnemann's original term was the more correct. The only excuse for calling excessively diluted medicines high is that the numerals that denote them are so."

Hahnemann continues: "I thank you for the duodecimo vials. There is more than an ample supply of them for my purpose, which is to send to patients at a distance a globule for olfaction in them. I enclose herewith a small quantity of globules from my little store. Should you go to Leipsic, get some good confectioner (or, better, one of his best workmen) to make half a pound of similar globules, and send Gross as many of them as I send to you to-day."

In a letter written December, 1826, to the same man, he says:‡ "The new symptoms that have now appeared are evidently caused by the *Calcarea*, because they have occurred within the limits of its duration of action. It has not acted quite unsuitably, not strikingly unfavorably. You will do well to let it act for thirty-six days, and then give her the enclosed powder (two globules of *Lycopodium* iv.) moistening them first with two or three drops of water."

Again, in 1827, he says of *Calcarea:*‖ "In metrorrhagias *Calcarea* in small doses is the chief remedy. If we attend carefully to the symptoms in the selection of an antipsoric remedy, we shall see in the first twelve to eighteen days how far it will serve us. If it causes any important new symptoms, we are as much justified in changing it for another antipsoric remedy as if it should aggravate excessively the symptoms it is intended to cure; this is owing to the dose having been too strong, which we shall see within twelve or eighteen days. Another antipsoric remedy must then be substituted, and we must not feel

---

* *Hom. World*, Vol. xxiv., p. 362.
† *Hom. World*, Vol. xxiv., p. 311.
‡ *Hom World.* Vol. xxiv., p. 364.
‖ *Hom. World*, Vol. xxiv., p. 366.

surprised if, even after the latter, the disease continues some time longer."

In another letter to Stapf, dated September 28, 1829, he says:* "I have thought of two medicines for your patient (antipsorics), viz., for her severe nausea and extreme weakness *Natrum muri-atium* (of which I send a globule ♀ for olfaction), and for her depression of spirits at other times *Conium mac.* x, at which you should only allow her to smell once, allowing both to act for from twelve to twenty days. As a rule I would counsel you not to employ the antipsorics for this patient, who has been brought so low by over-excitement, in any other way than by olfaction."

In a letter written to Dr. Schreeter, and dated September 12, 1829, Hahnemann says:† "I do not approve of your dynamizing the medicines higher (as for instance up to xii and xx). There must be some end to the thing; it cannot go on to infinity. By laying it down as a rule that all Homœopathic remedies be diluted and dynamized up to x, we have a uniform mode of procedure in the treatment of all Homœopathists, and when they describe a cure we can repeat it, as they and we operate with the same tools. In one word, we would do well to go forward uninterruptedly in the beaten path. Then our enemies will not be able to reproach us with having nothing fixed—no normal standard."

In paragraph 270 of the fifth edition of the "Organon" he says: "Two drops of the fresh vegetable juice mingled with equal parts of alcohol are diluted with ninety eight drops of *Alcohol* and potentized by means of two succussions whereby the first development of power is formed, and this process is repeated through twenty-nine more vials, each of which is filled three-quarters full with ninety-nine drops of *Alcohol*, and each succeeding vial is to be provided with one drop from the preceding vial (which has already been shaken twice) and is in its turn twice shaken, and in the same manner at last the thirtieth development of power (potentized decillionth dilution x) which is the one most generally used."

Thus in the letter to Schreeter, when he speaks of dynamizing up to x he means what is termed the thirtieth potency.

* *Hom. World*, Vol. xxv., p. 112.
† *Brit. Jour. Hom.*, Vol. v., p. 398. *Neue Archiv.*, Vol. ii., part 3, 1829.

Hahnemann, in prescribing one unchangeable and fixed dose for every one, seems to lose sight of the idiosyncrasies and differences of temperament, habits of life, etc., in patients. And it is very well assured that he did not confine himself to any such arbitrary rule as the thirtieth in every case. His pocket case tells a different story.

The constant aim with Hahnemann seemed to be to cure the patient with the smallest dose possible. His teachings and practice greatly varied in this respect; there are many things in the "Organon" that seem contradictory. But underlying every hypothesis is the plainly expressed wish to cure, and to cure as easily as he could.

As his experiments increased in potentization, and in the use of the higher potencies, he became convinced that the attenuation or potentization, or, as he called it, dynamization of drugs, invested them with a greater or spiritual power. In paragraph 269 of the "Organon," he says: "The Homœopathic system of medicine develops for its use, to a hitherto unheard of degree, the spirit-like medicinal powers of the crude substances by means of a process peculiar to it and which has hitherto never been tried, whereby only they all become penetratingly efficacious and remedial, even those that in the crude state give no evidence of the slightest medicinal power on the human body."

Again in paragraph 279: "The dose of the Homœopathically selected remedy can never be prepared so small that it shall not be stronger than the natural disease, and shall not be able to overpower, extinguish, cure it, at least in part, as long as it is capable of causing some, though but a slight preponderance of its own symptoms over those of the disease resembling it (slight Homœopathic aggravation, Par. 157, 160,) immediately after its ingestion."

The perfect method was to be able to determine just how much medicine would cure and at the same time leave the slightest possible medicinal aggravation.

This notion of reducing all medication to the thirtieth potency does not seem to have been followed by Hahnemann himself.

In speaking of the very minute doses he says in a note in the "Organon," fifth edition: "The doctrine of the divisibility of matter teaches us that we can not make a part so small that it shall cease to be something, and that it shall not share all the properties of the whole.

"If now the smallest possible part is powerful enough for the purpose for which you require it, would you employ a greater quantity than you require, in order not to run counter to traditional custom, and out of deference to the prejudices of those whose standard of measurement is imperfect? And what is the use of larger doses of medicines if the smallest possible quantities given on the Homœopathic principle suffice for the cure of diseases in the most rapid and permanent manner? The effect of the dose increases the greater the quantity of liquid it is dissolved in when given to the patient."

The dose of medicine was only to be repeated when the effect of the dose already given was exhausted.

CHAPTER LXXXIV.

POSOLOGY CONTINUED.

In all the directions for preparing drugs but two vehicles were recommended by Hahnemann, sugar of milk for triturations and alcohol for the attenuations. To this rule he always adhered. The dilutions were also all to be made in a separate vial, and succussions to be given to each.

In paragraph 288 of the "Organon," he mentions olfaction as a means of cure, saying: "It is especially in the form of vapor, by olfaction and inhalation of the medicinal aura that is always emanating from a globule impregnated with a medicinal fluid in a high development of power, and placed dry in a small vial, that the Homœopathic remedies act most surely and most powerfully. The Homœopathic physician allows the patient to hold the open mouth of the vial first in one nostril, and in the act of inspiration draw the air out of it into himself, and then if it is wished to give a stronger dose, smell in the same manner with the other nostril, more or less strongly, according to the strength it is intended the dose should be; he then corks up the vial and replaces it in his pocket case to prevent misuse of it, and unless he wish it, he has no occasion for an apothecary's assistance in his practice."

Hahnemann continues to speak of the undiminished power of the medicated globule after many years, and of being convinced that the action of medicine on the system is as strong by olfaction as by the ordinary method of the mouth.

In a letter to Stapf, dated February 15, 1830, he says, in speaking of the expected decision regarding the right of Homœopathic physicians to dispense their own medicines:*

"I learn from Von Brunnow that the question respecting the dispensing their medicines by Homœopathists will be determined by the Government in the beginning of February. Von Brunnow doubts if it will be settled in our favor. But, howsoever it may turn out, at all events we shall set heads and hearts in motion, and that in no small manner; and if they will not now do us justice they will in the end be forced to do so.

"How would it do if you were in the *Archiv* to recommend the Homœopaths, who are persecuted by the medical authorities for dispensing their own medicines to adopt a plan whereby they could elude all such laws, *e. g.*, that they should not allow their patients to take anything material, but only let them smell at a phial in their pocket-cases, so that the physician neither gives powders himself nor prescribes them from the drug shops. *La rareté du fait* would serve to maintain their patients' confidence; no authority could forbid this, and experience shows that acute as well as chronic diseases of all kinds can be happily and speedily cured by this means. This would be the speediest way to induce the governmental authorities to grant us the right to dispense our medicines, when they see that we can do without their permission. If I were in such a difficulty I would at once do this."

The following letter, probably written in 1831, is of interest, inasmuch as it bears upon the repetition of the dose in chronic diseases.†

Hahnemann's dictum always was that the proper dose should be allowed to act as long as its action lasted, before another dose was given. This we find illustrated in the letter:

"*My Dear Postmaster:* You have done well to enquire of me whether, in case of obvious (striking) amelioration of your salivary fistula, you should nevertheless take the new medicament? I answer: No! Continue so long entirely without medicine, living regularly, until the gland has been again getting worse for seven days. Then only begin with the new medicine.

"It is impossible in the various constitutions of the body to determine how long a given antipsoric drug may continue to act.

---

* *Hom. World*, Vol. xxv., p. 114.
† *The Organon*, Vol. ii., p. 172.

This much, however, is certain, that its action lasts as long as it does good and the disease does not again *continuously* increase."

He says to Schreter, in 1829:[*] "Your want of success in the cases you have recorded is certainly owing to the rapid changes of the remedies, the often unfitting dilution and dynamization, and the too large doses.

"Once you have spoilt matters with these three faults for about four weeks, it is very difficult to set them right again. My advice is that you bide rigorously by the precepts contained in my book on chronic diseases; and, if possible, go still further than I have done, in allowing a still longer period for the anti-psoric remedies to exhaust their action, in administering still smaller doses than I have advised, and in dynamizing all anti-psoric medicines up to thirty."

In 1832 was published, in Stapf's *Archiv*,[†] an article by one Herr Von Korsakoff, a noble and landed proprietor near Moscow, and a great dilettante upon the subject of Homœopathy,[‡] entitled: "Experiences on the Propagation of the Medicinal Power of Homœopathic Remedies, with Ideas on the Mode of Propagation." In this he advocated that the attenuation or potentization of remedies might be carried much higher than had hitherto been done; he potentized a remedy to the 1500th dynamization. He said that one medicated globule placed in a bottle in which were a thousand unmedicated globules would medicate the whole.

He claims to have medicated 13,500 globules with a single globule of *Sulphur* 30th. He thought that the material division of medicine ceased at the sixth dilution, and that after that the medicinal power was dynamic or spiritual.

There is a letter from Hahnemann in answer to these extravagances in the same number. He admits that the experiments are curious and says:[‖]

"I must say that these procedures seem to show chiefly how high one can go with the potentized attenuation of medicines without their action on the human health becoming *nil*. For this these experiments are of inestimable value; but for the Hom-

---

[*] *Brit. Jour. Hom.*, Vol. v., p. 397.

[†] *Archiv fur hom. Heilkunst*, Vol. xi., part 2, p. 87.

[‡] *Brit. Jour. Hom.*, Vol. v., p. 129.

[‖] Dudgeon's "Organon," p. 303.

œopathic treatment of patients it is expedient in the preparation of all kinds of medicines to remain stationary at the decillionth attenuation and potency, in order that Homœopathic practitioners may be able to promise themselves uniform results in their cures.''

Hahnemann did not altogether indorse this plan, although it is likely that he afterwards made use at times of the very high attenuations.

But certain of his followers, years later, notably Dr. Gross, made use of these high potencies. Dr. Gross induced one Herr Jenichen of Wismar, who was said to be a horse breaker, or trainer, to undertake the preparation of high potencies. He did so, making from the 100th up to the 60,000th potency. His preparations were declared by a certain part of the profession to be valuable. His method of attenuation was kept a profound secret. Dr. Dudgeon, in the *British Journal of Homœopathy*, gave a sketch of his life and explained his methods in preparing these so-called high potencies. He was a very powerful man and hence he was enabled by his vigorous shakes to greatly increase the strength of the medicine he was preparing. Contrary to the dictum of Hahnemann, who recommended but a limited number of succussions, Jenichen gave each remedy many thousand shakes, and is said to have worked five hours a day in their manufacture.*

In the pamphlet on the "Cure of Asiatic Cholera" he recommends drop doses of a strong solution of *Camphor* every five minutes, with *Camphor* also to be rubbed upon the skin.†

Two cases cured by Hahnemann were published in the *New Archives* for 1844, by Bœnninghausen. A girl of fourteen years had a sunstroke, and Hahnemann gave *Belladonna* as follows: One globule of the sixtieth potency dissolved in seven teaspoonfuls of water, of this solution one tablespoonful dissolved in one glass of water, and, after stirring, one teaspoonful of this latter solution was to be taken in the morning.

The next day a teaspoonful of this last-mentioned solution was dissolved in a second tumbler of water, and two to four teaspoonfuls were to be taken in the morning. Five days later one globule of *Belladonna* higher potency, dissolved in seven table-

---

* *Brit. Jour. Hom.*, Vol. x., p. 168. Dudgeon's Lectures, p. 353.
† "Lesser Writings," New York.

spoonfuls of water, one tablespoonful to be mixed in a tumbler of water and one teaspoonful to be taken every morning for six days. At intervals of some days *Hyos.* 30 and a high potency of *Sulphur* were also used.*

The other case mentioned was treated in much the same manner in regard to the potency and repetition of the dose.

In the second edition of the "Chronic Diseases," 1835, *Nitric acid* is recommended in the sixth, and in the preface to the third part, 1837, he says that when the thirtieth potency has become powerless the twenty-fourth should be used. He advises giving a dose daily of the medicine each time in a lower potency.

Dr. Romani, in 1845, published a historical eulogy upon Hahnemann, and in it is a letter written by Hahnemann to a Russian general living in Naples, whose son he was treating. It is dated at Coethen, August 31, 1833. He says:† "I forward seven globules; the patient is to take one every seven days, in the morning on an empty stomach. The globules are to be dissolved in a spoonful of water. When taking the globule marked one, the patient is to smell at the same time with both the nostrils at the tube marked S. He must smell at the tube C. when he takes globule three, and smell at the tube H. S. when he takes globule number five. He should only make one olfaction." It is probable that the medicine was in the tubes and not in the globules.

In January, 1843, Hahnemann wrote to Dr. Romani from Paris, prescribing for a patient with cancer of the tongue *Acidum muriaticum* thirtieth, one globule in fifteen spoonfuls of water and one of *Alcohol*, in a smooth bottle; this was to be shaken and a tablespoonful of this put in a tumbler containing ten spoonfuls of water. The patient was to take for two days a teaspoonful, the third and fourth days two teaspoonfuls, etc., increasing the doses.

In February, in another letter, Hahnemann sends Dr. Romani two globules of *Thuja*, "a very highly perfected dynamization, which will be fully described in the forthcoming sixth edition of my 'Organon.'" This was to be used in a similar manner.

In a letter dated October 10, 1829, addressed to his favorite nephew, Trinius, Hahnemann says:‡ "It is wonderful, but not

* Fincke on High Potencies, p. 118.
† *Brit. Jour. Hom.*, Vol. xiii., p. 147.
‡ *Brit. Jour. Hom.*, Vol. xxx., p. 297.

the less true, that the higher a medicine is refined and potentized the more permanent its efficacy. If the highly potentized medicine would not evaporate, it would be found as powerful as ever after the lapse of a generation.

"The powders you got from Neudietendorf, if kept in well-corked vials, will, so far as I know, retain their power unaltered *forever;* and if we moisten a globule the size of a hemp seed with the last dilution (x), for the purpose of allowing delicate patients to smell at it, in place of taking it (as is often necessary), such globules retain their medicinal power for many years, as I can testify, although the bottles in which they are contained may be often opened for olfaction.

"Such being the case, the Homœopathic practitioner prepares his medicines to last him all his life, by dropping six or eight drops of the last dilution (x) of each fluid medicine into a small, narrow, rather high vessel; as, for instance, a clean thimble, containing a number of finest sugar globules (three hundred of which weigh a grain), from four to five thousand. By this they will be more than saturated and impregnated with the medicine. The whole thimbleful of moistened globules is to be emptied on to a piece of paper and spread out by means of a thin bit of wood. In about a quarter of an hour they are dry, and must be kept in a wide-mouthed, well-corked bottle, and duly labeled. Of course the piece of paper and bit of wood must be always thrown away, and fresh ones used for each medicine. The thimble, too, must every time be washed and dried in the most careful manner, before using it for another medicine.

"In this way we obtain a supply of all Homœopathic and antipsoric medicines, which will retain their powers undiminished for an incalculable number of years. They are always ready for use, are sufficient for a lifelong practice, or even for stocking a hospital for life. I beg you will communicate what stands in this page to the other Homœopathists, especially to the docile Dr. Hermann, and believe me to remain,

"Yours,   "SAM. HAHNEMANN."

In a letter written to Dr. Lehmann on March 23, 1841, Hahnemann requests him to send the third trituration of a number of medicines, the list of which he encloses. Dr. Lehmann, who had been his assistant at Coethen, prepared his medicines up to the end of Hahnemann's life.*

---

* Preface "Lesser Writings," New York.

CHAPTER LXXXV.

POSOLOGY CONCLUDED.

In 1853, Dr. J. Chapman, writing to the London *Homœopathic Times*, says:* "My reason for addressing you is to prove what was the actual practice of Hahnemann during his residence in Paris, and to the close of his life. I have before me, while I write, the box of medicines he carried about with him during the time I have mentioned. It is a very small box, made to contain 160 tubes of globules; these tubes are very small, and each of them contains about fifty or sixty globules when filled. The corks were marked by Hahnemann himself with the names of the medicines and the number of the dilution of each.

"His characteristic handwriting would be recognized at once by any one familiar with it.

"Four of the tubes are missing, and one has a blank cork, so that there is evidence given from 155 tubes of the practice of Hahnemann in respect to the dilution, for it was from this box that he gave medicines to his patients.

"It may be conjectured that *Manganum* was contained in one of the missing tubes. As there are three dilutions of *Arnica*, *Arsenicum* and *Bryonia* there were probably three of *Aconite*, *Belladonna* and *Pulsatilla*, this would account for the three missing tubes. This, however, is mere conjecture.

"The dilutions he habitually used, it may be seen, were the sixth, ninth, twelfth, eighteenth, twenty-fourth and thirtieth. Hahnemann used at his house a larger box containing the same medicines and dilutions as those in the smaller.

"The Reverend Mr. Everest, the English friend of Hahnemann, has, I believe, one or more duplicate boxes containing the medicines corresponding to those in Hahnemann's box. He can supply the gaps of the four missing tubes." * * * *

THE MEDICINES AND DILUTIONS OF THEM HABITUALLY USED BY HAHNEMANN.

Acidum muriaticum, 30.
Acidum nitricum, 30.
Acidum phosphoricum, 30.
Acidum sulphuricum, 30.

Aconite, 12, 30.
Agaricus, 30.
Agnus castus, 18.
Alumina, 30.

* *Hom. Times*, Vol. iv., p. 685. Kirby's *Am. Jour. Hom.*, Vol. viii., p. 42.

Ambra grisea, 24.
. Ammonium carbonicum, 24.
Anacardium, 18.
Angustura, 30.
Antimonium crudum, 24.
Antimonium tart., 12.
Aranea diadema, 30.
Argentum, 24.
Arnica moutana, 6, 12, 30.
Arsenicum album, 9, 18, 30.
Asafœtida, 30.
Asarum Europeum, 30.
Aurum metallicum, 12, 30.
Baryta acetica, 30.
Baryta carbonica, 30.
Belladonna, 12, 30.
Bismuthum, 18.
Borax, 18.
Bovista, 24.
Bryonia, 6, 18, 30.
Caladium seguinum, 24.
Calcarea acetica, 24.
Calcarea carb., 30.
Camphor, 6, 24.
Cancer fluviatilis, 12.
Cannabis sativa, 12, 30.
Cantharis, 30.
Capsicum, 30.
Carbo animalis, 24.
Carbo vegetabilis, 12, 30.
Castoreum, 24.
Chamomilla, 12.
Chelidonium majus, 30.
China, 30.
Also a tube of China unnumbered.
Cicuta, 24.
Cina, 30.
Cinnabar, 24.
Clematis, 12.
Cocculus, 12.
Coffea cruda, 12, 30.
Colchicum, 18.
Colocynth, 30.
Conium maculatum, 24.
Copaiba, 24.
Corallium, 30.
Crocus sativus, 18.
Cuprum metallicum, 30.
Cyclamen, 24.
Digitalis, 24.
Drosera, 18.
Dulcamara, 24.
Euphorbium, 24.
Euphrasia, 12.
Ferrum metallicum, 24.
Filix mas., 18.
Graphites, 24.
Gratiola, 24.
Guaiacum, 30.
Helleborus niger, 24.

Hepar sulphuris, 18.
Hyoscyamus, 12.
Ignatia, 12.
Indigo. 30.
Iodium, 30.
Ipecacuanha, 12.
Jacea, 24.
Kali carbonicum, 30.
Kali hydriodicum, 24.
Lachesis, 30.
Lamium album, 24.
Ledum, 24.
Lycopodium, 30.
Magnesia carbonica, 24.
Magnesia muriatica, 24.
Menyanthes trifol., 24.
Mercurius corr., 24.
Mercurius sol., 30.
Mercurius vivus, 24.
Mezereum, 24.
Millefolium, 12.
Millep (thus on cork), 24.
Moschus, 24.
Natrum carb., 24.
Natrum muriaticum, 30.
Niccolum, 24.
Nitrum, 24.
Nux vomica, 12, 30.
Oleander, 24.
Oleum animale, 30.
Ol. terebinth, 30.
Opium, 12. 30.
Paris quadrifolia, 24.
Petroleum, 24.
Petrosilinum, 18.
Phellandrium, 24.
Phosphorus, 18.
Platina, 24.
Plumbum metallicum, 24.
Pulsatilla, 9, 30.
Ranunculus bulbosus, 18.
Rheum, 18.
Rhus tox, 12.
Ruta, 12.
Sabadilla, 18.
Sabina, 24.
Sambucus, 18.
Sarsaparilla, 24.
Secale corn, 18.
Selenium, 18.
Sepia, 30.
Silicea, not numbered, probably 30.
Spigelia, 24.
Spongia, 30.
Squilla, 30.
Stannum, 30.
Staphysagria, 24.
Stramonium, 24.
Strontiana, 30.
Sulphur, 30.

Tabacum, 12.	Veratrum, 30.
Teucrium marum, 18.	Verbascum, 18.
Thuja, 12.	Viola odor., 18.
Tinct. sulph., 24.	Uva ursi, 30.
Valerian, 18.	Zincum met., 30.

In the next number of the *Times*, Dr. Chapman says:* "Since my last letter I have seen two boxes of Homœopathic medicines, which Hahnemann selected for a patient in the years 1841–42. He died, as you know, in 1843. The larger box contains one hundred and fifty tubes; among them is *Arnica* 3, *Euphrasia* 6 and other low dilutions. None is higher than thirty. In this box the dilutions are three, six, nine, twelve, eighteen, twenty-four, thirty. I have what I consider the best possible authority for stating that Hahnemann used no medicine beyond the thirtieth dilution."

This letter caused some discussion among the London physicians. Dr. Chapman insisted that the box was the one used by Hahnemann and that he had its loan from a person to whom Hahnemann gave it only a few days previous to his death.

In the *Times* for July 30, 1853, the Reverend Mr. Everest, who probably knew more about Hahnemann than any man then living, published a letter to Dr. Luther, in which he says:†

"Hahnemann endeavored to find means to administer remedies in such a way that the least possible disturbance compatible with cure should result. To this end he made a great variety of experiments. The first in order was olfaction, and this he adopted in certain cases to the end of his life; I am not aware that he altogether abandoned it.

"But certain objections caused him to seek for some other means of moderating medicinal action. His next experiment was to dissolve three, two or one globule in a glass of water, and then, after carefully stirring, to put a dessert or teaspoonful of this into another glass.

"He still found, however, that in very many delicate constitutions too much excitement was produced even thus, when the medicine was accurately chosen; for if a medicine is not exactly harmonic to the case, its effects are, of course, much less, inasmuch as in that case it acts on a part of the organism not morbidly excited; and this remark will explain why so many prac-

---

* *Hom. Times*, Vol. iv., p. 700.
† *Hom. Times*, Vol. iv. p. 731.

ticers of the modern or 'improved Homœopathy' experience so few cases of aggravation, that is because they give medicines at random, and so do not touch the disturbed nerves at all.

"The attenuation was sometimes carried through two, three, four, five and six tumblers; but it was a very inconvenient proceeding, and it had none of that simplicity which Nature's laws generally have.

"He tried, in its order, the diminution of the number of shakes, but that seemed not to give the accurate result that he wanted. He tried many plans and made many experiments with one or two of which I am acquainted and others I have forgotten, if ever I heard them.

"The last, however, and the one that gave the most satisfactory results (I believe I may say that he was perfectly satisfied with them), was the plan I will now explain:

"Starting from the first spirituous tincture of any medicine, which I believe was the third from the commencement, and is, according to the ordinary notation, written 1, instead of adding one drop of this dynamization to one hundred drops of spirit of wine to make the next, and so continuing the dynamization by drops, he moistened a few globules of a fixed normal size with it, and taking in the first experiments, I believe, ten, but in the latter and more satisfactory ones only one globule of those so moistened he dissolved that in a minute drop of water, and then added one hundred drops of spirit of wine. Having shaken it (I forget how much) he moistened globules with this, and having dried them, put them into a tube in his medicine chest, well corked; these he labelled $\frac{0}{1}$. The next dynamization was procured by dissolving one globule of $\frac{0}{1}$ in a small drop of water, and adding one hundred drops of spirit of wine; with this he humected globules as before, and called that dynamization $\frac{0}{2}$. This proceeding was thus carried on until the tenth, which was labelled $\frac{0}{10}$. Originally I think he used the Roman characters, and called them $\frac{0}{ix}$, $\frac{0}{x}$, etc., but afterwards adhered for these preparations to the Arabic ciphers.

"The preparations so made were called *medicamens au globule* (which is the meaning of the o), to distinguish them from the old ones, which are marked with a small cross (x), and called *medicamens a la goutte* (medicines of the drop).

"He was so entirely satisfied with the gentle and kindly actions of these preparations that they would, I think, almost have superseded with him all other preparations. I possess many of the medicines so prepared for him; most of them are complete series from $\frac{0}{1}$ to $\frac{0}{10}$.

"I do not recollect that any were carried beyond 10, unless it was *Phosphorus*, which I think he made up to $\frac{0}{15}$.

"This is written from memory, but I believe the account is quite or nearly accurate. Hahnemann only confided to me the preparation of his globules (most of which I made myself for him). Another friend prepared the dynamizations. I trusted to memory, because Hahnemann has so often told me that the new edition of the 'Organon' would contain the whole account of that and many other most valuable discoveries, and I know that that edition was ready, because Hahnemann himself had intrusted to me to negotiate with a bookseller of Paris the publication of it." * * * * *

Dr. Luther also wrote on the subject, and expressed a wish that Madame Hahnemann be induced to publish the new edition of the "Organon" so that the latest ideas of Hahnemann on the dose might be given to the Homœopathic profession. This correspondence may also be found in *Kirby's American Journal of Homœopathy*, New York, Vol. viii.

There is no doubt that Hahnemann's constant effort was to make the dose of medicine as small as he possibly could and yet cure the patient, and it is most probable that could we obtain the annotations of the unpublished sixth edition of the "Organon," much light would be thrown on his latest opinions.

CHAPTER LXXXVI.

TRIAL OF MADAME HAHNEMANN FOR PRACTICING ILLEGALLY—
VISIT OF DR. I. T. TALBOT.

After Hahnemann's death Madame Hahnemann still continued to practice. In the *Allgemeine Zeitung* the following appears:* "The widow of Dr. Hahnemann announces that she will practice medicine, and on her card she has placed the legend: *Madame Hahnemann, docteur en medicine homeopathique.*"

As has previously been stated, before the death of the Master, Madame Hahnemann usually prescribed for the patients, asking, when needful, Hahnemann's advice. Afterwards the patients still continued to go to her as before. No one interfered with her for several years.

In 1847, through the instigation of M. Orfila, the Dean of the Medical Faculty of Paris, a process was brought against Madame Hahnemann in the courts for practicing without a diploma. The following account of her trial was taken from the stenographic reports and was published in the *Hygea:* †

"Paris, February 20, 1848. After Madame Hahnemann had given the President her name, age, etc., she was impeached on the counts of practicing medicine and pharmacy illegally; of distributing cards bearing the title of doctor of medicine. She denied these things. She said she neither was a physician nor did she keep a pharmacy; to the title of doctor she had a right from the Academy in Pennsylvania, without reference to her relations with Hahnemann; and that this school was the greatest Homœopathic school in the world. To the question as to her practice of medicine, her ability to practice, her medical learning, she replied that she was only a lay practitioner, an intermediary between doctors, whose standing the Faculty recognized. Madame Hahnemann then mentioned her advocate, who sat at her side, the eminent M. Chaix d'Est Ange, who would defend her.

---

* *Allg. hom. Zeitung*, Vol. xxv., January 29, 1844.

† *Hygea: Centralorgan fur die hom. oder specifi. Heilkunst.* Dr. Grieselich. Vol. i., new series, p. 245.

See also: "Compte-Rendu du Proces de Mme. Hahnemann, Docteur en Homœopathie. Question d'exercice de la Medicine. Paris: Bailliere. 1847."

"Witnesses whereby this would be proven of Madame Hahnemann were witnesses of the old school (the plaintiff was M. Orfila, Dean of the Faculty of Paris), and the death of one Madame Broggi was the cause of this prosecution.

"Doctors Deleau and Croserio, the agents of Madame Hahnemann, were also examined. The first one calls himself the assistant of Madame Hahnemann, and says that he goes to her office twice a week, sees the patients, examines them, and prescribes for them, that he confers with Madame Hahnemann, the heiress of the Hahnemannic system of medicine, and she tells him that her husband used to do so and so, under such and such circumstances, but that he advises Madame Hahnemann only in difficult cases. Dr. Deleau denies that Madame Hahnemann was Madame Broggi's physician, and says that he himself had been her physician. But since, as the President says, it was shown by the testimony of witnesses that Madame Broggi was treated directly by Madame Hahnemann, Dr. Deleau acknowledged that he was not always at the House of Ordination, that Madame Hahnemann was there then; that she keeps a memorandum book respecting the patients, noting down their symptoms, etc., and that on his return they were accustomed to talk over matters, but that he writes the prescriptions. He further says that although Madame Hahnemann had been her husband's secretary, she never visits patients unless he (Deleau) is with her. Dr. Croserio said substantially the same, and added that Hahnemann often said to him: 'My wife understands Homœopathy perfectly; she knows as much about it as I do.' He and Dr. Croserio regarded Madame Hahnemann as a fully competent physician, and they say that she is more familiar with Homœopathy than any of the physicians. They both denied that Madame Hahnemann had received any honorary degree, but said that she had received something of a like nature. One woman testified that a ring had been presented to Madame Hahnemann. An apothecary named Lethiere furnished medicines gratuitously upon the prescriptions of physicians.

"It was very evident that Madame Hahnemann practiced medicine, even physicians acknowledged her as the mistress. The requisitorium of Saillard, the Deputy of the Public Prosecutor, viewed the whole matter simply as a blunder. Hence the question, he maintained, is not whether Madame Hahnemann understands Homœopathy, or understands it better than all others, but whether she has a legal diploma? The American diploma was not such; and the law makes no distinction between medicine in general and Homœopathy. It was perfectly clear from the testimony of physicians that Madame Hahnemann practiced medicine daily; that Madame Broggi was examined by her, and that Madame Hahnemann prescribed for Madame Broggi, and that Madame Hahnemann visited the houses of patients in Versailles without being accompanied by Dr. Deleau. The Deputy declared that both physicians are persons thrust into the case in order to preserve the appearance of law. The whole requisitorium, which is not without a sarcastic side-cut, shows up the testimony of the three interested parties in all its nakedness. The pleading of the defendant's counsel, M. Chaix d'Est Ange, is one of those masterpieces of our lawyers who know how to bring assistance to their client from every nook and corner of expediency. While the public prosecutor did not meddle with Homœopathy, Chaix d'Est Ange made a medical harangue. He took the field against the old system of medicine, cited witty and ingenious passages from the writings of both the Old and New School of practitioners, and gave an epitome of Hahnemann's life and writings and of Homœopathy in general, just as a Homœopathist would have composed it.

"A lawyer's defence of a persecuted woman is not seen every day. Moreover a Frenchman is polite, and so there was no lack of eulogy of Madame Hahnemann; poems composed about her were produced in court, and letters were read in which the whole talk was about her tall and commanding figure and agreeable manners, as well as her accomplishments and intellectual attainments.

"As regards Madame Hahnemann's practice of medicine, her counsel added that after the death of Hahnemann, the Reformer of Medicine, his clients applied to the widow, who had received from her husband all his knowledge, and that she always treated them without taking any remuneration; and he remarked that Madame Broggi had suffered from aneurism of the heart, as was testified to by Drs. Deleau and Croserio; that the physician who was sent for found her dead, and that besides this Madame Broggi's condition had improved, and for this the patient had at one time fallen on her knees before Madame Hahnemann and entreated her to accept a ring. Madame Hahnemann refused to accept the ring which the would-be donor wished to place on her finger. The words, 'To my angel,' were inscribed in it. The lawyer exhibited the ring which was worth about forty or fifty francs. The letters which he read in his client's favor fill more than twelve pages. Drs. Deleau and Croserio had been recommended to the sick by Madame Hahnemann because they adhered more faithfully to the Hahnemannian doctrine than the other physicians. The members of the then existing Homœopathic Society could so much the rather bear this reproach because it depended upon the attainment of a definite purpose, which Madame Hahnemann was carrying out.

"Chaix d'Est-Ange argued that Madame Hahnemann was performing the most unselfish of human duties, that it would be an act of impiety to condemn her, and that she had been summoned before the Court purely out of a feeling of jealousy or envy on the part of the physicians of the old school. Madame Hahnemann waived the privilege of making any further explanations, and the Public Prosecutor then replied to the counsel for the defence in a speech of two hours duration. He kept in the foreground the fact that only Madame Hahnemann had attended Madame Broggi, and that she generally practiced medicine, for the two physicians played a subordinate role in the consultation office of Madame Hahnemann, they being mere 'men of straw.' The Public Prosecutor repeatedly broadened his accusation by charging illegal practice of pharmacy, since Lethiere was not an apothecary and Madame Hahnemann had delivered or dispensed the medicines.

"The clever rejoinder of the defendant's lawyer was of no avail, and Madame Hahnemann was fined one hundred francs for illegal practice of medicine and pharmacy and adjudged to pay the costs. Thus the trial ended. Every person visiting Paris can judge for himself whether Madame Hahnemann has ceased to practice medicine."

The next note, in the *Hygea*, is as follows: "Paris, March 1 (1848). The overthrow of the first heartless, but now headless, July Monarchy, may produce a very important change in the condition of Homœopathy. Orfila, the Dean of the Medical Faculty and the bitter enemy of Homœopathy, has taken his departure, and five members of the Provisional Government, Lamartine,

Bethmond, Marie, Cremieux and Louis Blanc, have for years been among the clientage of Homœopathic physicians."

Madame Hahnemann, in the defence at her trial, stated that she was the possessor of a diploma from the North American Academy of the Homœopathic Healing Art, of Allentown, Pa. We find by a letter, written in 1841 to some one of the members of that Faculty, which has been previously quoted, that Hahnemann asked this favor and honor for his wife, and in a letter to Hering, in 1842, he again speaks of this diploma as follows:*

"*Dear Friend and Colleague:* At the end of October of last year I wrote you a long letter about my beloved wife Melanie, in which I stated to you the reasons that caused me earnestly to wish to obtain for her, by your kindness, as soon as possible, a diploma as Doctor of Homœopathic Medicine from the Academy at Allentown. In your answer of 19th of July, 1841, you were so good as to approve of my request and to promise a speedy compliance with it.

"I now beg of you to write as soon as possible about it, for I cannot imagine to what I am to attribute your silence.

"Your most devoted friend,

"SAMUEL HAHNEMANN."

It appears from this that the diploma was not granted until some time in 1842. Now the Allentown Academy was not in active operation in 1842, and the diploma must have been sent to the lady by the members of the Faculty after the School of Medicine was discontinued.

It may be mentioned that at this time Madame Hahnemann resided at No. 48 Rue de Clichy.

With the change in the Government there was no more trouble, and Madame Hahnemann continued her professional life undisturbed. Perhaps no better glimpse of this life can be given than to publish the following interview: †

Dr. I. T. Talbot, of Boston, says: "In the winter of 1854-55 I called upon Madame Hahnemann. On my first visit I learned that she was at her country house, to be absent two weeks. The second time I was more fortunate, and on sending up my card as *from America* I was shown into a spacious, but rather dreary and scantily furnished reception room, the principal orna-

---

* *Hom. World,* Vol. xxvi., p. 120.

† *N. E. Med. Gazette,* Vol. ix., p. 80.

ment of which, aside from the mirrors and clock, the constant furniture of Parisian rooms, was a colossal marble bust of Hahnemann, by David. It was taken in the last year of his life, and undoubtedly idealized its subject. In a few moments a lady of middle age entered the room. She was tall and quite graceful; her hair slightly grey and in curls; her forehead high and intellectual. Her countenance impressed me as cold and austere, and her manner as courtly and forbidding. It was Madame Hahnemann. With her first salutation it was easy to see that she was a lady of unusual accomplishments and accustomed to meet strangers.

"When I referred to her illustrious husband and to the wide acceptance of his doctrines in America her coldness and austerity immediately vanished, and she became an interested and genial listener.

"She spoke freely and enthusiastically of Hahnemann, and said that his mind grew clearer and his reasoning powers more comprehensive in the last years of his life.

"When it was known that Hahnemann was in Paris, many visited her residence to see him, and here her devotion to him and his interests is unquestioned. She acted as his interpreter, scribe, apothecary and business agent; and it is fair to assume that his life was lengthened by her constant, unwearying attentions. 'When he died,' said she, 'I felt that my mission was ended.' But it seems that old patients came to her, knowing that she had a record of their cases as treated by Hahnemann, and new ones, hoping through her to derive some benefit from his transcendent ability. Eleven years had passed since his death, but I did not learn that she then engaged largely in professional work. Since that time, however, her practice has been quite extensive."

CHAPTER LXXXVII.

The following letter is addressed to Dr. Nichols, the editor of the *New England Medical Gazette*, by a lady who had known Madame Hahnemann, and at that time (1874) resided in Boston:*

"*Dear Sir:* It gives me pleasure to furnish at your request, for the *Gazette*, some reminiscences of Madame Hahnemann.

"It was my good fortune to meet her first during the autumn of 1867. Having need of a physician, I called at the apartment of. Dr. Bœnninghausen, only to learn that he was in Germany and Madame Hahnemann was treating his patients meanwhile. I had not known until then that the celebrated widow was living; but I now very gladly left a request that she would call at our rooms as soon as possible; two of my friends had been suddenly seized with violent fever. I shall never forget the untiring devotion and rare skill of Madame Hahnemann in the management of their cases. Once we had occasion to call her at midnight. We were *au quatrieme* (without an elevator), and as she came climbing up the many stairs I could not resist a half apology for her supposed fatigue. She turned quickly toward me, her expressive face crowned with its glory of silver white hair and beaming with life and vigor, and, with the bright naivete of a young girl, said, *Je suis encore jeune.*

"We all became strongly attached to her during those weeks of anxious watching; and when we were obliged to leave Paris she took under her especial care our brother, who remained behind, called herself his mother, and put forth all her skill and tenderness to avert from him any ill consequences of the fearful fever from which he was just emerging. I have thought I could do no better than to give you a few extracts from his letters written to me after my return home.

"Madame seemed disappointed when I told her how sick J—— was, in spite of her medicines, and said he ought, when he got home, to put himself under the care of a good physician, a

* *N. E. Medical Gazette*, Vol. ix., p. 81. (February, 1874.)

Hahnemannian, and have those tendencies thoroughly cured. She has the largest notions of what Homœopathy can do, even in eradicating evil tendencies, and leaving one, *ganz gesund*. Even inherited ills have no right to exist; it may take time to remove them, but the result is certain. She always had confirmed headaches till she knew Hahnemann, and he cured her in three years. I see her every week. She proposes to give me a sound head.

"I called on Madame a few days ago and spent an hour with her. Thinking I was to leave at once for Germany, she had hunted up an old photograph of herself for me. But it was very bad, had none of her benevolence; and at her promise to have some new ones taken soon and give me one, I did not take it. She told me much of her own life and that of her husband. She is French and a Catholic; she was born in Paris; became early interested in medicine, and determined to study.

"Through the exertions of a friend she was able, when quite a girl, to be admitted to the dissecting-rooms of the medical school, at times when the students were not there, and in some way which I did not understand she got the benefit of the lectures, too. For many years she studied in this way, and went over the same course which all Allopathic students take for their degree. But she said the more she studied, the more unsatisfactory medicine became. It was a mirage. Then she met Hahnemann; what he told her made all plain; he recognized her doubts and showed the truths to which they pointed.

"Hahnemann was then eighty, and she a girl, I don't know how old. He told her he had all his life looked for a *woman*, as Diogenes did for a man, and that he found what he sought in her. She married him, and as she expressed it, 'I was a servant to him, and his copyist, and kept his house, and studied with him, and it was paradise.' I wish you could have seen the dear old lady's enthusiasm. 'He was the most godlike man,' she said. 'No one ever had such a face or character.' I said, 'Then he was not old when you married him?' 'No,' said she, 'he had never drunk wine, ale, coffee nor tea; had never sinned against his body in any way, and was as fresh and young at eighty as most men twenty-five years younger.'

"She showed me an enormous book, giving the symptoms for Homœopathic medicines then known, which she said she and

her husband had compiled entirely by experiments on themselves.   I must come and see her every three or four days and
let her talk of Hahnemann.   I might read of him in books, but
no one could tell me what he was as she could.   I promised to
come often, and she said she wished to introduce me to her son-
in-law and daughter.

"Madame gives me sanction to spend a week or two in London; provides me with medicines; will see me when I return,
and if I have gained as much as I ought, will let me go back to
study.   Her care has been the wisest and kindest.   She gladly
makes clear to me the difficult problems of her husband's doctrines.

"Her description the other day of their wedded Homœopathic
bliss was amusing.   She told of their labors together, and how
Hahnemann had no secrets apart from her, and how 'all day we
worked at the same table, and at night his bed was here, mine
there, and when we waked in the night our talk was of medicine.
I didn't marry him for his property, but for enthusiasm.'

"He was rich, she his second wife; and the law allows the
wife, on the husband's death, half the property, the other half
goes to the children.   She gave up her half to the children by
the previous marriage, and she said: 'You would think they
would have been grateful, wouldn't you? but they were not.'
This is the only allusion she has ever made to me with reference
to the attacks upon her."

Dr. Neidhard, in an address before the Philadelphia County
Homœopathic Medical Society in 1869, mentions a visit to
Madame Hahnemann:

"During my stay in Paris I visited Madame Hahnemann several times, and was very kindly received.   She is now a lady of
venerable aspect, having a high forehead and pale complexion.
She does not seem to be on good terms with the Homœopathic
physicians of Paris.   'These men,' she said, 'think that because
they are called doctors they know something of medical science
and the cure of diseases, but they know nothing.'

"Tears came into her eyes when she spoke of Hahnemann.
She does not practice Homœopathy now.   Dr. Bœnninghausen,
the son of the late celebrated Von Bœnninghausen, has married
a relation* of Madame Hahnemann, and has his office at Madame
Hahnemann's house.

---

* Her adopted daughter.

"Madame Hahnemann spoke a great deal of the purity of Homœopathy and the malpractice of many Parisian Homœopathic physicians, mentioning a case where one of them gave fifty drops of *Aconite* 6th in one dose. Hahnemann, she said, deeply regretted, before his death, the abandonment by so many physicians of his wise and well tried maxims.

"Hahnemann's 'Organon' will appear this year. The reason of its non-appearance is a change of editors. It was very difficult to find a reliable editor. Dr. Stapf's letters to Hahnemann will also be published shortly.

"For our Philadelphia hospital fair Madame Hahnemann had promised to give me a silver cup from which Hahnemann drank his cocoa every morning. On leaving Paris, when I claimed my prize, reminding her of the promise, she excused herself on the ground of the family objecting to part with it.

"As to the insinuation made by some that Hahnemann became childish during his last years she strongly denied it. Instead of losing his memory and judgment, he was, during the last years of his life, more enlightened and deeply intelligent than ever."*

CHAPTER LXXXVIII.

RIVAL EDITIONS OF THE "ORGANON"—BY LUTZE—SUSS-HAHNEMANN—MADAME HAHNEMANN—OPINIONS OF THE PROFESSION.

The intended publication of a new edition of the "Organon," of which Dr. Neidhard speaks, resulted from the following circumstances:

When Hahnemann died he left, in his own handwriting, numerous annotations in a copy of the last edition of the "Organon" for a sixth edition, in which it is presumed he had propounded his later medical opinions. Although it was known by the friends of Hahnemann that such a book existed, it was not given to the world. As may be seen, Croserio in his letter mentions this fact and it is mentioned by others. After his.

* "Homœopathy in France, Germany and England in the year 1869."

death the MSS. remained in the hands of Madame Hahnemann and nothing was done about publishing it. In 1865 Dr. Arthur Lutze published at Coethen a sixth edition of the "Organon," interpolated with certain notes and suggestions of his own. He added the following new paragraph, advising the use of double and triple remedies:*

"Section 274 b. There are several compound cases of disease in which the administration of a double remedy is perfectly Homœopathic and truly rational; where, for instance, each of two medicines appears suited for the case of disease, but each from a different side; or where the case of disease depends on more than one of the three radical causes of chronic diseases discovered by me, as when in addition to psora we have to do with syphilis or sycosis also. Just as in very rapid acute diseases I give two or three of the most appropriate remedies in alternation; i. e., in cholera, *Cuprum* and *Veratrum;* or in croup, *Aconite, Hepar sulph.* and *Spongia;* so in chronic diseases I may give together two well-indicated Homœopathic remedies acting from different sides, in the smallest dose. I must here deprecate most distinctly all thoughtless mixtures or frivolous choice of two medicines, which would be analogous to Allopathic polypharmacy. I must also once again particularly insist that such rightly chosen Homœopathic double remedies must only be given in the most highly potentized and attenuated doses."

The following foot-note occurs on page 267 of Lutze's "Organon:" "This is the paragraph intended by our Master for the fifth edition of the 'Organon,' but suppressed by the senselessness of others, which I had the good fortune to discover, and which I deem it my duty to give to the world in this place, after having already published a chapter on the double remedies in my 'Lehrbuch der Homoopathie.' Dr. Julius Aegidi, at that time physician in ordinary to the Princess Frederica of Prussia, in Dusseldorf, sent Hahnemann the report of two hundred and thirty-three cases of cures effected by double remedies, and the reply of this great thinker, dated Coethen, 15th of June, 1833, of which I possess the original, runs thus:

"'*Dear Friend and Colleague:* Do not think that I am capable of rejecting any good thing from prejudice, or because it might cause alterations in my doctrine. My sole desire is for truth,

---

* *Brit. Jour. Hom.*, Vol. xxiii., p. 413; also Lutze's "Organon."

and I believe yours is also. Hence I am delighted that such a happy idea has occurred to you, and that you have kept it within its necessary limits; that two medicinal substances (in smallest dose, or by olfaction) should be given together only in a case where both seem Homœopathically suitable, but each from a different side. Under such circumstances the procedure is so consonant with the requirements of our art that nothing can be urged against it; on the contrary, Homœopathy must be congratulated on your discovery. I myself will take the first opportunity of putting it in practice, and I have no doubt that von Bœnninghausen is completely of our opinion and acts accordingly. I think, too, that both remedies should be given together; just as we take *Sulphur* and *Calcarea* together when we cause our patients to take or smell *Hepar sulph.* or *Sulphur* and *Mercury* when they take or smell *Cinnabar*. Permit me, then, to give your discovery to the world in the fifth edition of the 'Organon,' which will soon be published. Until then, however, I beg you to keep all to yourself, and try to get Mr. Jahr, whom I greatly esteem, to do the like. At the same time I there protest and earnestly warn against all abuse of the practice by a frivolous choice of two medicines to be used in combination.

"'Yours sincerely,

"'SAMUEL HAHNEMANN.'"

Lutze continues: "After State Councillor Dr. von Bœnninghausen, whose name has been several times honorably mentioned in this book, and our Master himself had tested this practice and found it good, he (Hahnemann) wrote the following letter, the original of which I also possess, to Dr. Aegidi, dated 19th August, 1833: 'I have devoted a special paragraph in the fifth edition of the "Organon" to your discovery of the administration of double remedies. I sent the manuscript yesterday evening to Arnold and enjoined him to print it soon and put the steel engraving of my portrait as a frontispiece. The race for priority is anxiously pursued. Thirty years ago I was weak enough to contend for it.

"'But for a long time past my only wish is that the world should gain the best, the most useful truth, let it come from me or from any other.'

"The foregoing paragraph is sanctioned by these expressions of the now enlightened spirit. In the Congress of Homœopathic medical men which took place soon afterwards on the 10th of August, 1833, the Master brought this new discovery before his disciples, but in place of finding willing listeners, he encountered opposition. The narrow mindedness and ignorance of these men went so far as to compare this true Homœopathic discovery to the polypharmacy of Allopathy, and they drew such a dismal picture to the hoary Master of the harm he would do to his doctrine thereby, that he allowed himself to be persuaded to recall the paragraph he had already sent to the printer, which an eager disciple of not the purest sort undertook to do, and thus the world was for many years deprived of this important discovery."

Dr. Lutze continues with examples of this double remedy, and signs his name at the end. In an editorial in the *British Journal of Homœopathy*, of July, 1865, the author says that the letters printed by Lutze are no doubt genuine and thus explains the matter:

Dr. Aegidi proposed to Hahnemann to administer a mixture of two highly-potentized remedies each corresponding to different parts of the disease. In the potentized state the medicines thus mixed would be incapable of chemical reaction, but would each act separately in its own sphere. Dr. Bœnninghausen approved of the idea and Hahnemann was induced to present the matter to the meeting of the Central Society for 1833. Hahnemann was persuaded that this would probably lead to the polypharmacy of the old school, and he decided to exclude this doctrine from the new edition of the "Organon." Hahnemann in no manner sanctioned alternation after this time.

Jahr afterwards mentioned Aegidi's discovery, and Aegidi answered Jahr in an article published in the *Archives* for 1834. He disavowed this method in 1857.

Hahnemann recommended alternation of remedies in the first edition of the "Organon." Paragraph 145 of this edition reads:* "It is only in some cases of ancient chronic diseases which are liable to no remarkable alterations, which have certain fixed and permanent fundamental symptoms, that two almost equally appropriate Homœopathic remedies may be successfully employed in alternation."

He gives as a reason that the number of remedies at that time

---

* "Organon der rationellen Heilkunde," Dresden, 1810, p. 119. Dudgeon's "Lectures on Homœopathy," London, 1854, p. 474.

proven was not large enough to produce in every case the exact similimum. In the "Chronic Diseases" Hahnemann mentions certain cases in which he alternated remedies in intermittent fever.

But it is very certain that Hahnemann's ideas upon alternation were different from those held by certain of his followers. His were rather those of rotation.

Hahnemann, instead of recommending alternation in the fifth edition of the "Organon," says in paragraph 272: "In no case is it requisite to administer more than one single, simple medicinal substance at one time."

In a note he says: "Some Homœopathists have made the experiment in cases where they deemed one remedy Homœopathically suitable for one portion of the symptoms of a case of disease, and a second for another portion, of administering both remedies at the same or at almost the same time; but I earnestly deprecate such a hazardous experiment, which can never be necessary, though it may sometimes seem to be of use." Paragraphs 273, 274 also treat of this matter.

Whatever Hahnemann wrote to Lutze or to Aegidi, or in whatever degree his spirit of experimentation and fairness led him to discuss the plan of alternation, it is very certain that he was not enthusiastic in the matter, and at best considered it a makeshift for careful study.

An interesting article on alternation, by Dr. Aug. Korndœrfer, may be found in the Hahnemannian Monthly for February and April, 1874.

This so-called sixth edition of the "Organon," edited and published by Lutze, contains many alterations from the original text, and many important parts are also suppressed. It called forth the opposition of the whole German Homœopathic Press and the German Homœopathic Societies protested against such a liberty on the part of Dr. Lutze.

A long article appeared in the *Allgemeine hom. Zeitung*, Vol. lxx. (April 10, 1865), declaring the book to be spurious and apochryphal and utterly repudiating it. This is signed by Drs. Bolle, Hirschel, Meyer, Cl. Muller.

In 1857 Dr. Aegidi had repudiated, in the *Allgemeine Zeitung*, the practice of alternation, although in his "Lehrbuch," in 1860, Lutze quoted him in its favor.

But on the appearance of this "Organon" both Dr. Aegidi and Dr. Bœnninghausen denied Lutze's assertions, as follows:*

"EXPLANATION.—The protest of the honored representatives of the Homœopathic press, of Germany, against the alleged sixth edition of the "Organon of the Healing Art," published in the *Allg. hom. Zeitung* of April 10, Hahnemann's birthday, having embraced the mention of my name, yet having omitted to mention that I also participate in the conviction in behalf of which the signers of the protest contend, that, years ago, I loudly and publicly made known my disapproval of the administration of so-called double remedies, as an abuse and a mischievous proceeding, I find myself compelled to publish my explanation as it originally appeared in the *Allg. hom. Zeitung*, 54, 12 (May 18, 1857), and thence copied in the *Neue Zeitschrift fur Homoopathische Klinik*, 11, 12 (June 15, 1857). It was in the following language:

"The undersigned finds himself compelled to join his voice in the reproaches that have been made, particularly of late, against the Homœopathic administration of so-called double remedies so much the more, inasmuch as it is he who is charged with having taken the initiative in this mode of acting which is the subject of reprobation. Entirely agreeing with all the arguments adduced against it by competent persons and the refutation of which must be impossible, the undersigned is compelled to make known emphatically and publicly his decided disapproval of such an abuse of our excellent and most serviceable art, as has been lately recommended in an apparently systematic manner and as a rule; to the end, that persons may forbear to take his supposed authority, as a sanction of a mode of treatment which, even as he (Stapf's *Archives*, 1834, 14) thought he might recommend a modification of it for very rare and exceptional cases, is very far from being the abuse and mischief which it is now made and being made.

"I add to this that I thoroughly agree with the contents of the above-mentioned protest; and that, in my opinion, the practice therein rebuked is not dealt with even as severely as in the interests of our science it should have been.

"AEGIDI.

"Freienwald, April 12, 1865."

---

* *Am. Hom. Review*, N. Y., Vol. v., p. 562.

Dr. Bœnninghausen wrote to Dr. Carroll Dunham regarding this affair as follows:

"MUNSTER, March 25, 1865.

" To DR. CARROLL DUNHAM, NEW YORK.

"*My Very Dear Friend and Colleague:* I have just to day received your letter of the 2d instant. The passage which you quote concerning the 'combined doses containing two different remedies' imposes on me the duty of replying without a moment's delay.

"It is true that during the years 1832 and 1833, at the instance of Dr. Aegidi, I made some experiments with combined doses, that the results were sometimes surprising, and that I spoke of the circumstance to Hahnemann, who after some experiments made by himself had entertained for awhile the idea of alluding to the matter in the fifth edition of the 'Organon,' which he was preparing in 1833. But this novelty appeared too dangerous for the new method of cure, and it was I who induced Hahnemann to express his disapproval of it in the fifth edition of the "Organon," 1833, in the note to paragraph 272. Since this period neither Hahnemann nor myself have made further use of these combined doses. Dr. Aegidi was not long in abandoning this method, which resembles too closely the procedures of Allopathy, opening the way to a relapse from the precious law of simplicity, a method, too, which is becoming every day more entirely superfluous from the augmentation of our Materia Medica.

"If, consequently, in our day, a Homœopathician takes it into his head to act according to experiments made thirty years ago, in the infancy of our science, and subsequently rebuked by unanimous vote, he clearly walks backwards, like a crab, and shows that he has not kept up with nor followed the progress of science.

"Supposing that it may interest you to know the origin of the above-mentioned method, I add the following: There was about this time (1832 and 1833), at Cologne, an old physician named Dr. Stoll, himself a constant invalid and hypochondriac, who, distrusting the old medical doctrine, but having only a superficial smattering of Homœopathy, had conceived the idea of dividing the remedies into two classes, the one of which should act upon the body and the other on the soul. He thought that these two kinds of medicine should be combined in a prescription in order to supplement each other.

"His method making some noise in Cologne, and Dr. Aegidi, then at Dusseldorf, having in vain endeavored to discover the essential secret of this novelty, the latter induced me to endeavor to find it out. I succeeded in doing so. Although the idea of Dr. Stoll was utterly devoid of foundation, it nevertheless induced us to make experiments in another way; namely, that above recited, but which, as I said before, was utterly rejected long, long ago. "Yours very sincerely,

"C. VON BŒNNINGHAUSEN."

The Homœopathic Medical College of Pennsylvania held a meeting on May 20, 1865, and entered a solemn protest against Lutze's book, which was declared "to be mutilated and perverted."

The Homœopathic profession in Europe and America refused to have anything to do with Lutze's edition of Hahnemann's "Organon."

CHAPTER LXXXIX.

THE RIVAL "ORGANONS" CONTINUED.

Not long after this an advertisement appeared in the German journals of a forthcoming sixth edition of the "Organon," to be edited by Dr. Suss-Hahnemann, the grandson of the Master. The preface was printed. It was intended to use the fourth edition of the "Organon," instead of the fifth, in the preparation of this book. The fourth edition contains many statements from Old School physicians regarding the favorable action of medicines Homœopathically, which are omitted in the fifth edition.

As soon as Dr. Suss-Hahnemann announced this edition Madame Hahnemann wrote the following letter to his publishers:

"PARIS, 23d April, 1865.

"MESSRS. REICHARDT AND ZANDER.

"*Gentlemen:* I perceive from No. 14 of the *Allgemeine hom. Zeitung*, of 3d April, that your firm is about to publish a new edition of Hahnemann's 'Organon,' edited by Dr. Suss, of London. I beg to inform you that the exclusive right to publish the said work belongs solely to me; and as I possess the manuscript sixth edition of the 'Organon,' written by my late husband's own hand, Dr. Suss's work can have no claim whatever to be considered genuine. You, as booksellers, are no doubt aware of the stringent laws of Germany protecting the copyright of literary works, and therefore this notice I hope will be sufficient to warn you against the sale of Dr. Suss's intended edition of the said work.

"I remain, gentlemen,

"Truly yours,

"MELANIE HAHNEMANN."

Madame Hahnemann also sent the following letter to the *Allgemeine hom. Zeitung* of May 1st:

"PARIS, 21st April, 1865.

"TO THE EDITOR OF THE *Allgemeine hom. Zeitung*.

"*Respected Sir:* To my great astonishment I perceive in No. 14 of the *Allg. hom. Zeit.*, for April 3d, that Dr. Lutze and Dr. Suss, of London, announce the publication of a sixth, considerably improved and enlarged edition of Hahnemann's 'Organon.' I alone have the right to publish the sixth edition of the 'Organon;' I alone possess the manuscript in my late husband's own handwriting of this important work; to me alone were communicated all the improvements which the author made in the 'Organon.' Dr. Lutze never saw Hahnemann, nor was he in any way connected with him.

"Dr. Suss, of London, saw Hahnemann twice only; the first time when a child of six years of age, and afterwards, when a student in Leipsic, the day before the death of my husband; it is, therefore, impossible he can have obtained from him anything new relating to Homœopathy.

"Now that it is pretended that something new is known, when it is intended to make a sort of romance of our holy 'Organon,' now is the time to publish the genuine and real 'Organon,' and I shall now send it to press. Just as no one dares to improve, take away from, or add to the Holy Gospel or the other Holy Scriptures, so no one should dare to make any alterations in the 'Organon,' the codex of human health; it must remain as its author created it, and it should only appear in its pure, unadulterated truth and genuineness.

"I urgently beg of you to allow this letter to appear without any alterations in the next number of the *Allg. Zeitung*.

"Your devotion to the true maxims of our beneficent doctrine and your sense of justice will induce you to grant me this favor, for which I thank you beforehand in my own name and in that of the true disciples of Hahnemann.

"Accept, esteemed doctor, the assurances of my most distinguished consideration.

"M. HAHNEMANN.

"*54 Faubourg St. Honore.*"

In reply to this letter Dr. Suss-Hahnemann sent to the editor of the *British Journal of Homœopathy* the following:

"1 WEST ST., FINSBURY CIRCUS, LONDON.

"TO THE EDITORS OF THE *British Journal of Homœopathy*.

"*Gentlemen :* You are no doubt aware that, in consequence of my grandfather's German works having gone completely out of print, I have considered it my duty, due alike to the memory of my departed great ancestor as to the cause of Homœopathy, to commence a reissue of his literary productions; the 'Organon,' as the most important work, has been taken in hand first, and my publishers in Berlin have announced its publication to be shortly completed.

"Madame Hahnemann seems, however, to have taken great umbrage at my proceedings; not only has she threatened to intimidate my publishers by empty threats of legal prosecutions, but she has also published herself, in the *Allgemeine hom. Zeitung* of May 1st, an article by which she unmistakably wishes to damage and lower my publication in the estimation of my medical brethren. If the facts stated by her had been correct, I would have remained most willingly silent, as I believe my own age or personal acquaintance with my late grandfather can not in the least deteriorate the value of the 'Organon,' which I have had faithfully reprinted from one of the previous editions, which was considered by Hahnemann himself the most complete (according to my late mother's assertion).

"In common fairness Madame Hahnemann should have waited until the work had been published, when it would have been time to criticise its correctness. My aunt, Hahnemann's youngest daughter, is still alive and in possession of quite as valuable manuscripts as Madame Hahnemann alleges she herself possesses, and being with her on the most affectionate terms of relationship, I have always received her willing and cordial assistance in all my literary pursuits.

"Madame Hahnemann seems particularly anxious to make it known amongst the Homœopathic profession that I saw my grandfather but twice in all my life, once when six years old and the second time on the eve of his death, strongly insisting therefrom that my edition of the 'Organon' ought not to be relied upon.

"Madame Hahnemann having had little communication with the family of her late husband, I do not expect her to know much about my humble self, but if she wishes to inform the world of my young days, I might expect her to be truthful and correct in her statements. I was brought up and educated by my late grandfather up to Mademoiselle d'Hervilly's sudden appearance in Coethen, when I was sent to Halle to school, and at the time of Madame Hahnemann's departure with my grandfather to Paris I was just eight years old; I was also present at my grandfather's sorrowful leave-taking in Halle from the members of his family who had accompanied him from Coethen to that place.

"Unfortunately, I was only present at the very last dying moments of my grandfather, not even on the eve of his death, although my late mother and I had arrived in Paris already a whole week previous to this sad event taking place; a circumstance Madame Hahnemann seems to have forgotten, as she does not mention it in her article. In spite of our most earnest entreaties, in spite of Hahnemann's own wish to see once more his favorite daughter, Madame Hahnemann resolutely and sternly refused us an interview with our dying parent, when he would have been still able to speak to us and to bless us. Now, in her eagerness, to damage any forthcoming edition of Hahnemann's works, Madame Hahnemann has betrayed a valuable secret by confessing to possess the manuscript sixth edition of the 'Organon.' 'Out of evil cometh good.' I feel highly gratified that I have thus indirectly rendered a service to the cause of Homœopathy; for Madame Hahnemann declares herself, after twenty-two years silence, ready to publish this manuscript. I hope she will soon do it; better late than never, although this neglect amounts almost to contempt of the whole Homœopathic medical profession.

"I am, gentlemen, your obedient servant,

"L. SUSS-HAHNEMANN.

"*May 30, 1865.*"

During the summer of 1865 the Faculty of the Homœopathic Medical College of Pennsylvania wrote to Madame Hahnemann stating that the previous English and American editions of the "Organon" were full of errors, and in order that a reliable edition might be obtained they offered to literally translate the manuscript of a sixth edition that was in her possession. When it is remembered that Drs. Hering, Raue and Lippe were at that time members of this Faculty, it can readily be understood that Madame Hahnemann could have no just reason for refusing these gentlemen the manuscript of the "Organon," supposed to have been left by Hahnemann.

Madame Hahnemann sent the following letter in reply:*

"C. HERING, M. D.

"*My Dear and Excellent Doctor and Friend:* I have received the letter which you and the physicians, who signed it, have collectively addressed to me concerning the literal translation of the 'Organon' into the English language, of which the original MS. is in my possession.

"I am very glad you will make this translation, because then I shall be certain it will be done with fidelity and perfection.

"It is certainly not from any indifference that I have delayed so long to say to you how much I approve of your proposition; this delay was caused by the desire that I might be able to announce the beginning of the printing of this book, of which I would immediately have sent you a copy.

"A first copy, though made in my house and from the MS. proved so faulty and incorrect that it was impossible to make any use of it.

"Like you, I would not permit that a single word of the sacred text should be changed. I have consequently been obliged to have a new copy made, and this time *in my presence*

Hahnemannian Monthly, Vol. i., p. 171.

and under my eyes. This copy is now making at such hours as I can superintend it; this will delay the finishing of it a little. As soon as it is completed and the printing commenced, I will send you the sheets as they are printed. They will be forwarded to you through Mr. Bigelow, my friend and your Ambassador at Paris. *   *   *   *   *   *   *

"I regret very much that you have not received my previous letters, which contained communications respecting some unpublished medicines, which would have interested you.

"Be kind enough to offer my compliments to the physicians who joined you in writing to me, and say to them that I honor and esteem them as faithful disciples who are intent to promulgate the true doctrine of the Master as he created and perfected it.

"Accept the expression of my admiration for your labors, and my best wishes for your health and happiness.

"M. HAHNEMANN.

"*Paris, 54 Faubourg St. Honore.*"

CHAPTER XC.

THE "ORGANON" CONTINUED—DR. BAYES'S OFFER FOR THE MSS.—CORRESPONDENCE BETWEEN MADAME HAHNEMANN AND DR. T. P. WILSON.

But the expected sheets of the "Organon" did not appear. Neither did Dr. Suss-Hahnemann publish his advertised edition.

Mention was occasionally made to visitors by Madame Hahnemann of the fact that the sixth edition was in her possession. And then came the Franco-German war, and in it, so she said, Madame Hahnemann lost her fortune.

In 1877, Dr. Bayes, in behalf of the London School of Homœopathy, wrote to Madame Hahnemann, asking if she would intrust some or all of the valuable records of Hahnemann, in her possession, to the London School for publication.* She replied to him that she had the sixth edition of the "Organon" finally corrected, and was willing to superintend its publication if the Homœopathic profession of England would raise for her a sum

* *Brit. Jour. Hom.*, Vol. xxxvi., p. 302.

the interest of which would be equivalent to the income she derived from her practice. This the British Homœopaths naturally thought rather exorbitant.

*M. Sanches, who took up the matter in behalf of Madame Hahnemann, said that the publication was delayed because Hahnemann suggested to her that delay might be wise until time should settle men's minds, and that she should fix her own time in the future. In answer to this a letter written to Dr. Hirschfeld by Hahnemann in March, 1843, is quoted: "I have resolved to retire from practice before I am forced to do so by the weakness of old age, and by God's grace I will bring out the sixth edition of my 'Organon,' which will be more complete than the others."

In 1877 Madame Hahnemann addressed the following letter to Dr. T. P. Wilson, the editor of the *Medical Advance:*†

"104 FAUBOURG ST. HONORE, PARIS,
"November 9, 1877.

"*M. le Docteur Wilson:* I regret that I did not receive your letter sooner. It came while I was away from Paris, which is but seldom. You ask me about the sixth edition of the 'Organon.' I wish to say that I have in my possession important unpublished papers written by my beloved husband, and confided to my care before his death. There is in them much that is new and of great value to the medical world, and no one but myself can arrange them in proper shape, for they were given me with full explanations by the great Founder of Homœopathy himself. What a grand volume these would make! What a large number of copies could be sold to the physicians of America, for in your country the doctrines of Homœopathy have taken strong and wide hold. Even the Allopathic school would seek it.

"I have all of Hahnemann's correspondence filed by his own hand and marked by notes. You see, my dear doctor, it will be a great work to get this mass of material out in the order Hahnemann desired. I alone can do it. Drs. Lippe and Hering, of Philadelphia, are informed of my desire. They know I lost all my property in the Franco Prussian war, and that I now have to make my living by the practice of medicine. Such being the fact, I have no time to attend to this great work.

* *Brit. Jour. Hom.*, Vol. xxxvii., p. 101-4.
† Cincinnati *Med. Advance*, Vol. v., pp. 404, 545.

"I do not wish to make any money out of the writings of Hahnemann. Those I have are my property, but I will freely give them to his followers and friends if I can have the opportunity. What I desire is assistance from the Homœopathic physicians of America. Do you not think they would subscribe for the book and remit to me so much in advance as would enable me to live without practicing my profession until I can get out the work? I have the energy and ability to do it, if only I can have the time. It would be a proud gift to lay in the hands of the profession, and no doctor but would be glad to see it in the hands of his patients. This matter was under advisement at the time the late Dr. Carroll Dunham was arranging the World's Homœopathic Convention, and but for his lamented death this project would now be already consummated. Dr. Dunham was greatly desirous to have these papers brought out. Now, my dear doctor, you have sufficient authority to undertake this matter of procuring subscribers. I know you cannot fail. America is a land of great undertakings. It is not like Europe, where everyone sticks to the old ways. Thanks to your liberty and the energy of your people who have so generously accepted the teachings of Hahnemann!

"I want the subscriptions taken in Hahnemann's name, and I am glad you appreciate the importance of the task. I am, doctor, with sentiments of high regard and fraternal consideration,   "Yours,

"M. HAHNEMANN."

The April number of the *Advance* contained the following letter:

"104 FAUBOURG ST. HONORE, PARIS,
"March 4, (1878).

"*M. le Docteur Wilson:* Upon referring to my letter written to you and published in your January number, I find that I am not correctly represented in the following phrase:

"Do you not think they would subscribe for the book and remit to me so much in advance as would enable me to live without practicing my profession until I can get out the work?

"What I desire is a subscription, which once organized will produce a fund sufficiently large to enable me to give my entire time to the works of Hahnemann, and obviate the necessity of my attempting to recover my practice, which, in the nature of things, I must lose while engaged in this work. I have never yet sold one of Hahnemann's works; I have only used them in order to meet my necessities. I ask only for a subscription from the doctors and their patients. Such a subscription, if properly managed, would in a little time produce a capital of considerable size without causing the doctors to give more than they wished. It is the surest means, the most delicate manner and the most honorable by which to obtain money in an affair of this kind. I wish to begin this work as soon as possible. In the course of a few months I will be able to give you the 'Organon' for printing. After that I will proceed to the other works which are equally of great importance. Present my thanks to the noble doctor who proffered aid in the sum of one hundred dollars (Breyfogle). I thank you all in the name of Hahnemann.

" With great esteem and consideration, I remain yours, dear doctor,

"M. HAHNEMANN."

Nothing resulted, although there was some further correspondence.

CHAPTER XCI.

DEATH OF MADAME HAHNEMANN—MADAME BŒNNINGHAUSEN
TO DR. T. P. WILSON—VISIT OF DR. J. A. CAMPBELL TO
MADAME BŒNNINGHAUSEN—LETTERS TO DR.
CAMPBELL.

Madame Hahnemann died of bronchial catarrh, like her husband, on May 27, 1878. The following editorial appeared in the *Medical Advance :**

" We are pained to announce the death of this distinguished lady, the wife of Dr. Samuel Hahnemann. She died, as will be seen, in Paris, on the 27th of last May. She was seventy-eight years old. Our readers are aware that since the death of Hahnemann, now some thirty years ago, Madame Hahnemann has been in possession of a large amount of unpublished manuscript, the work of her husband. From causes not worth while to mention here, they have been withheld from the profession. Negotia-

---

* Cincinnati *Med. Advance*, Vol. vi., p. 129.

tious have of late been pending for the purchase of the manuscripts with a view to their publication. In this work the medical profession of America has shown a lively interest. As will be seen by the subjoined letter there is hope that the scheme may be yet consummated. The following has just come to hand:

"'104 FAUBOURG ST. HONORE, PARIS, FRANCE,

"'June 5, 1878.

"'*M. le Docteur Wilson :* I announce to you the sad loss I have sustained in the death of my beloved mother, Madame Samuel Hahnemann. On the 27th of May she succumbed to a pulmonary catarrh from which she had suffered many years. I am her adopted daughter, and have had charge of her correspondence with you in reference to the unpublished manuscripts of Hahnemann, and I am quite disposed to complete the plan already proposed by you and accepted by her. It is now several months since she made me commence, under her supervision, the first copy in German of the sixth edition of the 'Organon.' I have already advanced a long way with the work, and happily I know her wishes exactly in regard to it.

"'Receive, Monsieur Doctor, my highest esteem,

"'S. BŒNNINGHAUSEN HAHNEMANN.'

"It will be remembered from our former correspondence published in the *Advance* that Madame Hahnemann proposed to make a gift of all Hahnemann's unpublished works 'to the Homœopathic physicians of America as a token of her appreciation of the regard they have always had for her distinguished husband.'

"In return for this it was proposed to raise a fund sufficiently large for its interest to support the donor during the balance of her life. Already considerable money had been subscribed, and but for the death of Madame Hahnemann the matter would have been placed in the hands of the American Institute of Homœopathy, and probably the plan completed under its direction. In this we have now been frustrated, and some negotiations must be entered upon to be reported on at some subsequent time.

"If Madame B.-Hahnemann proves to be what her letters indicate, we will have no special trouble in becoming possessed of the works in question. We solicit suggestions and advice upon the matter from our readers.—T. P. WILSON, M. D."

This was published in the July number of the *Advance*, and in the August number the following letter from Dr. J. A. Campbell may be found:

"*Editor Medical Advance:* When I left America bearing your letters of introduction to Madame Hahnemann, with authority to confer with her in reference to the unpublished manuscripts of her illustrious husband, I looked forward with much interest to the occasion which would take me into the personal presence of the one nearest the great founder of our system of practice; one almost to be venerated by reason of association; one who would be full of personal reminiscences, and one who would be surrounded on all sides by things which were with and were a part of Hahnemann's everyday life. But as you are probably already informed, Madame Hahnemann is now peacefully at rest by the side of her husband in the cemetery of Montmartre.

"I have had two interesting interviews with Madame Bœnninghausen, the adopted daughter of Madame Hahnemann and the wife of Dr. Carl Bœnninghausen. I know it will be of some interest to give a brief account of some of the facts thus obtained.

"Madame Hahnemann had suffered more or less for about two years with catarrh of the lungs (thus it was given me). No particular attention was given it, as it was not regarded as very serious. About eight days before she died it became much aggravated and she rapidly sank, and on the twenty-seventh of May died at the advanced age of seventy-eight.

"I sat by the side of Madame Bœnninghausen at the little table which Madame Hahnemann had just left as it were. Before me stood pictures in miniature of her, taken when young and fair. By its side one of Hahnemann.

"In the corner of the room stood the bed in which Madame Hahnemann had so recently died. And as one by one the relics of Hahnemann and his former life were placed before me it was to me, indeed, as if I felt his very presence. Here is a full, curly lock of his hair, once pure and white, but now golden with age; I could almost be superstitious and believe it an emblematic symbol by fate ordained—silver turned to precious gold. There was his pocket handkerchief, collar and neckerchief, the last worn by him and just as he left them.

"On one side was a large bundle of his correspondence from

patients, with marginal notes of the remedies prescribed. Before me hung a magnificent oil portrait of Hahnemann, painted when he was about sixty. In the corner stood a grand bust in marble (by David), the original of the many fine plaster casts. In fact, everything about me was Hahnemann and of Hahnemann.

"As the subject of Hahnemann's manuscripts and the sixth edition of the 'Organon' has been taken hold of with so much interest in America, a few facts on this topic will be in place here. Madame Bœnninghausen received me very cordially and has given me the fullest information possible upon the subject.

"She showed me an old edition of the 'Organon,' full of marginal notes, interlineations and additions made by Hahnemann. Madame B. says this has never been published. And this is to be the sixth edition promised. About three months before Madame Hahnemann's death Madame Bœnninghausen commenced to copy all of this into an intelligible form under the immediate supervision and direction of Madame Hahnemann herself.

"The death of the latter has necessarily caused a temporary suspension of the work, but Madame B. informs me that she will have it all completed in about three months. It is all in German, and rather difficult to decipher and understand unless previously instructed.

"This Madame B. claims to have been, and she informs me that she is following the general instructions given Madame Hahnemann by Hahnemann himself, and that she will faithfully and accurately transcribe it, and when finished will send it in this form to America for translation and publication.

"The other manuscript spoken of consists of a large number of letters from patients to Hahnemann, describing their symptoms, while on their margins are notes by Hahnemann of the remedies given, showing how he treated cases and what he gave. These letters make a bundle weighing about thirty pounds.

"Madame B. informs me that she has had many applications from Germany and from France by parties very desirous of obtaining these papers for publication, but she says that to America they must go. Such was Madame Hahnemann's desire, which she seconds with all her heart. She says that it is to America that Homœopathy must look for its best support and its proper promulgation, and that America is the nation for great enterprise and action. She further says that she intends to leave by will, to some properly constituted representative body in America, Hahnemann's original manuscript, his magnificent bust, and the grand portrait spoken of, and other mementoes connected with our great leader and his life history while here.

"And now how will America respond? How will she show that she is worthy of this distinction, as above all other nations the champion of the great cause? This is the question to be answed by the profession at large.

"A few words as to Madame Bœnninghausen. Madame Hahnemann was thirty-five years old when she married Hahnemann; just before he died, by his special request, Madame H. adopted Madame Bœnninghausen, then about five years of age. She is now the wife of Dr. Carl Bœnninghausen.*

"They all lived here together in Paris until the breaking out of the Franco-German war; they then went to Westphalia, where Dr. B. is at present attending to a large practice, going backwards and forwards from time to time. Madame B. was the constant companion of Madame Hahnemann and her main reliance, and thus she ought certainly better than any one else to understand the task before her.

"Fraternally yours,

"JAMES A. CAMPBELL, M. D.

"*Paris, June 22, 1878.*"

Dr. James A. Campbell, writing to the compiler of this book in 1893, says of this visit:

"*Dear Doctor:*

"Yours of August, 1893, in reference to my letter from Paris to Dr. Wilson in 1878 received. What the final disposition of the literary and other relics of Hahnemann was I am unable to say. As the letter tells, I went over, hoping to arrange with Madame Hahnemann in reference to the publication of the sixth edition of the 'Organon.' I arrived there just a few weeks after her death, and had all my dealings with Madame Bœnninghausen, the adopted daughter.

"Madame Hahnemann was, as you know, a *business woman*,

---

* The eldest son of Baron von Bœnninghausen.

close and grasping. She thought that great and rich America could and would *pay*, and pay well for this fifth edition ' Organon' with marginal notes all through, made by Hahnemann himself, and this was to be the sixth edition.

"She wanted $50,000. Madame Bœnninghausen also saw visions of wealth from the same source, but she put the price at $25,000.

"I assured her that such a proposition would never be entertained by the American Institute of Homœopathy, as it was entirely impossible to devote that amount for the purpose. I told her that without question she would be allowed to have *all* profits arising from the sale of the book, but beyond that we could not go.

"She told me it was her intention to give to the American Institute either the fine marble bust spoken of or the portrait of splendid proportions which hung in the same room. She even offered me Hahnemann's watch to take to the Institute, but I saw it was in a moment of hysterical impulse, and I refused to take it. She gave me several cameo heads of Hahnemann, suitable for a ring or scarf pin, to be presented to several well-known Homœopathists in America; one to Lippe, one to Helmuth, etc. I have one myself, also a ring set with the same cameo."

In a letter dated September 19, 1893, Dr. Campbell says:

"After my return, in 1878, I had some correspondence with Madame Bœnninghausen on the subject. Five of these letters I inclose. You may find something of interest in them. You will see that she was quite diplomatic in reference to the price for her wares, with me it was $25,000 that she named as the price. You will find that the part of her letters written in German are more satisfactory in respect to information. My conferences with her were in German, as that is her native tongue.

"JAMES A. CAMPBELL."

CHAPTER XCII.

LETTERS FROM MADAME BŒNNINGHAUSEN—MEETING OF HOMŒOPATHIC PHYSICIANS.

Space forbids publishing all the five letters mentioned. Most of them are written both in German and English in the same letter.

The first letter from Madame Bœnninghausen is as follows:

"PARIS, August 5, 1879.
."278 Faubourg. St. Germain.

"Dear Doctor:

"As I had the pleasure last year to make your personal acquaintance in Paris, and having been imbued with your great love and enthusiasm for our beautiful and beneficial Homœopathy, I believe I can give you a great pleasure to-day in making haste to announce that a copy of the sixth edition of the 'Organon' is now entirely finished and in such shape as to be given to the printer. At the same time knowing the friendly relations which you have with Dr. Wilson, of Cincinnati, I turn to you to express my astonishment at not having yet received an answer from him to my last letter, in which I begged him to make counter propositions relative or about the literary remains of Hahnemann, inasmuch as he did not accept my propositions, which are the same as were those of my mother. It is very sad that so much time is wasted, and yet it would be such an easy matter to arrange to give to the world this indispensable work, and that in the shortest possible time; it is the more sad if you bear in mind that it is but a question of money which stands in the way to the publishing of Hahnemann's writings. Of just as much importance in another direction are the series of books containing Hahnemann's clinical cases, which fill sixty large volumes, beginning with the nativity of Homœopathy and ending with the death of the great Master.

"The 'Organon' and the clinical cases supplement each other; in the 'Organon' Hahnemann shows the theory of his new doctrine, in the clinical cases he shows the practical appli-

cation at the sick bed, and how glorious the theory and practice
accord is documented in a telling manner in these works, and
for such work America cannot make any financial sacrifices, this
America which has done so much for science and especially for
Homœopathy, whose physicians owe their fortune almost altogether to this beautiful law of cure. If every Homœopathic
physician of America and their patients were to contribute only
a few dollars the amount necessary to secure these important
writings could easily be raised.   How happy would I be if my
financial condition was such as to permit me to give you all these
precious manuscripts of Hahnemann as a present; but, alas, you
have already been made acquainted, and that through my beloved mother herself, we lost our whole fortune in the war of
1871. Dr. Wilson told me at the time that he could, were my
mother yet amongst the living, easily raise the necessary funds
by subscription. Why should that not be possible after her
death? the value of the writings surely is the same and has not
been diminished by one jot. I entreat you, therefore, highly
honored doctor, to communicate with your colleague, Dr. Wilson,
as to the acquisition of Hahnemann's writings, and to let me
know the result of your endeavors by return mail.

"I think I have mentioned already to you that I have all
letters which were written by the patients to Hahnemann, 'many
thousands of letters' in my possession. In addition to these
letters Hahnemann not only mentioned a remedy which he prescribed in that given case with his own hand, but he added
many remarks.

"With high esteem, I am,
"Very sincerely yours,
"S. BŒNNINGHAUSEN HAHNEMANN.

The next letter is in both English and German.
"PARIS, 10th November, 1879.
"*My Dear Doctor:*
"I found your last and very kind letter on my return from a
short trip to Germany and I thank you very much for the inter-
est and friendship you express.

"Soon after the reception of your letter our mutual friend, Dr.
Wilson, wrote and told me that it will be his happiness at the next
session of the American Institute of Homœopathy, in his inaugu-

ral address as president, to lay before them the whole subject and recommend the appointment of a committee to take charge in the matter. He is a powerful man and in a position to gain the attention of all the Homœopathic physicians in his country, and if you'll aid me also with your influence, dear doctor, the success is sure beforehand.

"I thank you for the congratulation at the completion of the work; it is very desirable that it shall be published as soon as possible.

"I have sent Dr. Wilson my answers in reference to the subjects that we discussed in Paris, and I hope he will understand it because I wrote in French. * * * With assurances of esteem and sincere friendship,

"I remain, dear sir,

"Yours truly,

"S. BŒNNINGHAUSEN HAHNEMANN."

"PARIS, 23rd January, 1880.

"*My Dear Doctor:* I write to you again knowing with what skill and love you devoted yourself to the early publication of the writings of Hahnemann.

"Our mutual friend, Dr. Wilson, wrote to me about two months ago asking for permission to have an attorney examine Hahnemann's papers, in his name. He also would like to know the conditions under which I would deliver these to him. I immediately answered Dr. Wilson that I was quite willing to entertain his proposition as to the examination of the papers, as he decided, with the conditions. They are the same which I told you, my dear doctor, at your last visit, at your request. I am still without an answer to this letter and am afraid that the same may have been lost in transit. Owing to this delay I am compelled to make a journey to Germany in short time, but which journey I do not want to undertake until I am advised at about what time this attorney is to make the examination of Hahnemann's writings and will call on me to that effect, for as a matter of course I would have to be in Paris when he arrives, for without me he could do nothing. I entreat you, therefore, my dear doctor, to write for me to your friend, Dr. Wilson, and to find out the cause of his silence; would you do me that favor? and now a question honored doctor: I recollect that you told me, in answer to my question when you would come to Paris again, that you would do so in two or three years, and I recollect this answer with a great deal of pleasure, and I beg you to tell me whether you can hold out a hope that possibly I should have the pleasure of seeing you again already this year; I can assure you it would afford me great gratification to see you again.

"Hoping that you and your esteemed family are in the best of health, I beg to assure you, my dear doctor, of my high esteem and friendship.   I am,

"Very sincerely yours,

"S. BŒNNINGHAUSEN HAHNEMANN."

Dr. T. P. Wilson in his address as President of the American Institute of Homœopathy at the meeting held in Milwaukee, in 1880, kept his promise to Madame Bœnninghausen, and referred to the matter as follows:*   "It is well known to most of you that but a small part of the writings of Samuel Hahnemann has been given to the world.   His 'Materia Medica Pura,' his 'Chronic Diseases,' his 'Lesser Writings,' and, above all, his 'Organon of the Art of Healing' have long been the classics of our literature. I am credibly informed that a large amount of unpublished manuscript is yet in the hands of his heirs.   I have in my possession a pretty full catalogue of what those writings comprise. It has been thought desirable by many that these should be given to the world.   I am heartily of that opinion.   I would like to place in the hands of a committee such documents as have come into my possession in reference to this matter, and to have that committee report upon the subject at an early date."

Nothing more seems to have been done about the matter. The records of the Institute show the appointment of no committee.

Not long afterwards Dr. H. N. Guernsey went to Europe and visited Madame Bœnninghausen.   On his return a meeting was held at the house of Dr. Hering, in Philadelphia.

This meeting resulted in the following circular:

"At a meeting of Homœopathic physicians, held at the house of Dr. Hering, June 9th, 1880, for the purpose of procuring and publishing the MSS. of Hahnemann, Dr. H. N. Guernsey made the following report:

* Trans. Am. Inst. of Homœopathy, 1880, p. 32.

"Having just returned from Europe, where I made the acquaintance of Madame Bœnninghausen, Hahnemann's adopted daughter, the present possessor of the MSS., etc., and also of Peter Stuart, Esq., of Liverpool, a wealthy ship owner and an enthusiastic Homœopath, who has the entire confidence of Madame Bœnninghausen, I am able to make the following statement, viz.: The MSS. consist of:

"(1). The sixth edition of Hahnemann's 'Organon,' *in his own handwriting;* together with a copy thereof by the late Madame Hahnemann; this sixth edition contains many improvements which never have been published.

"(2). His case-books (nearly fifty in number), containing the records of his practice from the beginning of Homœopathy until his death.

"(3). His correspondence with his patients (weighing nearly sixty pounds).

"(4). His Repertorium, consisting of four volumes, containing an aggregate of 4,239 pages, fifty-two lines to the page.

"(5). A large number of letters from Drs. Stapf and Gross to Hahnemann.

"(6). Miscellaneous writings.

"(7). A bust of Hahnemann, with its crown of gold, sculptured by the celebrated David.

"Madame Bœnninghausen is exceedingly desirous that these precious writings should be published in America; circumstances, however, compel her to fix a price on them, and it has been arranged that for the sum of $10,000 and a royalty she will part with them.

"Mr. Stuart (with whom Dr. Berridge, of England, has been intimately acquainted for some years) proposes to send one of his sons to Paris as soon as the money is raised, and then and there receive in exchange the MSS., etc., and at once ship them to the United States.

"After the reading of this report, the meeting resolved itself into an organization for the furtherance of these ends, and the following physicians were appointed a committee with power to add to their number:

Edward Bayard, M. D., of New York.

E. W. Berridge, M. D., London, England, *Foreign Secretary*.

H. N. Guernsey, M. D., Philadelphia, *President*.

Constantine Hering, M. D., Philadelphia.

J. K. Lee, M. D., Philadelphia, *Vice-President.*

Ad. Lippe, M. D., Philadelphia, *Treasurer.*

Thos. Moore, M. D., Philadelphia, *Secretary.*

Thos. Skinner, M. D., Liverpool, England.

W. P. Wesselhoeft, M. D., Boston, Mass.

David Wilson, M. D., London, England.

"The importance of these works to all Homœopathic physicians cannot be overestimated. It now only remains for them to subscribe and collect the required amount, and so raise a worthy monument to that illustrious healer to whom they are indebted not only for the very reputation they possess, but also for health and perhaps life itself.

"All donations are to be sent to the Treasurer, Ad. Lippe, M. D., 1204 Walnut Street, Philadelphia, Penna., who will furnish acknowledgment for the same.

"The *immediate* attention of all the adherents of Homœopathy, whether lay or medical, is earnestly requested, as unless the sum of fifteen thousand dollars (being the estimated cost with the expenses of printing, etc.) is raised within a year the project will have to be abandoned, and all funds collected will be returned to the donors.

"H. N. GUERNSEY, M. D., *President.*

"THOMAS MOORE, M. D., *Secretary.*"

There were present at this meeting Drs. Constantine Hering, Henry N. Guernsey, Ad. Lippe, C. B. Knerr, J. K. Lee, Thos. Moore, Joseph C. Guernsey.

While it was the desire of all present that these valuable documents should be given to the Homœopathic profession, yet the sum demanded seemed very exorbitant. Some money was subscribed, but the matter was dropped.

It would seem that the willingness both of Madame Hahnemann and of her adopted daughter and heir to give to the Homœopathic profession of America the literary treasures left by Hahnemann depended greatly upon the amount of remuneration that would accrue to themselves.

Nothing was done after this by the profession in the United States. No action has since been taken in Europe. Madame Bœnninghausen at present (1894) resides at Munster, Germany,

and so far as is known to the compiler of this book still has
Hahnemann's unpublished papers in her possession and is likely
to keep them. In a letter lately received from a prominent
Homœopathic physician in Germany, he says: "This lady for
some reason is decidedly unkind to every suggestion concerning
her stepfather Hahnemann."

The truth about this so much talked of "sixth edition" is
that it is simply the fifth edition annotated by Hahnemann. He
never wrote a new edition after the fifth. Madame Hahnemann
must, at the time she was promising so much to the profession,
have known how impossible it was of fulfillment. When Dr.
Campbell visited Madame Bœnninghausen, after the death of
Madame Hahnemann, the truth was discovered.

However much Madame Hahnemann may have wished to do
for the benefit of the followers of her husband, it is quite within
the bounds of truth to say that she did not do it.

HAHNEMANN'S FAMILY.*

WIVES.

1. JOHANNA HENRIETTA LEOPOLDINE KUCHLER, daughter of Godfried Henry Kuchler, step-daughter of the apothecary Haseler, born June 7, 1762; married at Dessau, December 1, 1782; died at Coethen, March 31, 1830. Eleven children.

2. MELANIE D'HERVILLY, daughter of a painter of Savoy. He afterwards became blind and destitute, and Hahnemann cared for him. Adopted daughter of (the late Minister of Justice and President of the Executive Directory of the French Republic in the time of the Eighteenth Brumaire, 1799,) Louis Jerome Gohier. (M. Gohier died in 1830.) Born in 1800; married at Coethen, January 28, 1835; died at Paris, May 27, 1878. No children.

CHILDREN.
(All by first wife.)

1. HENRIETTE, born at Gommern in 1783; married Pastor Forster; lived in Dresdorf, near Sangerhausen, in the Thuringen Hartz Mountains. Had children: Louis, merchant; Robert, farmer; Angeline, who married Herr Stollberg; Adelheid, unmarried.

2. FRIEDRICH, born at Dresden, November 30, 1786; married in 1812; had but one child, a daughter, who married Rector Hohlfeld, of Dresden. Died about 1829.

3. WILHELMINE, born at Dresden about 1788; married Music Director Richter, of Gera; died about 1818; had one son, Hermann Friedrich Sigismund, who died at Coethen, May 13, 1866.

4. AMALIE, married Dr. Leopold Suss, by whom she had one son, Leopold Suss, who afterwards took the name Suss-Hahnemann, and who is now (1895) a Homœopathic physician in London. Married for second husband, Herr Liebe; lived in Paris and London; died in Coethen, December 7, 1857.†

---

*"Ein biographisches, Denkmal," p. 122, and Albrecht's "Leben und Wirken," p. 107.

† *All. hom. Zeitung*, Vol. lv, p. 144. (December 14, 1857.)

5. CAROLINE, died unmarried.   A writer in Schwabe's *Populaire Zeitschrift fur Homoopathie* in 1893 (Dr. Puhlmann) says: "A grown up daughter was murdered while he lived in Leipsic, and another daughter, Caroline, probably met her death in the same way, for she was found dead in a mill-pond near Coethen."

6 (7). TWINS: FREDERIKA, married Post and Clothing Inspector Dellbruck, in Stotteritz, near Leipsic.   7. A still born sister.

8. ERNST, born at Konigslutter in 1798; killed by a fall from a wagon when a babe, near Mulhausen.

9. ELEONORE, married to Herr Klemmen, afterwards to Dr. Wolff.

10. CHARLOTTE, born at Leipsic; lived with her father and died at Coethen unmarried, April 13, 1863.   (Died at Coethen, April 13, 1863, of paralysis of the lungs, Miss Charlotte Hahnemann.   She was the last surviving unmarried daughter of our great Master.—*Am. Hom. Rev.*, Vol. iii., p. 576. See *Allg. Zeitung.*)

Lutze's *Fliegende Blatter* for April 24, 1863, has: "On Monday evening at 11½ o'clock, the 13th April, 1863, died Fraulein Charlotte Hahnemann." ,

11. LOUISE, born at Leipsic; married Dr. Mossdorf; after his death she lived at Coethen with Charlotte.

BROTHERS AND SISTERS.

1. AUGUST HAHNEMANN, Field Apothecary in Austria.

2. CHARLOTTE HAHNEMANN, married for her first husband Pastor A. B. Trinius, of Eisleben; by whom one son, Bernard. For second husband she married General Superintendent Muller, of Eisleben.

3. MINNA HAHNEMANN, married M. Aubortin, of Stuttgart; his daughter married Von Landech, and lived at Rosswein.

BIBLIOGRAPHY.

LIST OF TRANSLATIONS MADE BY HAHNEMANN.

FROM THE ENGLISH.

1777. STEDTMANN'S PHYSIOLOGICAL ESSAYS AND OBSERVA-TIONS. Leipsic. Muller.

1777. NUGENT'S ESSAY ON HYDROPHOBIA. Leipsic. Muller.

1777. FALCONER ON WATER AND WARM BATHS. Leipsic. Hilscher.

1777. BALL'S MODERN PRACTICE OF PHYSIC. Leipsic. 2 vols.

1789. HISTORY OF THE LIVES OF ABELARD AND HELOISE. Leipsic. Weygand.

1790. INQUIRY INTO THE NATURE, CAUSES AND CURE OF CON-SUMPTION OF THE LUNGS. Leipsic. Weygand.

1790. A TREATISE ON THE MATERIA MEDICA. William Cullen. Leipsic. Schweikert. 2 vols.

1791. JOHN GRIGG'S ADVICE TO THE FEMALE SEX IN PREG-NANCY AND LYING IN WITH DIRECTIONS ON THE MANAGE-MENT OF CHILDREN. Leipsic. Weygand.

1790-91. ARTHUR YOUNG'S ANNALS OF AGRICULTURE. Leipsic. Crusius. 2 vols.

1791. DONALD MONRO'S MEDICAL AND PHARMACEUTICAL CHEMISTRY. Leipsic. 2 vols.

1791. EDWARD RIGBY'S CHEMICAL OBSERVATION ON SUGAR. Dresden. Walther.

1797-8. EDINBURGH DISPENSATORY. Leipsic. Fleischer. 2 vols.

1797-8. W. TAPLIN'S EQUERRY, OR MODERN VETERINARY MEDICINE. Leipsic. 2 vols.

1800. HOME'S PRACTICAL OBSERVATIONS ON THE CURE OF STRICTURES OF THE URETHRA BY CAUSTICS. Leipsic. Fleischer.

1800. THESAURUS MEDICAMINUM; A New Collection of Medical Pre-scriptions, Distributed into Twelve Classes, and Accompanied with Pharmaceutical Remarks, etc. Leipsic. Fleischer. (This is the book of which Hahnemann wrote a preface ridiculing the body of the book.)

FROM THE LATIN.

1806. ALBRECHT VON HALLER'S MATERIA MEDICA. Leipsic. Steinaker.

FROM THE FRENCH.

1784. DEMACHY'S ART OF MANUFACTURING CHEMICAL PROD-UCTS. With Struve's additions. Leipsic. Crusius. 2 vols.

1785. DEMACHY'S ART OF DISTILLING LIQUOR. Leipsic. Crusius. 2 vols.

1787. DEMACHY'S ART OF MANUFACTURING VINEGAR. With Annotations by Struve. Leipsic. Crusius.

1787. SIGNS OF THE PURITY AND ADULTERATIONS OF DRUGS. By J. B. van den Sande. Dresden. Walther.

1790–1. METHERIE'S ANALYTICAL ESSAY ON PURE AIR, AND THE DIFFERENT KINDS OF AIR. Leipsic. Crusius. 2 vols.

1796. HAND-BOOK FOR MOTHERS. J. J. Rousseau on the Education of Infants, under the above title: Leipsic. Fleischer. Second edition in 1804.

FROM THE ITALIAN.

1790. FABBRONI'S ART OF MAKING WINE. Leipsic. Barth.

ORIGINAL WRITINGS, BOOKS, ESSAYS AND MAGAZINE ARTICLES.

1779. INAUGURAL THESIS. Defended August 10, 1779. Erlangen. Ellrodtianis.

1782. SMALL ESSAYS published in Kreb's Journal. Quedlinburg.

1783. ARTICLES IN THE SAMMLUNG FOR PHYSICIANS. Leipsic. Weygand. 1783–7.

1784. DIRECTIONS FOR CURING OLD SORES AND ULCERS, Etc. Leipsic. Crusius.

1786. ON ARSENICAL POISONING, ITS TREATMENT AND JUDICIAL DETECTION. Leipsic. Crusius.

1787. TREATISE ON THE PREJUDICES EXISTING AGAINST COAL FIRES; and Mode of Improving this Combustible, and its Employment in Heating Bakers' Ovens. Dresden. Walther.

1787. ON THE DIFFICULTIES OF PREPARING SODA FROM POTASH AND KITCHEN SALT. In Crell's Annals of Chemistry.

1788. ON THE INFLUENCE OF CERTAIN GASES IN THE FERMENTATION OF WINE. In Crell's Annals of Chemistry. Vol. 1, pt. 4.

1788. ON THE WINE TEST FOR IRON AND LEAD. In Crell's Annals, vol. 1, pt. 4.

1788. CONCERNING BILE AND GALL STONES. In Crell's Annals, vol. 2, pt. 10.

1788. ESSAY ON A NEW AGENT IN THE PREVENTION OF PUTREFACTION. In Crell's Annals, vol. 2, pt. 12. Also Journal of Medicine. Paris. Vol. 81.

1789. UNSUCCESSFUL EXPERIMENTS WITH SOME NEW DISCOVERIES. In Crell's Annals of Chemistry, vol. 1, pt. 3.

1789. LETTER TO L. CRELL UPON BARYTA. In Crell's Annals of Chemistry, vol. 1, pt. 8.

1789. DISCOVERY OF A NEW CONSTITUENT IN PLUMBAGO In Crell's Annals, vol 2, pt. 10.

1789. OBSERVATIONS ON THE ASTRINGENT PROPERTIES OF PLANTS. In Crell's Annals, vol. 4, pt. 10.

1789. EXACT MODE OF PREPARING THE SOLUBLE MERCURY. In the New Literary Adviser for Physicians, Halle, 1789, and in Baldinger's New Magazine for Physicians, vol. 11, pt. 5.

1789. INSTRUCTIONS FOR SURGEONS RESPECTING VENEREAL DISEASES; TOGETHER WITH A NEW MERCURIAL PREPARATION. Leipsic. Crusius. Also in Dudgeon's translation of Lesser Writings.

1790. COMPLETE MODE OF PREPARING THE SOLUBLE MERCURY. Crell's Annals, vol. 2, pt. 8.

1790. NOTES TO CRELL ON VARIOUS SUBJECTS. Crell's Annals, vol. 1, pt. 3.

1791. INSOLUBILITY OF SOME METALS AND THEIR OXIDES, IN CAUSTIC AMMONIA. Crell's Annals, vol. 2, pt. 8.

1791. ON THE BEST METHOD OF PREVENTING SALIVATION AND THE DESTRUCTIVE EFFECTS OF MERCURY. Blumenbach's Medical Book, vol. 3, pt. 3.

1792. ON THE PREPARATION OF GLAUBER'S SALTS ACCORDING TO THE MODE OF BALLEN. Crell's Annals, pt. 1.

1792. ON THE ART OF TESTING WINE. Scherf's Archives of Medicine, vol. 3.

1792. THE FRIEND OF HEALTH. Vol. 1. Leipsic. Fleischer. Vol. 2. Leipsic. Crusius. Consists of a series of short essays on medical subjects. Dudgeon's Lesser Writings. Stapf's Kl. Med. Schrift.

1793-99. PHARMACEUTICAL LEXICON. Leipsic. Crusius. In 4 vols.

1793. REMARKS ON THE WIRTEMBURG AND HAHNEMANN'S WINE TEST. In the German Literary Gazette, No. 79.

1793. PREPARATION OF THE CASSEL YELLOW. Erfurt. Also in Act. Academ. Scient. Erfurt. 1794.

1794. ON HAHNEMANN'S TEST FOR WINE AND THE NEW LIQUOR PROBATORIUS FORTIOR. Tromsdorf's Journal of Pharmacy, vol. 2. Crell's Annals, vol. 1.

1795. ON CRUSTA LACTEA. Blumenbach's Med. Bibliothek, vol. 3.

1796. DESCRIPTION OF KLOCKENBRING DURING HIS INSANITY. In German Monthly Magazine, February, 1796. Lesser Writings.

1796. ESSAY ON A NEW PRINCIPLE FOR ASCERTAINING THE CURATIVE POWERS OF DRUGS. Hufeland's Journal for Practicing Physicians, vol. 2, pts. 3, 4. Lesser Writings. This was the first public announcement of the new principle of Homœopathy.

1797. SOMETHING ABOUT THE PULVERIZATION OF IGNATIA BEANS. In Tromsdorf's Journal of Pharmacy, vol. 5, pt. 1.

1797. ARE THE OBSTACLES TO THE ATTAINMENT OF SIMPLICITY AND CERTAINTY IN THE PRACTICE OF MEDICINE INSURMOUNTABLE? Hufeland's Journal, vol. 4. pt. 4. Lesser Writings. Brit. Jour. Hom., vol. 2.

1797. CASE OF RAPIDLY CURED COLICODYNIA. Hufeland's Journal, vol. 3, pt. 1. Dudgeon's Lesser Writings.

1798. ANTIDOTES TO SOME HEROIC VEGETABLE SUBSTANCES. Hufeland's Journal, vol. 5, pt. 1. Lesser Writings.

1798. SOME KINDS OF CONTINUED AND REMITTENT FEVERS. Hufeland's Journal, vol. 5, pt. 1. Lesser Writings.

1798. SOME PERIODICAL AND HEBDOMADAL DISEASES Hufeland's Journal, vol. 5, pt. 1. Lesser Writings.

1800 PREFACE TO THE THESAURUS MEDICAMINUM. Leipsic. Fleischer. Lesser Writings. (This is the preface in which he condemns the book.)

1801. OBSERVATIONS ON THE THREE CURRENT METHODS OF TREATMENT. Hufeland's Journal, vol. 11, pt. 4. Stapf's Kl. Med. Schrift.

1801. ESSAY ON SMALL DOSES OF MEDICINE AND OF BELLADONNA IN PARTICULAR. Hufeland's Journal, vol. 13, pt. 2. Lesser Writings.

1801. FRAGMENTARY OBSERVATIONS ON BROWN'S ELEMENTS OF MEDICINE. Hufeland's Journal, vol. 12, pt. 2. Lesser Writings.

1801. VIEW OF PROFESSIONAL LIBERALITY AT THE COMMENCEMENT OF THE NINETEENTH CENTURY. Reichs Anzeiger, No. 32. Lesser Writings.

1801. CURE AND PREVENTION OF SCARLET FEVER. Gotha. Becker. Edited by Buchner, and reprinted in 1844. Lesser Writings.

1803. ON A PROPOSED REMEDY FOR HYDROPHOBIA. In Reichs Anzeiger, No. 71. Lesser Writings.

1803. ON THE EFFECTS OF COFFEE. Leipsic. Steinacker. Lesser Writings; Am. Jour. Hom., June, 1835; Hom. Exam., Aug., 1840. Trans. into French by Brunnow, and published at Dresden, 1824; into Danish by Lund, Copenhagen, 1827; into Hungarian by Paul Balogh, Pesth, 1829; into Russian by Dr. A. Peterson; also into Spanish and Italian; in 1855 into English by Mrs. Epps, and published in a book, "Progress of Homœopathy," London, 1855. Trans. by W. L. Breyfogle, Louisville, Ky., 1875.

1805. FRAGMENTA DE VIRIBUS MEDICAMENTORUM POSITIVIS SIVE IN SANO CORPORE HUMANO OBSERVATIS. Leipsic. Barth. 2 parts. (The first collection of Drug Provings on the Healthy Body.) This was issued in one volume in 1834, edited by F. F. Quin, of London.

1805. ÆSCULAPIUS IN THE BALANCE. Dresden. Arnold. Lesser Writings. Brit. Jour. Hom., vol. 3. Hom. Pioneer. Schweikert's Zeitung, vol. 1, 1830. Trans. into Danish by Lund.

1806. OBJECTIONS TO PROPOSED SUBSTITUTES FOR CINCHONA, AND TO SUCCEDANEA IN GENERAL. In Reichs Anzeiger, No. 57. Lesser Writings.

1806. CONCERNING SUBSTITUTES FOR QUININE. Hufeland's Journal, vol. 23.

1806. WHAT ARE POISONS? WHAT ARE MEDICINES? Hufeland's Journal, vol. 24, pt. 3.

1806. SCARLET FEVER AND PUPURA MILIARIS, TWO DIFFERENT DISEASES. Hufeland's Journal, vol. 17, pt. 1.

1806. MEDICINE OF EXPERIENCE. Berlin. Wittig. Hufeland's Journal, vol 22, pt. 3. Lesser Writings. Brit. Jour. Hom., vol. 1.

1808. ON THE VALUE OF SPECULATIVE SYSTEMS OF MEDICINE, ESPECIALLY IN CONNECTION WITH THE VARIOUS SYSTEMS OF PRACTICE. Allgemeine Anzeiger. Lesser Writings. Brit. Jour. Hom., vol. 2. Hom. Exam., 1840. Am. Jour. Hom., Feb., 1835. Hom. Pioneer.

1808. EXTRACT FROM A LETTER TO A PHYSICIAN OF HIGH STANDING ON THE GREAT NECESSITY OF A REGENERATION IN MEDICINE. In Allgemeine Anzeiger, No. 343 Lesser Writings. Hom. Exam., Sept., 1840. Hom. Pioneer. (Letter to Hufeland.)

1808. INDICATIONS OF THE HOMŒOPATHIC EMPLOYMENT OF MEDICINES IN ORDINARY PRACTICE. Hufeland's Journal, vol. 26, pt. 2; also in first three editions of Organon. Dudgeon's trans of the Organon.

1808. ON THE PRESENT WANT OF FOREIGN MEDICINES. Allgemeine Anzeiger, No. 207. Lesser Writings.

1808. ON SUBSTITUTES FOR FOREIGN DRUGS, AND ON THE RECENT ANNOUNCEMENT OF THE MEDICAL FACULTY IN VIENNA RELATIVE TO THE SUPERFLUOUSNESS OF THE LATTER. Allgemeine Anzeiger, No. 327. Lesser Writings.

1808. OBSERVATIONS ON SCARLET FEVER. Allgemeine Anzeiger, No. 160. Lesser Writings.

1808. REPLY TO A QUESTION ABOUT THE PROPHYLACTIC FOR SCARLET FEVER. Hufeland's Journal, vol. 27, pt. 4.

1809. TO A CANDIDATE FOR THE DEGREE OF M. D. Allgemeine Anzeiger, No. 227. Lesser Writings.

1809. SIGNS OF THE TIMES IN THE ORDINARY SYSTEM OF MEDICINE. Allgemeine Anzeiger, No. 326 Lesser Writings.

1809. ON THE PREVAILING FEVER. Allgemeine Anzeiger, No. 261. Lesser Writings.

1810. ORGANON OF RATIONAL HEALING. Dresden. Arnold. 2d edition, 1819; 3d edition, 1824; 4th edition, 1829; 5th edition, 1833
Trans. into French by Brunnow, and published in Dresden by Arnold in 1824; 2d edition of same, 1832.
Into Hungarian in 1830, Pesth, Ottonal.
French translation by Dr. Jourdan, Paris, Bailliere, 1832; also in 1834; 3d edition of same, 1845; 4th, 1873.
In 1833 translated from the 4th German edition by Chas. H. Devriant, with notes by Sam'l Stratton. Dublin, London, Edinburgh.
Trans by Dr. Liedbeck into Swedish, Stockholm, 1836.
In 1840, into Russian by Wratzky; into Russian by Sarokin in 1887–90.
Into Spanish by Sanllehy, Madrid; into Spanish in 1853 by Valero.
Into Italian by Guranta, and also by Francesco Romano.
A 6th German edition was edited by Lutze, Coethen, 1865.
In 1849 by Dudgeon into English from the 5th edition. London, Headland.
In 1836 the 1st American from the British translation of 1833 was published by the Allentown Academy. 1843, 2d American edition, New York, Radde. 1849, 3d American edition, New York, Radde. 1869, 4th American edition, New York, Radde. In 1876 it was re-translated by Conrad Wesselhœft, of Boston, and published by Boericke & Tafel. This is the 5th American from the 5th German edition.
New edition by Dudgeon, with an Appendix. London, 1893.
Trans. by Fincke, Jour. of Homœopathics, New York, 1889. See, also Cal. Hom'th, vol. 9, p. 337.

1811. MATERIA MEDICA PURA. Dresden. Arnold. 6 vols. Vol. 1, 1811; vol. 2, 1816; vol. 3, 1817; vol. 4, 1818; vol. 5, 1819; vol. 6, 1821.
2d edition. Vol. 1, 1822; vol. 2, 1824; vol. 3, 1825; vol. 4, 1825; vol. 5, 1826; vol. 6, 1827.
3d edition, 1830. Vol. 2, 1833. Only two vols. were published of this edition.

In 1825 translated into Italian by Romani. Naples. Nobile.

In 1826 an edition in Latin was published in Leipsic by Brunnow, Stapf and Gross, containing also the Viribus.

Trans. in 1828 into French by Bigel. Varsovie. Into French by Jourdan in 1834, Paris, Bailliere. In 1877 by the Drs. Simon into French.

In 1840 Dr. Quin commenced a translation into English in London, but when vol. 1 was published it was destroyed by fire. No others were published.

Trans. by Hempel in 1846. New York. Radde.

A Hahnemann Materia Medica by Drysdale, Black, Dudgeon and Hughes, published in London in 1852; but 3 parts published.

Into Italian by Dadea in 1873. Turin. 2 vols.

1880. Trans. by Dudgeon. London. 2 vols. with additions by Hughes.

1880. Trans. by Arndt. Med. Counselor, vols. 3, 4, 5.

1812. DISSERTATION ON THE HELLEBORISM OF THE ANCIENTS. Leipsic. Tauchnitz. Thesis to the Faculty at Leipsic. Also in Lesser Writings.

1813. SPIRIT OF THE HOMŒOPATHIC DOCTRINE OF MEDICINE. In Allgemeine Anzeiger, March, 1813. Vol. 2 of Materia Medica Pura. Lesser Writings. As a pamphlet in New York by Hans Birch Gram in 1825. Trans. by Ad. Lippe in 1878, and published in The Organon, a Journal. Hom. Exam., Oct., 1840. Also trans. by G. M. Scott, London, Glasgow. 1838. Trans. by Lund into Danish.

1814. TREATMENT OF TYPHUS FEVER AT PRESENT PREVAILING. Allgemeine Anzeiger, No. 6. Lesser Writings.

1816. VENEREAL DISEASE AND ITS IMPROPER TREATMENT. Allgemeine Anzeiger, No. 211. Lesser Writings.

1816. TREATMENT OF BURNS. Answer to Dr. Dzondi. In Allgemeine Anzeiger, Nos. 156, 204. Lesser Writings.

1819. ON UNCHARITABLENESS TO SUICIDES. Allgemeine Anzeiger, No. 144. Lesser Writings.

1820. ON THE PREPARATION AND DISPENSING OF MEDICINES BY HOMŒOPATHIC PHYSICIANS. First published in Stapf's Lesser Writings of Hahnemann. Also Dudgeon's Lesser Writings.

1821. TREATMENT OF PUPURA MILIARIS. Allgemeine Anzeiger, No. 26. Lesser Writings.

1825. HOW MAY HOMŒOPATHY BE MOST CERTAINLY ERADICATED? Allgemeine Anzeiger, No. 227. Lesser Writings.

1825. INFORMATION FOR THE TRUTH SEEKER. Published in the Materia Medica Pura under the title: How Can Small Doses of Such Very Attenuated Medicines as Homœopathy Employs Still Possess Great Power? Allgemeine Anzeiger, No. 194. Lesser Writings. Hom. Pioneer. Brit. Jour. Hom., vol. 2.

1828. CHRONIC DISEASES, THEIR NATURE AND HOMŒOPATHIC TREATMENT. Dresden and Leipsic. Arnold. Vols. 1, 2, 3, 1828; vol. 4, 1830.

2d edition. Dusseldorf. Schaub. Vols. 1, 2, 1835; vol. 3, 1837; vol. 4, 1838; vol. 5, 1839.

Trans. into French by Jourdan. Paris, 1832. 2d edition of same 1846. Into French by Bigel. Edited by Des Guidi in 1832.

Into English from French edition by G. M. Scott. Glasgow, 1842.

Into Italian by Belluomini. Teramo. 1832-7. 4 vols.

In 1849 into Italian by Villannera. Madrid.

In 1845 by Hempel into English. New York. Radde. 5 vols.

Reprint of vol. 1 in Med. Advance, vol. 22. 1889.

In 1894 from 5th German edition into English by L. H. Tafel. Boericke & Tafel. Philadelphia.

1829. LETTERS BY HAHNEMANN TO DR. SCHRETER. New Archives of Stapf. Vol. 23.

1829. LETTER TO KORSAKOFF ABOUT IMPREGNATION OF GLOBULES WITH MEDICINE. Stapf's Archivs. Vol. 8, pt. 2. Lesser Writings.

1829. LESSER MEDICAL WRITINGS OF HAHNEMANN. Collected by Stapf. Dresden: Arnold. But for this book we should know but little of the essays of Hahnemann. These are for the most part translated and published in Dudgeon's edition of Lesser Writings, of which there is an English and an American edition.

1831. ALLOPATHY, A WORD OF WARNING TO SICK PERSONS. Leipsic. Baumgartner. Lesser Writings. Trans. into Danish by Lund.

1831. APPEAL TO THINKING PHILANTHROPISTS RESPECTING THE MODE OF PROPAGATION OF ASIATIC CHOLERA. Leipsic. Berger. Lesser Writings. Brit. Jour. Hom., Oct., 1849. S. W. Hom. Jour. and Rev., vol. 3.

1831. CURE OF ASIATIC CHOLERA. Coethen. Aug., 1831. Same. 2d edition. Leipsic. Gluck.

1831. LETTER ABOUT THE CURE OF CHOLERA. Berlin. Hirschwald. Trans. into Danish by Lund.

1831. CIRCULAR ON THE CHOLERA. Schweikert's Zeitung d. Natur. Heilkunst. Vol. 2.

1831. CURE AND PREVENTION OF ASIATIC CHOLERA. Stapf's Archivs. Vol. 11, pt. 1. Schweickert's Zeitung, Vol. 2.

1831. NOTES BY HAHNEMANN ON KORSAKOFF'S LETTER ON ATTENUATION OF HOMŒOPATHIC REMEDIES. Stapf's Archivs, vol. 11, pt. 2. Lesser Writings.

1832. SUMMONS TO THE HALF-HOMŒOPATHISTS OF LEIPSIC. N. W. Jour. Hom., vol. 4.

1832. CURE OF CHOLERA. Nurnburg. Stein.

1832. PREFACE TO BŒNNINGHAUSEN'S REPERTORY.

1843. INTRODUCTION TO THE PROVING OF ARSENIC. Brit. Jour. Hom., vol. 1.

1845. EXAMINATION OF THE SOURCES OF THE MATERIA MEDICA. Brit. Jour. Hom., vol 3.

1849. ON THE CONTAGIOUSNESS OF CHOLERA. Brit. Jour. Hom., Vol. 7.

1853. TREATMENT OF CHRONIC LOCAL DISEASE AND OF PHTHISIS. Brit. Jour. Hom., Vol. 11.

1863. ITCH INSECT. Brit. Jour. Hom., Vol. 21.

1850. STUDIES OF HOMŒOPATHIC MEDICINE. Hartung. Paris. 2 vols. Contains 12 essays and 14 letters by Hahnemann.

The full titles of these books can be found in my large work on Homœopathic Bibliography. Philada: Boericke & Tafel, 1892.

CPSIA information can be obtained
at www.ICGtesting.com
Printed in the USA
LVHW080956211019
634835LV00011B/85/P